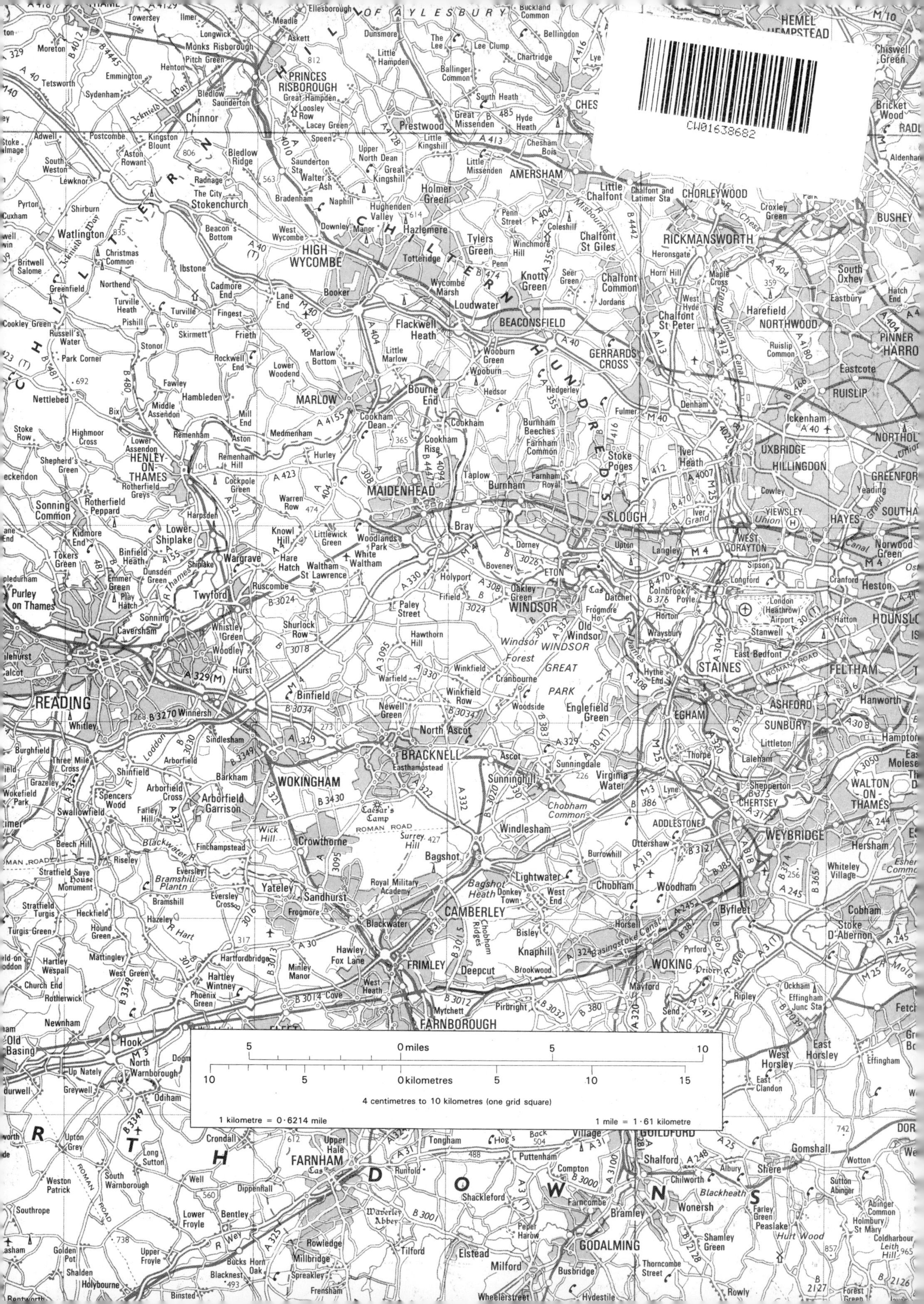

5 0 miles 5 10
10 5 0 kilometres 5 10 15
4 centimetres to 10 kilometres (one grid square)
1 kilometre = 0·6214 mile
1 mile = 1·61 kilometre
PRINCES RISBOROUGH
HIGH WYCOMBE
AMERSHAM
CHORLEYWOOD
RICKMANSWORTH
BEACONSFIELD
NORTHWOOD
GERRARDS CROSS
MARLOW
HENLEY-ON-THAMES
MAIDENHEAD
SLOUGH
UXBRIDGE
HILLINGDON
WINDSOR
READING
STAINES
WOKINGHAM
BRACKNELL
EGHAM
CAMBERLEY
WEYBRIDGE
WALTON-ON-THAMES
WOKING
FARNBOROUGH
FRIMLEY
FARNHAM
GODALMING
CHILTERN HILLS
CHILTERN HUNDREDS
NORTH DOWNS

COUNTY
STREET ATLAS

BERKSHIRE

COUNTY
STREET ATLAS

PHILIP'S

BERKSHIRE

COUNTY STREET ATLAS
BERKSHIRE

First Edition published 1990 by

Ordnance Survey
Romsey Road
Maybush
Southampton SO9 4DH

and

George Philip Ltd
59 Grosvenor Street
London W1X 9DA

ISBN 0 540 05596 4 (George Philip)
ISBN 0 319 00227 6 (Ordnance Survey)

To the best of the Publishers' knowledge, the information in this atlas was correct at the time of going to press. No responsibility can be accepted for any errors or their consequences.

The representation in this atlas of a road, track or path is no evidence of the existence of a right of way.

Printed in Great Britain by
Butler & Tanner Ltd, Frome and London

Contents

Key map	vi-vii
Administrative map	viii
Street maps	1-153
Index explanation and abbreviations	154
List of towns, villages and rural localities	155
Index	156

key to map symbols

- British Rail Station
- London Transport Station
- Private Railway Station
- Bus or Coach Station
- Police Station (may not be open 24hrs)
- Hospital with Casualty Facilities (may not be open 24hrs)
- Post Office
- Place of Worship
- Important Building
- P Parking
- 120 Adjoining page indicator

- Motorway and Dual Carriageway
- Main or through road
- A 27(T) Road numbers (Dept of Transport)
- Gate and obstruction to traffic (restrictions may not apply at all times and to all vehicles)
- Footpath
- Bridleway

The representation in this atlas of a road, track or path is no evidence of the existence of a right of way.

Amb Sta	Ambulance Station
Coll	College
FB	Foot Bridge
F Sta	Fire Station
LC	Level Crossing
Liby	Library
Mus	Museum
Sch	School
TH	Town Hall

The large letters and numbers around the edge of the maps are the referencing system.
An explanation of how to use the system for locating the position of street names appears on page 154

The small numbers identify the 1 kilometre National Grid lines.

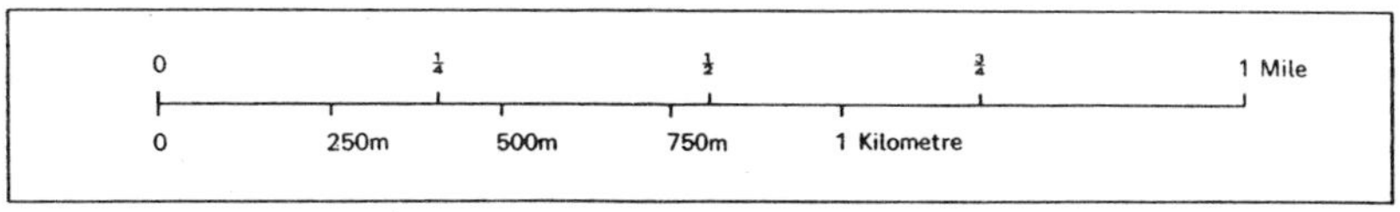

Scale of Maps is 3½ inches to 1 mile (1:18103)

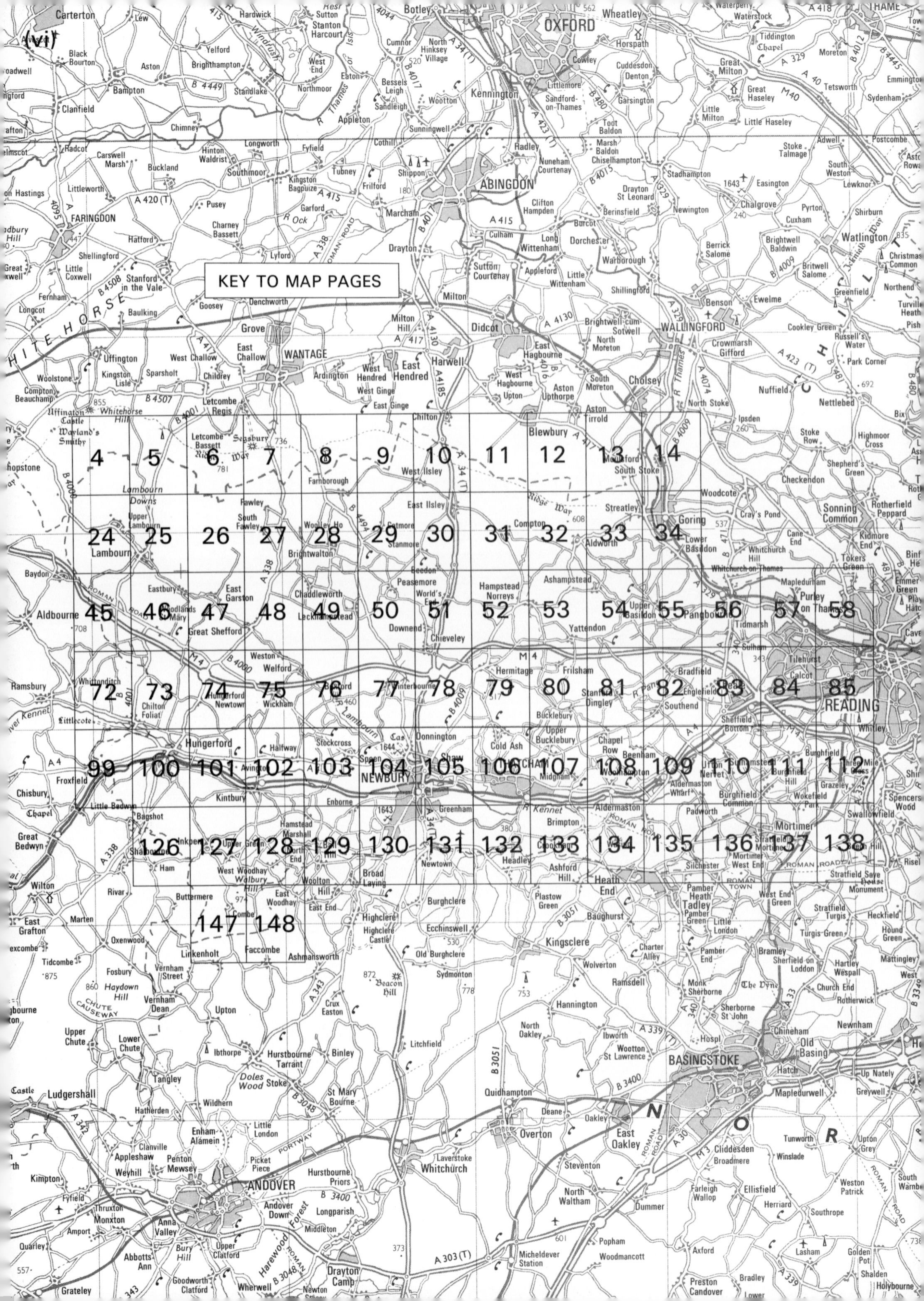
KEY TO MAP PAGES
4 5 6 7 8 9 10 11 12 13 14
24 25 26 27 28 29 30 31 32 33 34
45 46 47 48 49 50 51 52 53 54 55 56 57 58
72 73 74 75 76 77 78 79 80 81 82 83 84 85
99 100 101 102 103 104 105 106 107 108 109 110 111 112
126 127 128 129 130 131 132 133 134 135 136 137 138
147 148
OXFORD
ABINGDON
FARINGDON
WANTAGE
WALLINGFORD
NEWBURY
READING
BASINGSTOKE
ANDOVER
Didcot
Hungerford
Whitchurch

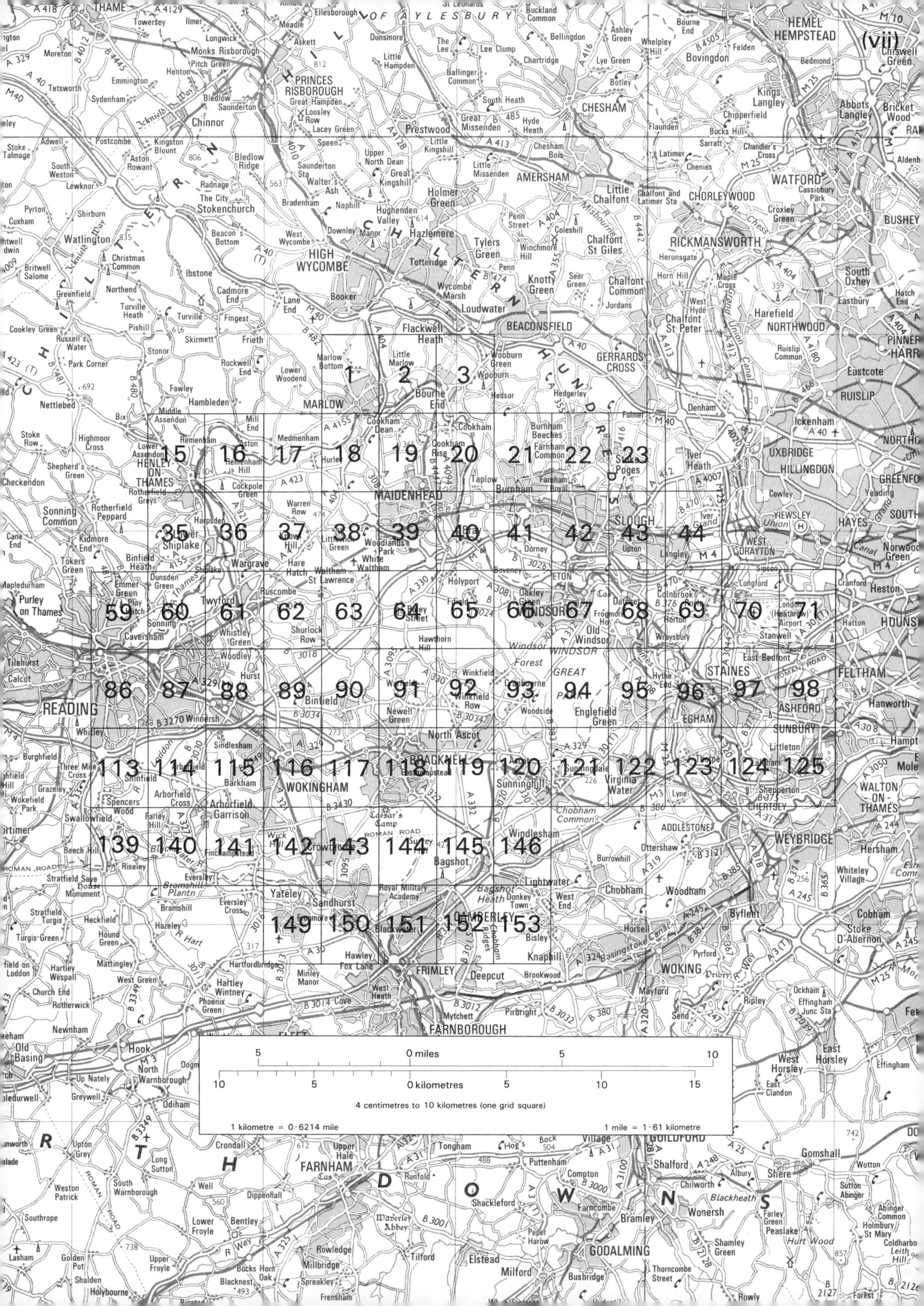

1 2 3
15 16 17 18 19 20 21 22 23
35 36 37 38 39 40 41 42 43 44
59 60 61 62 63 64 65 66 67 68 69 70 71
86 87 88 89 90 91 92 93 94 95 96 97 98
113 114 115 116 117 118 119 120 121 122 123 124 125
139 140 141 142 143 144 145 146
149 150 151 152 153
THAME
PRINCES RISBOROUGH
HEMEL HEMPSTEAD
CHESHAM
AMERSHAM
WATFORD
CHORLEYWOOD
RICKMANSWORTH
HIGH WYCOMBE
BEACONSFIELD
GERRARDS CROSS
NORTHWOOD
RUISLIP
MARLOW
HENLEY-ON-THAMES
MAIDENHEAD
SLOUGH
UXBRIDGE
HILLINGDON
HAYES
WINDSOR
STAINES
FELTHAM
READING
WOKINGHAM
BRACKNELL
EGHAM
ASHFORD
SUNBURY
CHERTSEY
WALTON-ON-THAMES
WEYBRIDGE
WOKING
CAMBERLEY
FRIMLEY
FARNBOROUGH
FARNHAM
GUILDFORD
GODALMING
5 0 miles 5 10
10 5 0 kilometres 5 10 15
4 centimetres to 10 kilometres (one grid square)
1 kilometre = 0·6214 mile
1 mile = 1·61 kilometre

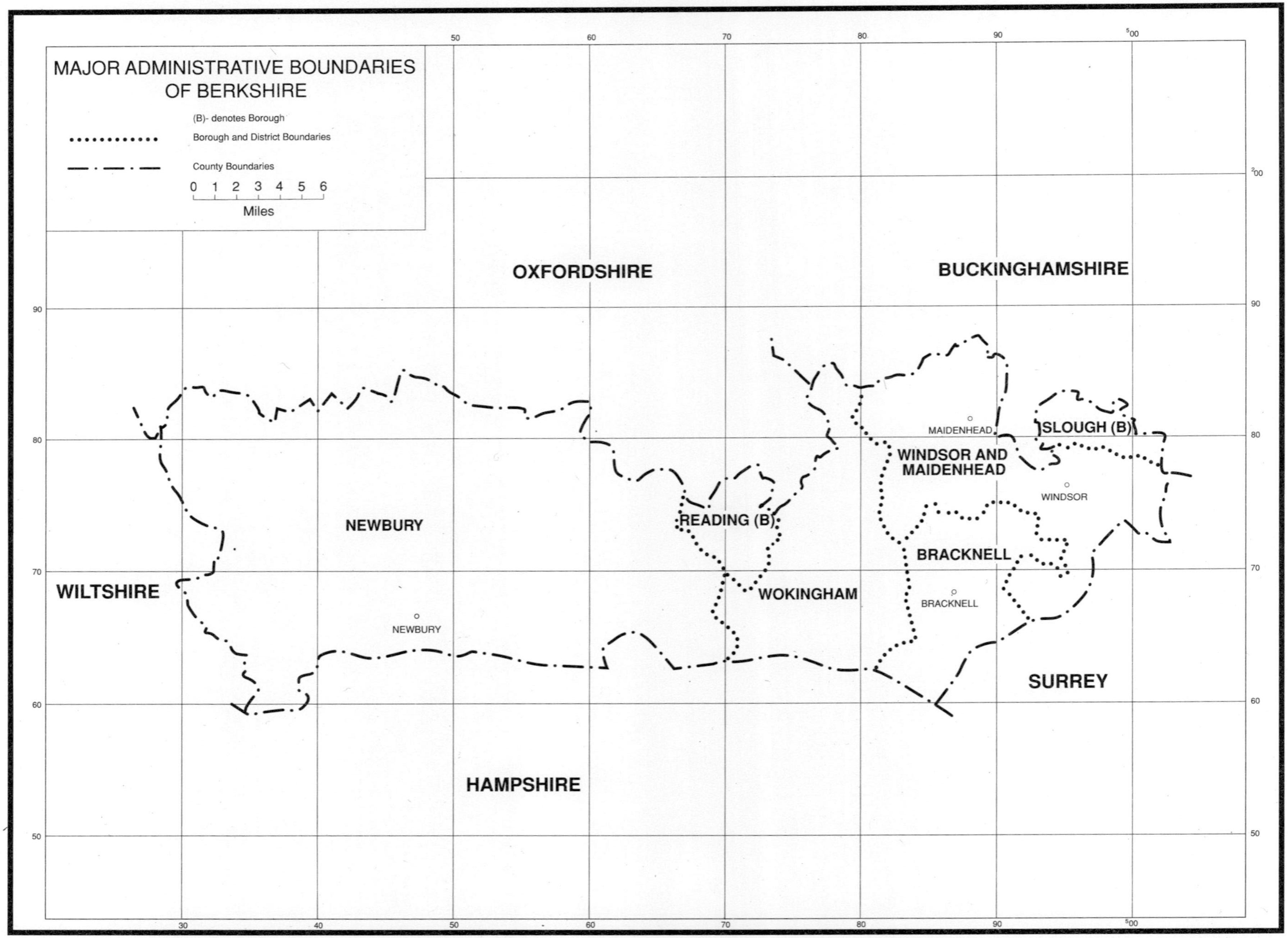
MAJOR ADMINISTRATIVE BOUNDARIES OF BERKSHIRE
(B)- denotes Borough
Borough and District Boundaries
County Boundaries
0 1 2 3 4 5 6
Miles
OXFORDSHIRE
BUCKINGHAMSHIRE
WILTSHIRE
NEWBURY
READING (B)
WOKINGHAM
WINDSOR AND MAIDENHEAD
MAIDENHEAD
SLOUGH (B)
WINDSOR
BRACKNELL
SURREY
HAMPSHIRE

not continued, see key diagram

2

18

not continued, see key diagram

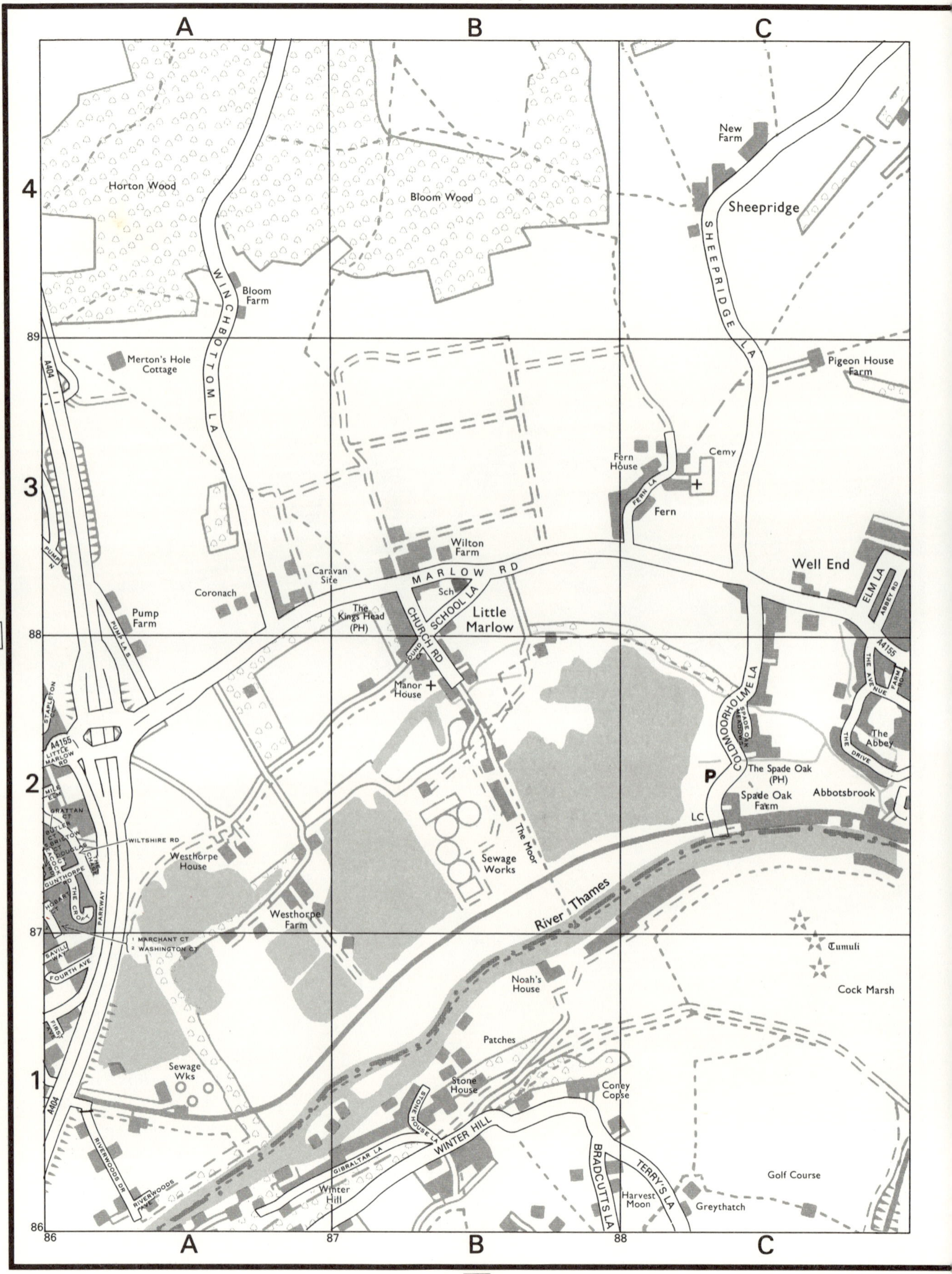

1

19

not continued, see key diagram

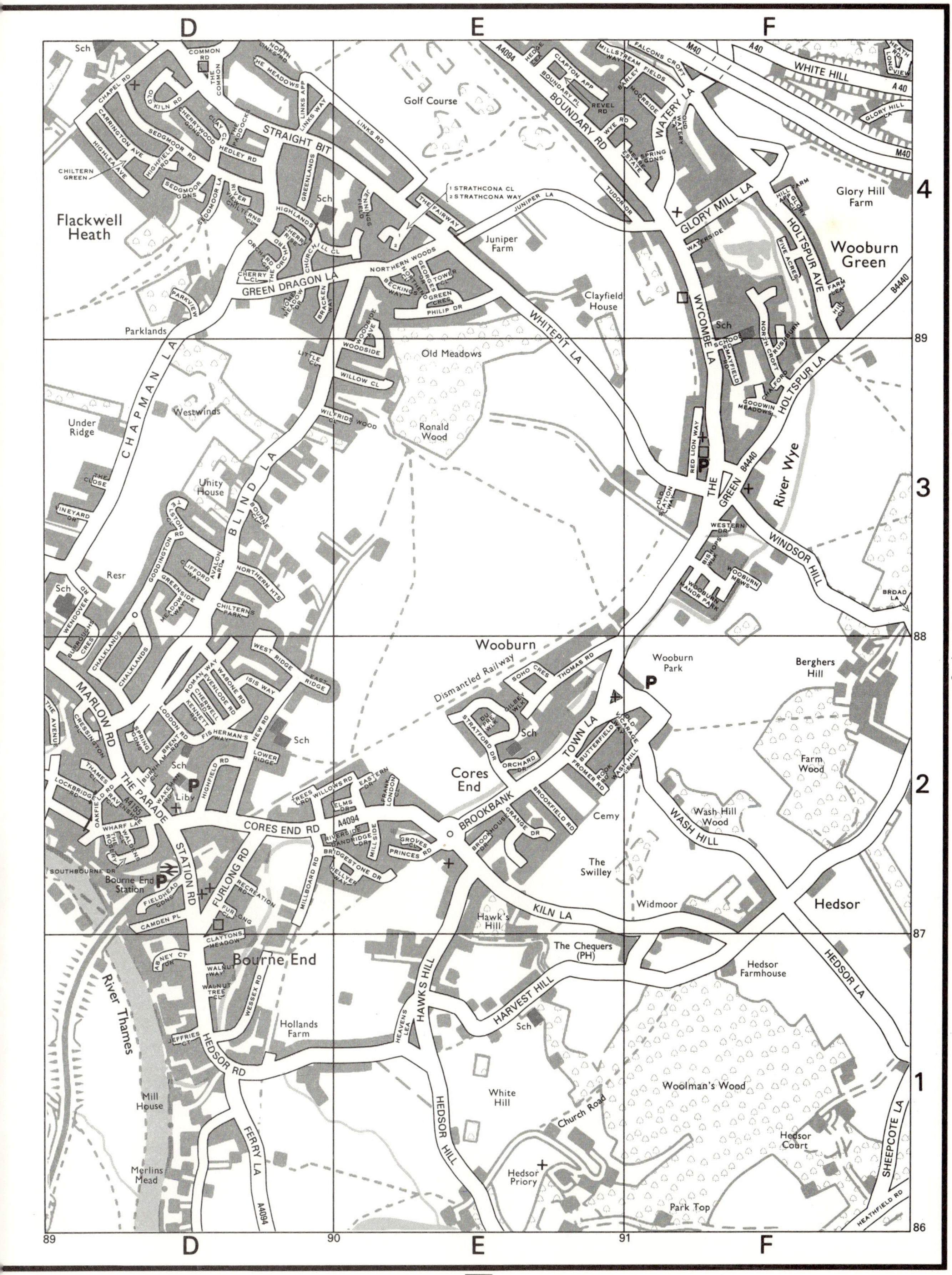

not continued, see key diagram

not continued, see key diagram

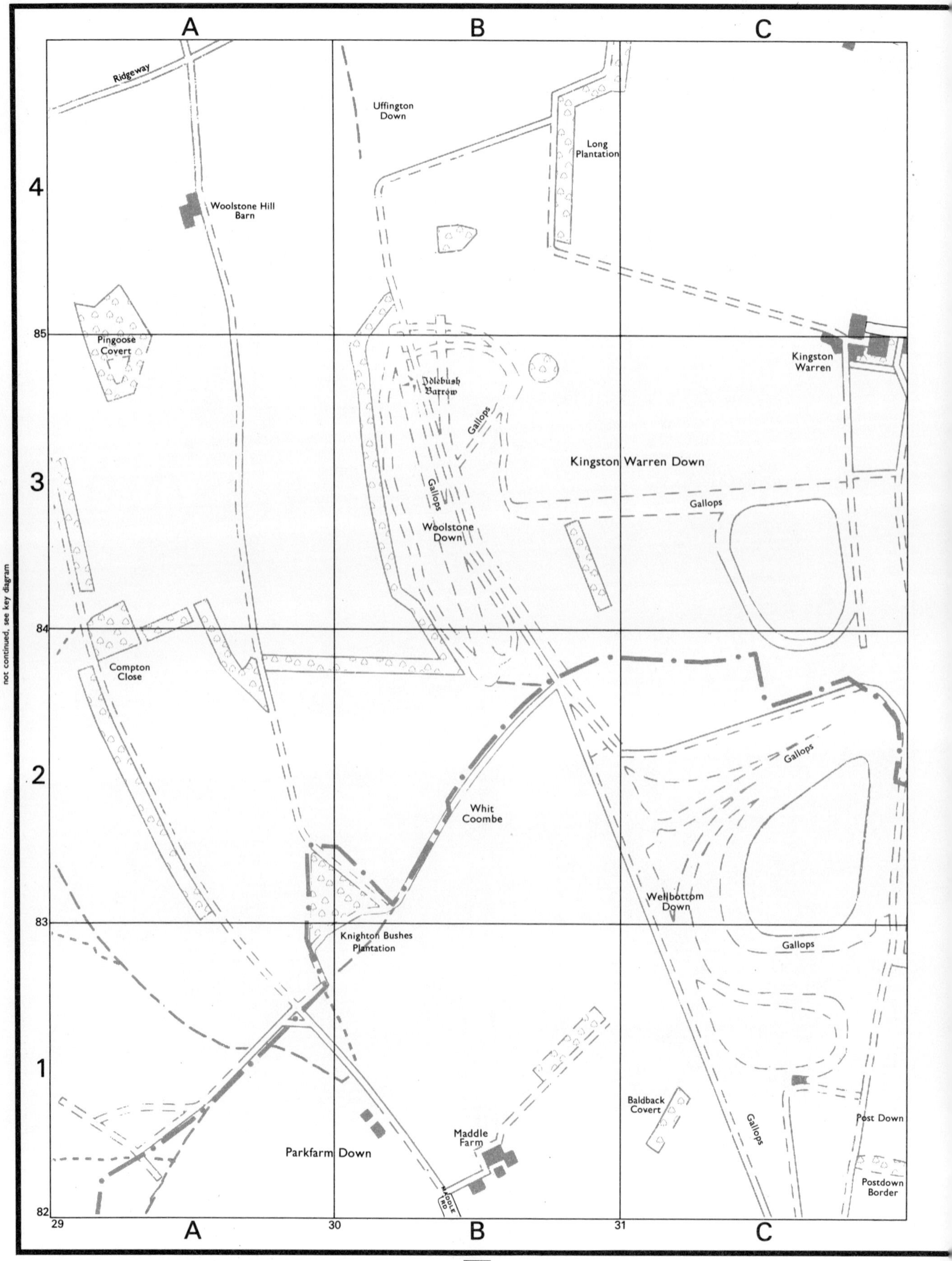

not continued, see key diagram

24

not continued, see key diagram

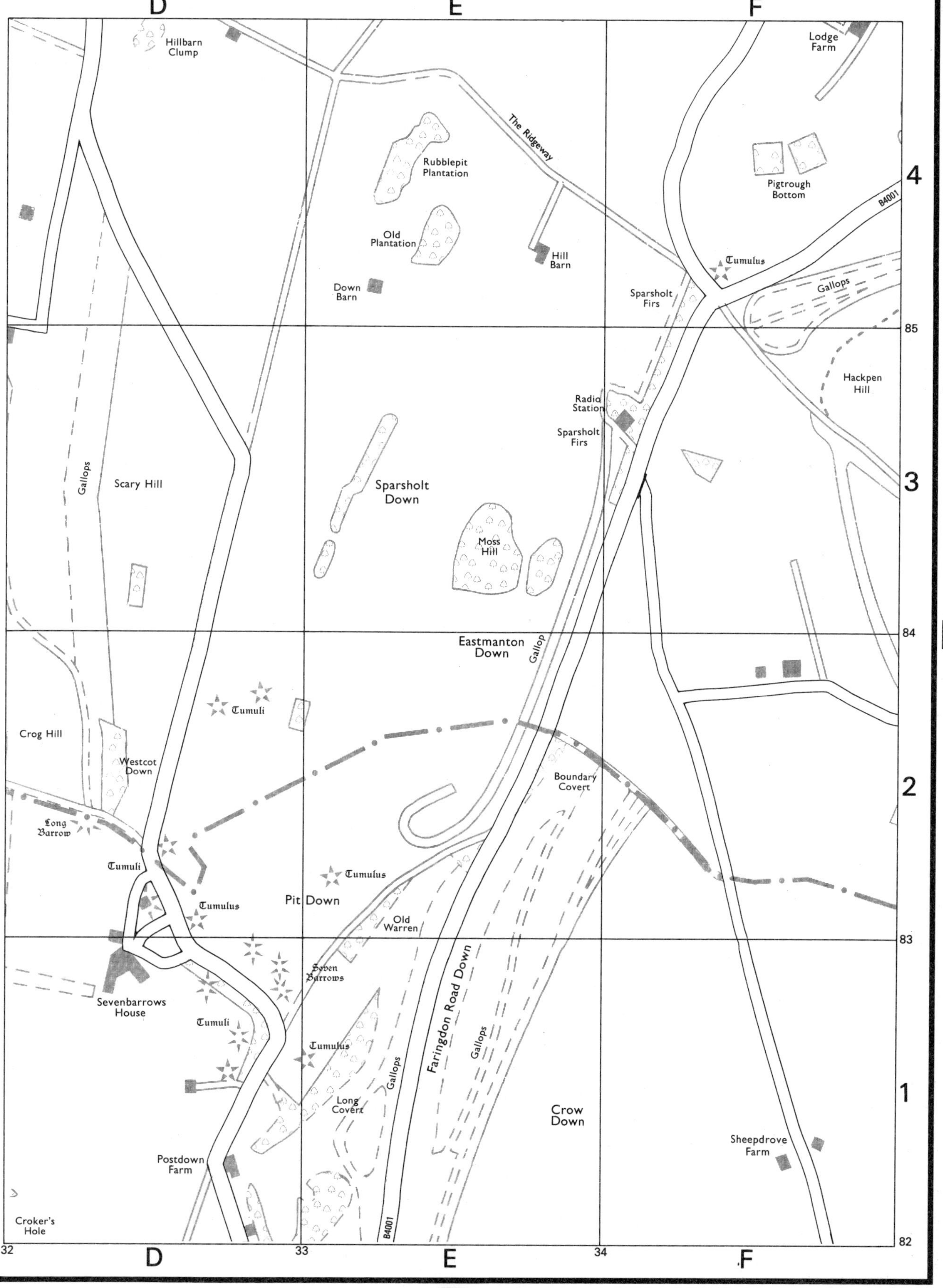

25

not continued, see key diagram

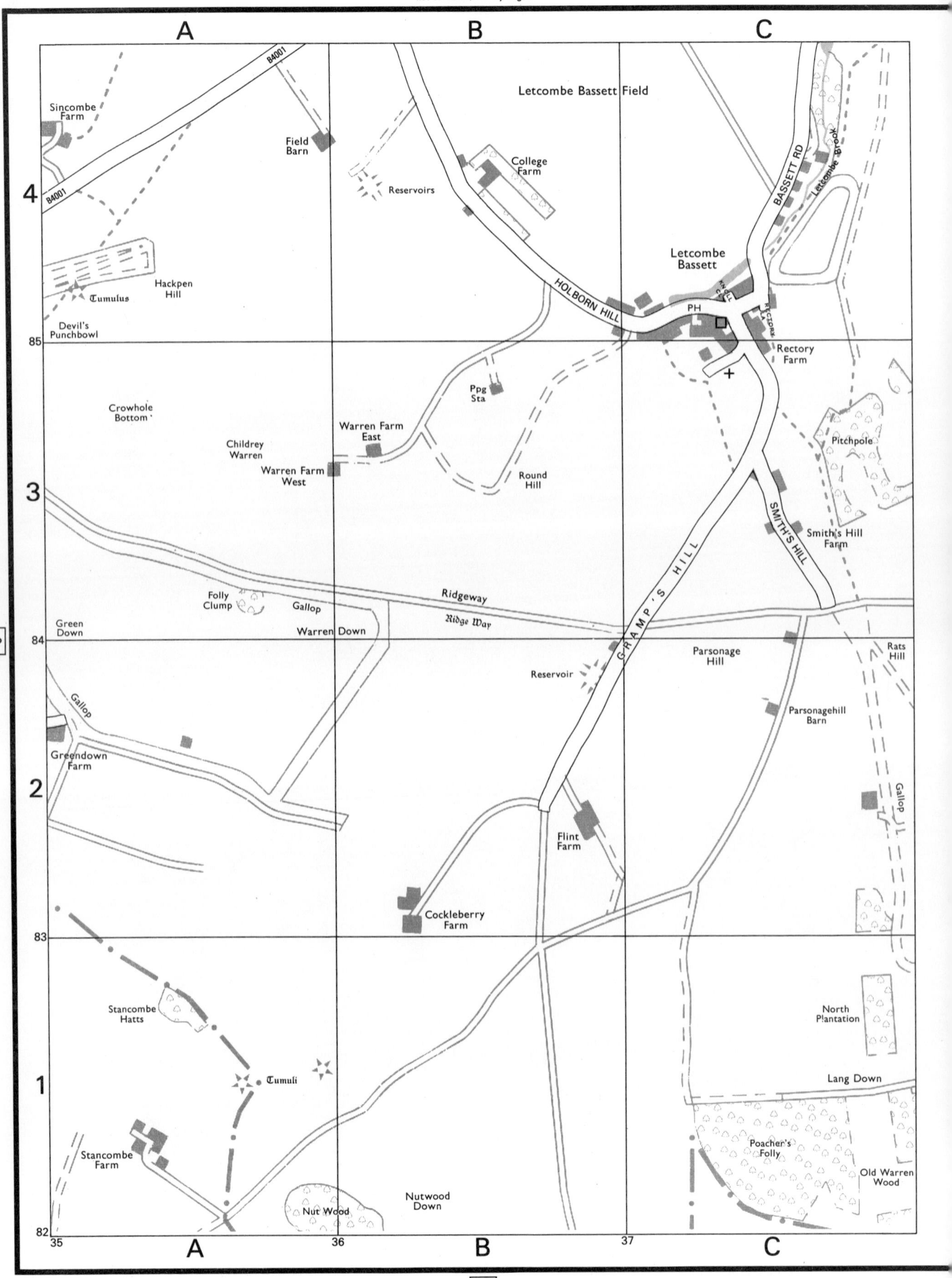

5

26

not continued, see key diagram

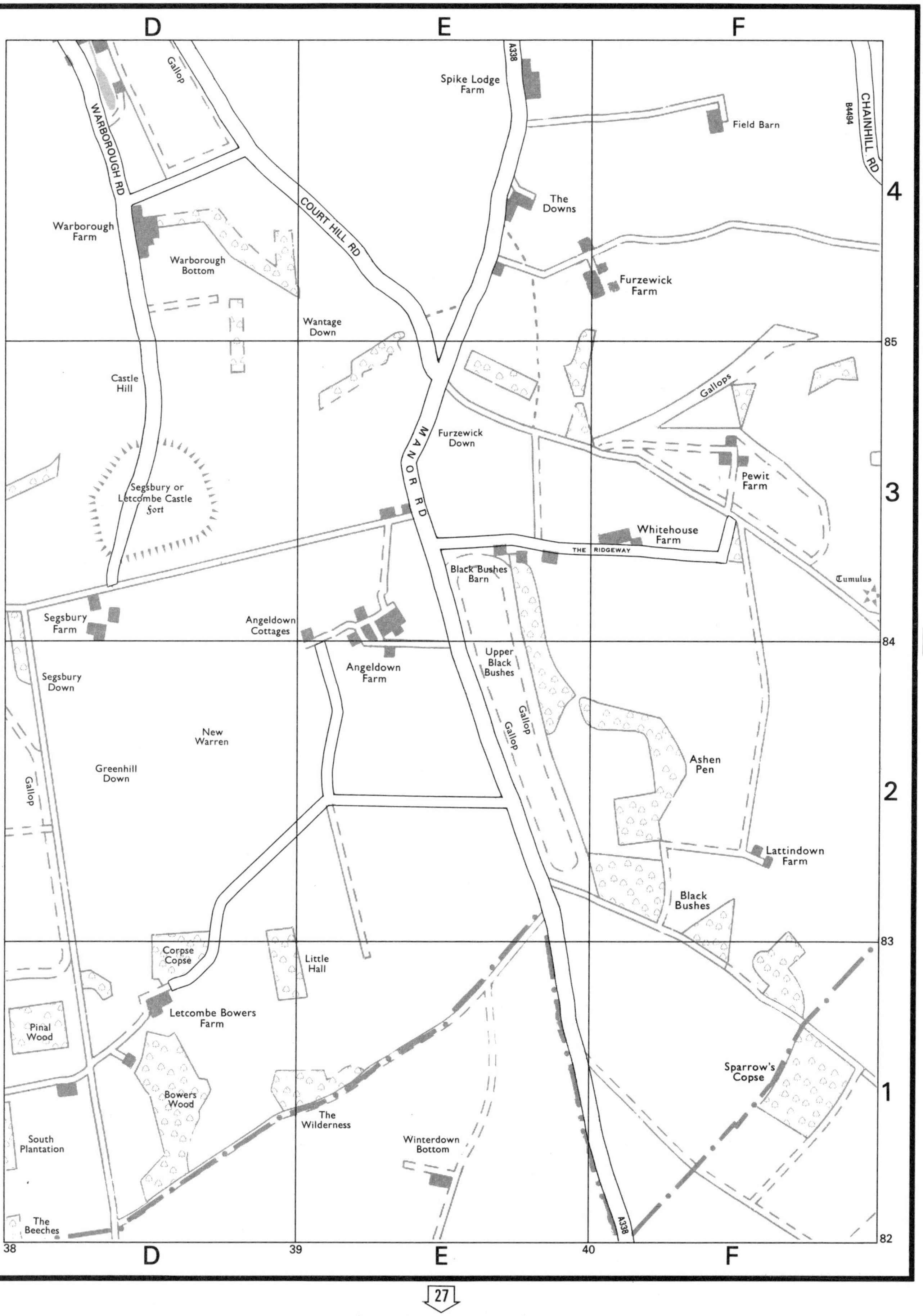

8

27

not continued, see key diagram

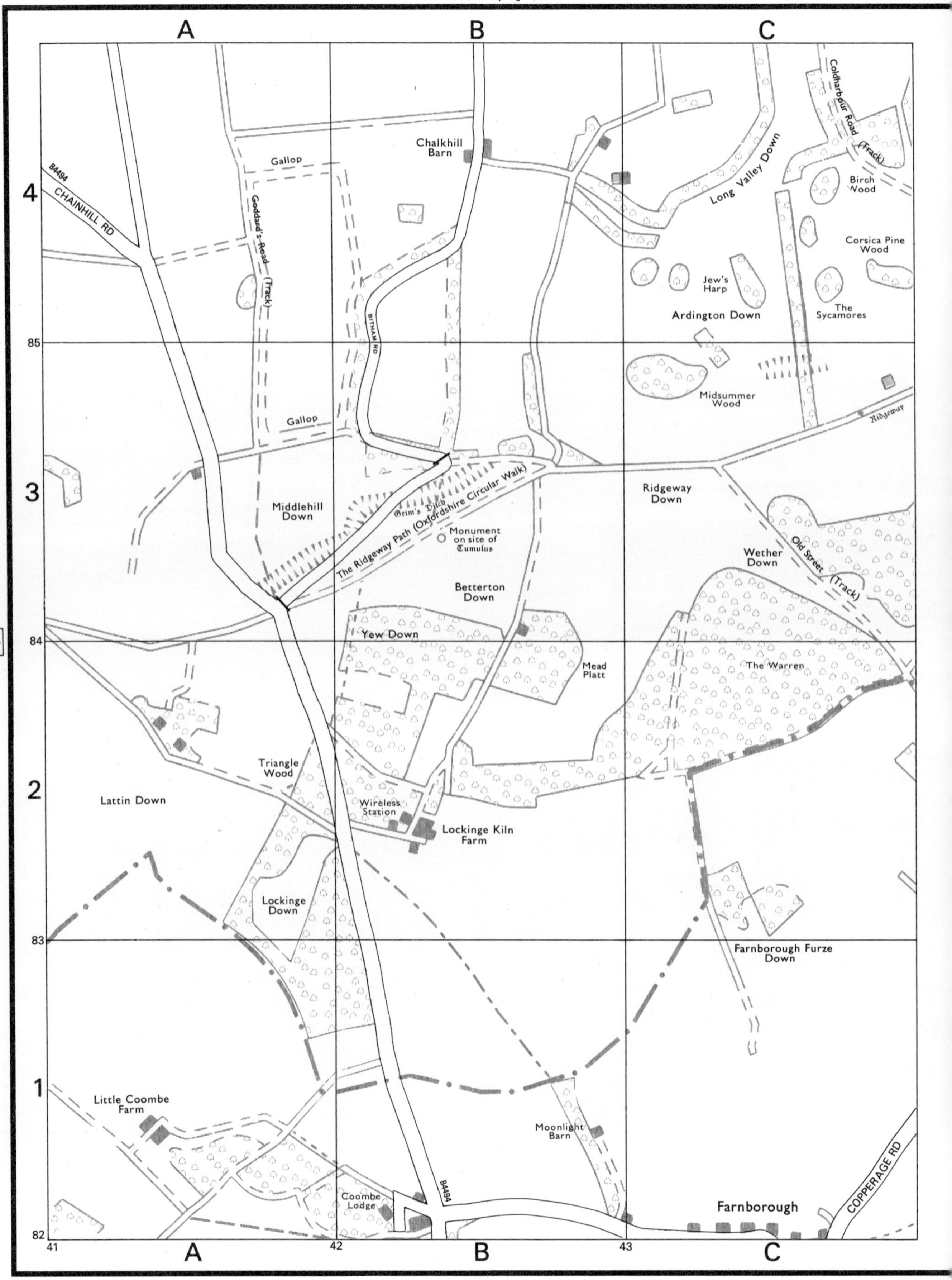

7

28

not continued, see key diagram

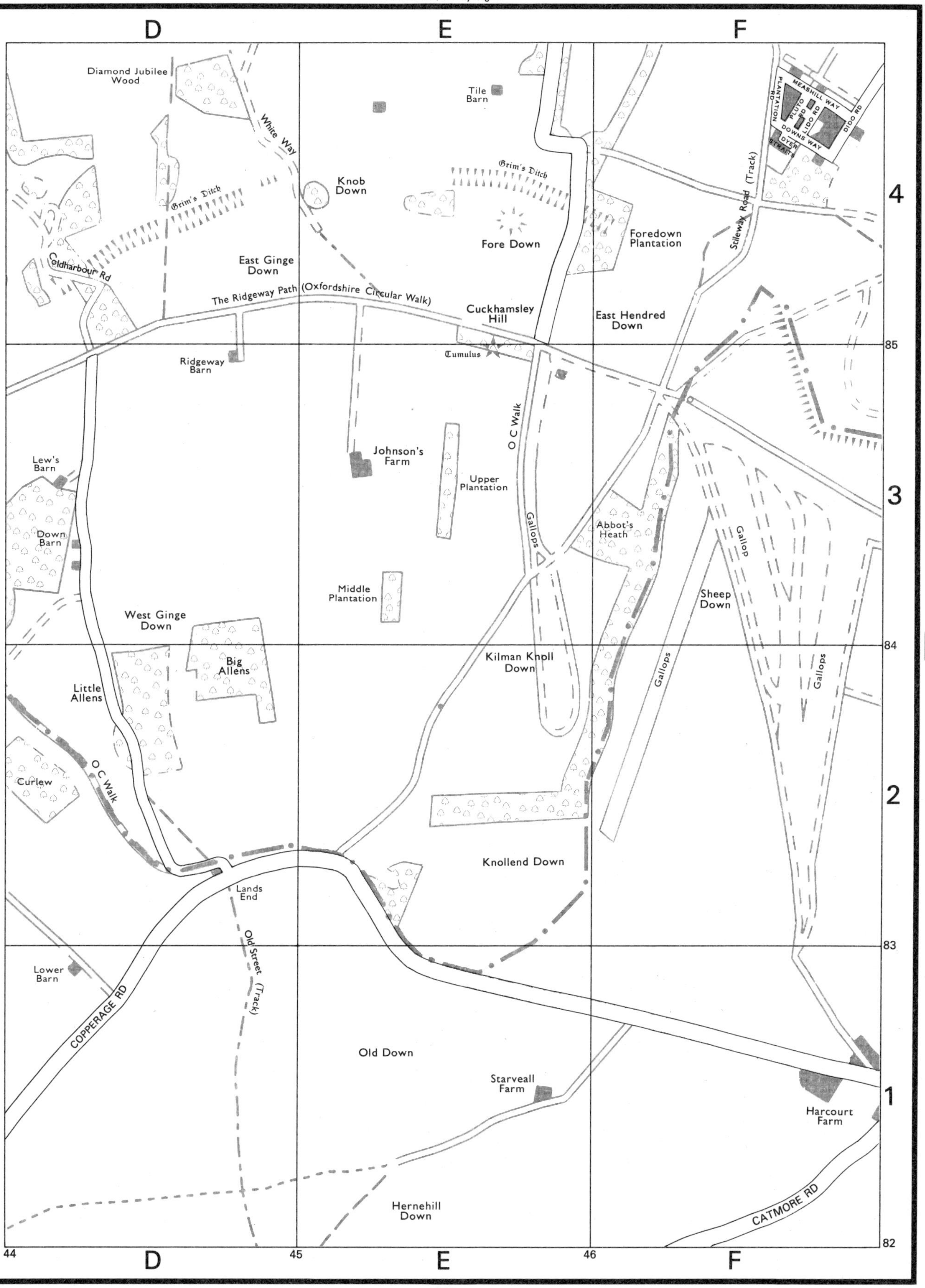

10

29

not continued, see key diagram

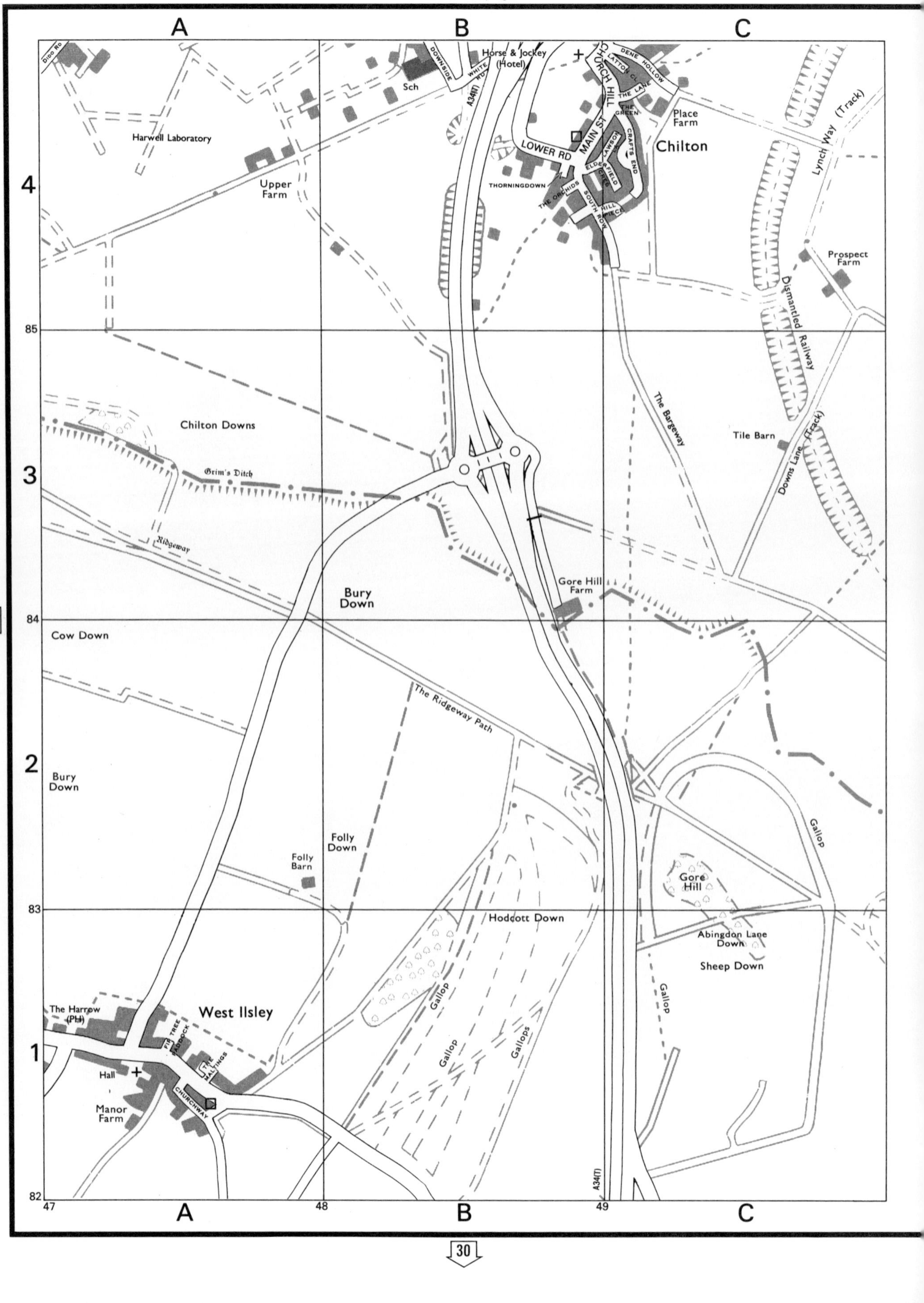

9

30

not continued, see key diagram

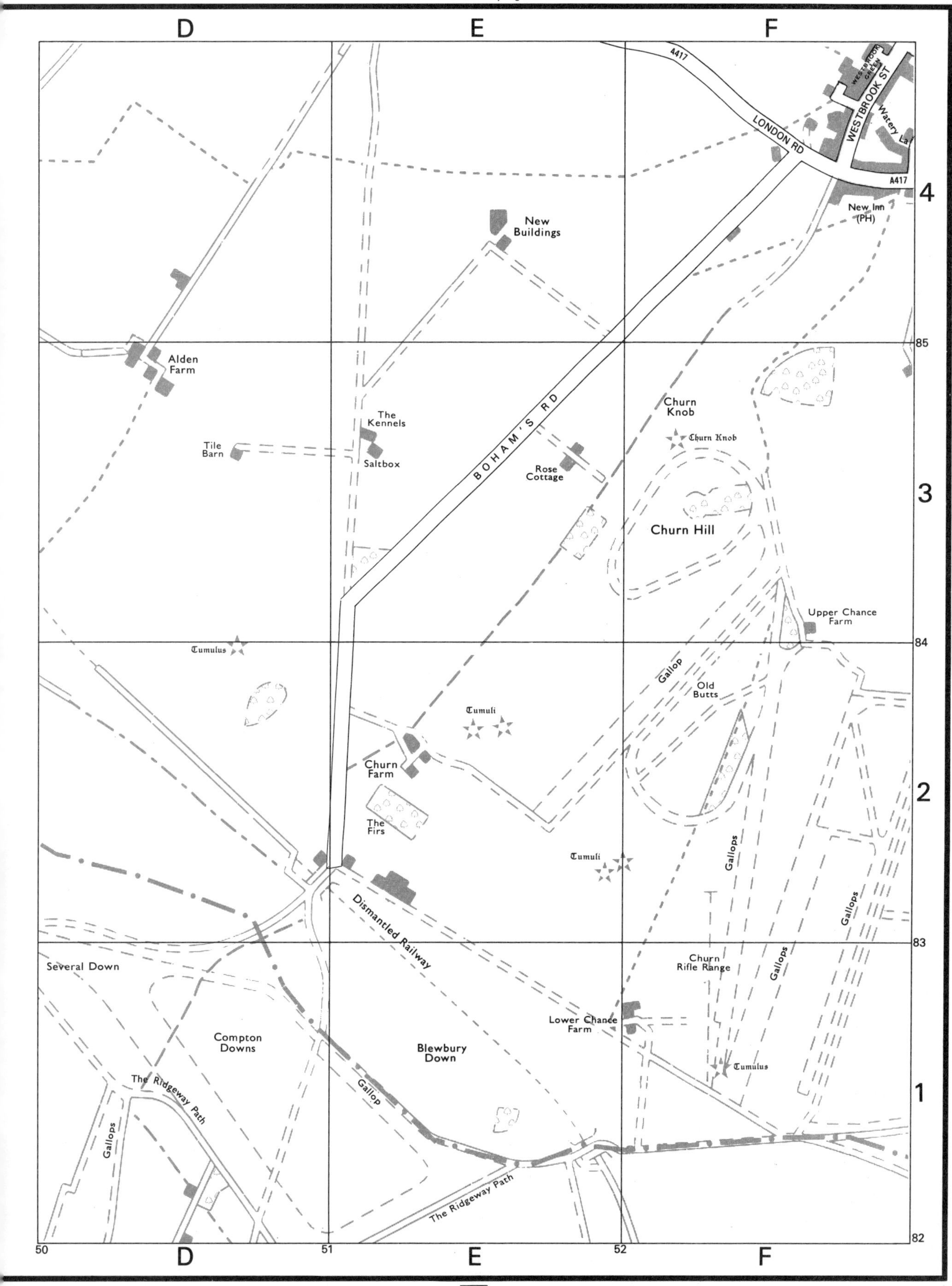

12

31

not continued, see key diagram

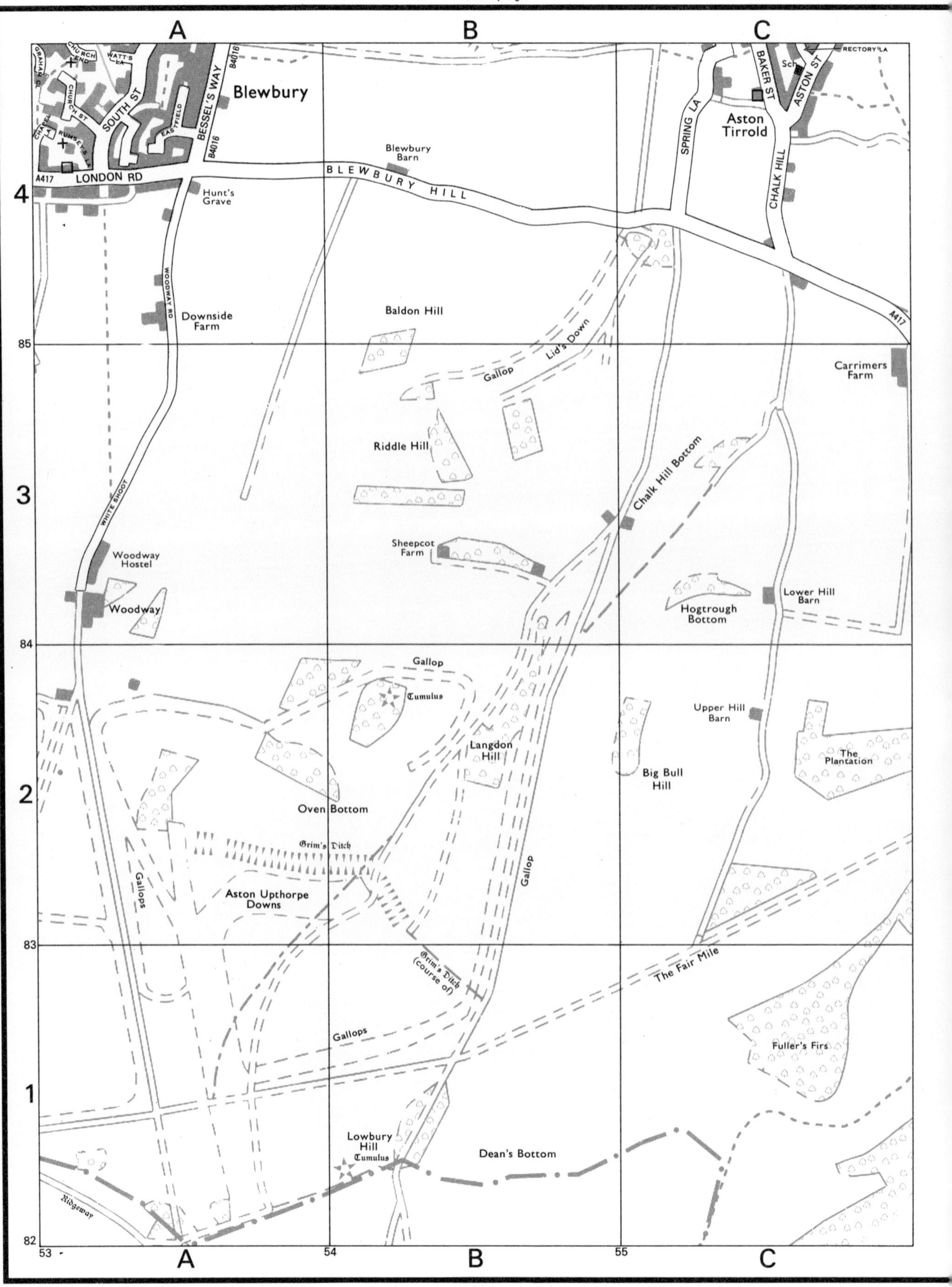

11

32

not continued, see key diagram

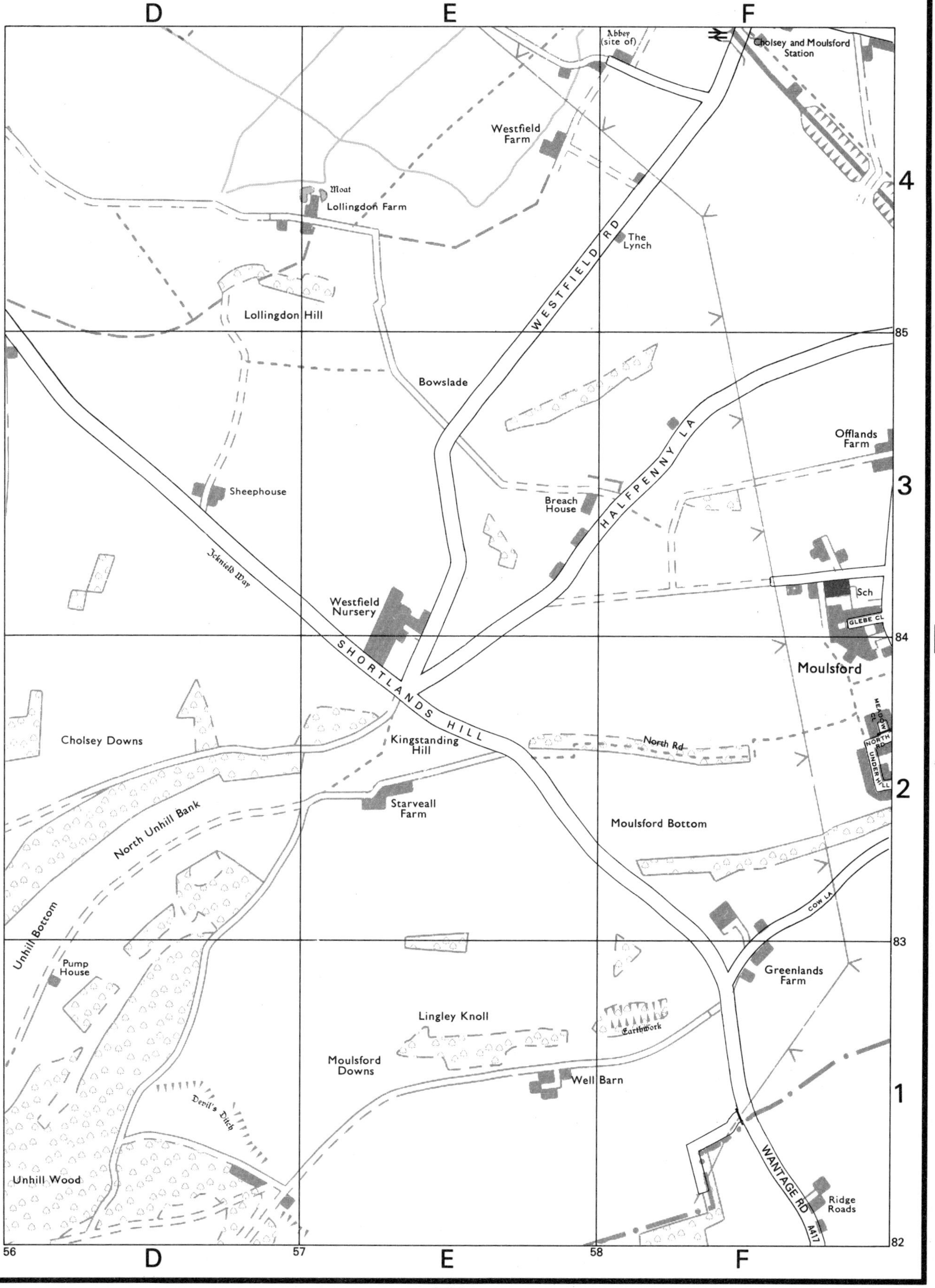

14

33

not continued, see key diagram

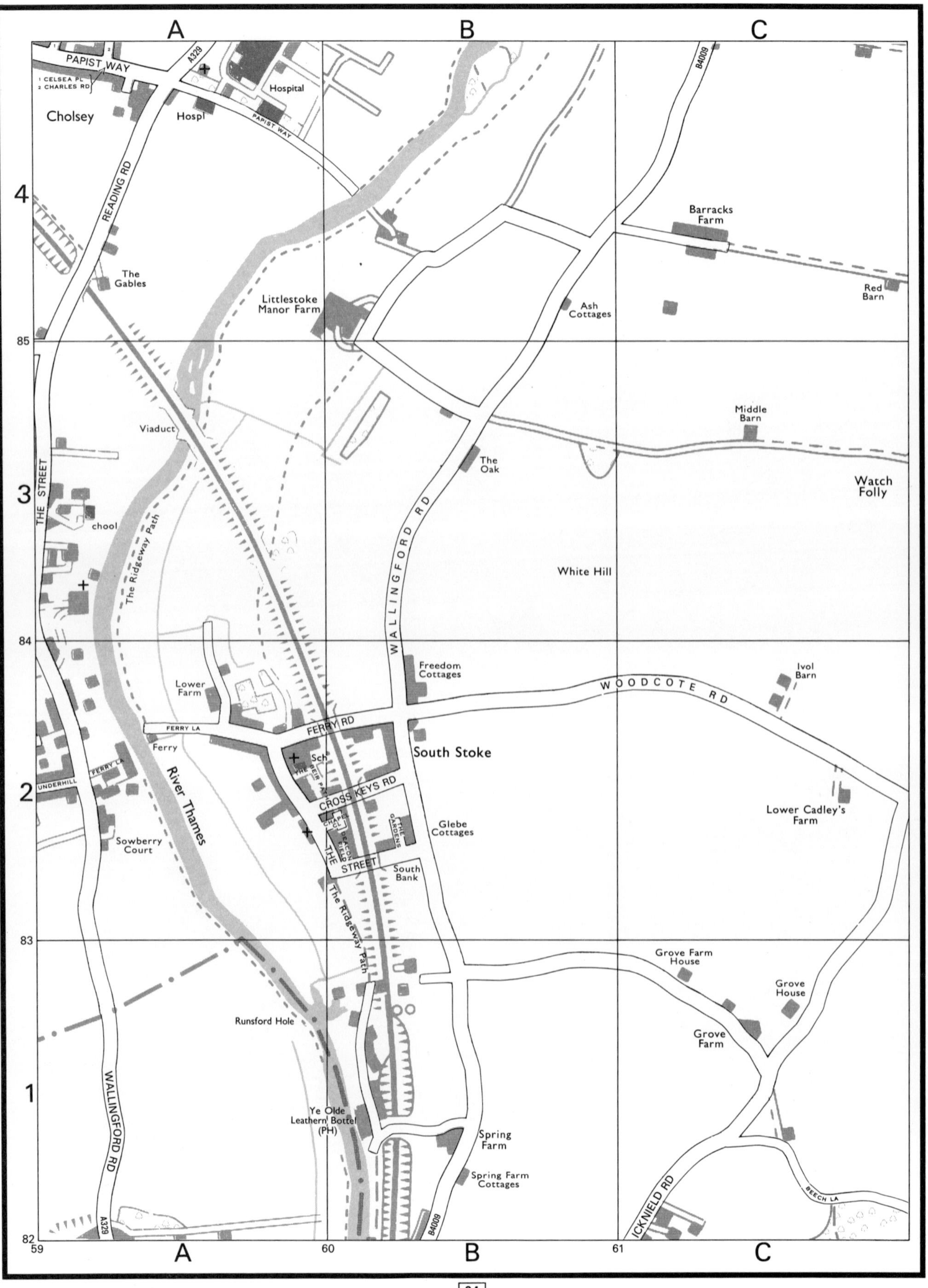

13

34

not continued, see key diagram

16

35

not continued, see key diagram

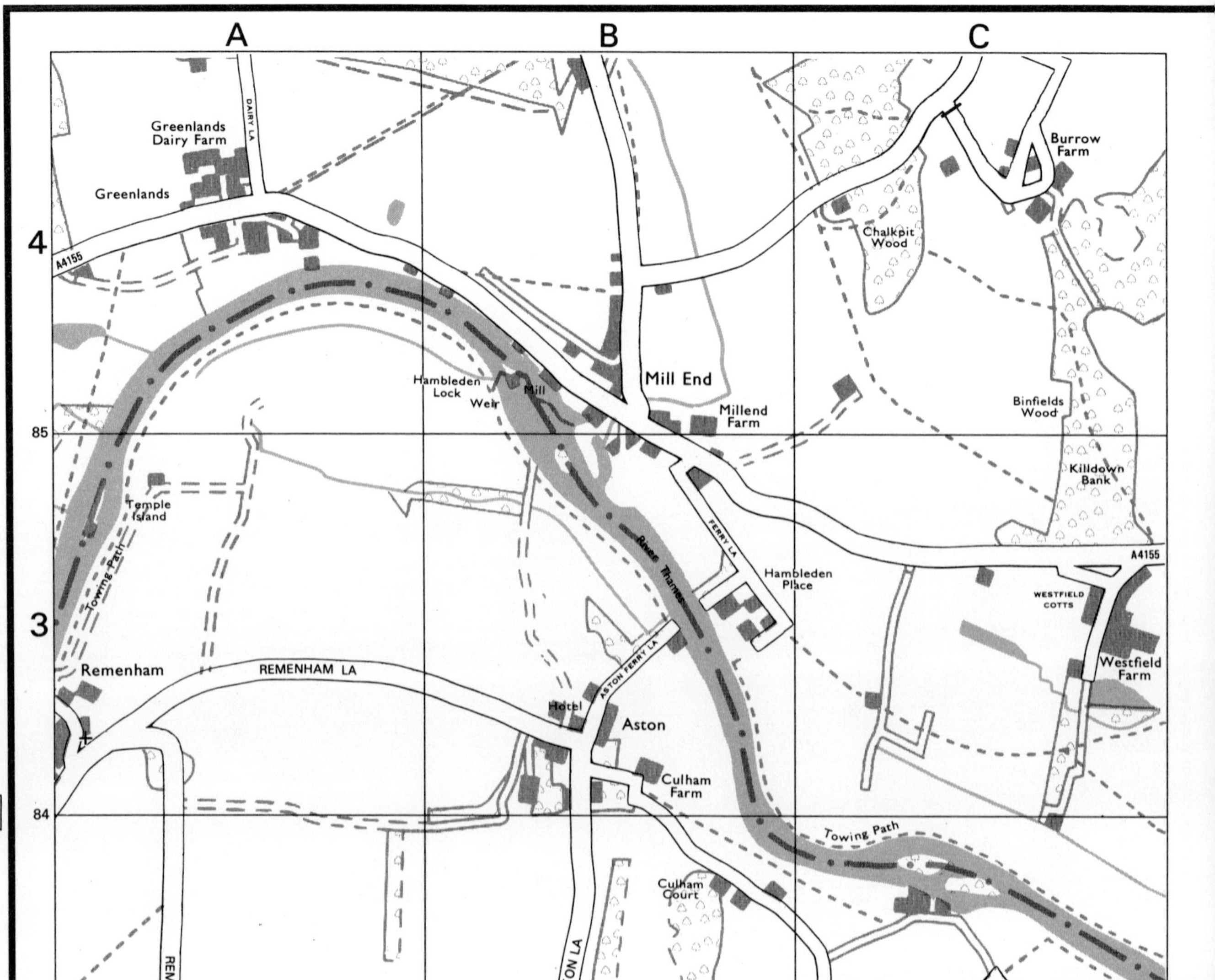

15

36

not continued, see key diagram

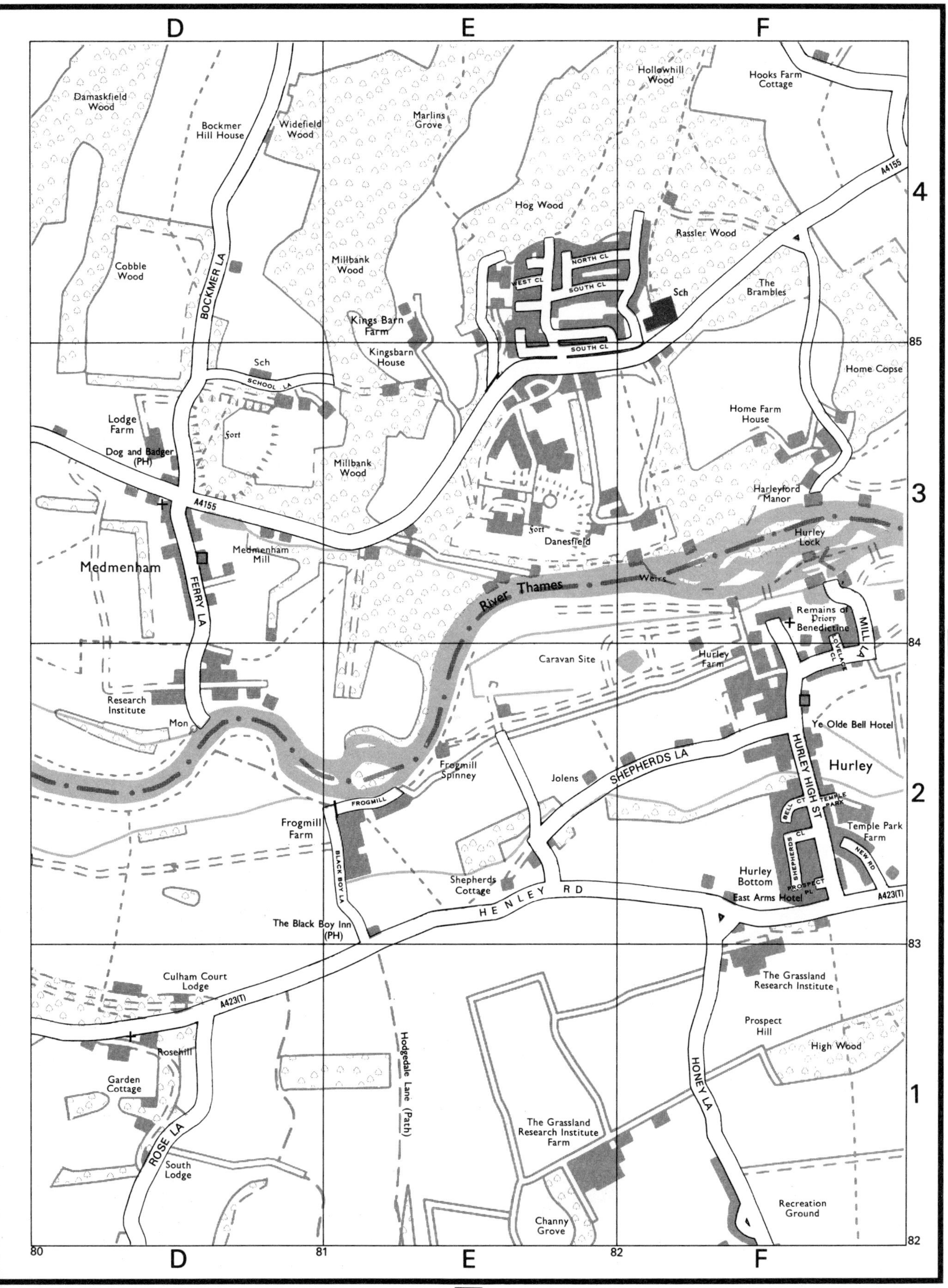

37

1

17

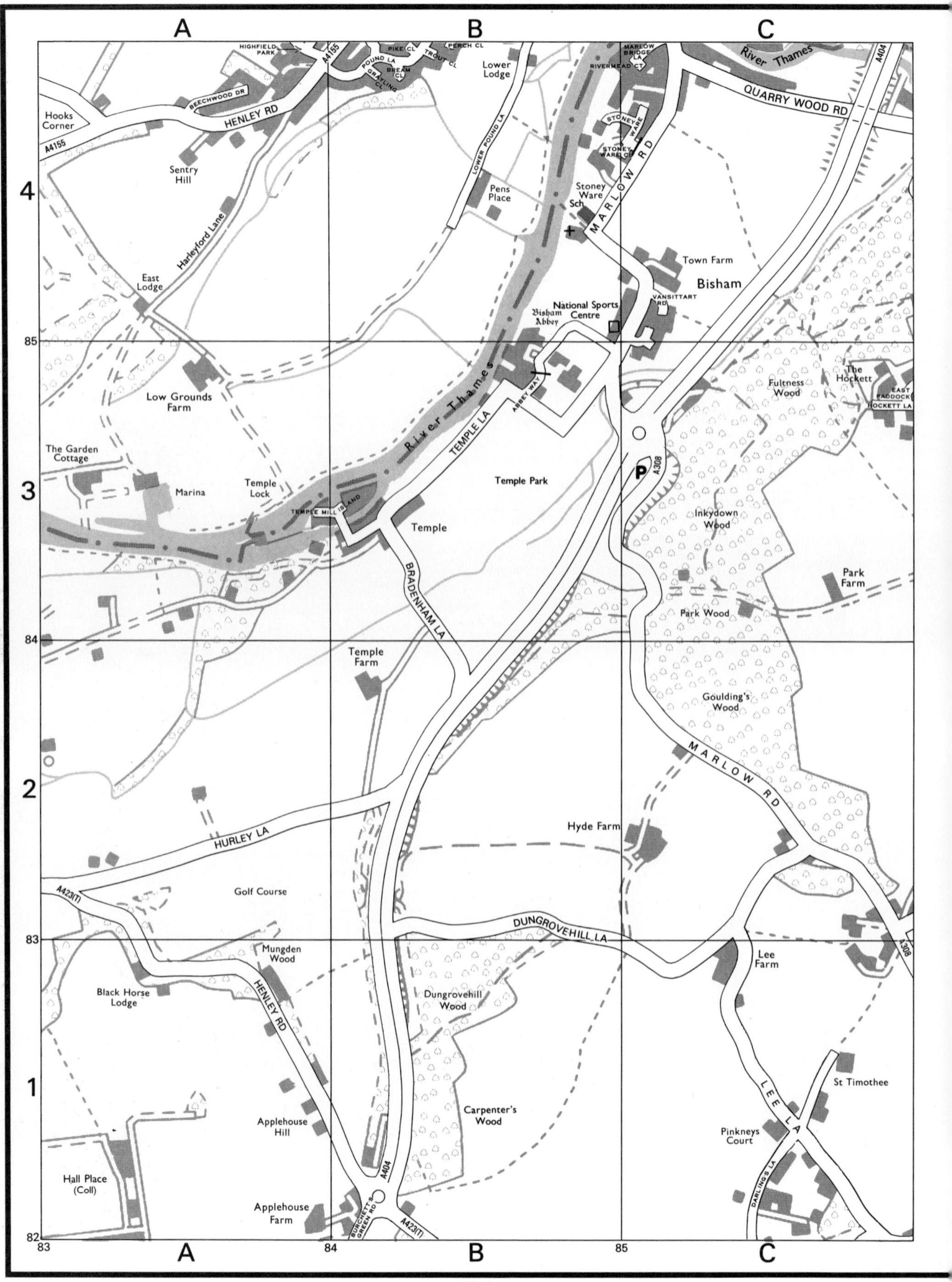
A
B
C
1
2
3
4
82
83
84
85
Hooks Corner
A4155
HIGHFIELD PARK
PIKE CL
PERCH CL
TROUT CL
POUND LA
BREAM CL
GRAYLING CL
BEECHWOOD DR
HENLEY RD
Sentry Hill
Harleyford Lane
East Lodge
Low Grounds Farm
The Garden Cottage
Marina
Temple Lock
TEMPLE MILL ISLAND
Temple
TEMPLE LA
River Thames
ABBEY WAY
Bisham Abbey
National Sports Centre
Lower Lodge
LOWER POUND LA
Pens Place
Stoney Ware
Sch
MARLOW BRIDGE LA
RIVERMEAD CT
STONEYWARE
STONEY WARE CL
MARLOW RD
Town Farm
Bisham
VANSITTART RD
QUARRY WOOD RD
A404
Fultness Wood
The Hockett
EAST PADDOCK
HOCKETT LA
A308
P
Temple Park
Inkydown Wood
Park Farm
Park Wood
BRADENHAM LA
Temple Farm
Goulding's Wood
HURLEY LA
Hyde Farm
Golf Course
A423(T)
DUNGROVEHILL LA
Mungden Wood
Black Horse Lodge
Dungrovehill Wood
Lee Farm
St Timothee
LEE LA
Carpenter's Wood
Applehouse Hill
Pinkneys Court
DARLINGS LA
Hall Place (Coll)
Applehouse Farm
BURCHETT'S GREEN RD
A423(T)

38

2

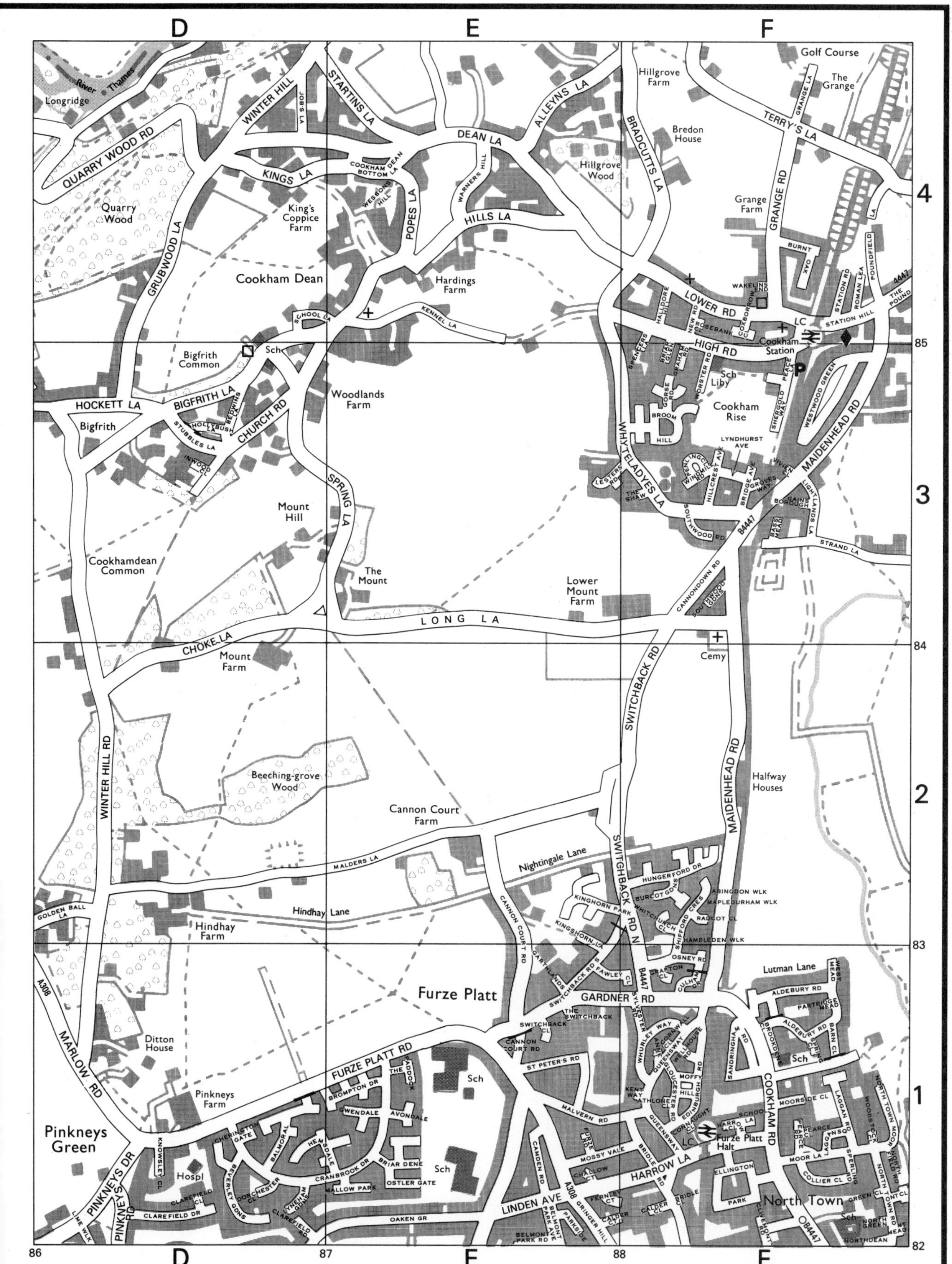
D
E
F
River Thames
Longridge
QUARRY WOOD RD
Quarry Wood
WINTER HILL
JOBS LA
STARTINS LA
ALLEYNS LA
DEAN LA
KINGS LA
COOKHAM DEAN BOTTOM LA
WESSONS HILL
WARNERS HILL
POPES LA
HILLS LA
King's Coppice Farm
Hillgrove Farm
Bredon House
Hillgrove Wood
BRADCUTTS LA
Golf Course
The Grange
GRANGE LA
TERRY'S LA
GRANGE RD
Grange Farm
BURNT OAK
STATION RD
ROMAN LEA
POUNDFIELD LA
THE POUND
STATION HILL
WAKELINS END
LOWER RD
HALLDORE HILL
NEW RD
COXBORROW CL
ROSEBANK CL
Cookham Station
LC
HIGH RD
GRUBWOOD LA
Cookham Dean
Hardings Farm
SCHOOL LA
KENNEL LA
Bigfrith Common
Sch
HOCKETT LA
Bigfrith
BIGFRITH LA
BEDWINS LA
HOLLYBUSH LA
STUBBLES LA
CHURCH RD
INWOOD CL
Woodlands Farm
SPENCERS RD
BRIAR GLEN
GRAHAM RD
GORSE RD
WORSTER RD
Sch
Liby
Cookham Rise
PEACE LA
SHERGOLD WAY
WESTWOOD GREEN
MAIDENHEAD RD
BROOM HILL
LYNDHURST AVE
WHYTELADYES LA
LESTERS RD
THE SHAW
PEARLINGS CL
WINDMILL RD
HILLCREST AVE
BRIDGE AVE
GROVES WAY
VIVIEN CL
LIGHTLANDS LA
GAINSBOROUGH
SOUTHWOOD RD
B4447
STRAND LA
SPRING LA
Mount Hill
Cookhamdean Common
The Mount
Lower Mount Farm
CANNONDOWN RD
SOUTHWOOD GDNS
LONG LA
CHOKE LA
Mount Farm
Cemy
SWITCHBACK RD
WINTER HILL RD
Beeching-grove Wood
MAIDENHEAD RD
Halfway Houses
Cannon Court Farm
MALDERS LA
Nightingale Lane
SWITCHBACK RD N
HUNGERFORD DR
BURCOT GDNS
ABINGDON WLK
MAPLEDURHAM WLK
KINGHORN PARK
WHITCHURCH CL
SHIFFORD CRES
RADCOT CL
Hindhay Lane
GOLDEN BALL LA
Hindhay Farm
CANNON COURT RD
KINGSHORN LA
HAMBLEDEN WLK
OSNEY RD
GARTHLANDS
SWITCHBACK RD S
FAWLEY CL
GRAFTON CL
CULHAM DR
Lutman Lane
WEST MEAD
ALDEBURY RD
PARTRIDGE MEAD
A308
Furze Platt
GARDNER RD
THE SWITCHBACK
SWITCHBACK CL
CANNON COURT RD
WHURLEY WAY
CORNWALL CL
QUEENSWAY
WELLHOUSE RD
SANDRINGHAM RD
BROOKDENE
BARN CL
MARLOW RD
Ditton House
FURZE PLATT RD
THE PADDOCK
Sch
ST PETER'S RD
MOFFY HILL
COOKHAM RD
Sch
MOORSIDE CL
LAGGAN RD
WOODSTOCK
NORTH TOWN MOOR
Pinkneys Farm
BROMPTON DR
GWENDALE
AVONDALE
MALVERN RD
KENT WAY
ATHLONE CL
GLOUCESTER RD
CONNAUGHT RD
HARROW LA
SCHOOL LA
Furze Platt Halt
PEARCE RD
LAGGAN SQ
Pinkneys Green
KNOWSLEY CL
CHERINGTON GATE
BALMORAL
HEMSDALE
CRANBROOK DR
BRIAR DENE
Sch
CAMDEN RD
MOSSY VALE
BRIDLE RD
ELLINGTON RD
MOOR LA
SPERLING RD
COLLIER CL
Hospl
PINKNEYS DR
PINKNEYS RD
CLAREFIELD RD
BEVERLEY GDNS
DORCHESTER CL
TYNEHAM GDNS
MALLOW PARK
OSTLER GATE
CHALLOW CT
FERNEY CT
BRIDLE CL
PARK
North Town
GREEN CL
NORTH TOWN CL
LIME WLK
CLAREFIELD DR
CLAREFIELD CL
OAKEN GR
LINDEN AVE
BELMONT PARK AVE
PARKSIDE
GRINGER HILL
CALDER CT
CALDER CL
CLIVEMONT RD
B4447
NORTH GREEN
NORTHDEAN
BELMONT PARK RD
4
85
3
84
2
83
1
82
86
87
88
D
E
F

20

39

3

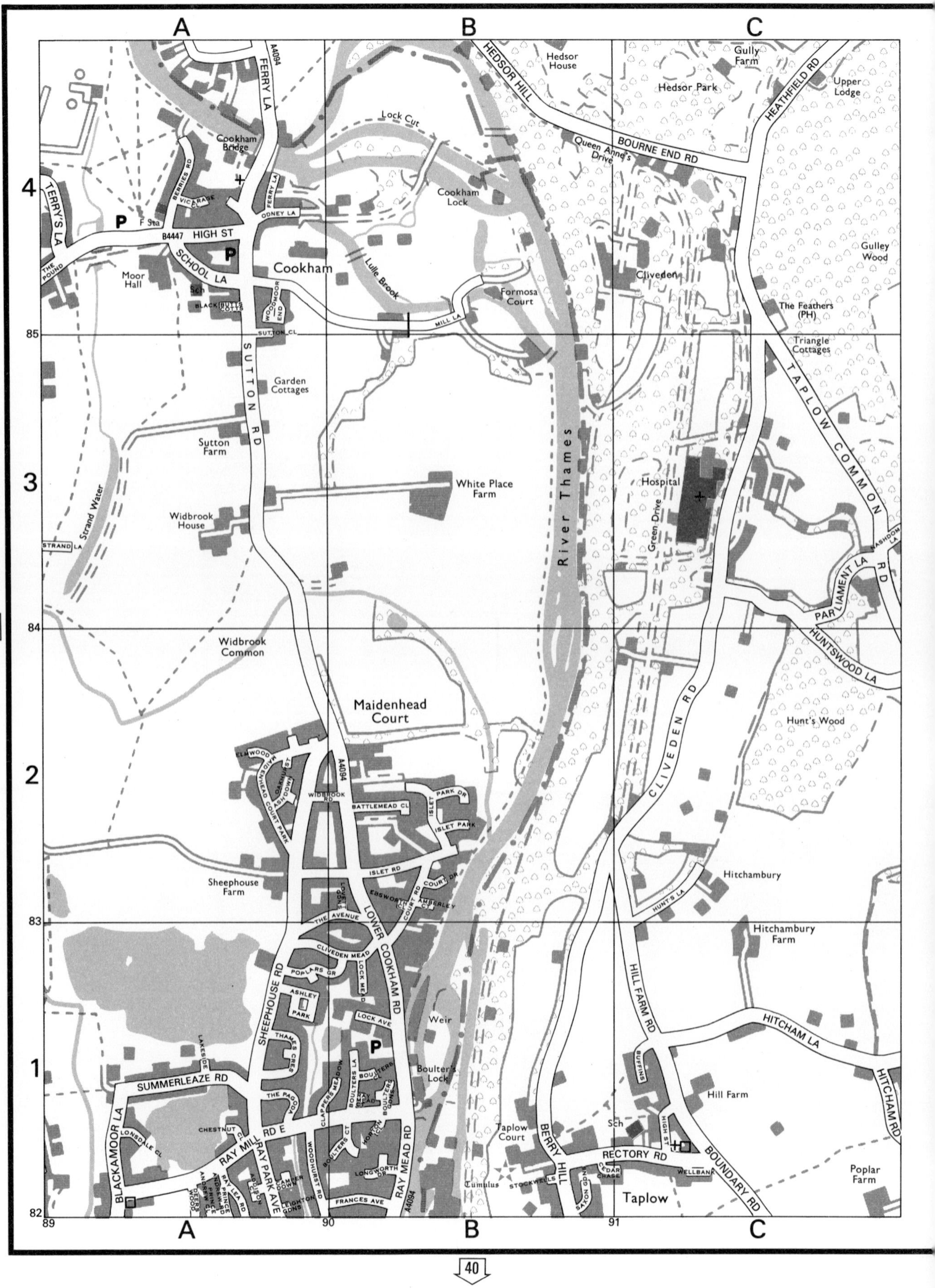
A
B
C
4
3
2
1
85
84
83
82
89
90
91
Cookham Bridge
Cookham
Hedsor House
Hedsor Park
Gully Farm
Upper Lodge
HEDSOR HILL
HEATHFIELD RD
BOURNE END RD
Queen Anne's Drive
Lock Cut
Cookham Lock
Lulle Brook
Formosa Court
MILL LA
Cliveden
Gulley Wood
The Feathers (PH)
Triangle Cottages
TAPLOW COMMON
FERRY LA
A4094
BERRIES RD
VICARAGE
ODNEY LA
TERRY'S LA
F Sta
B4447
HIGH ST
THE POUND
SCHOOL LA
Moor Hall
Sch
BLACK BUTTS COTTS
WOODMOOR END
SUTTON CL
SUTTON RD
Garden Cottages
Sutton Farm
Strand Water
STRAND LA
Widbrook House
White Place Farm
River Thames
Hospital
Green Drive
NASHDOM LA
PARLIAMENT LA
RD
HUNTSWOOD LA
Widbrook Common
Maidenhead Court
Hunt's Wood
CLIVEDEN RD
ELMWOOD
MAIDENHEAD COURT PARK
OAKHURST
ASHDOWN
WIDBROOK RD
BATTLEMEAD CL
ISLET PARK DR
ISLET PARK
ISLET RD
COURT DR
COURT RD
EBSWORTH CL
AMBERLEY CT
Sheephouse Farm
Hitchambury
HUNT'S LA
Hitchambury Farm
LOVETT GDNS
THE AVENUE
LOWER COOKHAM RD
CLIVEDEN MEAD
POPLARS GR
LOCK MEAD
ASHLEY PARK
SHEEPHOUSE RD
THAMES CRES
LOCK AVE
Weir
Boulter's Lock
HILL FARM RD
HITCHAM LA
BUFFINS
Hill Farm
HITCHAM RD
LAKESIDE
SUMMERLEAZE RD
THE PAGODA
CLAPPERS MEADOW
BOULTERS LA
BOULTERS CT
CHESTNUT CL
RAY MILL RD E
RAY PARK AVE
WOODHURST RD
HORTON CL
RAY MEAD RD
LONGWORTH DR
FRANCES AVE
LEIGHTON GDNS
BLACKAMOOR LA
LONSDALE CL
DEERSWOOD
RAY LEA RD
Taplow Court
Sch
BERRY HILL
RECTORY RD
HIGH ST
Tumulus
STOCKWELLS
CEDAR CHASE
SAXON GDNS
WELLBANK
BOUNDARY RD
Taplow
Poplar Farm

19

40

not continued, see key diagram

22

41

not continued, see key diagram

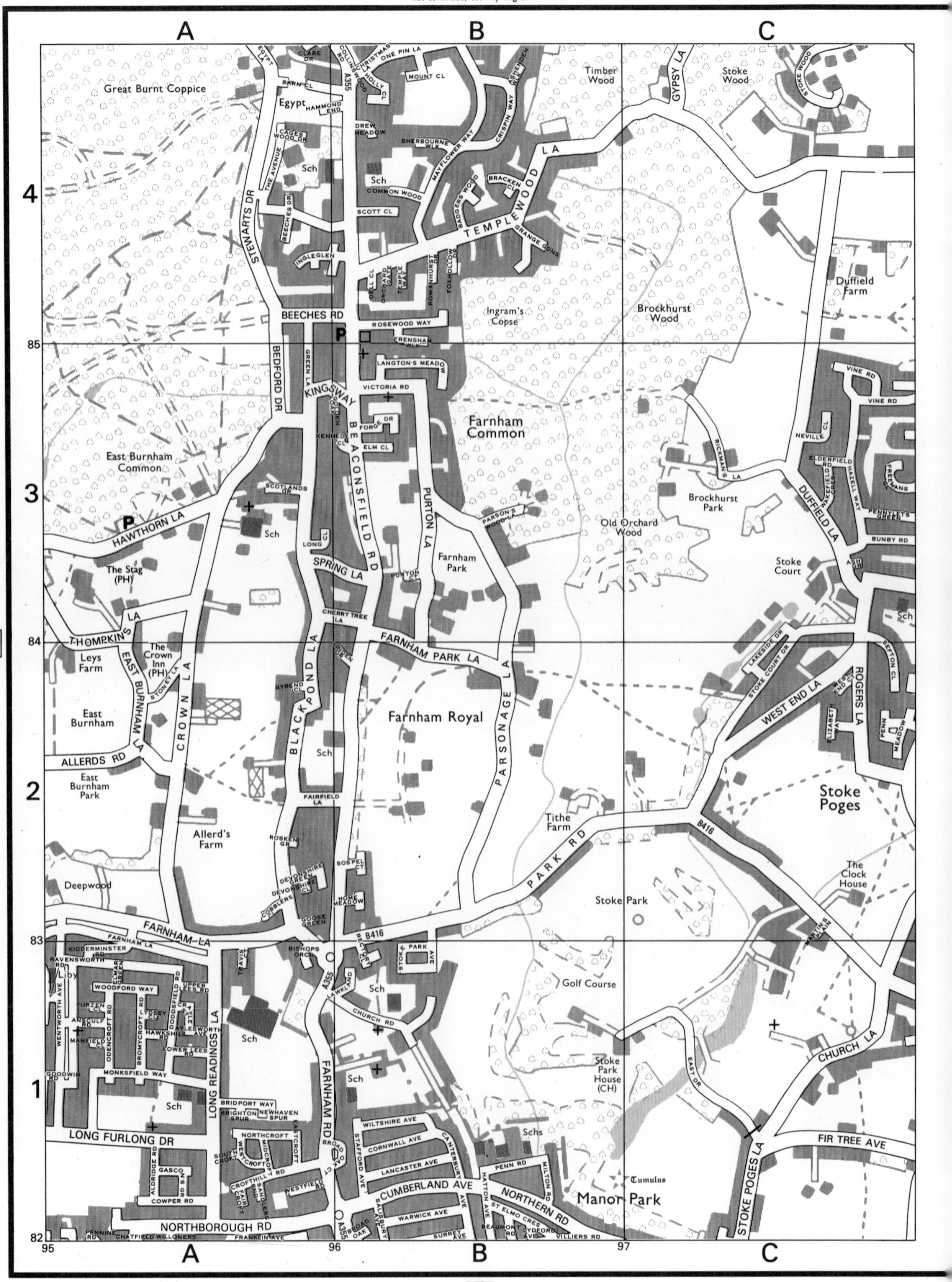

21

42

not continued, see key diagram

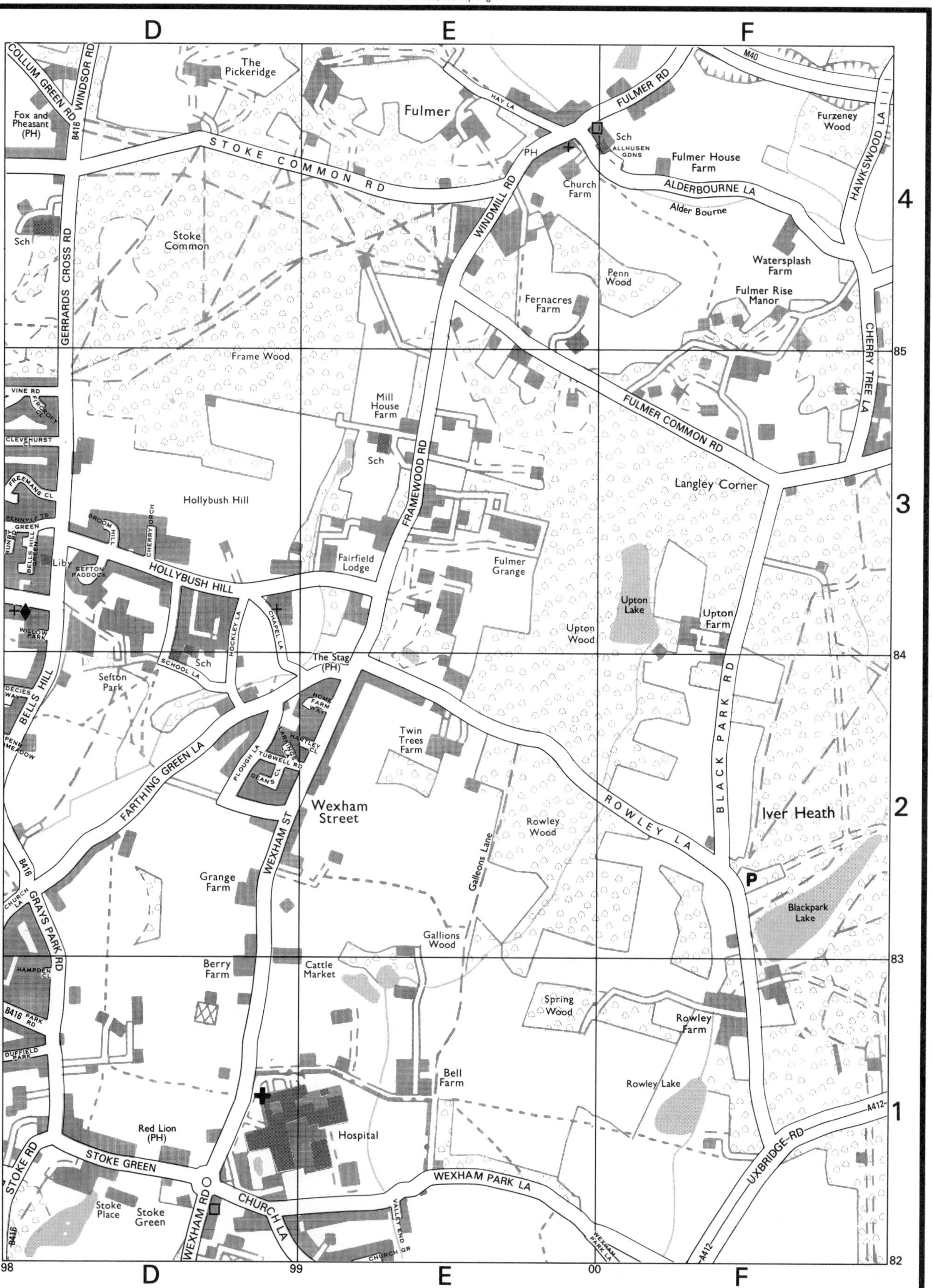

not continued, see key diagram

4

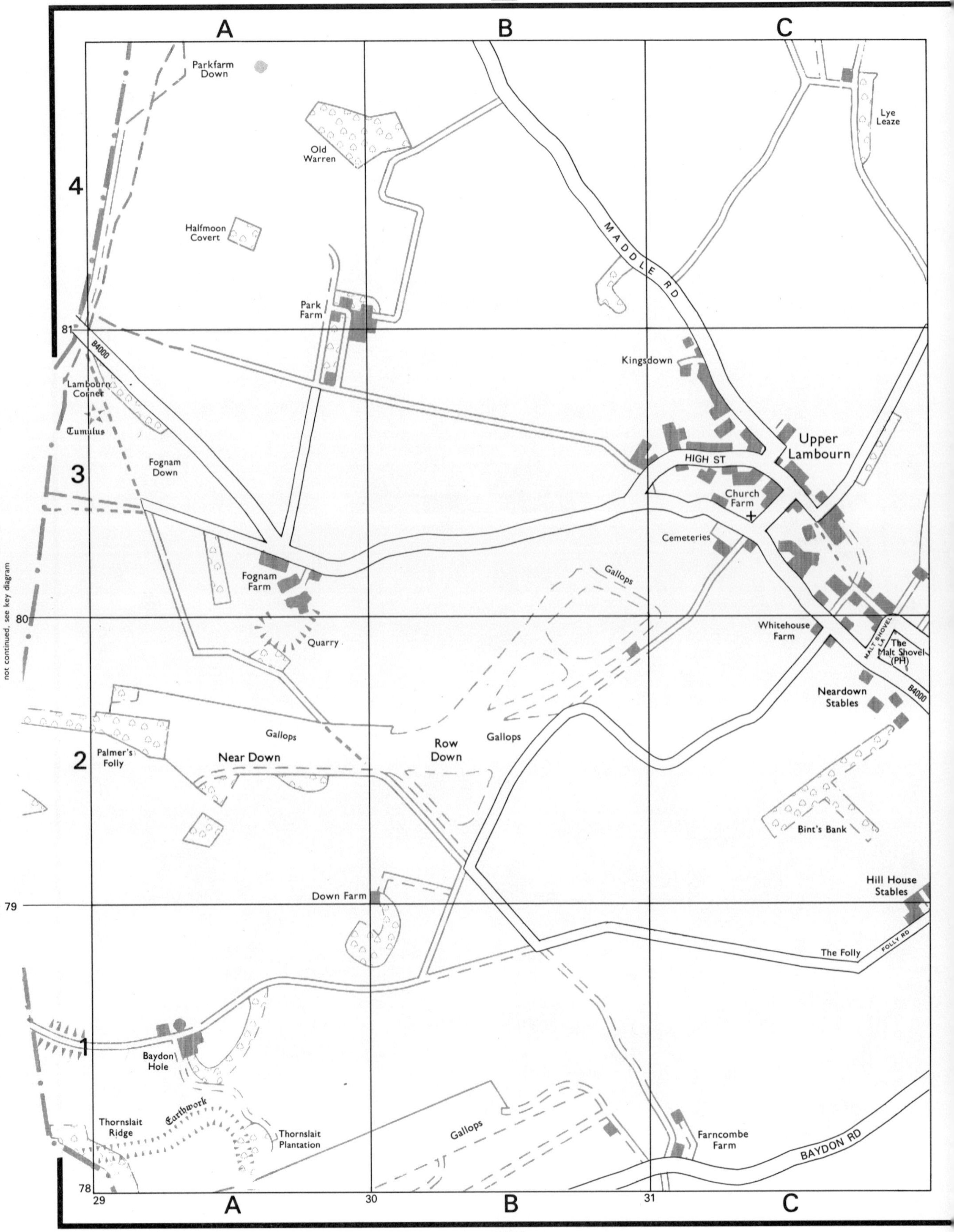
A
B
C
4
3
2
1
81
80
79
78
29
30
31
Parkfarm Down
Old Warren
Halfmoon Covert
Park Farm
MADDLE RD
Lye Leaze
Kingsdown
Upper Lambourn
HIGH ST
Church Farm
Cemeteries
B4000
Lambourn Corner
Tumulus
Fognam Down
Fognam Farm
Quarry
Gallops
Whitehouse Farm
MALT SHOVEL LA
The Malt Shovel (PH)
Neardown Stables
Palmer's Folly
Near Down
Row Down
Bint's Bank
Hill House Stables
Down Farm
The Folly
FOLLY RD
Baydon Hole
Earthwork
Thornslait Ridge
Thornslait Plantation
Farncombe Farm
BAYDON RD
not continued, see key diagram

45

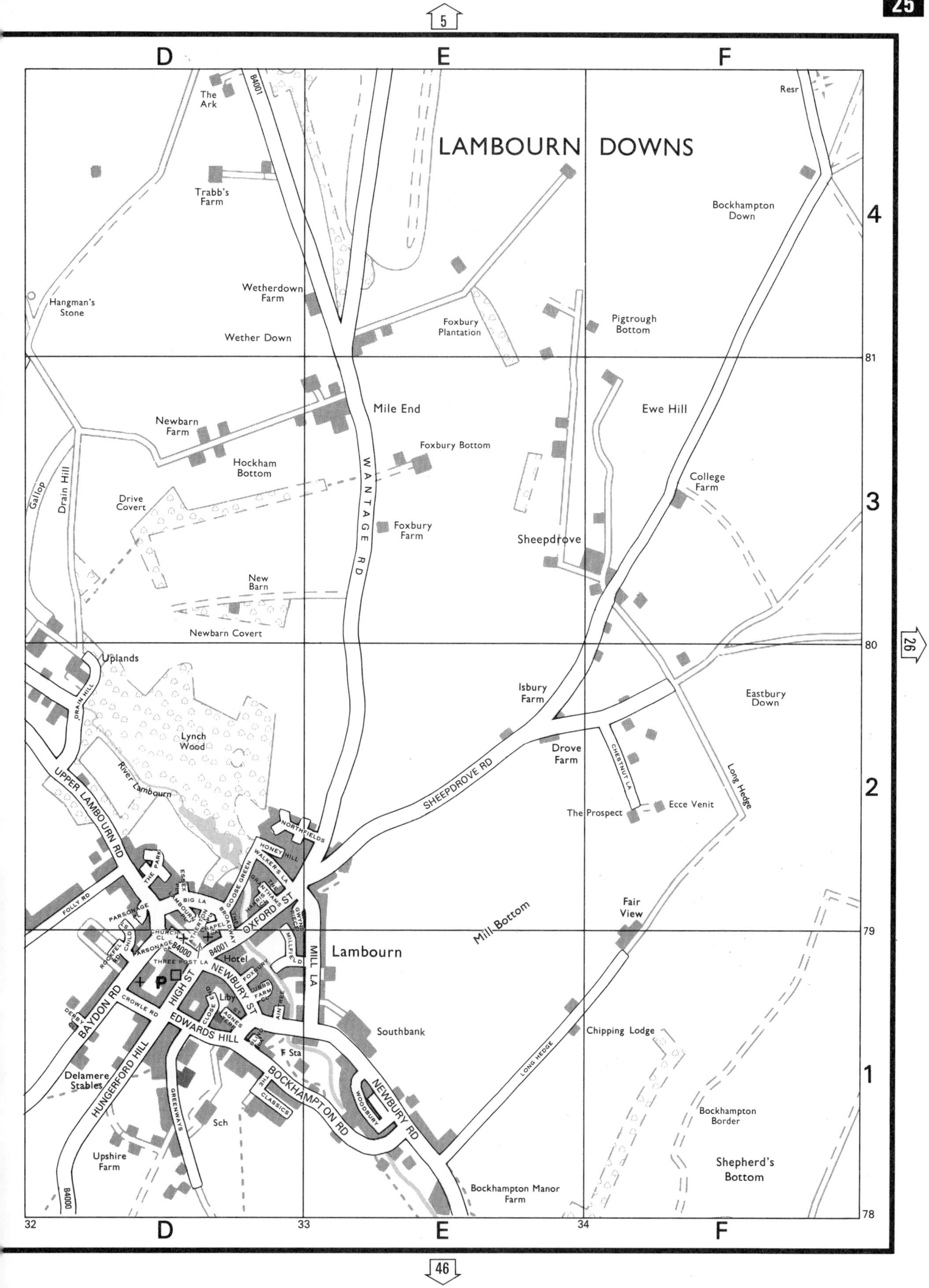
5
D
E
F
LAMBOURN DOWNS
B4001
The Ark
Trabb's Farm
Resr
Bockhampton Down
4
Wetherdown Farm
Hangman's Stone
Wether Down
Foxbury Plantation
Pigtrough Bottom
81
Mile End
Ewe Hill
Newbarn Farm
Foxbury Bottom
Hockham Bottom
WANTAGE RD
College Farm
Gallop
Drain Hill
Drive Covert
3
Foxbury Farm
Sheepdrove
New Barn
Newbarn Covert
80
26
Uplands
Isbury Farm
Eastbury Down
DRAIN HILL
Lynch Wood
Drove Farm
CHESTNUT LA
Long Hedge
UPPER LAMBOURN RD
River Lambourn
SHEEPDROVE RD
2
The Prospect
Ecce Venit
NORTHFIELDS
HONEY HILL
WALKER'S LA
THE PARK
GOOSE GREEN
BROADWAY
ESSEX
BIG LA
OXFORD ST
FOLLY RD
PARSONAGE PL
CHURCH CL
CHAPEL
B4000
B4001
Mill Bottom
Fair View
79
MILL LA
Lambourn
PARSONAGE LA
THREE POST LA
Hotel
NEWBURY ST
HIGH ST
BAYDON RD
CROWLE RD
DERBY
Liby
EDWARDS HILL
FOXBURY
Southbank
Chipping Lodge
F Sta
HUNGERFORD HILL
Delamere Stables
1
BOCKHAMPTON RD
NEWBURY RD
WOODBURY
THE CLASSICS
LONG HEDGE
GREENWAYS
Sch
Bockhampton Border
Upshire Farm
Shepherd's Bottom
Bockhampton Manor Farm
B4000
32
33
34
78
D
E
F
46

6

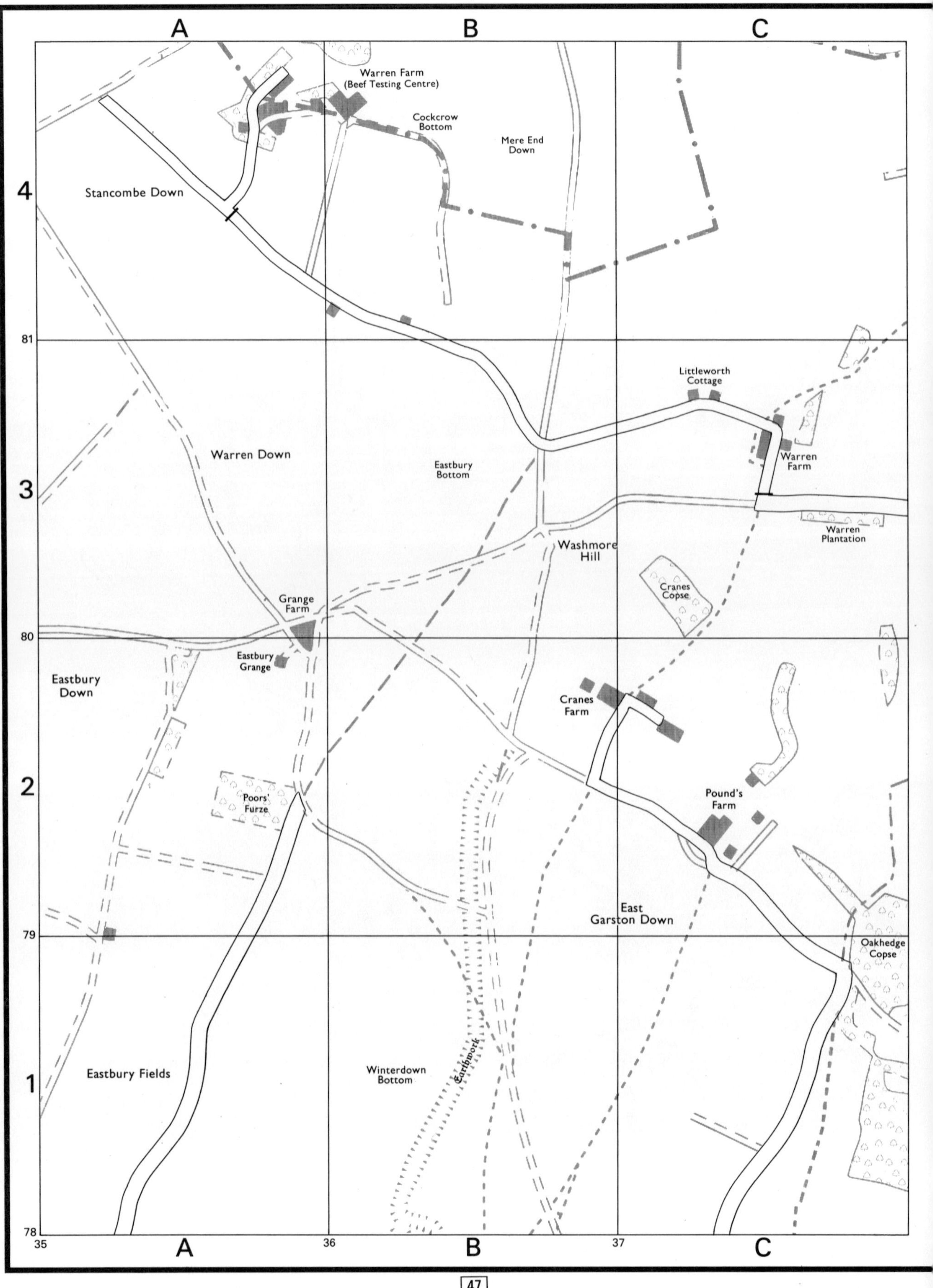
A
B
C
Warren Farm
(Beef Testing Centre)
Cockcrow
Bottom
Mere End
Down
Stancombe Down
4
81
Littleworth
Cottage
Warren Down
Eastbury
Bottom
Warren
Farm
3
Warren
Plantation
Washmore
Hill
Cranes
Copse
Grange
Farm
80
Eastbury
Grange
Eastbury
Down
Cranes
Farm
2
Poors'
Furze
Pound's
Farm
East
Garston Down
79
Oakhedge
Copse
Earthwork
1
Eastbury Fields
Winterdown
Bottom
78
35
36
37
A
B
C

25

47

7

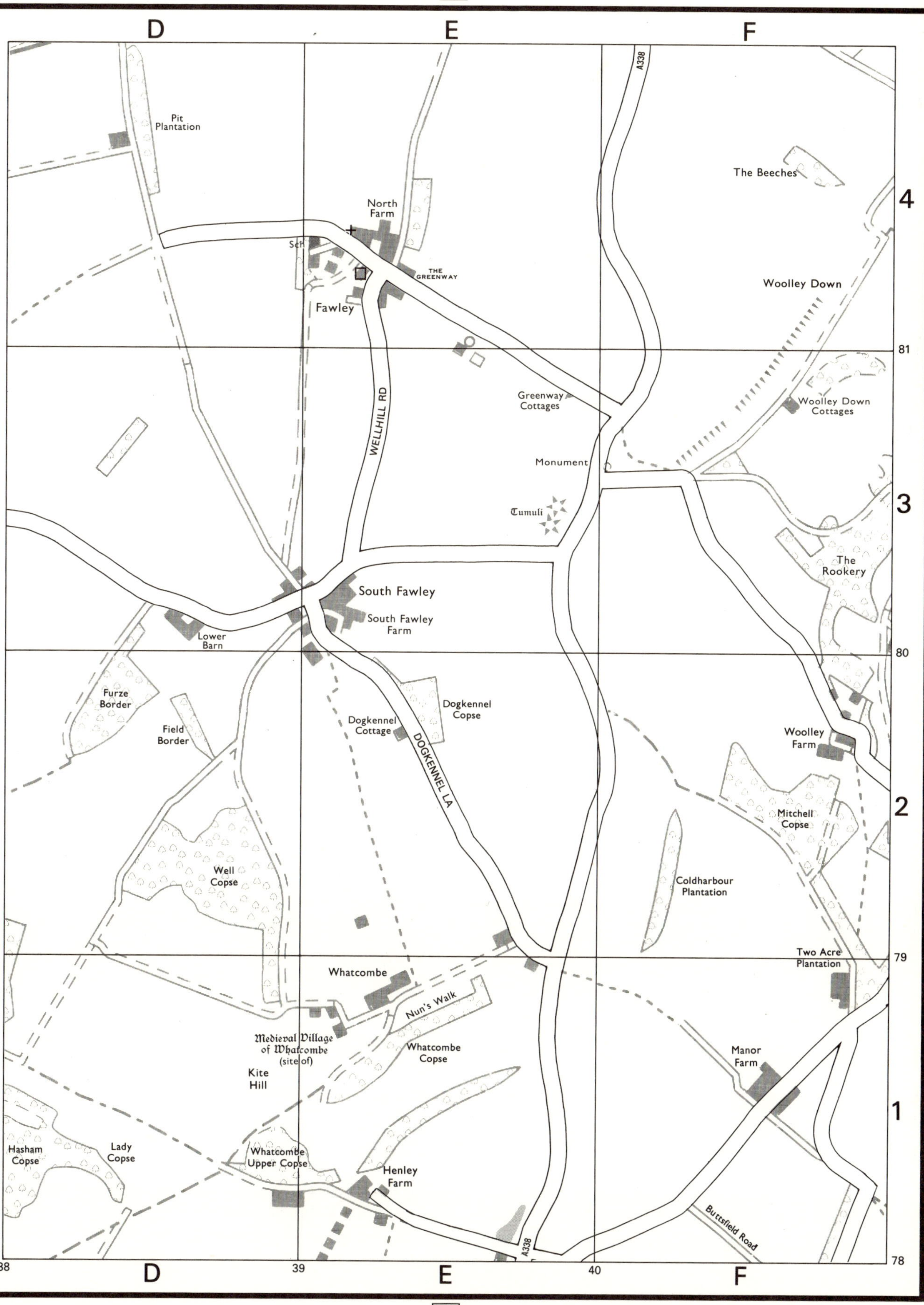
D
E
F
A338
Pit Plantation
The Beeches
North Farm
Sch
THE GREENWAY
Fawley
Woolley Down
4
81
WELLHILL RD
Greenway Cottages
Woolley Down Cottages
Monument
Tumuli
3
South Fawley
South Fawley Farm
The Rookery
Lower Barn
80
Furze Border
Dogkennel Copse
Dogkennel Cottage
Field Border
DOGKENNEL LA
Woolley Farm
2
Mitchell Copse
Well Copse
Coldharbour Plantation
Two Acre Plantation
79
Whatcombe
Nun's Walk
Medieval Village of Whatcombe (site of)
Whatcombe Copse
Kite Hill
Manor Farm
1
Hasham Copse
Lady Copse
Whatcombe Upper Copse
Henley Farm
Buttsfield Road
A338
38
39
40
78
D
E
F

28

48

8

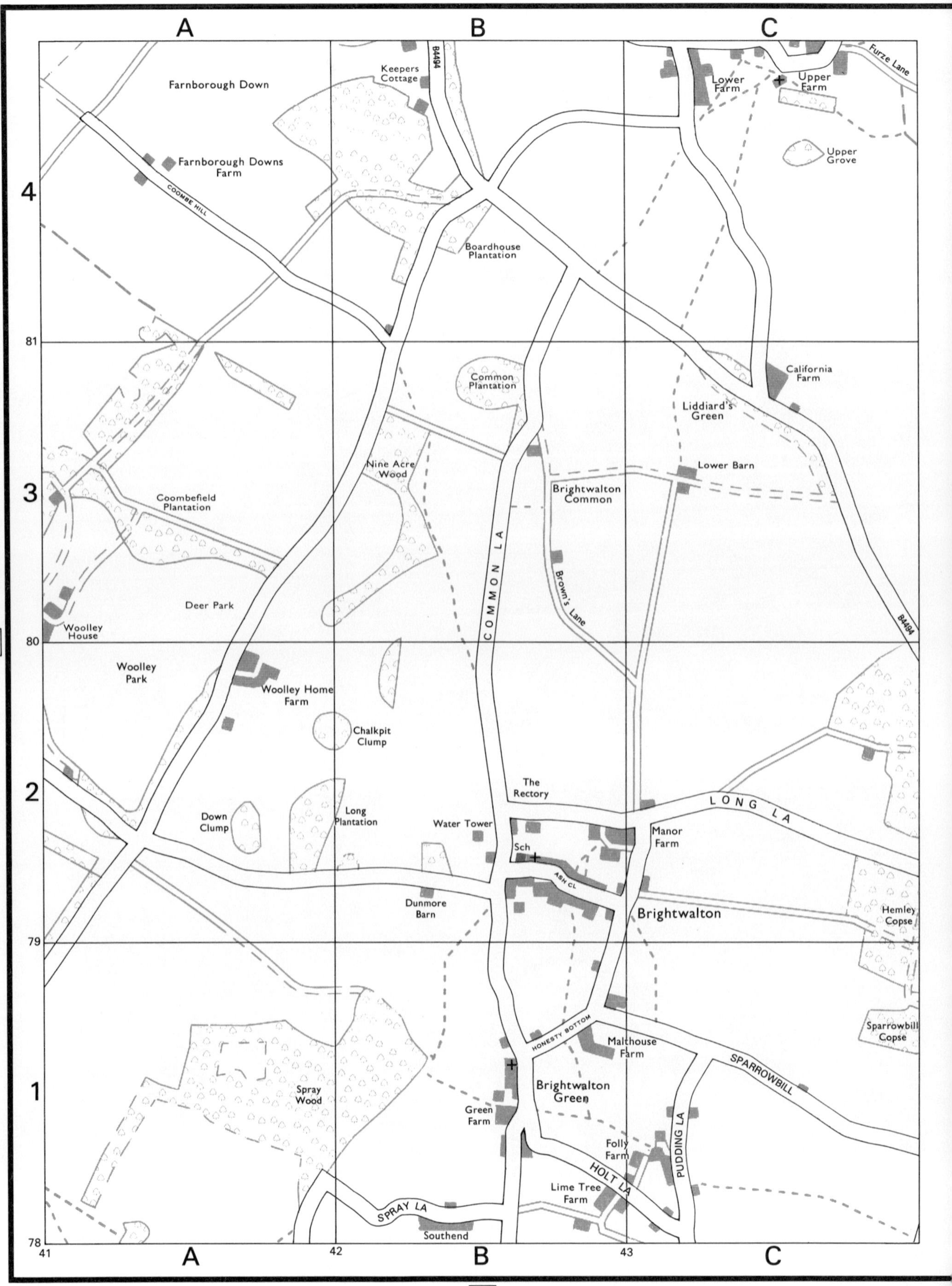
A
B
C
Farnborough Down
Keepers Cottage
B4494
Lower Farm
Upper Farm
Furze Lane
Farnborough Downs Farm
COOMBE HILL
Upper Grove
Boardhouse Plantation
Common Plantation
California Farm
Liddiard's Green
Nine Acre Wood
Lower Barn
Coombefield Plantation
Brightwalton Common
COMMON LA
Brown's Lane
Deer Park
Woolley House
B4494
Woolley Park
Woolley Home Farm
Chalkpit Clump
The Rectory
LONG LA
Down Clump
Long Plantation
Water Tower
Manor Farm
Sch
ASH CL
Dunmore Barn
Brightwalton
Hemley Copse
Sparrowbill Copse
HONESTY BOTTOM
Malthouse Farm
SPARROWBILL
Spray Wood
Brightwalton Green
Green Farm
PUDDING LA
Folly Farm
HOLT LA
Lime Tree Farm
SPRAY LA
Southend
4
3
2
1
81
80
79
78
41
42
43
A
B
C

27

49

9

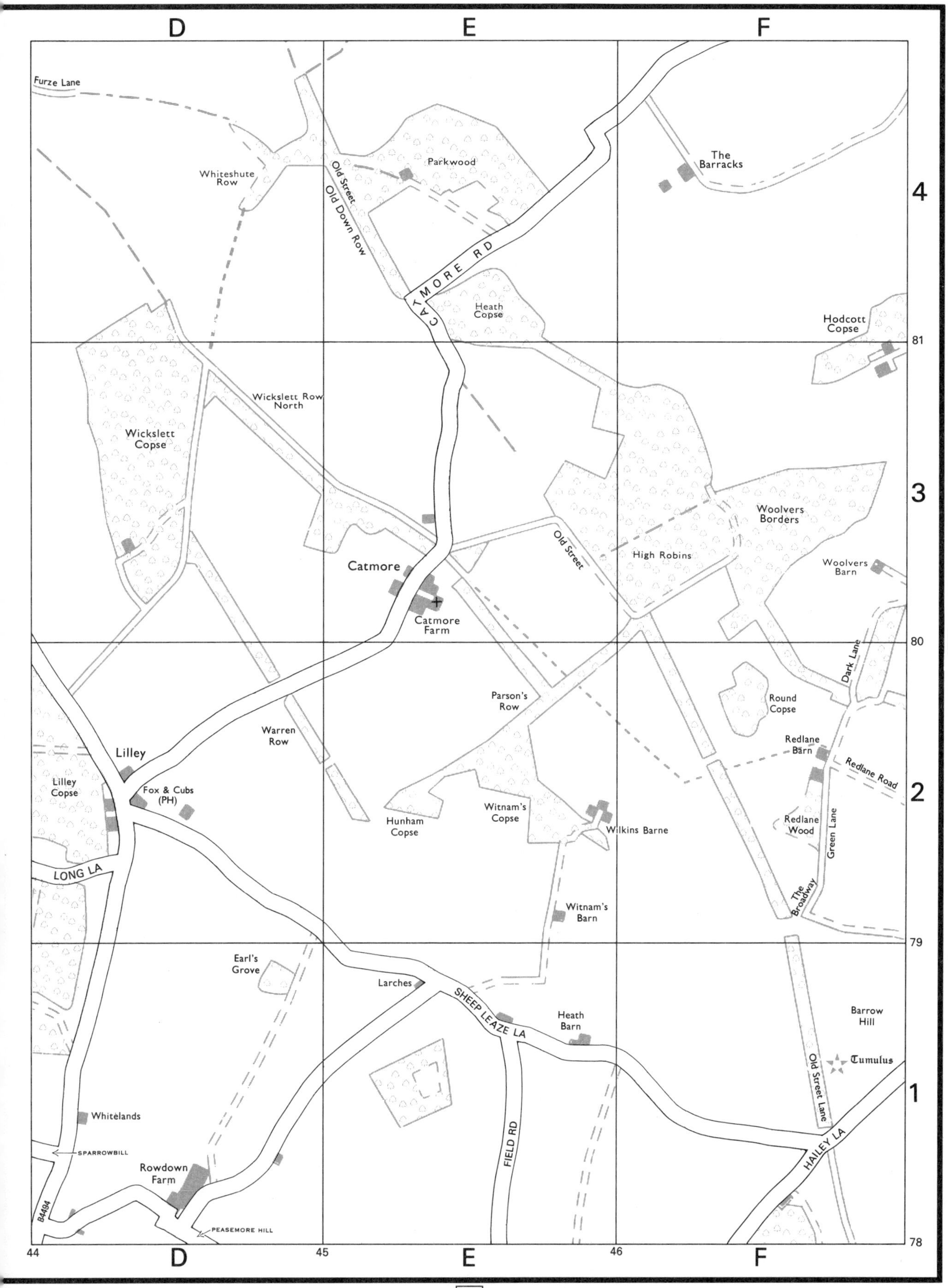
D
E
F
Furze Lane
Whiteshute Row
Parkwood
Old Street
Old Down Row
The Barracks
CATMORE RD
Heath Copse
Hodcott Copse
Wickslett Row North
Wickslett Copse
Woolvers Borders
Old Street
High Robins
Woolvers Barn
Catmore
Catmore Farm
Dark Lane
Parson's Row
Round Copse
Warren Row
Redlane Barn
Redlane Road
Lilley
Lilley Copse
Fox & Cubs (PH)
Witnam's Copse
Hunham Copse
Wilkins Barne
Redlane Wood
Green Lane
LONG LA
The Broadway
Witnam's Barn
Earl's Grove
Larches
SHEEP LEAZE LA
Heath Barn
Barrow Hill
Tumulus
Old Street Lane
Whitelands
FIELD RD
HAILEY LA
SPARROWBILL
Rowdown Farm
B4494
PEASEMORE HILL
4
3
2
1
81
80
79
78
44
45
46
D
E
F

30

50

10

29

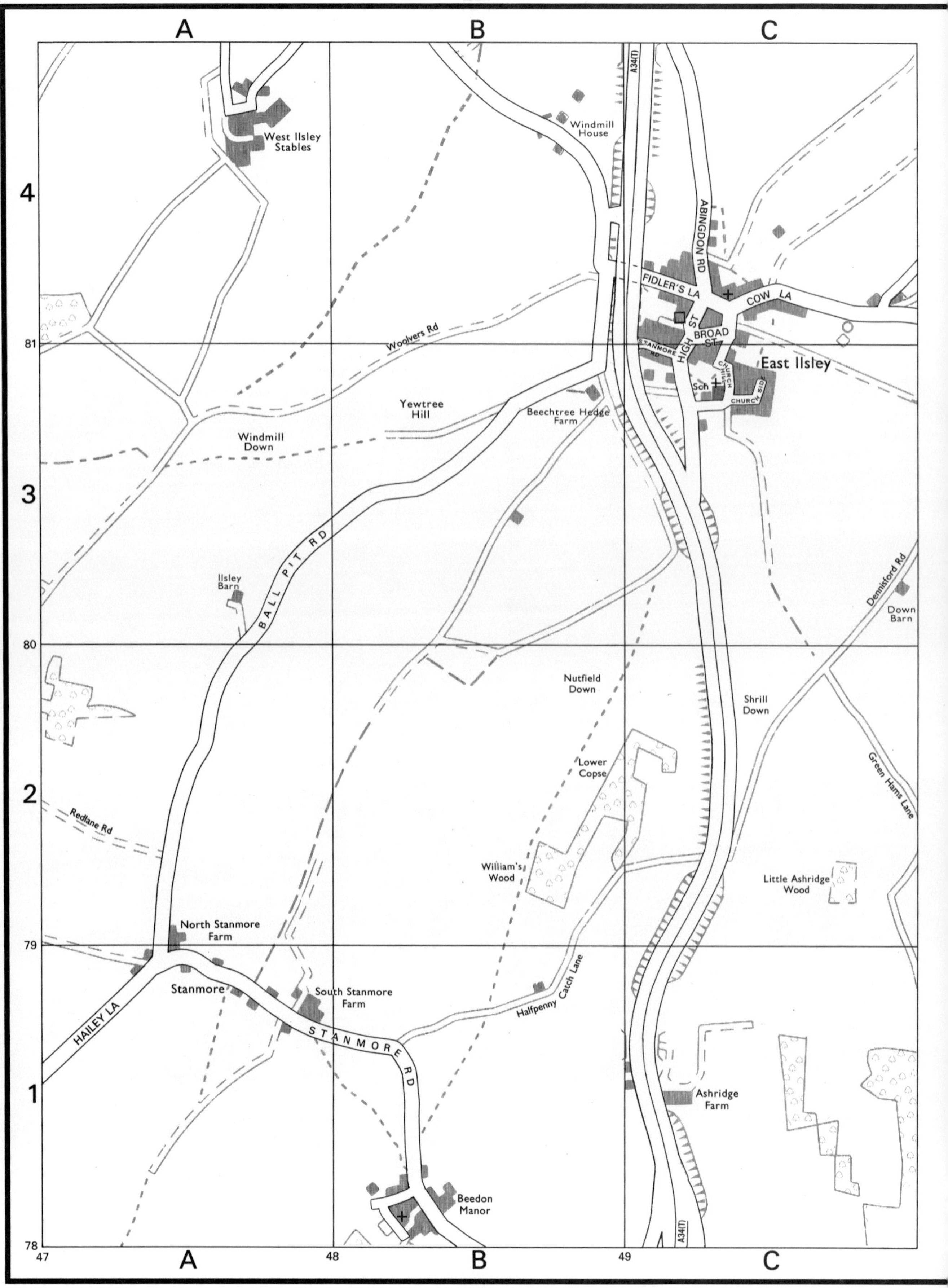
A
B
C
4
3
2
1
81
80
79
78
47
48
49
A34(T)
West Ilsley Stables
Windmill House
ABINGDON RD
FIDLER'S LA
COW LA
HIGH ST
BROAD ST
STANMORE RD
CHURCH
CHURCH SIDE
Sch
East Ilsley
Woolvers Rd
Yewtree Hill
Beechtree Hedge Farm
Windmill Down
BALL PIT RD
Ilsley Barn
Dennisford Rd
Down Barn
Nutfield Down
Shrill Down
Lower Copse
Green Hams Lane
Redlane Rd
William's Wood
Little Ashridge Wood
North Stanmore Farm
Stanmore
South Stanmore Farm
HAILEY LA
STANMORE RD
Halfpenny Catch Lane
Ashridge Farm
Beedon Manor

51

11

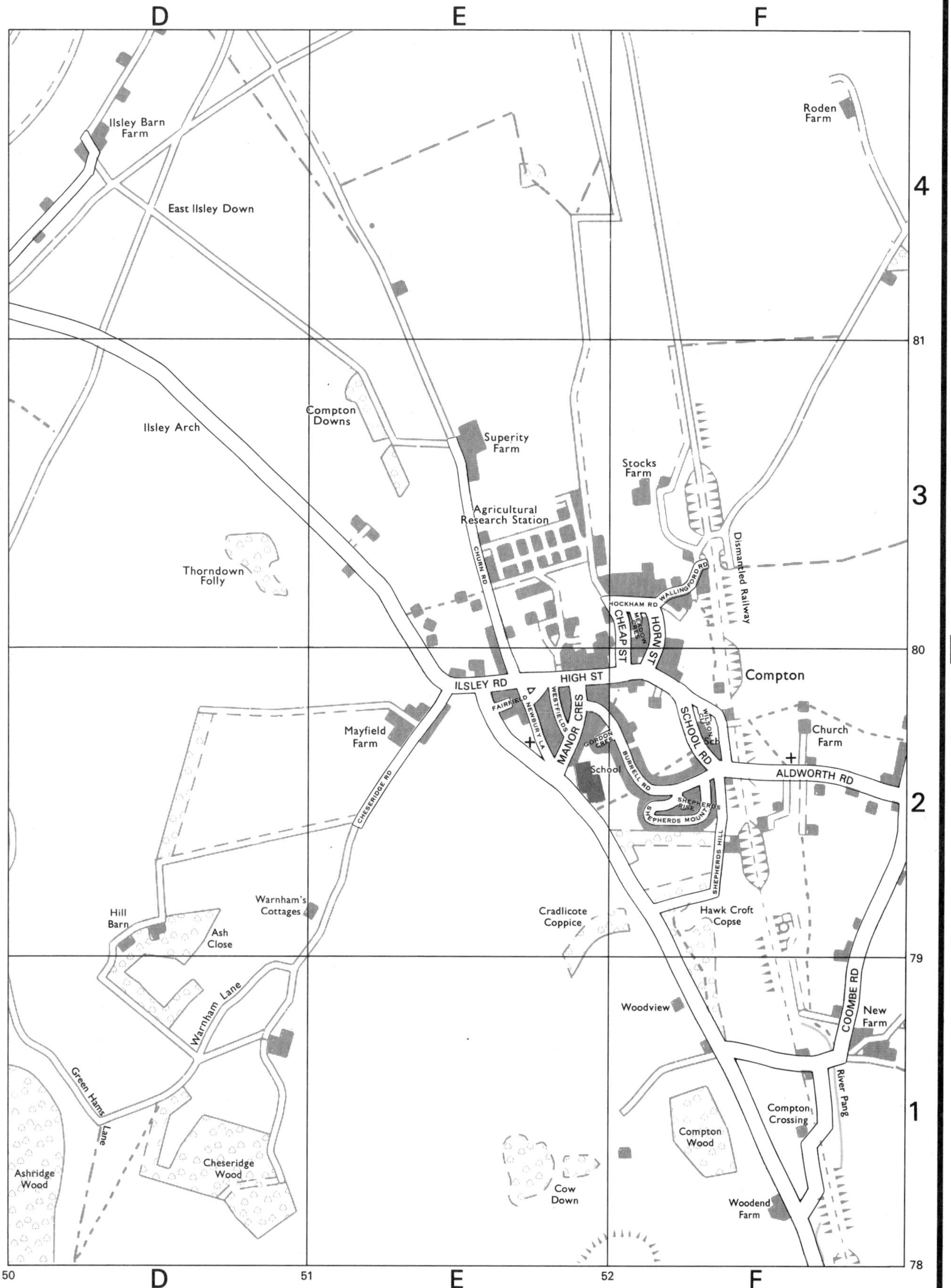
D
E
F
4
3
2
1
81
80
79
78
50
51
52
Ilsley Barn Farm
East Ilsley Down
Roden Farm
Compton Downs
Ilsley Arch
Superity Farm
Stocks Farm
Agricultural Research Station
CHURN RD
Thorndown Folly
Dismantled Railway
WALLINGFORD RD
HOCKHAM RD
CHEAP ST
HORN ST
Compton
ILSLEY RD
HIGH ST
FAIRFIELD
NEWBURY LA
WESTFIELDS
MANOR CRES
GORDON CRES
BURRELL RD
SCHOOL RD
WILSON CL
Sch
School
Church Farm
ALDWORTH RD
Mayfield Farm
CHESERIDGE RD
SHEPHERDS RISE
SHEPHERDS MOUNT
SHEPHERDS HILL
Hill Barn
Ash Close
Warnham's Cottages
Cradlicote Coppice
Hawk Croft Copse
Woodview
COOMBE RD
New Farm
Warnham Lane
Green Hams Lane
River Pang
Compton Crossing
Compton Wood
Ashridge Wood
Cheseridge Wood
Cow Down
Woodend Farm

32
52

12

31

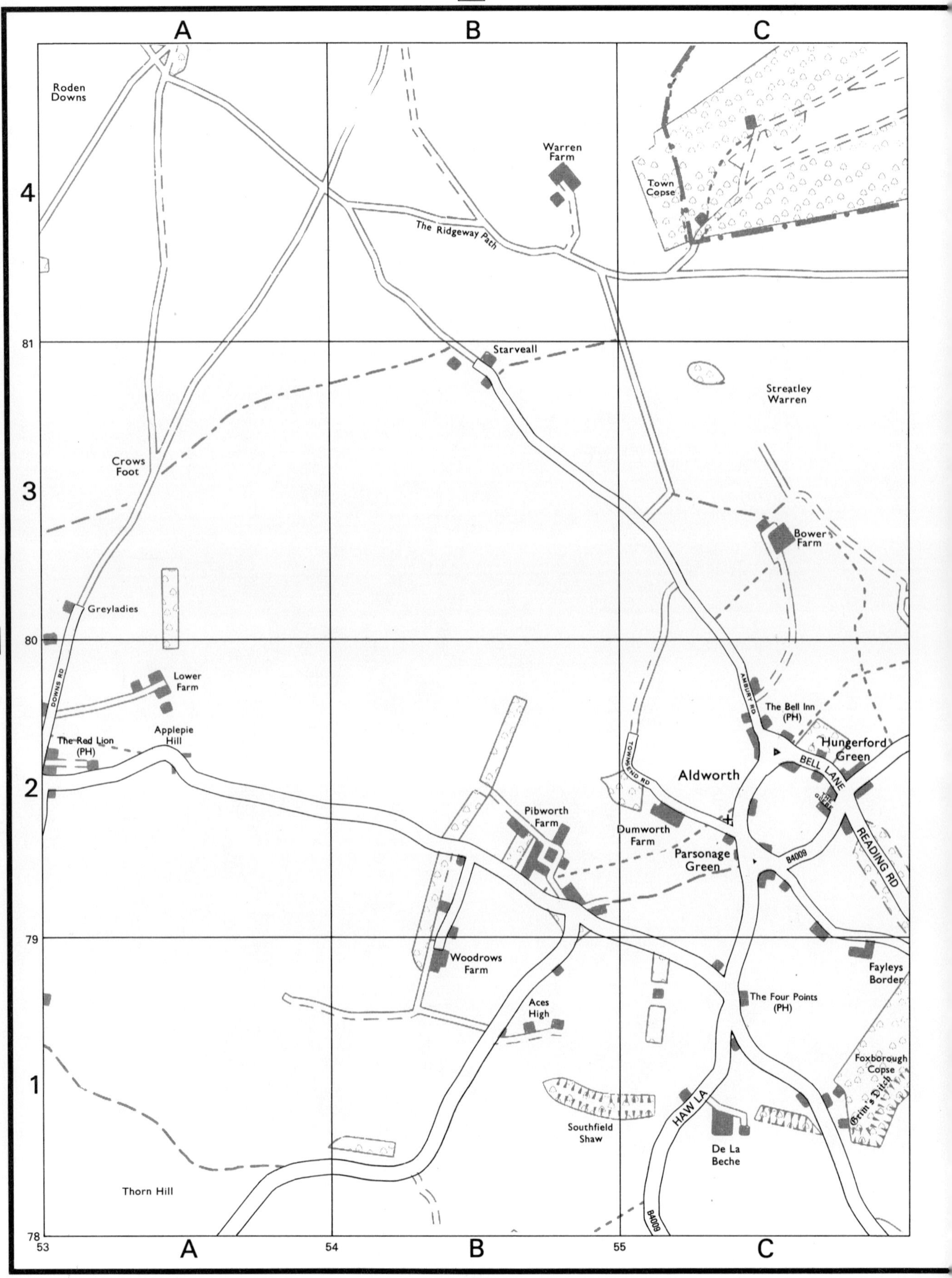
A
B
C
4
3
2
1
81
80
79
78
53
54
55
Roden Downs
Warren Farm
Town Copse
The Ridgeway Path
Starveall
Streatley Warren
Crows Foot
Bower Farm
Greyladies
DOWNS RD
Lower Farm
AMBURY RD
The Bell Inn (PH)
The Red Lion (PH)
Applepie Hill
Hungerford Green
BELL LANE
TOWNSEND RD
Aldworth
Pibworth Farm
Dumworth Farm
READING RD
Parsonage Green
B4009
Woodrows Farm
Fayleys Border
The Four Points (PH)
Aces High
Foxborough Copse
Grim's Ditch
HAW LA
Southfield Shaw
De La Beche
Thorn Hill
B4009

53

13

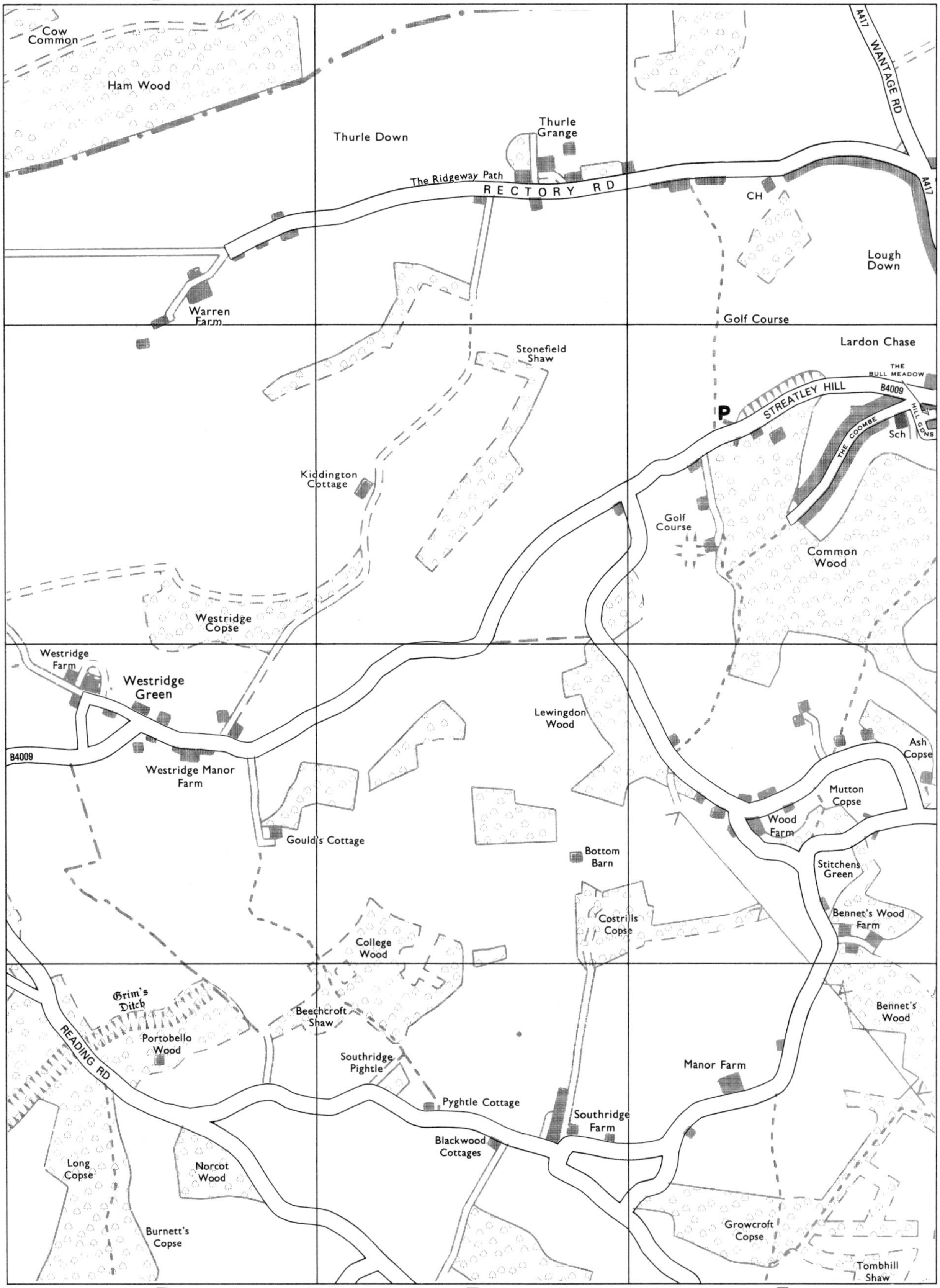
D
E
F
Cow Common
Ham Wood
Thurle Down
Thurle Grange
The Ridgeway Path
RECTORY RD
CH
A417
WANTAGE RD
A417
Lough Down
Warren Farm
Golf Course
81
Lardon Chase
Stonefield Shaw
THE BULL MEADOW
STREATLEY HILL
B4009
P
THE COOMBE
HILL GDNS
Sch
Kiddington Cottage
3
Golf Course
Common Wood
Westridge Copse
80
Westridge Farm
Westridge Green
Lewingdon Wood
Ash Copse
B4009
Westridge Manor Farm
Mutton Copse
2
Wood Farm
Gould's Cottage
Bottom Barn
Stitchens Green
Costrills Copse
Bennet's Wood Farm
College Wood
79
Grim's Ditch
Beechcroft Shaw
Bennet's Wood
Portobello Wood
READING RD
Southridge Pightle
Manor Farm
Pyghtle Cottage
Southridge Farm
1
Blackwood Cottages
Long Copse
Norcot Wood
Burnett's Copse
Growcroft Copse
Tombhill Shaw
4
56
57
58
78
D
E
F

34

54

14

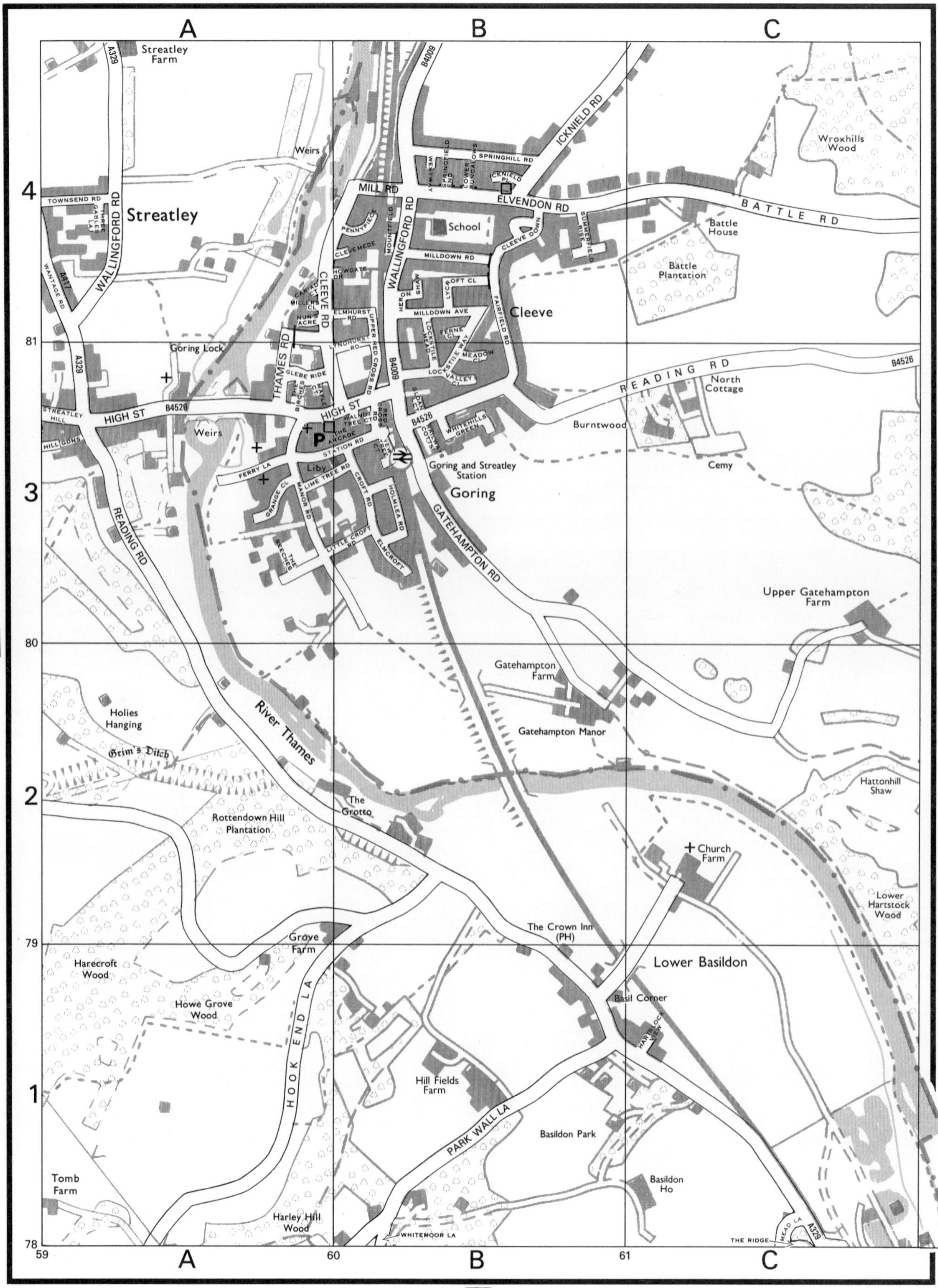
A
B
C
4
3
2
1
81
80
79
78
59
60
61
Streatley Farm
A329
B4009
Weirs
Wroxhills Wood
ICKNIELD RD
SPRINGHILL RD
WESTWAY
SPRINGFIELD END
LOWER BUNGALOWS
ICKNIELD PL
MILL RD
ELVENDON RD
BATTLE RD
TOWNSEND RD
THREE GABLES LA
WALLINGFORD RD
Streatley
School
PENNYPIECE
MOUNTFIELD
CLEEVEMEDE
CLEEVE DOWN
SUMMERFIELD RISE
Battle House
MILLDOWN RD
HOWGATE DR
Battle Plantation
CLEEVE RD
HERON SHAW
LYCROFT CL
FAIRFIELD RD
A417
WANTAGE RD
MILLERS CL
NUN'S ACRE
ELMHURST RD
UPPER RED CROSS RD
MILLDOWN AVE
Cleeve
THAMES RD
LYNDHURST RD
FERNE CL
LOCKSTILE MEAD
STILE WAY
Goring Lock
MEADOW CL
B4526
READING RD
GLEBE RIDE
THE BIRCHES
LOCKSTILE WAY
VALLEY CL
North Cottage
STREATLEY HILL
HIGH ST
B4526
HIGH ST
WALNUT TREE CT
RED CROSS
WHITEHILLS GREEN
HILL GDNS
Weirs
THE ARCADE
Burntwood
P
STATION RD
FERRY LA
Liby
Goring and Streatley Station
Cemy
LIME TREE RD
CROFT RD
HOLMLEA RD
GRANGE CL
MANOR RD
Goring
READING RD
GATEHAMPTON RD
LITTLE CROFT RD
THE BEECHES
ELMCROFT
Upper Gatehampton Farm
Gatehampton Farm
Holies Hanging
River Thames
Gatehampton Manor
Grim's Ditch
Hattonhill Shaw
The Grotto
Rottendown Hill Plantation
Church Farm
Lower Hartstock Wood
The Crown Inn (PH)
Grove Farm
Lower Basildon
Harecroft Wood
Basil Corner
Howe Grove Wood
HARTSLOCK VIEW
HOOK END LA
Hill Fields Farm
PARK WALL LA
Basildon Park
Tomb Farm
Basildon Ho
Harley Hill Wood
WHITEMOOR LA
THE RIDGE
MEAD LA
A329

33

55

15

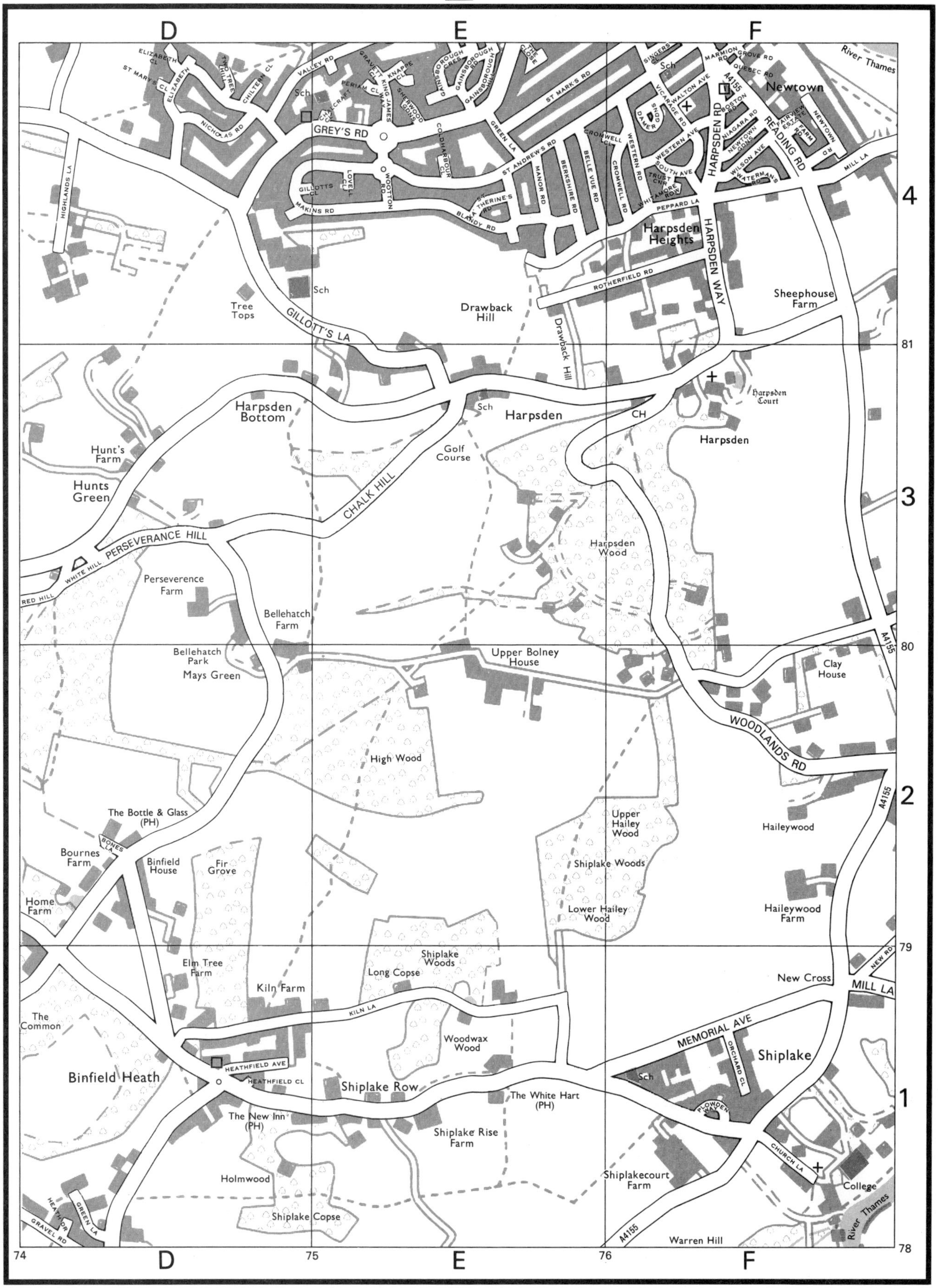
D
E
F
River Thames
Newtown
ELIZABETH CL
ELIZABETH
ST MARY'S CL
TWO TREE HILL
CHILTERN CL
NICHOLAS RD
VALLEY RD
Sch
GRAVETT CL
KING JAMES WAY
KNAPPE CL
PERIAM CL
SHERWOOD GDNS
CHECRAFT
GAINSBOROUGH CRES
GAINSBOROUGH RD
GAINSBOROUGH HILL
THE CLOSE
ST MARK'S RD
SINGERS CL
MARMION RD
GROVE RD
QUEBEC RD
WALTON AVE
VICARAGE RD
DAMER GDNS
A4155
BOSTON RD
NIAGARA RD
NEWTOWN GDNS
FAIRVIEW ESTATE
FARM RD
NEWTOWN RD
MILL LA
GREY'S RD
COLDHARBOUR CL
GREEN LA
CROMWELL CL
CROMWELL RD
WESTERN RD
WESTERN AVE
SOUTH AVE
TRUST CNR
WHITAMORE ROW
WILSON AVE
WATERMANS RD
HARPSDEN RD
READING RD
HIGHLANDS LA
GILLOTTS CL
LOVELL CL
WOOTTON RD
MAKINS RD
BLANDY RD
ST KATHERINE'S RD
ST ANDREW'S RD
MANOR RD
BERKSHIRE RD
BELLE VUE RD
PEPPARD LA
Harpsden Heights
HARPSDEN WAY
ROTHERFIELD RD
Tree Tops
GILLOTT'S LA
Drawback Hill
Drawback Hill
Sheephouse Farm
Harpsden Court
Harpsden Bottom
Harpsden
CH
Hunt's Farm
Hunts Green
Golf Course
CHALK HILL
PERSEVERANCE HILL
WHITE HILL
RED HILL
Harpsden Wood
Perseverence Farm
Bellehatch Farm
Bellehatch Park
Mays Green
Upper Bolney House
Clay House
A4155
WOODLANDS RD
High Wood
A4155
Haileywood
The Bottle & Glass (PH)
BONES LA
Bournes Farm
Binfield House
Fir Grove
Upper Hailey Wood
Shiplake Woods
Home Farm
Lower Hailey Wood
Haileywood Farm
Elm Tree Farm
Long Copse
Shiplake Woods
NEW RD
New Cross
MILL LA
Kiln Farm
KILN LA
The Common
MEMORIAL AVE
Woodwax Wood
ORCHARD CL
Shiplake
HEATHFIELD AVE
Binfield Heath
HEATHFIELD CL
Shiplake Row
Sch
The White Hart (PH)
PLOWDEN WAY
The New Inn (PH)
Shiplake Rise Farm
CHURCH LA
Holmwood
Shiplakecourt Farm
College
HEATH DR
GREEN LA
GRAVEL RD
Shiplake Copse
River Thames
A4155
Warren Hill
74
75
76
78
79
80
81
1
2
3
4

36

60

16

35

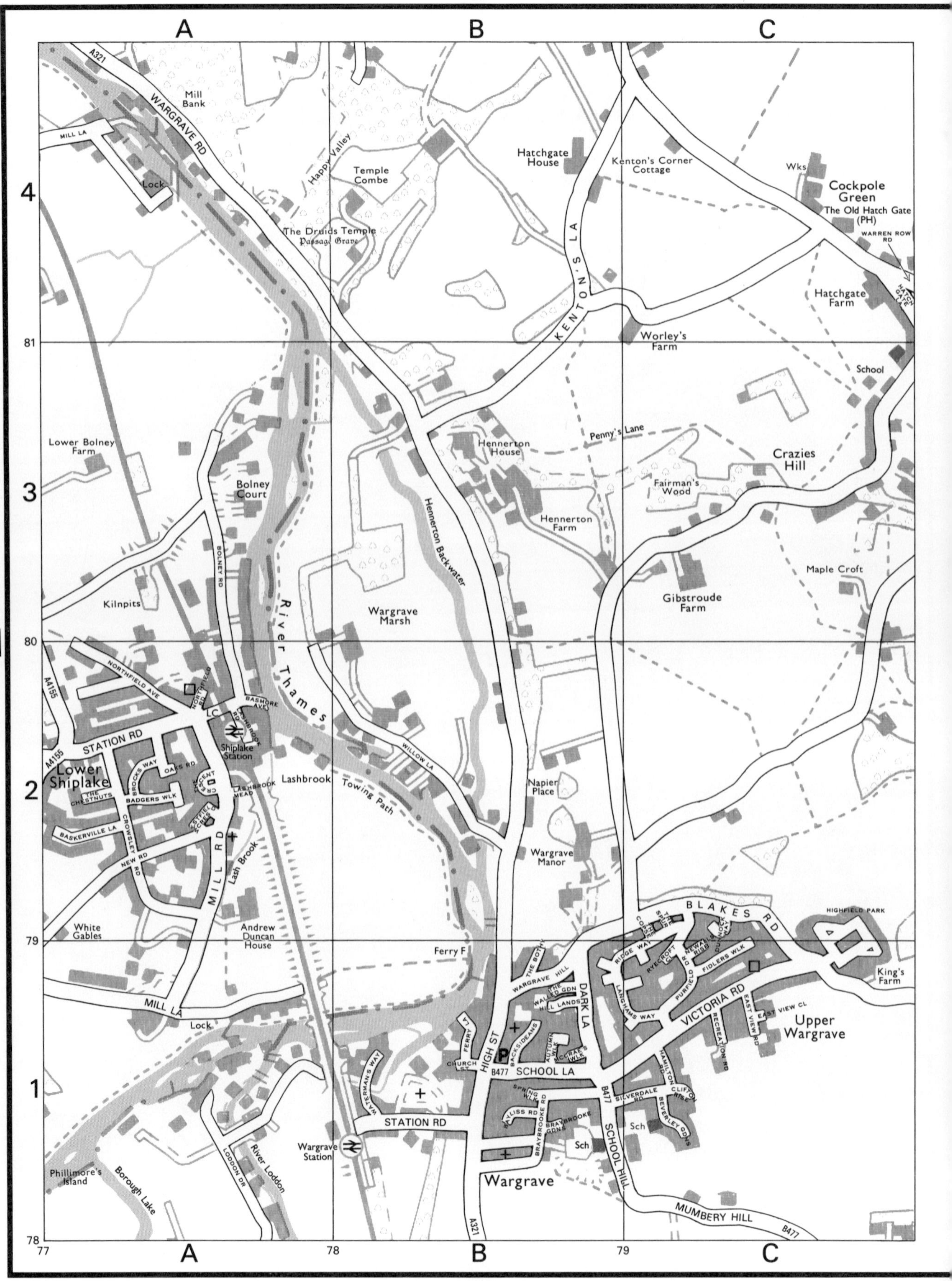
A
B
C
4
3
2
1
81
80
79
78
77
78
79
A321
WARGRAVE RD
Mill Bank
MILL LA
Lock
Happy Valley
Temple Combe
The Druids Temple
Passage Grave
Hatchgate House
Kenton's Corner Cottage
KENTON'S LA
Wks
Cockpole Green
The Old Hatch Gate (PH)
WARREN ROW RD
HATCH GATE
Hatchgate Farm
Worley's Farm
School
Lower Bolney Farm
Bolney Court
BOLNEY RD
Hennerton House
Penny's Lane
Crazies Hill
Fairman's Wood
Hennerton Farm
Hennerton Backwater
River Thames
Kilnpits
Wargrave Marsh
Gibstroude Farm
Maple Croft
A4155
NORTHFIELD AVE
NORTHFIELD RD
BASMORE AVE
LC
LASHBROOK RD
STATION RD
Shiplake Station
Lower Shiplake
BROCKS WAY
OAKS RD
THE CRESCENT
THE CHESTNUTS
BADGERS WLK
LASHBROOK MEAD
Lashbrook
Towing Path
WILLOW LA
Napier Place
BASKERVILLE LA
CROWSLEY RD
NEW RD
MILL RD
Lath Brook
Wargrave Manor
White Gables
Andrew Duncan House
Ferry F
MILL LA
Lock
BLAKES RD
HIGHFIELD PARK
THE BOTHY
WARGRAVE HILL
DARK LA
RIDGE WAY
RYECROFT CL
NEWALLS RISE
DUNNOCK WAY
FIDLERS WLK
PURFIELD DR
LANGHAMS WAY
VICTORIA RD
EAST VIEW CL
EAST VIEW RD
RECREATION RD
King's Farm
Upper Wargrave
HIGH ST
FERRY LA
CHURCH ST
BACKSIDEANS
AUTUMN WLK
B477
SCHOOL LA
HAMILTON RD
CLIFTON RISE
SILVERDALE RD
BEVERLEY GDNS
WATERMAN'S WAY
STATION RD
BAYLISS RD
BRAYBROOKE RD
BRAYBROOKE GDNS
Sch
SCHOOL HILL
Wargrave Station
Wargrave
Phillimore's Island
Borough Lake
LODDON DR
River Loddon
A321
MUMBERY HILL
B477

61

17

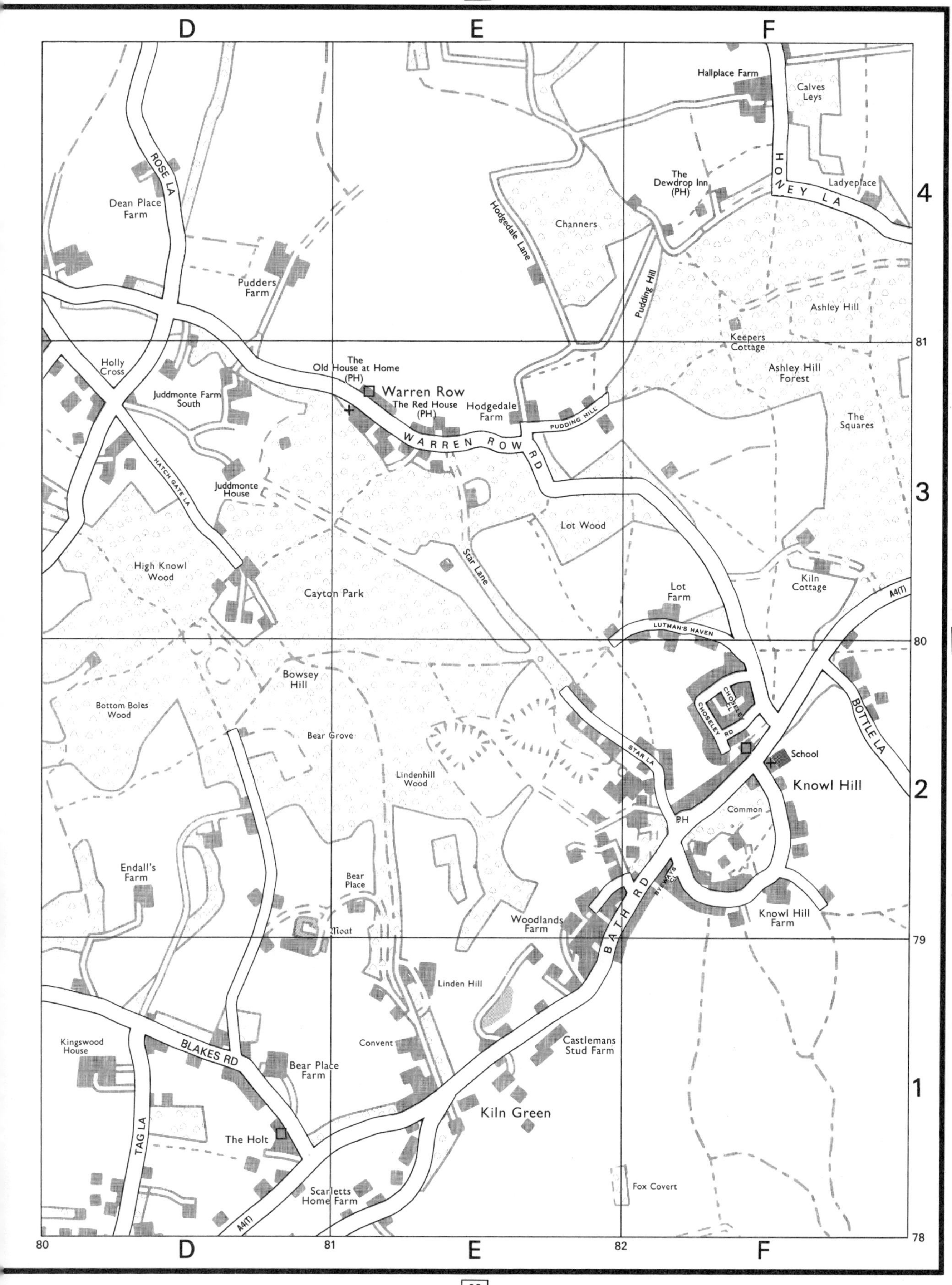

D
E
F
Hallplace Farm
Calves Leys
ROSE LA
HONEY LA
Ladyeplace
The Dewdrop Inn (PH)
Dean Place Farm
Hodgedale Lane
Channers
4
Pudders Farm
Pudding Hill
Ashley Hill
Keepers Cottage
81
Holly Cross
The Old House at Home (PH)
Warren Row
Ashley Hill Forest
Juddmonte Farm South
The Red House (PH)
Hodgedale Farm
PUDDING HILL
The Squares
WARREN ROW RD
HATCH GATE LA
Juddmonte House
3
Lot Wood
Star Lane
High Knowl Wood
Kiln Cottage
Cayton Park
Lot Farm
A4(T)
LUTMAN'S HAVEN
80
Bowsey Hill
Bottom Boles Wood
CHOSELEY CL
CHOSELEY RD
BOTTLE LA
Bear Grove
STAR LA
School
Lindenhill Wood
Knowl Hill
2
Common
PH
Endall's Farm
Bear Place
BATH RD
BYEWAYS CL
Knowl Hill Farm
Woodlands Farm
Moat
79
Linden Hill
Kingswood House
Convent
Castlemans Stud Farm
BLAKES RD
Bear Place Farm
1
Kiln Green
TAG LA
The Holt
Fox Covert
Scarletts Home Farm
A4(T)
78
80
81
82
D
E
F

38

62

18

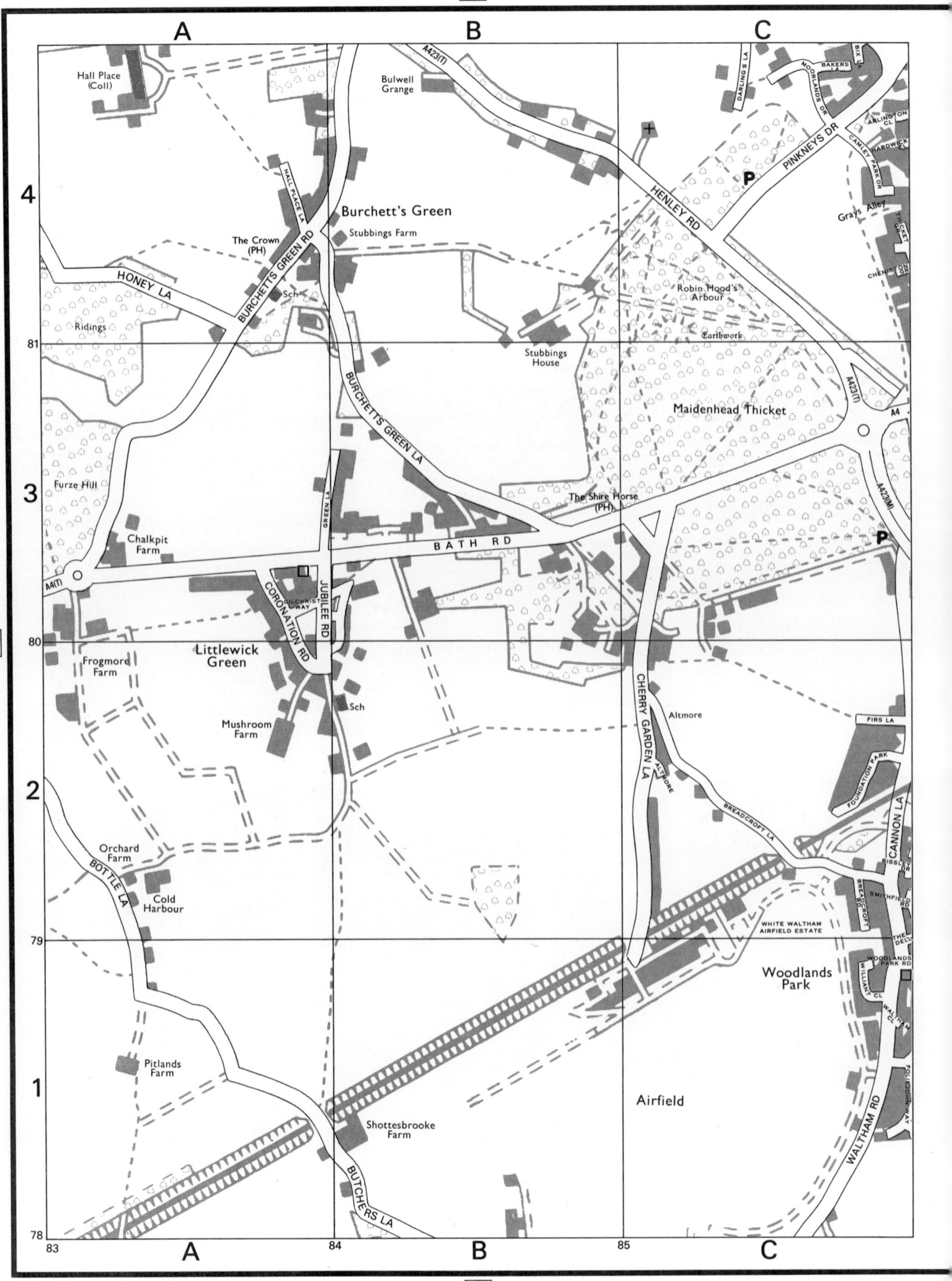
A
B
C
4
3
2
1
81
80
79
78
83
84
85
Hall Place (Coll)
Bulwell Grange
A423(T)
DARLING'S LA
MOORLANDS DR
BAKERS LA
BIX LA
ARLINGTON CL
HARDWICK CL
CAMLEY PARK DR
PINKNEYS DR
P
HENLEY RD
HALL PLACE LA
Burchett's Green
Stubbings Farm
The Crown (PH)
BURCHETTS GREEN RD
HONEY LA
Sch
Ridings
Grays Alley
THICKET GR
CHENISTON GR
Robin Hood's Arbour
Earthwork
Stubbings House
BURCHETTS GREEN LA
Maidenhead Thicket
A423(T)
A4
A423(M)
Furze Hill
GREEN LA
The Shire Horse (PH)
Chalkpit Farm
BATH RD
A4(T)
CORONATION RD
JUBILEE RD
GILCHRIST WAY
Littlewick Green
Frogmore Farm
Mushroom Farm
Sch
CHERRY GARDEN LA
Altmore
ALTMORE
FIRS LA
FOUNDATION PARK
CANNON LA
BREADCROFT LA
BISSLEY DR
SMITHFIELD RD
BREADCROFT
WHITE WALTHAM AIRFIELD ESTATE
THE DELL
WOODLANDS PARK RD
Woodlands Park
WILLIANT CL
WALTHAM CL
Orchard Farm
BOTTLE LA
Cold Harbour
Pitlands Farm
Airfield
Shottesbrooke Farm
FOLIEJON WAY
WALTHAM RD
BUTCHERS LA

37

63

19

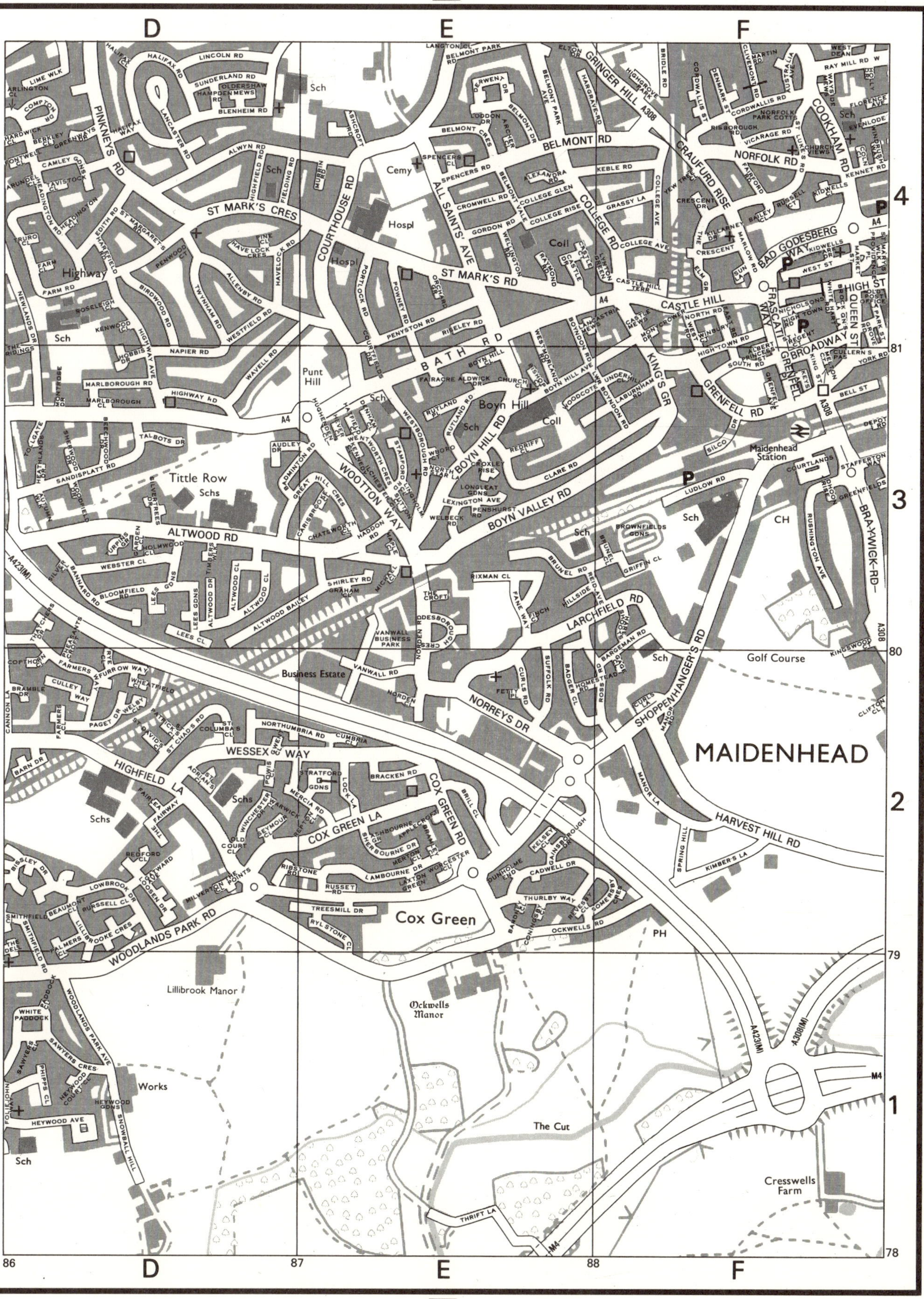

D
E
F
4
3
2
1
86
87
88
81
80
79
78
MAIDENHEAD
Cox Green
Boyn Hill
Highway
Tittle Row
Punt Hill
Maidenhead Station
Golf Course
Lillibrook Manor
Ockwells Manor
The Cut
Cresswells Farm
Works
Business Estate
VANWALL BUSINESS PARK
Cemy
Hospl
Coll
Sch
Schs
CH
PH
ST MARK'S CRES
ST MARK'S RD
BATH RD
CASTLE HILL
BELMONT RD
COLLEGE RD
CRAUFURD RISE
NORFOLK RD
COOKHAM RD
BAD GODESBERG WAY
HIGH ST
QUEEN ST
BROADWAY
FRASCATI WAY
GRENFELL RD
KING'S GR
BOYN HILL RD
BOYN VALLEY RD
WOOTTON WAY
ALTWOOD RD
ALTWOOD BAILEY
COURTHOUSE RD
ALL SAINTS' AVE
GRINGER HILL A308
PINKNEYS RD
HIGHWAY AVE
NAPIER RD
MARLBOROUGH RD
TALBOTS DR
SANDISPLATT RD
LARCHFIELD RD
SHOPPENHANGER'S RD
NORREYS DR
HARVEST HILL RD
WESSEX WAY
HIGHFIELD LA
COX GREEN LA
COX GREEN RD
WOODLANDS PARK RD
WOODLANDS PARK AVE
OCKWELLS RD
LUDLOW RD
BRAYWICK RD
RUSHINGTON AVE
SPRING HILL
KIMBER'S LA
THRIFT LA
SNOWBALL HILL
HEYWOOD AVE
A4
A308
A423(M)
A308(M)
M4

40

64

20

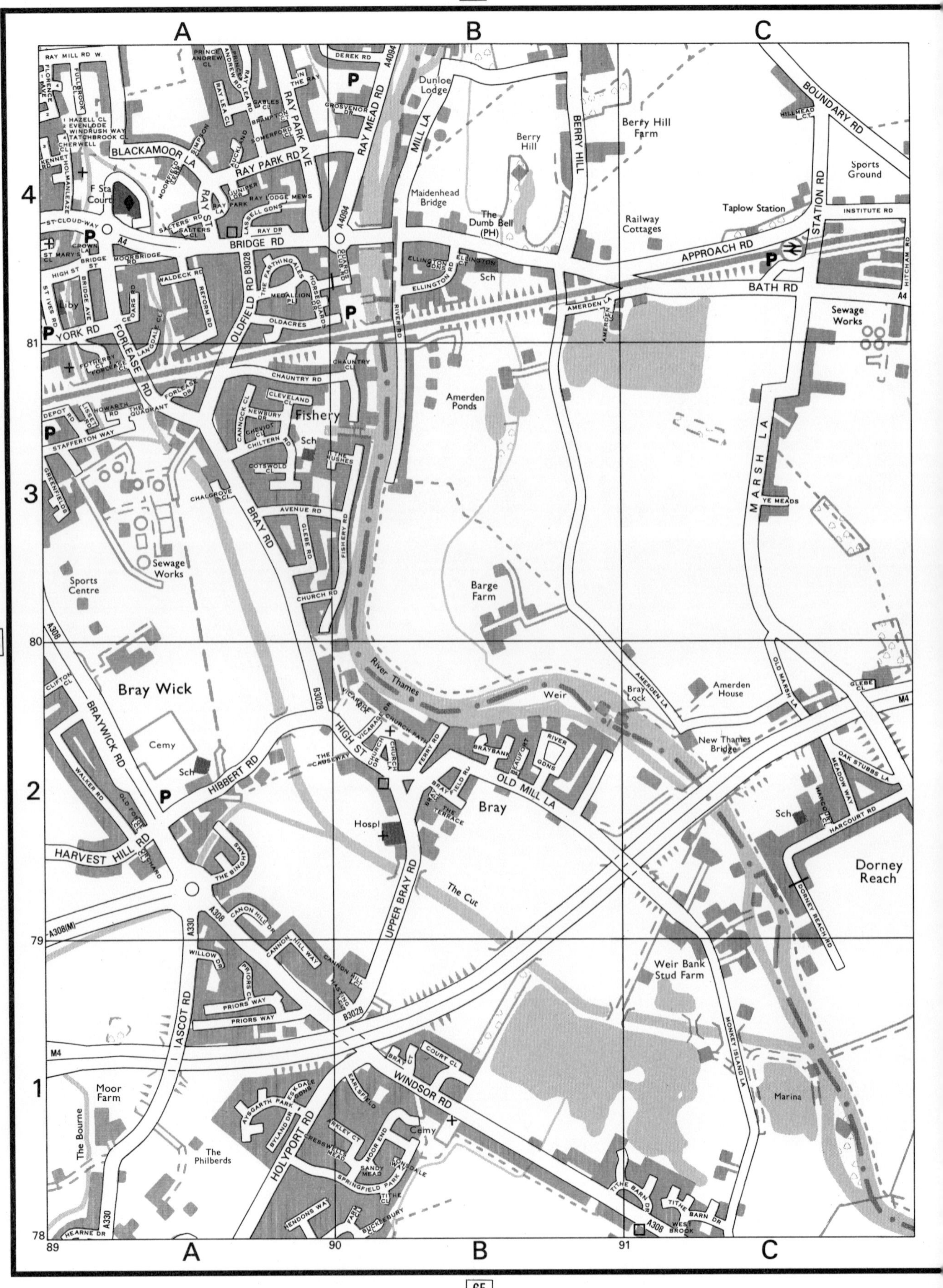
A
B
C
4
3
2
1
81
80
79
78
89
90
91
RAY MILL RD W
PRINCE ANDREW CL
DEREK RD
A4094
Dunloe Lodge
BERRY HILL
Berry Hill Farm
BOUNDARY RD
HILLMEAD CT
Sports Ground
Berry Hill
MILL LA
RAY MEAD RD
RAY PARK AVE
RAY PARK RD
BLACKAMOOR LA
HAZELL CL
EVENLODE
WINDRUSH WAY
TATCHBROOK CL
CHERWELL
FULLBROOK CL
KENNET
HOLMANLEAZE
F Sta
Court
ST CLOUD WAY
RAY ST
RAY DR
RAY LODGE MEWS
GROSVENOR DR
SOMERFORD CL
BRAMPTON CT
GABLES CL
Maidenhead Bridge
The Dumb Bell (PH)
Railway Cottages
Taplow Station
INSTITUTE RD
STATION RD
APPROACH RD
BATH RD
A4
BRIDGE RD
A4094
A4
ST MARY'S
HIGH ST
MOORBRIDGE RD
WALDECK RD
REFORM RD
OLDFIELD RD
B3028
THE FARTHINGALES
MEDALLION PL
HORSEGUARDS DR
OLDACRES
ELLINGTON GDNS
ELLINGTON RD
Sch
AMERDEN LA
HITCHAM RD
Sewage Works
Liby
BRIDGE AVE
ST IVES RD
YORK RD
FORLEASE RD
LANGDALE CL
FOTHERBY CT
FORCEACRE CL
CHAUNTRY CL
CHAUNTRY RD
RIVER RD
Amerden Ponds
DEPOT RD
HOWARTH RD
THE QUADRANT
STAFFERTON WAY
CLEVELAND CL
NEWBURY DR
CANNOCK CL
CHEVIOT CL
CHILTERN RD
Fishery
Sch
THE RUSHES
COTSWOLD CL
CHALGROVE CL
GREENFIELDS
AVENUE RD
GLEBE RD
FISHERY RD
BRAY RD
MARSH LA
YE MEADS
Sewage Works
Sports Centre
Barge Farm
CHURCH RD
A308
OLD MARSH LA
River Thames
Weir
Bray Lock
AMERDEN LA
Amerden House
GLEBE CL
M4
Bray Wick
CLIFTON CL
BRAYWICK RD
VICARAGE DR
VICARAGE WALK
CHURCH PATH
HIGH ST
FERRY RD
BRAYBANK
BEAUFORT GDNS
RIVER GDNS
New Thames Bridge
OAK STUBBS LA
MEADOW WAY
HARCOURT
HARCOURT RD
Cemy
Sch
HIBBERT RD
THE CAUSEWAY
CHURCH DR
CHURCH LA
BRAYFIELD RD
OLD MILL LA
THE TERRACE
Bray
WALKER RD
OLD FORGE CL
Hospl
Sch
Dorney Reach
DORNEY REACH RD
HARVEST HILL RD
ORCHARD
THE BINGHAMS
The Cut
A308(M)
A330
A308
CANON HILL DR
CANNON HILL WAY
CANNON HILL CL
HASTINGS
UPPER BRAY RD
WILLOW DR
ASCOT RD
PRIORS CL
PRIORS WAY
B3028
Weir Bank Stud Farm
MONKEY ISLAND LA
BRAY CT
COURT CL
WINDSOR RD
Moor Farm
The Bourne
AYSGARTH PARK
ESKDALE GDNS
EARLSFIELD
BYLAND DR
HOLYPORT RD
ARKLEY CT
CRESSWELLS MEAD
MOOR END
Cemy
SANDY MEAD
LONSDALE WAY
SPRINGFIELD PARK
TITHE CL
The Philberds
HENDONS WAY
FARM CL
BUCKLEBURY
TITHE BARN DR
WEST BROOK
Marina
HEARNE DR
A330
A308

39

65

21

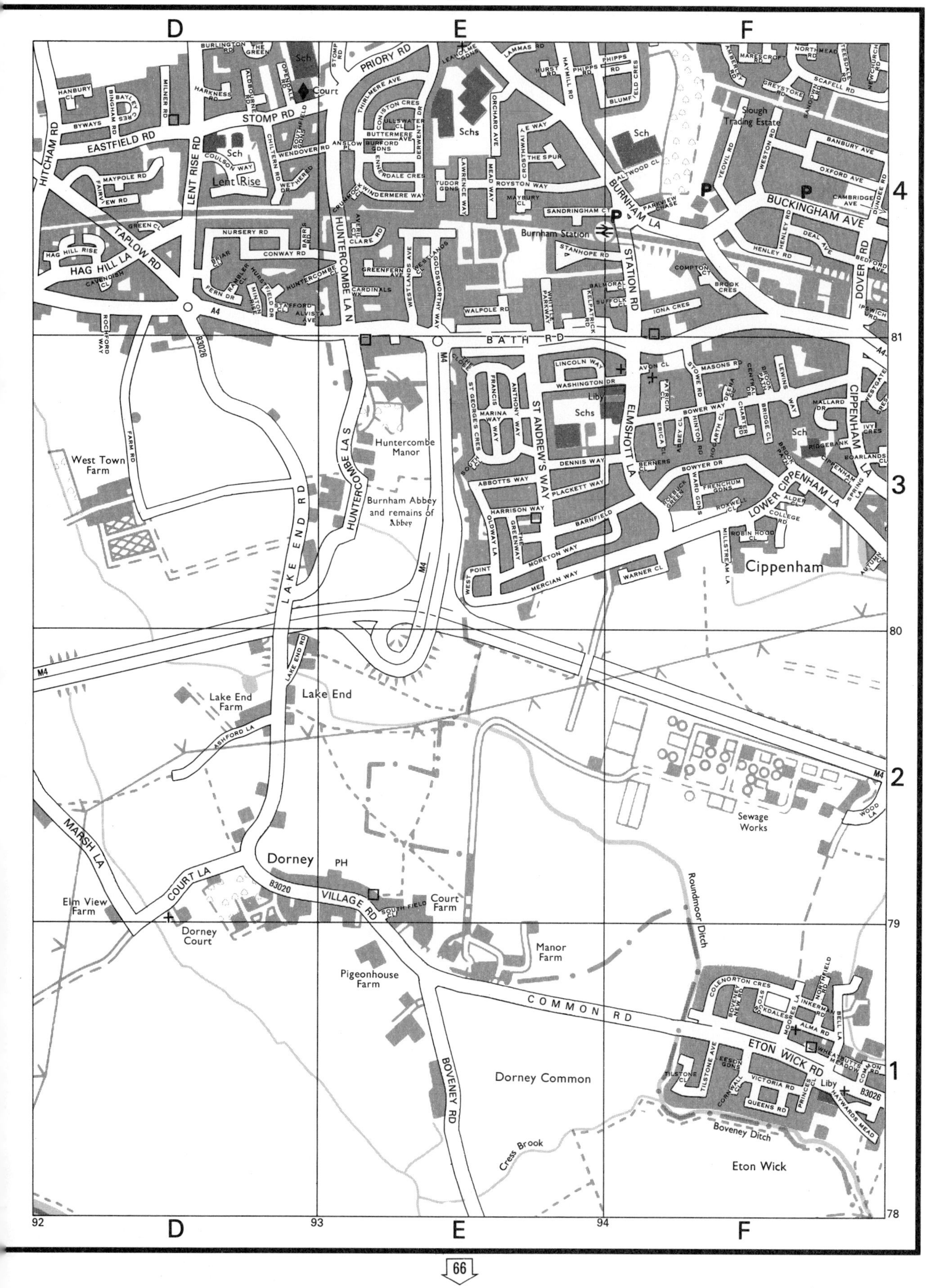
D
E
F
Sch
Court
STOMP RD
PRIORY RD
EASTFIELD RD
HITCHAM RD
LENT RISE RD
Lent Rise
HANBURY CL
BYWAYS
MAYPOLE RD
TAPLOW RD
HAG HILL LA
HAG HILL RISE
CAVENDISH CL
GREEN CL
NURSERY RD
CONWAY RD
HUNTERCOMBE LA N
WINDERMERE WAY
THIRLMERE AVE
CONISTON CRES
ULLSWATER CL
BUTTERMERE AVE
Schs
ORCHARD AVE
MEAD WAY
LAWRENCE WAY
ROYSTON WAY
THE SPUR
MAYBURY CL
LAMMAS RD
HAYMILL RD
PHIPPS RD
BLUMFIELD CRES
Sch
ALTWOOD CL
Slough Trading Estate
BURNHAM LA
SANDRINGHAM CT
Burnham Station
STANHOPE RD
STATION RD
WALPOLE RD
IONA CRES
BUCKINGHAM AVE
BANBURY AVE
OXFORD AVE
CAMBRIDGE AVE
HENLEY RD
DEAL AVE
DOVER RD
BEDFORD AVE
YEOVIL RD
WESTON RD
SCAFELL RD
GREYSTOKE RD
P
P
P
A4
BATH RD
81
B3026
M4
ROCHFORD WAY
FARM RD
West Town Farm
Huntercombe Manor
Burnham Abbey and remains of Abbey
HUNTERCOMBE LA S
LAKE END RD
ST ANDREW'S WAY
ELMSHOTT LA
LINCOLN WAY
WASHINGTON DR
Liby
Schs
DENNIS WAY
PLACKETT WAY
ABBOTTS WAY
HARRISON WAY
BARNFIELD
MORETON WAY
MERCIAN WAY
WEST POINT
WARNER CL
BOWYER DR
LOWER CIPPENHAM LA
CIPPENHAM LA
Sch
Cippenham
MILLSTREAM LA
3
80
M4
Lake End Farm
Lake End
ASHFORD LA
LAKE END RD
2
M4
Sewage Works
WOOD LA
MARSH LA
Dorney
PH
COURT LA
B3020
VILLAGE RD
Court Farm
Elm View Farm
Dorney Court
79
Manor Farm
Roundmoor Ditch
Pigeonhouse Farm
COMMON RD
BOVENEY RD
Dorney Common
ETON WICK RD
COLENORTON CRES
INKERMAN RD
ALMA RD
TILSTONE AVE
VICTORIA RD
QUEENS RD
Liby
B3026
HAYWARDS MEAD
1
Boveney Ditch
Cress Brook
Eton Wick
78
92
93
94
D
E
F

42

66

22

41

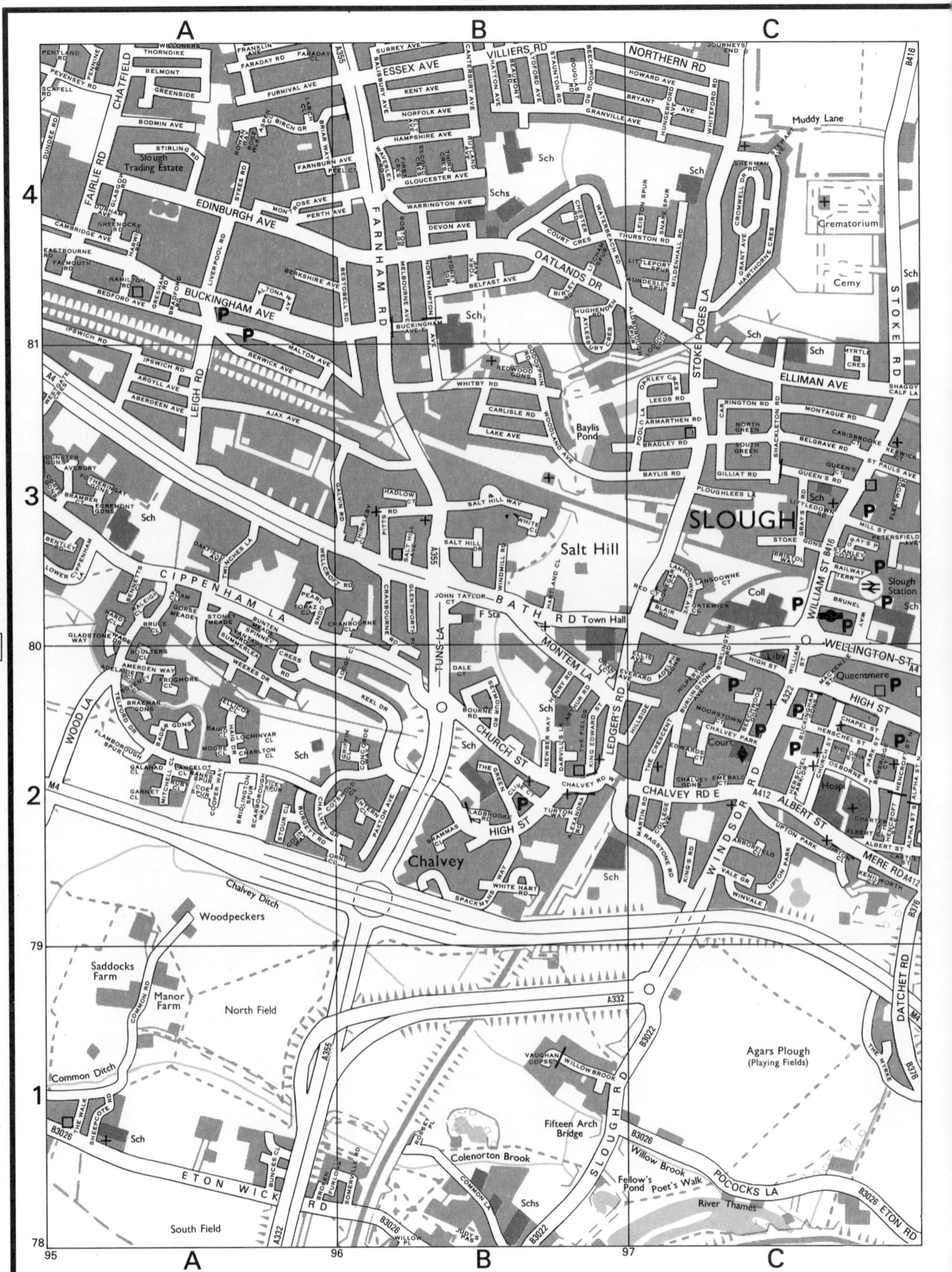
A
B
C
4
3
2
1
81
80
79
78
95
96
97
SLOUGH
Slough Trading Estate
Salt Hill
Baylis Pond
Chalvey
Crematorium
Cemy
Muddy Lane
Slough Station
Town Hall
Queensmere
Coll
Court
Liby
Hospl
F Sta
Sch
Schs
Woodpeckers
Saddocks Farm
Manor Farm
North Field
South Field
Common Ditch
Chalvey Ditch
Colenorton Brook
Fifteen Arch Bridge
Willow Brook
Fellow's Pond
Poet's Walk
River Thames
Agars Plough
(Playing Fields)
NORTHERN RD
VILLIERS RD
ESSEX AVE
FARNHAM RD
EDINBURGH AVE
BUCKINGHAM AVE
OATLANDS DR
STOKE POGES LA
ELLIMAN AVE
STOKE RD
CIPPENHAM LA
BATH RD
TUNS LA
MONTEM LA
LEDGER'S RD
CHURCH ST
HIGH ST
CHALVEY RD E
CHALVEY RD W
WINDSOR RD
ALBERT ST
MERE RD
WELLINGTON ST
WILLIAM ST
SLOUGH RD
POCOCKS LA
ETON WICK RD
ETON RD
DATCHET RD
COMMON RD
WOOD LA
LEIGH RD
FAIRLIE RD
CHATFIELD
LIVERPOOL RD
AJAX AVE
BERWICK AVE
MALTON AVE
IPSWICH RD
AVEBURY
WEEKES DR
KEEL DR
SPACKMANS WAY
WHITE HART RD
UPTON PARK
VALE GR
WINVALE
M4
A4
A355
A332
A412
B416
B3026
B3022
B376

67

23

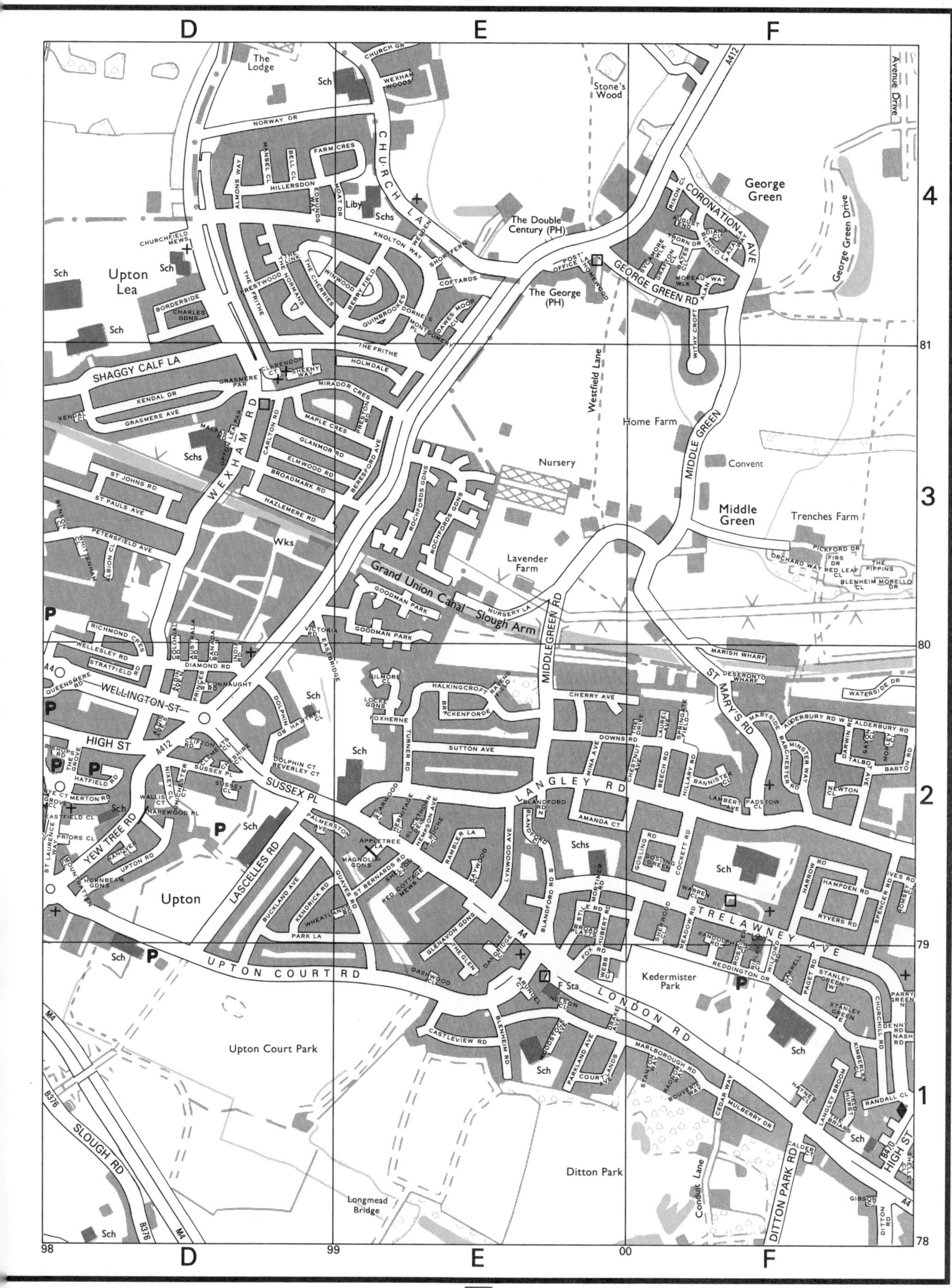
D
E
F
4
3
2
1
81
80
79
78
98
99
00
The Lodge
Sch
Stone's Wood
A412
Avenue Drive
NORWAY DR
CHURCH LA
WEXHAM WOODS
CHURCH GR
FARM CRES
MANSEL CL
BELL CL
ALMONS WAY
HILLERSDON
EDMUNDS WAY
MOAT DR
Liby
Schs
George Green
CORONATION AVE
RIXON CL
AUGUST END
BOIANA CL
LINCOLN CL
THORN DR
GRAFTON WLK
SYCAMORE WLK
BATES CL
MOREAU WLK
ALAN WAY
WITHY CROFT
GEORGE GREEN RD
George Green Drive
The Double Century (PH)
The George (PH)
POST OFFICE LA
HOMEWOOD
KNOLTON WAY
WELDEN
SHORTFERN
COFTARDS
DAWES MOOR CL
MONTGOMERY PL
DORNELS
QUINBROOKES
BERRYFIELD
WINWOOD
THE CHERRIES
THE NORMANS
THE LINK
PRESTWOOD
THE FRITHE
CHURCHFIELD MEWS
Upton Lea
BORDERSIDE
CHARLES GDNS
SHAGGY CALF LA
CLARENDON CT
SHEEHY WAY
HOLMDALE
GRASMERE PAR
KENDAL DR
KENDAL CL
GRASMERE AVE
MIRADOR CRES
MAPLE CRES
PRESTON RD
GLANMOR RD
ELMWOOD RD
BROADMARK RD
HAZLEMERE RD
BERESFORD AVE
CARLTON RD
WEXHAM RD
UPTON LEA PAR
MALPAS
Westfield Lane
Home Farm
MIDDLE GREEN
Convent
Nursery
Middle Green
Trenches Farm
ST JOHNS RD
ST PAULS AVE
BENSON
PETERSFIELD AVE
WHITTENHAM
ALBION CL
Wks
ROCHFORDS GDNS
Lavender Farm
PICKFORD DR
FIRS DR
ORCHARD WAY
RED LEAF CL
THE PIPPINS
BLENHEIM
MORELLO DR
Grand Union Canal Slough Arm
GOODMAN PARK
NURSERY LA
MIDDLEGREEN RD
VICTORIA RD
EASTBRIDGE
RICHMOND CRES
WELLESLEY RD
STRATFIELD RD
COLONIAL RD
AUSTRALIA AVE
CANADA RD
INDIA RD
DIAMOND RD
CONNAUGHT
A4
QUEENSMERE RD
WELLINGTON ST
PRINCES ST
ALPHA ST
MARISH WHARF
DESERONTO WHARF
ST MARY'S RD
WATERSIDE DR
GILMORE CL
HALKINGCROFT
RAVENSFIELD
LOCKE GDNS
BRACKENFORDE
FOXHERNE
TURNER RD
SUTTON AVE
CHERRY AVE
DOWNS RD
LAUREL AVE
SPRINGATE FIELD
CHESTNUT AVE
TREE DRIVE
MINA AVE
BEECH RD
HILLARY RD
BANNISTER CL
LAMBERT AVE
PADSTOW CL
MARYSIDE
BARCHESTER RD
MINSTER WAY
ALDERBURY RD W
ALDERBURY RD
DARWIN RD
TALBOT AVE
BARTON RD
NEWTON CL
DOLPHIN RD
HAWTREY CL
DOLPHIN CT
BEVERLEY CT
HIGH ST
BISHOPS CL
THE GROVE
HATFIELD RD
CLIFTON RD
CLEMENTS CL
SHIRE CL
SUSSEX PL
SUSSEX CL
CHICHESTER CL
NIXEY CL
WALLIS CT
HAREWOOD PL
MERTON RD
RYE CT
EASTFIELD CL
PRIORS CL
ST LAURENCE WAY
YEW TREE RD
TANGIER CT
UPTON RD
HORNBEAM GDNS
MOUNTBATTEN
P
Upton
LASCELLES RD
PALMERSTON AVE
BUCKLAND AVE
KENDRICK RD
QUAVES RD
WHEATLANDS RD
PARK LA
ST BERNARDS RD
MAGNOLIA GDNS
APPLETREE LA
RED COTTAGE MEWS
SHELTON
STARWOOD
HERMITAGE
HEMPSON AVE
LA ROCHE CL
RAMBLER LA
BAYWOOD
LYNWOOD AVE
BLANDFORD RD N
BLANDFORD CL
BLANDFORD RD S
LANGLEY RD
AMANDA CT
Schs
GOSLING RD
GOSLING GREEN
COCKETT RD
MORTIMER RD
STILE RD
HUBERT RD
BROAD PLATTS
FOX RD
WEBB CL
WARREN CL
SHERWOOD
MEADOW RD
RANDOLPH RD
ROSSETTI
KIRKE CL
WILFORD RD
REDDINGTON DR
TRELAWNEY AVE
HARROW RD
HAMPDEN RD
RYVERS RD
SPENCER RD
IVES RD
ROMSEY
GLENAVON GDNS
THE GLEN
DANDRIDGE CL
DASHWOOD CL
UPTON COURT RD
F Sta
ARUNDEL CT
NELSON CL
LONDON RD
DRAKE AVE
Kedermister Park
PAGET RD
STANLEY GREEN W
STANLEY GREEN E
CHURCHILL RD
PARRY GREEN N
DENNY RD
NASH RD
KIMBERLEY CL
M4
Upton Court Park
CASTLEVIEW RD
BLENHEIM RD
WOODSTOCK AVE
PARKLAND AVE
COURTLANDS
STANYON WAY
BADGER WAY
BOUVERIE WAY
MARLBOROUGH RD
CEDAR WAY
MULBERRY DR
HAYNES CL
LANGLEY BROOM
FIELD HURST
THE BRIARS
RANDALL CL
B470
HIGH ST
SHELLEY
B376
SLOUGH RD
Ditton Park
Longmead Bridge
Conduit Lane
DITTON PARK RD
CALDER CT
GIBSON CT
DITTON RD

44

68

not continued, see key diagram

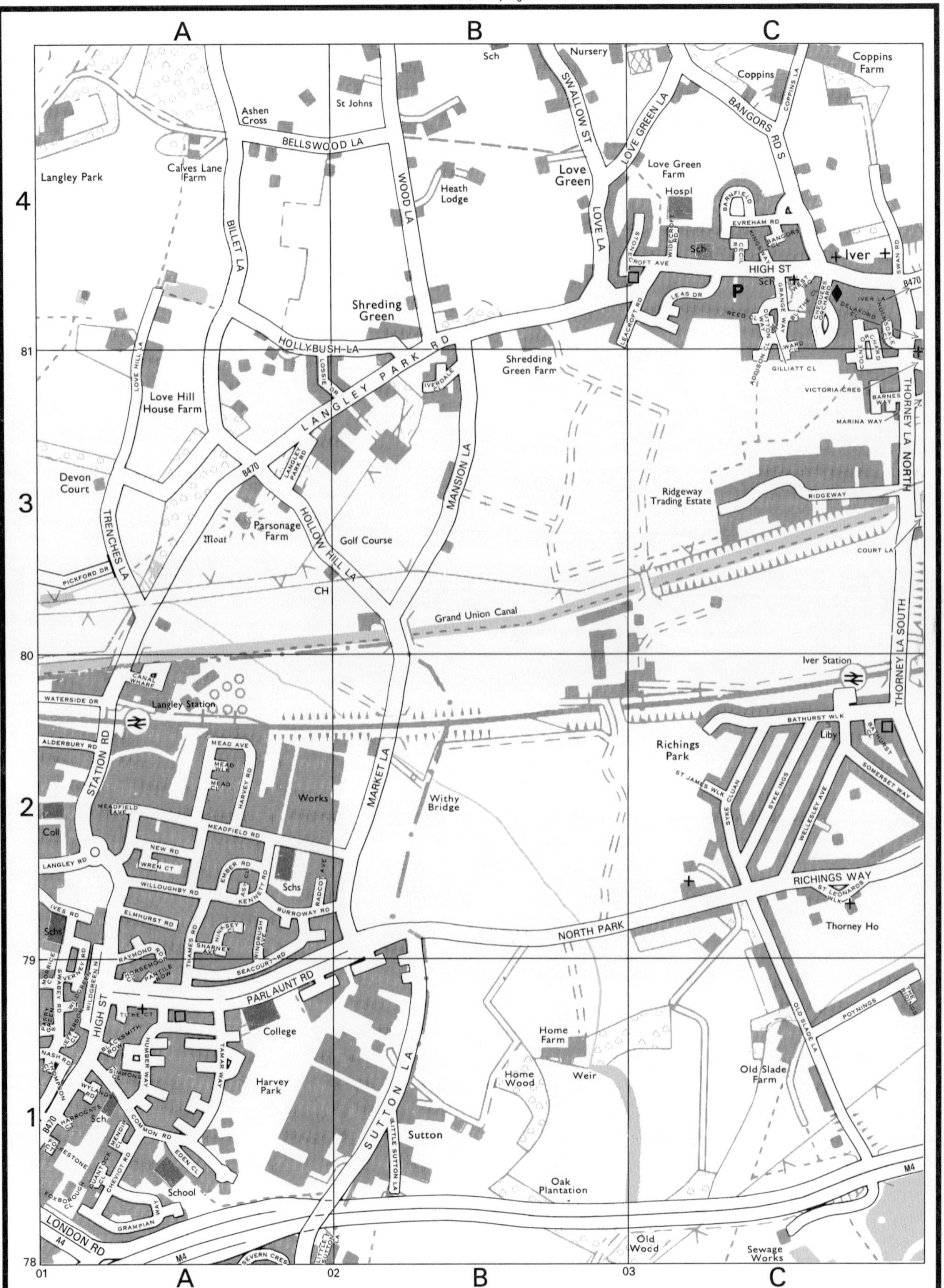

43

69

24

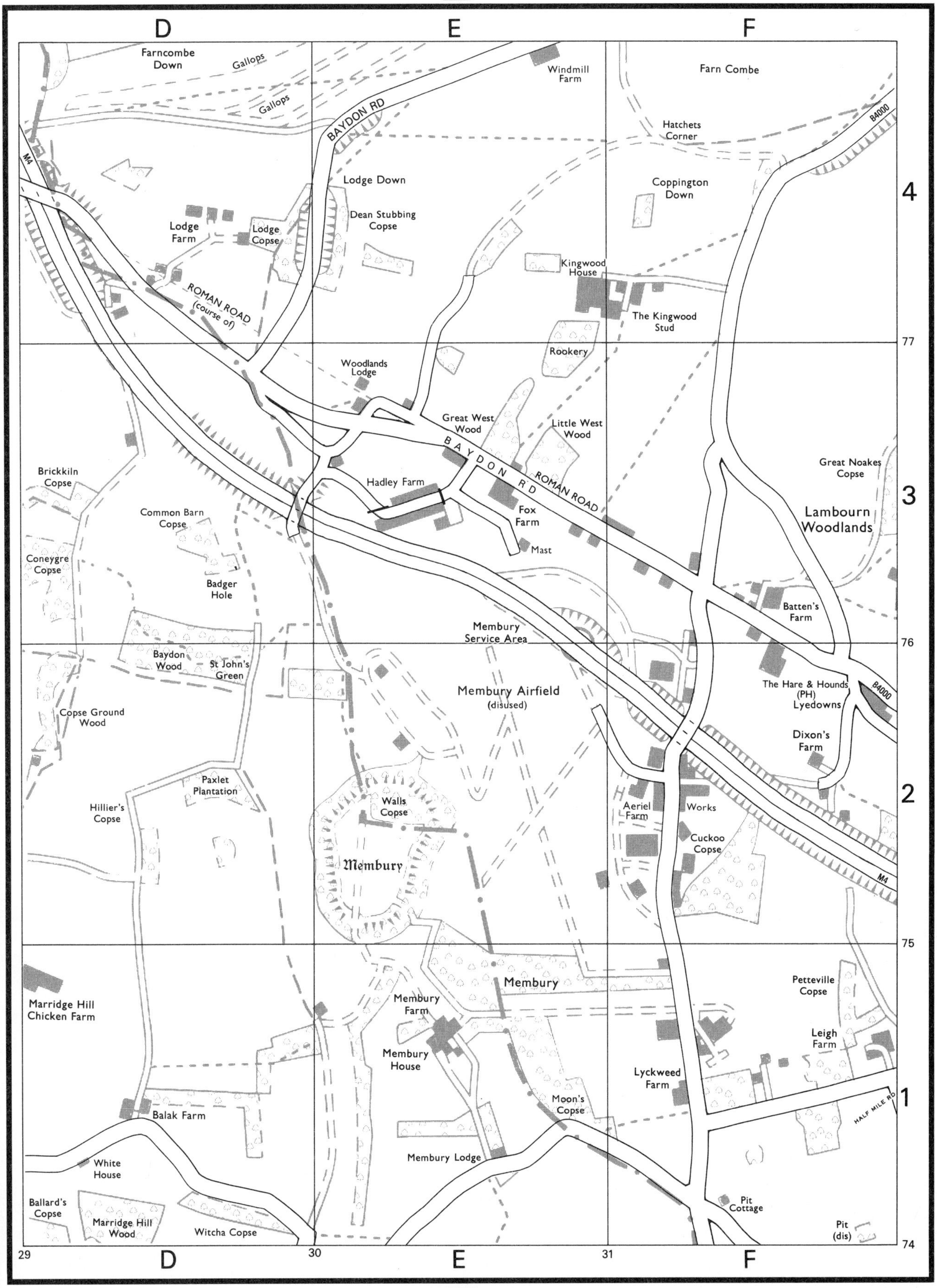
D
E
F
Farncombe Down
Gallops
Gallops
Windmill Farm
Farn Combe
BAYDON RD
Hatchets Corner
B4000
M4
Lodge Down
Coppington Down
4
Dean Stubbing Copse
Lodge Farm
Lodge Copse
Kingwood House
ROMAN ROAD (course of)
The Kingwood Stud
77
Rookery
Woodlands Lodge
Great West Wood
Little West Wood
BAYDON RD
Brickkiln Copse
Hadley Farm
ROMAN ROAD
Great Noakes Copse
Common Barn Copse
Fox Farm
3
Lambourn Woodlands
Coneygre Copse
Mast
Badger Hole
Batten's Farm
Membury Service Area
76
Baydon Wood
St John's Green
Membury Airfield (disused)
The Hare & Hounds (PH)
Lyedowns
B4000
Copse Ground Wood
Dixon's Farm
Paxlet Plantation
2
Hillier's Copse
Walls Copse
Aeriel Farm
Works
Cuckoo Copse
Membury
M4
75
Membury
Petteville Copse
Marridge Hill Chicken Farm
Membury Farm
Leigh Farm
Membury House
Lyckweed Farm
1
Moon's Copse
HALF MILE RD
Balak Farm
Membury Lodge
White House
Ballard's Copse
Pit Cottage
Marridge Hill Wood
Witcha Copse
Pit (dis)
74
29
30
31
D
E
F

46

72

25

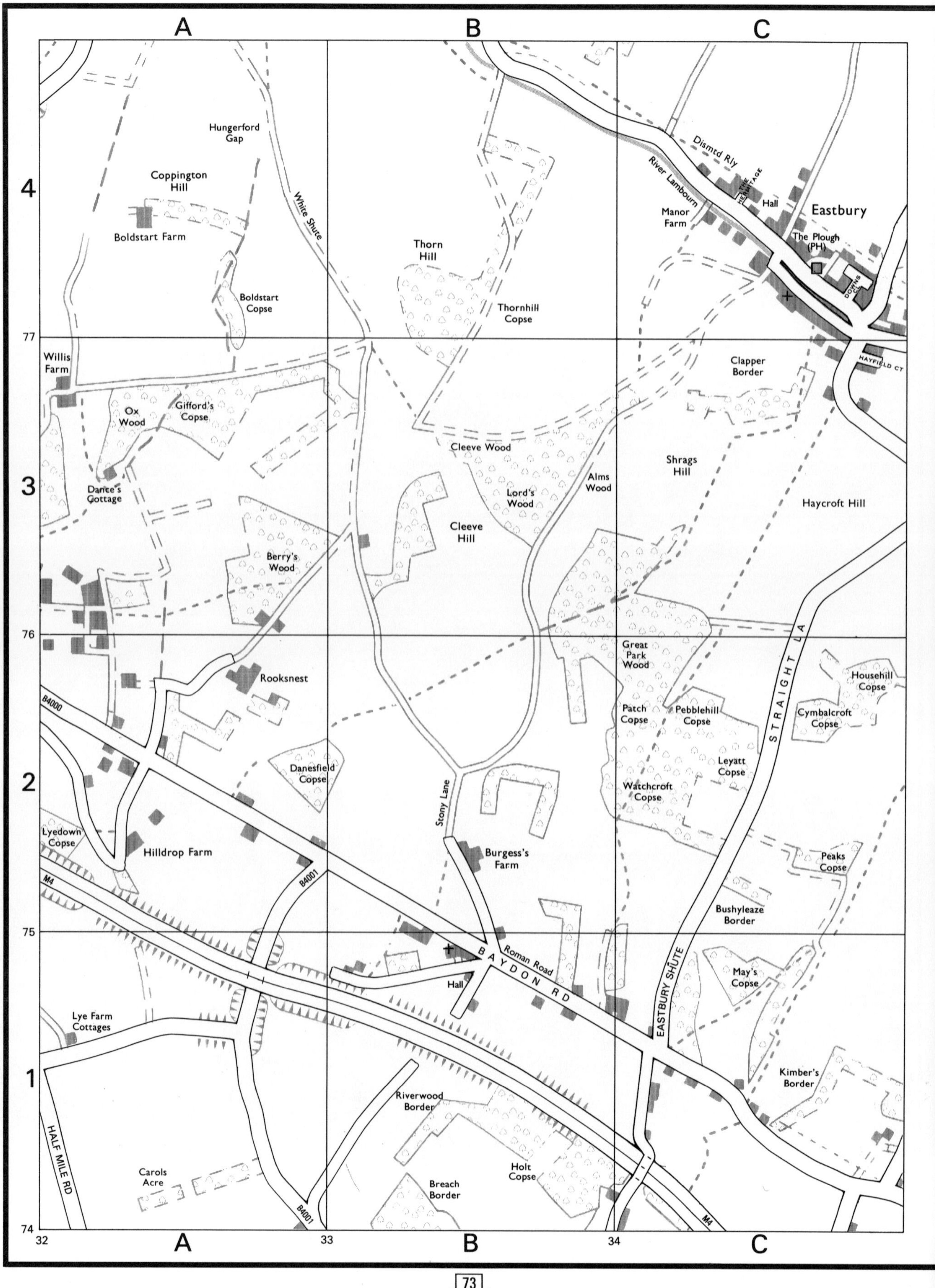
A
B
C
4
3
2
1
77
76
75
74
32
33
34
Hungerford Gap
Coppington Hill
Boldstart Farm
Boldstart Copse
White Shute
Thorn Hill
Thornhill Copse
Dismtd Rly
River Lambourn
THE HERMITAGE
Hall
Manor Farm
Eastbury
The Plough (PH)
DOWNS CL
HAYFIELD CT
Willis Farm
Ox Wood
Gifford's Copse
Dance's Cottage
Clapper Border
Cleeve Wood
Lord's Wood
Alms Wood
Shrags Hill
Haycroft Hill
Cleeve Hill
Berry's Wood
Rooksnest
Great Park Wood
Househill Copse
Cymbalcroft Copse
Patch Copse
Pebblehill Copse
Leyatt Copse
STRAIGHT LA
B4000
Danesfield Copse
Stony Lane
Watchcroft Copse
Lyedown Copse
Hilldrop Farm
Burgess's Farm
Peaks Copse
M4
B4001
Bushyleaze Border
Roman Road
BAYDON RD
Hall
May's Copse
EASTBURY SHUTE
Lye Farm Cottages
Kimber's Border
Riverwood Border
HALF MILE RD
Carols Acre
Holt Copse
Breach Border
B4001
M4

45

73

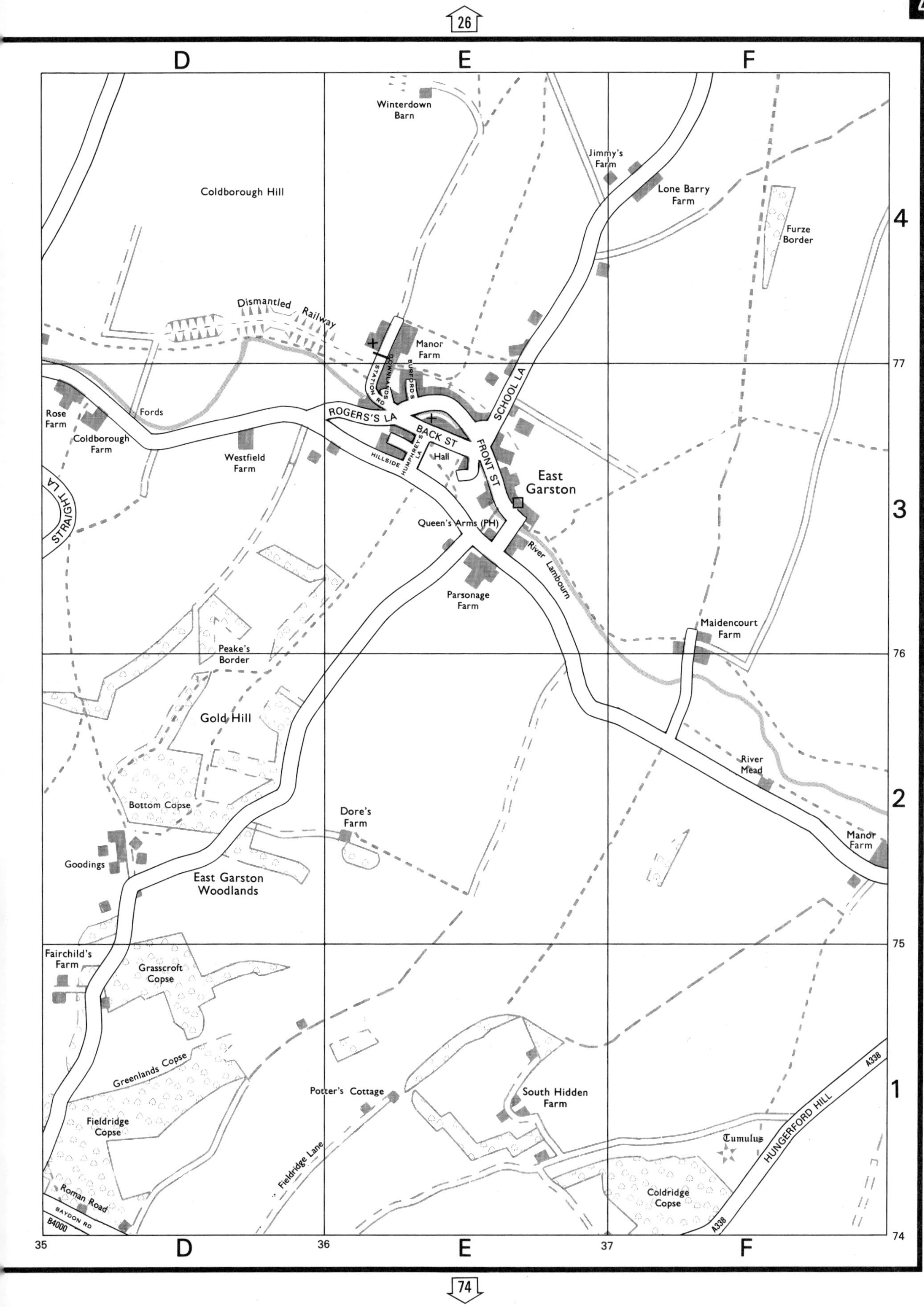
26
D
E
F
Winterdown Barn
Coldborough Hill
Jimmy's Farm
Lone Barry Farm
Furze Border
4
Dismantled Railway
Manor Farm
DOWNLANDS
STATION RD
BUMFORDS
SCHOOL LA
77
Rose Farm
Fords
ROGERS'S LA
BACK ST
Coldborough Farm
Westfield Farm
HILLSIDE
HUMPHREY'S LA
Hall
FRONT ST
East Garston
STRAIGHT LA
3
Queen's Arms (PH)
River Lambourn
Parsonage Farm
Maidencourt Farm
Peake's Border
76
48
Gold Hill
River Mead
2
Bottom Copse
Dore's Farm
Manor Farm
Goodings
East Garston Woodlands
75
Fairchild's Farm
Grasscroft Copse
Greenlands Copse
A338
1
Potter's Cottage
South Hidden Farm
HUNGERFORD HILL
Fieldridge Copse
Cumulus
Fieldridge Lane
Roman Road
Coldridge Copse
BAYDON RD
B4000
A338
74
35
36
37
74

27

47

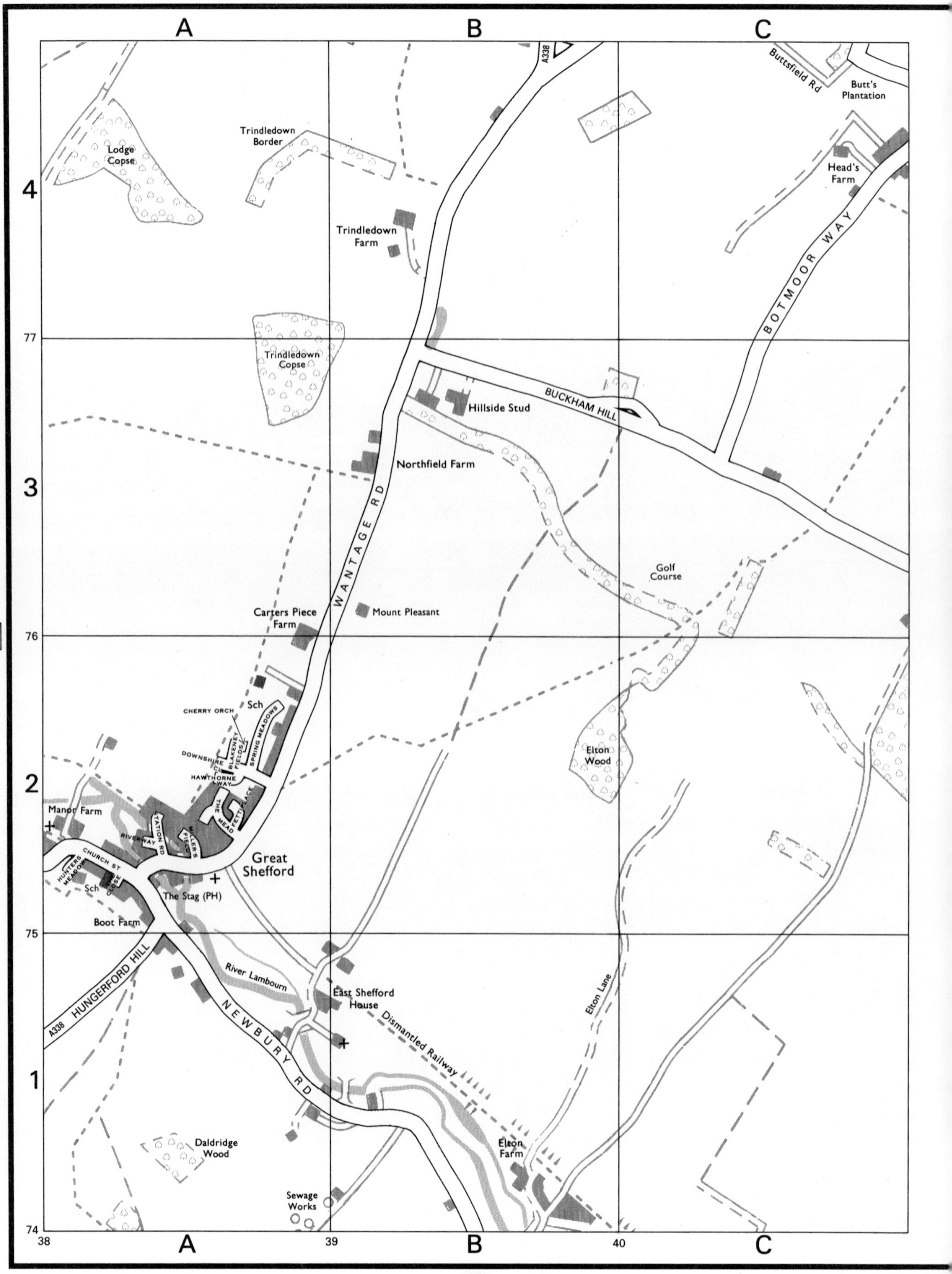
A
B
C
4
3
2
1
77
76
75
74
38
39
40
A338
Buttsfield Rd
Butt's Plantation
Lodge Copse
Trindledown Border
Head's Farm
Trindledown Farm
BOTMOOR WAY
Trindledown Copse
BUCKHAM HILL
Hillside Stud
Northfield Farm
WANTAGE RD
Golf Course
Carters Piece Farm
Mount Pleasant
Sch
CHERRY ORCH
SPRING MEADOWS
BLAKENEY FIELDS
DOWNSHIRE CL
HAWTHORNE WAY
Elton Wood
THE MEAD
PETTI PLACE
Manor Farm
STATION RD
MILLERS FIELD
RIVERWAY
CHURCH ST
HUNTERS MEADOW
Great Shefford
Sch
The Stag (PH)
Boot Farm
HUNGERFORD HILL
A338
River Lambourn
East Shefford House
NEWBURY RD
Dismantled Railway
Elton Lane
Daldridge Wood
Elton Farm
Sewage Works

75

28

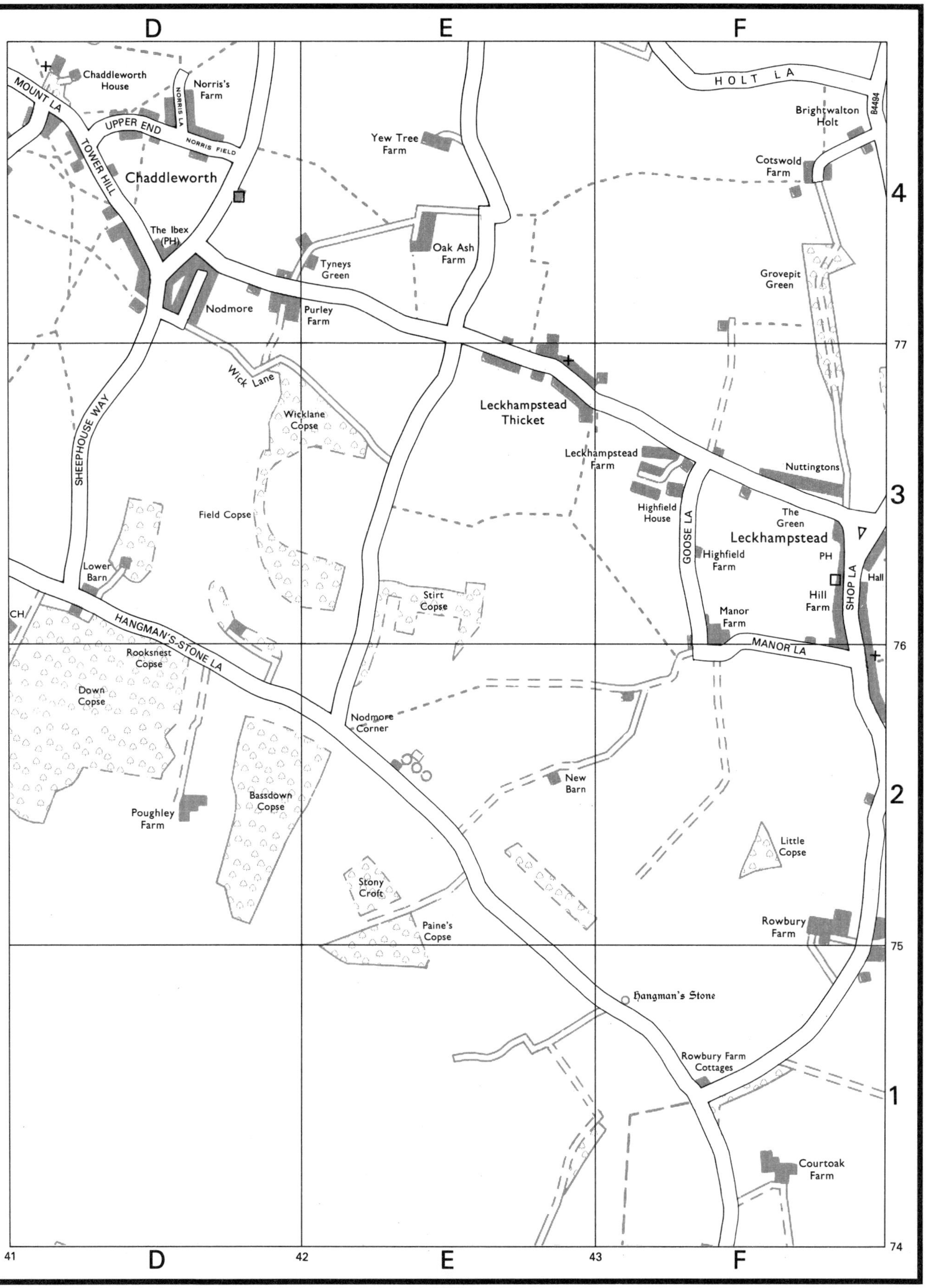
D
E
F
Chaddleworth House
Norris's Farm
MOUNT LA
NORRIS LA
UPPER END
NORRIS FIELD
TOWER HILL
Chaddleworth
The Ibex (PH)
Nodmore
Yew Tree Farm
Oak Ash Farm
Tyneys Green
Purley Farm
HOLT LA
B4494
Brightwalton Holt
Cotswold Farm
Grovepit Green
4
77
Wick Lane
Wicklane Copse
SHEEPHOUSE WAY
Leckhampstead Thicket
Leckhampstead Farm
Nuttingtons
Highfield House
3
Field Copse
The Green
Leckhampstead
GOOSE LA
Highfield Farm
PH
SHOP LA
Hall
Lower Barn
Stirt Copse
Hill Farm
CH
HANGMAN'S-STONE LA
Manor Farm
MANOR LA
76
Rooksnest Copse
Down Copse
Nodmore Corner
New Barn
2
Poughley Farm
Bassdown Copse
Little Copse
Stony Croft
Paine's Copse
Rowbury Farm
75
Hangman's Stone
Rowbury Farm Cottages
1
Courtoak Farm
74
41
42
43

50

76

29

49

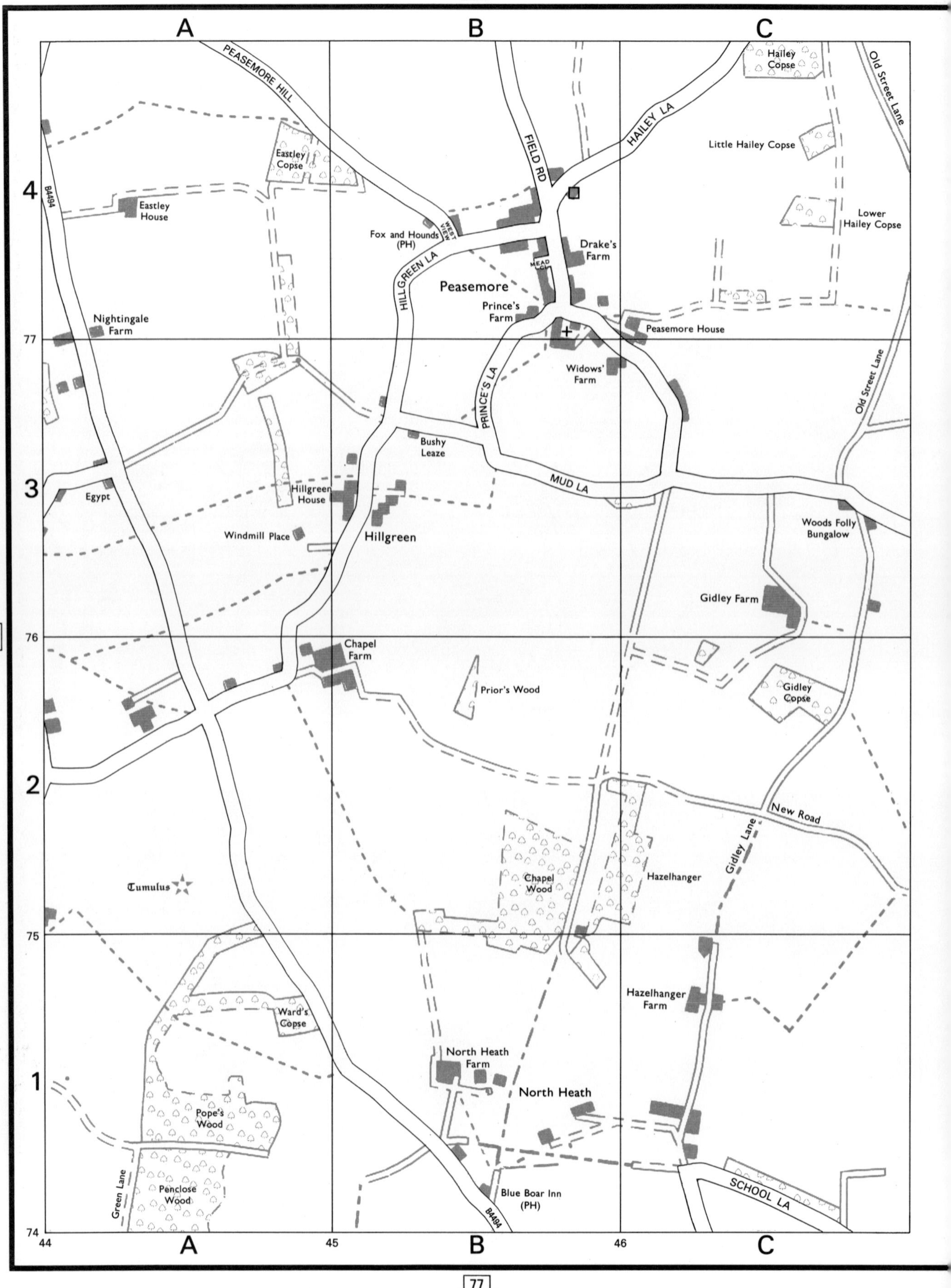
A
B
C
PEASEMORE HILL
FIELD RD
HAILEY LA
Hailey Copse
Old Street Lane
Little Hailey Copse
Eastley Copse
4
B4494
Eastley House
Fox and Hounds (PH)
WEST VIEW
Drake's Farm
Lower Hailey Copse
HILLGREEN LA
MEAD CL
Peasemore
Prince's Farm
Nightingale Farm
Peasemore House
77
PRINCE'S LA
Widows' Farm
Old Street Lane
Bushy Leaze
3
Egypt
Hillgreen House
MUD LA
Woods Folly Bungalow
Windmill Place
Hillgreen
Gidley Farm
76
Chapel Farm
Prior's Wood
Gidley Copse
2
New Road
Gidley Lane
Chapel Wood
Hazelhanger
Tumulus
75
Hazelhanger Farm
Ward's Copse
1
North Heath Farm
North Heath
Pope's Wood
Green Lane
Penclose Wood
Blue Boar Inn (PH)
SCHOOL LA
B4494
74
44
45
46
A
B
C

77

30

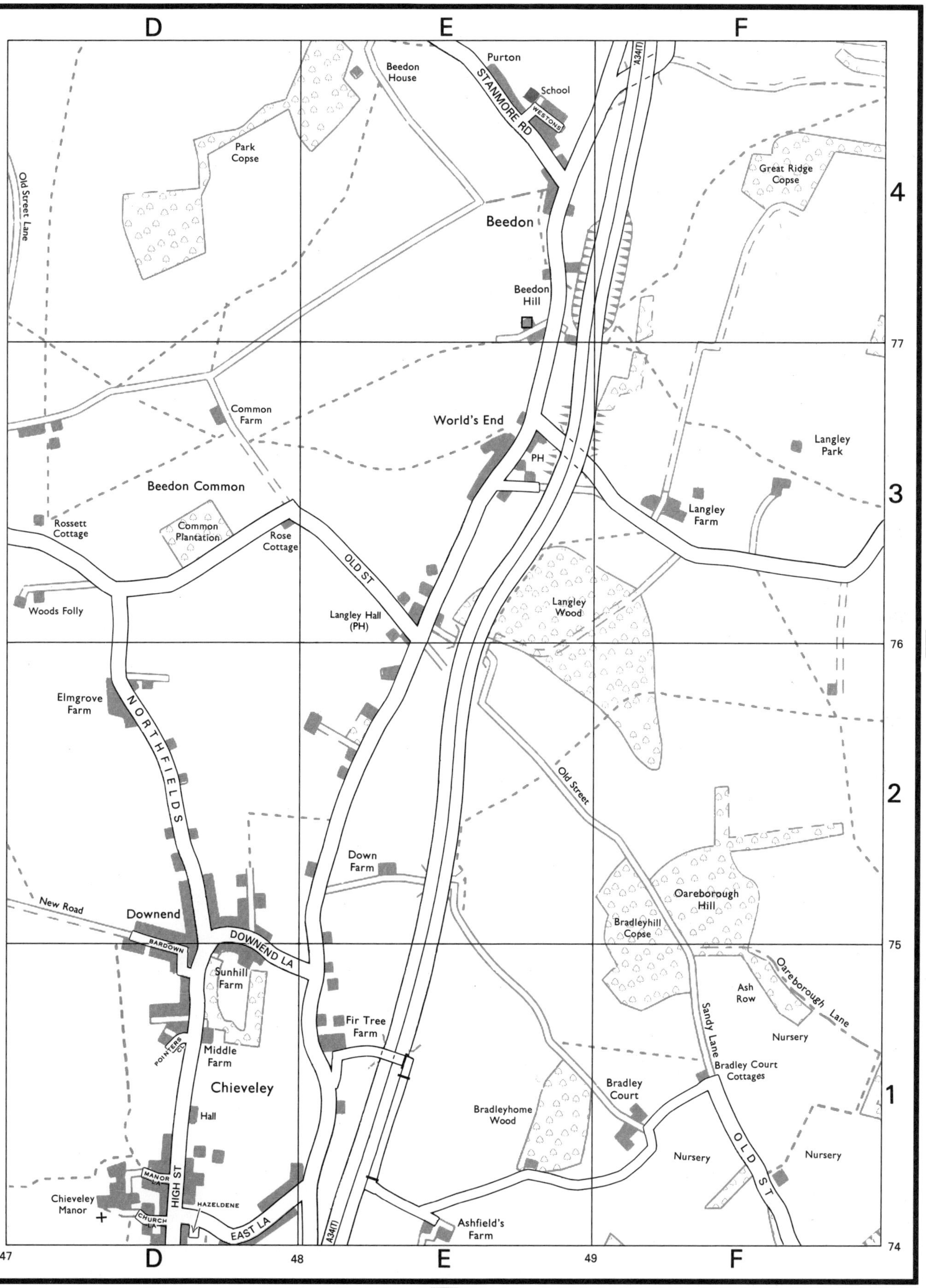

D
E
F
Purton
Beedon House
School
STANMORE RD
WESTONS
A34(T)
Park Copse
Old Street Lane
Great Ridge Copse
4
Beedon
Beedon Hill
77
Common Farm
World's End
Langley Park
PH
Beedon Common
3
Langley Farm
Rossett Cottage
Common Plantation
Rose Cottage
OLD ST
Langley Wood
Woods Folly
Langley Hall (PH)
76
Elmgrove Farm
NORTHFIELDS
Old Street
2
Down Farm
New Road
Oareborough Hill
Downend
Bradleyhill Copse
BARDOWN
DOWNEND LA
75
Oareborough Lane
Sunhill Farm
Ash Row
Sandy Lane
Fir Tree Farm
Nursery
POINTERS CL
Middle Farm
Bradley Court Cottages
Chieveley
Bradley Court
1
Bradleyhome Wood
Hall
Nursery
OLD ST
Nursery
MANOR LA
Chieveley Manor
HIGH ST
HAZELDENE
CHURCH LA
EAST LA
A34(T)
Ashfield's Farm
74
47
48
49

52

78

31

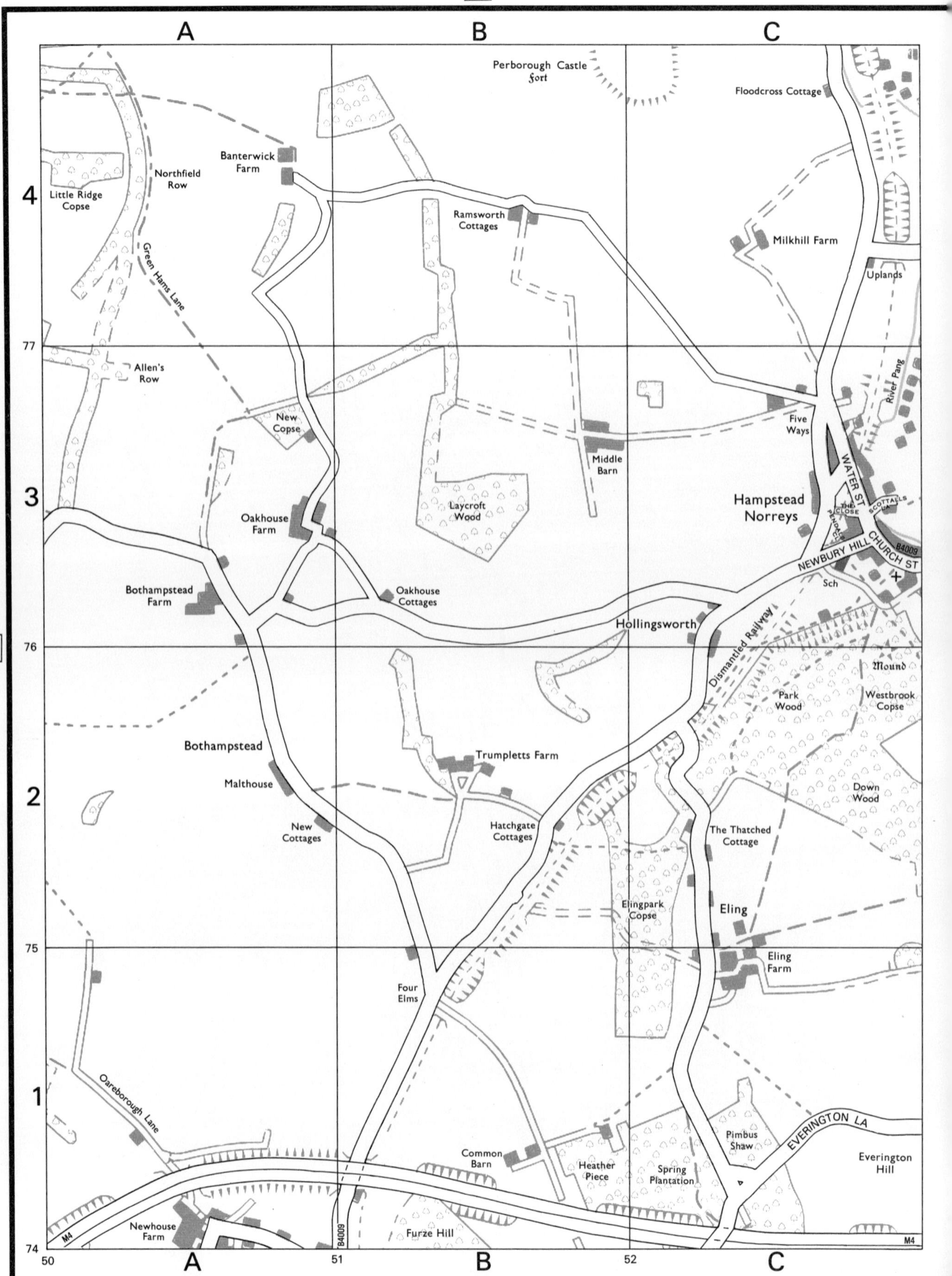
A
B
C
Perborough Castle
Fort
Floodcross Cottage
Banterwick Farm
Northfield Row
Little Ridge Copse
Ramsworth Cottages
Milkhill Farm
Uplands
Green Hams Lane
Allen's Row
River Pang
New Copse
Five Ways
Middle Barn
WATER ST
Hampstead Norreys
THE CLOSE
SCOTTALLS LA
Laycroft Wood
Oakhouse Farm
B4009
NEWBURY HILL
CHURCH ST
Bothampstead Farm
Oakhouse Cottages
Sch
Hollingsworth
Dismantled Railway
Mound
Park Wood
Westbrook Copse
Bothampstead
Trumpletts Farm
Malthouse
Down Wood
New Cottages
Hatchgate Cottages
The Thatched Cottage
Elingpark Copse
Eling
Eling Farm
Four Elms
Oareborough Lane
Pimbus Shaw
EVERINGTON LA
Everington Hill
Common Barn
Heather Piece
Spring Plantation
Newhouse Farm
Furze Hill
M4
B4009
4
3
2
1
77
76
75
74
50
51
52

51

79

32

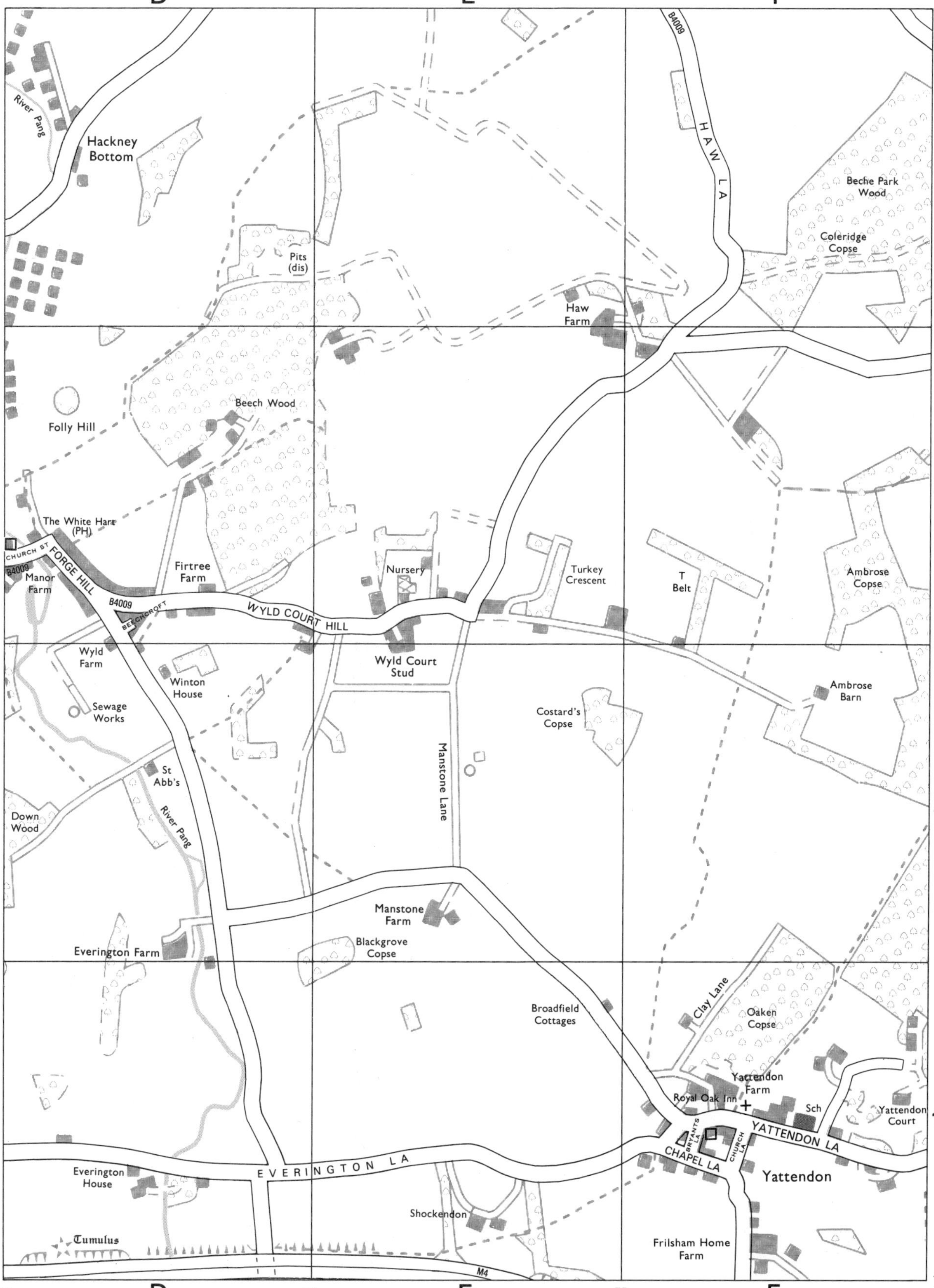
D
E
F
4
3
2
1
77
76
75
74
53
54
55
River Pang
Hackney Bottom
Pits (dis)
Haw Farm
HAW LA
B4009
Beche Park Wood
Coleridge Copse
Beech Wood
Folly Hill
The White Hart (PH)
CHURCH ST
FORGE HILL
Manor Farm
Firtree Farm
BEECHCROFT
WYLD COURT HILL
Nursery
Turkey Crescent
T Belt
Ambrose Copse
Wyld Farm
Wyld Court Stud
Winton House
Sewage Works
Ambrose Barn
Costard's Copse
St Abb's
Manstone Lane
Down Wood
Manstone Farm
Blackgrove Copse
Everington Farm
Broadfield Cottages
Clay Lane
Oaken Copse
Yattendon Farm
Royal Oak Inn
Sch
Yattendon Court
BRYANTS LA
CHURCH LA
YATTENDON LA
CHAPEL LA
Yattendon
EVERINGTON LA
Everington House
Shockendon
Tumulus
Frilsham Home Farm
M4

54

80

33

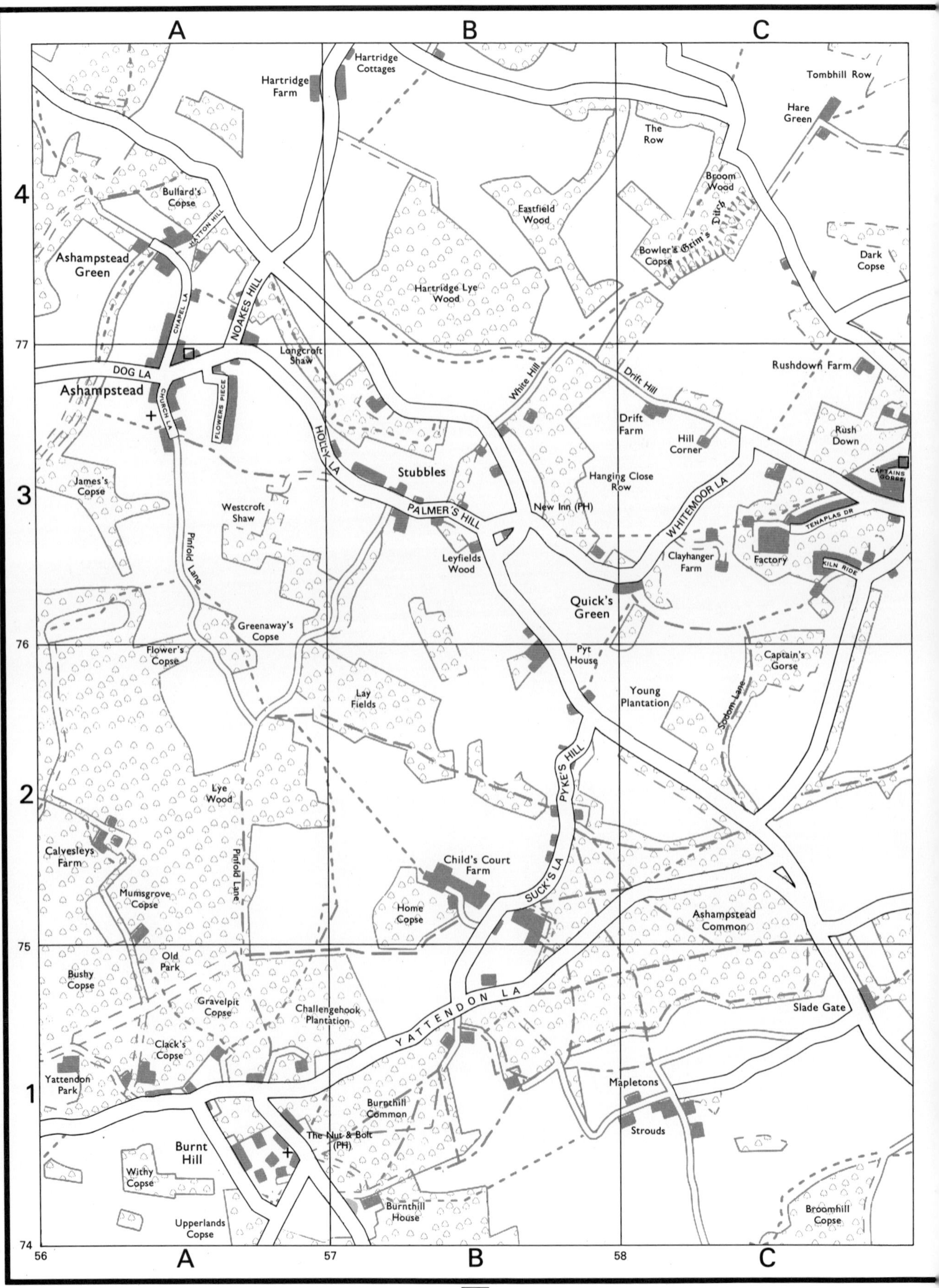
A
B
C
4
3
2
1
77
76
75
74
56
57
58
Hartridge Farm
Hartridge Cottages
Tombhill Row
Hare Green
The Row
Broom Wood
Bullard's Copse
HATTON HILL
Eastfield Wood
Grim's Ditch
Bowler's Copse
Dark Copse
Ashampstead Green
CHAPEL LA
NOAKES HILL
Hartridge Lye Wood
Longcroft Shaw
Rushdown Farm
DOG LA
Ashampstead
CHURCH LA
FLOWERS PIECE
White Hill
Drift Hill
Drift Farm
Hill Corner
Rush Down
CAPTAINS GORSE
HOLLY LA
Stubbles
Hanging Close Row
James's Copse
Westcroft Shaw
PALMER'S HILL
New Inn (PH)
WHITEMOOR LA
TENAPLAS DR
Pinfold Lane
Leyfields Wood
Clayhanger Farm
Factory
KILN RIDE
Quick's Green
Greenaway's Copse
Flower's Copse
Pyt House
Captain's Gorse
Young Plantation
Lay Fields
Sodom Lane
PYKE'S HILL
Lye Wood
Calvesleys Farm
Child's Court Farm
Pinfold Lane
Mumsgrove Copse
SUCK'S LA
Home Copse
Ashampstead Common
Old Park
Bushy Copse
Gravelpit Copse
Challengehook Plantation
YATTENDON LA
Slade Gate
Clack's Copse
Yattendon Park
Mapletons
Burnthill Common
Strouds
Burnt Hill
The Nut & Bolt (PH)
Withy Copse
Burnthill House
Broomhill Copse
Upperlands Copse

53

81

34

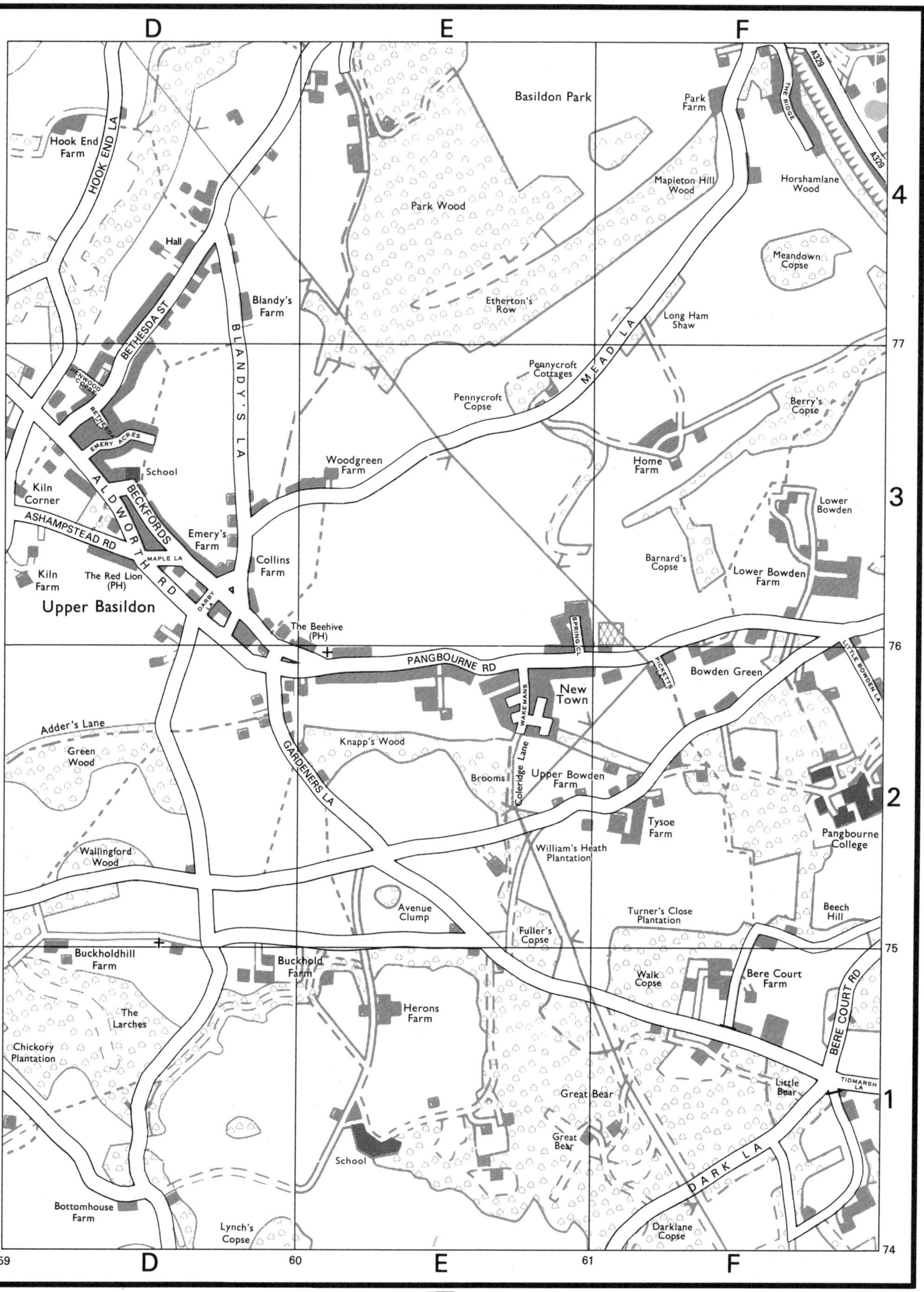
D
E
F
Basildon Park
Park Farm
A329
THE RIDGE
Hook End Farm
HOOK END LA
Mapleton Hill Wood
Horshamlane Wood
Park Wood
4
Hall
Meandown Copse
Blandy's Farm
Etherton's Row
BETHESDA ST
BLANDY'S LA
Long Ham Shaw
MEAD LA
77
HENWOOD COPSE
Pennycroft Cottages
Pennycroft Copse
Berry's Copse
BETHESDA CL
EMERY ACRES
School
Woodgreen Farm
Home Farm
Kiln Corner
ALDWORTH RD
BECKFORDS
3
Lower Bowden
ASHAMPSTEAD RD
Emery's Farm
MAPLE LA
Collins Farm
Barnard's Copse
Lower Bowden Farm
Kiln Farm
The Red Lion (PH)
DARBY LA
Upper Basildon
The Beehive (PH)
SPRING CL
76
PANGBOURNE RD
PICKETTS LA
Bowden Green
LITTLE BOWDEN LA
WAKEMANS
New Town
Adder's Lane
Knapp's Wood
GARDENERS LA
Green Wood
Coleridge Lane
Brooms
Upper Bowden Farm
2
Tysoe Farm
Pangbourne College
William's Heath Plantation
Wallingford Wood
Avenue Clump
Beech Hill
Turner's Close Plantation
Fuller's Copse
75
Buckholdhill Farm
Buckhold Farm
Walk Copse
Bere Court Farm
BERE COURT RD
Herons Farm
The Larches
Chickory Plantation
TIDMARSH LA
Little Bear
1
Great Bear
Great Bear
School
DARK LA
Bottomhouse Farm
Lynch's Copse
Darklane Copse
74
59
60
61
D
E
F

56

82

not continued, see key diagram

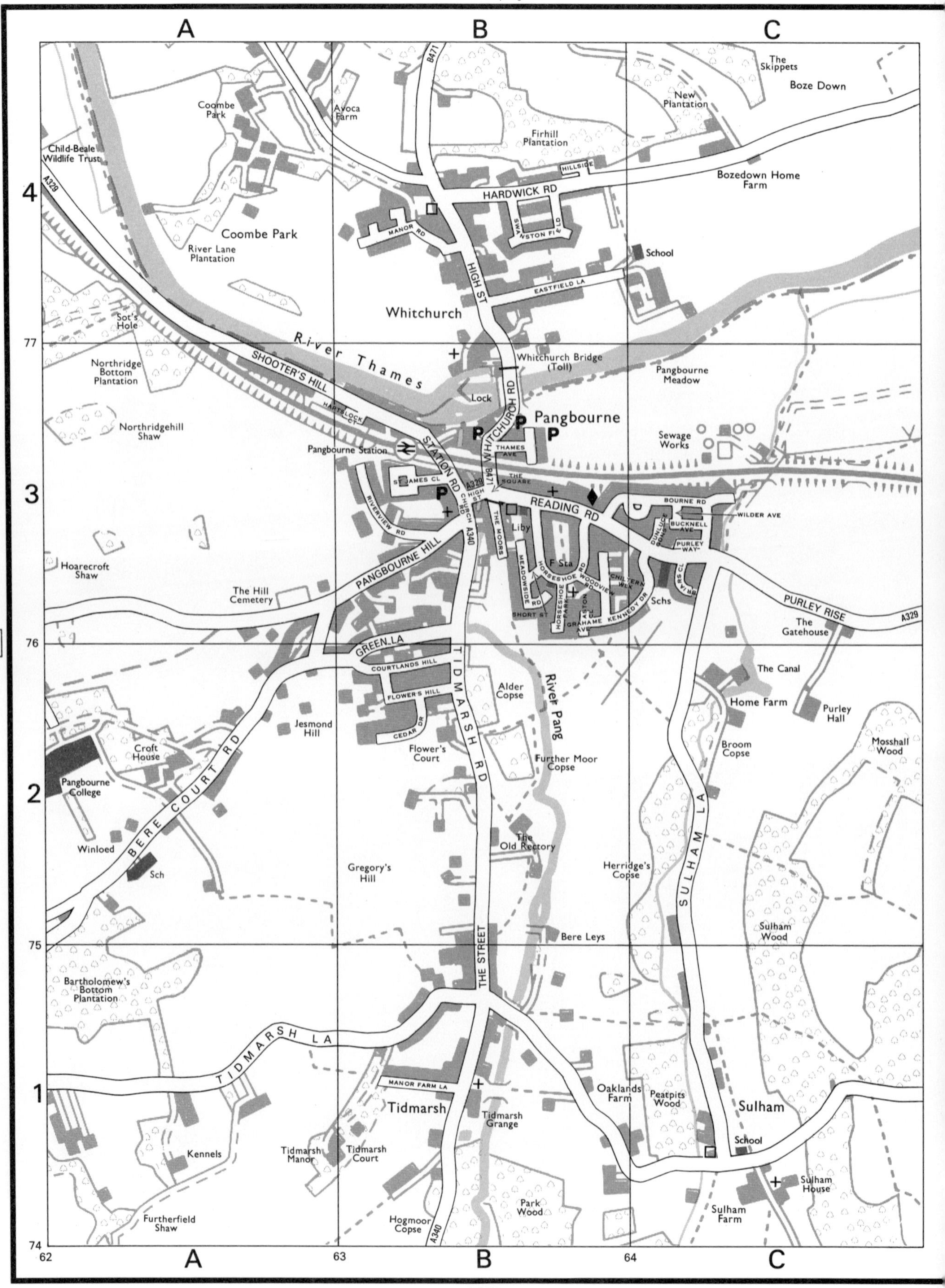

55

83

not continued, see key diagram

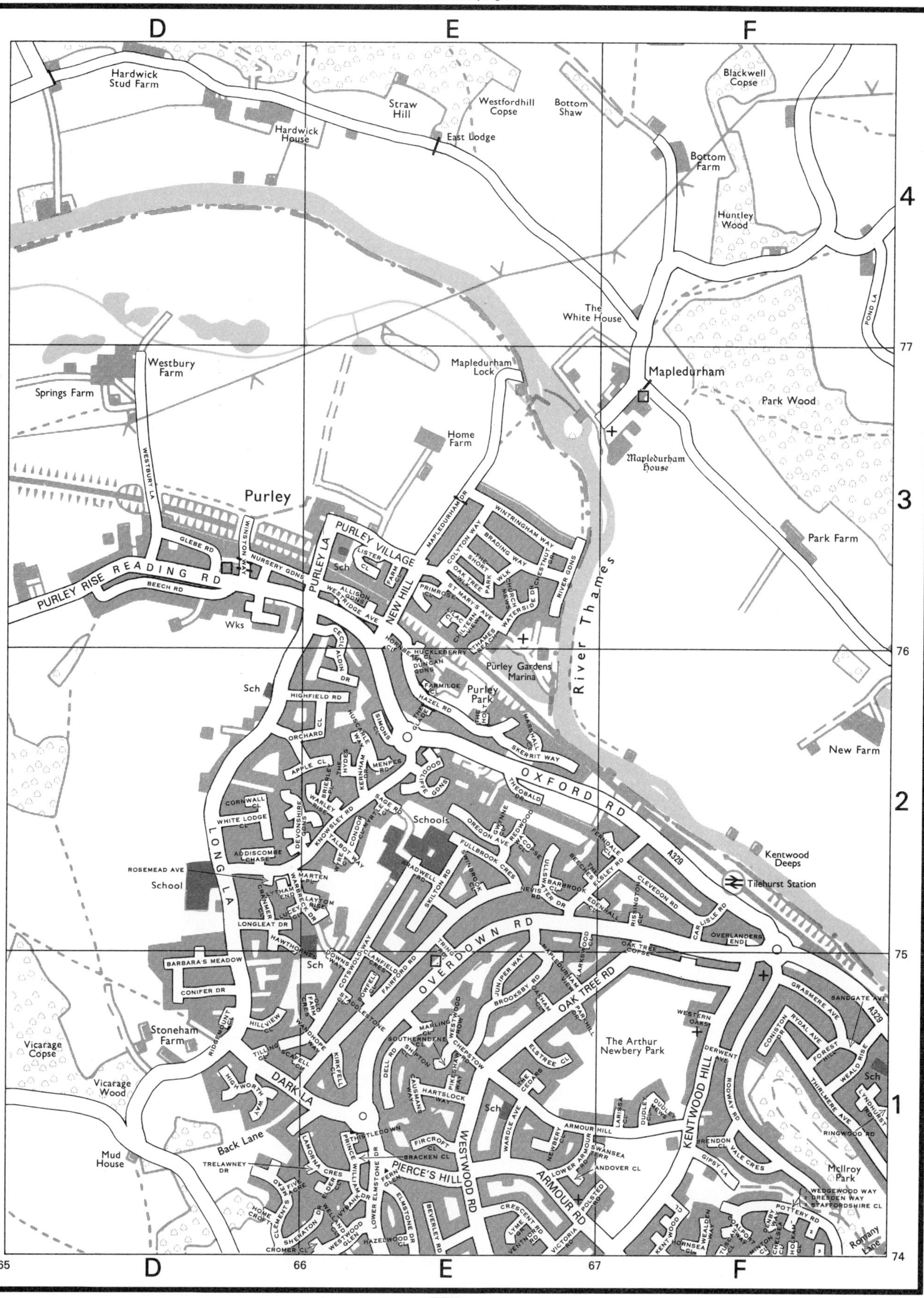

58

84

not continued, see key diagram

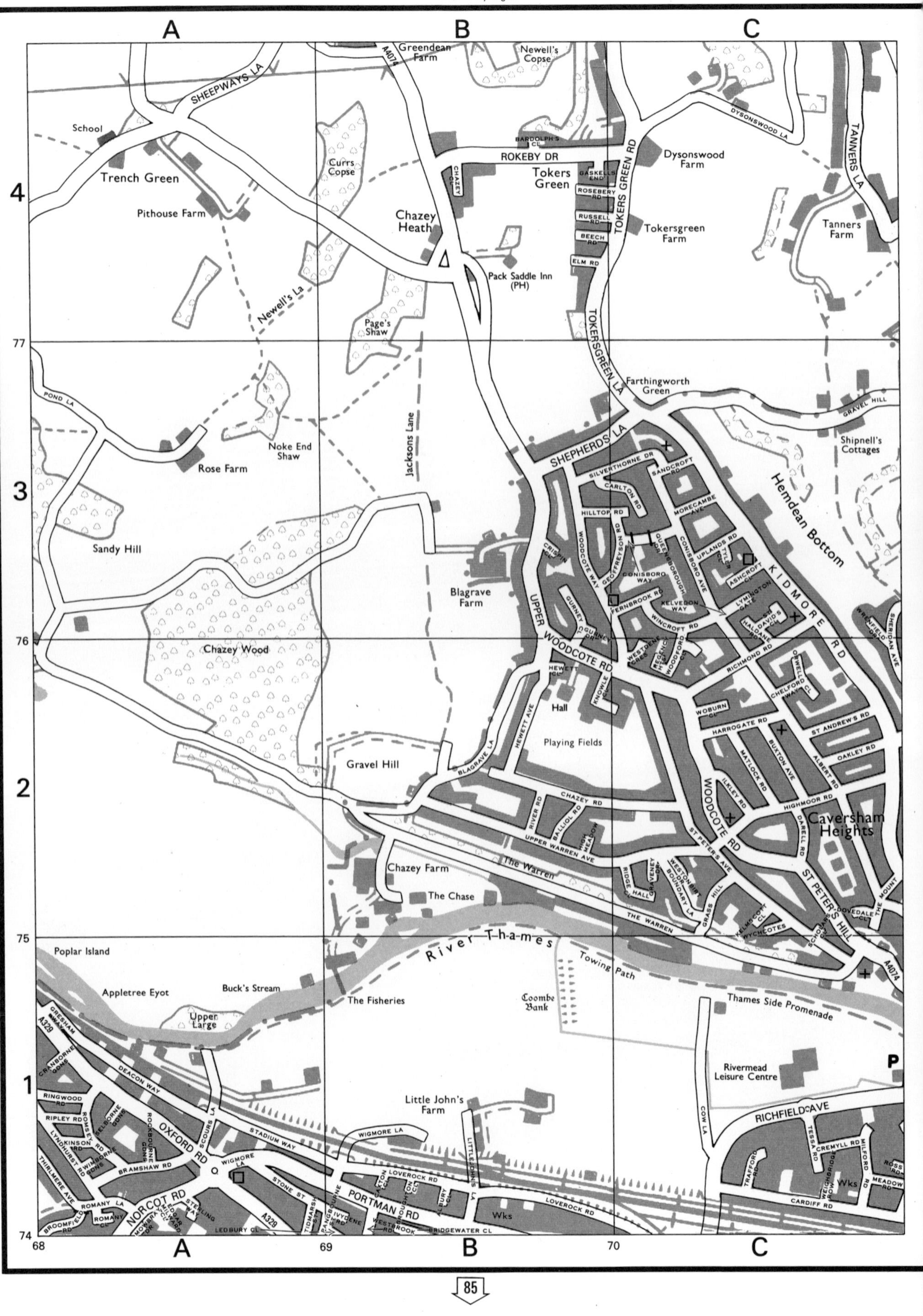

57

not continued, see key diagram

60

35

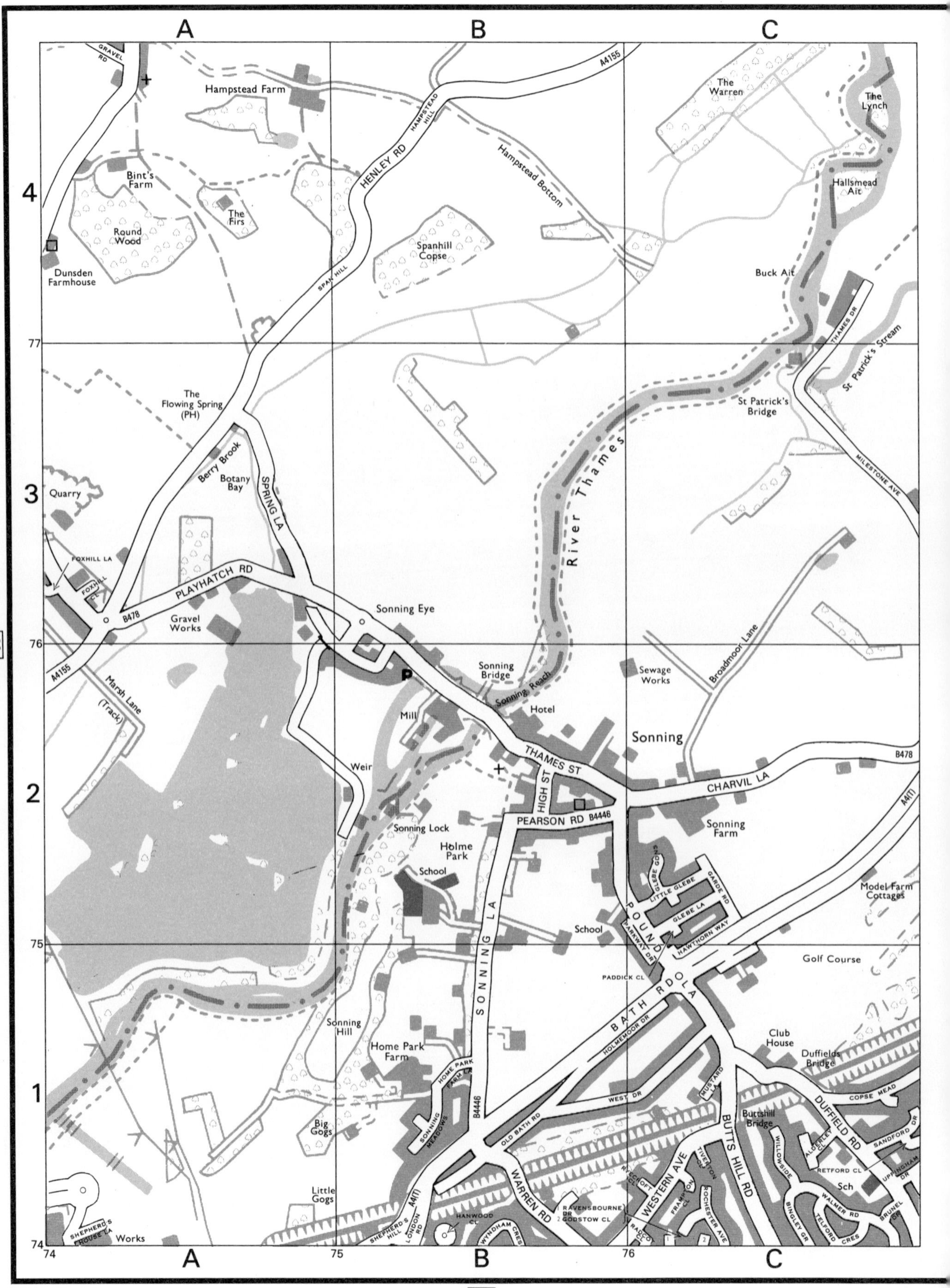
A
B
C
4
3
2
1
77
76
75
74
Hampstead Farm
Bint's Farm
Round Wood
The Firs
Dunsden Farmhouse
Spanhill Copse
Hampstead Bottom
HENLEY RD
HAMPSTEAD HILL
SPAN HILL
A4155
GRAVEL RD
The Warren
The Lynch
Hallsmead Ait
Buck Ait
THAMES DR
St Patrick's Stream
St Patrick's Bridge
MILESTONE AVE
The Flowing Spring (PH)
Berry Brook
Botany Bay
SPRING LA
Quarry
FOXHILL LA
FOXHILL CL
PLAYHATCH RD
B478
Gravel Works
Sonning Eye
River Thames
Marsh Lane (Track)
Sonning Bridge
Sonning Reach
Hotel
Sewage Works
Broadmoor Lane
Sonning
Mill
Weir
THAMES ST
HIGH ST
CHARVIL LA
PEARSON RD
B4446
Sonning Lock
Holme Park
School
Sonning Farm
GLEBE GDNS
LITTLE GLEBE
GARDE RD
GLEBE LA
HAWTHORN WAY
POUND LA
PARKWAY DR
Model Farm Cottages
SONNING LA
School
PADDICK CL
Golf Course
BATH RD
A4(T)
HOLMEMOOR DR
Sonning Hill
Home Park Farm
HOME PARK FARM LA
Club House
Duffields Bridge
WEST DR
MUSTARD LA
COPSE MEAD
DUFFIELD RD
Buttshill Bridge
BUTTS HILL RD
SANDFORD DR
SONNING MEADOWS
OLD BATH RD
Big Gogs
ALDERLEY CL
WILLOWSIDE
RETFORD CL
UPPINGHAM DR
Sch
WARREN RD
WESTERN AVE
TIVERTON
RAYCROFT CL
FRAMPTON CL
ROCHESTER AVE
BINGLEY GR
WALMER RD
TELFORD CRES
BRUNEL DR
Little Gogs
LONDON RD
SHEPHERD'S HILL
HANWOOD CL
WYNDHAM CRES
RAVENSBOURNE DR
GODSTOW CL
RADCOT CL
SHEPHERD'S HOUSE LA
Works

59

87

36

D
E
F
4
3
2
1
77
76
75
74
78
79
Borough Marsh
Borough Lake
LODDON DR
St Patrick's Stream
Sewage Works
Pumping Stations
Sheeplands Farm
MUMBERY HILL
B477
BATH RD
A4(T)
A3032
A321
WARGRAVE RD
School
Nursery
MALVERN WAY
NEW RD
Northfields
CHASESIDE AVE
CARLILE GDNS
AMBERLEY DR
HILLTOP RD
HERON DR
WESTVIEW DR
Loddon Park Farm
NEW BATH RD
YEWHURST CL
Works
WILLOW DR
LONGFIELD RD
PENNFIELDS
MIDDLEFIELDS
LONDON RD
NORTHBURY LA
Northbury Farm
NEW RD
Ruscombe
Bridge Farm
River Loddon
WHITE CRES
Sch
NORTHBURY AVE
ST JAMES CL
LODDON HALL RD
WALTHAM RD
B3024
Charvil
SYCAMORE DR
MILTON WAY
CHURCH LA
Twyford
LINCOLN GDNS
HERMITAGE DR
WENSLEY CL
B3024
RUSCOMBE RD
RUSCOMBE LA
RUSCOMBE PARK
MILESTONE AVE
ST PATRICK'S AVE
PARK VIEW DR N
KINGSLEY CL
Charvil Farm
EDWARD RD
White Bridge
OLD BATH RD
PINE GR
ORCHARD ESTATE
CHARVIL HOUSE RD
FAIRWAY
GINGELLS FARM RD
THORNBERS WAY
A3032
THE GROVE
SPRINGFIELD PARK
STANLAKE LA
Works
HIGH ST
CHURCH ST
Liby
Mill
POLEHAMPTON CL
CHAPEL ROW
Ruscombe Down
MILESTONE CRES
PARK VIEW DR S
CHEVIOT DR
MENDIP CL
CLEVELAND
CHILTERN DR
WALTHAM RD
WAGTAIL CL
BROOK ST
STATION RD
B3018
KILOWNA CL
WHITMORE DR
WENLOCK EDGE
PENNINE WAY
QUANTOCK CL
A321
BYRON RD
Stanlake Park
PH
A3032
A4(T)
BATH RD
Twyford Station
PADDOCK HTS
Ruscombe Turn
WINCHCOMBE RD
BOLWELL CL
BROAD HINTON
Charvil Hill
FOXES WLK
THE HAWTHORNS
PARK LA
Old River
COLLETON DR
VERNEY CL
Sch
WESSEX GDNS
WOODPECKER CL
HARRISON CL
1 SWANSCOURT
2 KINGFISHER CT
MALLARD CL
B3018
Stanlake Bridge
HURST RD
BROADWATER RD
HURST PARK RD
The Land's End (PH)
LANDSEND LA
WAINGELS RD
BEGGARS HILL RD
Giddy Bridge (FB)
Copper Bridge (FB)
Hogmoor Lane
COPSE MEAD
Sch
Bird Sanctuary
BROADWATER LA
POPLAR LA
SHIPLEY CL
DENMARK AVE
PERTH CL
1 RETFORD CL
2 CHURCH RD
3 BRANDON AVE
Ashenbury Park
Southcot Ditch
Whistley Bridge
B3030
Whistley Green
Ward's Cross
HOGMOOR LA
ROTHWELL GDNS
Whistley Court Farm
A321
TIPPINGS LA
B3030
LODGE RD
HINTON RD

62

88

37

61

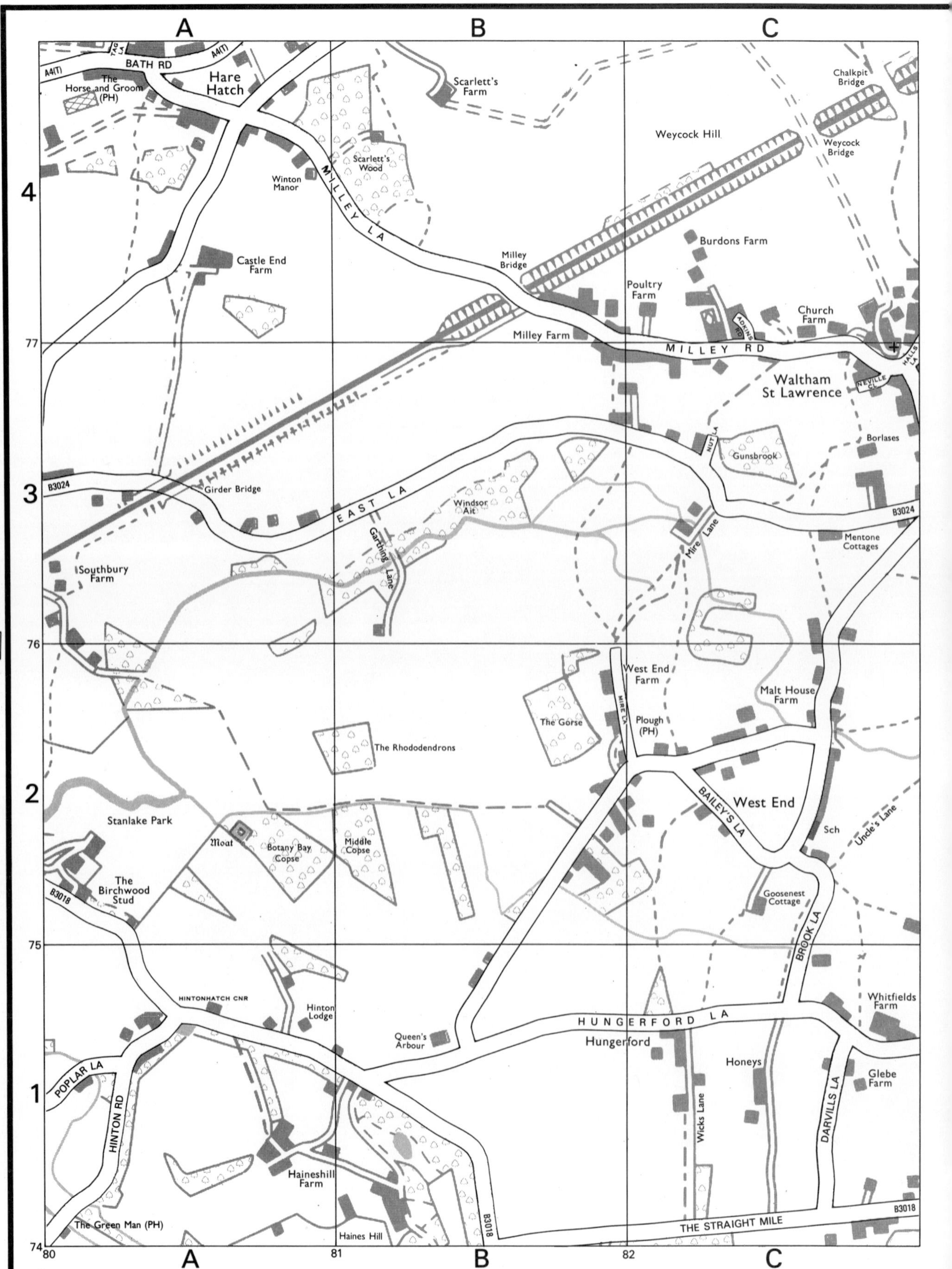

A
B
C
4
3
2
1
77
76
75
74
80
81
82
BATH RD
A4(T)
TAG LA
The Horse and Groom (PH)
Hare Hatch
Scarlett's Farm
Chalkpit Bridge
Weycock Hill
Weycock Bridge
Scarlett's Wood
Winton Manor
MILLEY LA
Castle End Farm
Milley Bridge
Burdons Farm
Poultry Farm
Church Farm
ADKINS RD
Milley Farm
MILLEY RD
HALLS LA
NEVILLE CL
Waltham St Lawrence
NUT LA
Gunsbrook
Borlases
B3024
Girder Bridge
EAST LA
Windsor Ait
Garthing Lane
Mire Lane
Mentone Cottages
Southbury Farm
West End Farm
Malt House Farm
MIRE LA
The Gorse
Plough (PH)
The Rhododendrons
BAILEY'S LA
West End
Stanlake Park
Moat
Botany Bay Copse
Middle Copse
Sch
Uncle's Lane
The Birchwood Stud
B3018
Goosenest Cottage
BROOK LA
HINTONHATCH CNR
Hinton Lodge
Whitfields Farm
HUNGERFORD LA
Queen's Arbour
Hungerford
POPLAR LA
Honeys
Glebe Farm
HINTON RD
Wicks Lane
DARVILLS LA
Haineshill Farm
The Green Man (PH)
Haines Hill
THE STRAIGHT MILE

89

38

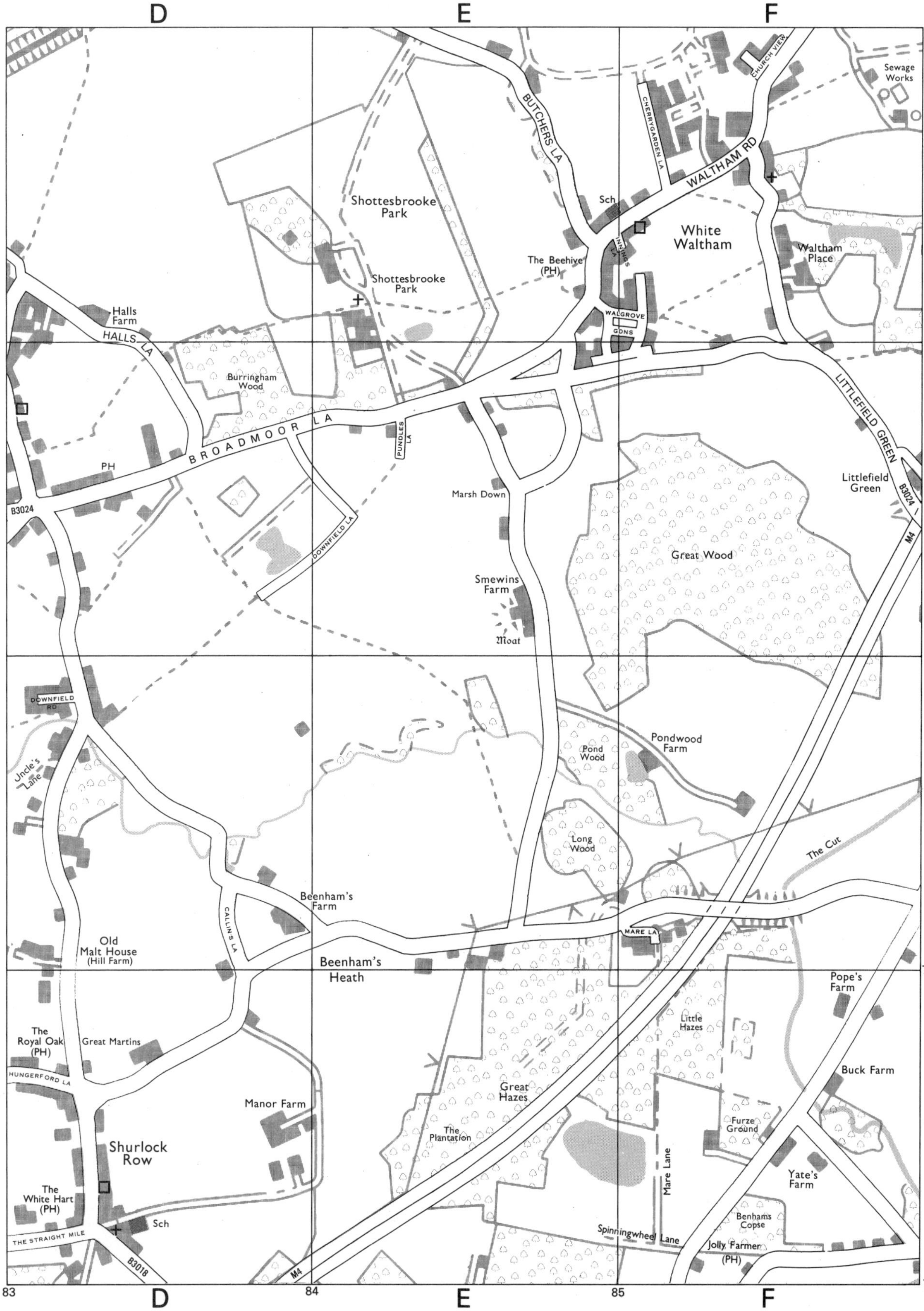
D
E
F
Shottesbrooke Park
Shottesbrooke Park
BUTCHERS LA
CHERRYGARDEN LA
CHURCH VIEW
WALTHAM RD
Sch
White Waltham
The Beehive (PH)
Waltham Place
Sewage Works
WALGROVE GDNS
Halls Farm
HALLS LA
Burringham Wood
BROADMOOR LA
PUNDLES LA
PH
B3024
DOWNFIELD LA
Marsh Down
LITTLEFIELD GREEN
Littlefield Green
Great Wood
M4
Smewins Farm
Moat
DOWNFIELD RD
Uncle's Lane
Pond Wood
Pondwood Farm
Long Wood
The Cut
Beenham's Farm
CALLIN'S LA
MARE LA
Old Malt House (Hill Farm)
Beenham's Heath
Pope's Farm
The Royal Oak (PH)
Great Martins
HUNGERFORD LA
Little Hazes
Buck Farm
Manor Farm
Great Hazes
The Plantation
Furze Ground
Shurlock Row
Mare Lane
Yate's Farm
The White Hart (PH)
Sch
THE STRAIGHT MILE
B3018
Spinningwheel Lane
Benhams Copse
Jolly Farmer (PH)
4
3
2
1
77
76
75
74
83
84
85

64

90

39

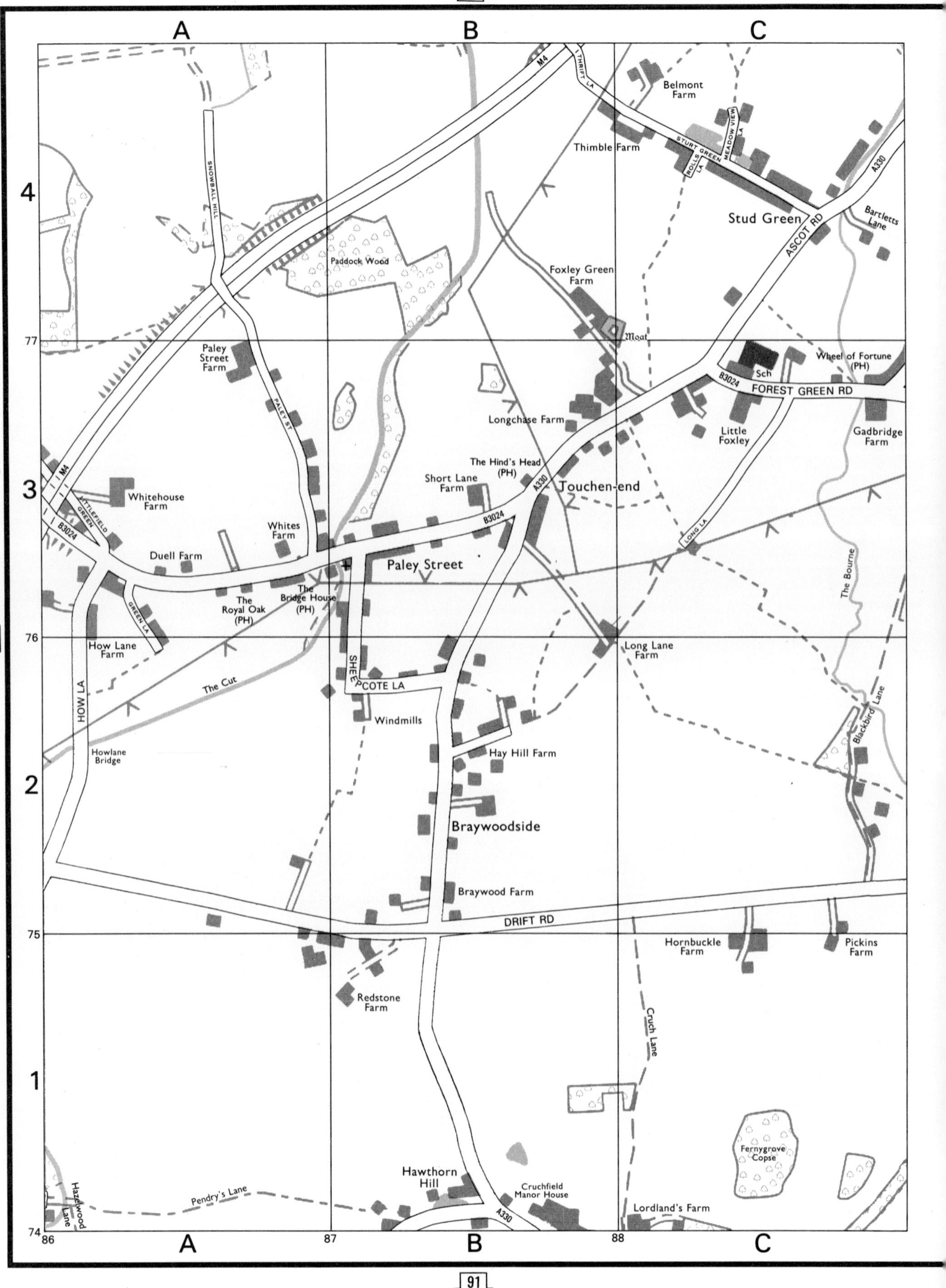
A
B
C
M4
THRIFT LA
Belmont Farm
SNOWBALL HILL
Thimble Farm
STURT GREEN
MEADOW VIEW
LA
ROLLS LA
A330
4
Stud Green
ASCOT RD
Bartletts Lane
Paddock Wood
Foxley Green Farm
77
Moat
Paley Street Farm
Wheel of Fortune (PH)
Sch
B3024
FOREST GREEN RD
PALEY ST
Longchase Farm
Little Foxley
Gadbridge Farm
The Hind's Head (PH)
Short Lane Farm
A330
Touchen-end
3
Whitehouse Farm
LITTLEFIELD GREEN
M4
B3024
B3024
Whites Farm
LONG LA
Duell Farm
Paley Street
The Bourne
The Royal Oak (PH)
The Bridge House (PH)
GREEN LA
76
How Lane Farm
SHEEPCOTE LA
Long Lane Farm
The Cut
HOW LA
Windmills
Blackbird Lane
Howlane Bridge
Hay Hill Farm
2
Braywoodside
Braywood Farm
DRIFT RD
75
Hornbuckle Farm
Pickins Farm
Redstone Farm
Cruch Lane
1
Fernygrove Copse
Hazelwood Lane
Hawthorn Hill
Pendry's Lane
Cruchfield Manor House
A330
Lordland's Farm
74
86
87
88
A
B
C

63

91

40

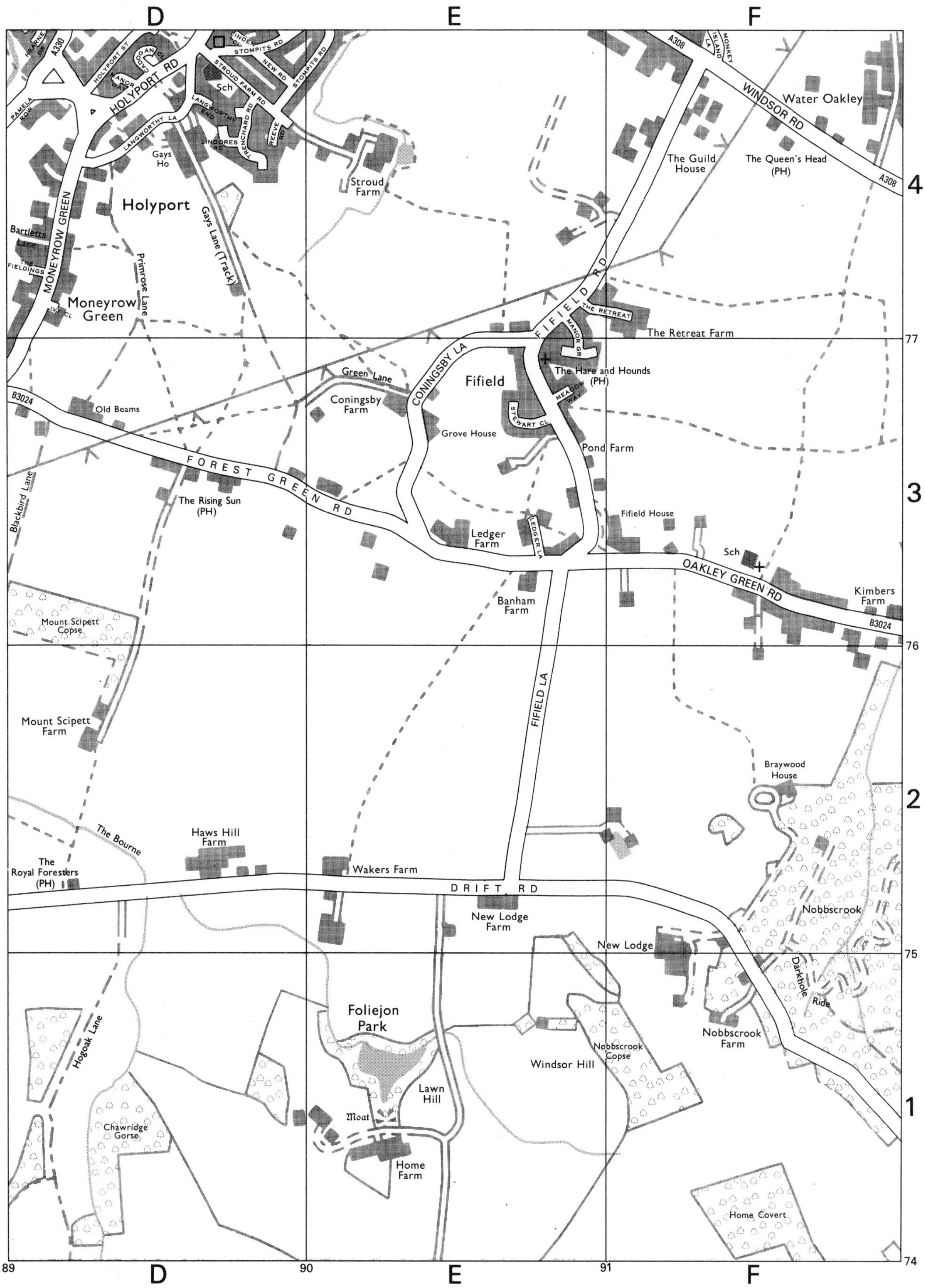
D
E
F
A330
HOLYPORT ST
HOLYPORT RD
STOMPITS RD
NEW RD
STROUD FARM RD
TRENCHARD RD
REEVE RD
LINDORES RD
LANGWORTHY END
LANGWORTHY LA
PAMELA ROW
Sch
Gays Ho
Holyport
Stroud Farm
Bartletts Lane
THE FIELDINGS
MONEYROW GREEN
Primrose Lane
Gays Lane (Track)
Moneyrow Green
IVY CL
A308
WINDSOR RD
ISLAND LA
MONKEY
Water Oakley
The Guild House
The Queen's Head (PH)
FIFIELD RD
THE RETREAT
The Retreat Farm
MANOR GR
The Hare and Hounds (PH)
MEADOW WAY
STEWART CL
Fifield
CONINGSBY LA
Green Lane
Coningsby Farm
Grove House
Pond Farm
B3024
Old Beams
FOREST GREEN RD
The Rising Sun (PH)
Blackbird Lane
Ledger Farm
LEDGER LA
Fifield House
Sch
OAKLEY GREEN RD
Kimbers Farm
Banham Farm
Mount Scipett Copse
Mount Scipett Farm
FIFIELD LA
Braywood House
The Bourne
Haws Hill Farm
The Royal Foresters (PH)
Wakers Farm
DRIFT RD
New Lodge Farm
New Lodge
Nobbscrook
Darkhole Ride
Foliejon Park
Nobbscrook Farm
Hogoak Lane
Nobbscrook Copse
Windsor Hill
Lawn Hill
Moat
Chawridge Gorse
Home Farm
Home Covert
4
3
2
1
77
76
75
74
89
90
91

66

92

41

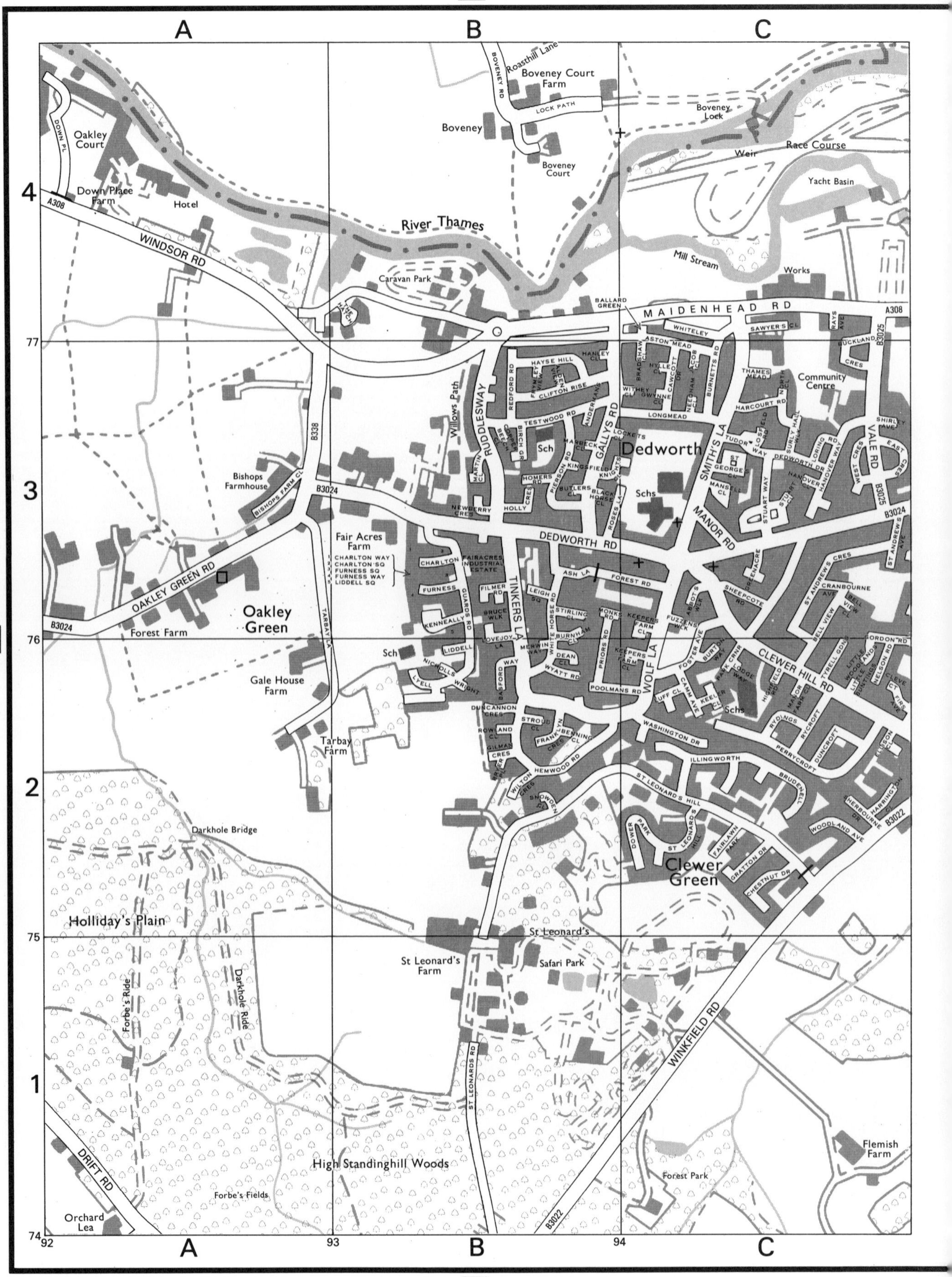
A
B
C
4
3
2
1
77
76
75
74
92
93
94
Roasthill Lane
BOVENEY RD
Boveney Court Farm
LOCK PATH
Boveney
Boveney Court
Boveney Lock
Weir
Race Course
Yacht Basin
DOWN PL
Oakley Court
Down Place Farm
Hotel
A308
WINDSOR RD
River Thames
Mill Stream
Works
Caravan Park
BALLARD GREEN
MAIDENHEAD RD
WHITELEY
SAWYER'S CL
RAYS AVE
BUCKLAND CRES
Community Centre
THAMES MEAD
HAYSE HILL
HANLEY CL
CLIFTON RISE
TESTWOOD RD
REDFORD RD
RUDDLESWAY
Willows Path
B338
GALLYS RD
LONGMEAD
SMITH'S LA
HARCOURT RD
Dedworth
Sch
Schs
LOCKETS
KINGSFIELD
BUTLERS CL
BLACK HORSE CL
ROSES LA
HOMERS RD
HOLLY CRES
NEWBERRY CRES
MARTIN CL
BIRCH GR
TUDOR WAY
DEDWORTH DR
ST GEORGES CL
MANSELL CL
STUART WAY
VALE RD
SHIRLEY AVE
EAST CRES
WEST CRES
B3025
B3024
Bishops Farmhouse
BISHOPS FARM CL
MANOR RD
DEDWORTH RD
Fair Acres Farm
CHARLTON WAY
CHARLTON SQ
FURNESS SQ
FURNESS WAY
LIDDELL SQ
CHARLTON
FAIRACRES INDUSTRIAL ESTATE
FURNESS
KENNEALLY
GUARDS RD
FILMER RD
BRUCE WLK
LOVEJOY LA
TINKERS LA
LEIGH SQ
ASH LA
FOREST RD
STIRLING CL
MONKS RD
KEEPERS FARM CL
FUZZENS WLK
ABBOTS WLK
SHEEPCOTE RD
GREENACRE
ST ANDREW'S CRES
ST ANDREWS AVE
CRANBOURNE AVE
BELL VIEW
BELL VIEW CL
GORDON RD
OAKLEY GREEN RD
Oakley Green
B3024
Forest Farm
TARBAY LA
Sch
LIDDELL
NICHOLLS
WRIGHT
LYELL
MERWIN WAY
WHITE HORSE RD
BURNHAM CL
DEAN CL
WYATT RD
PRIORS RD
KEEPERS FARM CL
WOLF LA
POOLMANS RD
FOSTER AVE
BURTON WAY
PARK CRNR
LODGE WAY
CLEWER HILL RD
TYRELL GDNS
NELSON RD
Gale House Farm
BASFORD WAY
DUNCANNON CRES
ROWLAND CL
GILMAN CRES
STROUD CL
FRANKLYN CRES
BENNING CL
WASHINGTON DR
UFF CL
KEELER CL
Schs
MAJOR CL
RYDINGS
RYCROFT
DUNCROFT
PERRYCROFT
ELLISON CL
Tarbay Farm
HEMWOOD RD
WILTON CRES
SNOWDEN
ILLINGWORTH
BRUDENELL
ST LEONARD'S HILL
HARRINGTON CL
SHERBOURNE DR
WOODLAND AVE
B3022
Darkhole Bridge
DOWER PARK
ST LEONARD'S HILL
FAIRLAWN PARK
GRATTON DR
CHESTNUT DR
Clewer Green
Holliday's Plain
St Leonard's
Safari Park
St Leonard's Farm
Forbe's Ride
Darkhole Ride
ST LEONARDS RD
WINKFIELD RD
Flemish Farm
High Standinghill Woods
DRIFT RD
Forest Park
Forbe's Fields
Orchard Lea
B3022

65

93

42

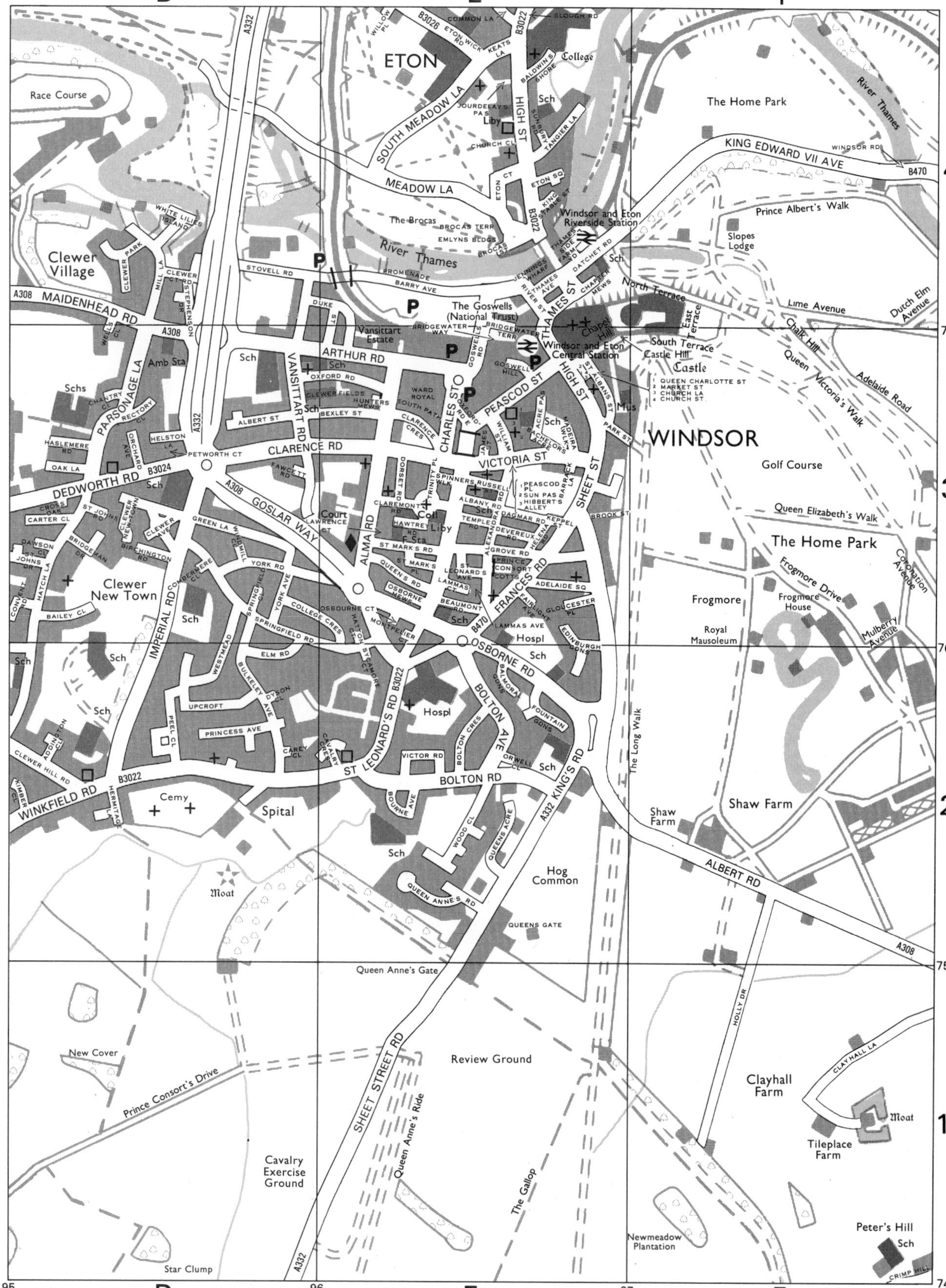
D
E
F
ETON
College
Race Course
The Home Park
River Thames
KING EDWARD VII AVE
WINDSOR RD
B470
SOUTH MEADOW LA
HIGH ST
MEADOW LA
The Brocas
BROCAS TERR
EMLYNS BLDGS
Windsor and Eton Riverside Station
Prince Albert's Walk
Slopes Lodge
Clewer Village
WHITE LILIES ISLAND
A308 MAIDENHEAD RD
STOVELL RD
PROMENADE
BARRY AVE
The Goswells (National Trust)
Vansittart Estate
North Terrace
Lime Avenue
Dutch Elm Avenue
East Terrace
Chapel Hill
Windsor and Eton Central Station
South Terrace
Castle Hill
Castle
Chalk Hill
Queen Victoria's Walk
Adelaide Road
ARTHUR RD
OXFORD RD
PARSONAGE LA
Amb Sta
VANSITTART RD
CHARLES ST
PEASCOD ST
THAMES ST
WINDSOR
CLARENCE RD
DEDWORTH RD
B3024
VICTORIA ST
SHEET ST
Golf Course
Queen Elizabeth's Walk
The Home Park
GOSLAR WAY
A308
Court
Coll
Liby
F Sta
ALMA RD
FRANCES RD
Clewer New Town
IMPERIAL RD
Frogmore
Frogmore Drive
Frogmore House
Royal Mausoleum
Coronation Avenue
Mulberry Avenue
OSBORNE RD
Hospl
BOLTON AVE
ST LEONARD'S RD
B3022
WINKFIELD RD
BOLTON RD
KING'S RD
A332
The Long Walk
Cemy
Spital
Shaw Farm
ALBERT RD
Moat
Hog Common
QUEEN ANNE'S RD
QUEENS GATE
Queen Anne's Gate
HOLLY DR
Review Ground
New Cover
Prince Consort's Drive
SHEET STREET RD
Clayhall Farm
CLAYHALL LA
Moat
Tileplace Farm
Cavalry Exercise Ground
Queen Anne's Ride
The Gallop
Newmeadow Plantation
Peter's Hill
Star Clump
CRIMP HILL
4
3
2
1
77
76
75
74
95
96
97

94

68

43

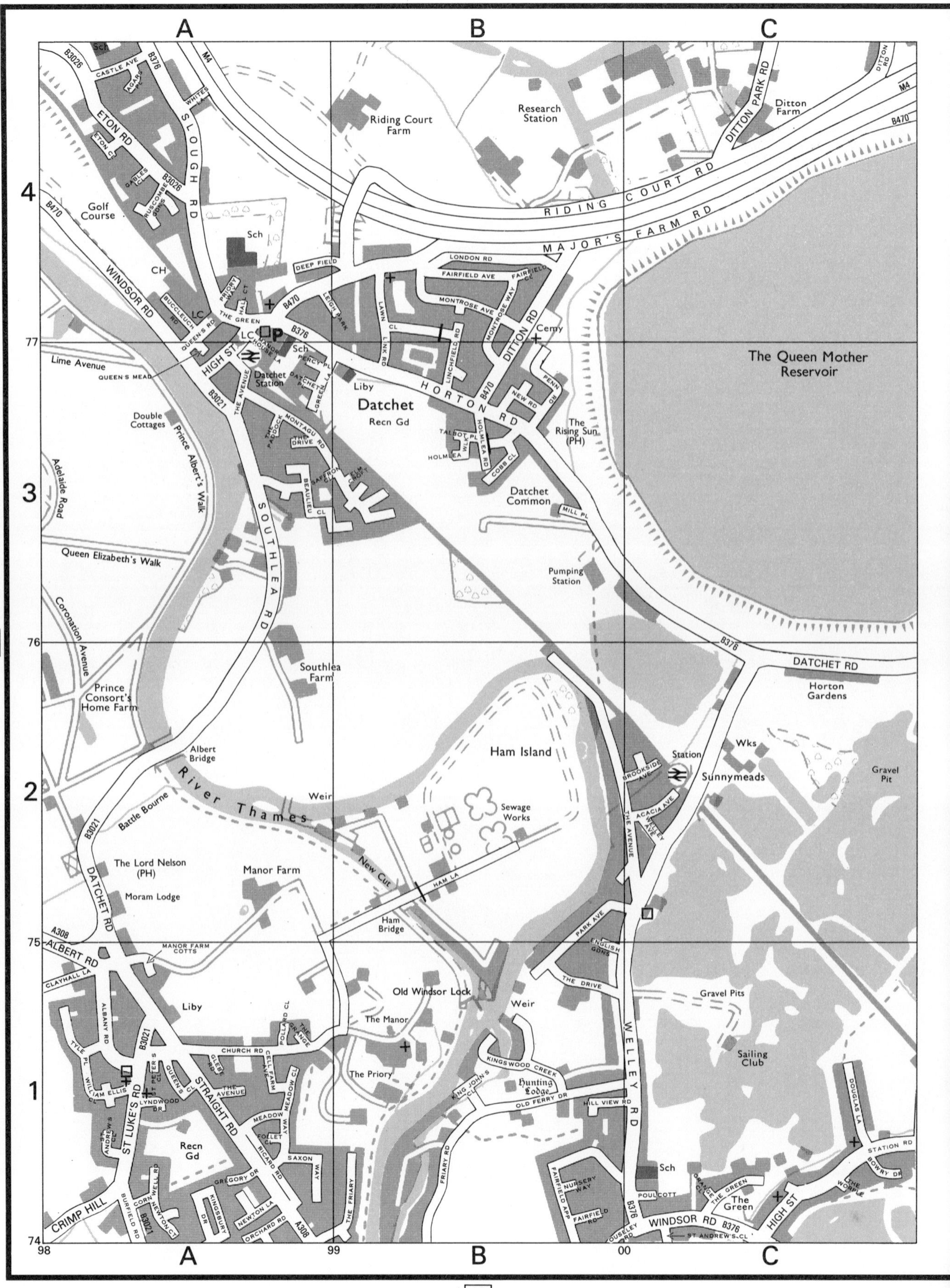
A
B
C
4
3
2
1
77
76
75
74
98
99
00
Riding Court Farm
Research Station
Ditton Farm
DITTON PARK RD
DITTON RD
M4
B470
RIDING COURT RD
MAJOR'S FARM RD
Golf Course
Sch
CH
LC
SLOUGH RD
ETON RD
CASTLE AVE
B3026
B376
WINDSOR RD
DEEP FIELD
LONDON RD
FAIRFIELD AVE
MONTROSE AVE
MONTROSE WAY
LEIGH PARK
LAWN CL
LINK RD
LINCHFIELD RD
Cemy
THE GREEN
HIGH ST
QUEEN'S RD
BUCCLEUCH RD
Lime Avenue
QUEEN'S MEAD
Datchet Station
Liby
Datchet
Recn Gd
HORTON RD
NEW RD
PENN RD
The Rising Sun (PH)
TALBOT PL
HOLMLEA RD
HOLMLEA
COBB CL
Datchet Common
MILL PL
The Queen Mother Reservoir
Double Cottages
Prince Albert's Walk
Adelaide Road
THE AVENUE
MONTAGU RD
THE DRIVE
SAFFRON CL
ELM CROFT
BEAULIEU CL
SOUTHLEA RD
B3021
Queen Elizabeth's Walk
Coronation Avenue
Pumping Station
B376
DATCHET RD
Horton Gardens
Southlea Farm
Prince Consort's Home Farm
Albert Bridge
Ham Island
Station
Sunnymeads
Wks
Gravel Pit
BROOKSIDE AVE
ACACIA AVE
WELLEY AVE
Weir
River Thames
Battle Bourne
Sewage Works
The Lord Nelson (PH)
Manor Farm
New Cut
HAM LA
Moram Lodge
DATCHET RD
Ham Bridge
PARK AVE
ENGLISH GDNS
THE DRIVE
A308
ALBERT RD
MANOR FARM COTTS
CLAYHALL LA
Liby
Old Windsor Lock
Weir
Gravel Pits
WELLEY RD
Sailing Club
The Manor
The Priory
CHURCH RD
KINGSWOOD CREEK
Hunting Lodge
OLD FERRY DR
KING JOHN'S CL
HILL VIEW RD
STRAIGHT RD
ST LUKE'S RD
Recn Gd
GREGORY DR
MEADOW WAY
SAXON WAY
THE FRIARY
FRIARY RD
NURSERY WAY
FAIRFIELD APP
FAIRFIELD RD
Sch
POULCOTT
THE GREEN
The Green
HIGH ST
WINDSOR RD
ST ANDREW'S CL
DOUGLAS LA
STATION RD
BOWRY DR
THE WORPLE
CRIMP HILL
BURFIELD RD
NEWTON LA
ORCHARD RD
KINGSBURY DR
A308

67

95

44

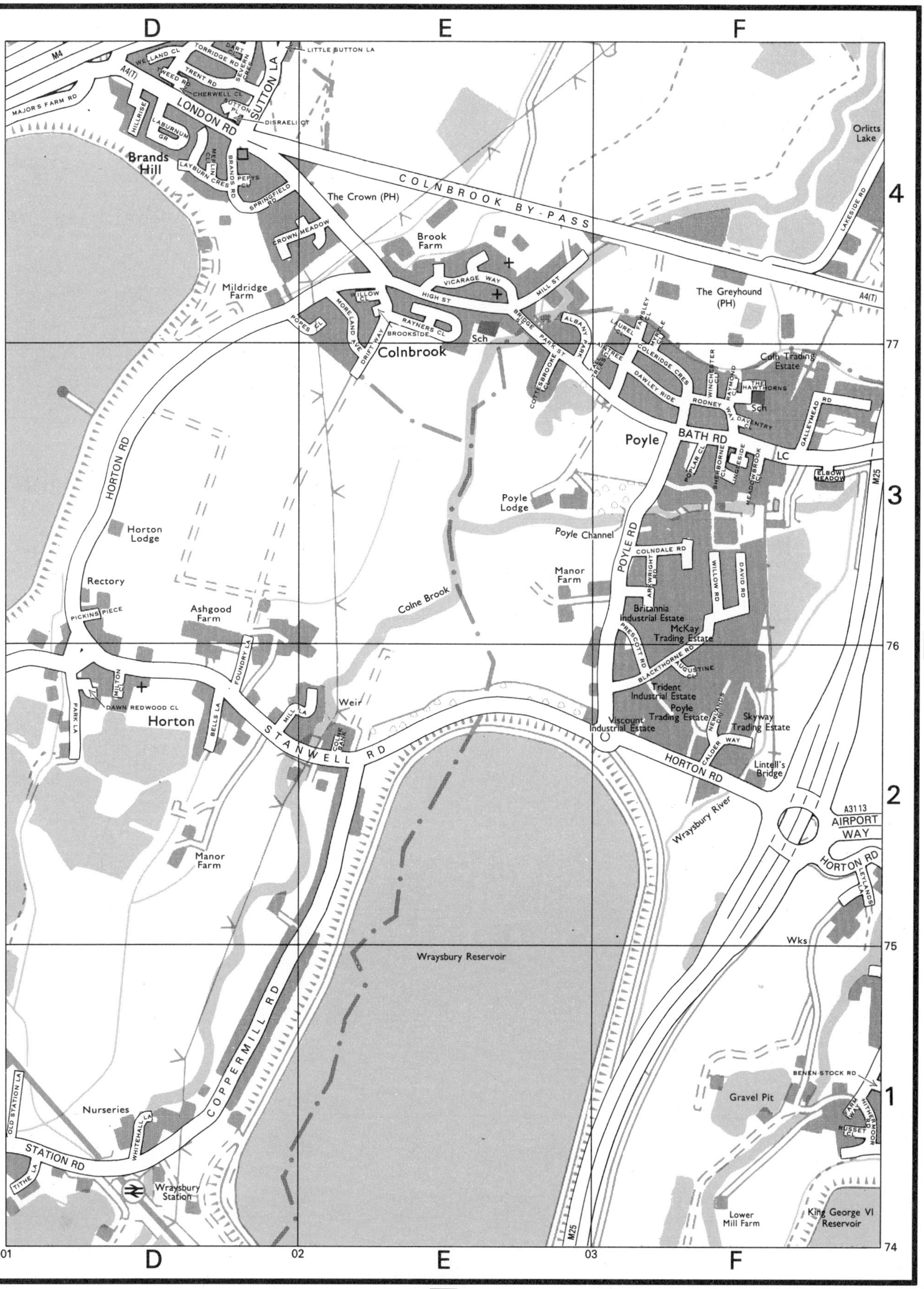
D
E
F
M4
A4(T)
MAJOR'S FARM RD
WELLAND CL
TORRIDGE RD
DART
SEVERN CRES
TWEED RD
TRENT RD
CHERWELL CL
SUTTON LA
SUTTON PL
LITTLE SUTTON LA
LONDON RD
DISRAELI CT
HILLRISE
LABURNUM GR
MERLIN CL
BRANDS RD
LAYBURN CRES
PEPYS CL
SPRINGFIELD RD
Brands Hill
COLNBROOK BY-PASS
The Crown (PH)
CROWN MEADOW
Brook Farm
VICARAGE WAY
MILL ST
HIGH ST
WILLOW CL
Mildridge Farm
POPES CL
MORELAND AVE
DRIFT WAY
RAYNERS CL
BROOKSIDE
Sch
Colnbrook
BRIDGE ST
PARK ST
ALBANY PARK
COTTESBROOKE CL
AINTREE
LAUREL
FAIRSLEY
MYRTLE CL
COLERIDGE CRES
DAWLEY RIDE
WINCHESTER CL
RAYMOND
RODNEY WAY
THE HAWTHORNS
DAVENTRY
GALLEYMEAD RD
The Greyhound (PH)
A4(T)
Orlitts Lake
LAKESIDE RD
Coln Trading Estate
Poyle
BATH RD
POPLAR CL
SHERBORNE CL
INGLESIDE
MEADOWBROOK CL
LC
ELBOW MEADOW
M25
HORTON RD
Horton Lodge
Rectory
PICKINS PIECE
Ashgood Farm
Poyle Lodge
Poyle Channel
POYLE RD
COLNDALE RD
ARKWRIGHT RD
WILLOW RD
DAVID RD
Manor Farm
Colne Brook
Britannia Industrial Estate
McKay Trading Estate
PRESCOTT RD
BLACKTHORNE RD
AUGUSTINE CL
Trident Industrial Estate
Poyle Trading Estate
Viscount Industrial Estate
Skyway Trading Estate
NEWLANDS DR
CALDER WAY
Lintell's Bridge
HORTON RD
FOUNDRY LA
MILTON CL
DAWN REDWOOD CL
PARK LA
Horton
BELLS LA
MILL LA
Weir
COLNE BANK
STANWELL RD
Wraysbury River
A3113
AIRPORT WAY
HORTON RD
LEYLANDS LA
Manor Farm
Wks
Wraysbury Reservoir
COPPERMILL RD
OLD STATION LA
Nurseries
WHITEHALL LA
STATION RD
TITHE LA
Wraysbury Station
BENEN-STOCK RD
Gravel Pit
FARM WAY
WITHEYMOOR RD
RUSSET CL
Lower Mill Farm
King George VI Reservoir
M25
4
3
2
1
77
76
75
74
01
02
03

70

96

not continued, see key diagram

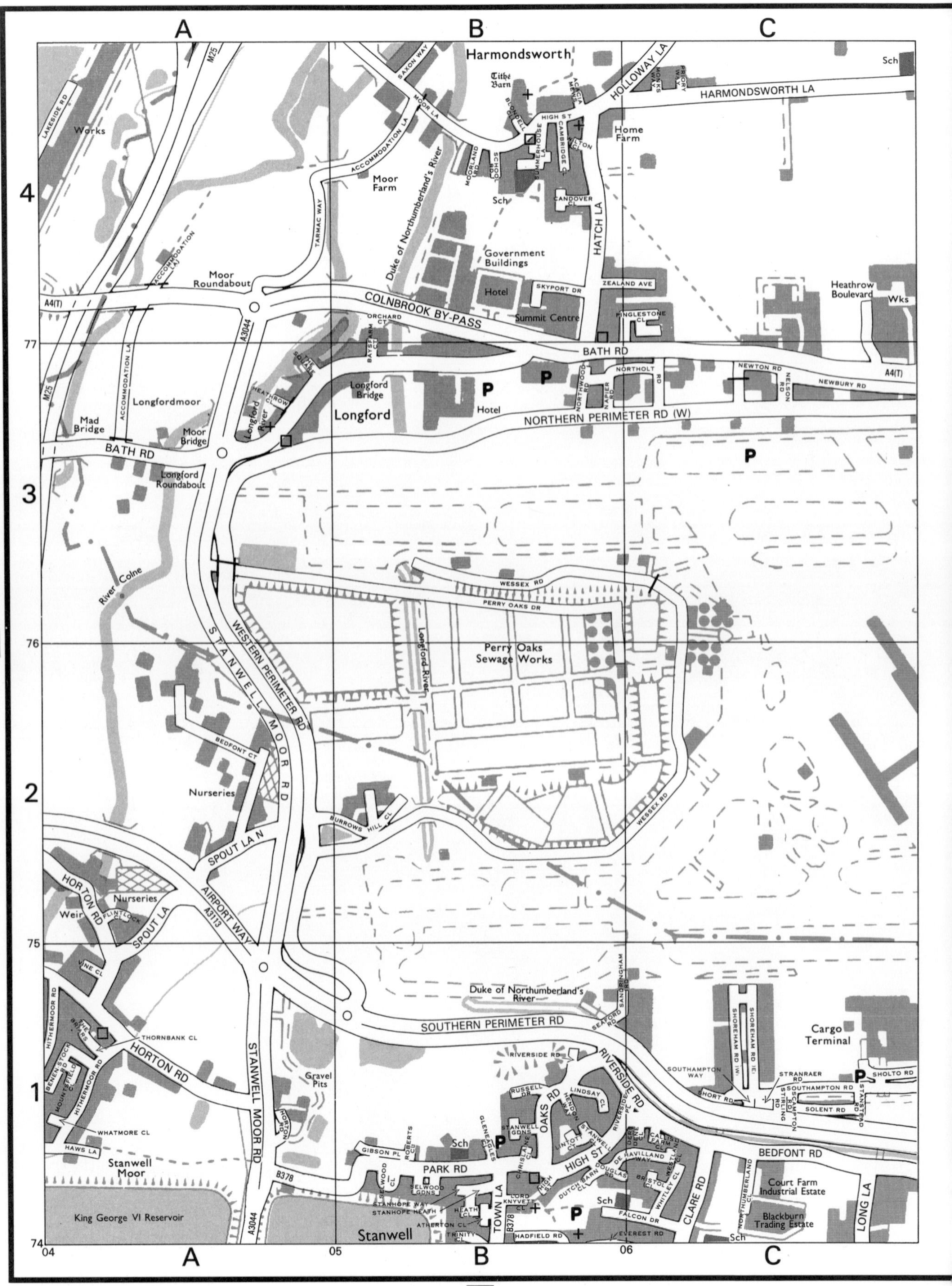

69

not continued, see key diagram

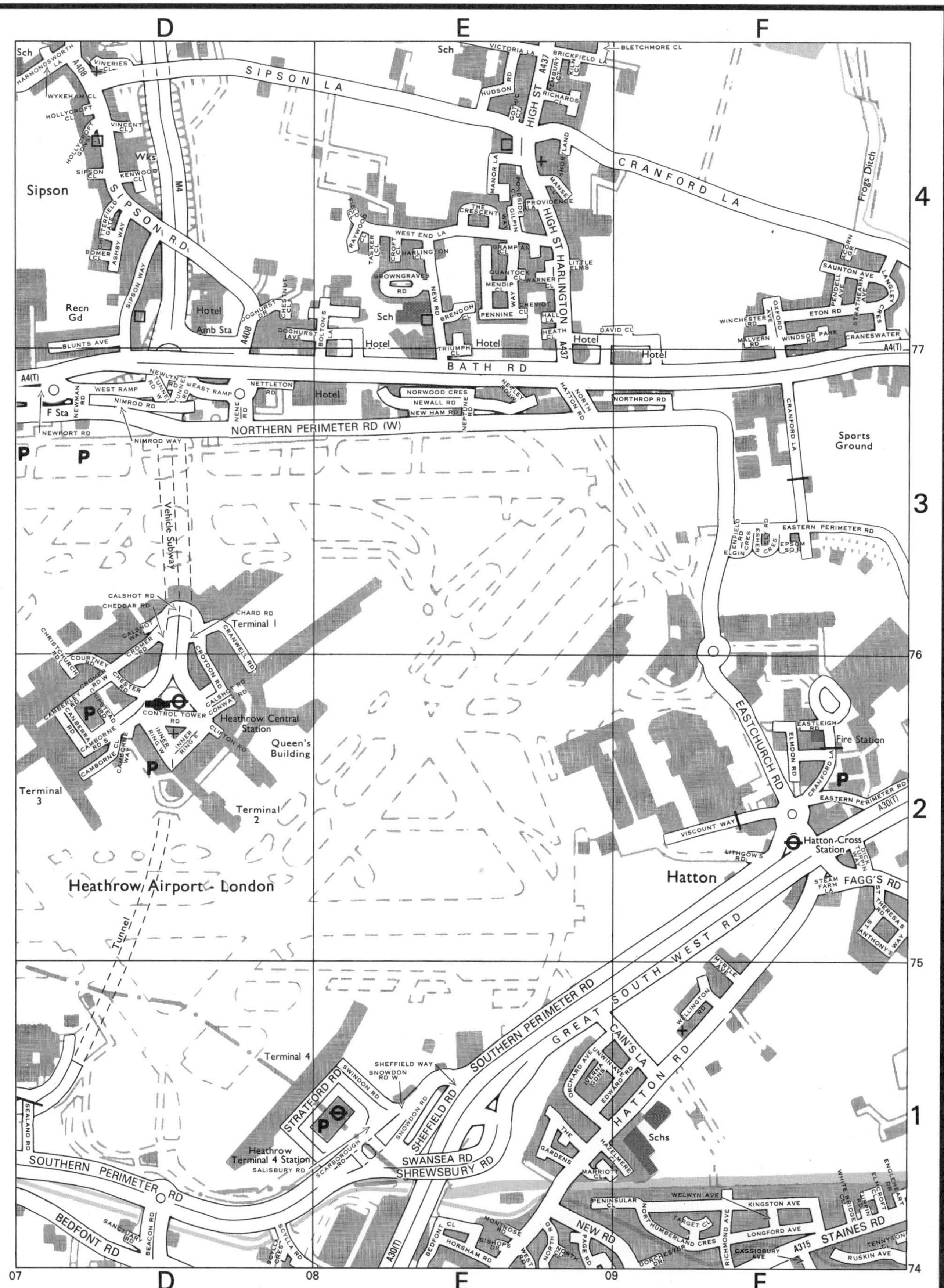

not continued, see key diagram

98

45

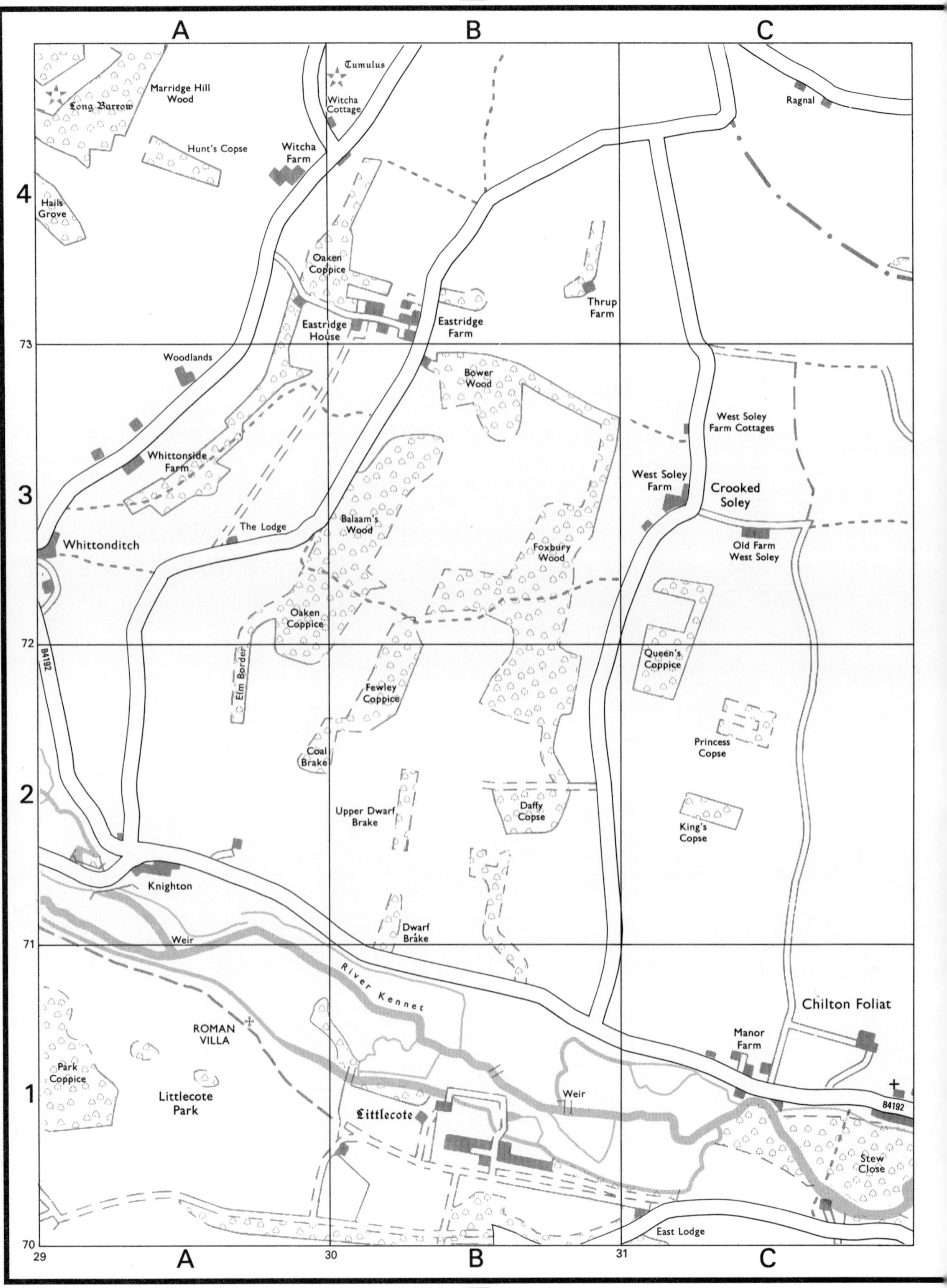
A
B
C
Tumulus
Marridge Hill Wood
Long Barrow
Witcha Cottage
Ragnal
Hunt's Copse
Witcha Farm
4
Hails Grove
Oaken Coppice
Thrup Farm
Eastridge House
Eastridge Farm
73
Woodlands
Bower Wood
West Soley Farm Cottages
Whittonside Farm
West Soley Farm
Crooked Soley
3
The Lodge
Balaam's Wood
Whittonditch
Foxbury Wood
Old Farm West Soley
Oaken Coppice
72
B4192
Elm Border
Queen's Coppice
Fewley Coppice
Princess Copse
Coal Brake
2
Upper Dwarf Brake
Daffy Copse
King's Copse
Knighton
Dwarf Brake
Weir
71
River Kennet
Chilton Foliat
ROMAN VILLA
Manor Farm
Park Coppice
Littlecote Park
Weir
Littlecote
B4192
Stew Close
East Lodge
70
29
30
31
not continued, see key diagram

99

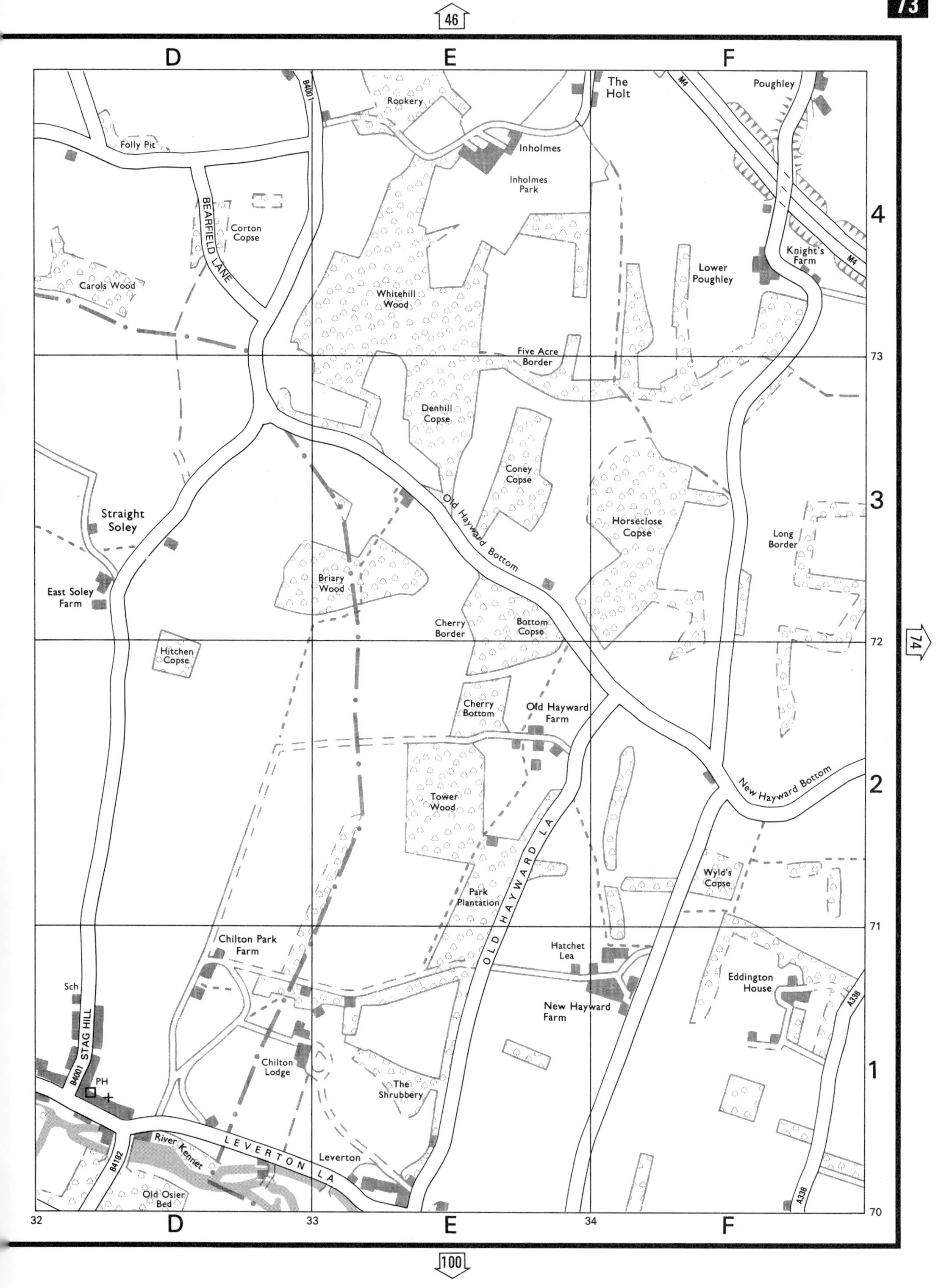
46
D
E
F
The Holt
Poughley
Rookery
B4001
M4
Folly Pit
Inholmes
Inholmes Park
BEARFIELD LANE
Corton Copse
4
Knight's Farm
Lower Poughley
Carols Wood
Whitehill Wood
Five Acre Border
73
Denhill Copse
Coney Copse
Horseclose Copse
3
Straight Soley
Old Hayward Bottom
Long Border
Briary Wood
East Soley Farm
Cherry Border
Bottom Copse
72
74
Hitchen Copse
Cherry Bottom
Old Hayward Farm
2
New Hayward Bottom
Tower Wood
Park Plantation
OLD HAYWARD LA
Wyld's Copse
71
Chilton Park Farm
Hatchet Lea
Eddington House
Sch
New Hayward Farm
A338
STAG HILL
Chilton Lodge
1
B4001
PH
The Shrubbery
B4192
River Kennet
LEVERTON LA
Leverton
Old Osier Bed
A338
70
32
33
34
100

47

73

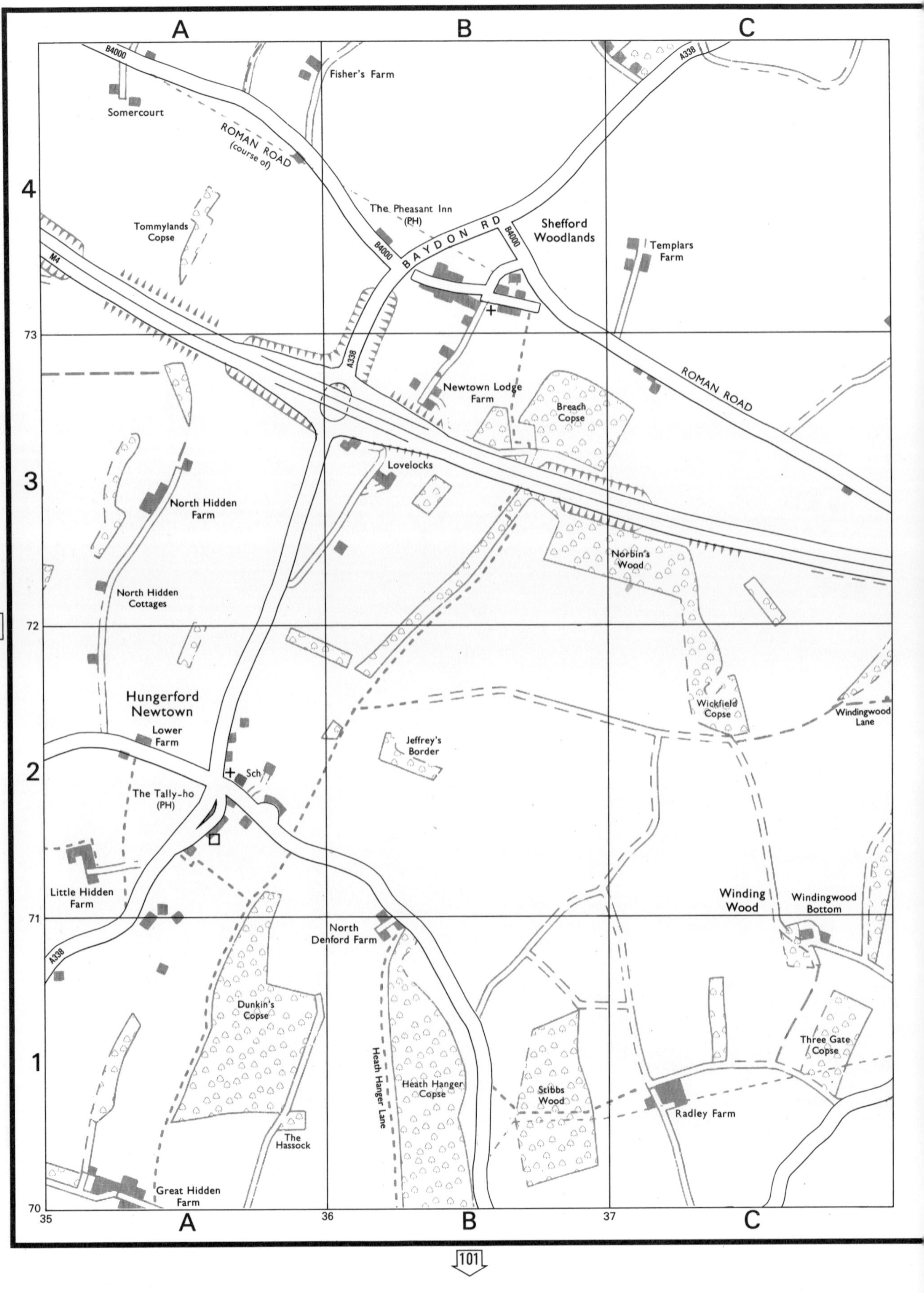
A
B
C
4
3
2
1
73
72
71
70
35
36
37
B4000
A338
M4
Somercourt
Fisher's Farm
ROMAN ROAD
(course of)
Tommylands
Copse
The Pheasant Inn
(PH)
BAYDON RD
Shefford
Woodlands
Templars
Farm
Newtown Lodge
Farm
Breach
Copse
ROMAN ROAD
Lovelocks
North Hidden
Farm
Norbin's
Wood
North Hidden
Cottages
Hungerford
Newtown
Lower
Farm
Jeffrey's
Border
Wickfield
Copse
Windingwood
Lane
Sch
The Tally-ho
(PH)
Little Hidden
Farm
Winding
Wood
Windingwood
Bottom
North
Denford Farm
Dunkin's
Copse
Heath Hanger Lane
Heath Hanger
Copse
Stibbs
Wood
Three Gate
Copse
Radley Farm
The
Hassock
Great Hidden
Farm

101

48

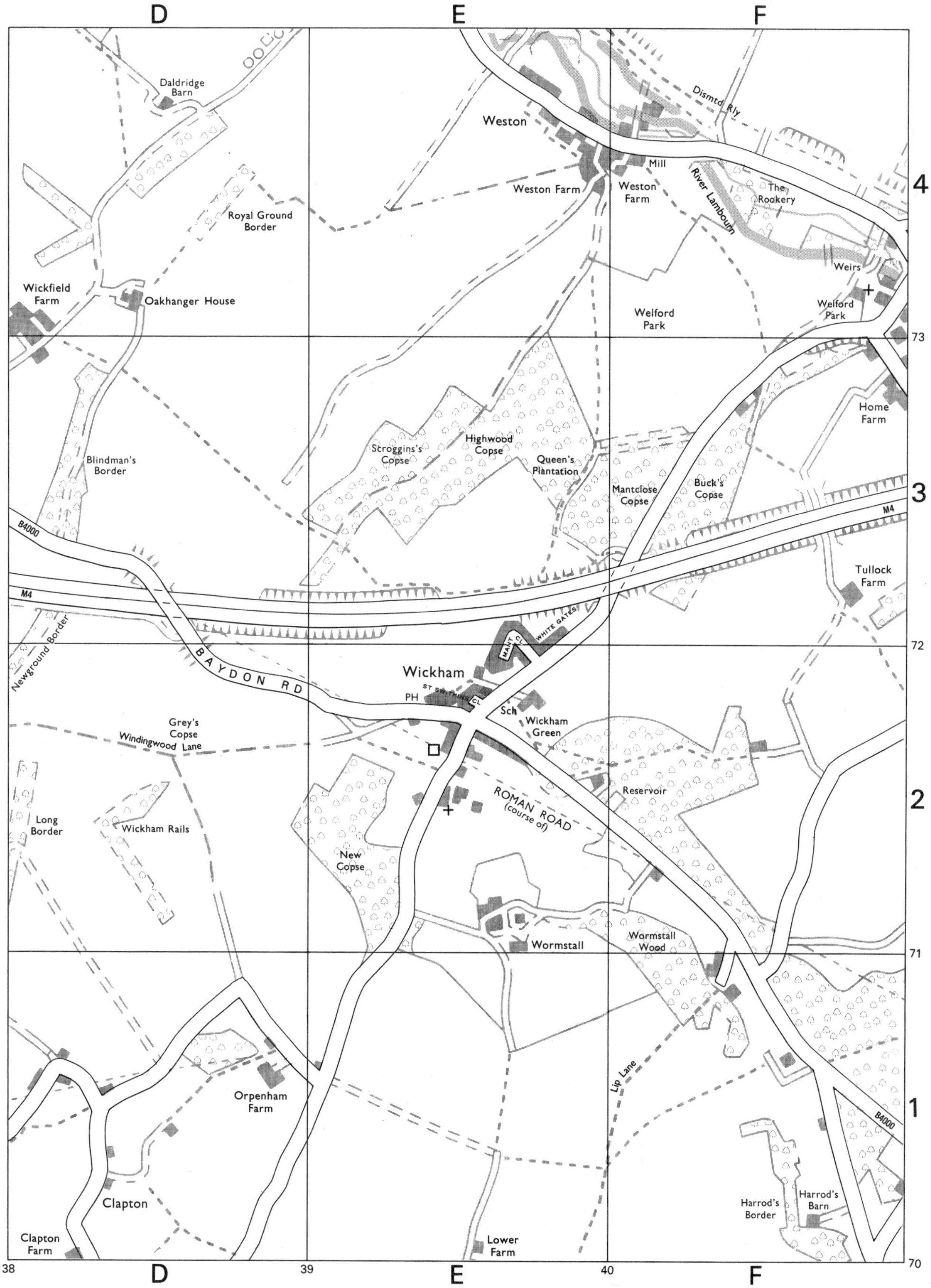
D
E
F
Daldridge Barn
Weston
Dismtd Rly
Mill
Weston Farm
Weston Farm
River Lambourn
The Rookery
Royal Ground Border
Weirs
Wickfield Farm
Oakhanger House
Welford Park
Welford Park
4
73
Home Farm
Blindman's Border
Scroggins's Copse
Highwood Copse
Queen's Plantation
Mantclose Copse
Buck's Copse
3
B4000
M4
M4
Tullock Farm
Newground Border
WHITE GATES
MANT CL
72
BAYDON RD
Wickham
PH
ST SWITHINS CL
Sch
Wickham Green
Grey's Copse
Windingwood Lane
Reservoir
ROMAN ROAD (course of)
2
Long Border
Wickham Rails
New Copse
Wormstall
Wormstall Wood
71
Lip Lane
Orpenham Farm
1
B4000
Clapton
Harrod's Border
Harrod's Barn
Clapton Farm
Lower Farm
38
39
40
70
D
E
F

76

102

49

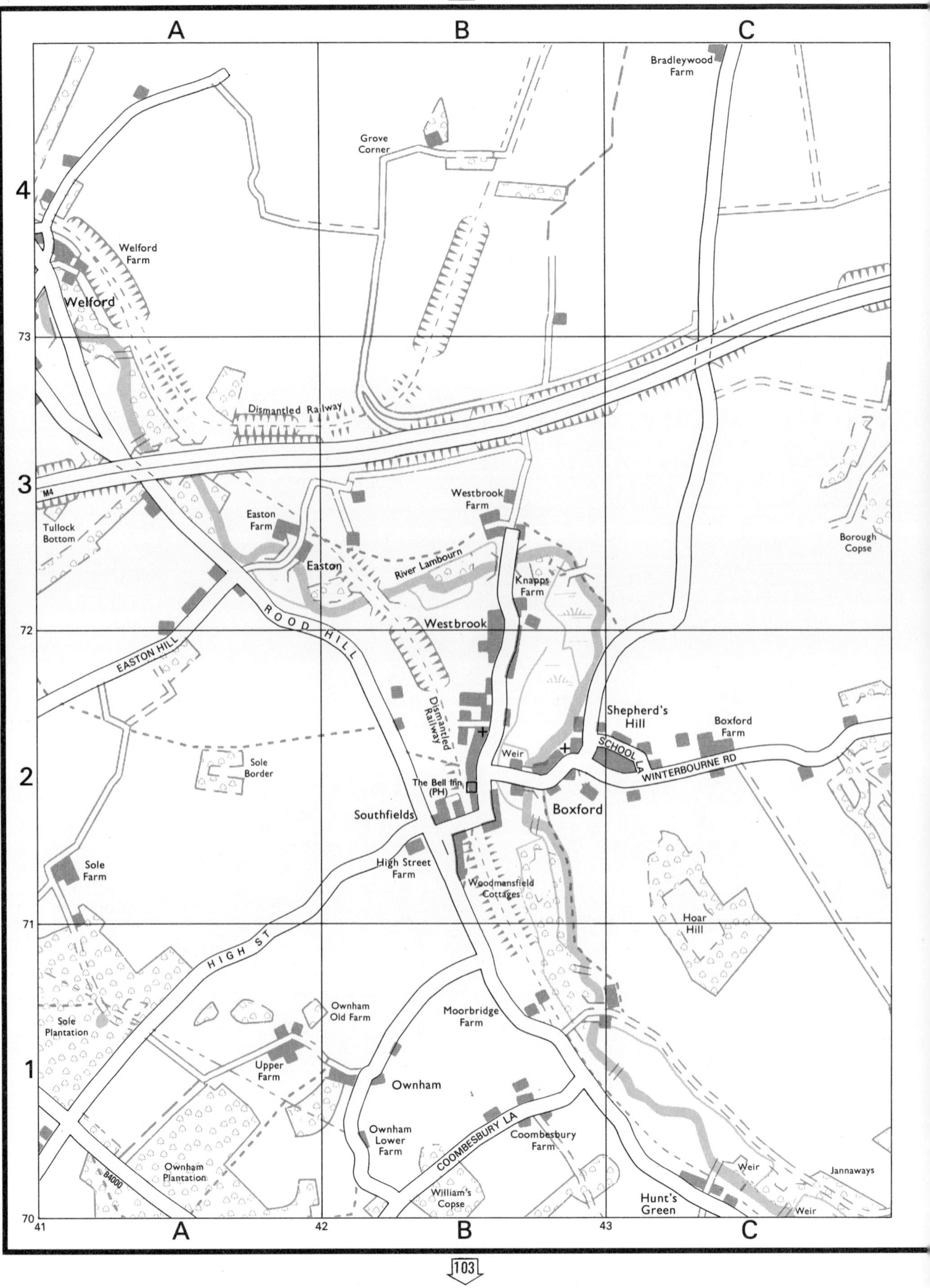
A
B
C
4
3
2
1
73
72
71
70
41
42
43
Bradleywood Farm
Grove Corner
Welford Farm
Welford
Dismantled Railway
M4
Tullock Bottom
Easton Farm
Easton
Westbrook Farm
River Lambourn
Knapps Farm
Westbrook
ROOD HILL
EASTON HILL
Borough Copse
Dismantled Railway
Shepherd's Hill
Boxford Farm
SCHOOL LA
WINTERBOURNE RD
Weir
Sole Border
The Bell Inn (PH)
Boxford
Southfields
Sole Farm
High Street Farm
Woodmansfield Cottages
Hoar Hill
HIGH ST
Ownham Old Farm
Moorbridge Farm
Sole Plantation
Upper Farm
Ownham
Ownham Lower Farm
Coombesbury Farm
COOMBESBURY LA
B4000
Ownham Plantation
William's Copse
Weir
Jannaways
Hunt's Green
Weir

75

103

50

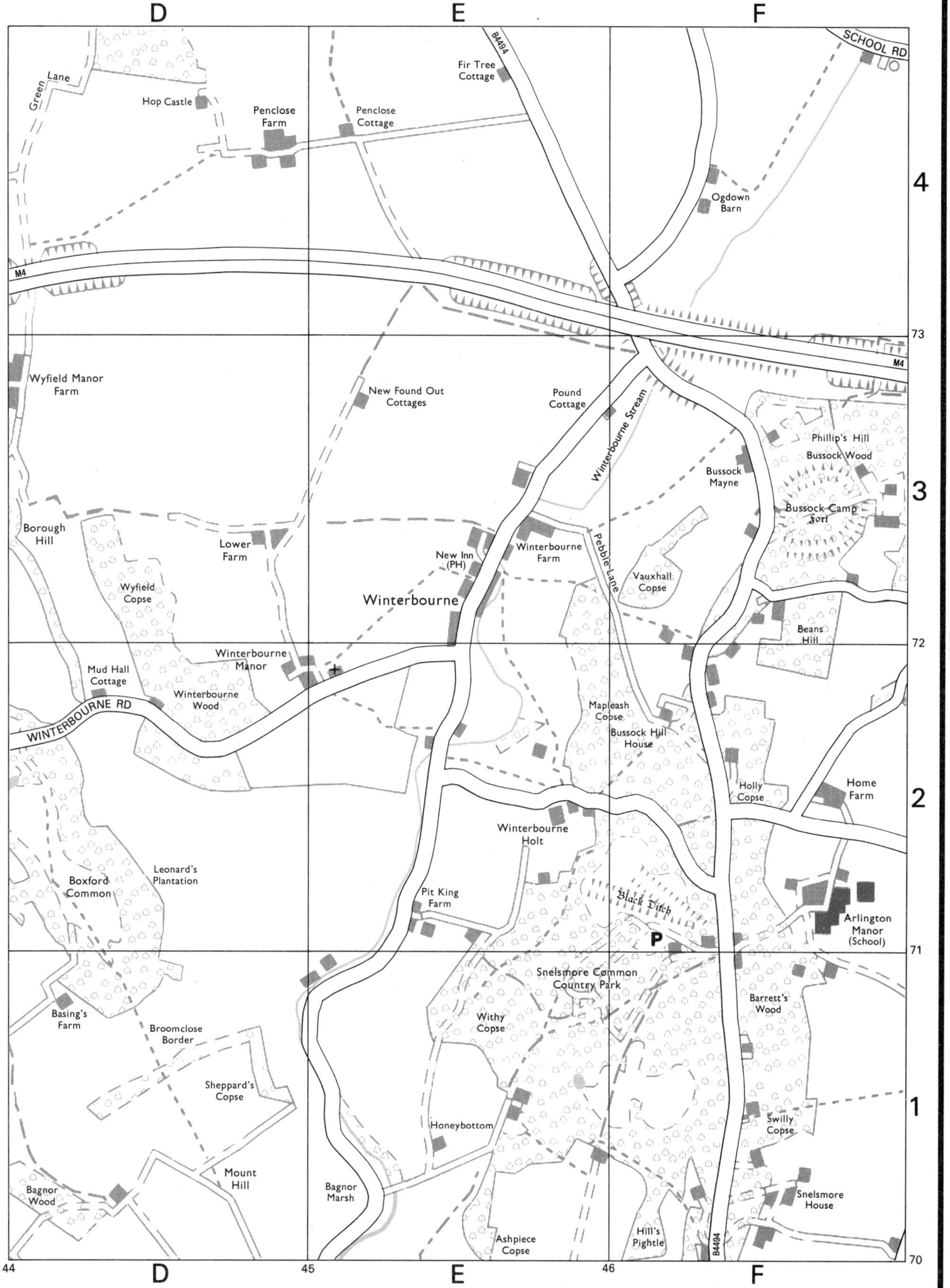

D
E
F
SCHOOL RD
B4494
Fir Tree Cottage
Green Lane
Hop Castle
Penclose Farm
Penclose Cottage
Ogdown Barn
4
M4
73
Wyfield Manor Farm
New Found Out Cottages
Pound Cottage
Winterbourne Stream
Phillip's Hill
Bussock Wood
Bussock Mayne
3
Bussock Camp Fort
Borough Hill
Lower Farm
New Inn (PH)
Winterbourne Farm
Pebble Lane
Vauxhall Copse
Wyfield Copse
Winterbourne
Beans Hill
72
Winterbourne Manor
Mud Hall Cottage
Winterbourne Wood
WINTERBOURNE RD
Mapleash Copse
Bussock Hill House
Home Farm
Holly Copse
2
Winterbourne Holt
Leonard's Plantation
Boxford Common
Pit King Farm
Black Ditch
Arlington Manor (School)
P
71
Snelsmore Common Country Park
Barrett's Wood
Basing's Farm
Withy Copse
Broomclose Border
Sheppard's Copse
1
Honeybottom
Swilly Copse
Mount Hill
Bagnor Marsh
Bagnor Wood
Snelsmore House
Hill's Pightle
Ashpiece Copse
B4494
70
44
45
46
D
E
F

78

104

51

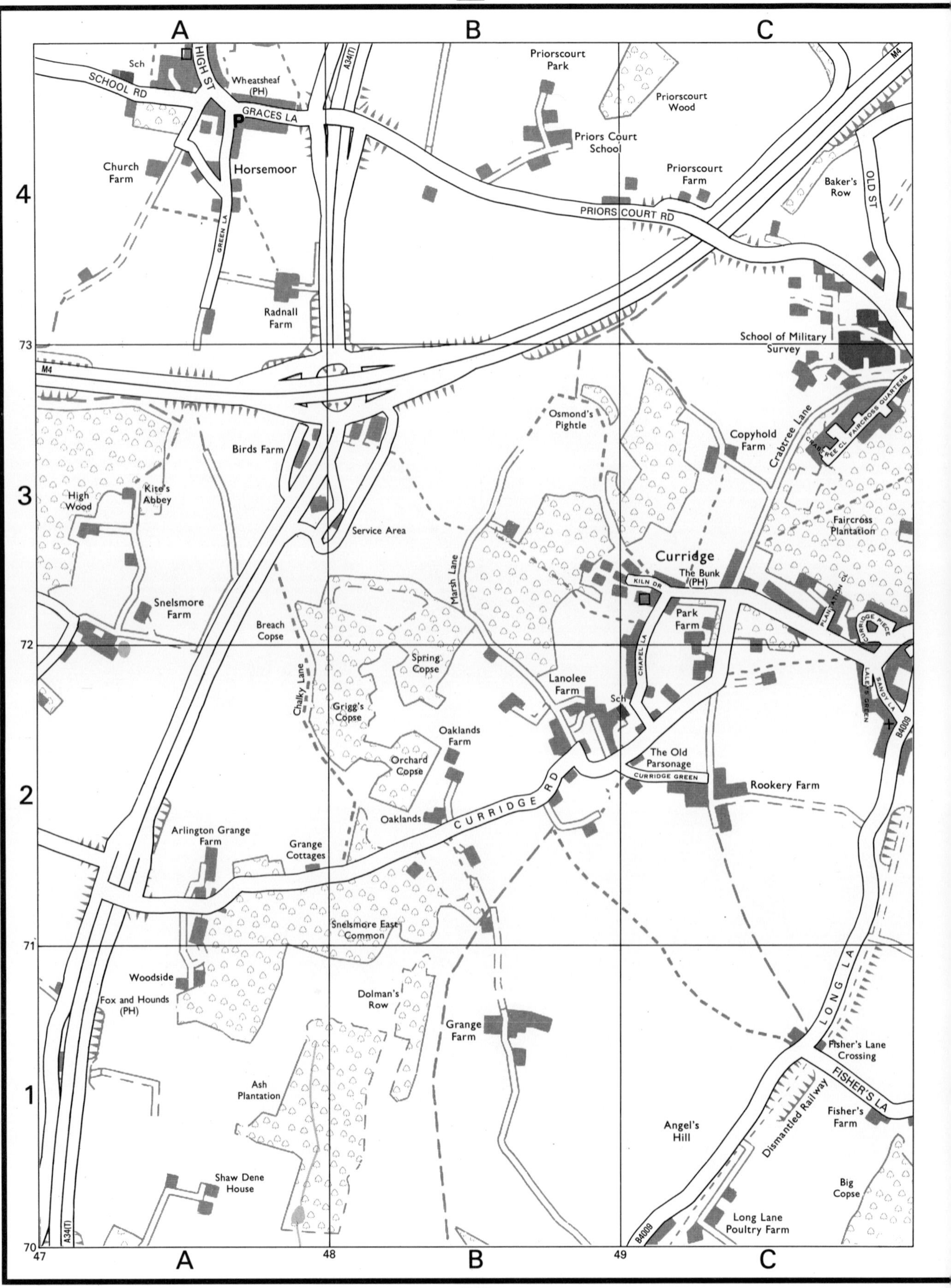
A
B
C
Sch
SCHOOL RD
HIGH ST
Wheatsheaf (PH)
GRACES LA
A34(T)
Priorscourt Park
Priorscourt Wood
Priors Court School
Priorscourt Farm
PRIORS COURT RD
M4
Church Farm
Horsemoor
GREEN LA
Baker's Row
OLD ST
Radnall Farm
School of Military Survey
Osmond's Pightle
Copyhold Farm
Crabtree Lane
FAIRCROSS QUARTERS
Birds Farm
Kite's Abbey
High Wood
Service Area
Faircross Plantation
Curridge
KILN DR
The Bunk (PH)
Marsh Lane
Snelsmore Farm
Breach Copse
Park Farm
PLANTATION CL
CURRIDGE PIECE
Spring Copse
CHAPEL LA
Lanolee Farm
Sch
SANDY LA
Chalky Lane
Grigg's Copse
Oaklands Farm
Orchard Copse
B4009
The Old Parsonage
CURRIDGE GREEN
Rookery Farm
CURRIDGE RD
Oaklands
Arlington Grange Farm
Grange Cottages
Snelsmore East Common
Woodside
Fox and Hounds (PH)
Dolman's Row
Grange Farm
LONG LA
Fisher's Lane Crossing
FISHER'S LA
Ash Plantation
Angel's Hill
Dismantled Railway
Fisher's Farm
Shaw Dene House
Big Copse
Long Lane Poultry Farm
4
3
2
1
73
72
71
70
47
48
49

77

105

52

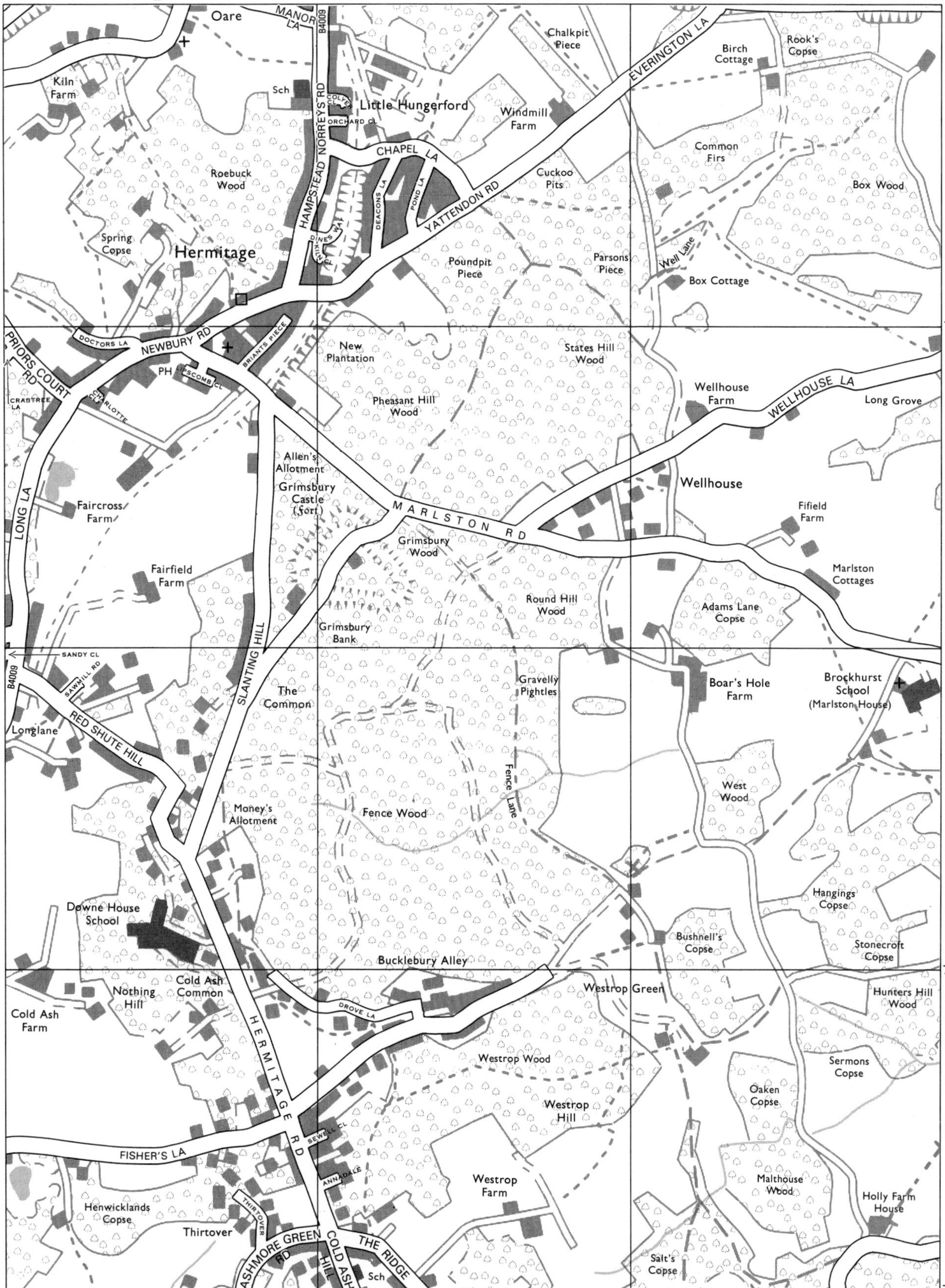
D
E
F
Oare
MANOR LA
B4009
Kiln Farm
Sch
Little Hungerford
COLYER CL
ORCHARD CL
HAMPSTEAD NORREYS RD
Chalkpit Piece
EVERINGTON LA
Birch Cottage
Rook's Copse
Windmill Farm
CHAPEL LA
Common Firs
Roebuck Wood
Cuckoo Pits
Box Wood
DEACONS LA
POND LA
YATTENDON RD
Spring Copse
Hermitage
Poundpit Piece
Parsons Piece
Well Lane
Box Cottage
DOCTORS LA
NEWBURY RD
PRIORS COURT RD
BRIANTS PIECE
New Plantation
States Hill Wood
PH
LIPSCOMB CL
CRABTREE LA
CHARLOTTE CL
Pheasant Hill Wood
Wellhouse Farm
WELLHOUSE LA
Long Grove
Allen's Allotment
Wellhouse
LONG LA
Grimsbury Castle (fort)
Faircross Farm
MARLSTON RD
Fifield Farm
Grimsbury Wood
Fairfield Farm
Marlston Cottages
Round Hill Wood
Adams Lane Copse
SLANTING HILL
Grimsbury Bank
SANDY CL
B4009
SAWHILL RD
Gravelly Pightles
Boar's Hole Farm
Brockhurst School (Marlston House)
The Common
Longlane
RED SHUTE HILL
Fence Lane
West Wood
Money's Allotment
Fence Wood
Downe House School
Hangings Copse
Bushnell's Copse
Stonecroft Copse
Bucklebury Alley
Nothing Hill
Cold Ash Common
Westrop Green
Hunters Hill Wood
Cold Ash Farm
DROVE LA
HERMITAGE RD
Westrop Wood
Sermons Copse
Oaken Copse
Westrop Hill
FISHER'S LA
SEWELL CL
ANNADALE
Westrop Farm
Malthouse Wood
Holly Farm House
Henwicklands Copse
THIRTOVER
Thirtover
ASHMORE GREEN RD
COLD ASH HILL
THE RIDGE
Sch
Salt's Copse
4
3
2
1
73
72
71
70
50
51
52

80

106

53

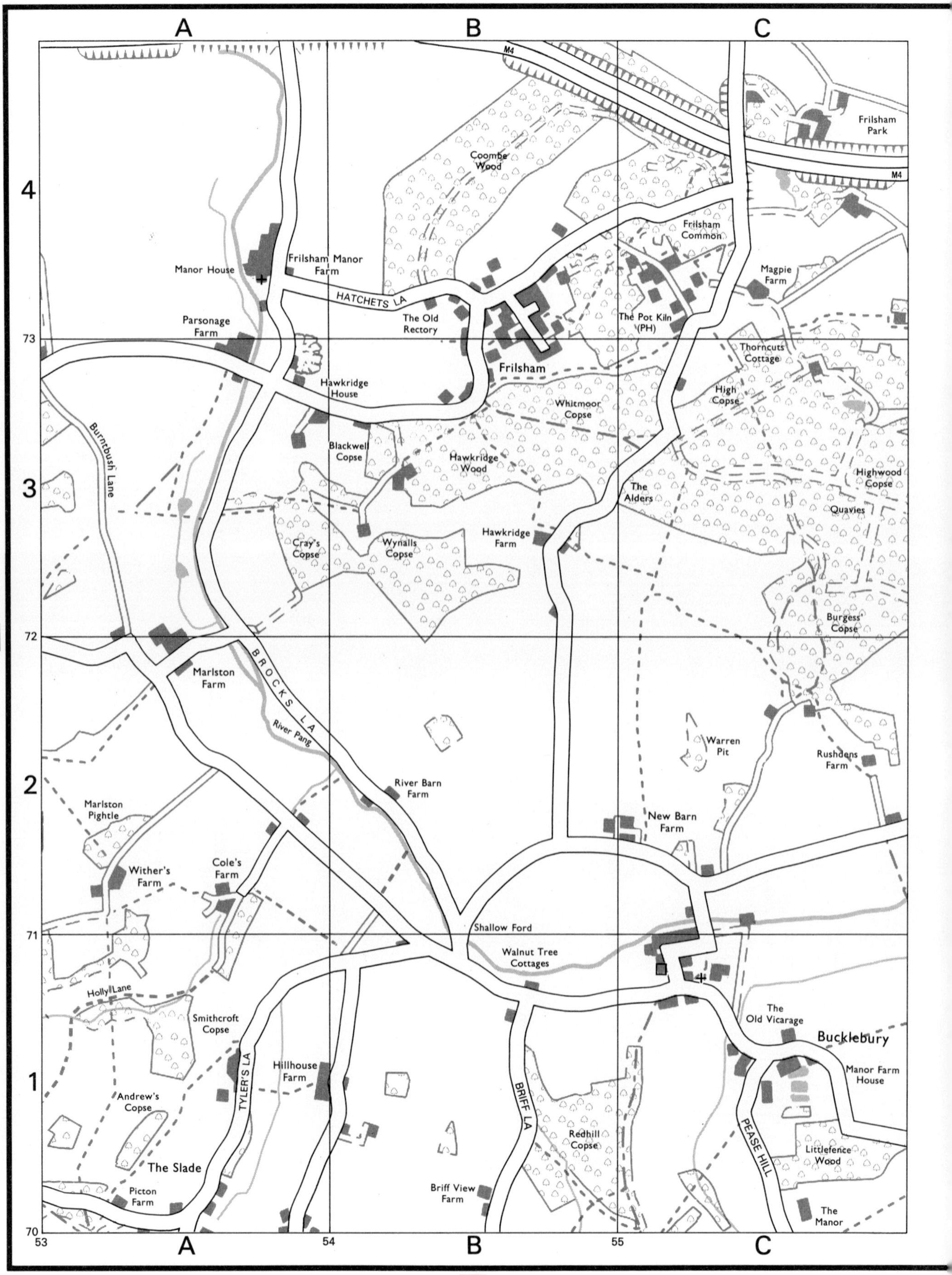
A
B
C
4
3
2
1
73
72
71
70
53
54
55
M4
Coombe Wood
Frilsham Park
Manor House
Frilsham Manor Farm
Hatchets La
The Old Rectory
Frilsham Common
Magpie Farm
The Pot Kiln (PH)
Parsonage Farm
Thorncuts Cottage
Frilsham
Hawkridge House
Whitmoor Copse
High Copse
Burntbush Lane
Blackwell Copse
Hawkridge Wood
Highwood Copse
The Alders
Quavies
Cray's Copse
Wynalls Copse
Hawkridge Farm
Burgess' Copse
Marlston Farm
Brocks La
River Pang
Warren Pit
Rushdens Farm
River Barn Farm
Marlston Pightle
New Barn Farm
Wither's Farm
Cole's Farm
Shallow Ford
Walnut Tree Cottages
Holly Lane
Smithcroft Copse
The Old Vicarage
Bucklebury
Hillhouse Farm
Manor Farm House
Tyler's La
Briff La
Andrew's Copse
Redhill Copse
Pease Hill
Littlefence Wood
The Slade
Picton Farm
Briff View Farm
The Manor

79

107

54

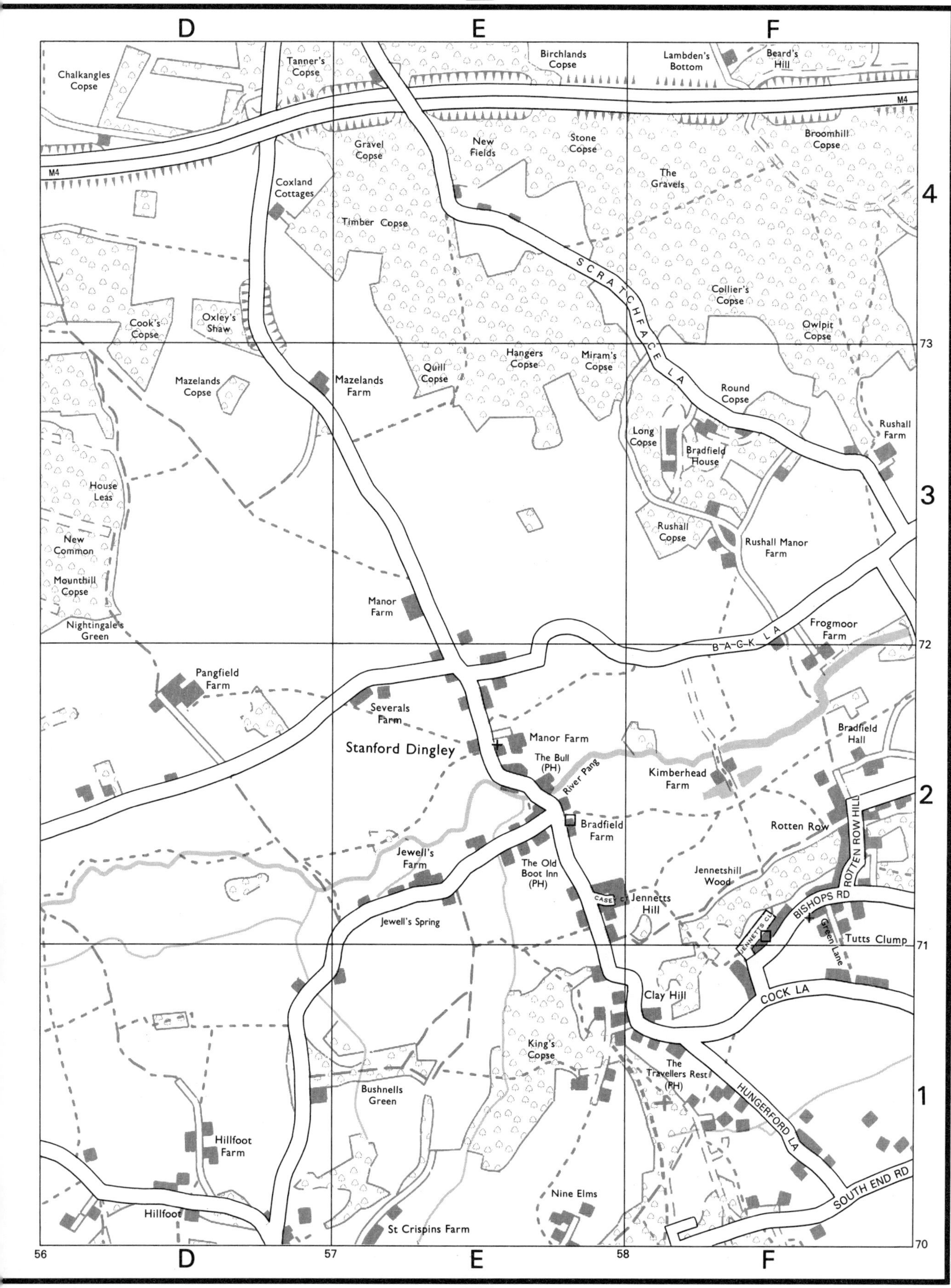
D
E
F
Chalkangles Copse
Tanner's Copse
Birchlands Copse
Lambden's Bottom
Beard's Hill
M4
Broomhill Copse
Gravel Copse
New Fields
Stone Copse
The Gravels
Coxland Cottages
Timber Copse
4
SCRATCHFACE LA
Collier's Copse
Cook's Copse
Oxley's Shaw
Owlpit Copse
73
Hangers Copse
Miram's Copse
Quill Copse
Mazelands Copse
Mazelands Farm
Round Copse
Rushall Farm
Long Copse
Bradfield House
House Leas
3
Rushall Copse
Rushall Manor Farm
New Common
Mounthill Copse
Manor Farm
Nightingale's Green
Frogmoor Farm
BACK LA
72
Pangfield Farm
Severals Farm
Bradfield Hall
Manor Farm
Stanford Dingley
The Bull (PH)
River Pang
Kimberhead Farm
2
ROTTEN ROW HILL
Bradfield Farm
Rotten Row
Jewell's Farm
The Old Boot Inn (PH)
Jennetshill Wood
CASEY CT
Jennetts Hill
BISHOPS RD
Jewell's Spring
JENNETTS CL
Green Lane
Tutts Clump
71
COCK LA
Clay Hill
King's Copse
The Travellers Rest (PH)
Bushnells Green
HUNGERFORD LA
1
Hillfoot Farm
SOUTH END RD
Nine Elms
Hillfoot
St Crispins Farm
70
56
57
58

82

108

55

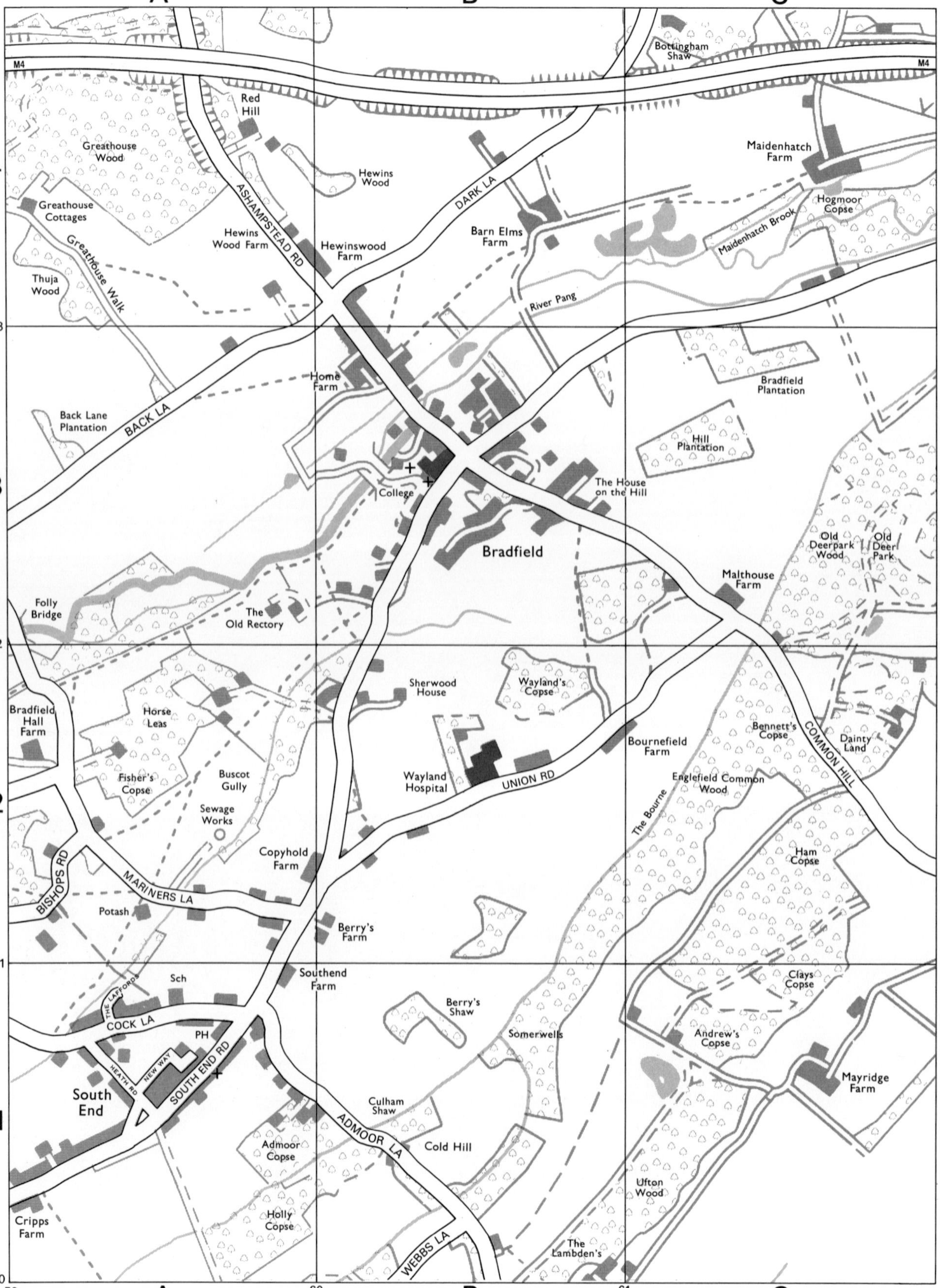
A
B
C
M4
M4
Bottingham Shaw
Red Hill
Greathouse Wood
Hewins Wood
Maidenhatch Farm
Hogmoor Copse
Greathouse Cottages
ASHAMPSTEAD RD
DARK LA
Barn Elms Farm
Maidenhatch Brook
Hewins Wood Farm
Hewinswood Farm
Greathouse Walk
Thuja Wood
River Pang
Home Farm
Bradfield Plantation
Back Lane Plantation
BACK LA
Hill Plantation
College
The House on the Hill
Bradfield
Old Deerpark Wood
Old Deer Park
Malthouse Farm
Folly Bridge
The Old Rectory
Sherwood House
Wayland's Copse
Bradfield Hall Farm
Horse Leas
Bennett's Copse
Dainty Land
Bournefield Farm
COMMON HILL
Fisher's Copse
Buscot Gully
Wayland Hospital
UNION RD
Englefield Common Wood
The Bourne
Sewage Works
Copyhold Farm
Ham Copse
BISHOPS RD
MARINERS LA
Potash
Berry's Farm
Southend Farm
Sch
Clays Copse
THE LAFFORDS
Berry's Shaw
COCK LA
PH
Somerwells
Andrew's Copse
HEATH RD
NEW WAY
SOUTH END RD
Mayridge Farm
South End
Culham Shaw
ADMOOR LA
Admoor Copse
Cold Hill
Ufton Wood
Cripps Farm
Holly Copse
WEBBS LA
The Lambden's
4
73
3
72
2
71
1
70
59
60
61

81

109

56

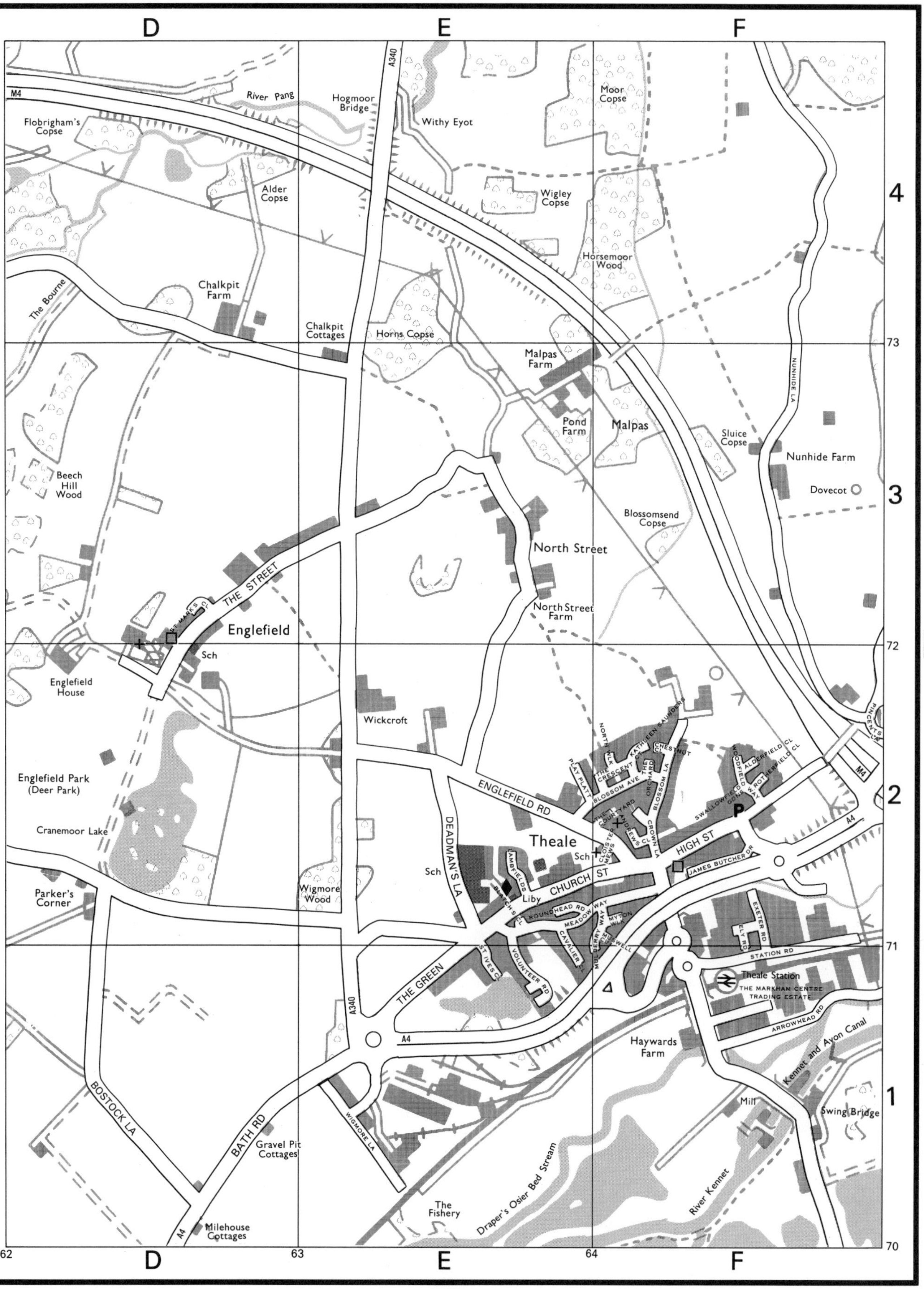
D
E
F
M4
River Pang
Hogmoor Bridge
Withy Eyot
Flobrigham's Copse
Moor Copse
Alder Copse
Wigley Copse
Horsemoor Wood
Chalkpit Farm
The Bourne
Chalkpit Cottages
Horns Copse
Malpas Farm
A340
Pond Farm
Malpas
Sluice Copse
Nunhide Farm
Dovecot
NUNHIDE LA
Beech Hill Wood
Blossomsend Copse
North Street
North Street Farm
THE STREET
ST MARKS CL
Englefield
Sch
Englefield House
Wickcroft
Englefield Park (Deer Park)
Cranemoor Lake
ENGLEFIELD RD
DEADMAN'S LA
Theale
Sch
Liby
CHURCH ST
HIGH ST
JAMES BUTCHER DR
A4
M4
PINCENTS LA
Parker's Corner
Wigmore Wood
THE GREEN
Theale Station
THE MARKHAM CENTRE TRADING ESTATE
STATION RD
ARROWHEAD RD
Haywards Farm
Kennet and Avon Canal
Mill
Swing Bridge
BOSTOCK LA
BATH RD
Gravel Pit Cottages
WIGMORE LA
Draper's Osier Bed Stream
River Kennet
The Fishery
Milehouse Cottages
4
3
2
1
73
72
71
70
62
63
64

84

110

57

83

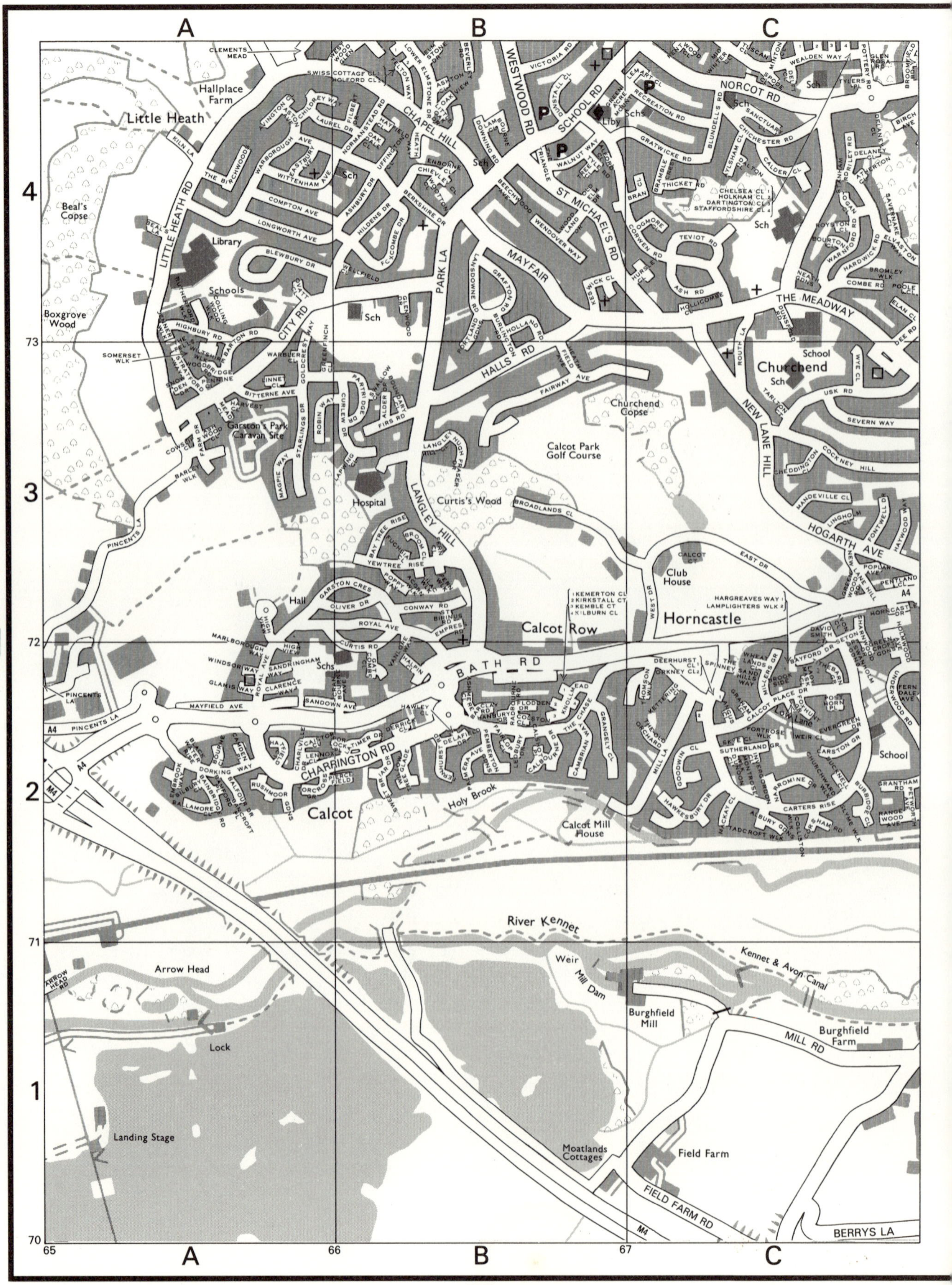
A
B
C
4
3
2
1
73
72
71
70
65
66
67
Little Heath
Hallplace Farm
Clements Mead
Beal's Copse
Boxgrove Wood
Library
Schools
Sch
Schs
Liby
Hospital
Hall
Garston's Park Caravan Site
Curtis's Wood
Calcot Park Golf Course
Churchend Copse
Churchend
School
Club House
Horncastle
Calcot Row
Calcot
Holy Brook
Calcot Mill House
River Kennet
Kennet & Avon Canal
Arrow Head
Lock
Landing Stage
Weir
Mill Dam
Burghfield Mill
Burghfield Farm
Moatlands Cottages
Field Farm
LITTLE HEATH RD
CITY RD
CHAPEL HILL
PARK LA
WESTWOOD RD
SCHOOL RD
ST MICHAEL'S RD
MAYFAIR
HALLS RD
NORCOT RD
THE MEADWAY
NEW LANE HILL
HOGARTH AVE
LANGLEY HILL
BATH RD
PINCENTS LA
MAYFIELD AVE
CHARRINGTON RD
MILL RD
FIELD FARM RD
BERRYS LA
A4
M4

111

58

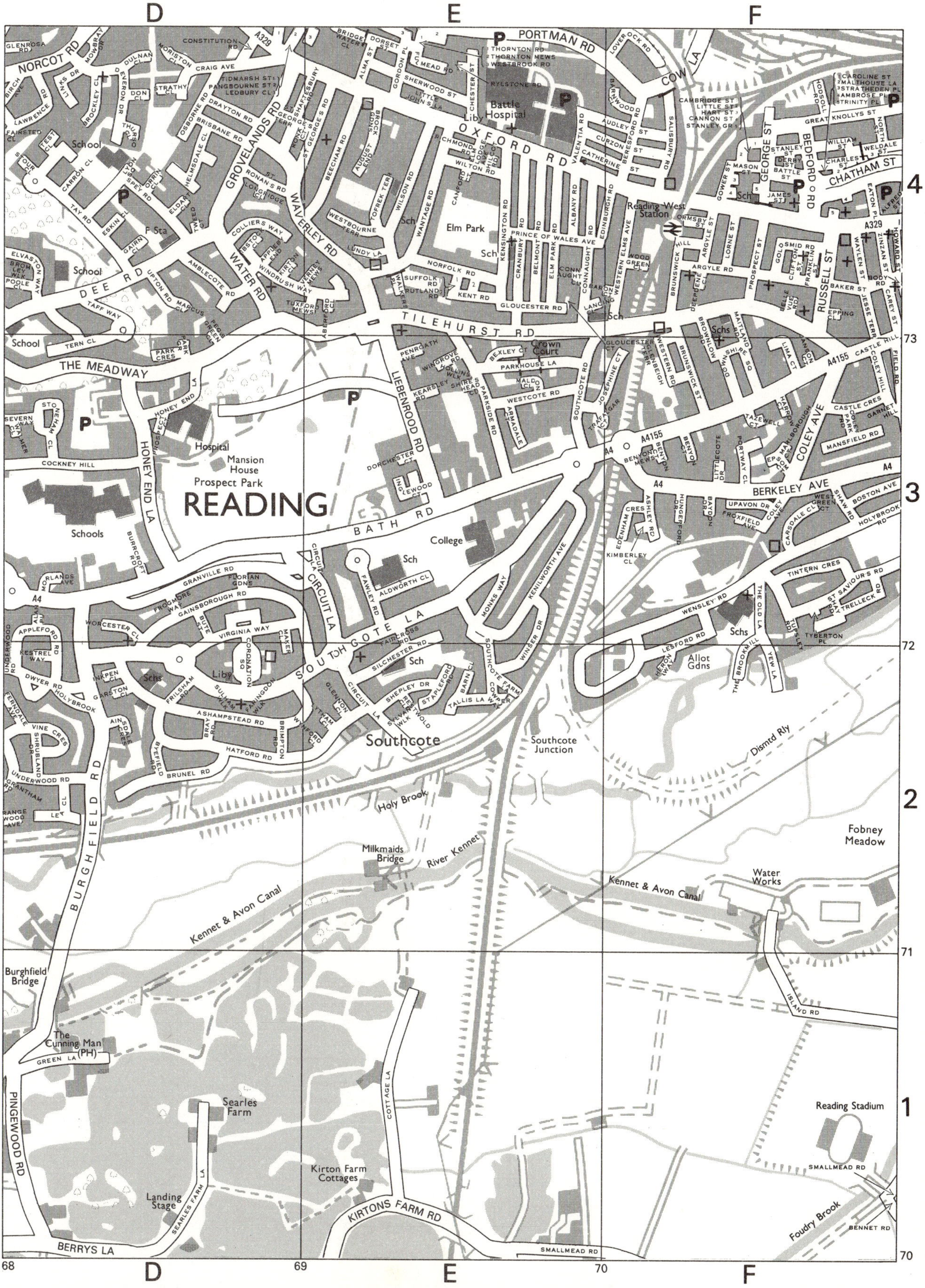

D
E
F
READING
Prospect Park
Mansion House
Hospital
Battle Hospital
Elm Park
Reading West Station
Crown Court
College
Southcote
Southcote Junction
Dismtd Rly
Holy Brook
Milkmaids Bridge
River Kennet
Kennet & Avon Canal
Water Works
Fobney Meadow
Burghfield Bridge
The Cunning Man (PH)
Searles Farm
Kirton Farm Cottages
Landing Stage
Reading Stadium
Foudry Brook
Allot Gdns
OXFORD RD
TILEHURST RD
BATH RD
THE MEADWAY
DEE RD
WATER RD
WAVERLEY RD
GROVELANDS RD
NORCOT RD
HONEY END LA
COCKNEY HILL
BURGHFIELD RD
PINGEWOOD RD
BERRYS LA
GREEN LA
KIRTONS FARM RD
COTTAGE LA
SMALLMEAD RD
ISLAND RD
BENNET RD
SOUTHCOTE LA
CIRCUIT LA
LIEBENROOD RD
BERKELEY AVE
COLEY AVE
CASTLE HILL
RUSSELL ST
GEORGE ST
BEDFORD RD
CHATHAM ST
PORTMAN RD
COW LA
A329
A4
A4155
1
2
3
4
68
69
70
71
72
73

86

112

59

85

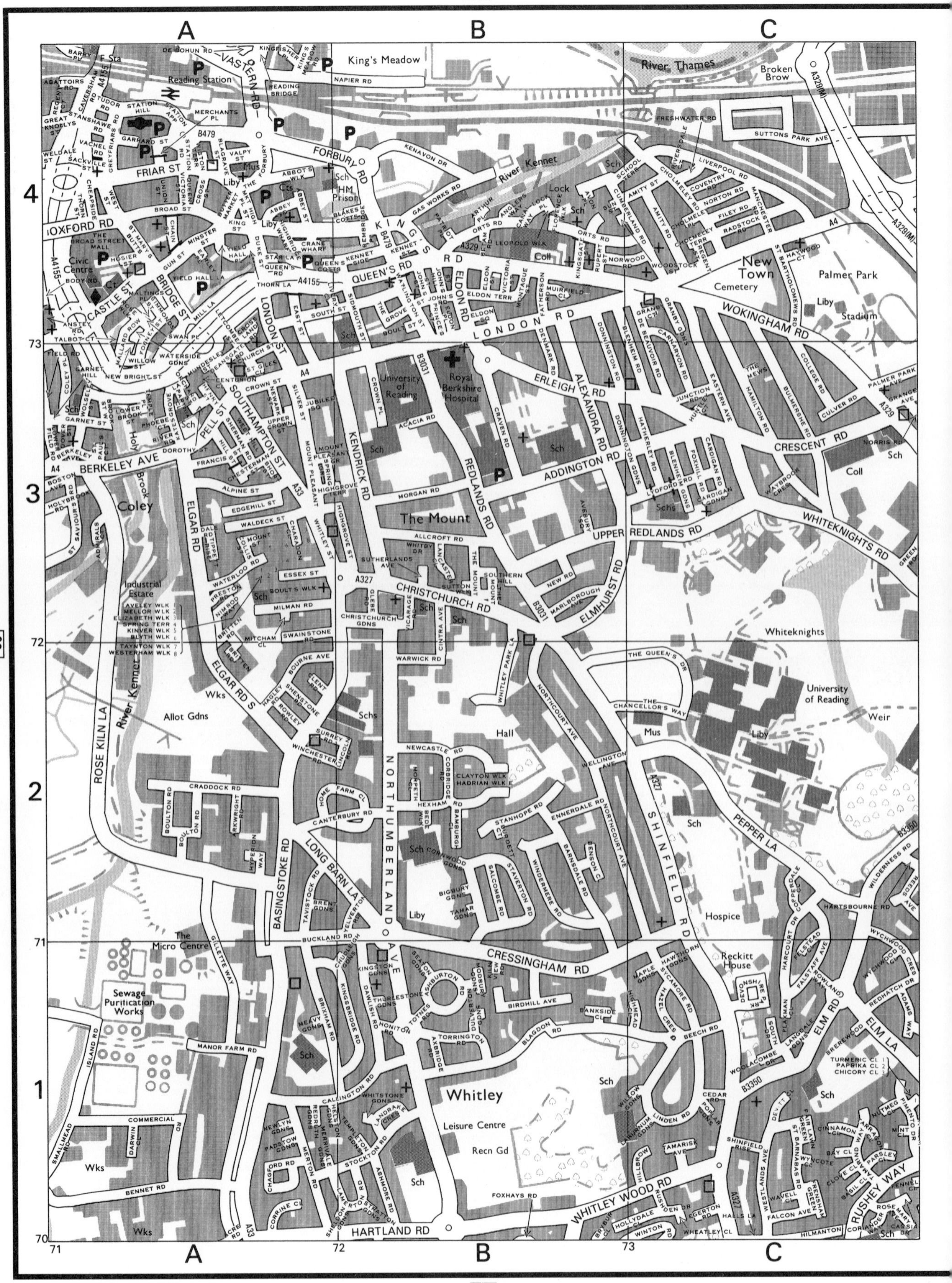

A
B
C
4
3
2
1
73
72
71
70
71
72
73
King's Meadow
River Thames
Broken Brow
Reading Station
Reading Bridge
Vastern Rd
Napier Rd
Forbury Rd
Kenavon Dr
River Kennet
Gas Works Rd
Friar St
Oxford Rd
Broad St
The Broad Street Mall
Civic Centre
Castle St
Bridge St
London St
Queen's Rd
Kennet Side
Kings Rd
Eldon Rd
London Rd
HM Prison
Lock
Coll
Sch
Liby
Mus
Cts
New Town
Cemetery
Palmer Park
Stadium
Wokingham Rd
Cumberland Rd
Liverpool Rd
Suttons Park Ave
Freshwater Rd
A329(M)
A4
A4155
A329
B479
B3031
A327
A33
B3350
Southampton St
Pell St
Berkeley Ave
Coley
Elgar Rd
University of Reading
Royal Berkshire Hospital
Kendrick Rd
Redlands Rd
Erleigh Rd
Alexandra Rd
Addington Rd
Crescent Rd
Whiteknights Rd
Upper Redlands Rd
The Mount
Christchurch Rd
Elmhurst Rd
Industrial Estate
Aveley Wlk 1
Mellor Wlk 2
Elizabeth Wlk 3
Spring Terr 4
Kinver Wlk 5
Blyth Wlk 6
Taynton Wlk 7
Westerham Wlk 8
Whiteknights
The Queen's Dr
The Chancellor's Way
University of Reading
Weir
Hall
Mus
Wks
Allot Gdns
Rose Kiln La
Elgar Rd S
Northumberland Ave
Northcourt Ave
Wellington Ave
Shinfield Rd
Pepper La
Basingstoke Rd
Long Barn La
Craddock Rd
Hospice
Reckitt House
The Micro Centre
Sewage Purification Works
Cressingham Rd
Buckland Rd
Manor Farm Rd
Gillette Way
Commercial Rd
Bennet Rd
Island Rd
Smallmead
Whitley
Leisure Centre
Recn Gd
Whitley Wood Rd
Foxhays Rd
Hartland Rd
Elm Rd
Elm La
Rushey Way
Wilderness Rd
Hartsbourne Rd

113

60

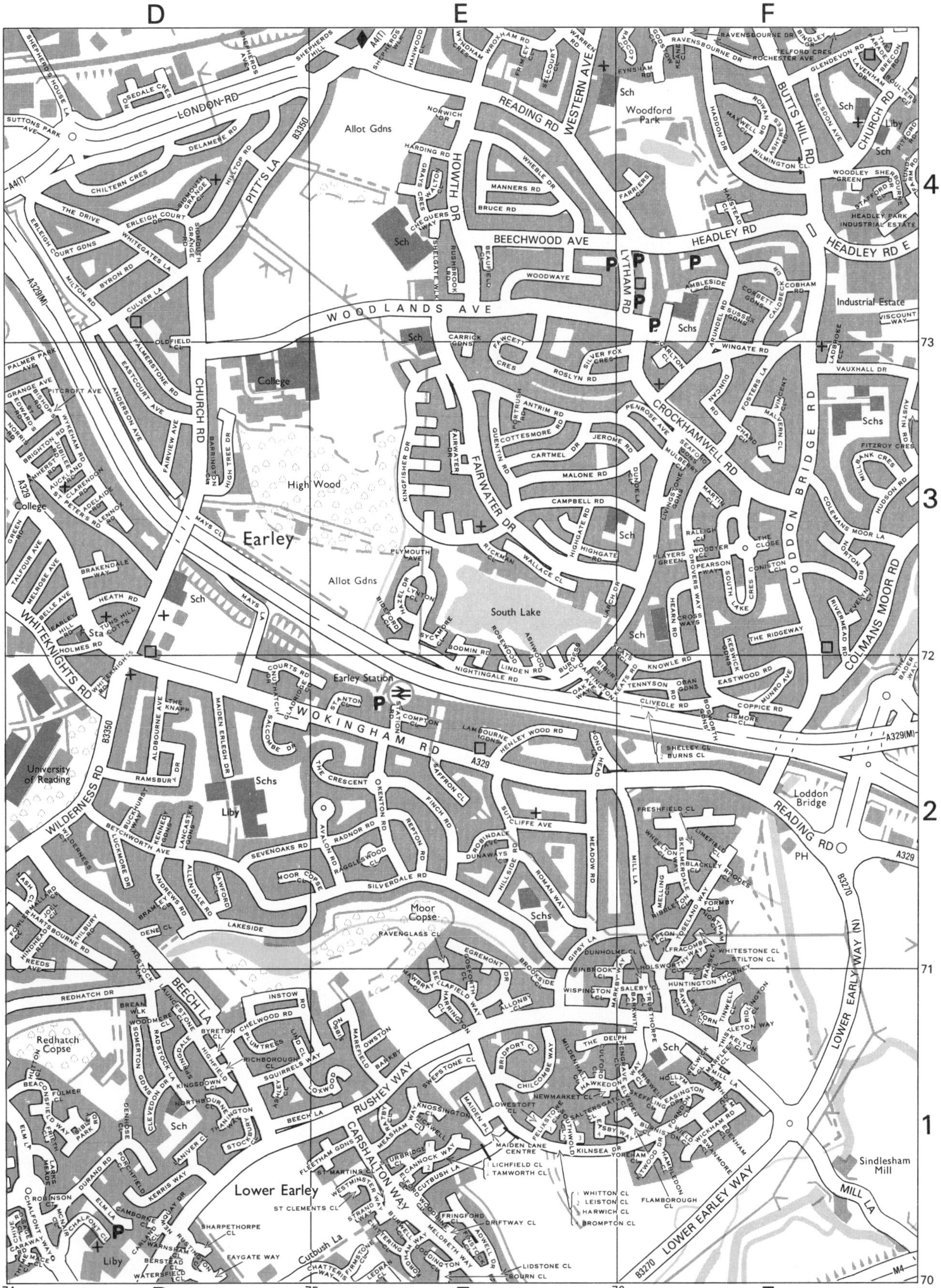

D
E
F
4
3
2
1
73
72
71
70
74
75
76
LONDON RD
SUTTONS PARK AVE
SHEPHERDS HOUSE LA
SHEPHERDS AVE
SHEPHERDS HILL
ROSEDALE CRES
DELAMERE RD
CHILTERN CRES
A4(T)
THE DRIVE
ERLEIGH COURT GDNS
ERLEIGH COURT DR
WHITEGATES LA
SIDMOUTH GRANGE
HILLTOP RD
PITT'S LA
B3350
MILTON RD
BYRON RD
CULVER LA
A329(M)
OLDFIELD CL
PALMERSTONE RD
EASTCOURT AVE
ANDERSON AVE
FAIRVIEW AVE
CHURCH RD
BARRINGTON CL
HIGH TREE DR
PALMER PARK AVE
GRANGE AVE
PITCROFT AVE
BRIGHTON RD
WYKEHAM RD
AMHERST RD
AUCKLAND RD
CLARENDON RD
ADELAIDE RD
ST PETERS RD
LENNOX RD
A329
College
GREEN RD
TALFOUR AVE
MELROSE AVE
BELLE AVE
BRAKENDALE WAY
HEATH RD
TUNS HILL COTTS
Sta
HOLMES RD
WHITEKNIGHTS RD
Earley
MAYS CL
MAYS LA
Sch
Allot Gdns
NORWICH DR
HARDING RD
GRAYS CRES
WALTON
CHEQUERS WAY
HOWTH DR
RUSHBROOK RD
SHELGATE WLK
Sch
WOODLANDS AVE
College
High Wood
Allot Gdns
PLYMOUTH AVE
HAZEL DR
LYNTON
SYCAMORE
BODMIN RD
NIGHTINGALE RD
LINDEN RD
ROSEWOOD
ASHWOOD
South Lake
KINGFISHER DR
FAIRWATER DR
CARRICK GDNS
FAWCETT CRES
ROSLYN RD
SILVER FOX CRES
PORTRUSH RD
ANTRIM RD
QUENTIN RD
COTTESMORE RD
CARTMEL DR
JEROME RD
MALONE RD
CAMPBELL RD
DUNDELA
HIGHGATE RD
RICKMAN CL
WALLACE CL
LARCH DR
BURGESS
WROXHAM RD
WYNDHAM CRES
HANWOOD CL
FRIMLEY CL
SELCOURT CL
WARREN RD
READING RD
WESTERN AVE
WHEBLE DR
MANNERS RD
BRUCE RD
BEECHWOOD AVE
BEAUFIELD CL
WOODWAYE
LYTHAM RD
P
Sch
Woodford Park
FARRIERS CL
HALSTEAD CL
HEADLEY RD
HEADLEY RD E
RAVENSBOURNE DR
BINGLEY GR
TELFORD CRES
ROCHESTER AVE
GLENDEVON RD
LAVENHAM DR
BUTTS HILL RD
HADDON DR
MAXWELL CL
ROWAN DR
ASHTREE CL
WILMINGTON CL
SELSDON AVE
CHURCH RD
Liby
Sch
WOODLEY GREEN
SHERBOURNE DR
STAFFORD CL
HEADLEY PARK INDUSTRIAL ESTATE
Industrial Estate
VISCOUNT WAY
AMBLESIDE CL
ARUNDEL RD
SUSSEX GDNS
CORBETT GDNS
CALDBECK DR
COBHAM RD
Schs
WINGATE RD
VAUXHALL DR
CROCKHAMWELL RD
PENROSE AVE
SEAFORD GDNS
MULBERRY
DUNCAN RD
FOSTERS LA
VINCENT RD
MALVERN CL
CHARD CL
LOQQDON BRIDGE RD
Schs
AUSTIN RD
FITZROY CRES
MILLBANK CRES
COLEMANS MOOR LA
HUDSON RD
NORTON RD
RIVERMEAD RD
EVELYN CL
COLMANS MOOR RD
LIVINGSTONE GDNS
MARTIN CL
RALEIGH CL
PLAYERS GREEN
WOODYER CL
DROVERS WAY
PEARSON WAY
SOUTH LAKE CRES
THE CLOSE
CONISTON CL
HEARN RD
CROSS WAYS
KESWICK GDNS
THE RIDGEWAY
KNOWLE RD
TENNYSON
OBAN GDNS
EASTWOOD RD
MUNRO AVE
COPPICE RD
LISMORE
BOSWORTH GDNS
CLIVEDLE RD
KEATS RD
SHELLEY CL
BURNS CL
Earley Station
COURTS RD
STANTON CL
STATION RD
COMPTON CL
WOKINGHAM RD
LAMBOURNE GDNS
HENLEY WOOD RD
POND HEAD LA
THE KNAPP
ALDBOURNE AVE
MAIDEN ERLEGH DR
SALCOMBE DR
THE CRESCENT
OKENTON RD
SAFFRON CL
FINCH RD
University of Reading
WILDERNESS RD
RAMSBURY DR
Schs
Liby
BUCKHURST
KENNEDY GDNS
LANCASTER GDNS
BETCHWORTH AVE
LUCKMORE DR
ANDREWS RD
ALLENDALE RD
CRAWFORD CL
SEVENOAKS RD
AVALON RD
RADNOR RD
REPTON RD
RAGGLESWOOD CL
MOOR COPSE CL
SILVERDALE RD
ROBINDALE AVE
DUNAWAYS CL
HILLSIDE RD
SUTCLIFFE AVE
ROMAN WAY
MEADOW RD
MILL LA
LAKESIDE
Moor Copse
RAVENGLASS CL
Schs
BRAMLEY CL
DENE CL
HARTSBOURNE RD
HILBURY
FOWLER CL
JOEL CL
ASH CL
REEDS AVE
Loddon Bridge
READING RD
PH
A329
B3270
FRESHFIELD CL
LIMEFIELD CL
WHEELTON CL
SKELMERSDALE WAY
BLACKLEY CL
RHODES CL
MELLING CL
RIBBLETON CL
TOSELAND WAY
FORMBY CL
GIPSY LA
DUNHOLME CL
ILFRACOMBE WAY
WHITESTONE CL
STILTON CL
HOLSWORTHY CL
LOWER EARLY WAY (N)
EGREMONT DR
BROOKSIDE
ALLONBY CL
MAWBRAY CL
GOSFORTH CL
HARRINGTON CL
BINBROOK CL
WISPINGTON CL
SALEBY CL
MARKBY WAY
HUNTINGTON CL
THORNEY CL
TINWELL CL
REDHATCH DR
BEECH LA
RADSTOCK LA
BREAN WLK
WOODMERE CL
Redhatch Copse
SOMERTON GDNS
CLEVEDON DR
BYRETON CL
CHELWOOD RD
PLUMTREES
RICHBOROUGH CL
SQUIRRELS WAY
KINGSDOWN CL
NORTHBOURNE CL
INSTOW RD
MAREFIELD
OWSTON
BARKBY
RUSHEY WAY
SWEPSTONE CL
ASHLEY CL
OXWOOD
BEECH LA
BRIDPORT CL
CHILCOMBE WAY
THE DELPH
NEWMARKET CL
HAWKEDON WAY
SALTERSGATE CL
LOWESTOFT CL
MAIDEN PL
KNOSSINGTON CL
CARSHALTON WAY
MEASHAM WAY
FEIXSTOWE CL
SOUTHWOLD
KILNSEA DR
EASBY WAY
YOREHAM CL
EASINGTON DR
HAMBLEDON CL
SWANMORE CL
WICKHAM RD
MILL LA
Sch
MAIDEN LANE CENTRE
LICHFIELD CL
TAMWORTH CL
WHITTON CL
LEISTON CL
HARWICH CL
BROMPTON CL
FLAMBOROUGH CL
LOWER EARLEY WAY
B3270
Sindlesham Mill
MILL LA
M4
Lower Earley
ST CLEMENTS CL
FLEETHAM GDNS
ST MARTINS CL
CANNOCK WAY
CUTBUSH LA
WESTMINSTER WAY
STRAND WAY
WOODBINE CL
FRINGFORD CL
DRIFTWAY CL
MELDRETH WAY
CHATTERIS WAY
Cutbush La
LIDSTONE CL
BOURN CL
ELM LA
CHALFONT WAY
ROBINSON CL
DURAND RD
PORCHFIELD CL
KERRIS WAY
CAMBORNE CL
SHARPETHORPE CL
FAYGATE WAY
WARNSHAM CL
BERSTEAD CL
WATERSFIELD CL
Liby
P
Sch
FULMER CL
BEACONSFIELD WAY
ELM LA
RUSTINGTON CL

88

114

61

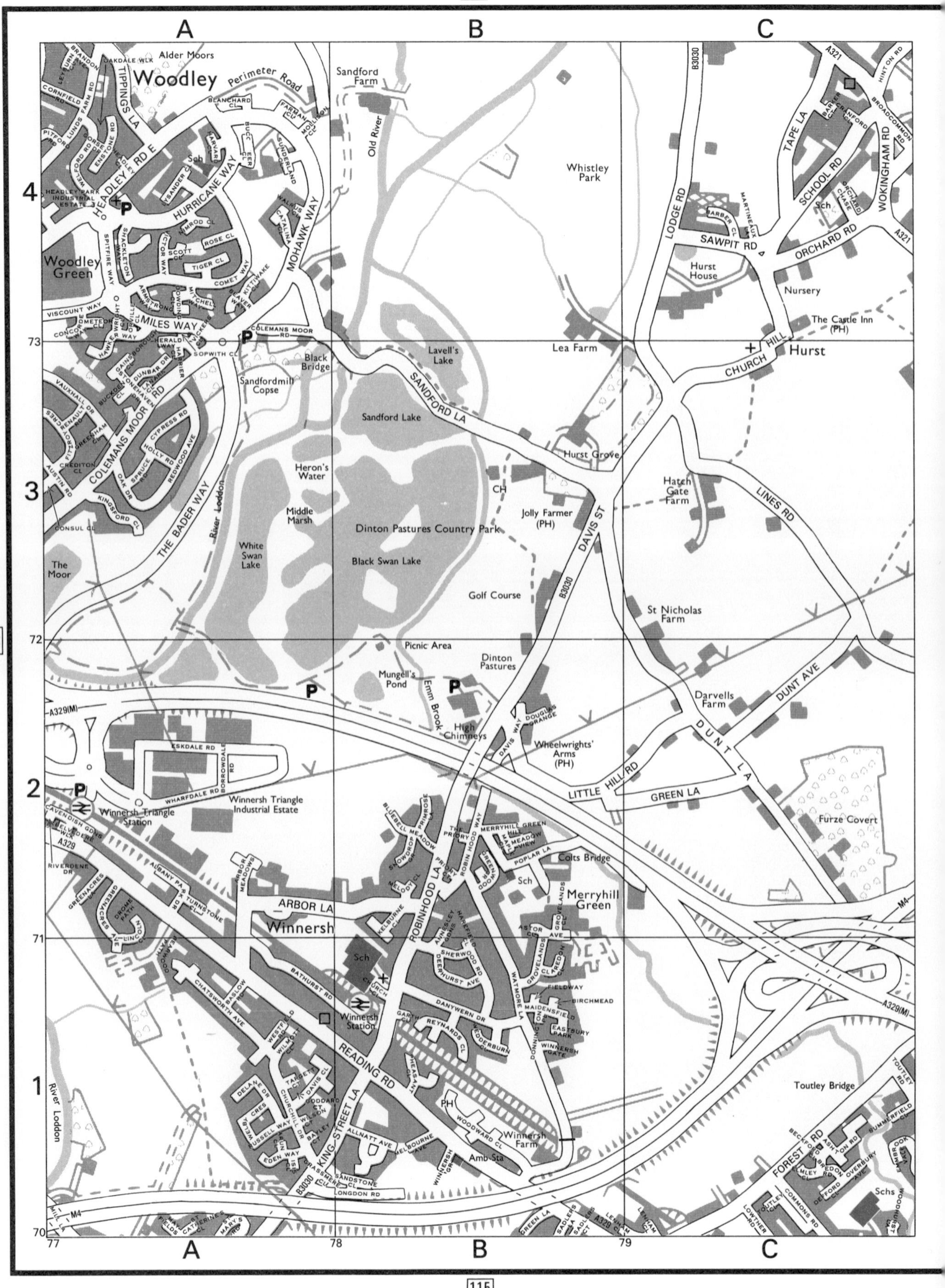
A
B
C
4
3
2
1
73
72
71
70
77
78
79
Woodley
Alder Moors
Perimeter Road
Sandford Farm
Old River
Whistley Park
Woodley Green
Headley Park Industrial Estate
Tippings La
Headley Rd E
Hurricane Way
Mohawk Way
Miles Way
Viscount Way
Colemans Moor Rd
Sopwith Cl
Black Bridge
Sandfordmill Copse
Lavell's Lake
Sandford Lake
Sandford La
Heron's Water
Middle Marsh
White Swan Lake
Dinton Pastures Country Park
Black Swan Lake
The Bader Way
River Loddon
The Moor
Lodge Rd
Sawpit Rd
Hurst House
Nursery
The Castle Inn (PH)
Church Hill
Hurst
Lea Farm
Hurst Grove
Hatch Gate Farm
Lines Rd
Jolly Farmer (PH)
Davis St
B3030
Golf Course
St Nicholas Farm
Picnic Area
Dinton Pastures
Mungell's Pond
Emm Brook
High Chimneys
Wheelwrights' Arms (PH)
Darvells Farm
Dunt Ave
Dunt La
Little Hill Rd
Green La
Furze Covert
A329(M)
Eskdale Rd
Wharfdale Rd
Borrowdale Rd
Winnersh Triangle Industrial Estate
Winnersh Triangle Station
A329
Albany Park Dr
Turnstone
Arbor La
Winnersh
Robinhood La
Merryhill Green
Colts Bridge
Poplar La
Watmore La
Sch
Winnersh Station
Reading Rd
King Street La
Danywern Dr
Reynards Cl
Chatsworth Ave
Winnersh Farm
Amb Sta
Longdon Rd
M4
Toutley Bridge
Forest Rd
Schs
Wokingham Rd
School Rd
Orchard Rd
Tape La
A321
Broadcommon Rd

87

115

62

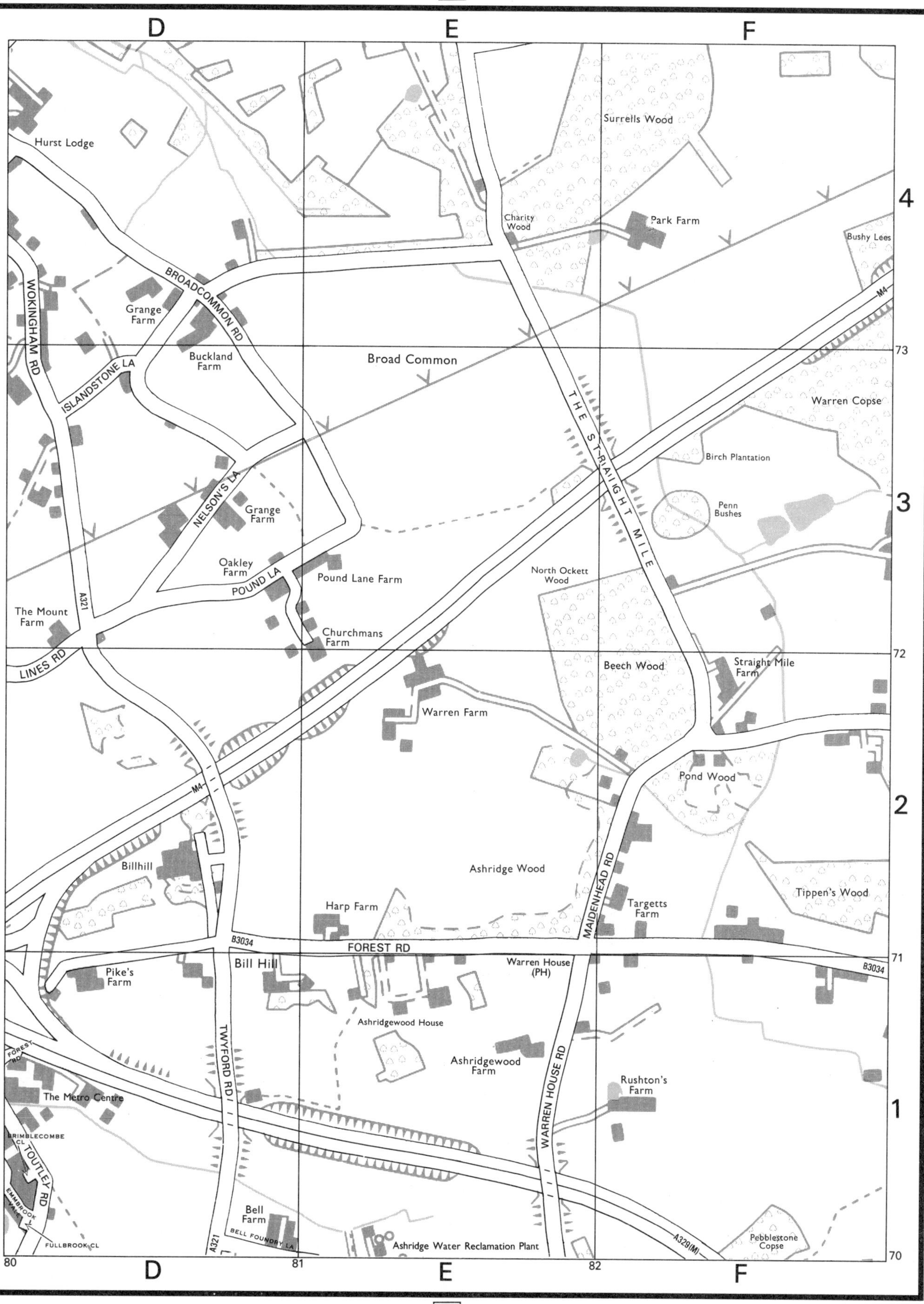
D
E
F
Hurst Lodge
Surrells Wood
Charity Wood
Park Farm
Bushy Lees
BROADCOMMON RD
WOKINGHAM RD
Grange Farm
Buckland Farm
ISLANDSTONE LA
Broad Common
THE STRAIGHT MILE
Warren Copse
Birch Plantation
NELSON'S LA
Grange Farm
Penn Bushes
Oakley Farm
POUND LA
Pound Lane Farm
North Ockett Wood
A321
The Mount Farm
Churchmans Farm
LINES RD
Beech Wood
Straight Mile Farm
Warren Farm
Pond Wood
M4
Billhill
Ashridge Wood
MAIDENHEAD RD
Harp Farm
Targetts Farm
Tippen's Wood
B3034
FOREST RD
Warren House (PH)
Pike's Farm
Bill Hill
Ashridgewood House
Ashridgewood Farm
FOREST RD
The Metro Centre
TWYFORD RD
WARREN HOUSE RD
Rushton's Farm
BRIMBLECOMBE CL
TOUTLEY RD
EMMBROOK VALE
FULLBROOK CL
Bell Farm
BELL FOUNDRY LA
A321
Ashridge Water Reclamation Plant
A329(M)
Pebblestone Copse
4
3
2
1
73
72
71
70
80
81
82

90

116

63

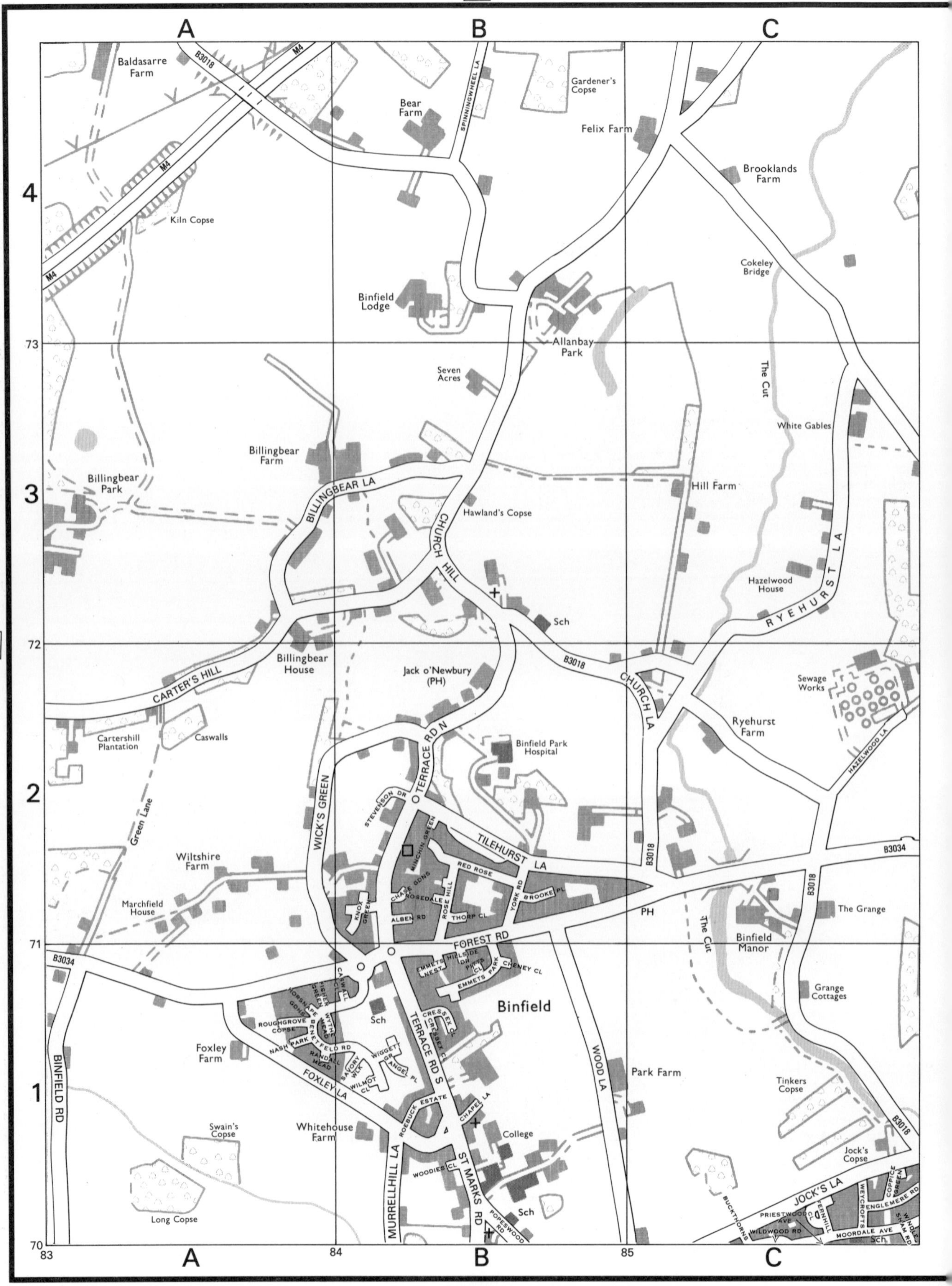
A
B
C
4
3
2
1
73
72
71
70
83
84
85
Baldasarre Farm
B3018
M4
Bear Farm
SPINNINGWHEEL LA
Gardener's Copse
Felix Farm
Brooklands Farm
Kiln Copse
Cokeley Bridge
Binfield Lodge
Allanbay Park
Seven Acres
The Cut
White Gables
Billingbear Farm
Billingbear Park
BILLINGBEAR LA
CHURCH HILL
Hawland's Copse
Hill Farm
Hazelwood House
RYEHURST LA
Sch
Billingbear House
CARTER'S HILL
Jack o'Newbury (PH)
CHURCH LA
Sewage Works
Ryehurst Farm
Cartershill Plantation
Caswalls
TERRACE RD N
Binfield Park Hospital
HAZELWOOD LA
Green Lane
WICK'S GREEN
STEVENSON DR
TILEHURST LA
B3034
Wiltshire Farm
RED ROSE
ROSE HILL
YORK RD
BROOKE PL
ROSEDALE
ALBEN RD
THORP CL
KNOX GREEN
PH
B3018
The Grange
Marchfield House
FOREST RD
Binfield Manor
CHENEY CL
EMMETS PARK
Binfield
Grange Cottages
TERRACE RD S
Foxley Farm
FOXLEY LA
WOOD LA
Park Farm
BINFIELD RD
ROUGHGROVE COPSE
NASH PARK
RANDALL MEAD
BENETFELD RD
Tinkers Copse
ROEBUCK ESTATE
CHAPEL LA
College
Swain's Copse
Whitehouse Farm
MURRELLHILL LA
WOODIES CL
ST MARKS RD
Jock's Copse
JOCK'S LA
Long Copse
POPESWOOD RD
Sch
BUCKHORNS
PRIESTWOOD AVE
WILDWOOD RD
FERNHILL CL
WEYCROFTS
ENGLEMERE RD
MOORDALE AVE
COPPICE GREEN
Sch

89

117

64

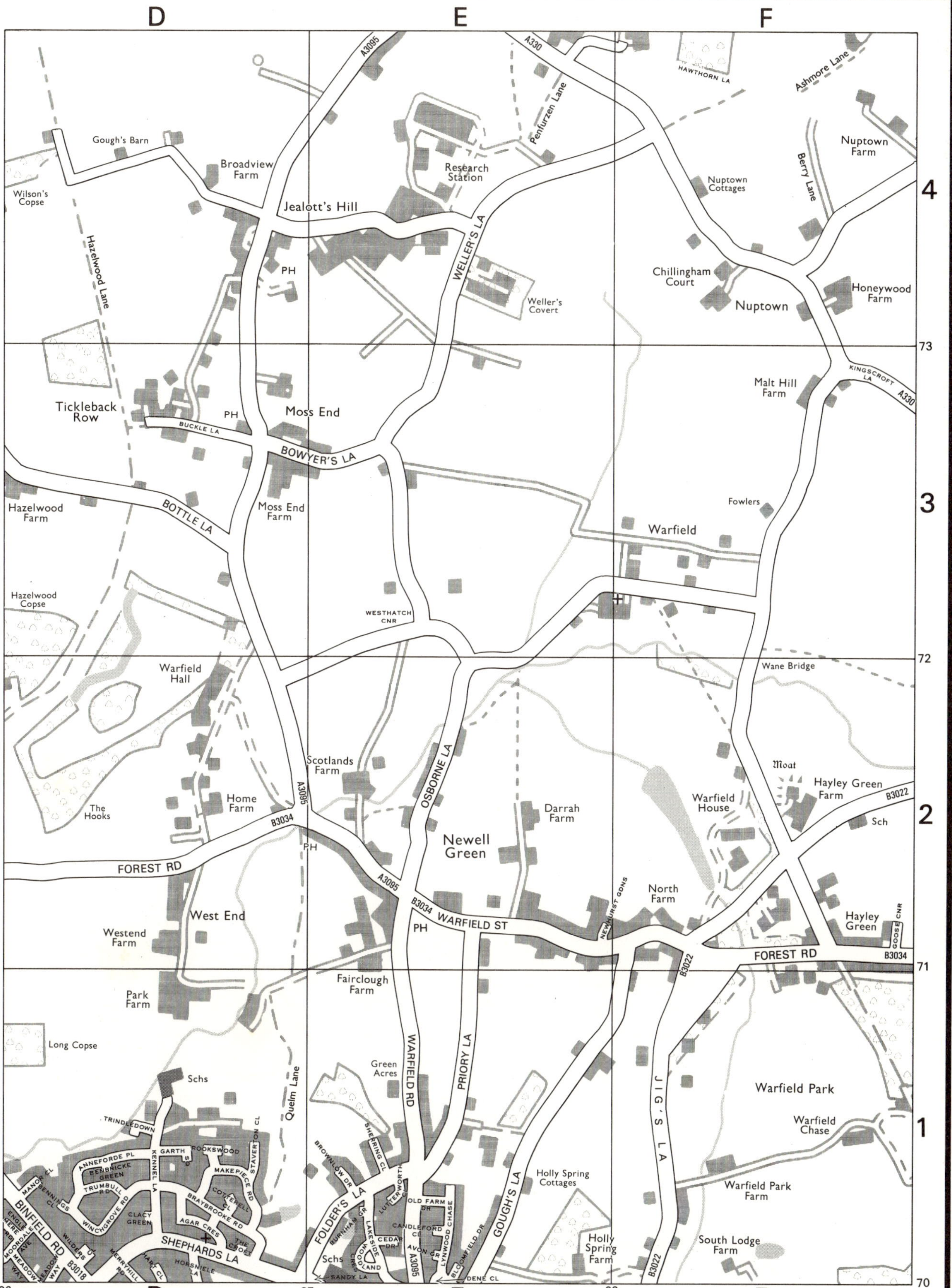
D
E
F
Gough's Barn
Broadview Farm
Wilson's Copse
Jealott's Hill
Research Station
Penfurzen Lane
A330
A3095
Hawthorn La
Ashmore Lane
Nuptown Farm
Berry Lane
Nuptown Cottages
Weller's La
Weller's Covert
PH
Hazelwood Lane
Chillingham Court
Nuptown
Honeywood Farm
4
73
Kingscroft La
Malt Hill Farm
Tickleback Row
PH
Moss End
Buckle La
Bowyer's La
Hazelwood Farm
Bottle La
Moss End Farm
Fowlers
Warfield
3
Hazelwood Copse
Westhatch Cnr
72
Warfield Hall
Wane Bridge
Moat
Scotlands Farm
Osborne La
Hayley Green Farm
B3022
Home Farm
The Hooks
Darrah Farm
Warfield House
2
Sch
B3034
PH
Newell Green
Forest Rd
A3095
West End
Newhurst Gdns
North Farm
Westend Farm
B3034 Warfield St
PH
Hayley Green
Goose Cnr
Forest Rd
B3034
71
Park Farm
Fairclough Farm
B3022
Long Copse
Green Acres
Warfield Rd
Priory La
Jig's La
Warfield Park
Schs
Quelm Lane
Warfield Chase
1
Trindledown
Garth Sq
Rookswood
Staverton Cl
Anneforde Pl
Benbricke Green
Kennel La
Makepiece Rd
Manor Cl
Bennings Cl
Trumbull Rd
Cotterell Cl
Braybrooke Rd
Winchgrove Rd
Clacy Green
Agar Cres
The Croft
Binfield Rd
Shephards La
Wilders Cl
Merryhill Rd
Hart Cl
Horsneile La
B3018
Brownlow Dr
Shering Cl
Folder's La
Burnham Gr
Lakeside
Woodland Cres
Lutterworth
Old Farm Dr
Candleford Cl
Cedar Dr
Avon Gr
Lynwood Chase
Bloomfield Dr
Gough's La
Holly Spring Cottages
Holly Spring Farm
Warfield Park Farm
South Lodge Farm
B3022
A3095
Schs
Sandy La
Dene Cl
70
86
87
88
D
E
F

92

118

65

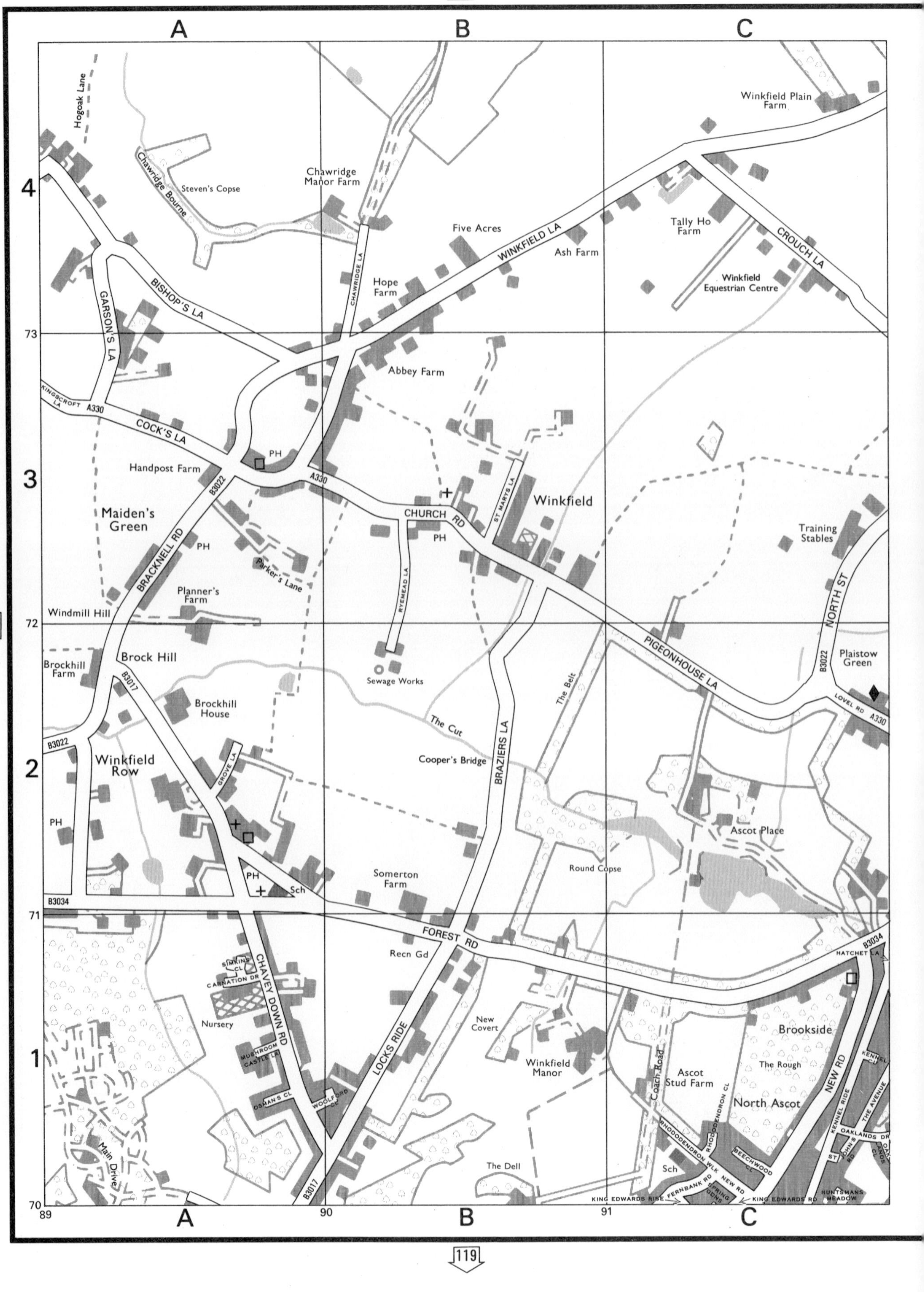
A
B
C
Hogoak Lane
Chawridge Bourne
Steven's Copse
Chawridge Manor Farm
Winkfield Plain Farm
Tally Ho Farm
Five Acres
Ash Farm
WINKFIELD LA
CROUCH LA
Winkfield Equestrian Centre
Hope Farm
CHAWRIDGE LA
BISHOP'S LA
GARSON'S LA
Abbey Farm
KINGSCROFT LA
A330
COCK'S LA
PH
Handpost Farm
B3022
Maiden's Green
CHURCH RD
ST MARYS LA
Winkfield
Training Stables
BRACKNELL RD
Parker's Lane
RYEMEAD LA
Planner's Farm
Windmill Hill
NORTH ST
PIGEONHOUSE LA
Plaistow Green
Brockhill Farm
Brock Hill
B3017
Sewage Works
The Belt
LOVEL RD
Brockhill House
The Cut
BRAZIERS LA
Winkfield Row
GROVE LA
Cooper's Bridge
Ascot Place
Round Copse
Somerton Farm
Sch
B3034
FOREST RD
Recn Gd
HATCHET LA
SIMKINS CL
CARNATION DR
CHAVEY DOWN RD
Nursery
New Covert
Brookside
LOCKS RIDE
MUSHROOM CASTLE LA
Winkfield Manor
Coach Road
Ascot Stud Farm
The Rough
NEW RD
KENNEL CL
KENNEL RIDE
THE AVENUE
OSMAN'S CL
WOOLFORD CL
RHODODENDRON CL
North Ascot
OAKLANDS DR
Main Drive
RHODODENDRON WLK
BEECHWOOD CL
ST JOHN'S RD
The Dell
Sch
NEW RD
SPRING GDNS
FERNBANK RD
KING EDWARDS RISE
KING EDWARDS RD
HUNTSMANS MEADOW
B3017
4
73
3
72
2
71
1
70
89
90
91

91

119

66

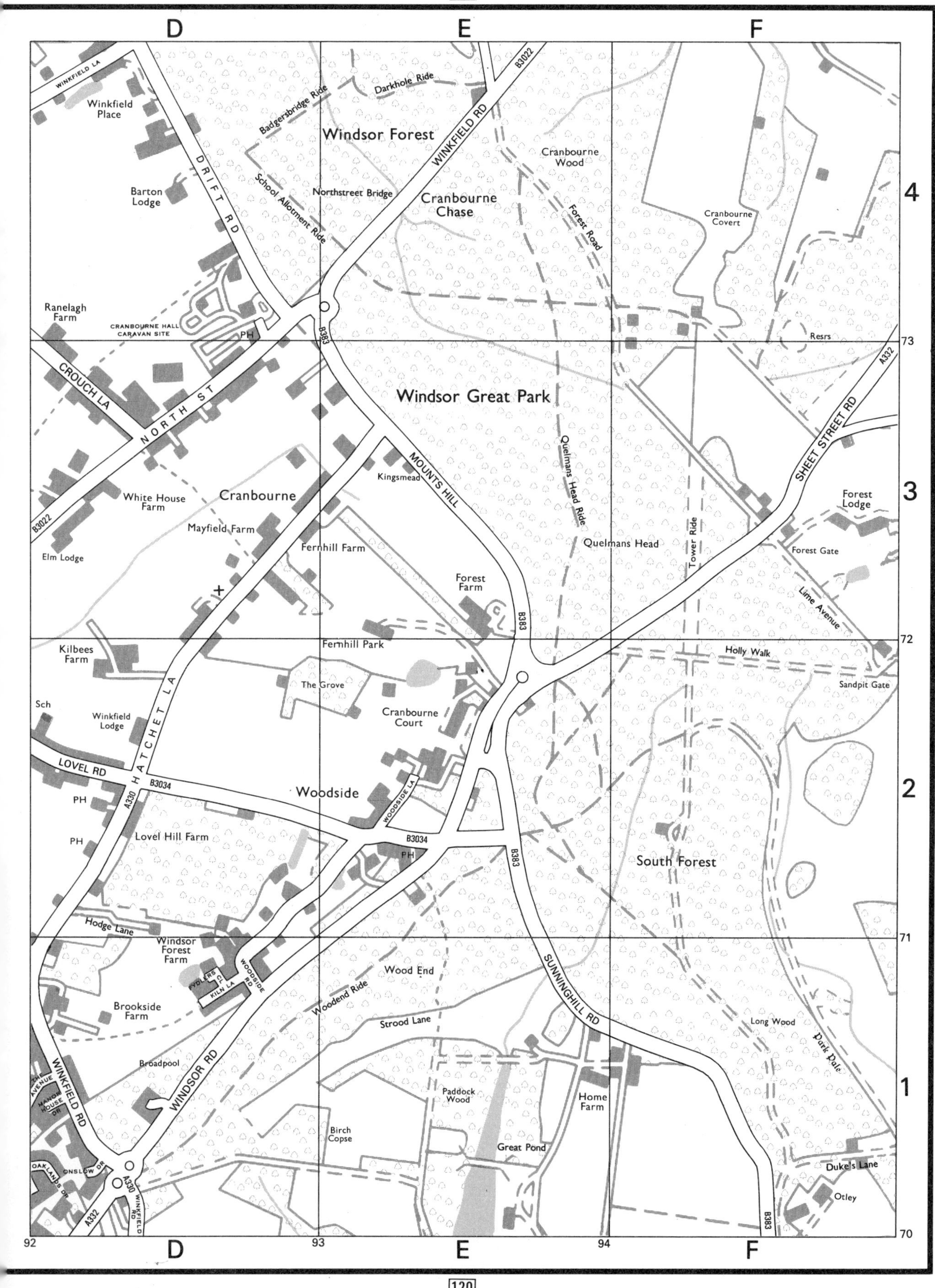
D
E
F
Winkfield Place
Winkfield La
Badgersbridge Ride
Darkhole Ride
Windsor Forest
Winkfield Rd
B3022
Drift Rd
Barton Lodge
School Allotment Ride
Northstreet Bridge
Cranbourne Chase
Cranbourne Wood
Forest Road
Cranbourne Covert
Ranelagh Farm
Cranbourne Hall Caravan Site
PH
B383
Resrs
Crouch La
North St
Windsor Great Park
A332
Sheet Street Rd
Mounts Hill
Kingsmead
Quelmans Head Ride
White House Farm
Cranbourne
Mayfield Farm
B3022
Elm Lodge
Fernhill Farm
Quelmans Head
Tower Ride
Forest Lodge
Forest Gate
Forest Farm
Lime Avenue
Kilbees Farm
Fernhill Park
Holly Walk
The Grove
Sandpit Gate
Sch
Winkfield Lodge
Hatchet La
Cranbourne Court
Lovel Rd
B3034
Woodside
Woodside La
A330
PH
PH
Lovel Hill Farm
B3034
PH
South Forest
Hodge Lane
Windsor Forest Farm
Fydlers Cl
Kiln La
Woodside Rd
Wood End
Sunninghill Rd
Woodend Ride
Brookside Farm
Strood Lane
Long Wood
Park Pale
Broadpool
Winkfield Rd
The Avenue
Manor House Dr
Windsor Rd
Paddock Wood
Home Farm
Birch Copse
Great Pond
Oaklands Dr
Onslow Dr
A330
A332
Winkfield Rd
Duke's Lane
Otley
B383
4
3
2
1
73
72
71
70
92
93
94
D
E
F

94

120

67

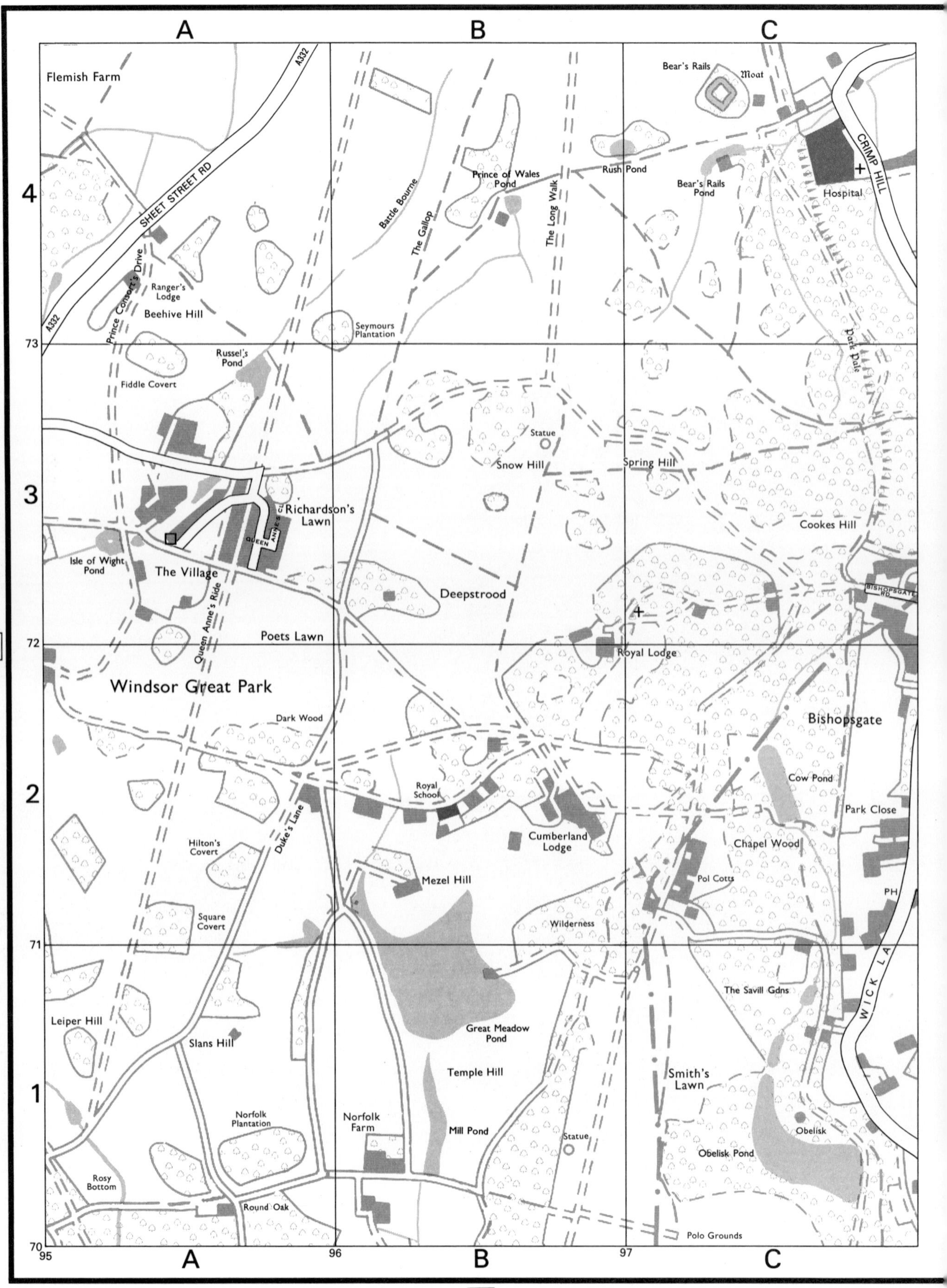
A
B
C
Flemish Farm
A332
SHEET STREET RD
Bear's Rails
Moat
Rush Pond
Bear's Rails Pond
CRIMP HILL
Hospital
Prince of Wales Pond
Bardle Bourne
The Gallop
The Long Walk
Prince Consort's Drive
Ranger's Lodge
Beehive Hill
Seymours Plantation
Dark Pale
Russel's Pond
Fiddle Covert
Statue
Snow Hill
Spring Hill
Richardson's Lawn
QUEEN ANNE'S
Cookes Hill
Isle of Wight Pond
The Village
Queen Anne's Ride
Deepstrood
BISHOPSGATE RD
Poets Lawn
Royal Lodge
Windsor Great Park
Dark Wood
Bishopsgate
Cow Pond
Royal School
Park Close
Hilton's Covert
Duke's Lane
Cumberland Lodge
Chapel Wood
Mezel Hill
Pol Cotts
PH
Square Covert
Wilderness
The Savill Gdns
WICK LA
Leiper Hill
Great Meadow Pond
Slans Hill
Temple Hill
Smith's Lawn
Norfolk Plantation
Norfolk Farm
Mill Pond
Statue
Obelisk
Obelisk Pond
Rosy Bottom
Round Oak
Polo Grounds
4
3
2
1
73
72
71
70
95
96
97

93

121

68

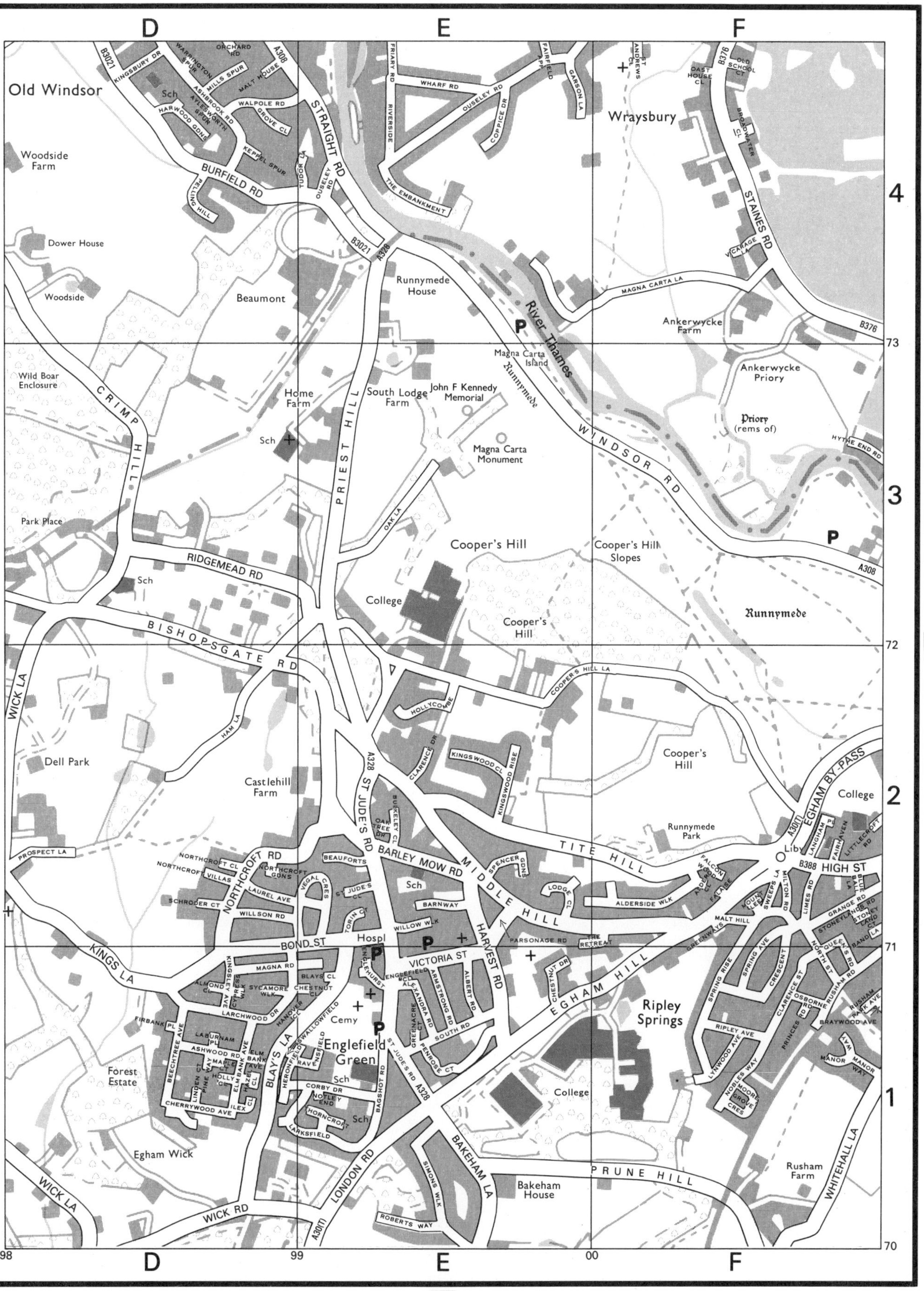
D
E
F
4
3
2
1
73
72
71
70
98
99
00
Old Windsor
Woodside Farm
Dower House
Woodside
Beaumont
Wild Boar Enclosure
Home Farm
Sch
Park Place
CRIMP HILL
RIDGEMEAD RD
BISHOPSGATE RD
WICK LA
HAM LA
Dell Park
Castlehill Farm
PROSPECT LA
KINGS LA
Forest Estate
Egham Wick
WICK RD
LONDON RD
A30(T)
BURFIELD RD
PELLING HILL
KEPPEL SPUR
WALPOLE RD
GROVE CL
MALT HOUSE
KINGSBURY DR
HARWOOD GDNS
B3021
A308
STRAIGHT RD
TUDOR LA
OUSELEY RD
ORCHARD RD
FRIARY RD
RIVERSIDE
WHARF RD
OUSELEY RD
COPPICE DR
FAIRFIELD APP
GARSON LA
ST ANDREWS CL
THE EMBANKMENT
A328
Runnymede House
South Lodge Farm
John F Kennedy Memorial
Magna Carta Monument
Magna Carta Island
Runnymede
River Thames
PRIEST HILL
OAK LA
Cooper's Hill
College
Cooper's Hill Slopes
WINDSOR RD
Wraysbury
OAST HOUSE CL
B376
OLD SCHOOL CT
BROADWATER CL
STAINES RD
VICARAGE LA
MAGNA CARTA LA
Ankerwycke Farm
Ankerwycke Priory
Priory (rems of)
HYTHE END RD
A308
Runnymede
COOPER'S HILL LA
HOLLYCOMBE
CLARENCE DR
KINGSWOOD CL
KINGSWOOD RISE
Runnymede Park
EGHAM BY-PASS
College
Lib
B388
HIGH ST
TITE HILL
MIDDLE HILL
ALDERSIDE WLK
LODGE CL
SPENCER GDNS
ST JUDE'S RD
BARLEY MOW RD
NORTHCROFT RD
NORTHCROFT CL
NORTHCROFT VILLAS
NORTHCROFT GDNS
BEAUFORTS
LAUREL AVE
SCHRODER CT
WILLSON RD
Sch
BARNWAY
WILLOW WLK
BOND ST
Hospl
VICTORIA ST
HARVEST RD
PARSONAGE RD
THE RETREAT
EGHAM HILL
CHESTNUT DR
MALT HILL
MAGNA RD
BLAYS CL
SYCAMORE WLK
CHESTNUT CL
ALMOND CL
LARCHWOOD DR
FIRBANK PL
LABURNAM
ASHWOOD RD
BEECHTREE AVE
CHERRYWOOD AVE
ILEX CL
BLAY'S LA
Cemy
Englefield Green
CORBY DR
NOTLEY END
HORNCROFT
LARKSFIELD
BAGSHOT RD
ARMSTRONG RD
ALBERT RD
SOUTH RD
PENROSE CT
Ripley Springs
College
BAKEHAM LA
SIMONS WLK
ROBERTS WAY
Bakeham House
PRUNE HILL
SPRING RISE
SPRING AVE
CRESCENT
CLARENCE ST
RIPLEY AVE
LYNWOOD AVE
NOBLES WAY
MOORE GROVE CRES
PRINCES RD
RUSHAM RD
BRAYWOOD AVE
MANOR WAY
Rusham Farm
WHITEHALL LA
NORTH ST
LIMES RD
MILTON RD
GRANGE RD
STONEYLANDS RD

96

122

69

95

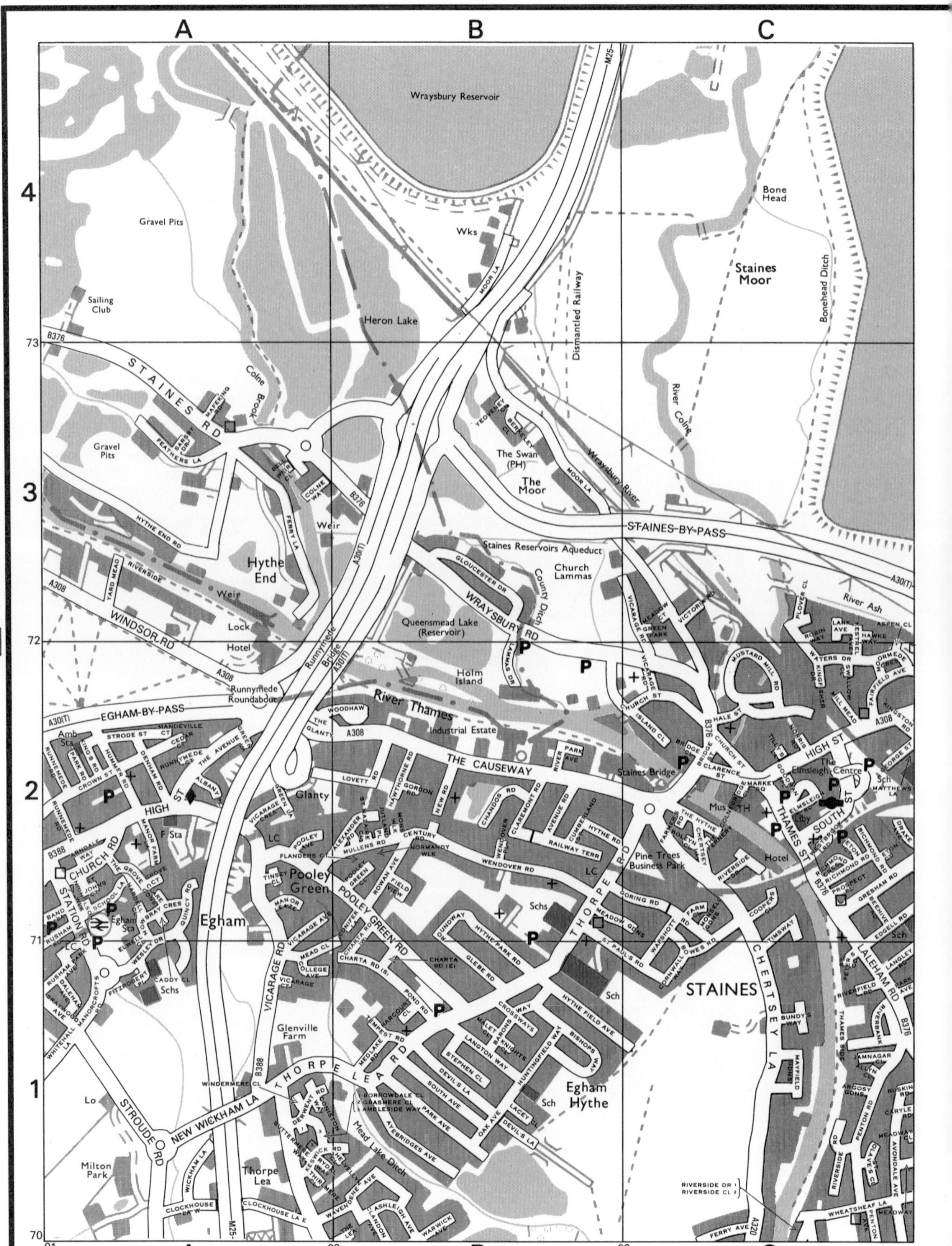
A
B
C
4
3
2
1
73
72
71
70
01
02
03
Wraysbury Reservoir
M25
Gravel Pits
Wks
Staines Moor
Bone Head
Bonehead Ditch
Sailing Club
Heron Lake
MOOR LA
Dismantled Railway
B376
STAINES RD
Colne Brook
MAFEKING
SAXBY
FEATHERS LA
Gravel Pits
BELLE WEIR CL
COLNE WAY
FERRY LA
YEOVENEY CL
BERKELEY CL
The Swan (PH)
The Moor
MOOR LA
Wraysbury River
River Colne
STAINES-BY-PASS
A30(T)
HYTHE END RD
Weir
Hythe End
YARD MEAD
RIVERSIDE
A308
WINDSOR RD
Weir
Lock
Hotel
Staines Reservoirs Aqueduct
GLOUCESTER DR
WRAYSBURY RD
County Ditch
Church Lammas
Queensmead Lake (Reservoir)
LAMMAS DR
Holm Island
VICARAGE RD
MEADOW CL
GREEN PARK
VICTORIA RD
River Ash
PLOVER CL
LARK AVE
ASPEN CL
ROBIN WAY
HAWKE WAY
MUSTARD MILL RD
WATERS DR
ORMEDE CRES
FAIRFIELD AVE
KINGFISHER DR
SWALLOW CL
MILL MEAD
KINGSTON RD
Runnymede Bridge
A30(T)
Runnymede Roundabout
EGHAM-BY-PASS
River Thames
WOODHAW
THE GLANTY
A308
Industrial Estate
ISLAND CL
CHURCH ST
HALE ST
B376
Amb Sta
MANDEVILLE CT
STRODE ST
CEDAR
RUNNYMEDE
KINGS RD
PARK RD
HUMMER RD
DENHAM RD
RUNNYMEDE CT
THE AVENUE
GREEN
CROWN ST
ALBANY
HIGH ST
LOVETT RD
HAWTHORNE RD
GORDON RD
NEW RD
THE CAUSEWAY
RIVER PARK AVE
Staines Bridge
BRIDGE ST
CLARENCE ST
MARKET
HIGH ST
The Elmsleigh Centre
GEORGE ST
Sch
MATTHEWS LA
Glanty
VICARAGE CRES
CHANDOS RD
CLAREMONT RD
AVENUE RD
CUMBERLAND
HYTHE RD
RAILWAY TERR
Mus
TH
THAMES ST
ELMSLEIGH
Cl
Lby
SOUTH ST
B388
ARNDALE WAY
CHURCH RD
MANOR FARM
F Sta
POOLEY AVE
FLANDERS CT
MULLENS RD
CENTURY RD
NORMANDY WLK
WENDOVER RD
WENDOVER RD
Pine Trees Business Park
THE HYTHE
RIVERSIDE DR
Hotel
RICHMOND RD
DRAKE
THE GROVE
LC
Pooley Green
TINSEY CL
ROWAN AVE
FIELD VIEW
LC
THORPE RD
CORING RD
FARM CL
ST JOHNS
STATION RD
Egham Sta
BRAY CRES
QUINCY RD
MANOR FARM
POOLEY GREEN RD
Schs
MEADOW GDNS
COOPERS CL
GRESHAM RD
PROSPECT CL
B376
RUSHAM RD
Egham
VICARAGE AVE
CONIFER
CHARTA RD
HYTHE PARK RD
ST PAUL'S RD
WARSHOTT RD
CORNWALL
TIMSWAY
EDGELL RD
Sch
BAND
ELWELL
WESLEY DR
CADDY CL
Schs
FITZROBERT
MANORCROFTS RD
VICARAGE RD
MEAD CL
COLLEGE AVE
CHARTA RD (S)
CHARTA RD (E)
GLEBE RD
CHERTSEY LA
STAINES
LALEHAM RD
LANGLEY
RUSHAM PARK AVE
DALEHAM AVE
WHITEHALL LA
GLENWOOD AVE
POND RD
HARCOURT CL
CROSSWAYS
HYTHE FIELD AVE
Sch
RIVERFIELD
RIVERBANK
B376
THAMES SIDE
BUNDYS WAY
MAYFIELD GDNS
Glenville Farm
TEMPEST RD
MEDLAKE RD
LANGTON WAY
STEPHEN CL
HUNTINGFIELD WAY
BISHOPS WAY
JAMNAGAR CL
ALLYN CL
RUSKIN
WINDERMERE CL
THORPE LEA RD
DEVILS LA
Egham Hythe
ARGOSY GDNS
Lo
STROUDE RD
NEW WICKHAM LA
1 BORROWDALE CL
2 GRASMERE CL
3 AMBLESIDE WAY
SOUTH AVE
PARK AVE
OAK AVE
LACEY CL
Sch
DEVIL'S LA
PENTON RD
CARYLE
MEADWAY
AVONDALE AVE
RIVERSIDE RD
BUTTERMERE WAY
KESWICK RD
RYDAL WAY
Mead Lake Ditch
AVEBRIDGES AVE
Milton Park
WICKHAM LA
Thorpe Lea
WAVENDENE AVE
ASHLEIGH AVE
WARWICK AVE
CLANDON AVE
RIVERSIDE DR 1
RIVERSIDE CL 2
WHEATSHEAF LA
PENTON
MEADWAY
CLOCKHOUSE LA W
CLOCKHOUSE LA E
M25
FERRY AVE
A320

123

70

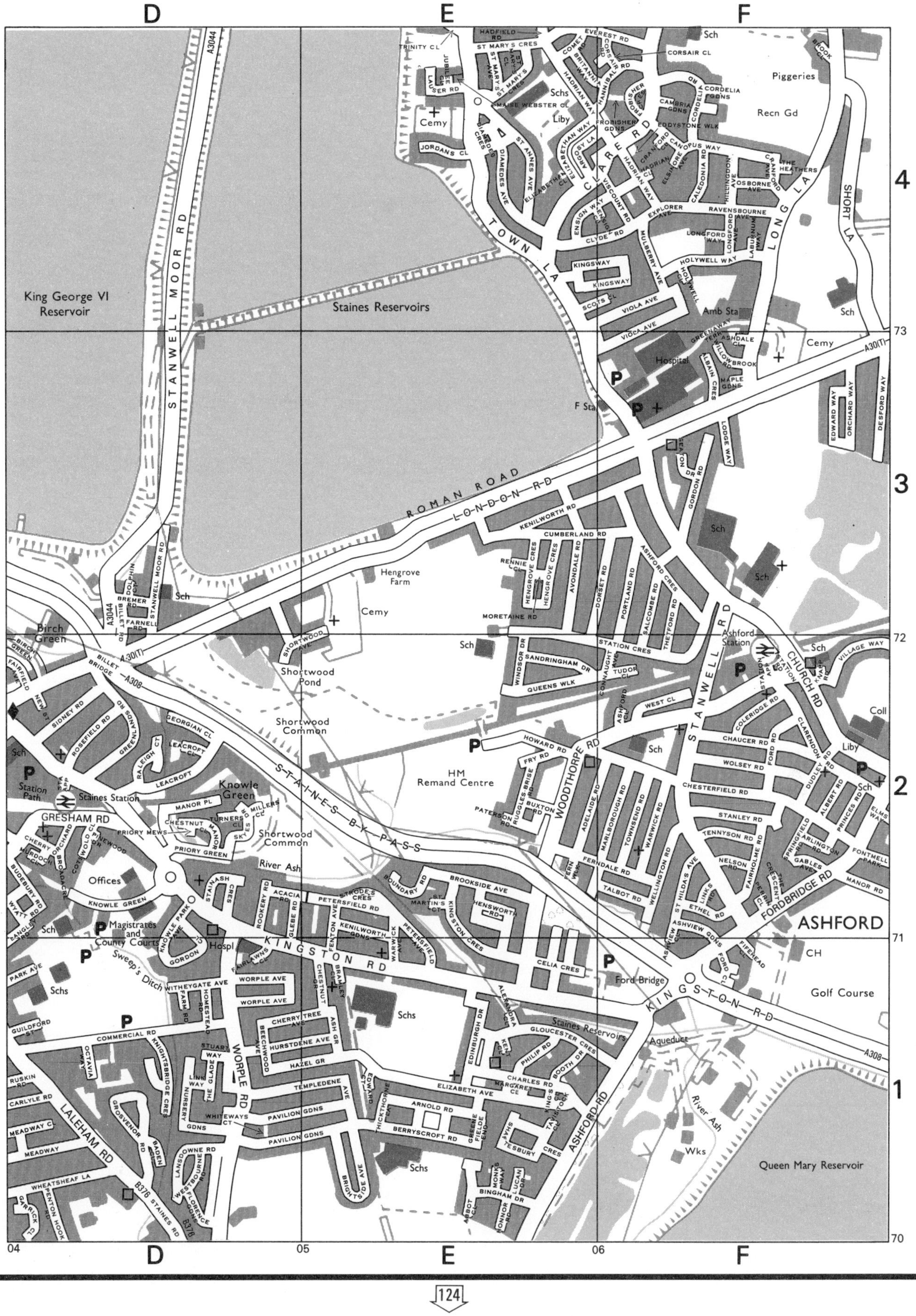
D
E
F
4
3
2
1
73
72
71
70
04
05
06
King George VI Reservoir
Staines Reservoirs
STANWELL MOOR RD
A3044
Piggeries
Recn Gd
Cemy
Schs
Liby
Sch
TOWN LA
LONG LA
SHORT LA
CLARE RD
HADFIELD RD
EVEREST RD
CORSAIR CL
TRINITY CL
ST MARYS CRES
JUBILEE CL
LAUSER RD
MAISE WEBSTER CL
JORDANS CL
DIAMEDES AVE
ST ANNES AVE
ELIZABETHAN WAY
HADRIAN WAY
FROBISHER GDNS
EDDYSTONE WLK
CAMBRIA GDNS
CORDELIA GDNS
CANOPUS WAY
CALEDONIA RD
OSBORNE AVE
THE HEATHERS
EXPLORER AVE
RAVENSBOURNE AVE
LONGFORD WAY
CLYDE RD
KINGSWAY
SCOTS CL
VIOLA AVE
MULBERRY AVE
HOLYWELL WAY
Amb Sta
Hospital
ASHDALE CL
WILLOWBROOK
MAPLE GDNS
ALBAIN CRES
F Sta
Cemy
A30(T)
EDWARD WAY
ORCHARD WAY
DESFORD WAY
LODGE WAY
GORDON RD
ROMAN ROAD
LONDON RD
KENILWORTH RD
CUMBERLAND RD
RENNIE CL
HENGROVE CRES
AVONDALE RD
DORSET RD
PORTLAND RD
SALCOMBE RD
ASHFORD CRES
THETFORD RD
MORETAINE RD
Hengrove Farm
Cemy
Sch
DOLPHIN CL
BREMER RD
BILLET RD
FARNELL RD
Birch Green
BILLET BRIDGE
A308
SHORTWOOD AVE
Shortwood Pond
Shortwood Common
STATION CRES
SANDRINGHAM DR
WINDSOR DR
QUEENS WLK
CONNAUGHT AVE
TUDOR CL
WEST CL
STANWELL RD
Ashford Station
CHURCH RD
VILLAGE WAY
Coll
Liby
HOWARD RD
FRY RD
HM Remand Centre
WOODTHORPE RD
ADELAIDE RD
MARLBOROUGH RD
TOWNSEND RD
WARWICK RD
CHAUCER RD
WOLSEY RD
CHESTERFIELD RD
STANLEY RD
TENNYSON RD
CLARENDON RD
DUDLEY RD
ALBERT RD
PRINCES RD
ELMS WAY
FONTMELL PARK
MANOR RD
FORDBRIDGE RD
NELSON RD
FAIRHOLME RD
ASHFORD
SIDNEY RD
ROSEFIELD RD
GEORGIAN CL
LEACROFT
RALEIGH CT
Staines Station
Station Path
GRESHAM RD
Knowle Green
MANOR PL
PRIORY MEWS
PRIORY GREEN
Shortwood Common
STAINES BY PASS
River Ash
Offices
KNOWLE GREEN
Magistrates and County Courts
Hospl
Sweep's Ditch
STAINASH CRES
ROOKERY RD
ACACIA RD
GLEBE RD
PETERSFIELD RD
BOUNDARY RD
BROOKSIDE AVE
KINGSTON CRES
HENSWORTH RD
FERNDALE RD
TALBOT RD
WELLINGTON RD
ST HILDAS AVE
ETHEL RD
ASHVIEW GDNS
FIFEHEAD CL
KINGSTON RD
CELIA CRES
Ford Bridge
CH
Golf Course
A308
Aqueduct
Staines Reservoirs
River Ash
Wks
Queen Mary Reservoir
WITHEYGATE AVE
WORPLE AVE
WORPLE RD
CHERRY TREE AVE
HURSTDENE AVE
HAZEL GR
TEMPLEDENE AVE
Schs
ALEXANDRA RD
EDINBURGH DR
GLOUCESTER CRES
PHILIP RD
CHARLES RD
ELIZABETH AVE
ASHFORD RD
PARK AVE
Schs
GUILDFORD ST
COMMERCIAL RD
KNIGHTSBRIDGE CRES
OCTAVIA WAY
RUSKIN AVE
CARLYLE RD
MEADWAY CL
MEADWAY
LALEHAM RD
GROSVENOR RD
BADEN CL
WHEATSHEAF LA
FENTON HOOK
LANSDOWNE RD
WESTBOURNE RD
FLORENCE RD
B376 STAINES RD
PAVILION GDNS
ARNOLD RD
BERRYSCROFT RD
Schs
BRIGHTSIDE AVE
BINGHAM DR
MONKS WAY
LUCAN DR
ABBOT CL
TESBURY CL
TAVISTOCK

98

124

71

97

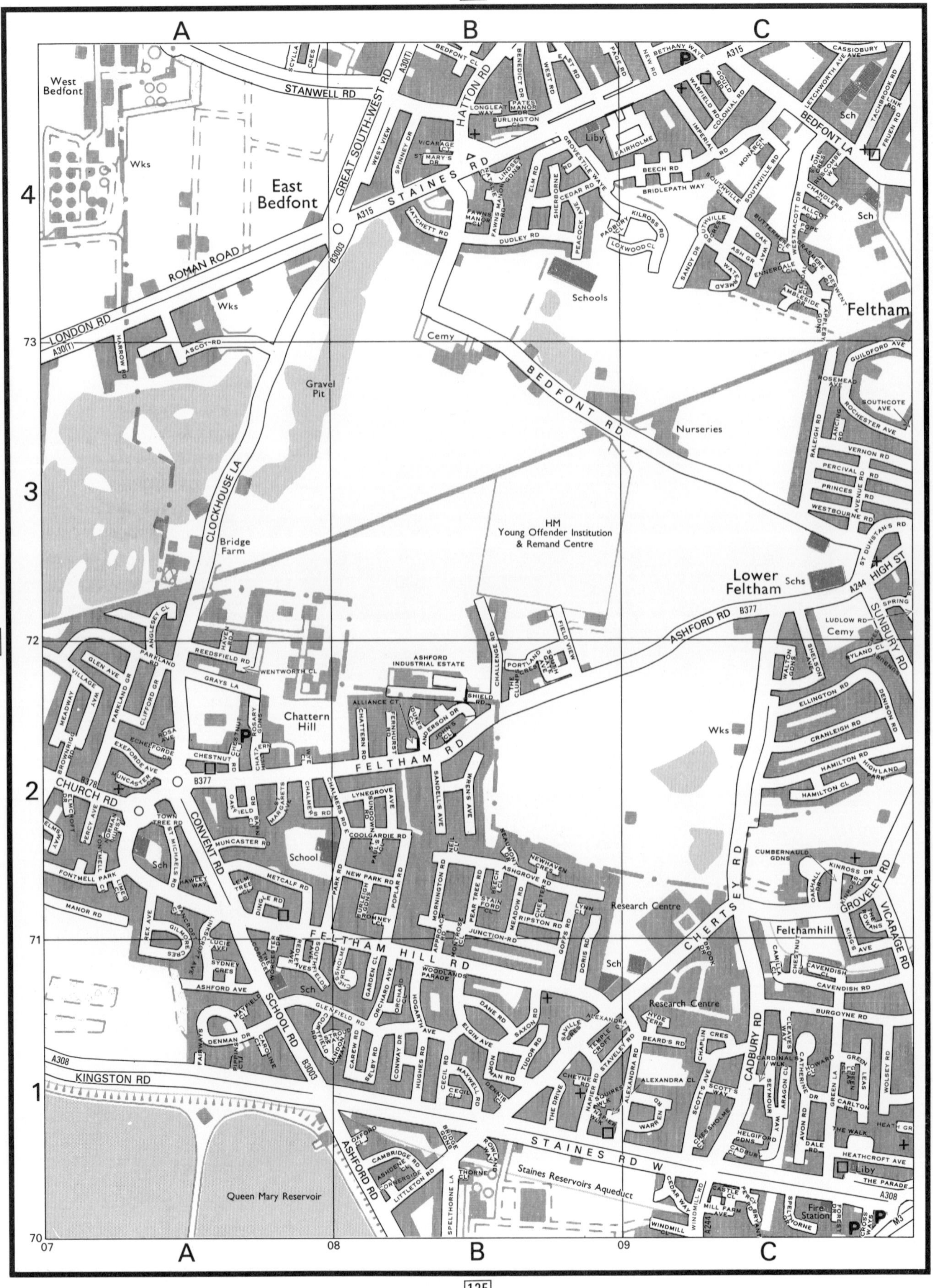
West Bedfont
East Bedfont
Wks
STANWELL RD
ROMAN ROAD
LONDON RD
GREAT SOUTH-WEST RD
STAINES RD
HATTON RD
BEDFONT LA
BEDFONT RD
Feltham
Cemy
Gravel Pit
Schools
Nurseries
HM
Young Offender Institution
& Remand Centre
Bridge Farm
CLOCKHOUSE LA
Lower Feltham
Schs
ASHFORD RD
HIGH ST
SUNBURY RD
ASHFORD INDUSTRIAL ESTATE
Chattern Hill
FELTHAM RD
FELTHAM HILL RD
CHURCH RD
CONVENT RD
SCHOOL RD
School
Sch
Research Centre
CHERTSEY RD
Feltham hill
VICARAGE RD
GROVELEY RD
CADBURY RD
KINGSTON RD
STAINES RD W
Queen Mary Reservoir
Staines Reservoirs Aqueduct
ASHFORD RD
Liby
Fire Station
A
B
C
4
3
2
1
73
72
71
70
07
08
09

125

72

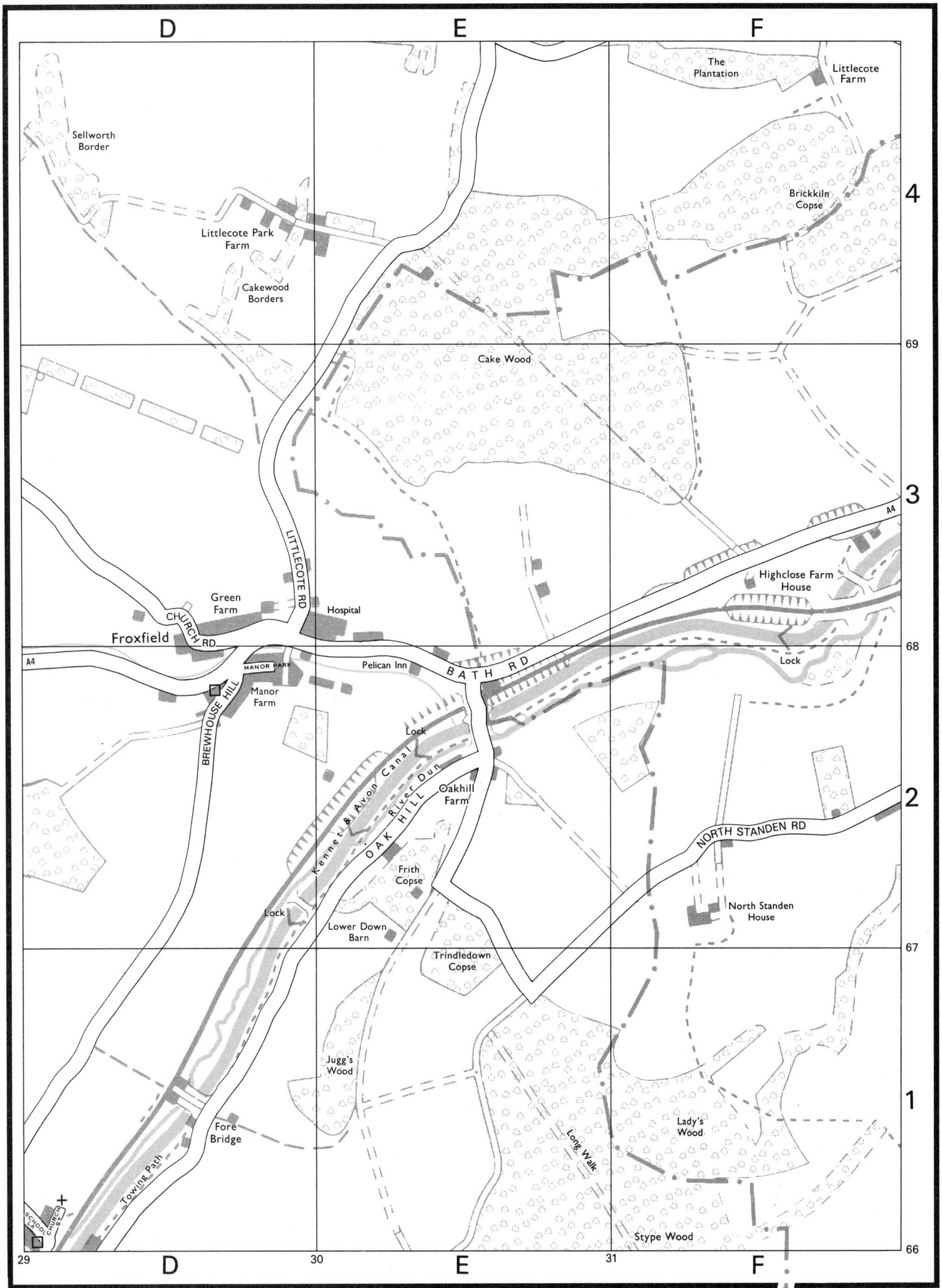

100

not continued, see key diagram

73

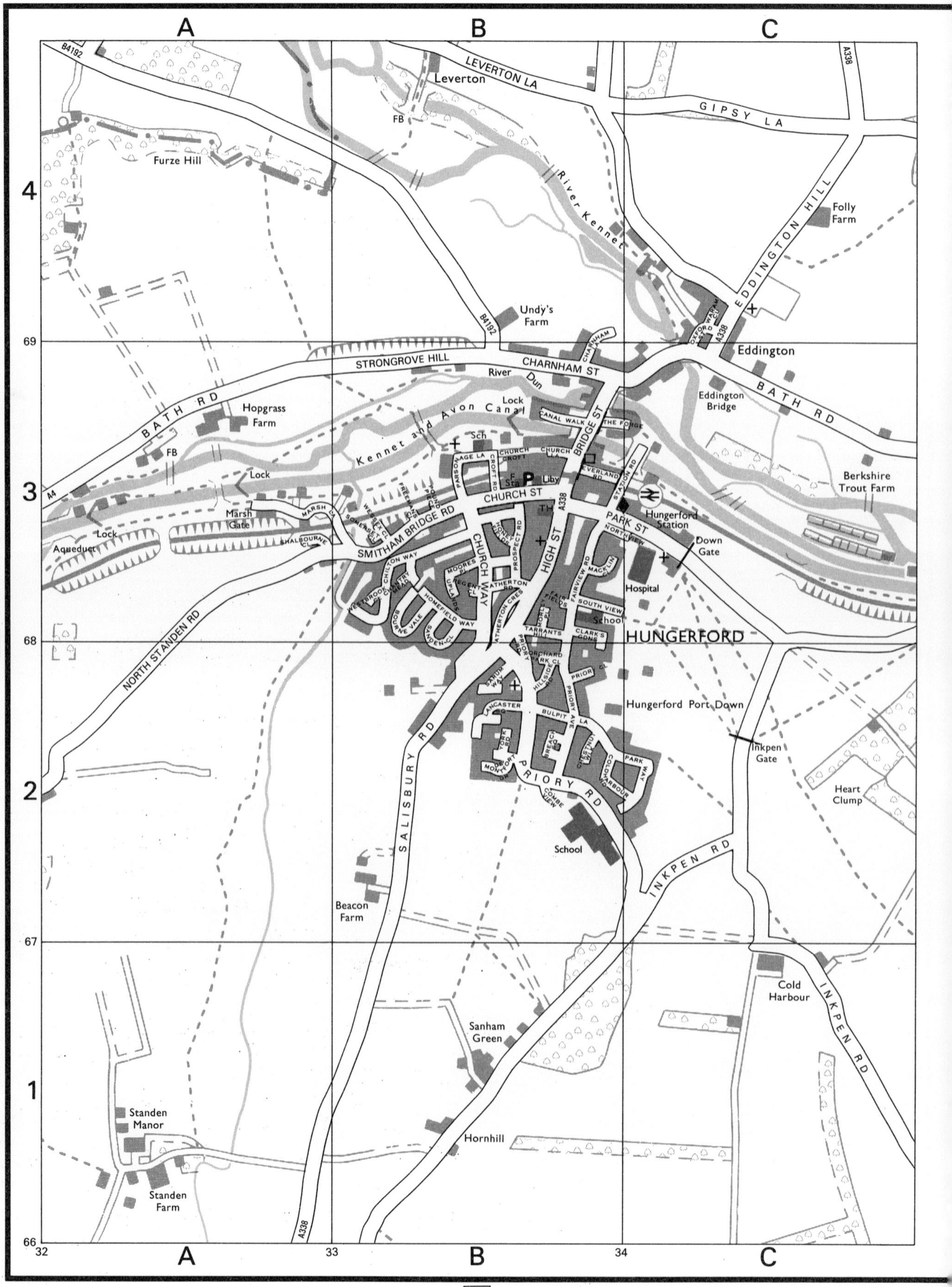

A
B
C
Leverton
LEVERTON LA
GIPSY LA
A338
B4192
FB
Furze Hill
River Kennet
4
Folly Farm
EDDINGTON HILL
Undy's Farm
69
STRONGROVE HILL
CHARNHAM ST
CHARNHAM CL
Eddington
BATH RD
River Dun
Lock
Hopgrass Farm
Eddington Bridge
Kennet and Avon Canal
CANAL WALK
THE FORGE
BRIDGE ST
FB
Lock
Sch
CHURCH CROFT
CHURCH LA
EVERLAND RD
STATION RD
Berkshire Trout Farm
3
A4
Marsh Gate
MARSH LA
CHURCH ST
Liby
TH
HIGH ST
Hungerford Station
PARK ST
Lock
Aqueduct
SHALBOURNE CL
SMITHAM BRIDGE RD
CHILTON WAY
CHURCH WAY
Down Gate
Hospital
ATHERTON RD
SOUTH VIEW
School
68
HUNGERFORD
NORTH STANDEN RD
HOMEFIELD WAY
SANDEN CL
BOURNE VALE
CLARK'S GDNS
PRIOR CL
Hungerford Port Down
LANCASTER SQ
BULPIT LA
PRIORY AVE
SALISBURY RD
Inkpen Gate
PARK WAY
2
PRIORY RD
Heart Clump
School
INKPEN RD
Beacon Farm
67
Cold Harbour
INKPEN RD
Sanham Green
1
Standen Manor
Hornhill
Standen Farm
A338
66
32
33
34

99

126

74

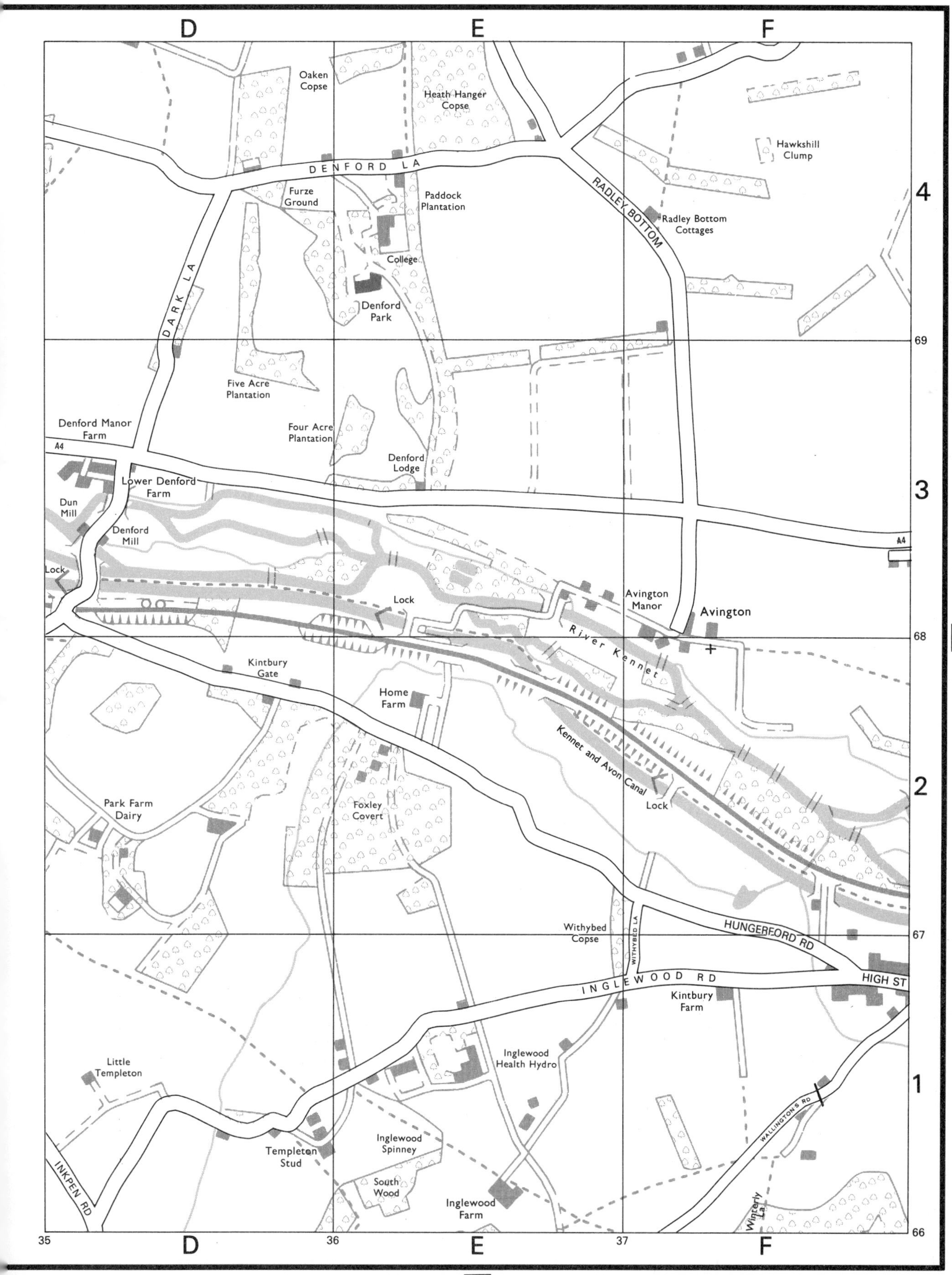
D
E
F
Oaken Copse
Heath Hanger Copse
Hawkshill Clump
DENFORD LA
Furze Ground
Paddock Plantation
RADLEY BOTTOM
Radley Bottom Cottages
College
DARK LA
Denford Park
Five Acre Plantation
Denford Manor Farm
Four Acre Plantation
Denford Lodge
A4
Lower Denford Farm
Dun Mill
Denford Mill
Lock
Lock
Avington Manor
Avington
River Kennet
Kintbury Gate
Home Farm
Kennet and Avon Canal
Lock
Park Farm Dairy
Foxley Covert
Withybed Copse
WITHYBED LA
HUNGERFORD RD
INGLEWOOD RD
HIGH ST
Kintbury Farm
Inglewood Health Hydro
Little Templeton
WALLINGTON'S RD
Templeton Stud
Inglewood Spinney
South Wood
Inglewood Farm
INKPEN RD
Winterly La
4
3
2
1
69
68
67
66
35
36
37

102

127

75

101

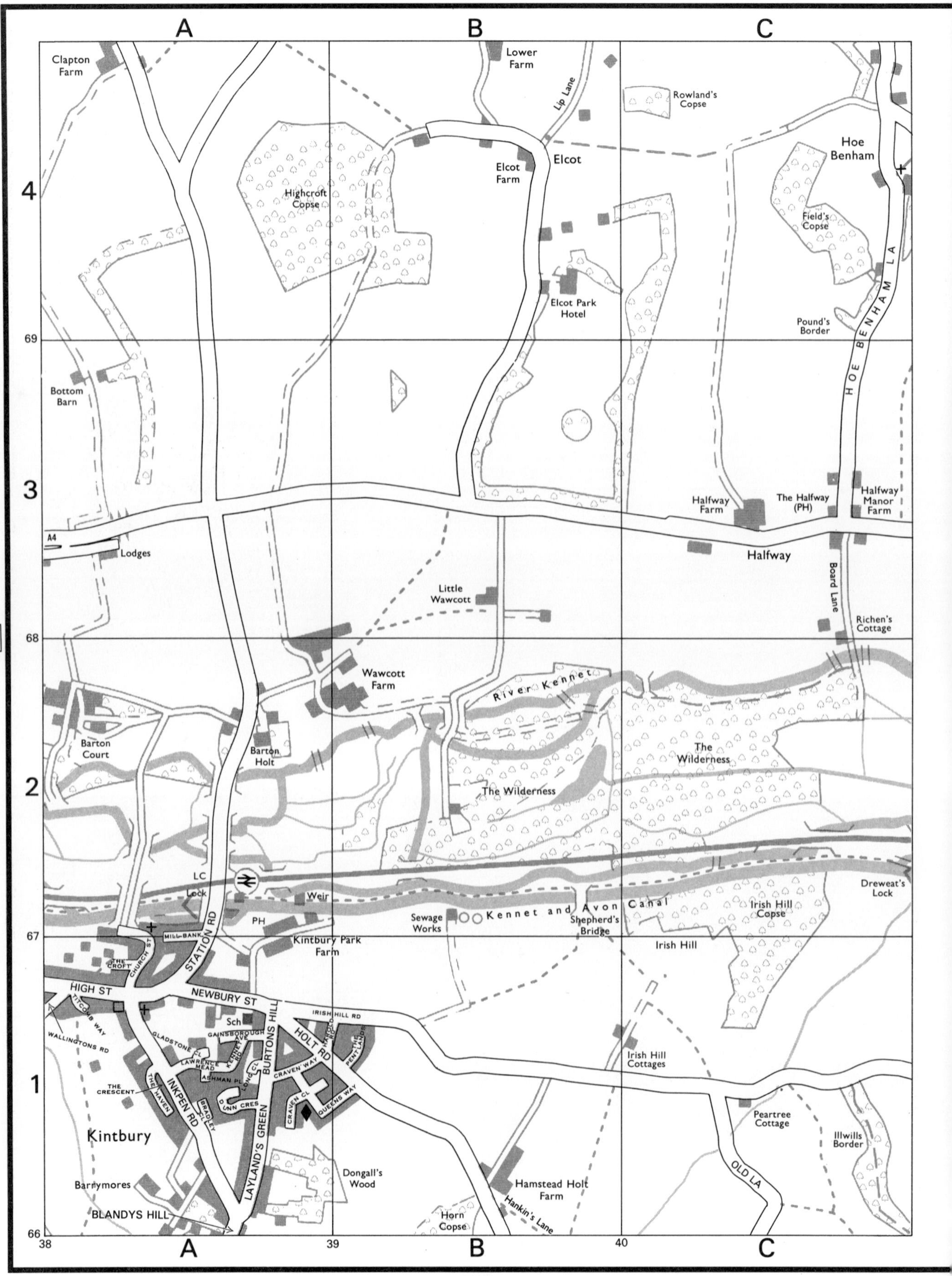

A
B
C
Clapton Farm
Lower Farm
Lip Lane
Rowland's Copse
Hoe Benham
Elcot
Elcot Farm
Highcroft Copse
Field's Copse
Elcot Park Hotel
Pound's Border
HOE BENHAM LA
4
69
Bottom Barn
3
Halfway Farm
The Halfway (PH)
Halfway Manor Farm
A4
Lodges
Halfway
Board Lane
Little Wawcott
Richen's Cottage
68
Wawcott Farm
River Kennet
Barton Court
Barton Holt
The Wilderness
The Wilderness
2
LC
Lock
Weir
PH
Sewage Works
Kennet and Avon Canal
Shepherd's Bridge
Irish Hill Copse
Dreweat's Lock
67
MILL BANK
THE CROFT
CHURCH ST
STATION RD
Kintbury Park Farm
Irish Hill
HIGH ST
NEWBURY ST
TITCOMB WAY
WALLINGTONS RD
Sch
IRISH HILL RD
BURTONS HILL
HOLT RD
GLADSTONE CL
GAINSBOROUGH
LAWRENCE MEAD
ASHMAN PL
CRAVEN WAY
QUEENS WAY
CRAVEN CL
DUNN CRES
THE CRESCENT
THE HAVEN
INKPEN RD
BRADLEY
LAYLAND'S GREEN
Irish Hill Cottages
1
Peartree Cottage
Illwills Border
Kintbury
Barrymores
Dongall's Wood
Hamstead Holt Farm
OLD LA
BLANDYS HILL
Horn Copse
Hankin's Lane
66
38
39
40

128

76

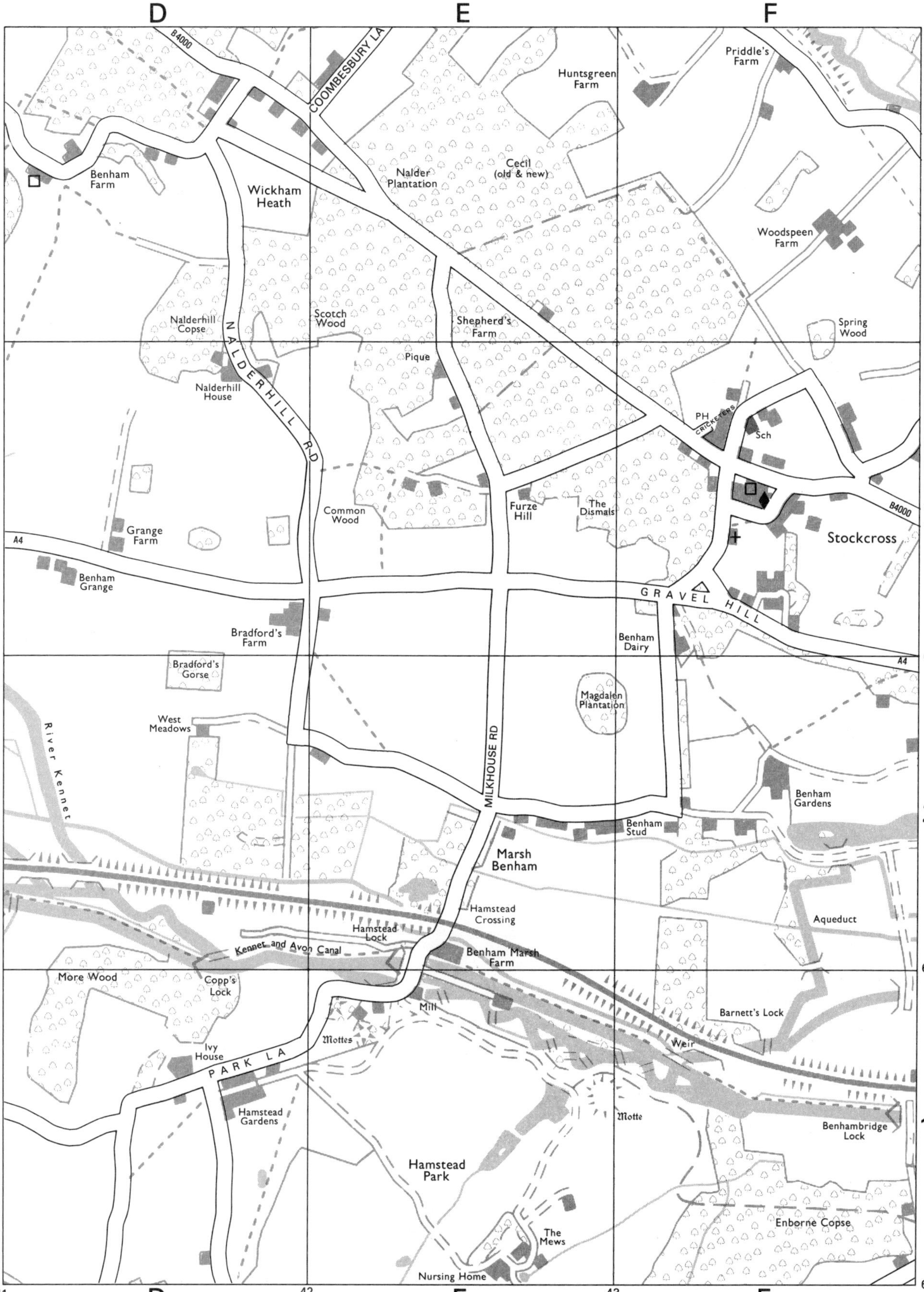

D
E
F
B4000
COOMBESBURY LA
Huntsgreen Farm
Priddle's Farm
Benham Farm
Wickham Heath
Nalder Plantation
Cecil (old & new)
4
Woodspeen Farm
Nalderhill Copse
NALDERHILL RD
Scotch Wood
Shepherd's Farm
Spring Wood
69
Pique
Nalderhill House
PH
CRICKETERS
Sch
Common Wood
Furze Hill
The Dismals
3
B4000
Grange Farm
A4
Stockcross
Benham Grange
GRAVEL HILL
Bradford's Farm
Benham Dairy
68
A4
Bradford's Gorse
Magdalen Plantation
West Meadows
River Kennet
MILKHOUSE RD
Benham Gardens
2
Benham Stud
Marsh Benham
Hamstead Crossing
Aqueduct
Hamstead Lock
Kennet and Avon Canal
Benham Marsh Farm
67
More Wood
Copp's Lock
Mill
Barnett's Lock
Mottes
Weir
Ivy House
PARK LA
Motte
1
Hamstead Gardens
Benhambridge Lock
Hamstead Park
Enborne Copse
The Mews
Nursing Home
66
41
42
43
D
E
F

104

129

77

103

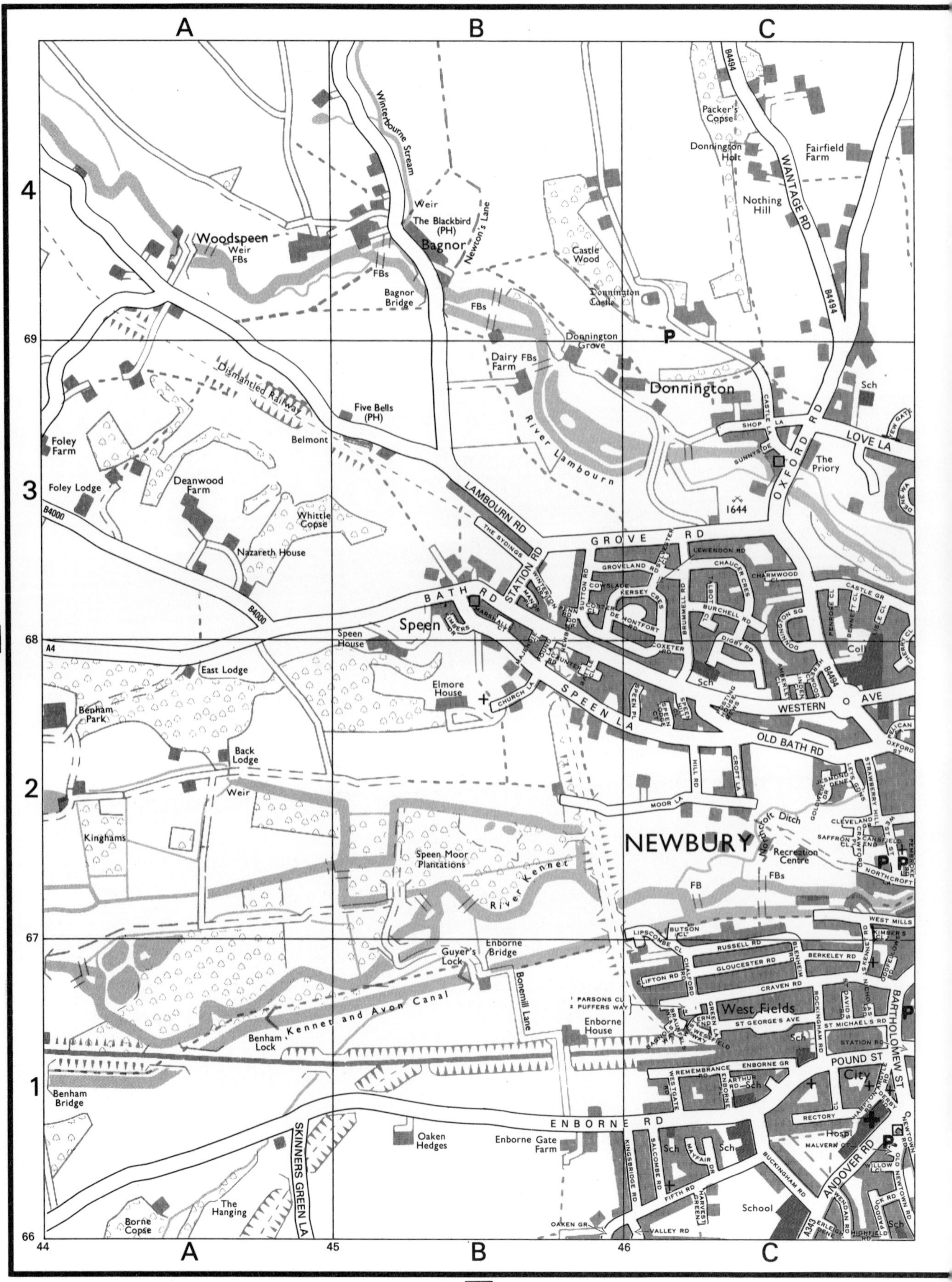
A
B
C
4
3
2
1
69
68
67
66
44
45
46
Winterbourne Stream
Weir
The Blackbird (PH)
Bagnor
Newton's Lane
Woodspeen
Weir FBs
FBs
Bagnor Bridge
FBs
Packer's Copse
Donnington Holt
Fairfield Farm
Nothing Hill
WANTAGE RD
B4494
Castle Wood
Donnington Castle
Donnington Grove
P
Dairy Farm
FBs
Donnington
Sch
Dismantled Railway
Five Bells (PH)
Belmont
Foley Farm
Foley Lodge
Deanwood Farm
Whittle Copse
Nazareth House
B4000
River Lambourn
SHOP LA
CASTLE LA
OXFORD RD
LOVE LA
SUNNYSIDE
The Priory
1644
LAMBOURN RD
THE SYDINGS
STATION RD
GROVE RD
LEWENDON RD
GROVELAND RD
CHAUCER CRES
CHARNWOOD CL
COWSLADE
KERSEY CRES
BRUMMELL RD
CASTLE GR
PENROSE CL
BENNETT CL
BURCHELL RD
DE MONTFORT
COXETER RD
DIGBY RD
DONNINGTON SQ
BATH RD
Speen
MARSHALLS CL
Speen House
A4
East Lodge
Elmore House
CHURCH LA
SPEEN LA
Sch
WESTERN AVE
Coll
Benham Park
Back Lodge
OLD BATH RD
HILL RD
CROFT LA
MOOR LA
Weir
Kinghams
NEWBURY
Northcroft Ditch
Recreation Centre
Speen Moor Plantations
River Kennet
FB
FBs
P
P
NORTHCROFT LA
WEST MILLS
BUTSON CL
LIPSCOMBE CL
RUSSELL RD
BERKELEY RD
GLOUCESTER RD
CLIFTON RD
CRAVEN RD
Guyer's Lock
Enborne Bridge
Bonemill Lane
1 PARSONS CL
2 PUFFERS WAY
West Fields
BARTHOLOMEW ST
Kennet and Avon Canal
Benham Lock
Enborne House
ST GEORGE'S AVE
ST MICHAELS RD
STATION RD
Sch
POUND ST
ENBORNE GR
City
Benham Bridge
ENBORNE RD
Sch
RECTORY
Hospl
P
Oaken Hedges
Enborne Gate Farm
Sch
Sch
SKINNERS GREEN LA
KINGSBRIDGE RD
SALCOMBE RD
FIFTH RD
BUCKINGHAM RD
ANDOVER RD
School
The Hanging
Borne Copse
OAKEN GR
VALLEY RD
A343
Sch

130

78

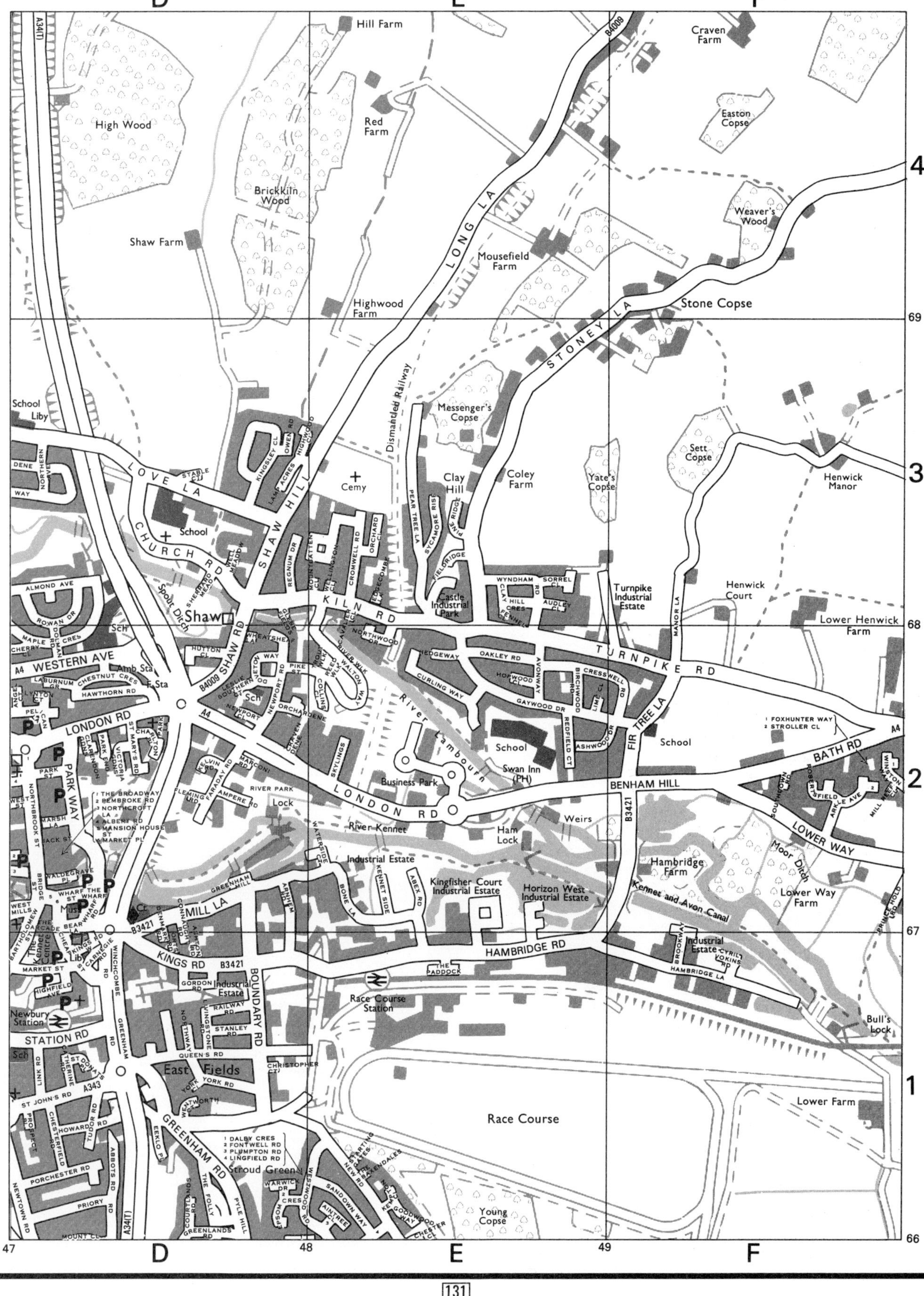

D
E
F
Hill Farm
Craven Farm
High Wood
Red Farm
Easton Copse
Brickkiln Wood
Weaver's Wood
Shaw Farm
Mousefield Farm
Highwood Farm
Stone Copse
LONG LA
STONEY LA
B4009
A34(T)
Dismantled Railway
Messenger's Copse
School
Liby
Sett Copse
Clay Hill
Coley Farm
Yate's Copse
Henwick Manor
Cemy
LOVE LA
CHURCH RD
SHAW HILL
School
Shaw
Spout Ditch
Turnpike Industrial Estate
Henwick Court
Lower Henwick Farm
Castle Industrial Park
KILN RD
TURNPIKE RD
MANOR LA
WESTERN AVE
Amb Sta
F Sta
LONDON RD
PARK WAY
River Lambourn
School
Swan Inn (PH)
Business Park
School
FIR TREE LA
BENHAM HILL
BATH RD
1 FOXHUNTER WAY
2 STROLLER CL
LOWER WAY
Weirs
Ham Lock
River Kennet
Lock
Industrial Estate
Kingfisher Court Industrial Estate
Horizon West Industrial Estate
Hambridge Farm
Moor Ditch
Lower Way Farm
Kennet and Avon Canal
MILL LA
HAMBRIDGE RD
Industrial Estate
HAMBRIDGE LA
KINGS RD
B3421
Industrial Estate
BOUNDARY RD
Race Course Station
Bull's Lock
Newbury Station
STATION RD
East Fields
Race Course
Lower Farm
GREENHAM RD
1 DALBY CRES
2 FONTWELL RD
3 PLUMPTON RD
4 LINGFIELD RD
Stroud Green
Young Copse
The Kennet Centre
1 THE BROADWAY
2 PEMBROKE RD
3 NORTHCROFT LA
4 ALBERT RD
5 MANSION HOUSE ST
6 MARKET PL
4
3
2
1
69
68
67
66
47
48
49

106

131

79

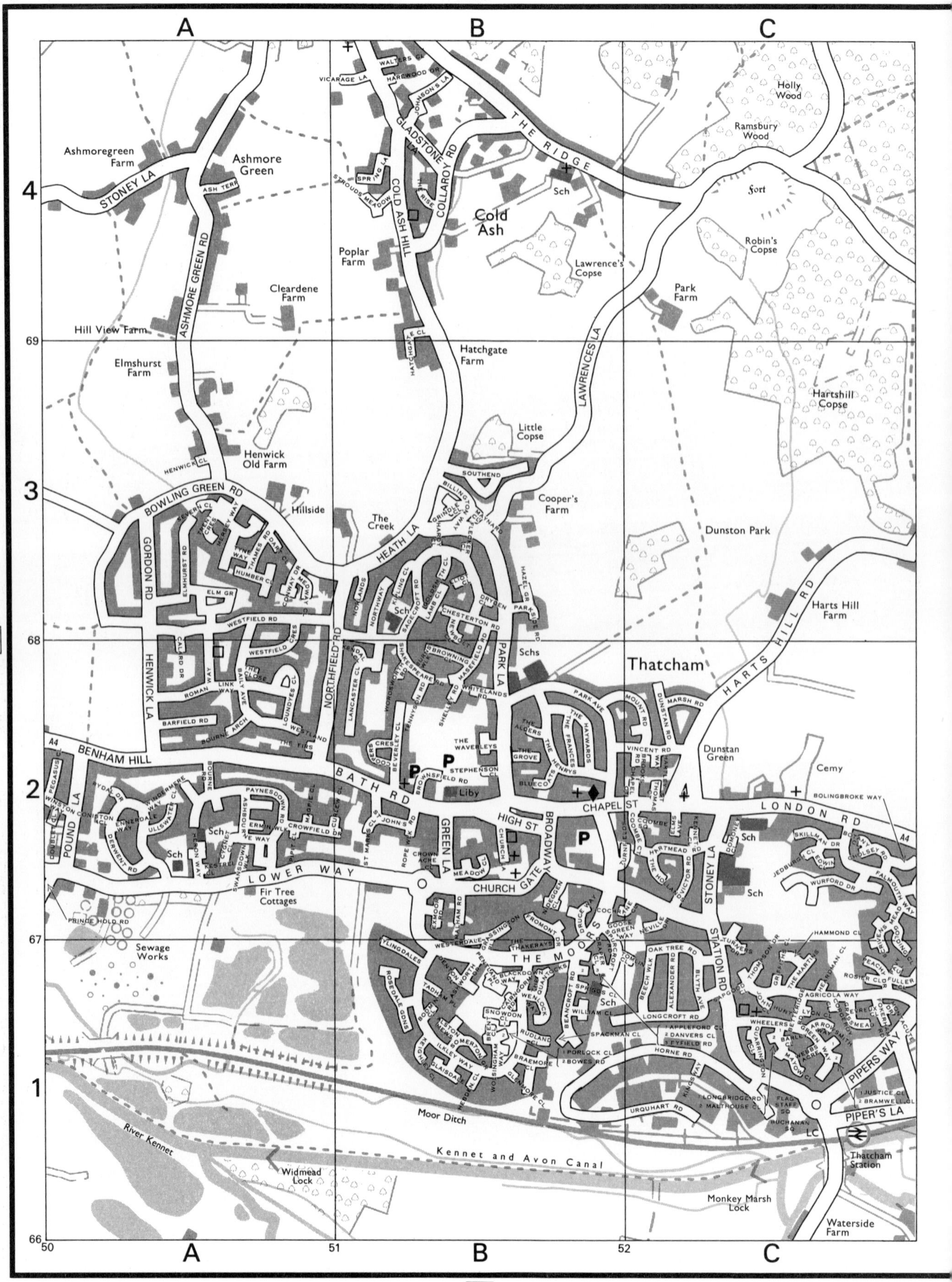
A
B
C
4
3
2
1
69
68
67
66
50
51
52
Ashmoregreen Farm
Ashmore Green
STONEY LA
ASH TERR
ASHMORE GREEN RD
Cleardene Farm
Hill View Farm
Elmshurst Farm
Henwick Old Farm
HENWICK CL
Hillside
BOWLING GREEN RD
VICARAGE LA
WALTERS CL
HAREWOOD DR
JOHNSON'S LA
GLADSTONE LA
SPRING LA
STROUDS MEADOW
COLD ASH HILL
COLLAROY RD
THE RIDGE
Sch
Cold Ash
Poplar Farm
Lawrence's Copse
HATCHGATE CL
Hatchgate Farm
LAWRENCES LA
Little Copse
SOUTHEND
Cooper's Farm
Holly Wood
Ramsbury Wood
Fort
Robin's Copse
Park Farm
Hartshill Copse
Dunston Park
Harts Hill Farm
HARTS HILL RD
The Creek
HEATH LA
GORDON RD
ELMHURST RD
THAMES RD
HUMBER CL
CONWAY DR
MEDWAY
ELM GR
WESTFIELD RD
WESTFIELD CRES
HENWICK LA
CALARD DR
ROMAN WAY
LINK WAY
BAILY AVE
THE CLOSE
LOUNDYES CL
WESTLAND
BARFIELD RD
BOURNE ARCH
THE FIRS
NORTHFIELD RD
NORTHWAY
NORLANDS
KIPLING CL
SAGECROFT RD
LAMB CL
CHESTERTON RD
BROWNING CL
MASEFIELD RD
SHAKESPEARE RD
LANCASTER CL
WORDSWORTH RD
TENNYSON RD
SHELLEY RD
WHITELANDS RD
PARK LA
Schs
Thatcham
PARK AVE
MOUNT RD
DUNSTAN RD
MARSH RD
THE ALGERS
THE FRANCES
THE HAYWARDS
THE HENRYS
THE GROVE
BLUECOATS
VINCENT RD
THOMAS LA
Dunstan Green
Cemy
THE WAVERLEYS
STEPHENSON CL
BEVERLEY CL
BROWNSFIELD RD
Liby
A4
BENHAM HILL
BATH RD
PEGASUS CL
POUND LA
WINSTON WAY
CONISTON CL
RYDAL DR
WINDERMERE WAY
ULLSWATER CL
DERWENT RD
ENNERDALE WAY
Sch
PAYNESDOWN RD
ASHBOURNE WAY
ERMIN WLK
CROWFIELD CL
KESTREL WAY
SWANSDOWN WAY
ST MARKS CL
ST JOHN'S RD
ROPE WLK
CROWN ACRE
GREEN LA
MEADOW CL
HIGH ST
CHURCH LA
BROADWAY
CHURCH GATE
CHAPEL ST
LONDON RD
BOLINGBROKE WAY
COOMBE CT
HARTMEAD RD
VICTOR RD
STONEY LA
SKILLMAN DR
JEDBURGH CL
EDWIN CL
WURFORD DR
CHOLSEY RD
FALMOUTH WAY
LOWER WAY
Fir Tree Cottages
PRINCE HOLD RD
Sewage Works
FROMONT DR
COCHRANE CL
NEVILLE CL
THE THAKERAYS
THE MOORS
WESTERDALE
YLINGDALES
ROSEDALE GDNS
TADHAM
DENTON
ASHWORTH DR
SNOWDON CL
RUDLAND CL
BRAEMORE CL
WOOSINGHAM WAY
ILKLEY WAY
GLAISDALE
HEBDEN CL
BEANCROFT RD
WILLIAM CL
OAK TREE RD
BEECH WLK
ALEXANDER RD
BLYTH AVE
LONGCROFT RD
STATION RD
Sch
1 APPLEFORD CL
2 DANVERS CL
3 FYFIELD RD
SPACKMAN CL
1 PORLOCK CL
2 BOWES RD
HORNE RD
KINGSWAY
URQUHART RD
1 LONGRIDGE RD
2 MALTHOUSE CL
THOMPSON DR
GRIFFITHS CL
THE MARTINS
HAMMOND CL
HERIDIAN CL
AGRICOLA WAY
ROSIER CL
FULLER CL
WHEELERS GREEN WAY
HERONS MEAD
PIPERS WAY
1 JUSTICE CL
2 BRAMWELL CL
PIPER'S LA
FLAG STAFF SQ
BUCHANAN SQ
LC
Thatcham Station
Moor Ditch
River Kennet
Kennet and Avon Canal
Widmead Lock
Monkey Marsh Lock
Waterside Farm

105

132

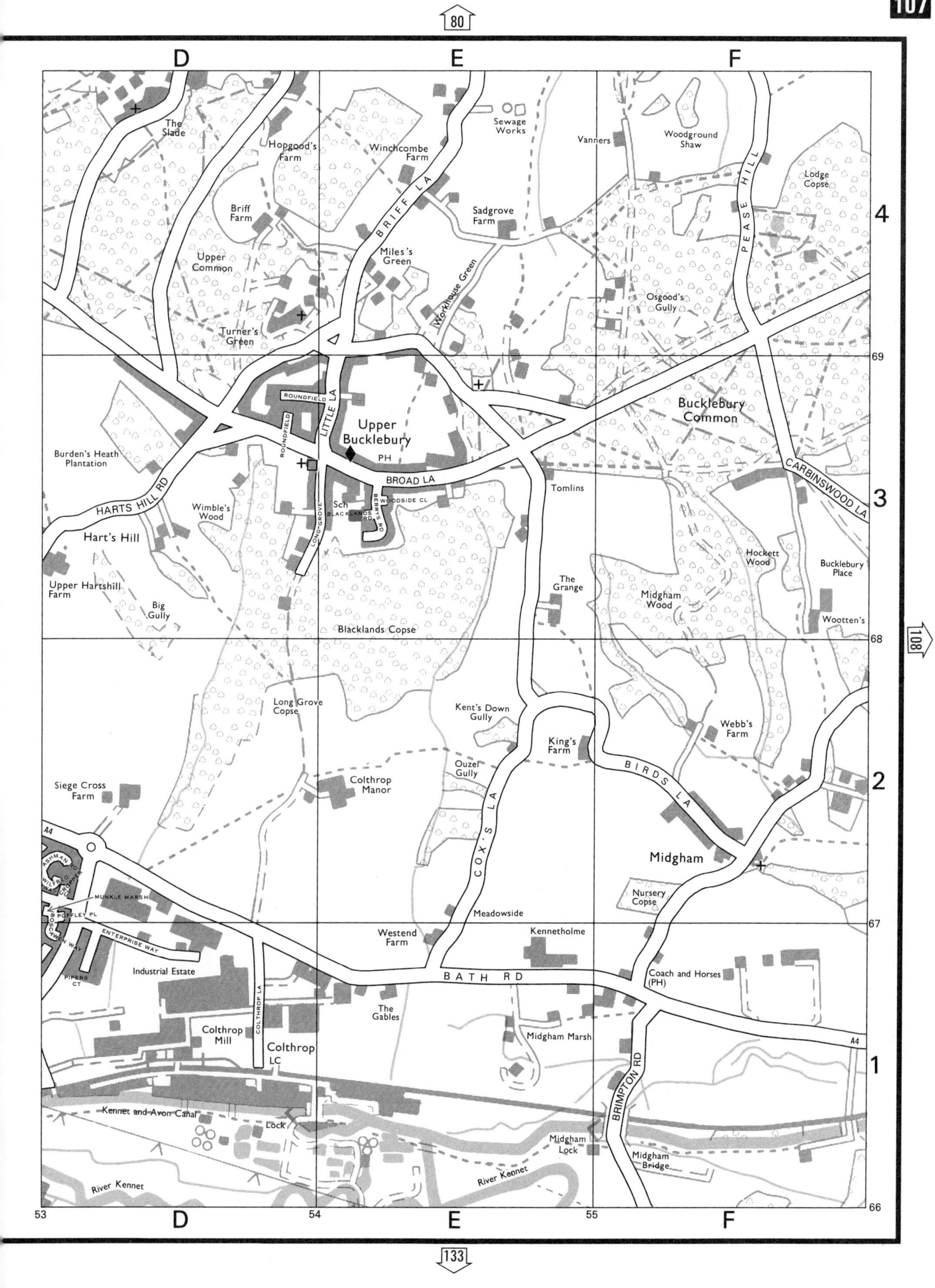
80
D
E
F
The Slade
Hopgood's Farm
Winchcombe Farm
Sewage Works
Vanners
Woodground Shaw
Lodge Copse
Briff Farm
BRIFF LA
Sadgrove Farm
PEASE HILL
Upper Common
Miles's Green
Workhouse Green
Osgood's Gully
Turner's Green
ROUNDFIELD
LITTLE LA
Upper Bucklebury
Bucklebury Common
PH
Burden's Heath Plantation
BROAD LA
CARBINSWOOD LA
HARTS HILL RD
Tomlins
Wimble's Wood
Sch
WOODSIDE CL
BLACKLANDS RD
BERRYS RD
LONG GROVE
Hart's Hill
Hockett Wood
Bucklebury Place
Upper Hartshill Farm
The Grange
Midgham Wood
Big Gully
Wootten's
Blacklands Copse
Long Grove Copse
Kent's Down Gully
Webb's Farm
King's Farm
BIRDS LA
Ouzel Gully
Siege Cross Farm
Colthrop Manor
COX'S LA
A4
Midgham
MUNKLE MARSH
POFFLEY PL
ENTERPRISE WAY
Nursery Copse
Meadowside
Westend Farm
Kennetholme
Industrial Estate
PIPERS CT
BATH RD
Coach and Horses (PH)
COLTHROP LA
The Gables
Colthrop Mill
Colthrop
LC
Midgham Marsh
BRIMPTON RD
Kennet and Avon Canal
Lock
Midgham Lock
Midgham Bridge
River Kennet
River Kennet
53
54
55
66
67
68
69
1
2
3
4
108
133

81

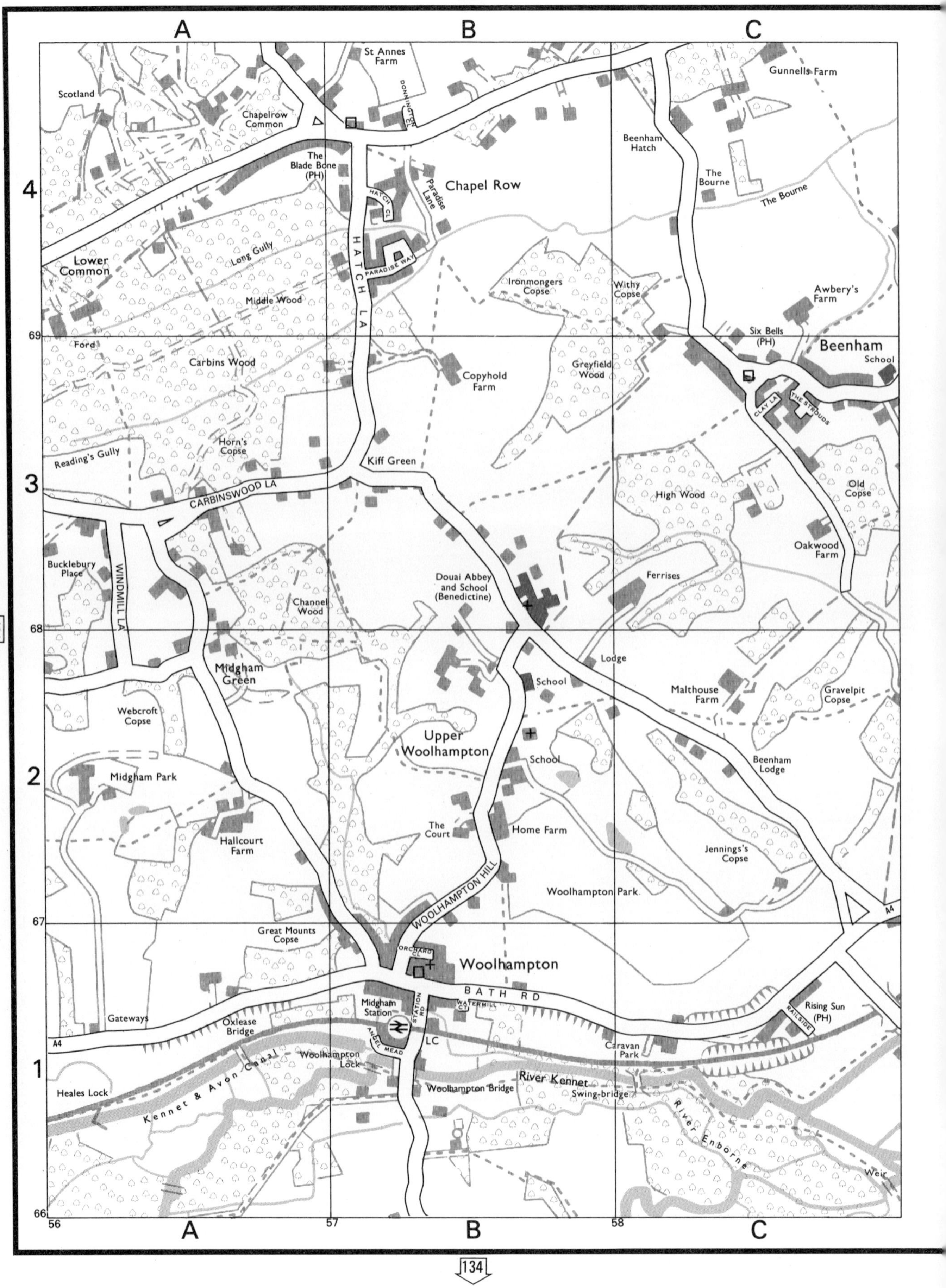

A
B
C
4
3
2
1
69
68
67
66
56
57
58
St Annes Farm
Gunnells Farm
Scotland
Chapelrow Common
DONNINGTON CL
Beenham Hatch
The Blade Bone (PH)
Chapel Row
Paradise Lane
HATCH CL
The Bourne
The Bourne
HATCH LA
Lower Common
Long Gully
PARADISE WAY
Middle Wood
Ironmongers Copse
Withy Copse
Awbery's Farm
Ford
Carbins Wood
Copyhold Farm
Greyfield Wood
Six Bells (PH)
Beenham
School
CLAY LA
THE STROUDS
Reading's Gully
Horn's Copse
Kiff Green
CARBINSWOOD LA
High Wood
Old Copse
Oakwood Farm
Bucklebury Place
WINDMILL LA
Channel Wood
Douai Abbey and School (Benedictine)
Ferrises
Midgham Green
Lodge
School
Malthouse Farm
Gravelpit Copse
Webcroft Copse
Upper Woolhampton
School
Beenham Lodge
Midgham Park
Hallcourt Farm
The Court
Home Farm
WOOLHAMPTON HILL
Jennings's Copse
Woolhampton Park
A4
Great Mounts Copse
ORCHARD CL
Woolhampton
BATH RD
Rising Sun (PH)
RAILSIDE
Gateways
Oxlease Bridge
Midgham Station
STATION RD
WATERMILL CT
ANGEL MEAD
LC
Caravan Park
A4
Woolhampton Lock
Kennet & Avon Canal
River Kennet
Heales Lock
Woolhampton Bridge
Swing-bridge
River Enborne
Weir

107

134

82

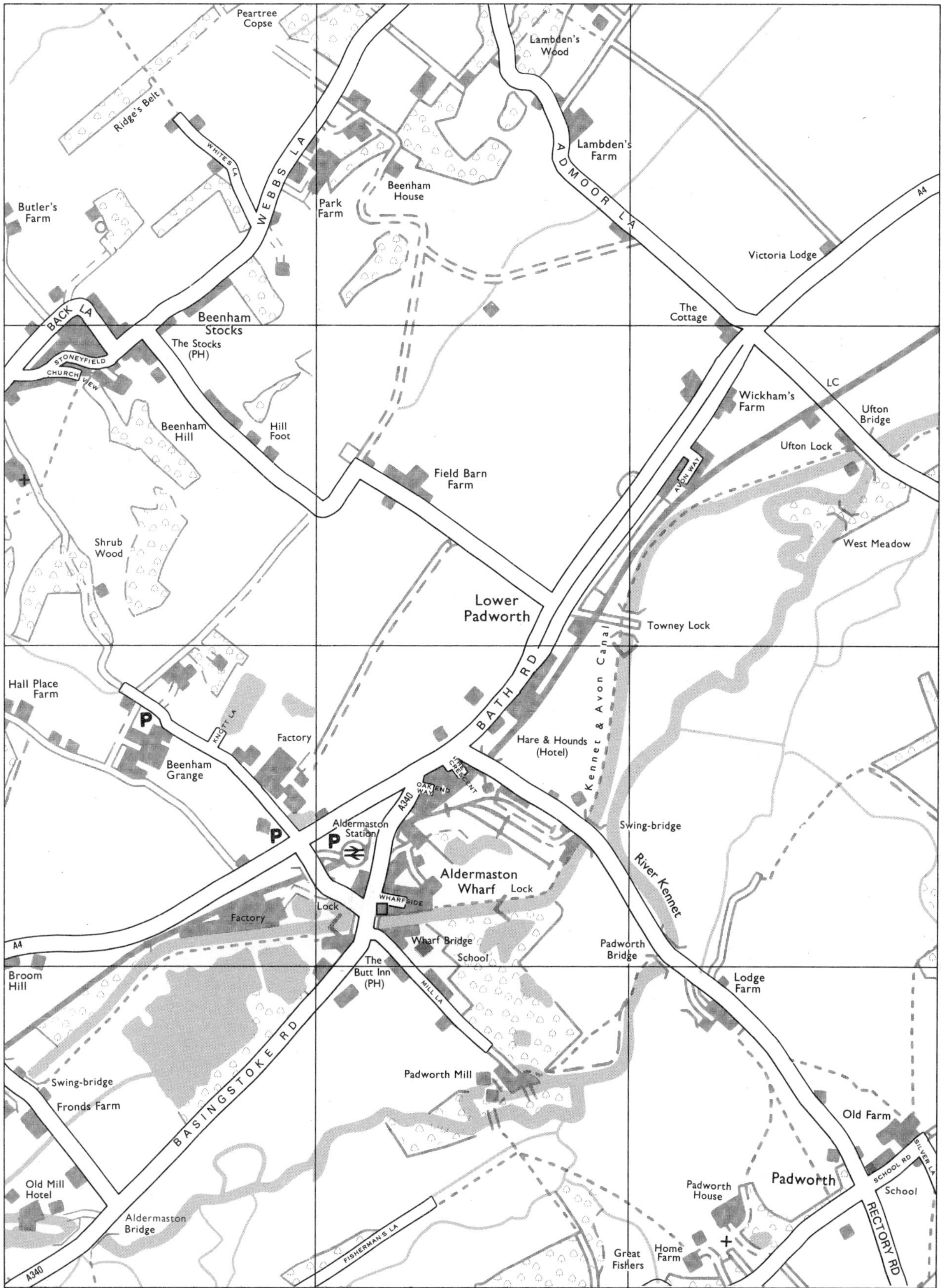
D
E
F
Peartree Copse
Lambden's Wood
Ridge's Belt
WHITE'S LA
WEBBS LA
Lambden's Farm
ADMOOR LA
Butler's Farm
Park Farm
Beenham House
4
A4
Victoria Lodge
BACK LA
Beenham Stocks
The Cottage
69
The Stocks (PH)
STONEYFIELD
CHURCH VIEW
LC
Wickham's Farm
Ufton Bridge
Beenham Hill
Hill Foot
Ufton Lock
Field Barn Farm
AVON WAY
3
Shrub Wood
West Meadow
Lower Padworth
Towney Lock
68
Hall Place Farm
BATH RD
Kennet & Avon Canal
KNOTT LA
Factory
Hare & Hounds (Hotel)
Beenham Grange
THE CRESCENT
OAK END WAY
A340
2
Aldermaston Station
Swing-bridge
River Kennet
Aldermaston Wharf
Lock
WHARFSIDE
Factory
Lock
Wharf Bridge
Padworth Bridge
A4
School
67
Broom Hill
The Butt Inn (PH)
Lodge Farm
MILL LA
BASINGSTOKE RD
Padworth Mill
Swing-bridge
Fronds Farm
Old Farm
1
SCHOOL RD
SILVER LA
Padworth
School
Old Mill Hotel
Padworth House
RECTORY RD
Aldermaston Bridge
FISHERMAN'S LA
Great Fishers
Home Farm
A340
66
59
60
61
D
E
F

110

135

83

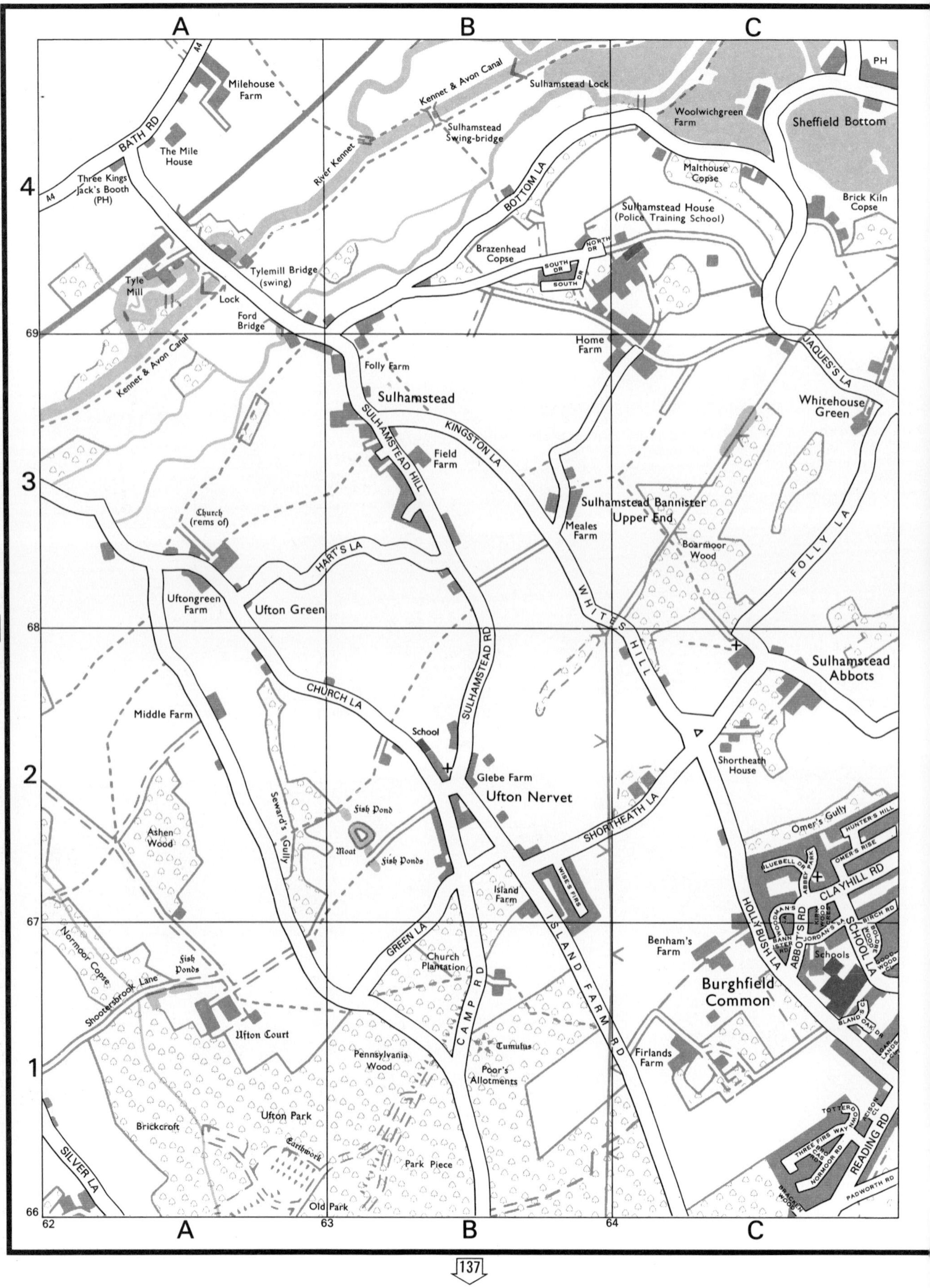
A
B
C
Milehouse Farm
BATH RD
A4
The Mile House
Three Kings Jack's Booth (PH)
Kennet & Avon Canal
Sulhamstead Lock
River Kennet
Sulhamstead Swing-bridge
Woolwichgreen Farm
Sheffield Bottom
PH
Malthouse Copse
Brick Kiln Copse
BOTTOM LA
Sulhamstead House (Police Training School)
Brazenhead Copse
NORTH DR
SOUTH DR
SOUTH DR
Tyle Mill
Lock
Tylemill Bridge (swing)
Ford Bridge
Home Farm
JAQUES'S LA
Folly Farm
Sulhamstead
Whitehouse Green
SULHAMSTEAD HILL
KINGSTON LA
Field Farm
Church (rems of)
Sulhamstead Bannister Upper End
Meales Farm
Boarmoor Wood
FOLLY LA
HART'S LA
Uftongreen Farm
Ufton Green
WHITES HILL
Sulhamstead Abbots
CHURCH LA
SULHAMSTEAD RD
Middle Farm
School
Shortheath House
Glebe Farm
Ufton Nervet
Seward's Gully
Fish Pond
Moat
Fish Ponds
Ashen Wood
SHORTHEATH LA
Omer's Gully
HUNTER'S HILL
OMER'S RISE
BLUEBELL DR
ABBEY PARK
CLAYHILL RD
WISES FIRS
Island Farm
HOLLYBUSH LA
ABBOT'S RD
SCHOOL LA
BIRCH RD
JORDAN'S LA
Schools
Normoor Copse
Fish Ponds
GREEN LA
Church Plantation
ISLAND FARM RD
Benham's Farm
Burghfield Common
Shootersbrook Lane
CAMP RD
BLAND'S CL
OAK DR
Ufton Court
Cumulus
Pennsylvania Wood
Poor's Allotments
Firlands Farm
TOTTERDOWN
MORRISON CL
THREE FIRS WAY
NORMOOR RD
READING RD
Ufton Park
Brickcroft
Earthwork
SILVER LA
Park Piece
Old Park
BRACKEN WOOD
PADWORTH RD
4
3
2
1
69
68
67
66
62
63
64
109

137

84

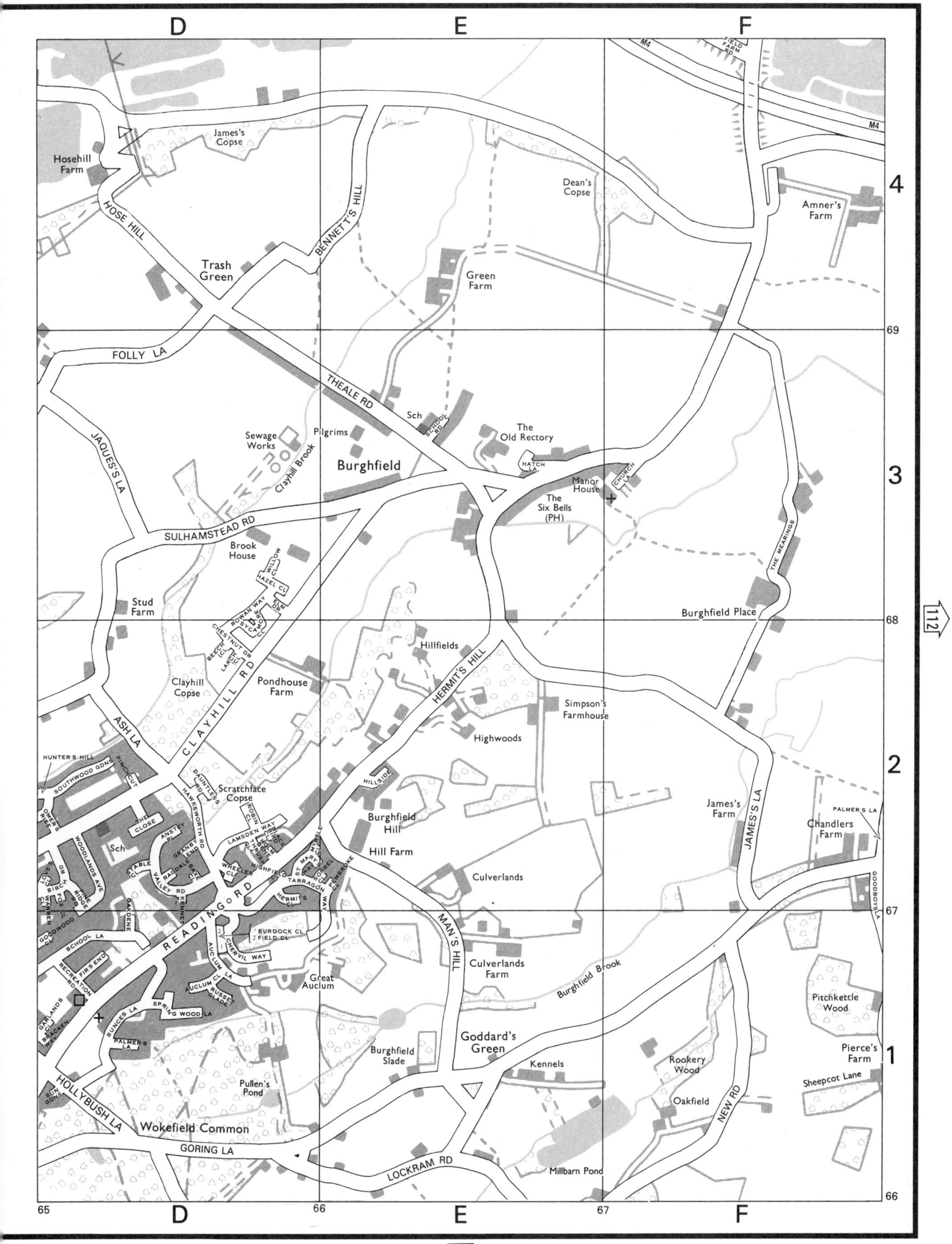
D
E
F
M4
FIELD FARM RD
James's Copse
Hosehill Farm
HOSE HILL
BENNETT'S HILL
Dean's Copse
Amner's Farm
4
Trash Green
Green Farm
FOLLY LA
69
THEALE RD
Sch
SCHOOL RD
JAQUES'S LA
Sewage Works
Pilgrims
The Old Rectory
Clayhill Brook
Burghfield
HATCH LA
CHURCH LA
Manor House
3
The Six Bells (PH)
SULHAMSTEAD RD
Brook House
WILLOW CL
HAZEL CL
THE MEARINGS
Stud Farm
ROWAN WAY
SYCAMORE CL
ELM DR
Burghfield Place
68
CHESTNUT DR
BEECH CL
LARCH CL
Hillfields
Clayhill Copse
Pondhouse Farm
HERMIT'S HILL
CLAYHILL RD
ASH LA
Simpson's Farmhouse
Highwoods
HUNTERS HILL
PINCHCUT
SOUTHWOOD GDNS
BAUNTLESS RD
Scratchface Copse
HILLSIDE
2
HAWKSWORTH RD
ROBIN
James's Farm
JAMES'S LA
PALMER'S LA
Chandlers Farm
THE CLOSE
ANSTEY PL
LAMSDEN WAY
Burghfield Hill
Sch
WOODLANDS AVE
GRANBY END
RAGDALE END
MYRTLE CL
Hill Farm
STABLE CL
WHEELER CL
HIGHFIELD CL
TARRAGON WAY
SORREL CL
PEMBROKE
Culverlands
BIRCH
PINE RIDGE
VALLEY RD
KENNET PL
HERMIT'S CL
GOODBOYS LA
OAKDENE
READING RD
67
GOODWOOD
SCHOOL LA
MAN'S HILL
BURDOCK CL
FIELD CL
CHERVIL WAY
AUCLUM CL
Culverlands Farm
FIRS END
RECREATION RD
Great Auclum
Burghfield Brook
Pitchkettle Wood
AUCLUM CL
RUSSET GLADE
SPRING WOOD LA
GARLANDS CL
BUNCES LA
BRACKEN WAY
Goddard's Green
Pierce's Farm
PALMER'S LA
Burghfield Slade
1
Kennels
Rookery Wood
Sheepcot Lane
HOLLYBUSH LA
Pullen's Pond
Oakfield
NEW RD
Wokefield Common
GORING LA
LOCKRAM RD
Millbarn Pond
66
65
66
67
112

85

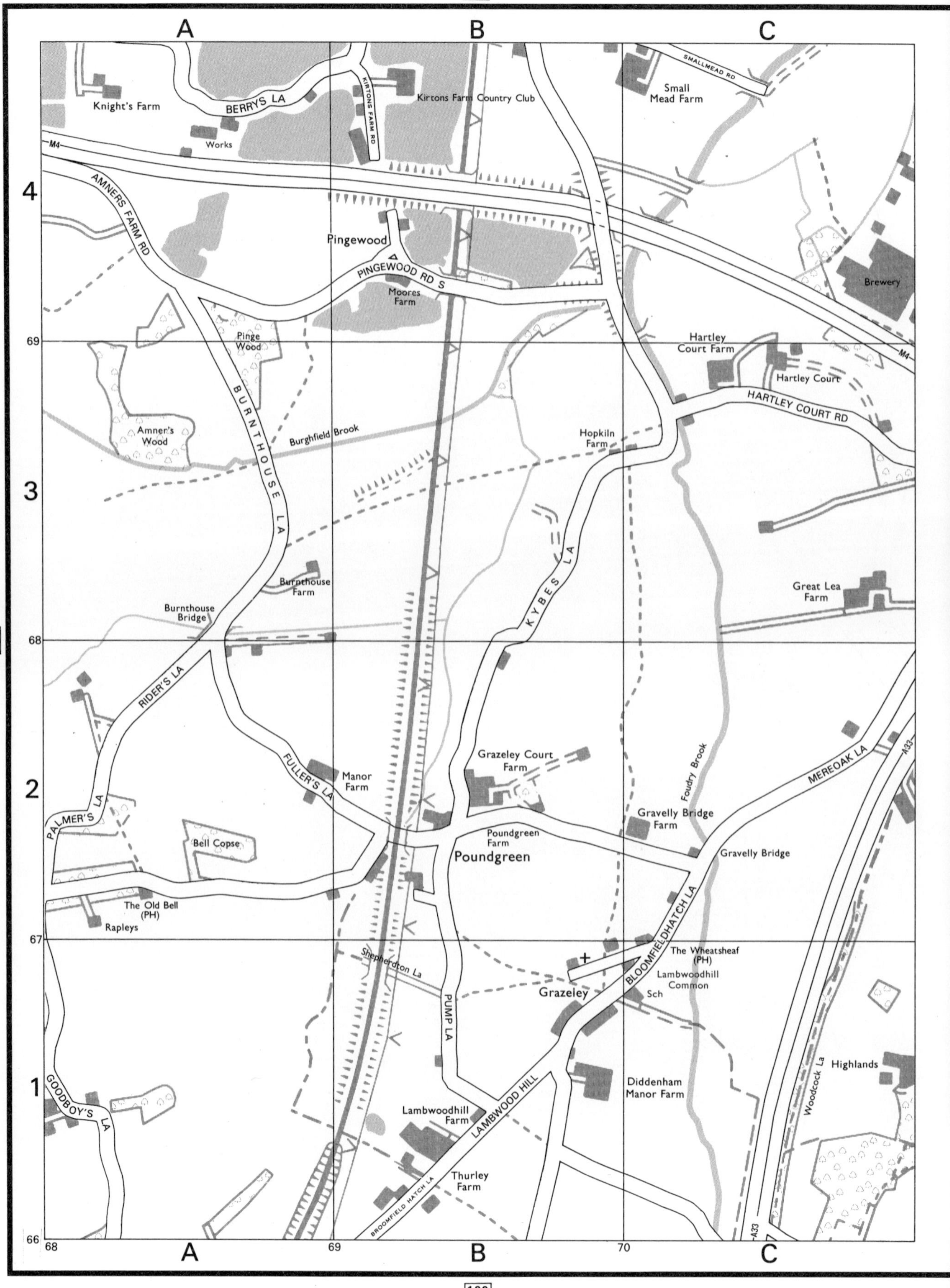

A
B
C
4
3
2
1
69
68
67
66
70
Knight's Farm
BERRYS LA
KIRTONS FARM RD
Kirtons Farm Country Club
SMALLMEAD RD
Small Mead Farm
Works
M4
AMNERS FARM RD
Pingewood
PINGEWOOD RD S
Moores Farm
Brewery
Pinge Wood
BURNTHOUSE LA
Hartley Court Farm
Hartley Court
HARTLEY COURT RD
Amner's Wood
Burghfield Brook
Hopkiln Farm
Burnthouse Farm
Burnthouse Bridge
KYBES LA
Great Lea Farm
RIDER'S LA
FULLER'S LA
Manor Farm
Grazeley Court Farm
Foudry Brook
MEREOAK LA
A33
PALMER'S LA
Bell Copse
Poundgreen Farm
Poundgreen
Gravelly Bridge Farm
Gravelly Bridge
The Old Bell (PH)
Rapleys
BLOOMFIELDHATCH LA
The Wheatsheaf (PH)
Lambwoodhill Common
Shepherdton La
PUMP LA
Grazeley
Sch
GOODBOY'S LA
LAMBWOOD HILL
Diddenham Manor Farm
Woodcock La
Highlands
Lambwoodhill Farm
Thurley Farm
BROOMFIELD HATCH LA

111

138

86

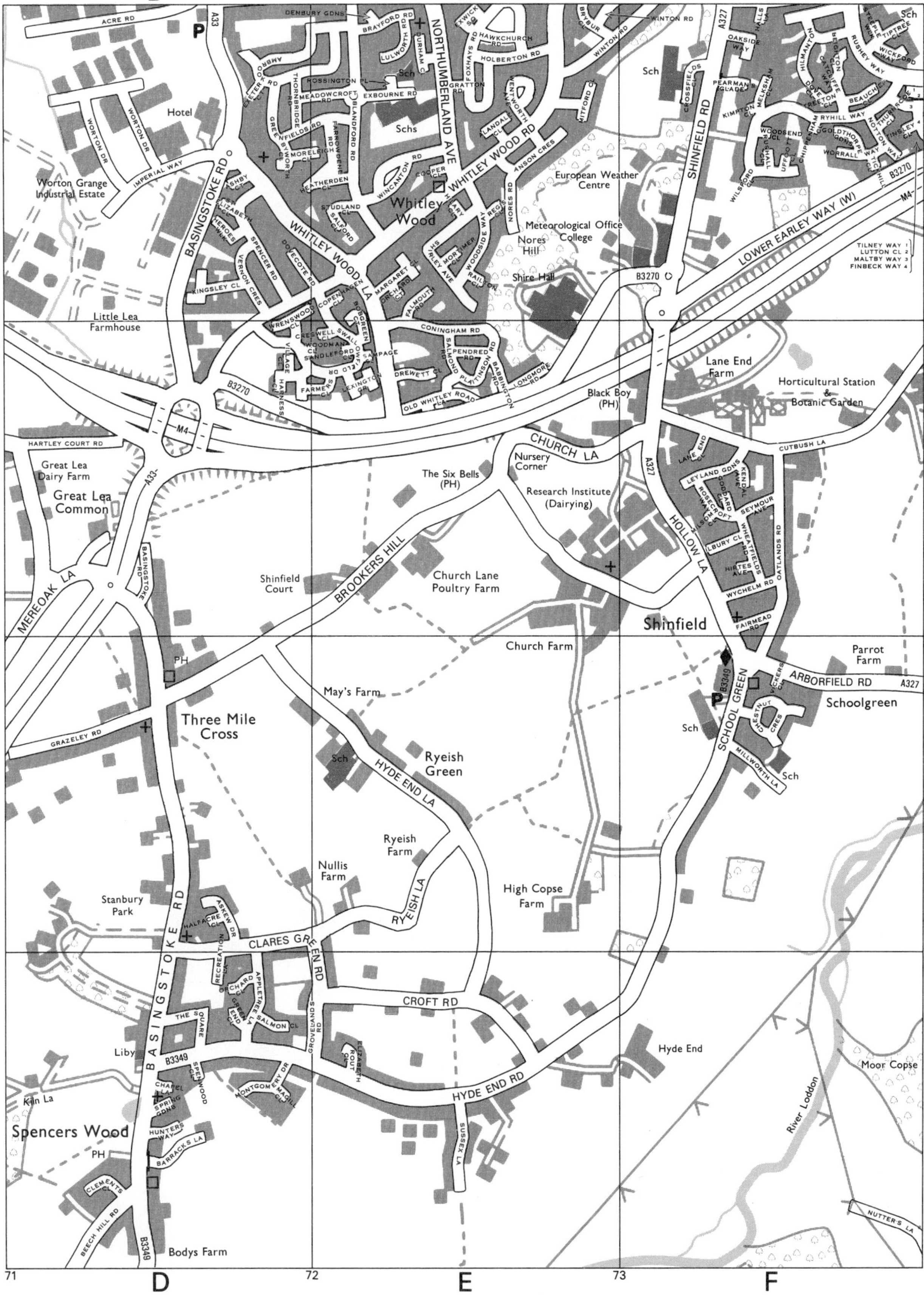
D
E
F
Worton Grange Industrial Estate
Hotel
Little Lea Farmhouse
Whitley Wood
Schs
Sch
European Weather Centre
Meteorological Office College
Nores Hill
Shire Hall
Lane End Farm
Horticultural Station & Botanic Garden
Black Boy (PH)
Great Lea Dairy Farm
Great Lea Common
The Six Bells (PH)
Nursery Corner
Research Institute (Dairying)
Shinfield Court
Church Lane Poultry Farm
Shinfield
Church Farm
Parrot Farm
Schoolgreen
May's Farm
Three Mile Cross
Ryeish Green
Ryeish Farm
Nullis Farm
Stanbury Park
High Copse Farm
Hyde End
Moor Copse
River Loddon
Spencers Wood
Bodys Farm
Liby
PH
Kiln La
ACRE RD
WORTON DR
IMPERIAL WAY
BASINGSTOKE RD
WHITLEY WOOD LA
WHITLEY WOOD RD
NORTHUMBERLAND AVE
SHINFIELD RD
LOWER EARLEY WAY (W)
B3270
M4
A33
A327
HARTLEY COURT RD
MEREOAK LA
CHURCH LA
BROOKERS HILL
HOLLOW LA
ARBORFIELD RD
SCHOOL GREEN
B3349
GRAZELEY RD
HYDE END LA
RYEISH LA
CLARES GREEN RD
CROFT RD
HYDE END RD
SUSSEX LA
BEECH HILL RD
NUTTER'S LA
MILLWORTH LA
CUTBUSH LA
TILNEY WAY 1
LUTTON CL 2
MALTBY WAY 3
FINBECK WAY 4
4
3
2
1
69
68
67
66
71
72
73

114

139

87

113

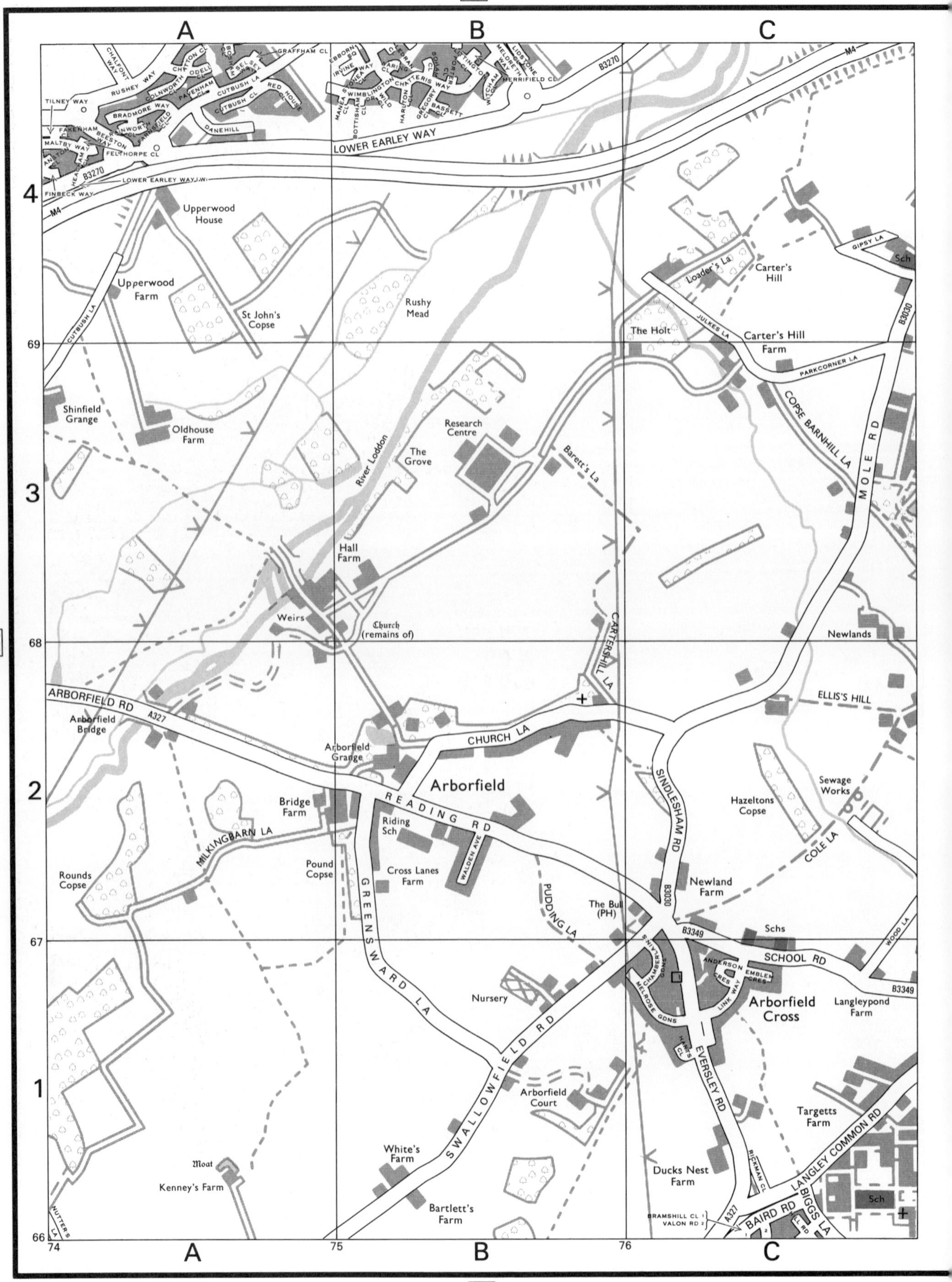
A
B
C
4
3
2
1
69
68
67
66
74
75
76
M4
B3270
LOWER EARLEY WAY
LOWER EARLEY WAY J.W.
TILNEY WAY
RUSHEY WAY
BRADMORE WAY
COLNWORTH CL
CHATTON CL
ODELL
PAVENHAM CL
CUTBUSH LA
CUTBUSH CL
RED HOUSE
GRAFFHAM CL
DANEHILL
FELTHORPE CL
FINBECK WAY
MALTBY WAY
FAKENHAM
BEESTON
EBBORN
IRVINE
WIMBLINGTON
CHATTERIS WAY
BASSETT
MELDRETH
LIDSTONE
HERRIFIELD CL
MANEA
BOTTISHAM CL
HARLTON CL
GREGORY CL
WITCHAM
Upperwood House
Upperwood Farm
St John's Copse
Rushy Mead
CUTBUSH LA
Shinfield Grange
Oldhouse Farm
Research Centre
The Grove
River Loddon
Hall Farm
Weirs
Church (remains of)
ARBORFIELD RD
A327
Arborfield Bridge
Arborfield Grange
CHURCH LA
Arborfield
READING RD
Bridge Farm
Riding Sch
MILKINGBARN LA
Rounds Copse
Pound Copse
Cross Lanes Farm
WALDEN AVE
GREENSWARD LA
PUDDING LA
The Bull (PH)
Nursery
SWALLOWFIELD RD
Arborfield Court
White's Farm
Bartlett's Farm
Moat
Kenney's Farm
NUTTERS LA
Loader's La
Carter's Hill
GIPSY LA
Sch
B3030
The Holt
JULKES LA
Carter's Hill Farm
PARKCORNER LA
COPSE BARNHILL LA
MOLE RD
Barett's La
CARTERSHILL LA
Newlands
ELLIS'S HILL
SINDLESHAM RD
Hazeltons Copse
Sewage Works
COLE LA
Newland Farm
B3349
Schs
SCHOOL RD
WOOD LA
ANDERSON CRES
EMBLEN CRES
LINK WAY
MELROSE GDNS
Arborfield Cross
Langleypond Farm
EVERSLEY RD
Targetts Farm
LANGLEY COMMON RD
Ducks Nest Farm
RICKMAN CL
BRAMSHILL CL 1
VALON RD 2
A327
BAIRD RD
BIGGS LA

140

88

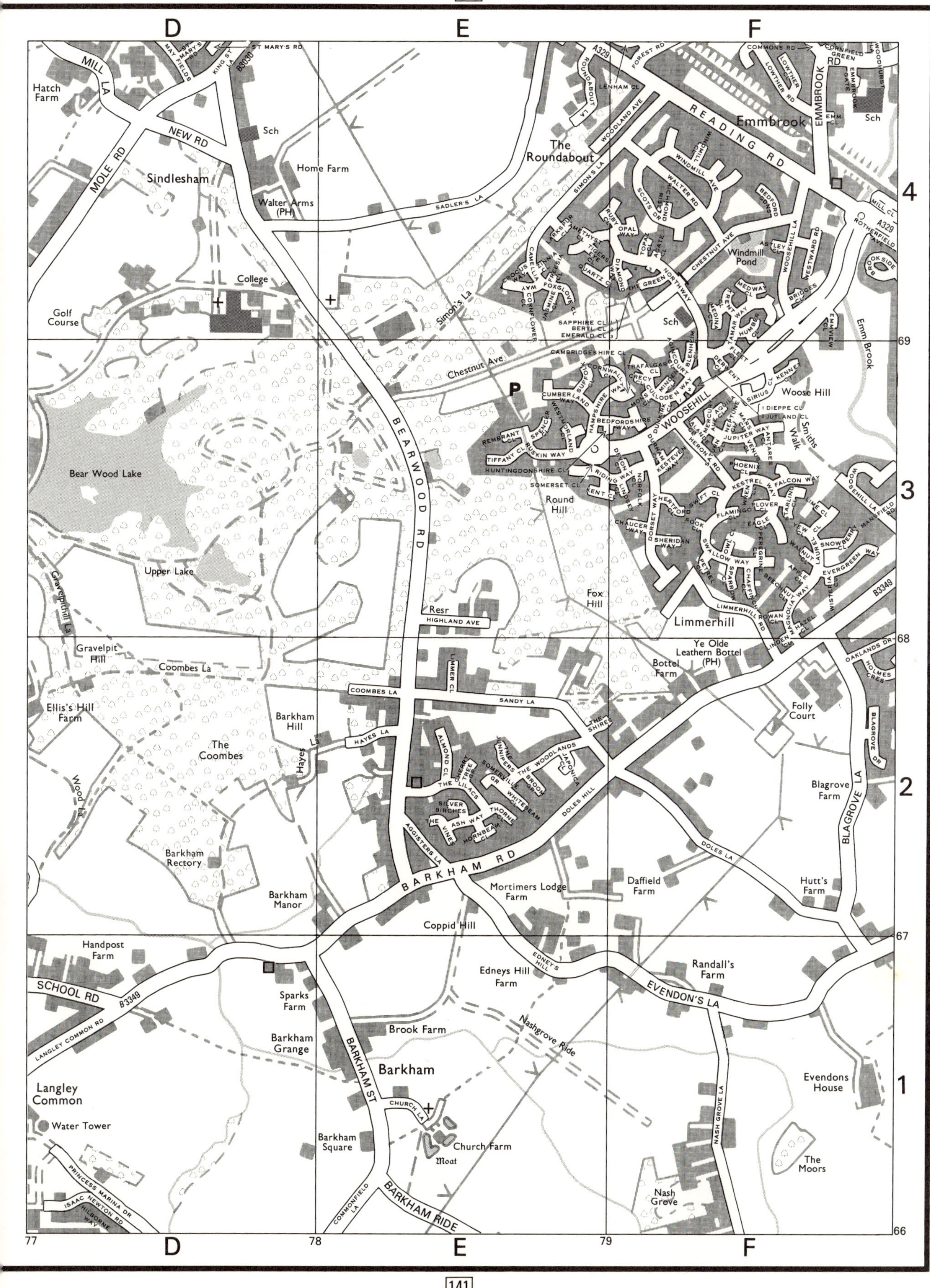

D
E
F
4
3
2
1
69
68
67
66
77
78
79
Hatch Farm
MILL LA
MOLE RD
NEW RD
Sindlesham
Sch
Home Farm
Walter Arms (PH)
SADLER'S LA
College
Golf Course
ST MARY'S RD
KING ST LA
B3030
A329
ROUNDABOUT LA
FOREST RD
LENHAM CL
WOODLAND AVE
READING RD
Emmbrook
EMMBROOK RD
COMMONS RD
LOWTHER RD
The Roundabout
SIMON'S LA
Simon's La
WINDMILL AVE
WALTER RD
RICHMOND RISE
SCOTS DR
BEDFORD GDNS
CHESTNUT AVE
Chestnut Ave
Windmill Pond
NORTHWAY
WOOSEHILL LA
WESTWARD RD
ROTHERFIELD AVE
MILL CL
Sch
CAMBRIDGESHIRE CL
SAPPHIRE CL
BERYL CL
EMERALD CL
CUMBERLAND WAY
WESTMORLAND
REMBRANT CL
TIFFANY CL
RUSKIN WAY
HUNTINGDONSHIRE CL
SOMERSET CL
BEDFORDSHIRE WAY
HAMPSHIRE WAY
WOOSEHILL
Woose Hill
Smiths Walk
Emm Brook
EMMVIEW CL
1 DIEPPE CL
2 JUTLAND CL
JUPITER WAY
PHOENIX CL
KESTREL WAY
FALCON WAY
Round Hill
Fox Hill
Limmerhill
LIMMERHILL RD
B3349
BEARWOOD RD
Bear Wood Lake
Upper Lake
Resr
HIGHLAND AVE
Gravelpitchill La
Gravelpit Hill
Coombes La
Ellis's Hill Farm
The Coombes
Barkham Hill
HAYES LA
Hayes La
Wood La
COOMBES LA
LIMMER CL
SANDY LA
THE SHIRES
Ye Olde Leathern Bottel (PH)
Bottel Farm
Folly Court
OAKLANDS DR
BLAGROVE DR
Blagrove Farm
BLAGROVE LA
DOLES HILL
DOLES LA
BARKHAM RD
AGGISTERS LA
Barkham Rectory
Barkham Manor
Mortimers Lodge Farm
Daffield Farm
Hutt's Farm
Coppid Hill
Handpost Farm
SCHOOL RD
B3349
LANGLEY COMMON RD
Sparks Farm
Barkham Grange
Edneys Hill Farm
EDNEY'S HILL
Randall's Farm
EVENDON'S LA
Brook Farm
Nashgrove Ride
BARKHAM ST
Barkham
CHURCH LA
Langley Common
Water Tower
Barkham Square
Church Farm
Moat
Evendons House
NASH GROVE LA
The Moors
Nash Grove
PRINCESS MARINA DR
ISAAC NEWTON RD
HILBORNE WAY
COMMONFIELD LA
BARKHAM RIDE

116

141

89

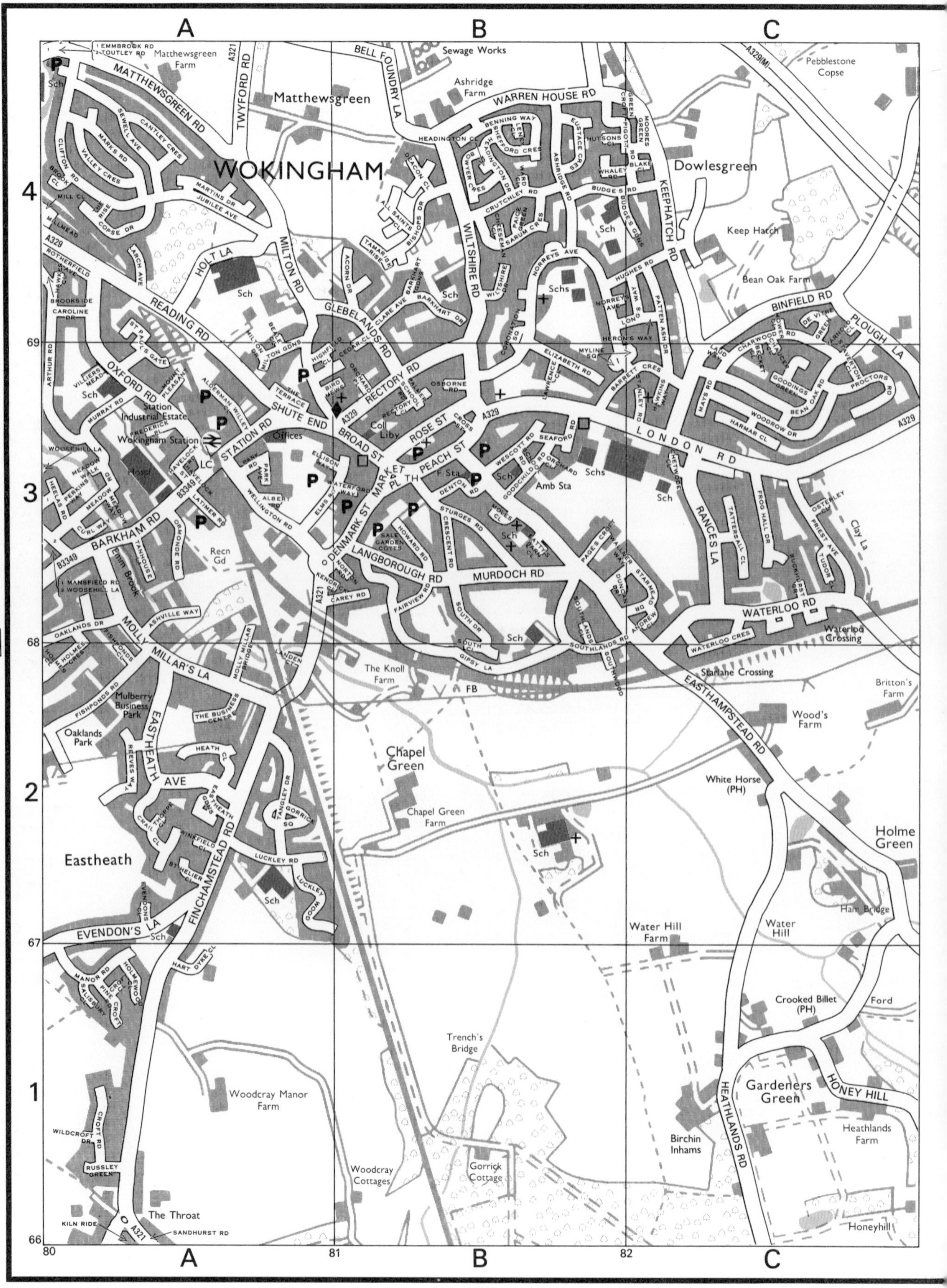
A
B
C
4
3
2
1
69
68
67
66
80
81
82
WOKINGHAM
Matthewsgreen
Matthewsgreen Farm
Sewage Works
Ashridge Farm
Pebblestone Copse
Dowlesgreen
Keep Hatch
Bean Oak Farm
MATTHEWSGREEN RD
TWYFORD RD
BELL FOUNDRY LA
WARREN HOUSE RD
KEEPHATCH RD
WILTSHIRE RD
MILTON RD
HOLT LA
READING RD
GLEBELANDS RD
RECTORY RD
BINFIELD RD
PLOUGH LA
LONDON RD
OXFORD RD
SHUTE END
STATION RD
BROAD ST
ROSE ST
PEACH ST
MARKET PL
DENMARK ST
LANGBOROUGH RD
MURDOCH RD
BARKHAM RD
WATERLOO RD
RANCES LA
ELIZABETH RD
NORREYS AVE
SOUTHLANDS RD
GIPSY LA
MOLLY MILLAR'S LA
EASTHEATH AVE
FINCHAMPSTEAD RD
EVENDON'S LA
EASTHAMPSTEAD RD
HEATHLANDS RD
HONEY HILL
Wokingham Station
Station Industrial Estate
Hospl
Offices
Coll Liby
Recn Gd
Sch
Schs
Amb Sta
F Sta
Mulberry Business Park
THE BUSINESS CENTRE
Oaklands Park
Eastheath
The Knoll Farm
Chapel Green
Chapel Green Farm
Starlane Crossing
Waterloo Crossing
Britton's Farm
Wood's Farm
White Horse (PH)
Holme Green
Ham Bridge
Water Hill
Water Hill Farm
Crooked Billet (PH)
Ford
Gardeners Green
Heathlands Farm
Birchin Inhams
Trench's Bridge
Woodcray Manor Farm
Woodcray Cottages
Gorrick Cottage
The Throat
Honeyhill
Clay La
KILN RIDE
SANDHURST RD
A321
A329
A329(M)
B3349
FB
LC

115

142

90

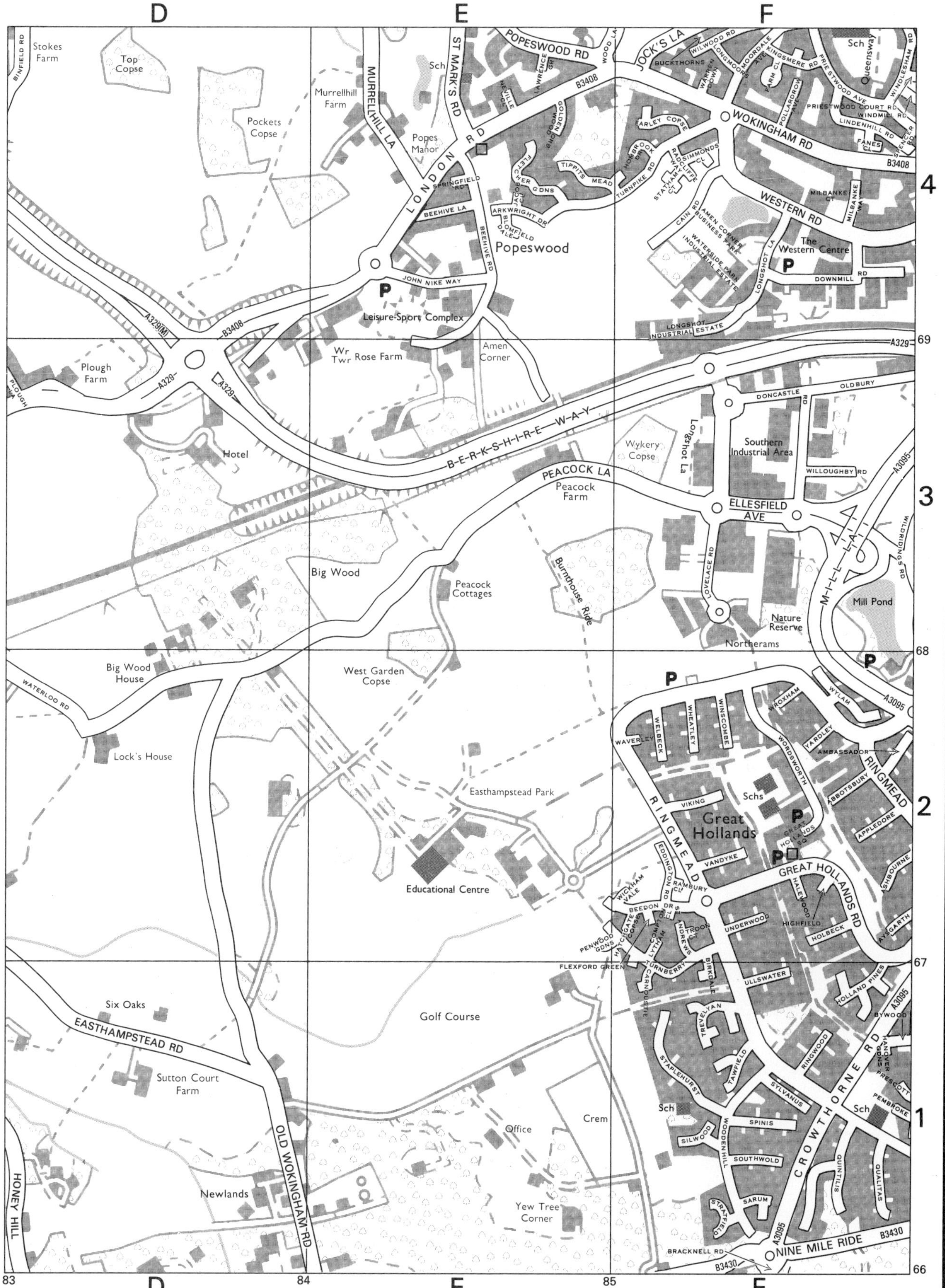
D
E
F
Stokes Farm
Top Copse
Pockets Copse
Murrellhill Farm
MURRELLHILL LA
ST MARK'S RD
Sch
Popes Manor
POPESWOOD RD
LONDON RD
B3408
Popeswood
Leisure-Sport Complex
JOHN NIKE WAY
BEEHIVE LA
BEEHIVE RD
SPRINGFIELD RD
ARKWRIGHT DR
TIPPITS MEAD
FARLEY COPSE
TURNPIKE RD
JOCK'S LA
WOKINGHAM RD
WESTERN RD
The Western Centre
LONGSHOT LA
DOWNMILL RD
LONGSHOT INDUSTRIAL ESTATE
AMEN CORNER BUSINESS PARK
WATERSIDE PARK INDUSTRIAL ESTATE
MILBANKE CT
Queensway
PRIESTWOOD AVE
PRIESTWOOD COURT RD
WINDMILL RD
LINDENHILL RD
FANES CL
4
A329(M)
A329
Plough Farm
Wr Twr
Rose Farm
Amen Corner
Hotel
B-E-R-K-S-H-I-R-E-W-A-Y
Wykery Copse
Longshot La
DONCASTLE RD
OLDBURY
Southern Industrial Area
WILLOUGHBY RD
PEACOCK LA
Peacock Farm
ELLESFIELD AVE
A3095
3
69
Big Wood
Peacock Cottages
Burnthouse Ride
LOVELACE RD
M-I-L-L LA
Mill Pond
Nature Reserve
Northerams
WILDRIDINGS RD
68
Big Wood House
WATERLOO RD
West Garden Copse
Lock's House
Easthampstead Park
Educational Centre
WAVERLEY
WELBECK
WHEATLEY
WINSCOMBE
WROXHAM
WORDSWORTH
WYLAM
YARDLEY
AMBASSADOR
RINGMEAD
ABBOTSBURY
APPLEDORE
VIKING
Schs
Great Hollands
VANDYKE
GREAT HOLLANDS RD
GREAT HOLLANDS SQ
EDDINGTON RD
RAMBURY CL
WICKHAM VALE
BEEDON DR
HALEWOOD
HIGHFIELD
HOLBECK
AYSGARTH
ASHBOURNE
UNDERWOOD
TROON CT
PENWOOD GDNS
FLEXFORD GREEN
TURNBERRY
BIRKDALE
CARNOUSTIE
ULLSWATER
HOLLAND PINES
BYWOOD
2
67
Six Oaks
EASTHAMPSTEAD RD
Golf Course
Sutton Court Farm
TREVELYAN
TAWFIELD
STAPLEHURST
RINGWOOD
SYLVANUS
CROWTHORNE RD
Sch
SPINIS
SILWOOD
WOODEN HILL
SOUTHWOLD
QUINTILIS
QUALITAS
PEMBROKE
PRESCOTT
Office
Crem
OLD WOKINGHAM RD
HONEY HILL
Newlands
Yew Tree Corner
SARUM
STRATFIELD
NINE MILE RIDE
B3430
BRACKNELL RD
1
66
83
84
85

118

143

91

117

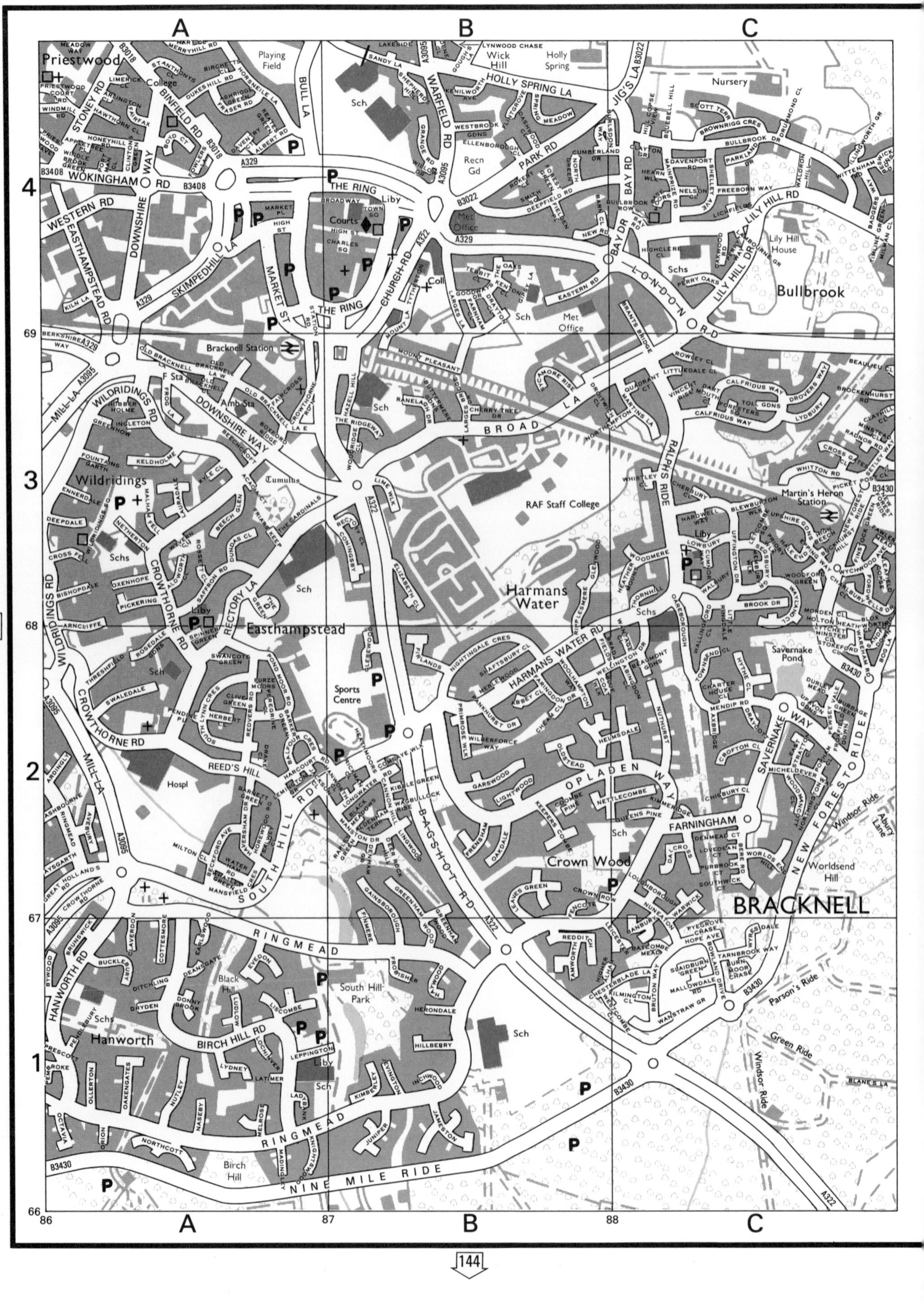
A
B
C
4
3
2
1
69
68
67
66
86
87
88
Priestwood
College
Playing Field
BULL LA
Sch
WARFIELD RD
Wick Hill
Holly Spring
HOLLY SPRING LA
JIG'S LA B3022
Nursery
STONEY RD
BINFIELD RD
WOKINGHAM RD
WESTERN RD
EASTHAMPSTEAD RD
DOWNSHIRE WAY
SKIMPEDHILL LA
MARKET ST
THE RING
Liby
Courts
CHURCH RD
Coll
Met Office
Recn Gd
PARK RD
BAY RD
BAY DR
LONDON RD
EASTERN RD
Schs
LILY HILL RD
LILY HILL DR
Lily Hill House
Bullbrook
BULLBROOK DR
BERKSHIRE WAY
Bracknell Station
MILL LA
WILDRIDINGS RD
F Sta
Amb Sta
BROAD LA
MOUNT PLEASANT
THE RIDGEWAY
RANELAGH DR
CALFRIDUS WAY
RALPHS RIDE
Wildridings
Tumulus
THE CARDINALS
RAF Staff College
Martin's Heron Station
Harmans Water
Easthampstead
RECTORY LA
CROWTHORNE RD
Sports Centre
HARMANS WATER RD
Savernake Pond
SAVERNAKE WAY
NEW FOREST RIDE
Hospl
REED'S HILL
SOUTH HILL RD
BAGSHOT RD
OPLADEN WAY
FARNINGHAM
Crown Wood
Windsor Ride
Abury Lane
Worldsend Hill
BRACKNELL
RINGMEAD
HANWORTH RD
Black Hill
South Hill Park
BIRCH HILL RD
Hanworth
Parson's Ride
Green Ride
Windsor Ride
BLANE'S LA
Birch Hill
NINE MILE RIDE
B3430
A3095
A322
A329
B3408
B3018

144

92

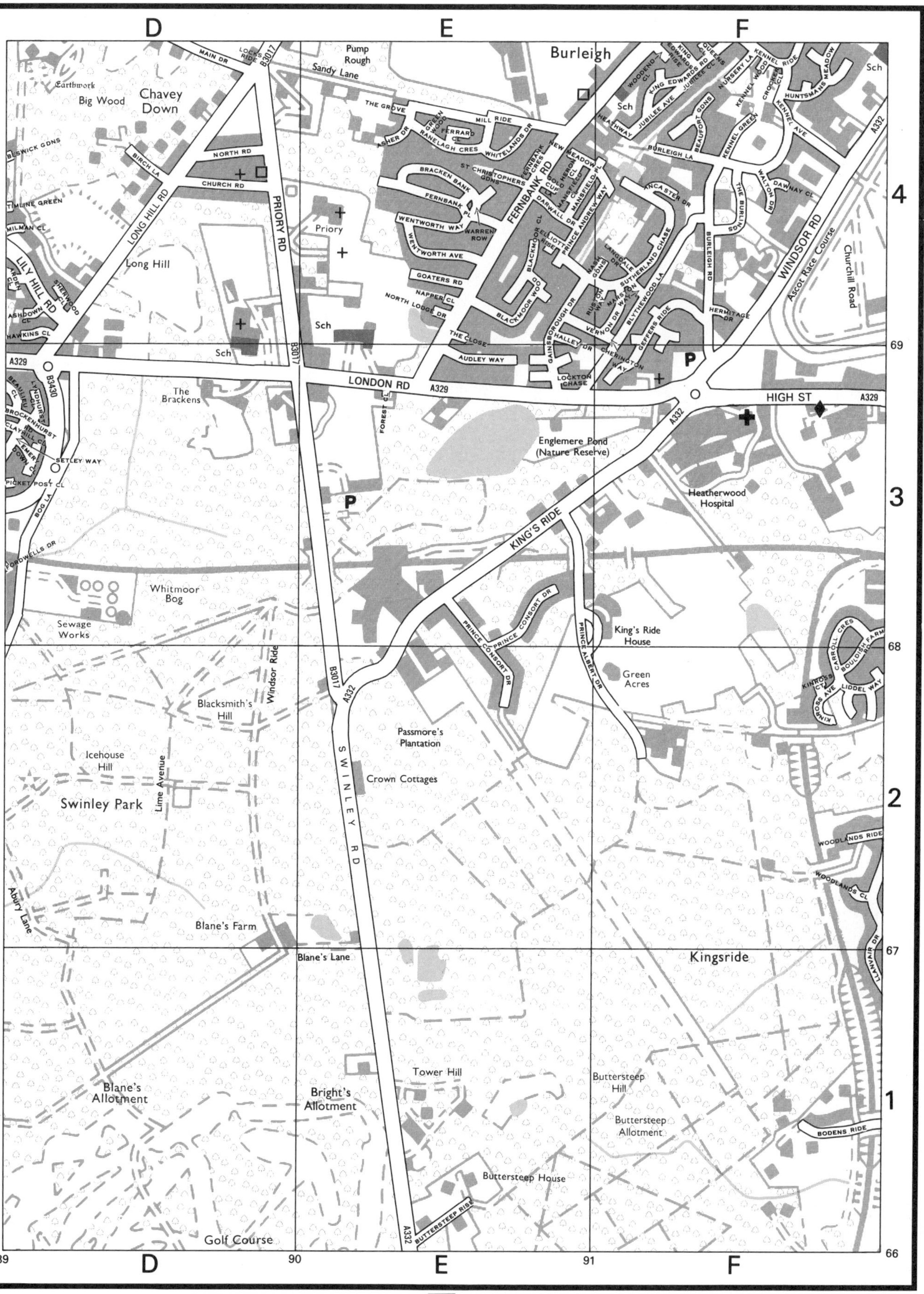
D
E
F
Pump Rough
Sandy Lane
Burleigh
Earthwork
Big Wood
Chavey Down
MAIN DR
LOCKS RIDE
B3017
BESWICK GDNS
BIRCH LA
NORTH RD
CHURCH RD
TIMLINE GREEN
LONG HILL RD
PRIORY RD
Priory
Long Hill
MILMAN CL
LILY HILL RD
SHERWOOD CL
ASHDOWN CL
HAWKINS CL
Sch
THE GROVE
GREEN WOOD
FERRARD CL
MILL RIDE
ASHER DR
RANELAGH CRES
WHITELANDS DR
ST CHRISTOPHERS GDNS
BRACKEN BANK
FERNBANK PL
FERNBANK RD
FERNBANK CRES
WENTWORTH WAY
WARREN ROW
WENTWORTH AVE
GOATERS RD
NAPPER CL
NORTH LODGE DR
THE CLOSE
AUDLEY WAY
NEW MEADOW
HERON CL
MANSFIELD PL
DARWALL DR
BLACKMOOR CL
BLACKMOOR WOOD
ELLIOTT RISE
PRINCE ANDREW WAY
GAINSBOROUGH DR
HALLEY DR
LOCKTON CHASE
LANCASTER DR
LANGDALE DR
SUTHERLAND CHASE
BLYTHEWOOD LA
VERNON DR
MARSTON WAY
GEFFERS RIDE
CHERINGTON WAY
WOODEND CL
KING EDWARDS RISE
KING EDWARDS RD
QUEENS RD
JUBILEE CL
JUBILEE AVE
HEATHWAY
NURSERY LA
KENNEL RIDE
KENNEL WOOD
CROCKER CL
HUNTSMANS MEADOW
BEAUFORT GDNS
KENNEL GREEN
KENNEL AVE
BURLEIGH LA
THE BURLINGS
WALTON DR
DAWNAY CL
BURLEIGH RD
HERMITAGE DR
WINDSOR RD
A332
Ascot Race Course
Churchill Road
P
4
69
A329
B3430
LONDON RD
HIGH ST
The Brackens
FOREST CL
BEAULIEU CL
LYNDHURST RD
BROCKENHURST RD
CLAYHILL CL
EMERY DOWN CL
SETLEY WAY
PICKET POST CL
BOG LA
Englemere Pond (Nature Reserve)
Heatherwood Hospital
3
FORDWELLS DR
KING'S RIDE
Whitmoor Bog
Sewage Works
PRINCE CONSORT DR
PRINCE ALBERT DR
King's Ride House
Green Acres
68
CARROLL CRES
BOULDISH FARM RD
KINROSS CT
KINROSS AVE
LIDDEL WAY
Windsor Ride
Blacksmith's Hill
Icehouse Hill
Lime Avenue
Swinley Park
Passmore's Plantation
Crown Cottages
SWINLEY RD
2
WOODLANDS RIDE
WOODLANDS CL
Abury Lane
Blane's Farm
Blane's Lane
Kingsride
67
LLANVAIR DR
Blane's Allotment
Bright's Allotment
Tower Hill
Buttersteep Hill
Buttersteep Allotment
1
BODENS RIDE
Buttersteep House
BUTTERSTEEP RISE
Golf Course
89
90
91
66

120

145

93

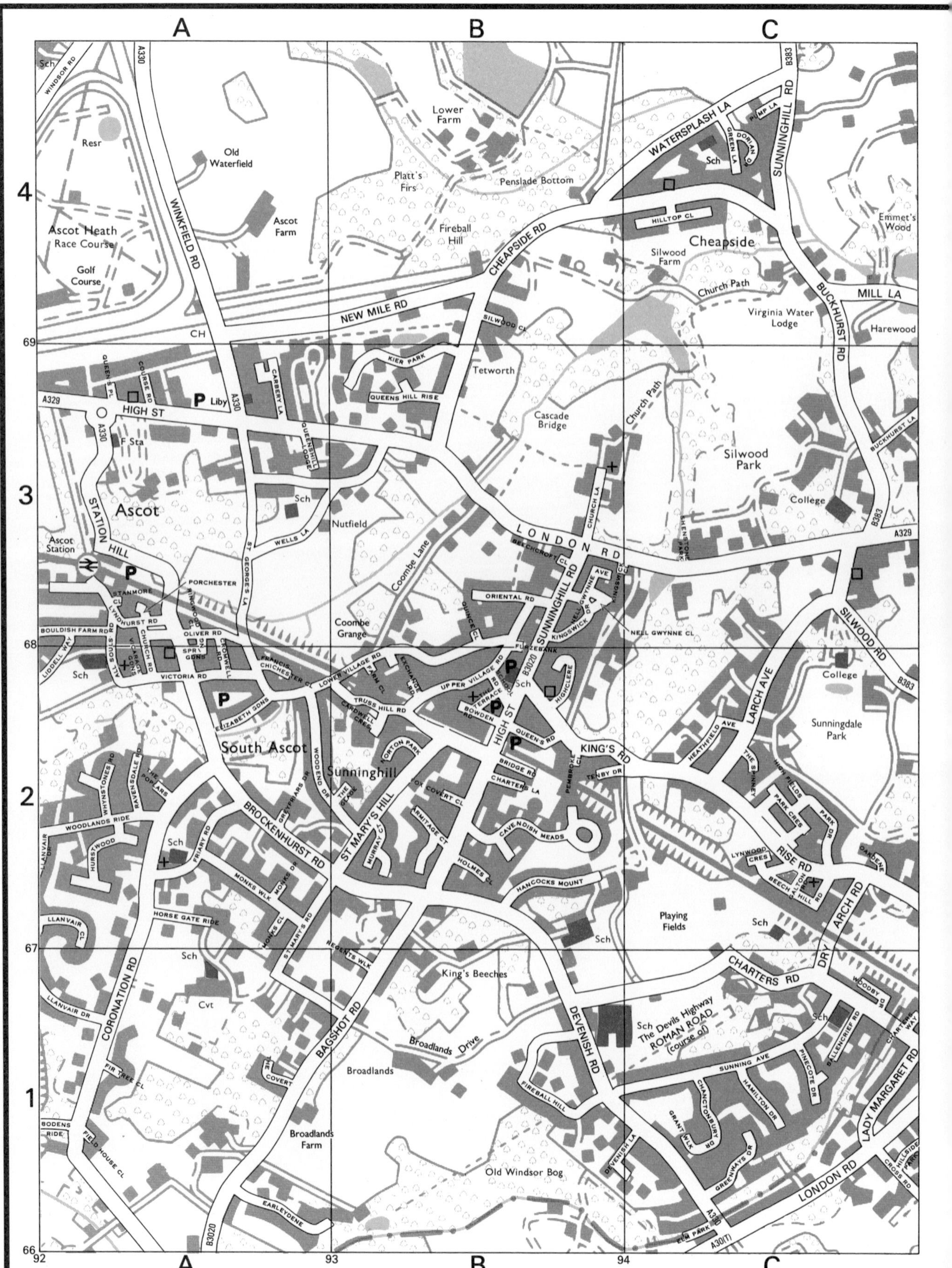
A
B
C
4
3
2
1
69
68
67
66
92
93
94
Sch
WINDSOR RD
A330
Resr
Old Waterfield
Lower Farm
Platt's Firs
Penslade Bottom
WATERSPLASH LA
PUMP LA
GREEN LA
DORIAN
SUNNINGHILL RD
B383
Ascot Heath
Race Course
Golf Course
WINKFIELD RD
Ascot Farm
Fireball Hill
CHEAPSIDE RD
HILLTOP CL
Cheapside
Silwood Farm
Emmet's Wood
Church Path
MILL LA
BUCKHURST RD
Virginia Water Lodge
Harewood
NEW MILE RD
CH
SILWOOD CL
KIER PARK
Tetworth
QUEENS PL
COURSE RD
CARBERY LA
QUEENS HILL RISE
A329
HIGH ST
P
Liby
F Sta
Cascade Bridge
Church Path
QUEENSHILL LODGE
Silwood Park
BUCKHURST LA
Ascot
STATION HILL
Sch
Nutfield
WELLS LA
ST GEORGES LA
College
CHURCH LA
LONDON RD
BEECHCROFT CL
SHENSTONE PARK
Ascot Station
PORCHESTER
STANMORE
Coombe Lane
ORIENTAL RD
QUINCE CL
SUNNINGHILL RD
B3020
NELL GWYNNE AVE
KINGSWICK DR
NELL GWYNNE CL
SILWOOD RD
LYNDHURST RD
RINGWOOD CL
Coombe Grange
BOULDISH FARM RD
OLIVER RD
CROMWELL
FURZEBANK
LIDDELL WAY
ALL SOULS RD
VICARAGE GDNS
CHURCH RD
SPRING GDNS
FRANCIS CHICHESTER CL
LOWER VILLAGE RD
EXCHANGE RD
FARM CL
UPPER VILLAGE RD
SCHOOL
HIGHCLERE
College
B383
VICTORIA RD
ELIZABETH GDNS
TRUSS HILL RD
CARDWELL CRES
THE TERRACE
BOWDEN RD
HIGH ST
QUEEN'S RD
KING'S RD
HEATHFIELD AVE
LARCH AVE
Sunningdale Park
South Ascot
NORTON PARK
Sunninghill
PEMBROKE CL
TENBY DR
THE SPINNEY
HIGH FIELDS
BRIDGE RD
CHARTERS LA
ST MARY'S HILL
FOX COVERT CL
PARK CRES
PARK DR
WOODEND DR
GREYFRIARS DR
THE GLADE
BROCKENHURST RD
ARMITAGE CT
CAVENDISH MEADS
PINEHURST
RAVENSDALE RD
THE POPLARS
WOODLANDS RIDE
LLANVAIR
HURSTWOOD
Sch
FRIARY RD
MURRAY CT
HOLMES CL
LYNWOOD CRES
RISE RD
BEECH HILL RD
OAKDENE
MONKS WLK
MONKS DR
HANCOCKS MOUNT
DRY ARCH RD
LLANVAIR CL
HORSE GATE RIDE
MONKS CL
ST MARY'S RD
Playing Fields
Sch
Sch
Sch
REGENTS WLK
CHARTERS RD
WOODBY DR
CORONATION RD
King's Beeches
LLANVAIR DR
Cvt
DEVENISH RD
Sch
The Devils Highway
ROMAN ROAD
(course of)
Sch
BALLENCRIEF RD
CHARTERS WAY
BAGSHOT RD
Broadlands Drive
SUNNING AVE
PINECOTE DR
FIR TREE CL
THE COVERT
Broadlands
FIREBALL HILL
CHANCTONBURY DR
HAMILTON DR
LADY MARGARET RD
GRANT WLK
BODENS RIDE
FIELD HOUSE CL
Broadlands Farm
DEVENISH LA
GREENWAYS DR
HILLSIDE
CROSS RD
Old Windsor Bog
LONDON RD
EARLEYDENE
A330
B3020
ELM PARK
A30(T)

119

146

94

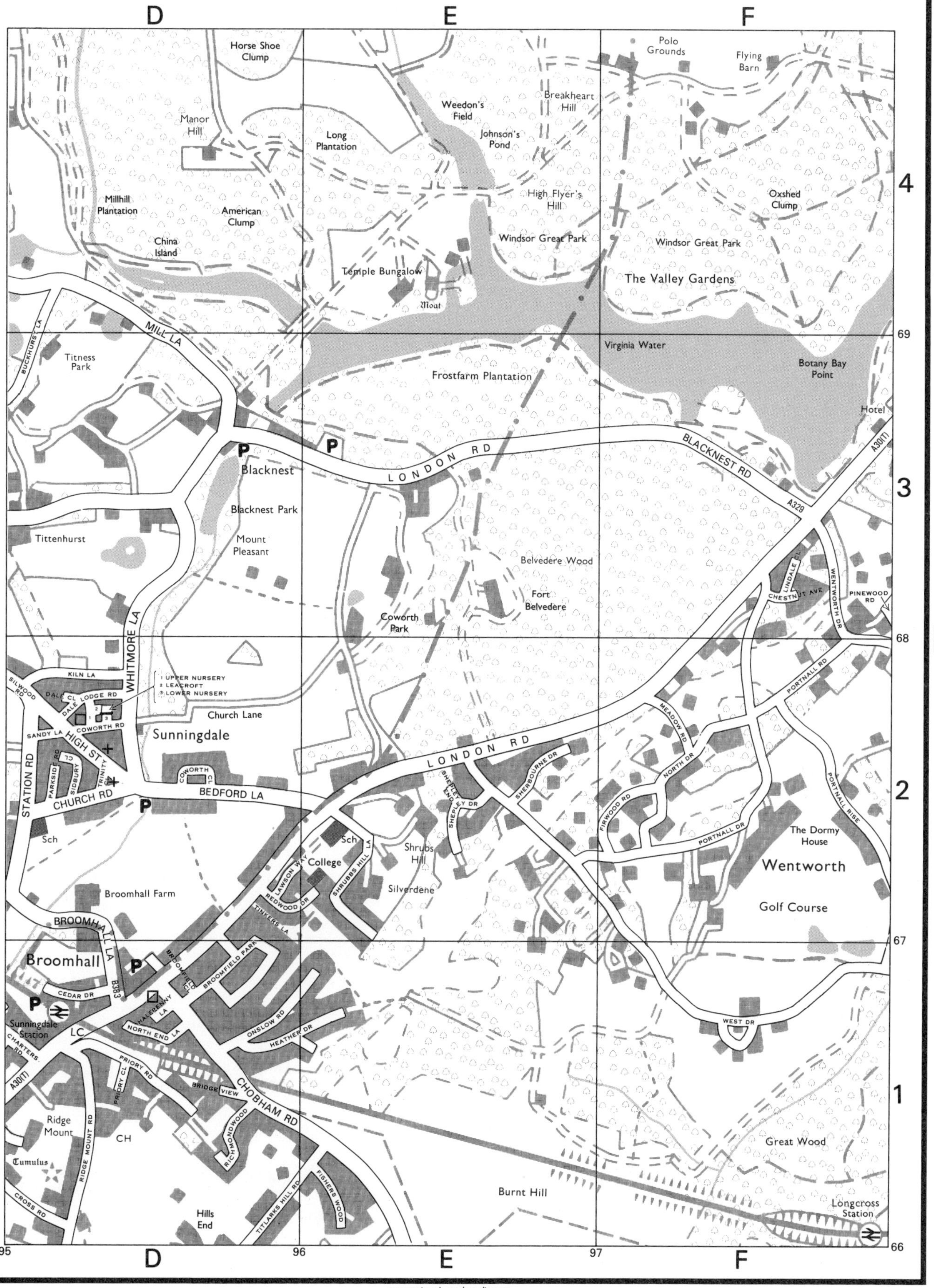

122

not continued, see key diagram

95

121

not continued, see key diagram

96

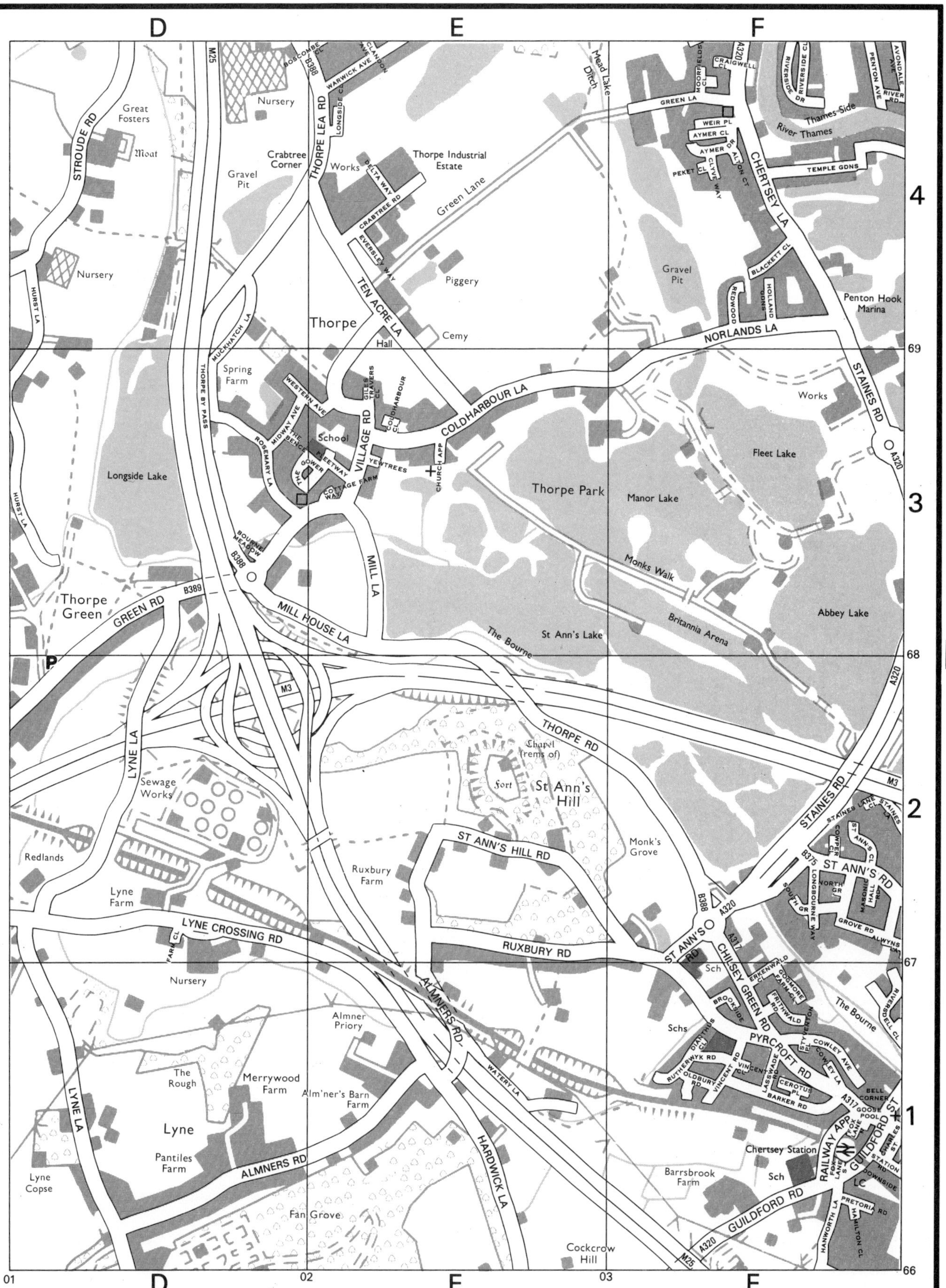

124

not continued, see key diagram

97

123

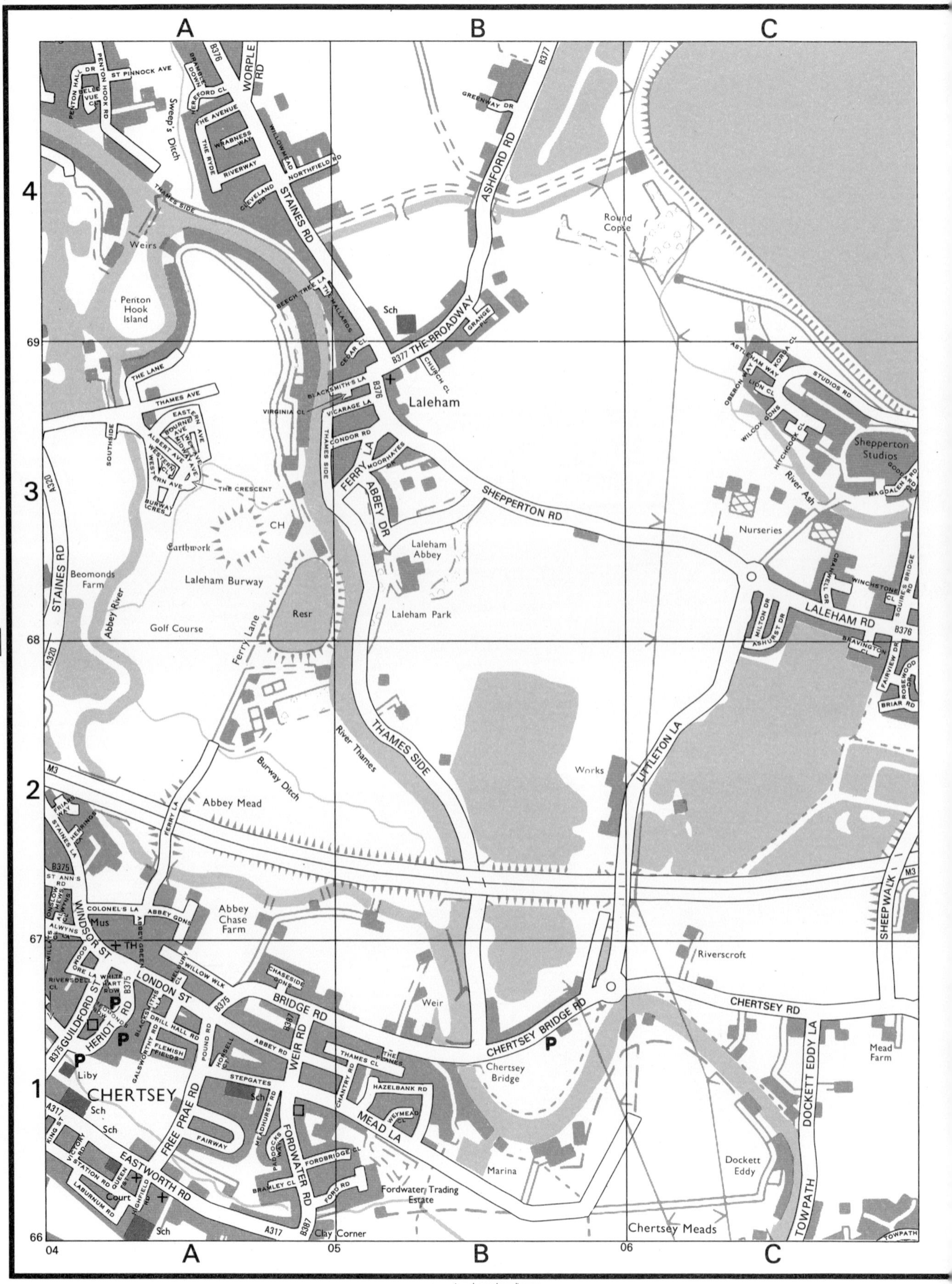

not continued, see key diagram

98

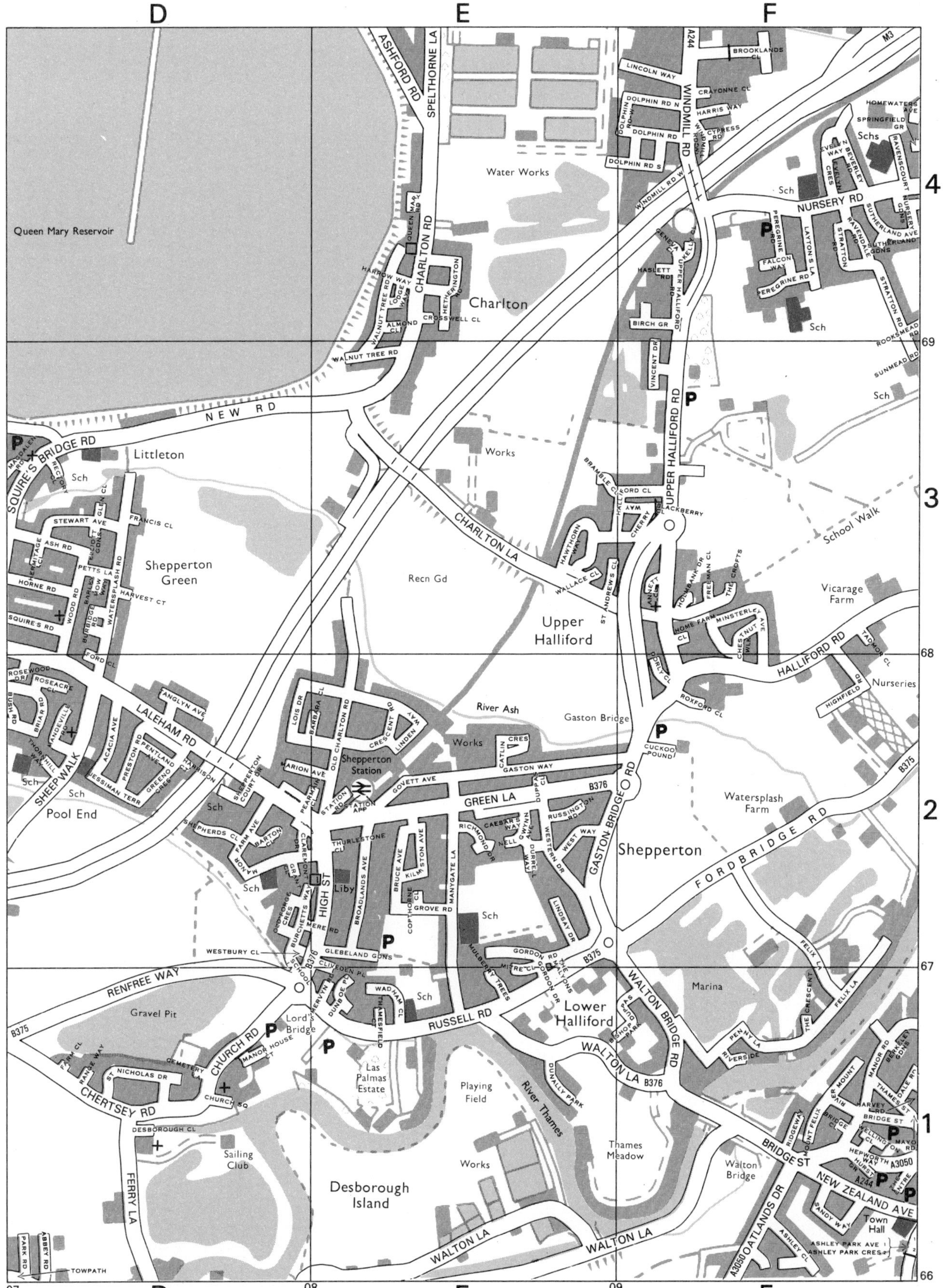

not continued, see key diagram

not continued, see key diagram

100

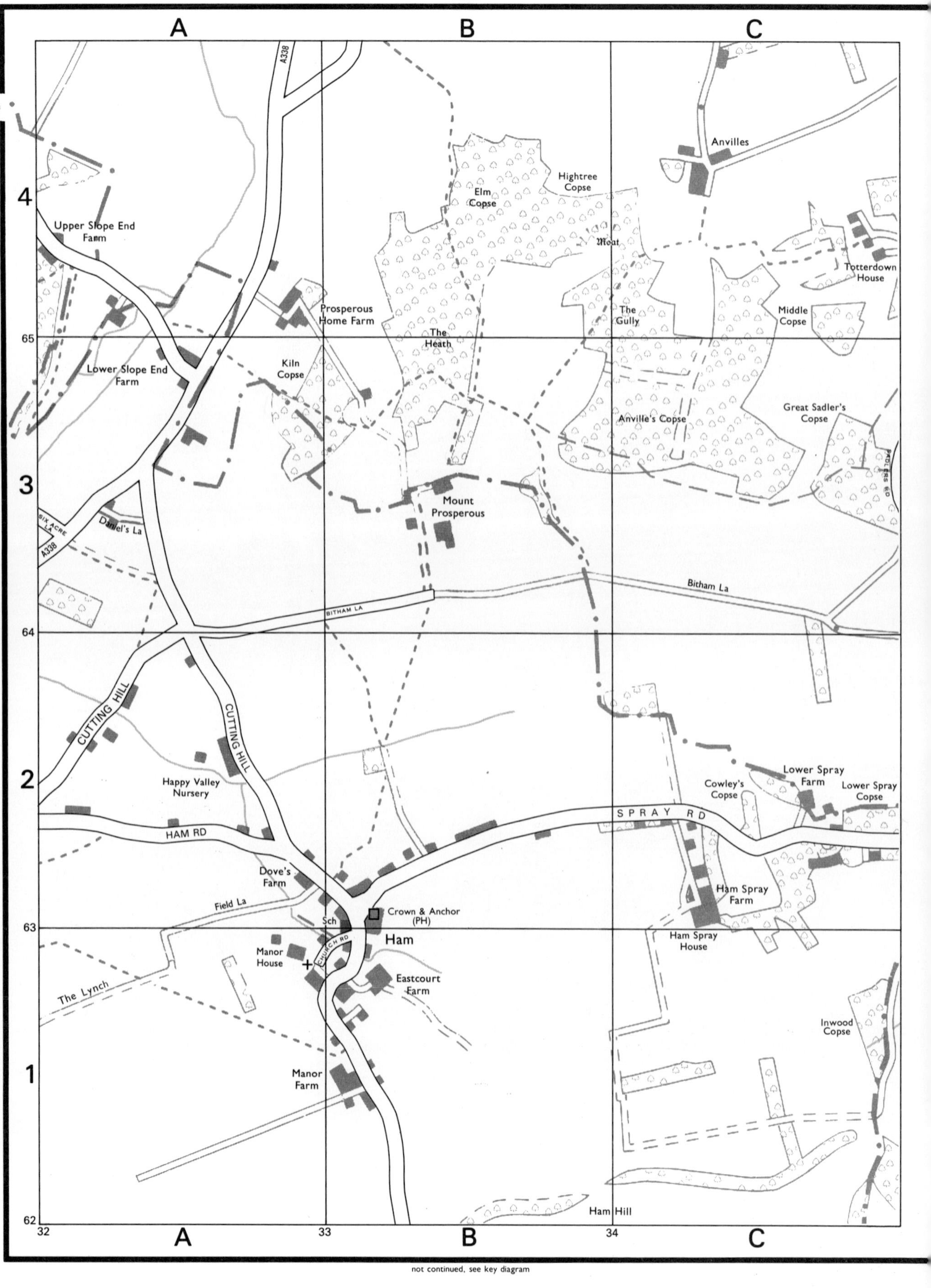

not continued, see key diagram

not continued, see key diagram

101

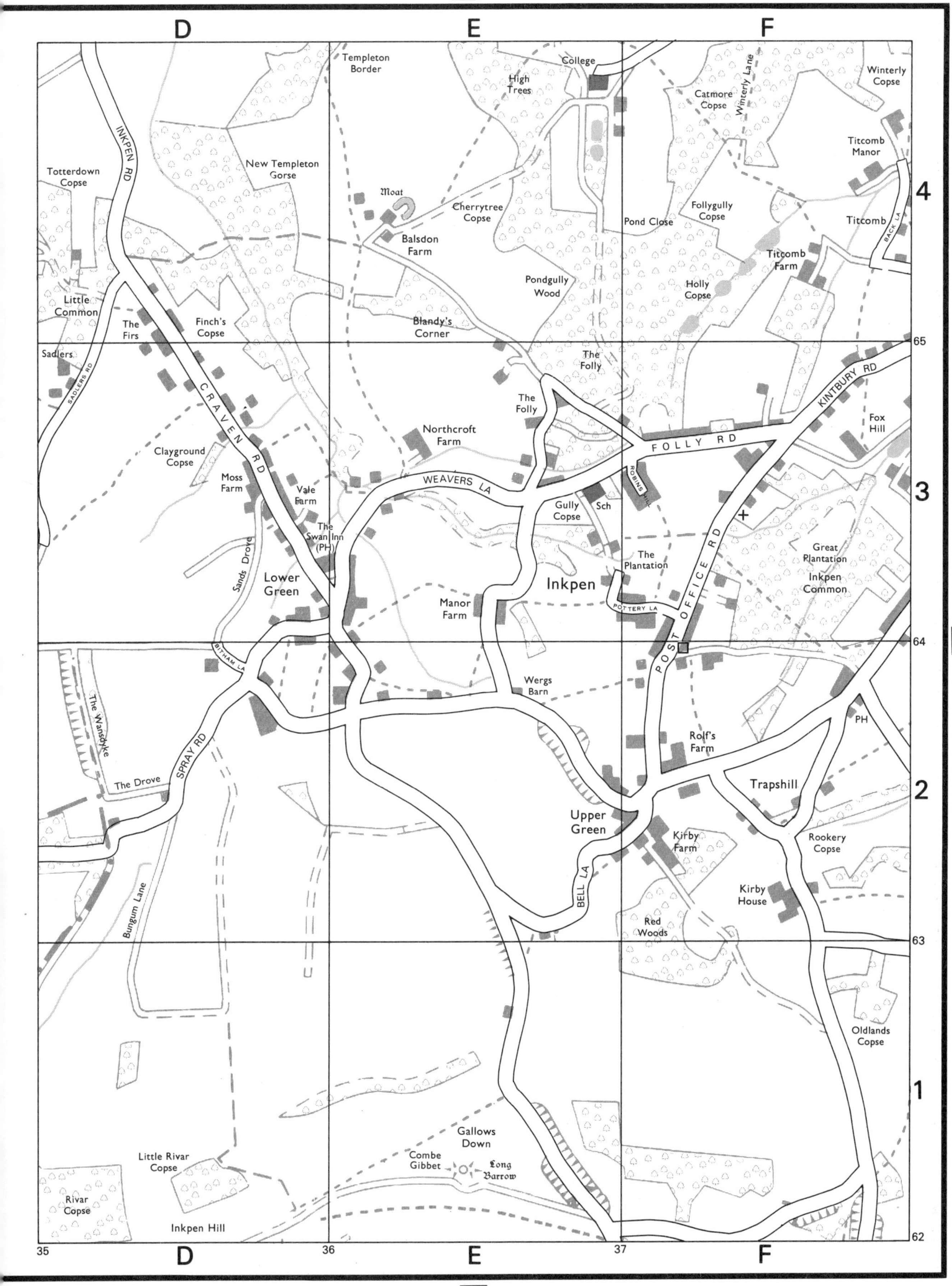

D
E
F
Templeton Border
College
High Trees
Winterly Copse
Catmore Copse
Winterly Lane
Titcomb Manor
INKPEN RD
Totterdown Copse
New Templeton Gorse
Moat
Cherrytree Copse
Pond Close
Follygully Copse
Titcomb
BACK LA
Balsdon Farm
Titcomb Farm
Pondgully Wood
Holly Copse
Little Common
The Firs
Finch's Copse
Blandy's Corner
Sadlers
SADLERS RD
The Folly
KINTBURY RD
CRAVEN RD
The Folly
Fox Hill
Northcroft Farm
FOLLY RD
Clayground Copse
Moss Farm
Vale Farm
WEAVERS LA
ROBINS HILL
Gully Copse
Sch
The Swan Inn (PH)
Sands Drove
The Plantation
Great Plantation
Lower Green
Inkpen
POST OFFICE RD
Inkpen Common
Manor Farm
POTTERY LA
BITHAM LA
Wergs Barn
The Wansdyke
PH
SPRAY RD
Rolf's Farm
The Drove
Trapshill
Upper Green
Kirby Farm
Rookery Copse
BELL LA
Bungum Lane
Kirby House
Red Woods
Oldlands Copse
Gallows Down
Little Rivar Copse
Combe Gibbet
Long Barrow
Rivar Copse
Inkpen Hill
4
3
2
1
65
64
63
62
35
36
37
D
E
F

128

147

102

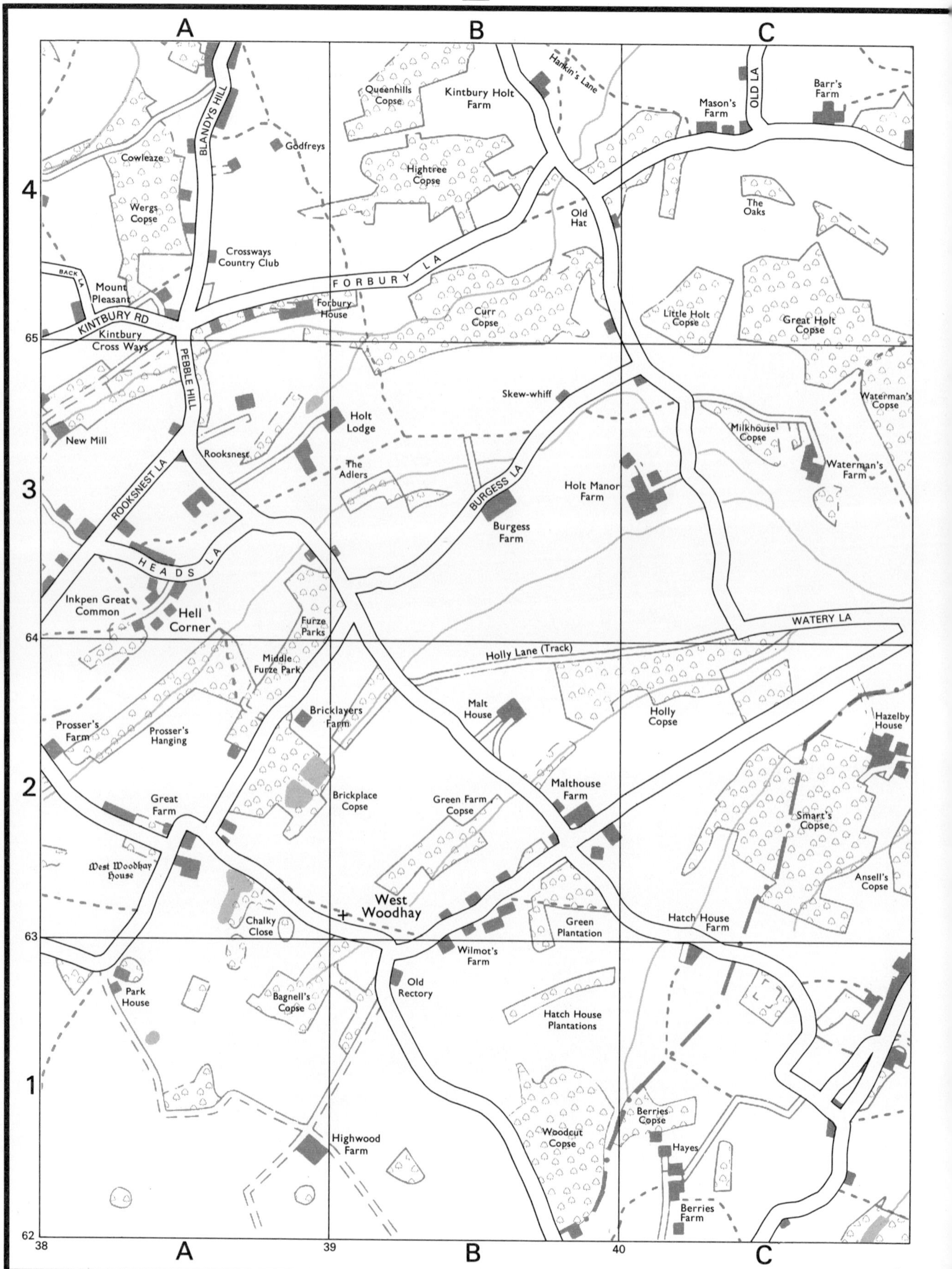

A
B
C
4
3
2
1
65
64
63
62
38
39
40
Queenhills Copse
Kintbury Holt Farm
Hankin's Lane
OLD LA
Barr's Farm
Mason's Farm
BLANDYS HILL
Godfreys
Cowleaze
Hightree Copse
The Oaks
Wergs Copse
Old Hat
Crossways Country Club
BACK LA
Mount Pleasant
FORBURY LA
KINTBURY RD
Forbury House
Curr Copse
Little Holt Copse
Great Holt Copse
Kintbury Cross Ways
PEBBLE HILL
Skew-whiff
Waterman's Copse
Holt Lodge
Milkhouse Copse
New Mill
Rooksnest
The Adlers
Waterman's Farm
ROOKSNEST LA
BURGESS LA
Holt Manor Farm
Burgess Farm
HEADS LA
Inkpen Great Common
Hell Corner
Furze Parks
WATERY LA
Holly Lane (Track)
Middle Furze Park
Malt House
Holly Copse
Hazelby House
Bricklayers Farm
Prosser's Farm
Prosser's Hanging
Malthouse Farm
Great Farm
Brickplace Copse
Green Farm Copse
Smart's Copse
West Woodhay House
Ansell's Copse
West Woodhay
Chalky Close
Green Plantation
Hatch House Farm
Wilmot's Farm
Park House
Old Rectory
Bagnell's Copse
Hatch House Plantations
Berries Copse
Woodcut Copse
Highwood Farm
Hayes
Berries Farm

127

148

103

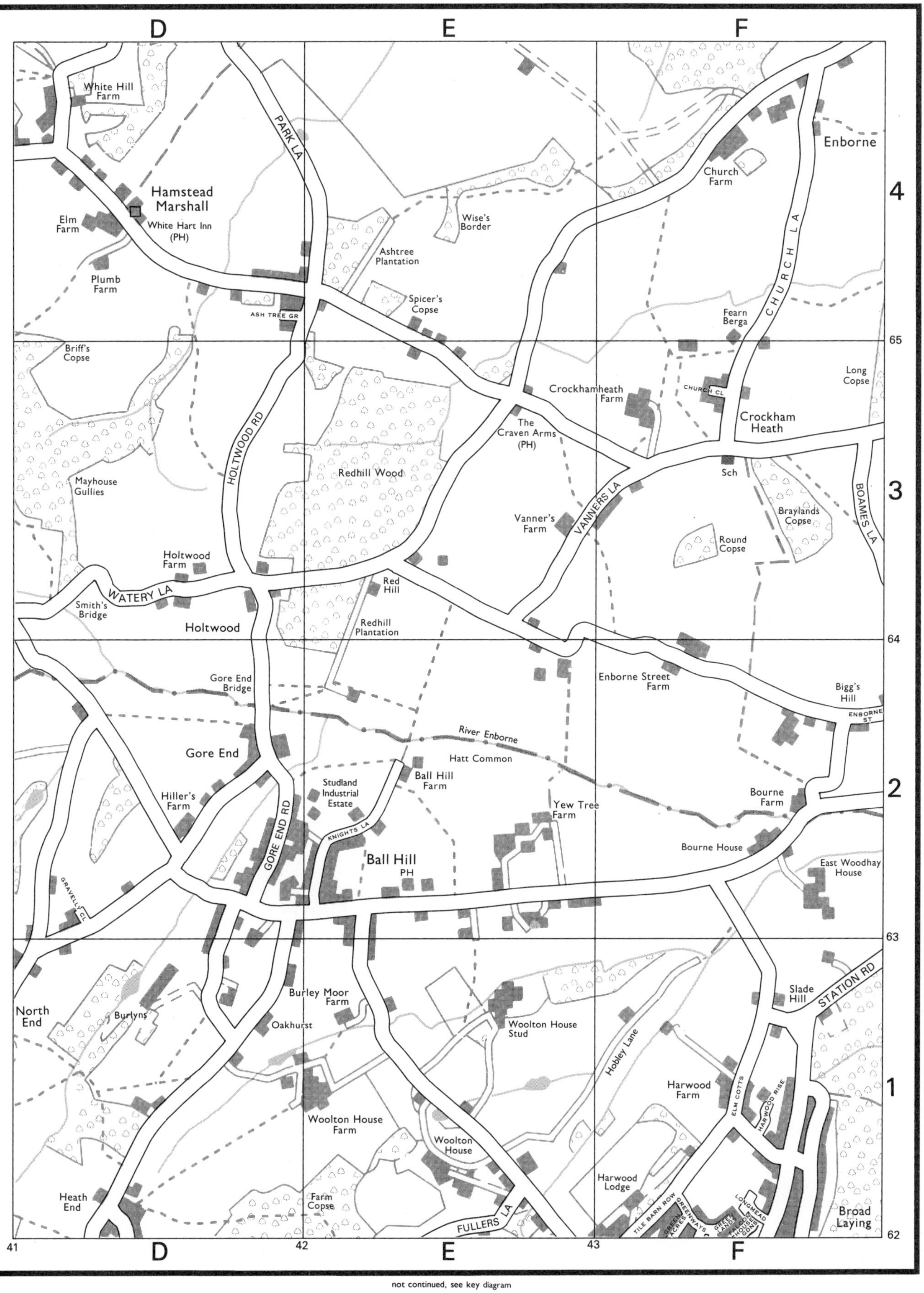
D
E
F
White Hill Farm
PARK LA
Hamstead Marshall
Elm Farm
White Hart Inn (PH)
Plumb Farm
Ashtree Plantation
Wise's Border
Spicer's Copse
ASH TREE GR
Church Farm
Enborne
CHURCH LA
Fearn Berga
Briff's Copse
Long Copse
Crockhamheath Farm
CHURCH CL
Crockham Heath
The Craven Arms (PH)
HOLTWOOD RD
Redhill Wood
Mayhouse Gullies
Sch
VANNERS LA
Vanner's Farm
Braylands Copse
BOAMES LA
Round Copse
Holtwood Farm
WATERY LA
Red Hill
Smith's Bridge
Holtwood
Redhill Plantation
Gore End Bridge
Enborne Street Farm
Bigg's Hill
ENBORNE ST
River Enborne
Gore End
Hatt Common
Ball Hill Farm
Studland Industrial Estate
Hiller's Farm
Yew Tree Farm
Bourne Farm
GORE END RD
KNIGHTS LA
Ball Hill
PH
Bourne House
East Woodhay House
GRAVELLY CL
Slade Hill
STATION RD
Burley Moor Farm
North End
Burlyns
Oakhurst
Woolton House Stud
Hobley Lane
Harwood Farm
ELM COTTS
HARWOOD RISE
Woolton House Farm
Woolton House
Harwood Lodge
Heath End
Farm Copse
FULLERS LA
TILE BARN ROW
GREENWAYS
GREEN ACRES
LONGMEAD
Broad Laying
4
3
2
1
65
64
63
62
41
42
43

130

104

129

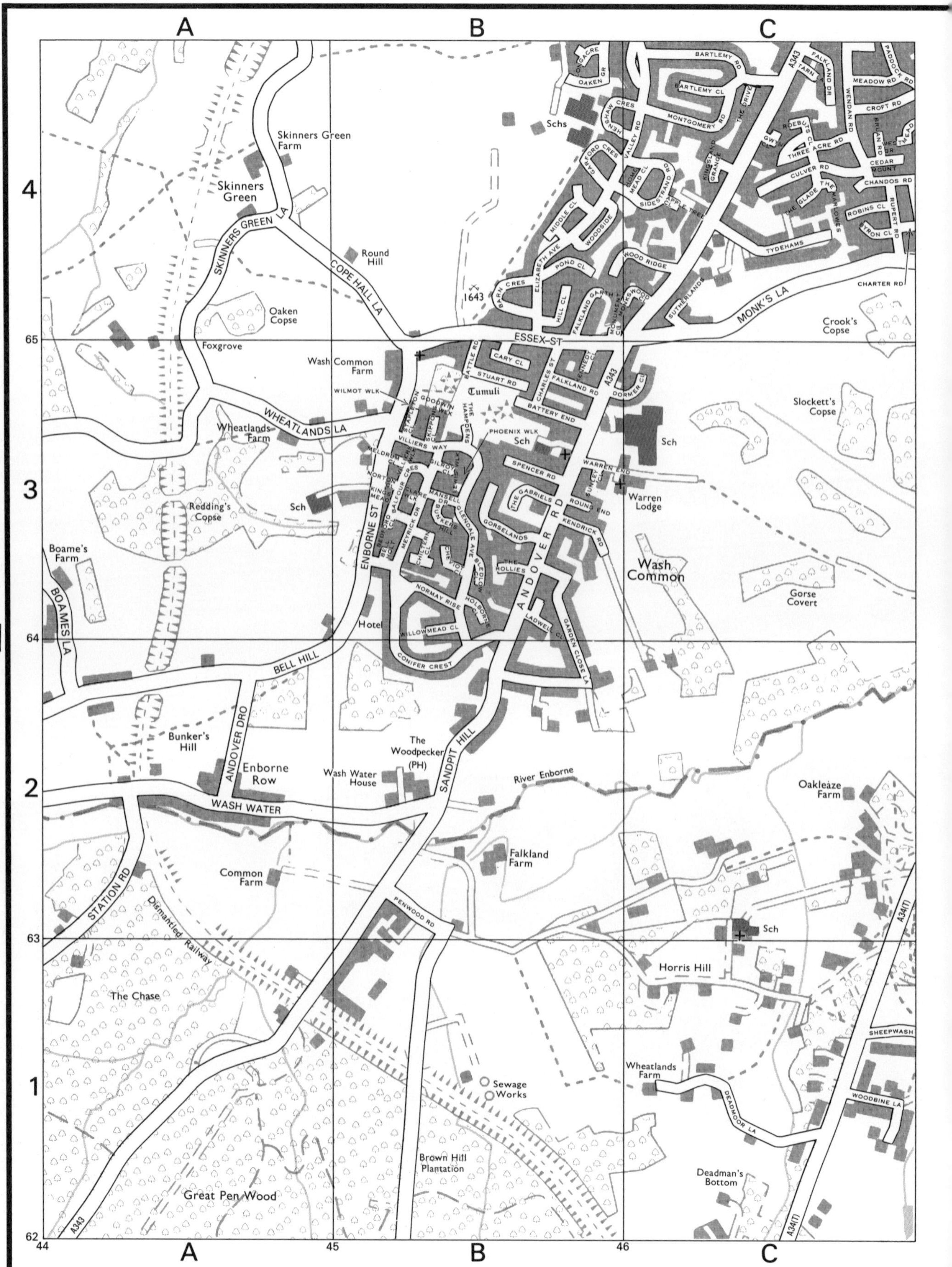
A
B
C
4
3
2
1
65
64
63
62
44
45
46
Skinners Green Farm
Skinners Green
SKINNERS GREEN LA
Round Hill
COPE HALL LA
Oaken Copse
Foxgrove
Wash Common Farm
WILMOT WLK
WHEATLANDS LA
Wheatlands Farm
Redding's Copse
Sch
Boame's Farm
BOAMES LA
BELL HILL
Hotel
Bunker's Hill
ANDOVER DRO
Enborne Row
WASH WATER
Wash Water House
The Woodpecker (PH)
SANDPIT HILL
River Enborne
Falkland Farm
Common Farm
STATION RD
Dismantled Railway
PENWOOD RD
The Chase
Sewage Works
Brown Hill Plantation
Great Pen Wood
A343
Schs
1643
ESSEX ST
CARY CL
STUART RD
FALKLAND RD
CHARLES ST
BATTERY END
DORMER CL
A343
Cumuli
PHOENIX WLK
Sch
SPENCER RD
WARREN END
Warren Lodge
ROUND END
THE GABRIELS
KENDRICK RD
GORSELANDS
THE ROLLIES
ANDOVER RD
LADWELL CL
GARDEN CLOSE LA
ENBORNE ST
NORMAY RISE
HOLBORNE
WILLOWMEAD CL
CONIFER CREST
BATTLE RD
STAPLETON
GOODWIN WLK
THE HAMPDENS
VILLIERS WAY
MELDRUM
NORTH
KINGS MEAD
CHILTERN CL
CHEVIOT
GLENDALE AVE
LEDBURY
BUNKERS HILL
MANSELL DR
BALFOUR CRES
CLARE
MEYRICK DR
BEDFORD
Wash Common
Gorse Covert
Slockett's Copse
Sch
Crook's Copse
MONK'S LA
CHARTER RD
SUTHERLANDS
WOOD RIDGE
MONUMENT CL
MONKSWOOD CL
FALKLAND GARTH
HILL CL
POND CL
ELIZABETH AVE
BARN CRES
MIDDLE CL
WOODSIDE
GARFORD CRES
VALLEY RD
HENSHAW CRES
MONTGOMERY RD
BARTLEMY RD
BARTLEMY CL
THE DRIVE
LONGACRE
OAKEN GR
SIDESTRAND RD
APPLE TREE
KINGSLAND GRANGE
TYDEHAMS
THE GLADE
THE MARLOWES
ROBINS CL
RUPERT RD
BYRON CL
CHANDOS RD
CEDAR MOUNT
CULVER RD
THREE ACRE RD
ROEBUTS CL
GWYN CL
CROFT RD
MEADOW RD
PADDOCK RD
FALKLAND DR
TARN LA
WENDAN RD
BRUAN RD
Oakleaze Farm
Sch
Horris Hill
A34(T)
SHEEPWASH
WOODBINE LA
Wheatlands Farm
DEADMOOR LA
Deadman's Bottom

105

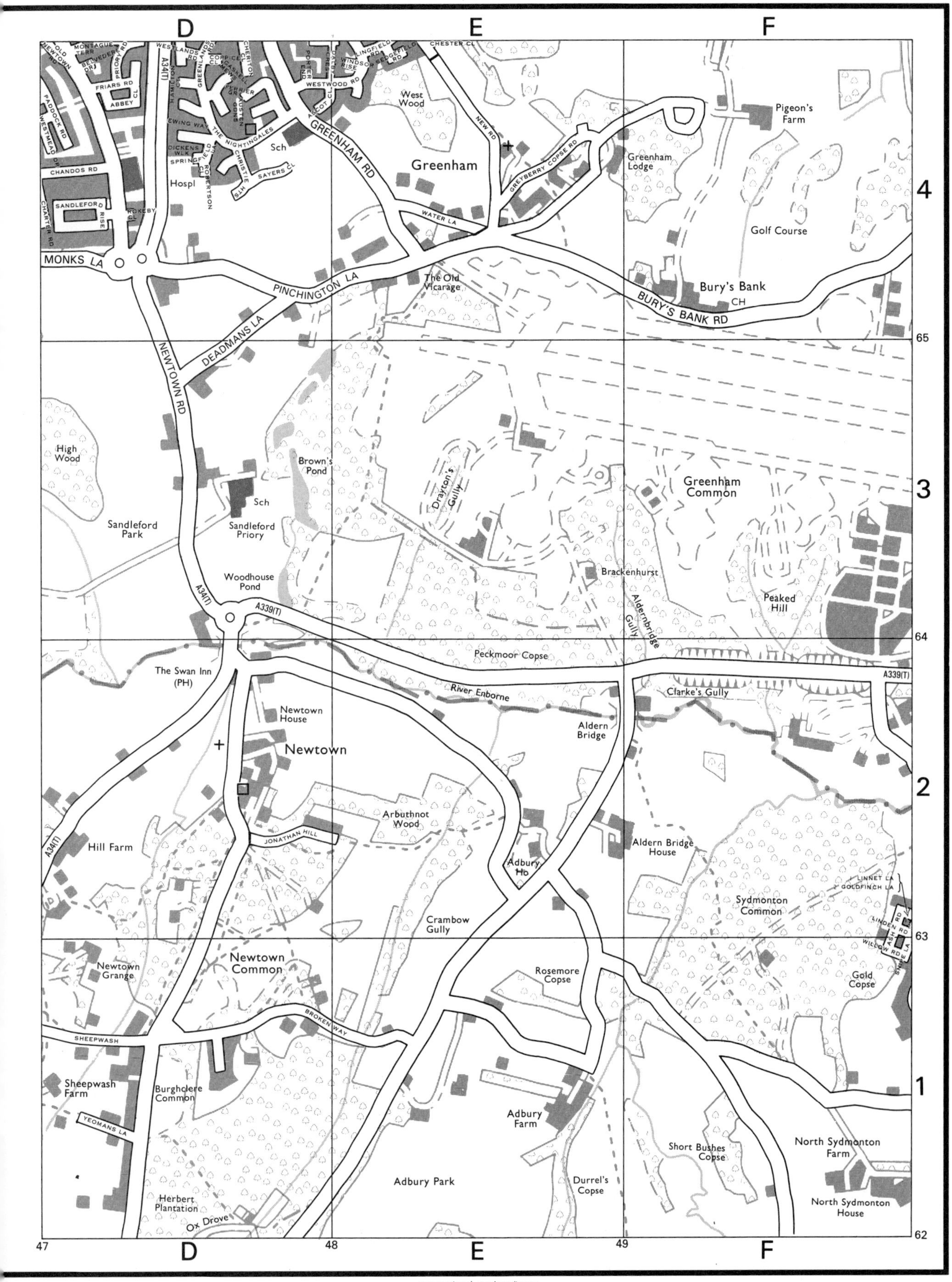

132

not continued, see key diagram

106

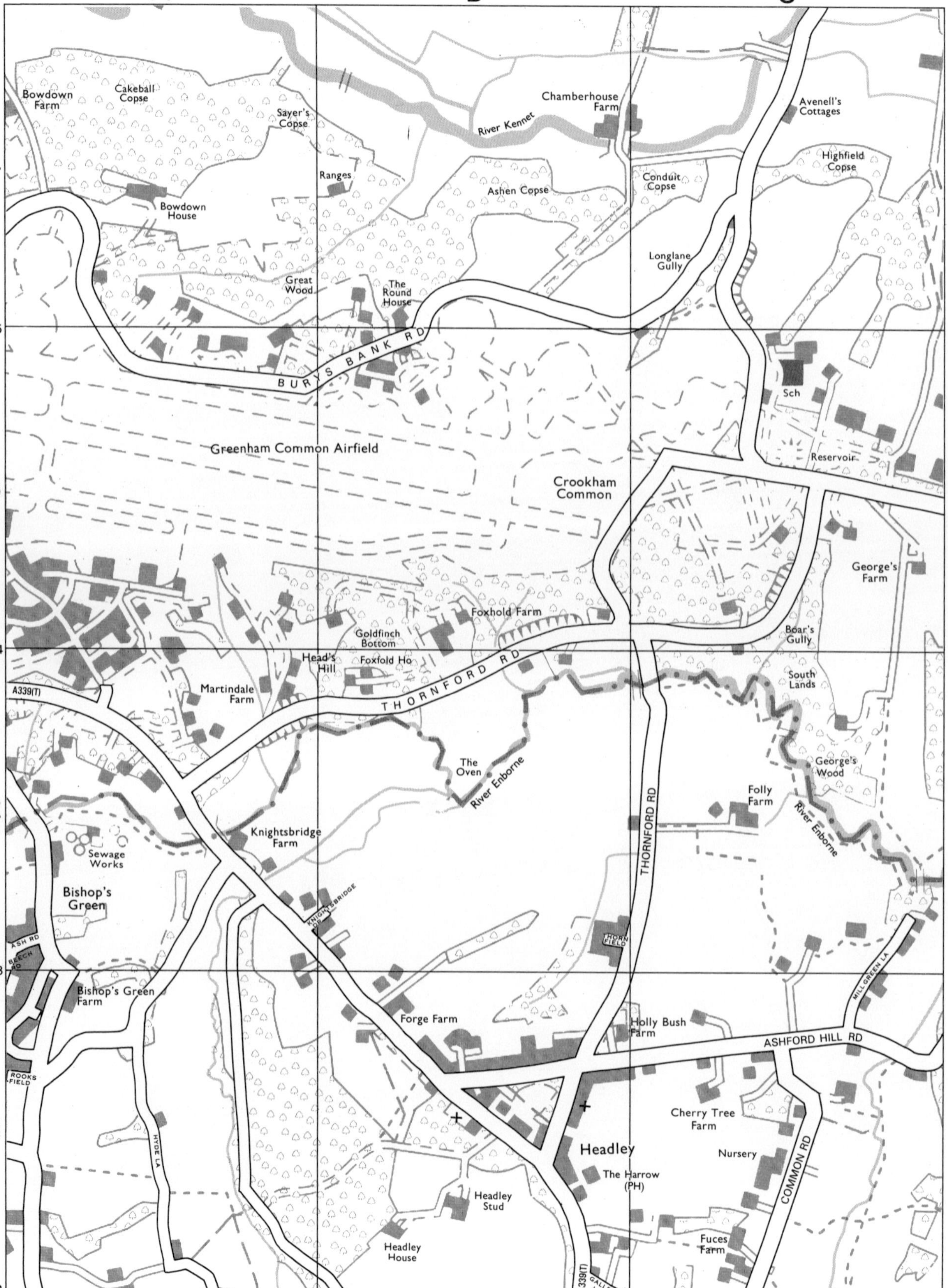

131

not continued, see key diagram

107

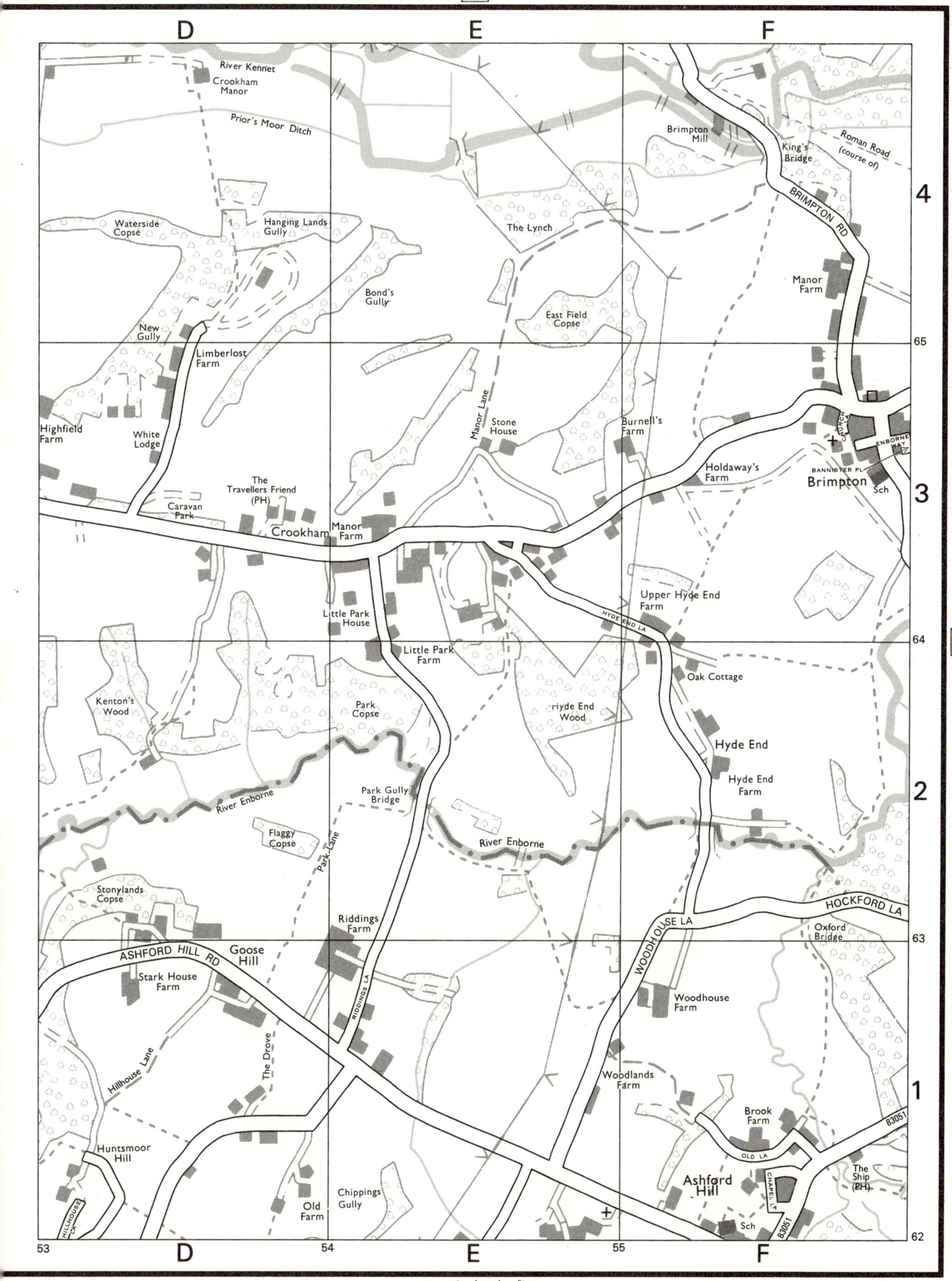
D
E
F
River Kennet
Crookham Manor
Prior's Moor Ditch
Brimpton Mill
King's Bridge
Roman Road (course of)
BRIMPTON RD
4
Waterside Copse
Hanging Lands Gully
The Lynch
Bond's Gully
Manor Farm
East Field Copse
New Gully
Limberlost Farm
65
Manor Lane
Stone House
Burnell's Farm
Highfield Farm
White Lodge
CHURCH LA
ENBORNE WAY
BANNISTER PL
Holdaway's Farm
Brimpton
Sch
The Travellers Friend (PH)
Caravan Park
Crookham
Manor Farm
3
Upper Hyde End Farm
HYDE END LA
Little Park House
Little Park Farm
64
Oak Cottage
Kenton's Wood
Park Copse
Hyde End Wood
Hyde End
Hyde End Farm
River Enborne
Park Gully Bridge
2
Flaggy Copse
Park Lane
River Enborne
Stonylands Copse
HOCKFORD LA
Riddings Farm
WOODHOUSE LA
Oxford Bridge
63
ASHFORD HILL RD
Goose Hill
Stark House Farm
RIDDINGS LA
Woodhouse Farm
The Drove
Hillhouse Lane
Woodlands Farm
1
Brook Farm
B3051
OLD LA
Huntsmoor Hill
The Ship (PH)
CHAPEL LA
Ashford Hill
Chippings Gully
Old Farm
HILLHOUSE LA
Sch
B3051
62
53
54
55
D
E
F

134

108

133

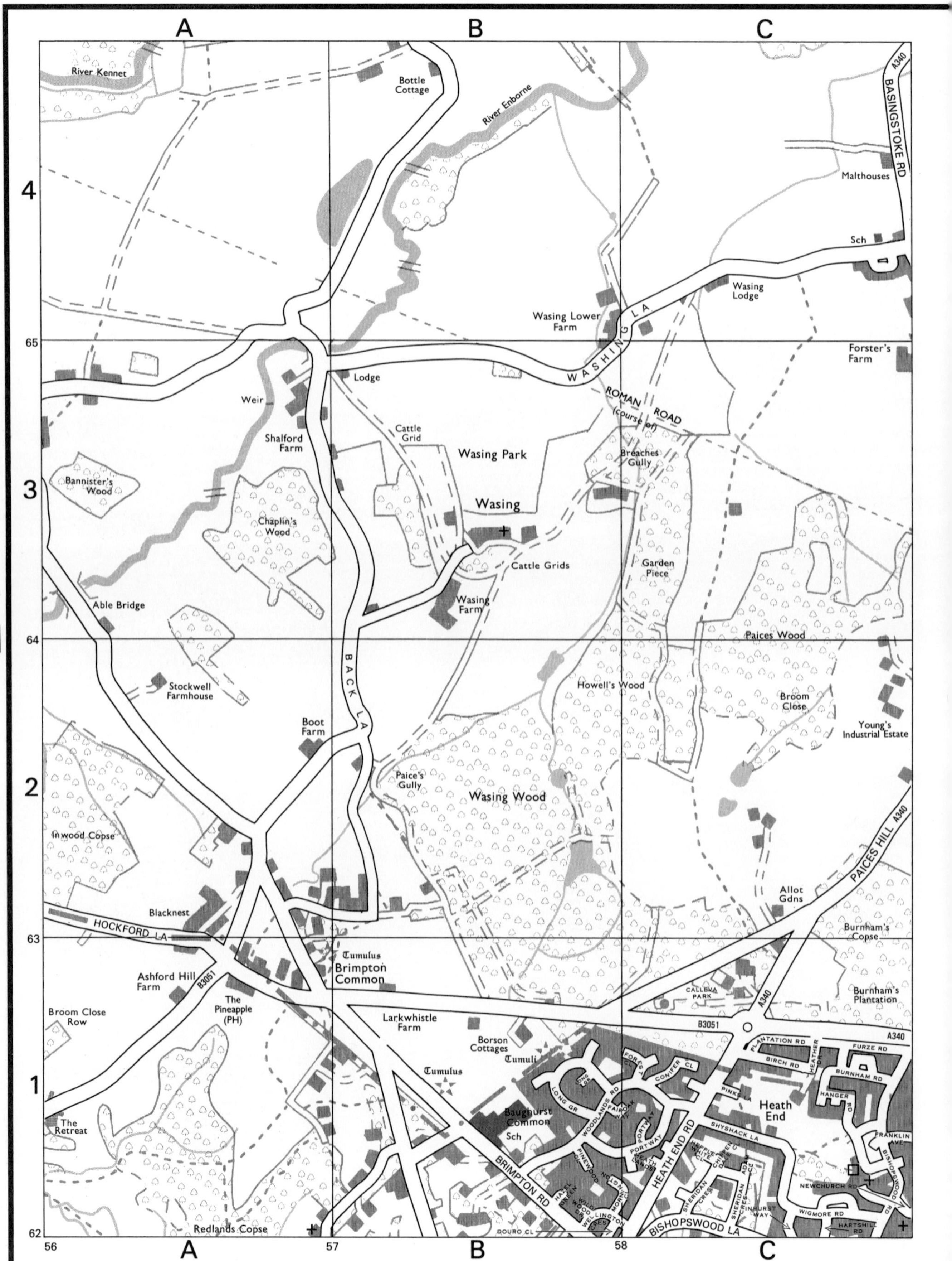

not continued, see key diagram

109

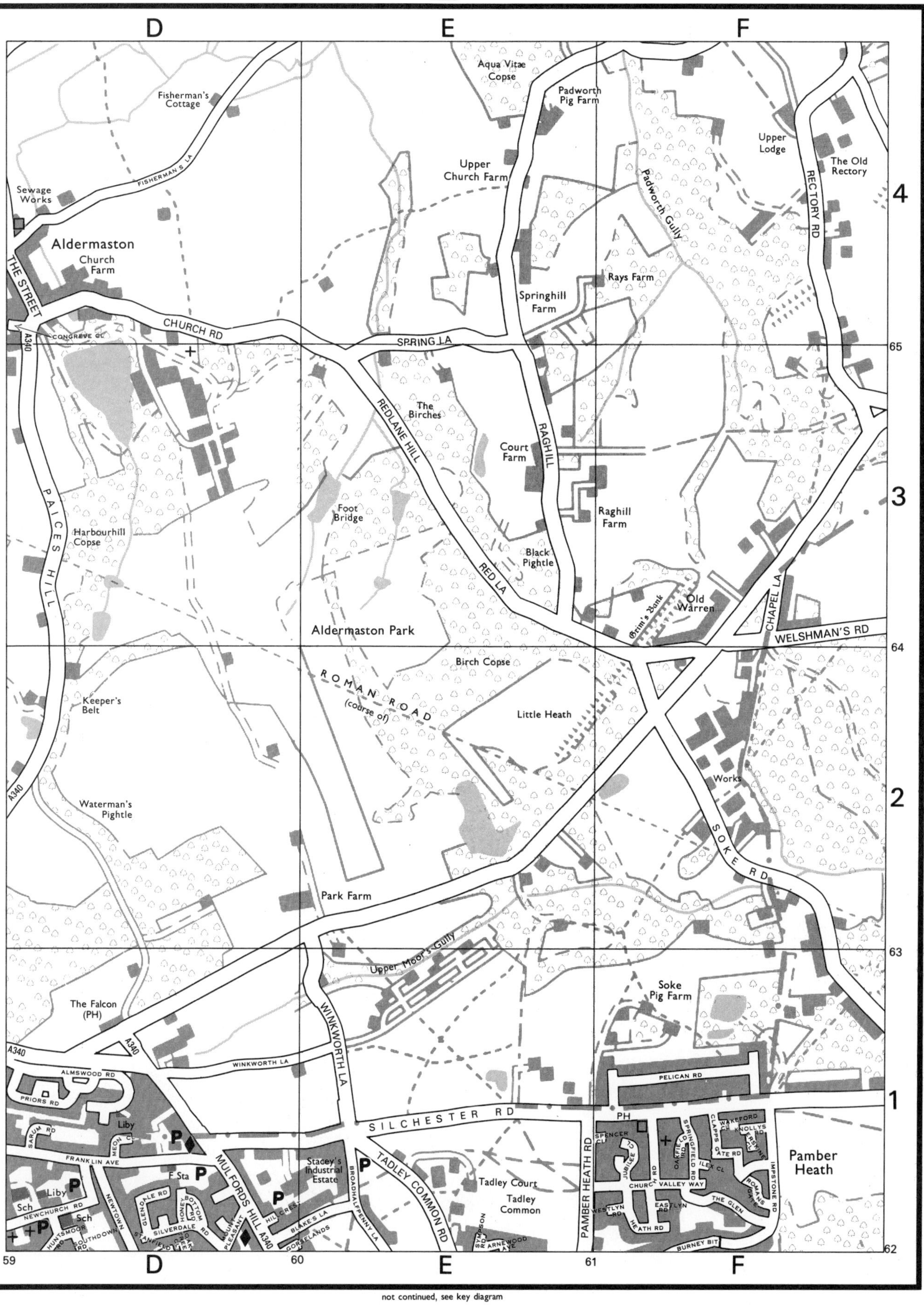
D
E
F
4
3
2
1
65
64
63
62
59
60
61
Aqua Vitae Copse
Fisherman's Cottage
Padworth Pig Farm
Upper Lodge
The Old Rectory
Upper Church Farm
Sewage Works
FISHERMAN'S LA
Padworth Gully
RECTORY RD
Aldermaston
Church Farm
THE STREET
Rays Farm
Springhill Farm
CHURCH RD
CONGREVE CL
A340
SPRING LA
REDLANE HILL
The Birches
Court Farm
RAGHILL
PAICES HILL
Foot Bridge
Raghill Farm
Harbourhill Copse
Black Pightle
RED LA
CHAPEL LA
Old Warren
Grim's Bank
Aldermaston Park
WELSHMAN'S RD
Birch Copse
ROMAN ROAD
(course of)
Keeper's Belt
Little Heath
Works
Waterman's Pightle
SOKE RD
Park Farm
Upper Moor's Gully
Soke Pig Farm
The Falcon (PH)
WINKWORTH LA
ALMSWOOD RD
PELICAN RD
PRIORS RD
SILCHESTER RD
PH
Liby
SARUM RD
MEON CL
FRANKLIN AVE
MULFORDS HILL
F Sta
Stacey's Industrial Estate
TADLEY COMMON RD
Tadley Court
Tadley Common
PAMBER HEATH RD
SPENCER CL
JUBILEE CL
OAKFIELD RD
SPRINGFIELD RD
CLAPPS GATE RD
WAKEFORD CL
KNOLLYS RD
ILEX CL
ROMANS GATE
IMPSTONE RD
Pamber Heath
CHURCH VALLEY WAY
THE GLEN
EASTLYN RD
WESTLYN RD
HEATH RD
BURNEY BIT
Sch
NEWCHURCH RD
HUNTSMOOR RD
SOUTHDOWN RD
NEWTOWN
SILVERDALE RD
HONEY BOTTOM RD
MOUNT PLEASANT
HILL CREST
BLAKE'S LA
GORSELANDS
BROADHALFPENNY LA
ARNEWOOD AVE
SIMPSON RD

136

110

135

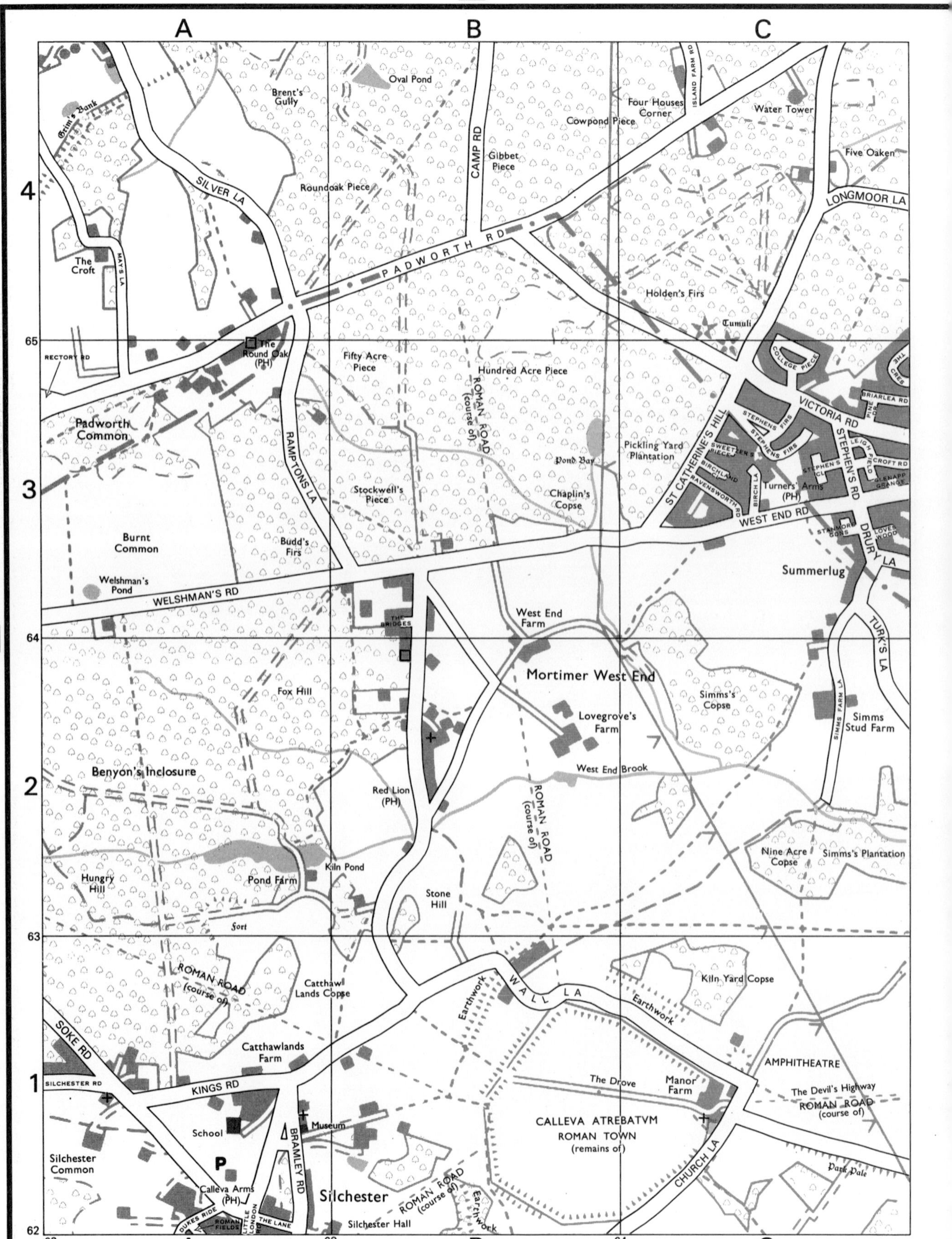

A
B
C
4
3
2
1
65
64
63
62
62
63
64
Grim's Bank
Brent's Gully
Oval Pond
Four Houses Corner
ISLAND FARM RD
Cowpond Piece
Water Tower
Five Oaken
CAMP RD
Gibbet Piece
SILVER LA
Roundoak Piece
LONGMOOR LA
The Croft
MAYS LA
PADWORTH RD
Holden's Firs
Tumuli
RECTORY RD
The Round Oak (PH)
Fifty Acre Piece
Hundred Acre Piece
COLLEGE PIECE
THE CRES
BRIARLEA RD
PINE RD
VICTORIA RD
ROMAN ROAD (course of)
Padworth Common
RAMPTONS LA
Pickling Yard Plantation
ST CATHERINE'S HILL
STEPHENS FIRS
SWEETZEN'S PIECE
BIRCHLAND
STEPHEN'S RD
LEIGH FIELD
CROFT RD
GLENAPP GRANGE
Pond Bay
Chaplin's Copse
RAVENSWORTH RD
BIRCH LA
Turners' Arms (PH)
Stockwell's Piece
WEST END RD
STANMORE
LOVES WOOD
DRURY LA
Burnt Common
Budd's Firs
Summerlug
Welshman's Pond
WELSHMAN'S RD
THE BRIDGES
West End Farm
TURK'S LA
Mortimer West End
Fox Hill
Simms's Copse
Lovegrove's Farm
SIMMS FARM LA
Simms Stud Farm
Benyon's Inclosure
West End Brook
Red Lion (PH)
ROMAN ROAD (course of)
Nine Acre Copse
Simms's Plantation
Hungry Hill
Kiln Pond
Pond Farm
Stone Hill
Fort
ROMAN ROAD (course of)
Catthaw Lands Copse
Earthwork
WALL LA
Kiln Yard Copse
Earthwork
SOKE RD
Catthawlands Farm
AMPHITHEATRE
SILCHESTER RD
KINGS RD
The Drove
Manor Farm
The Devil's Highway
ROMAN ROAD (course of)
School
Museum
BRAMLEY RD
CALLEVA ATREBATVM
ROMAN TOWN
(remains of)
Silchester Common
P
Calleva Arms (PH)
CHURCH LA
Park Pale
Silchester
ROMAN ROAD (course of)
Earthwork
DUKES RIDE
ROMAN FIELDS
LITTLE LONDON RD
THE LANE
Silchester Hall

111

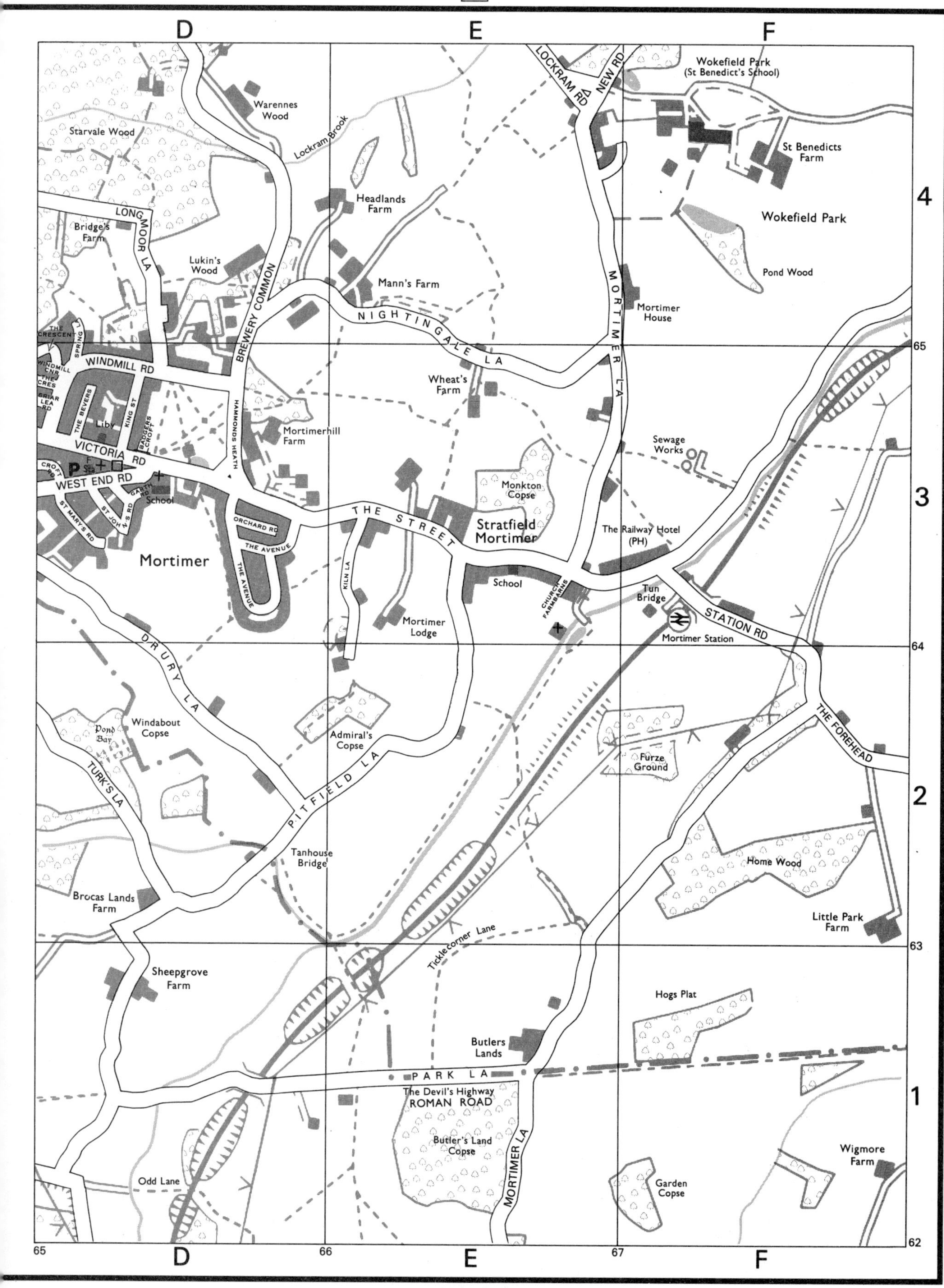
D
E
F
Warennes Wood
Starvale Wood
Lockram Brook
LOCKRAM RD
NEW RD
Wokefield Park (St Benedict's School)
St Benedicts Farm
Headlands Farm
Wokefield Park
LONG MOOR LA
Bridge's Farm
Lukin's Wood
BREWERY COMMON
Mann's Farm
Pond Wood
MORTIMER LA
Mortimer House
NIGHTINGALE LA
THE CRESCENT
SPRING LA
WINDMILL RD
THE BEVERS
KING ST
BADGERS CROFT
Wheat's Farm
Liby
HAMMONDS HEATH
Mortimerhill Farm
VICTORIA RD
Sewage Works
WEST END RD
GARTH RD
CROFT RD
Sta
School
ST MARY'S RD
ST JOHN'S RD
ORCHARD RD
THE AVENUE
THE STREET
Monkton Copse
Stratfield Mortimer
The Railway Hotel (PH)
Mortimer
KILN LA
School
CHURCH FARMBARNS
Tun Bridge
STATION RD
Mortimer Station
Mortimer Lodge
DRURY LA
Windabout Copse
Pond Bay
Admiral's Copse
THE FOREHEAD
Furze Ground
TURK'S LA
PITFIELD LA
Tanhouse Bridge
Home Wood
Brocas Lands Farm
Little Park Farm
Ticklecorner Lane
Sheepgrove Farm
Hogs Plat
Butlers Lands
PARK LA
The Devil's Highway ROMAN ROAD
Butler's Land Copse
MORTIMER LA
Wigmore Farm
Odd Lane
Garden Copse
4
3
2
1
65
64
63
62
65
66
67

138

112

137

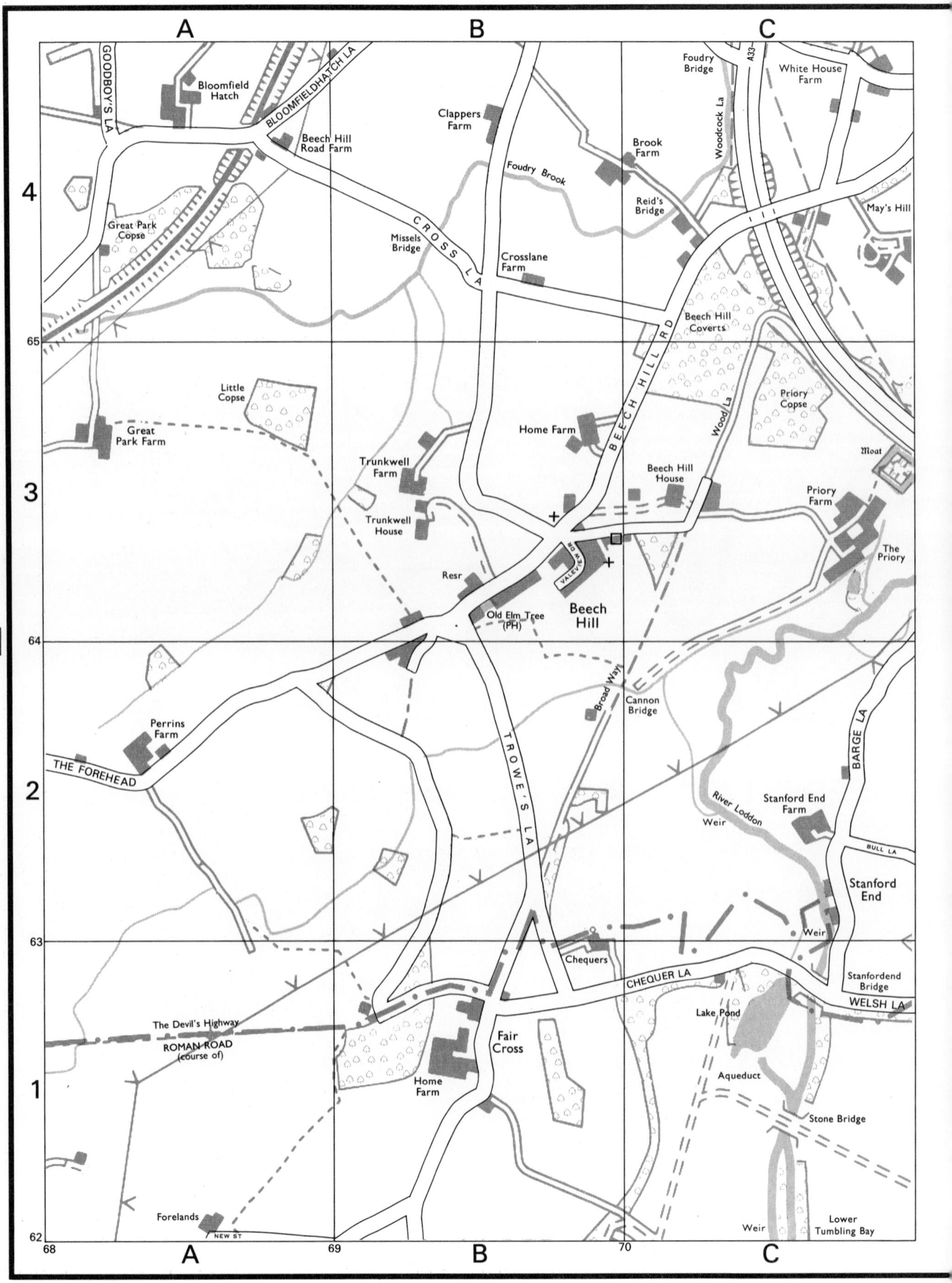

not continued, see key diagram

113

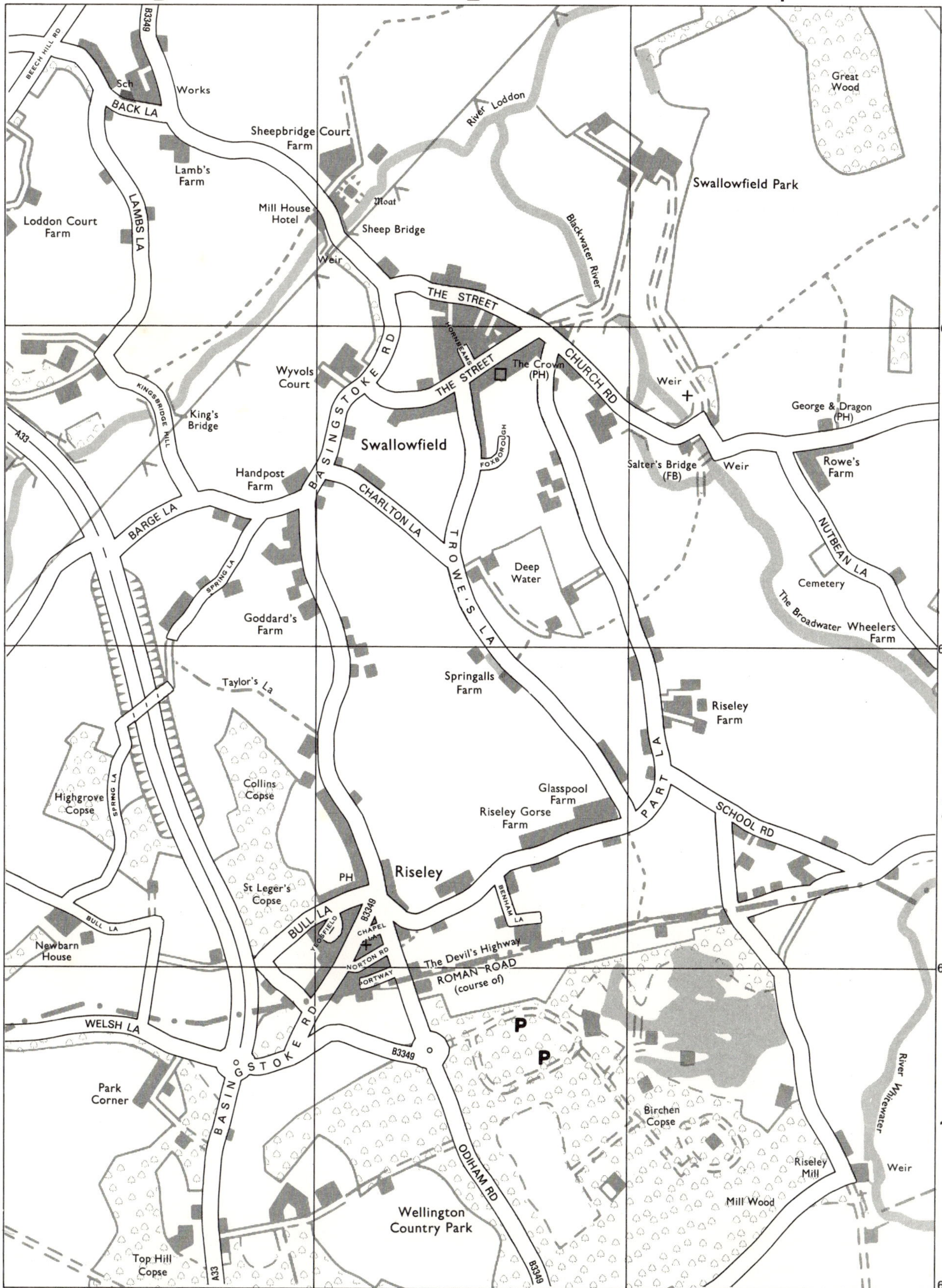

140

not continued, see key diagram

114

139

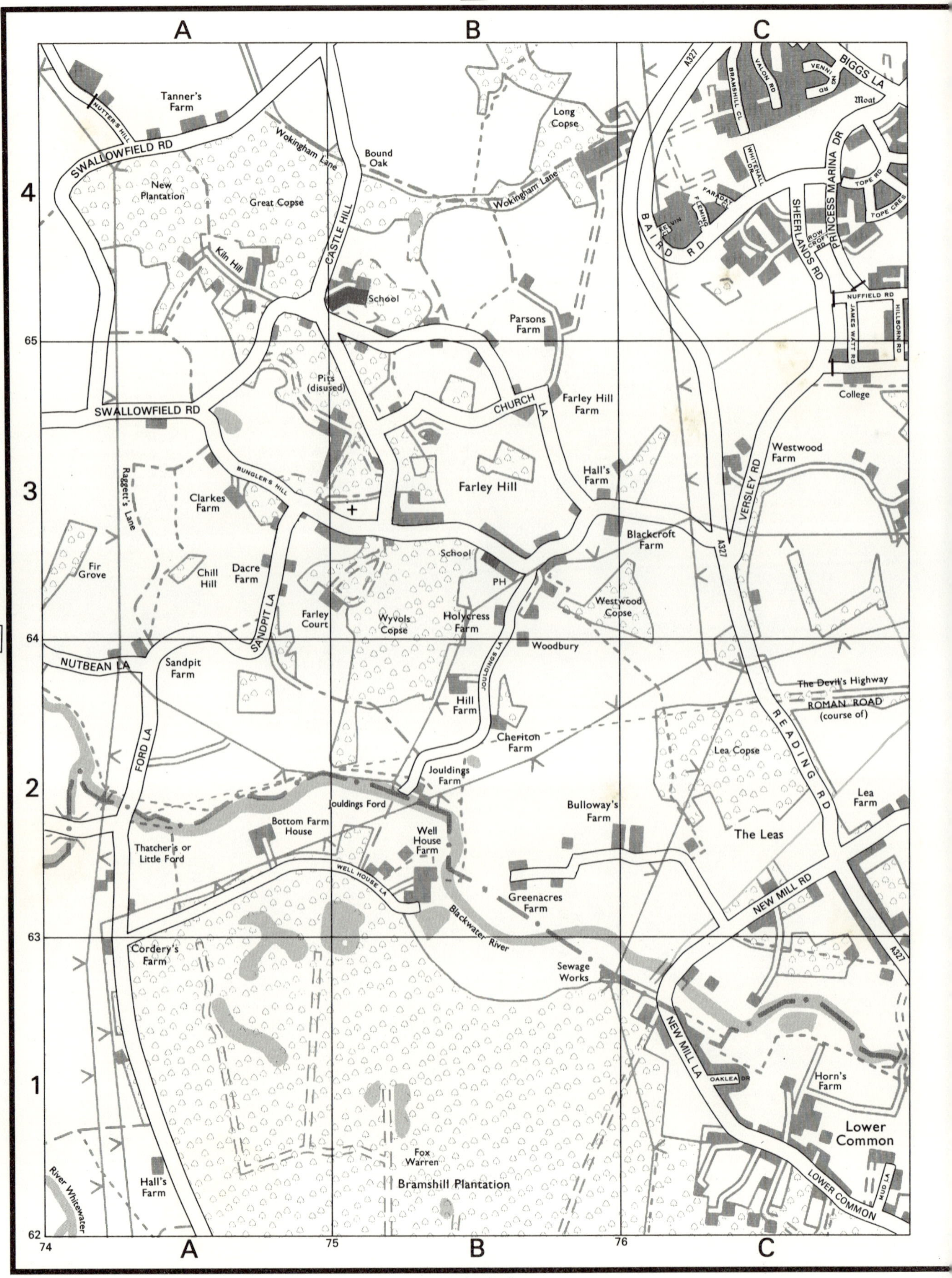

not continued, see key diagram

115

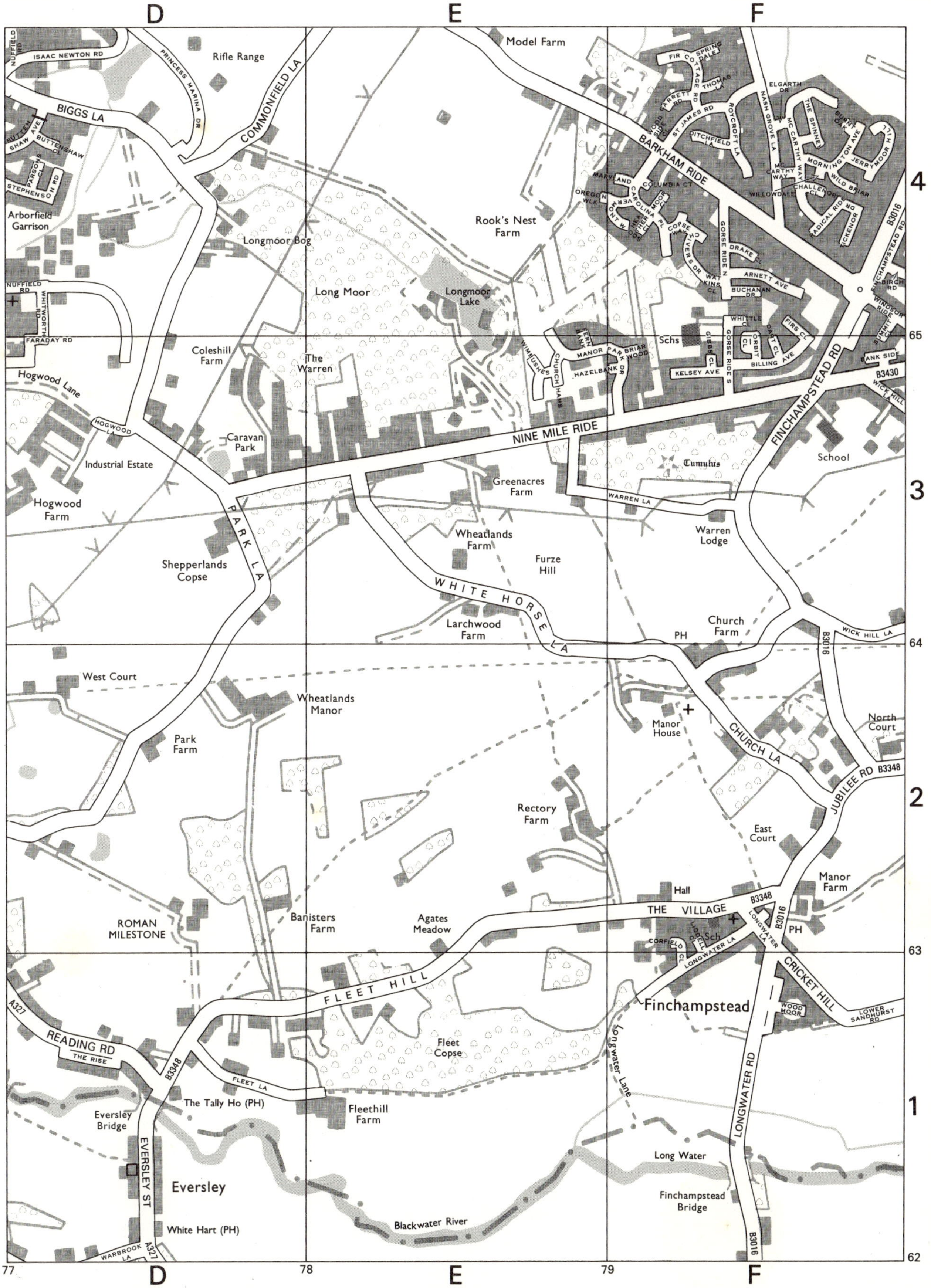

D
E
F
Model Farm
Rifle Range
ISAAC NEWTON RD
PRINCESS MARINA DR
COMMONFIELD LA
BIGGS LA
Arborfield Garrison
Longmoor Bog
Long Moor
Longmoor Lake
Rook's Nest Farm
BARKHAM RIDE
Schs
Coleshill Farm
The Warren
Hogwood Lane
HOGWOOD LA
Caravan Park
Industrial Estate
Hogwood Farm
NINE MILE RIDE
FINCHAMPSTEAD RD
School
Cumulus
Greenacres Farm
WARREN LA
Warren Lodge
PARK LA
Shepperlands Copse
Wheatlands Farm
Furze Hill
WHITE HORSE LA
Larchwood Farm
Church Farm
PH
WICK HILL LA
West Court
Wheatlands Manor
Park Farm
Manor House
CHURCH LA
North Court
JUBILEE RD
B3348
Rectory Farm
East Court
Manor Farm
Hall
THE VILLAGE
B3016
ROMAN MILESTONE
Banisters Farm
Agates Meadow
Sch
CRICKET HILL
FLEET HILL
Finchampstead
LOWER SANDHURST RD
A327
READING RD
THE RISE
Fleet Copse
Longwater Lane
LONGWATER RD
FLEET LA
The Tally Ho (PH)
Fleethill Farm
Eversley Bridge
EVERSLEY ST
Long Water
Eversley
Finchampstead Bridge
Blackwater River
White Hart (PH)
WARBROOK LA
4
3
2
1
65
64
63
62
77
78
79

142

116

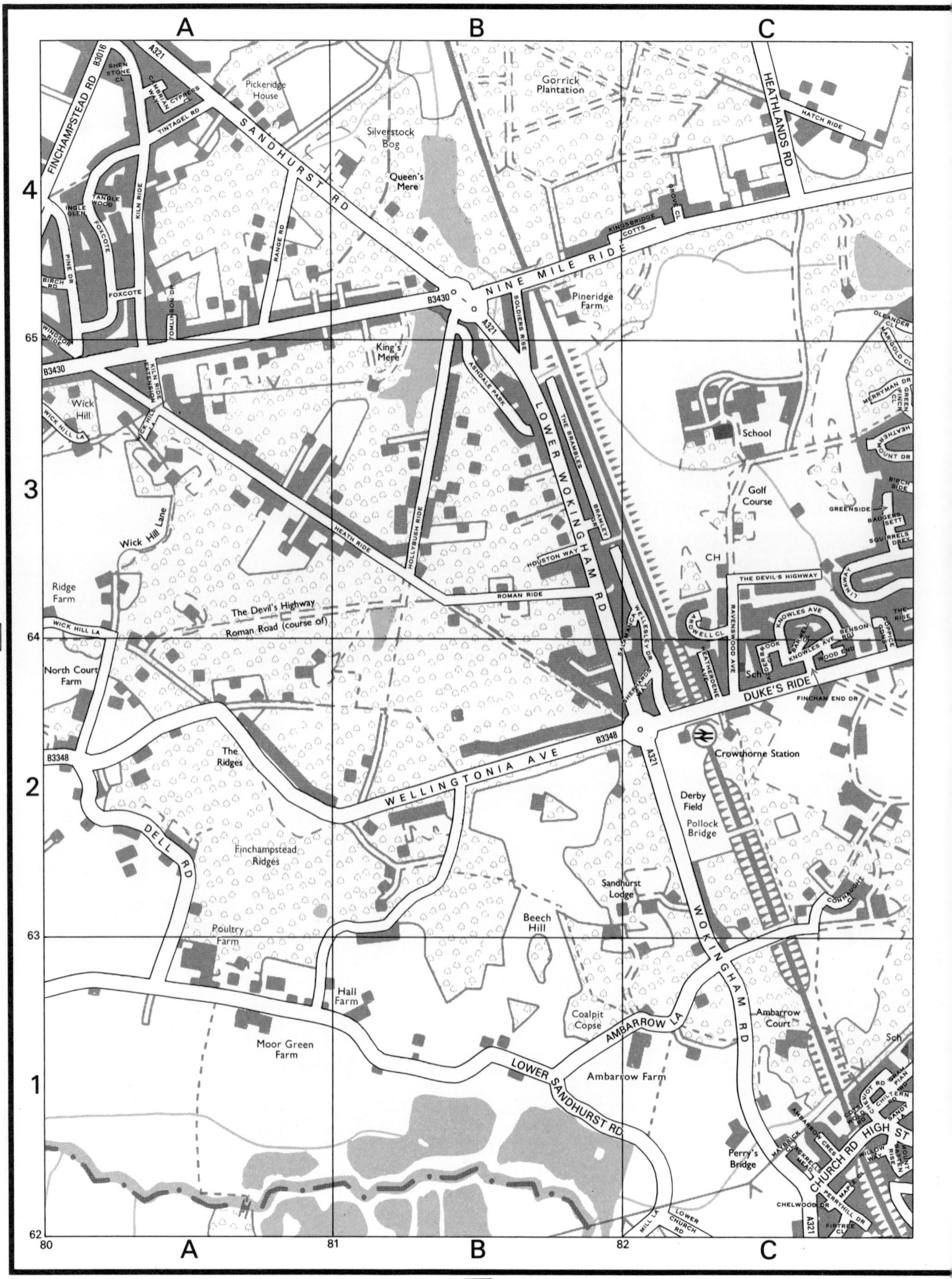

A
B
C
4
3
2
1
65
64
63
62
80
81
82
FINCHAMPSTEAD RD
B3016
A321
SANDHURST RD
Pickeridge House
Silverstock Bog
Queen's Mere
Gorrick Plantation
HEATHLANDS RD
HATCH RIDE
KINGSBRIDGE COTTS
NINE MILE RIDE
B3430
SOLDIERS RISE
Pineridge Farm
TINTAGEL RD
CYPRESS
KILN RIDE
TANGLE WOOD
INGLE GLEN
FOXCOTE
PINE DR
BIRCH RD
RANGE RD
TOMLINSON DR
WINDSOR RIDE
KILN RIDE EXTENSION
King's Mere
ASHDALE PARK
LOWER WOKINGHAM RD
THE BRAMBLES
Wick Hill
WICK HILL LA
School
Golf Course
CH
HEATH RIDE
HOLLYBUSH RIDE
HOUSTON WAY
ROMAN RIDE
Wick Hill Lane
Ridge Farm
The Devil's Highway
Roman Road (course of)
THE DEVIL'S HIGHWAY
RAVENSWOOD AVE
KNOWLES AVE
WOOD END
DUKE'S RIDE
FINCHAM END DR
WELLESLEY DR
SHEPPARDS WAY
HEATHERDENE AVE
North Court Farm
B3348
WELLINGTONIA AVE
Crowthorne Station
Derby Field
Pollock Bridge
The Ridges
DELL RD
Finchampstead Ridges
Sandhurst Lodge
Beech Hill
WOKINGHAM RD
Poultry Farm
Hall Farm
Coalpit Copse
AMBARROW LA
Ambarrow Court
Moor Green Farm
LOWER SANDHURST RD
Ambarrow Farm
Perry's Bridge
CHURCH RD
HIGH ST
AMBARROW CRES
CHELWOOD DR
PERRYHILL DR
MILL LA
LOWER CHURCH RD
Sch

141

149

117

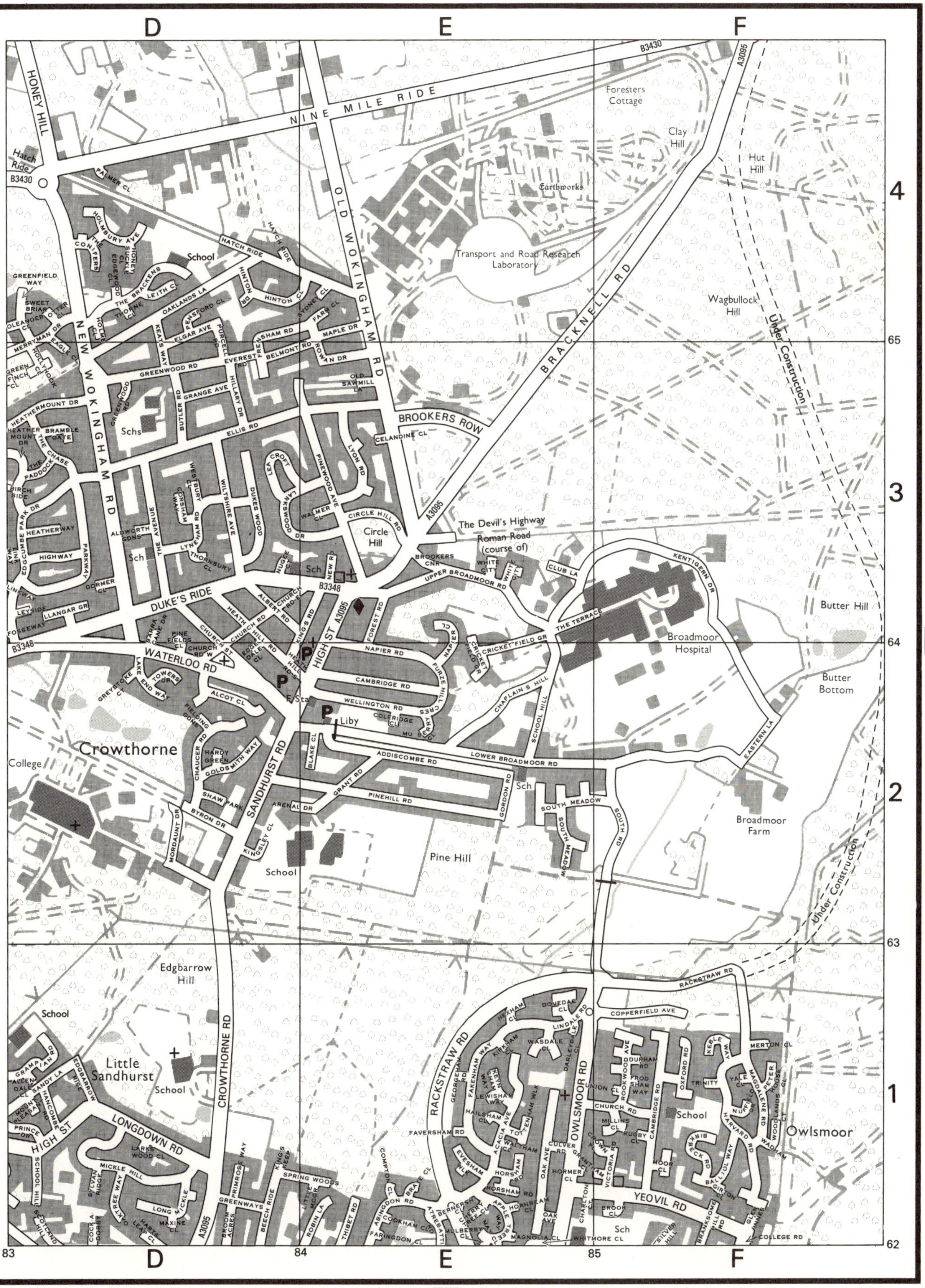
D
E
F
NINE MILE RIDE
B3430
HONEY HILL
Hatch Ride
Foresters Cottage
Clay Hill
Hut Hill
Earthworks
Transport and Road Research Laboratory
OLD WOKINGHAM RD
BRACKNELL RD
A3095
Wagbullock Hill
Under Construction
4
65
School
HATCH RIDE
NEW WOKINGHAM RD
BROOKERS ROW
Schs
Sch
3
The Devil's Highway Roman Road (course of)
Circle Hill
BROOKERS CNR
UPPER BROADMOOR RD
KENTIGERN DR
THE TERRACE
Butter Hill
DUKE'S RIDE
B3348
WATERLOO RD
HIGH ST
NAPIER RD
CAMBRIDGE RD
WELLINGTON RD
CRICKET FIELD GR
Broadmoor Hospital
64
144
Butter Bottom
F Sta
Liby
Crowthorne
College
ADDISCOMBE RD
LOWER BROADMOOR RD
EASTERN LA
SANDHURST RD
PINEHILL RD
GORDON RD
SOUTH MEADOW
SOUTH RD
2
Broadmoor Farm
Pine Hill
School
63
Edgbarrow Hill
School
RACKSTRAW RD
COPPERFIELD AVE
CROWTHORNE RD
OWLSMOOR RD
Little Sandhurst
School
1
Owlsmoor
School
LONGDOWN RD
HIGH ST
YEOVIL RD
Sch
COLLEGE RD
83
84
85
62

150

118

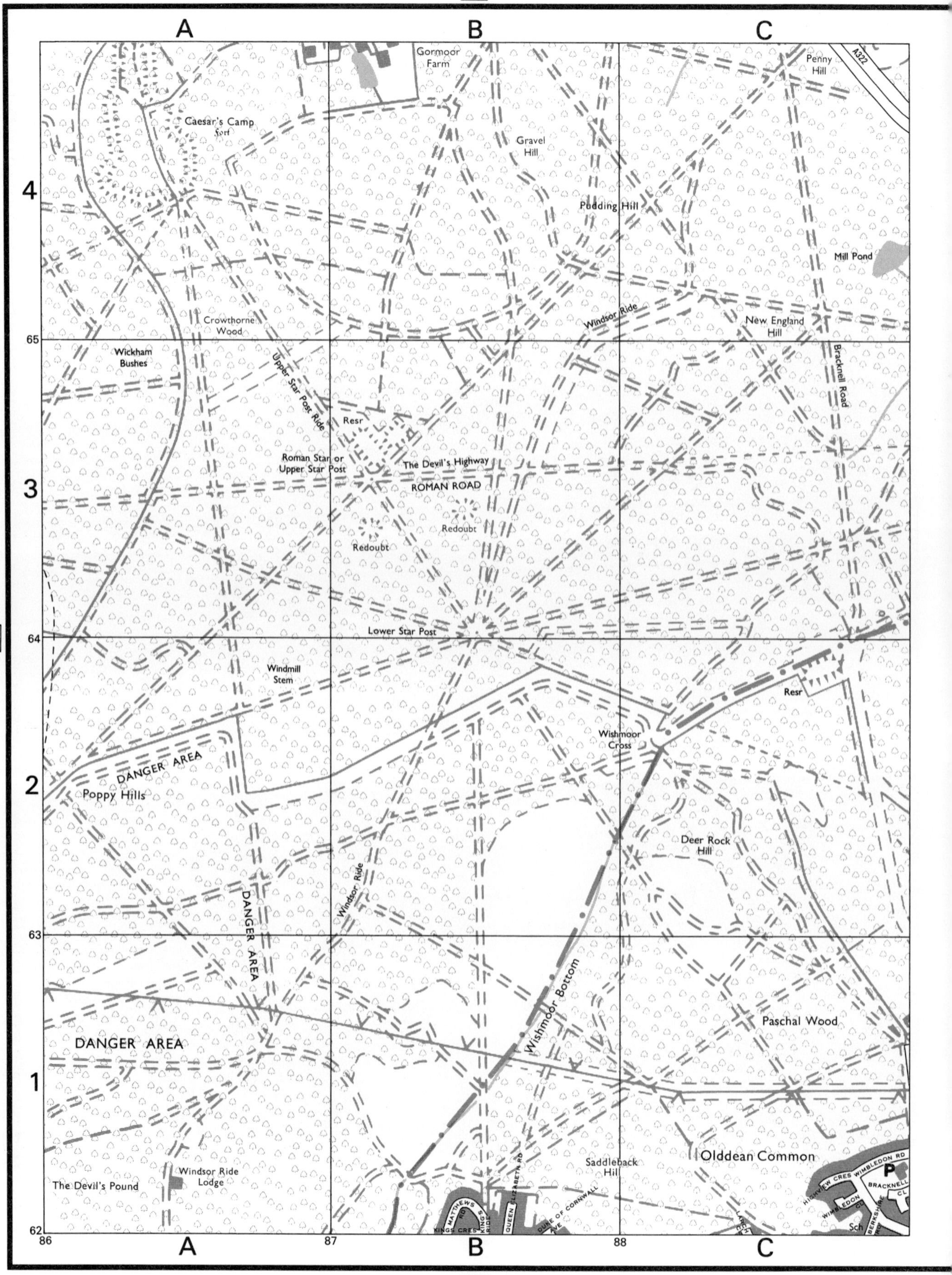
A
B
C
4
3
2
1
65
64
63
62
86
87
88
Gormoor Farm
Penny Hill
A322
Caesar's Camp
fort
Gravel Hill
Pudding Hill
Mill Pond
Windsor Ride
New England Hill
Crowthorne Wood
Wickham Bushes
Upper Star Post Ride
Bracknell Road
Resr
Roman Star or Upper Star Post
The Devil's Highway
ROMAN ROAD
Redoubt
Redoubt
Lower Star Post
Windmill Stem
Resr
Wishmoor Cross
DANGER AREA
Poppy Hills
Deer Rock Hill
Windsor Ride
DANGER AREA
Wishmoor Bottom
Paschal Wood
DANGER AREA
Olddean Common
Saddleback Hill
Windsor Ride Lodge
The Devil's Pound
MATTHEWS RD
KINGS CRES
QUEEN ELIZABETH RD
DUKE OF CORNWALL AVE
WIMBLEDON RD
HIGHVIEW CRES
BRACKNELL
WIMBLEDON CL
BERKSHIRE
P
Sch

143

151

119

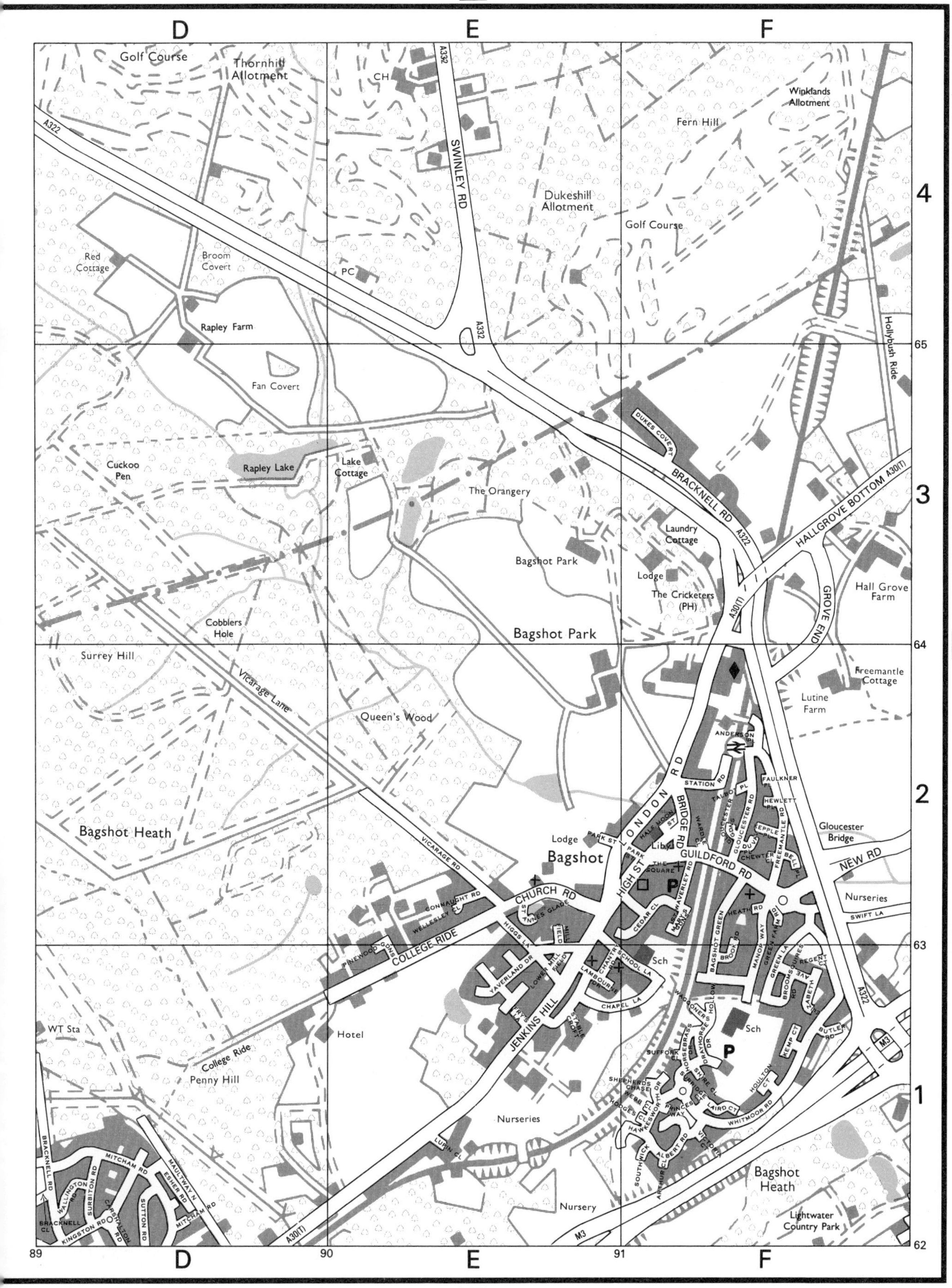
D
E
F
Golf Course
Thornhill Allotment
CH
A332
SWINLEY RD
Winklands Allotment
Fern Hill
A322
4
Dukeshill Allotment
Golf Course
Red Cottage
Broom Covert
PC
Rapley Farm
A332
Hollybush Ride
65
Fan Covert
DUKES COVERT
Cuckoo Pen
Rapley Lake
Lake Cottage
The Orangery
BRACKNELL RD
HALLGROVE BOTTOM A30(T)
3
A322
Laundry Cottage
Bagshot Park
Lodge
The Cricketers (PH)
A30(T)
GROVE END
Hall Grove Farm
Cobblers Hole
Bagshot Park
64
Surrey Hill
Vicarage Lane
Freemantle Cottage
Lutine Farm
Queen's Wood
ANDERSON
STATION RD
LONDON RD
BRIDGE RD
FAULKNER
HEWLETT PL
2
Gloucester Bridge
Bagshot Heath
VICARAGE RD
Lodge
PARK ST
Liby
GUILDFORD RD
NEW RD
Bagshot
HIGH ST
THE SQUARE
Nurseries
CHURCH RD
CONNAUGHT RD
WELLESLEY CL
ST ANNES GLADE
CEDAR CL
SWIFT LA
HIGGS LA
HEATH RD
63
PINEWOOD GDNS
COLLEGE RIDE
YAVERLAND DR
LOWER MILL FIELD
LAMBOURNE DR
SCHOOL LA
Sch
BAGSHOT GREEN
BROOK RD
MANOR WAY
GREEN LA
BROOMSQUIRES RD
REGENT CT
JENKINS HILL
CHAPEL LA
WAGGONERS HOLLOW
A322
WT Sta
Hotel
Sch
BUTLER RD
M3
College Ride
Penny Hill
SUFFOLK CL
P
KEMP CT
HOULTON CT
1
SHEPHERDS CHASE
LAIRD CT
WHITMOOR RD
Nurseries
HAWKESWORTH DR
ALBERT RD
VICTORIA CT
BRACKNELL RD
MITCHAM RD
MAULTWAY N
ESHER RD
SURBITON RD
WALLINGTON RD
CARSHALTON RD
SUTTON RD
MITCHAM RD
BRACKNELL CL
KINGSTON RD
LUPIN CL
SOUTHWICK
ARTHUR CL
Bagshot Heath
Nursery
Lightwater Country Park
A30(T)
M3
62
89
90
91
D
E
F

146

152

120

145

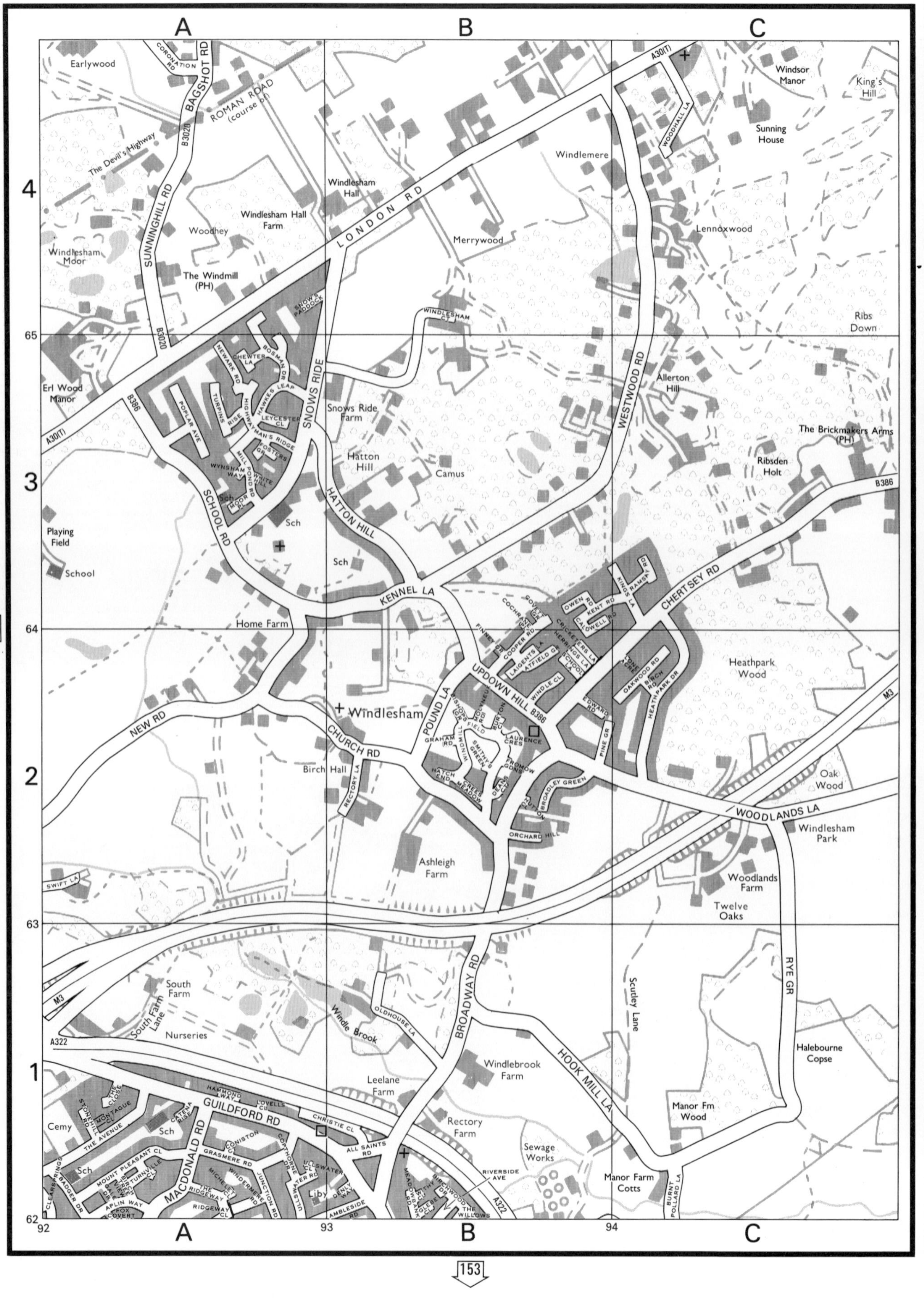
A
B
C
4
3
2
1
65
64
63
62
92
93
94
Earlywood
CORONATION RD
BAGSHOT RD
ROMAN ROAD (course of)
The Devil's Highway
B3020
SUNNINGHILL RD
Windlesham Moor
Woodhey
Windlesham Hall Farm
Windlesham Hall
The Windmill (PH)
LONDON RD
A30(T)
WOODHALL LA
Windsor Manor
King's Hill
Sunning House
Windlemere
Merrywood
Lennoxwood
Ribs Down
WINDLESHAM CT
SNOWS PADDOCK
Erl Wood Manor
B386
NEWARK RD
CHEWTER LA
BOSMAN DR
HAWKES LEAP
HIGHWAYMAN'S RIDGE
LEYCESTER CL
TURPINS RISE
POPLAR AVE
FOSTERS GR
MILL POND RD
WYNSHAM WAY
WHITE HILL
MOOR CL
SNOWS RIDE
Snows Ride Farm
Hatton Hill
Camus
WESTWOOD RD
Allerton Hill
The Brickmakers Arms (PH)
Ribsden Holt
SCHOOL RD
Sch
Playing Field
School
HATTON HILL
KENNEL LA
Home Farm
CHERTSEY RD
RAMSAY RD
KINGS LA
OWEN RD
KENT RD
CALDWELL RD
COCHRANE PL
CRICKETERS LA
HERRINGS LA
COOPER RD
FINNEY DR
LAIGENTS LA
ATFIELD GR
SCHOOL LA
WINDLE CL
UPDOWN HILL
LONE CRES
OAKWOOD RD
BIRCH RD
HEATHPARK DR
EDWARD RD
PINE GR
Heathpark Wood
M3
NEW RD
Windlesham
POUND LA
CHURCH RD
GRAHAM RD
WINDMILL FIELD
SMITHY'S GREEN
LAURENCE CRES
THOROLD GDNS
HATCH END
CREEK MEADOW
BROADLEY GREEN
ORCHARD HILL
Birch Hall
RECTORY LA
Ashleigh Farm
WOODLANDS LA
Oak Wood
Windlesham Park
Woodlands Farm
Twelve Oaks
SWIFT LA
South Farm
South Farm Lane
Nurseries
Windle Brook
OLDHOUSE LA
BROADWAY RD
Scutley Lane
RYE GR
A322
HOOK MILL LA
Halebourne Copse
Windlebrook Farm
Leelane Farm
Rectory Farm
Sewage Works
Manor Fm Wood
Manor Farm Cotts
BURNT POLLARD LA
HAMMOND WAY
LOVELLS CL
GUILDFORD RD
CHRISTIE CL
ALL SAINTS RD
Cemy
STONEHILL RD
THE CLOSE
MONTAGUE CL
CATENA RISE
THE AVENUE
MACDONALD RD
CONISTON CT
GRASMERE RD
COPTHORNE DR
MOUNT PLEASANT CL
Sch
WINDERMERE RD
JUNCTION RD
ULLSWATER RD
Liby
MICHELET CL
THE RIDGEWAY
RIDGEWAY CL
APLIN WAY
FOX COVERT
CLEARSPRINGS
BADGER DR
AMBLESIDE RD
MEADOWBANK
BIRCHWOOD DR
THE WILLOWS
RIVERSIDE AVE

153

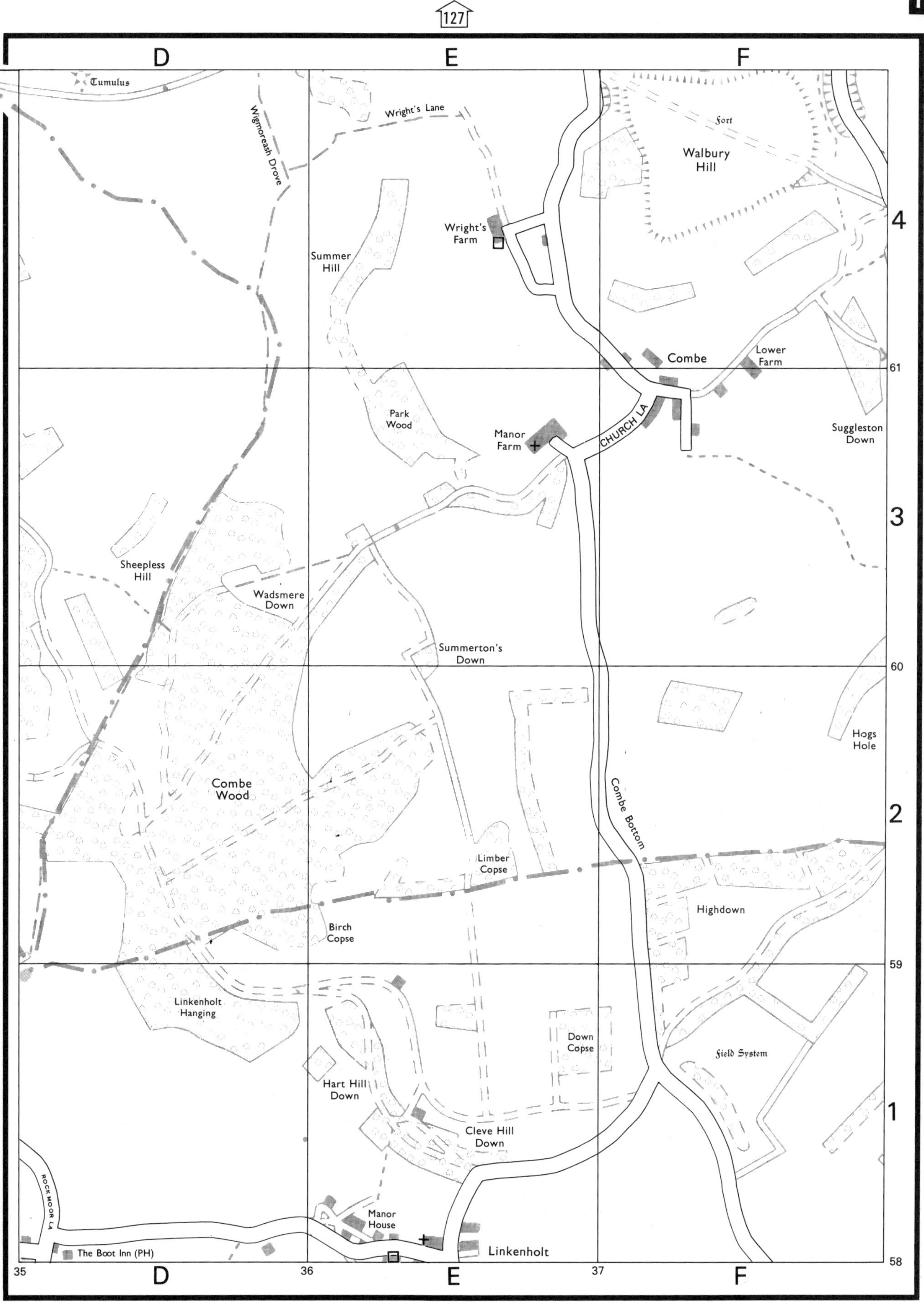

not continued, see key diagram

128

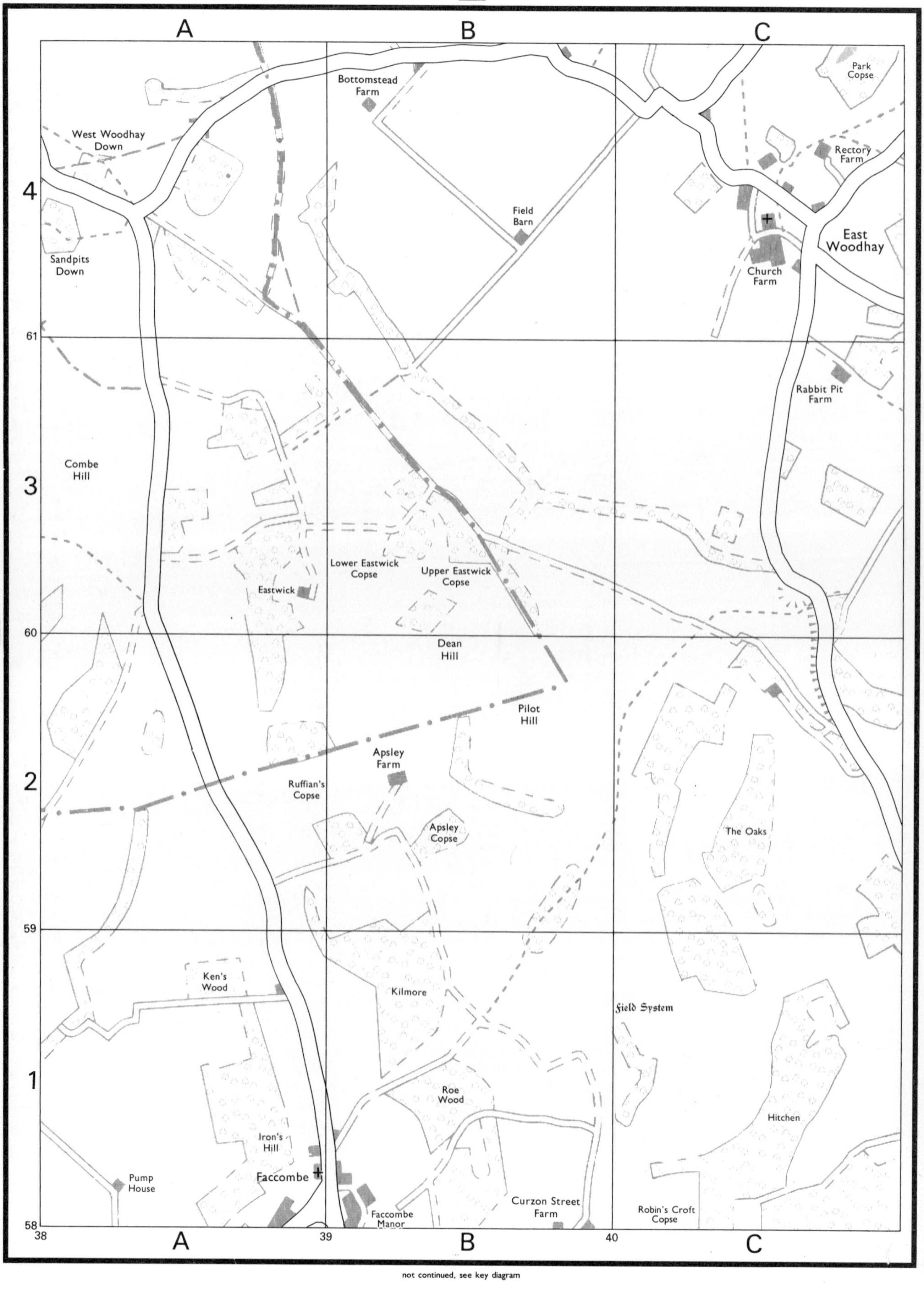

147

not continued, see key diagram

142

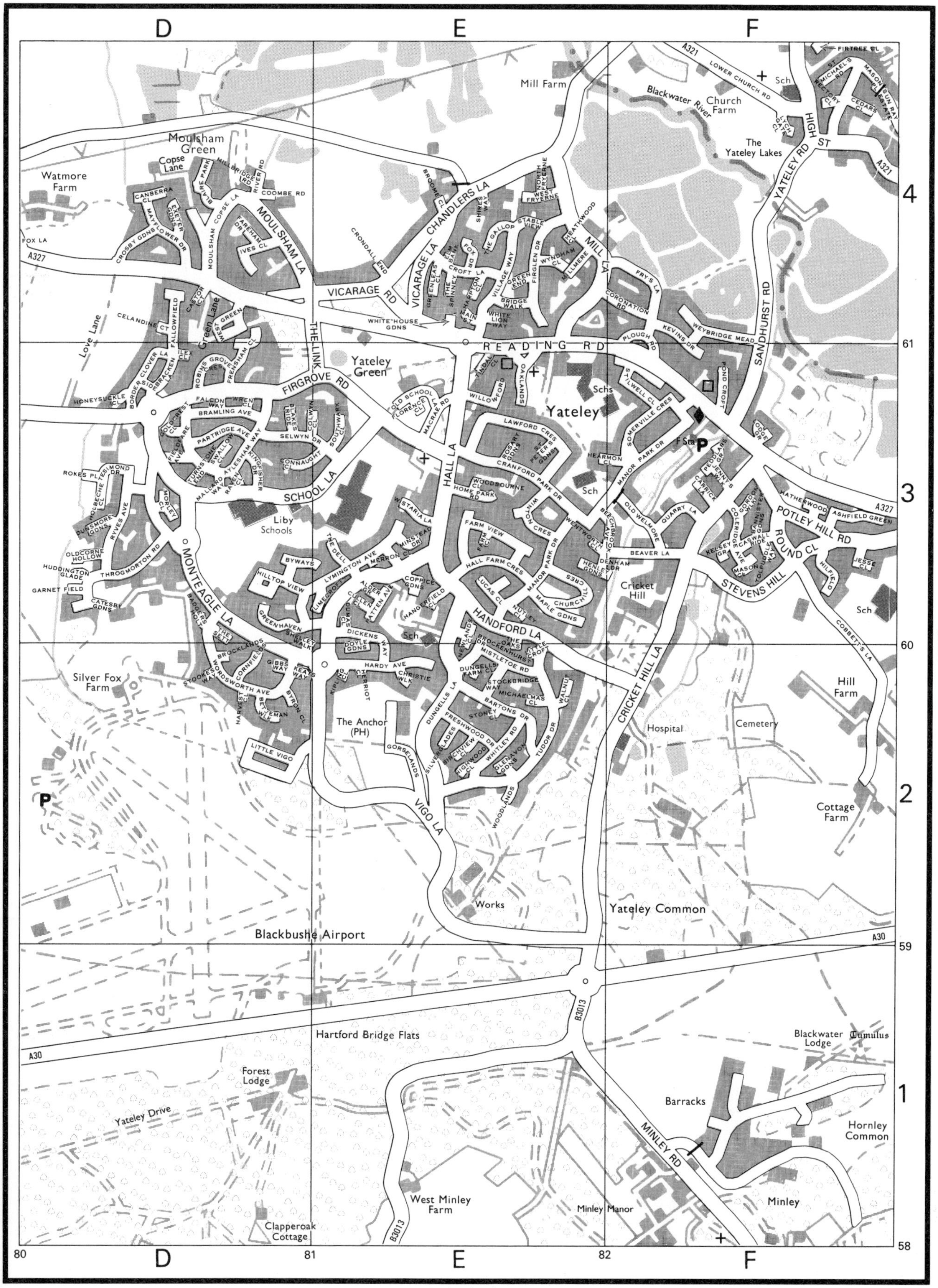

150

not continued, see key diagram

143

149

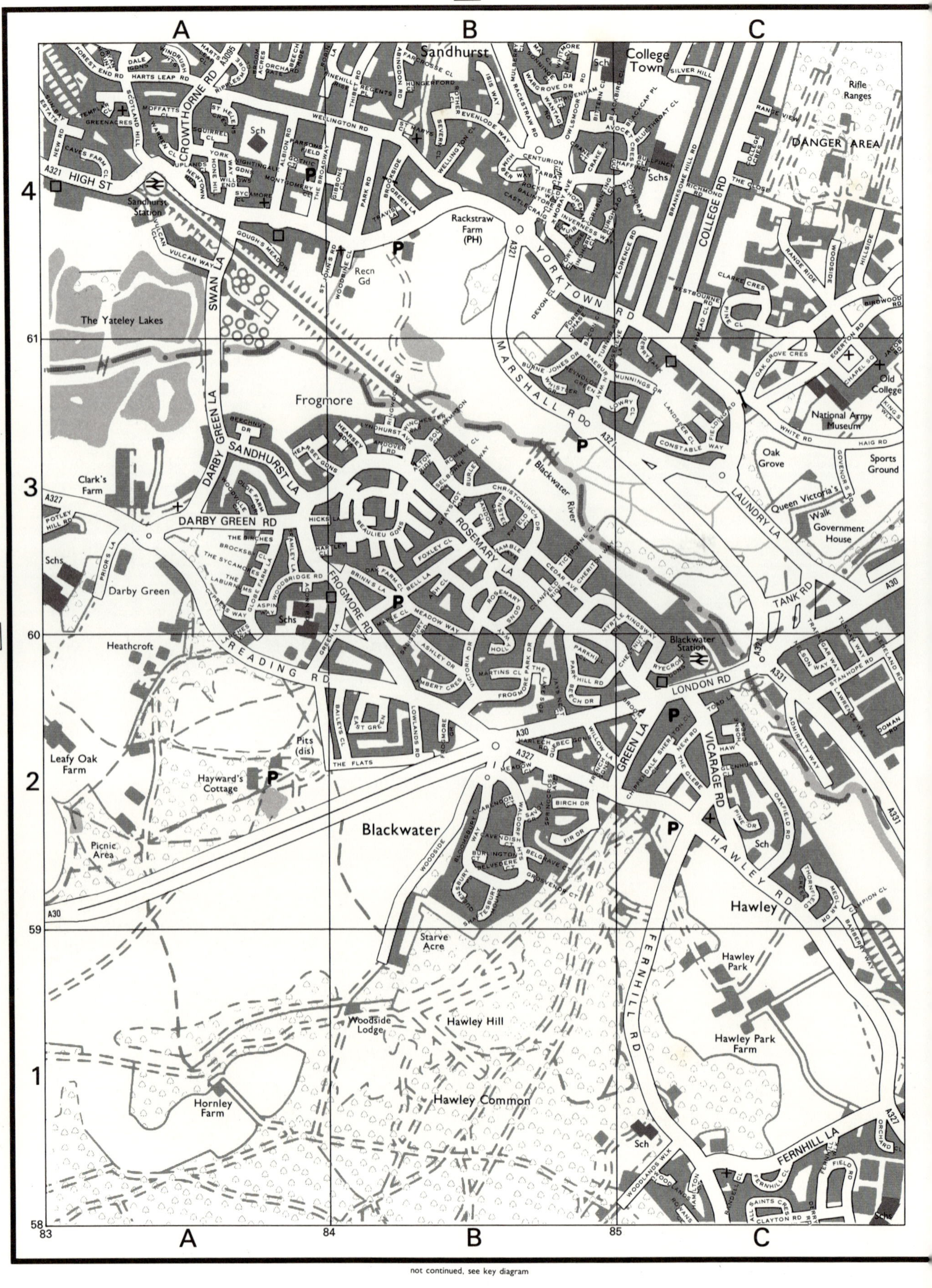
A
B
C
Sandhurst
College Town
Rifle Ranges
DANGER AREA
4
HIGH ST
Sandhurst Station
Sch
Schs
Rackstraw Farm (PH)
Recn Gd
YORKTOWN RD
COLLEGE RD
CROWTHORNE RD
WELLINGTON RD
SWAN LA
The Yateley Lakes
61
Frogmore
MARSHALL RD
Old College
National Army Museum
Oak Grove
Sports Ground
Blackwater River
3
Clark's Farm
DARBY GREEN LA
SANDHURST LA
DARBY GREEN RD
ROSEMARY LA
LAUNDRY LA
Queen Victoria's Walk
Government House
Darby Green
TANK RD
FROGMORE RD
60
Heathcroft
READING RD
Blackwater Station
LONDON RD
A30
A321
A327
A331
Pits (dis)
Leafy Oak Farm
Hayward's Cottage
2
Blackwater
GREEN LA
VICARAGE RD
HAWLEY RD
Picnic Area
Hawley
59
Starve Acre
FERNHILL RD
Hawley Park
Woodside Lodge
Hawley Hill
Hawley Park Farm
1
Hornley Farm
Hawley Common
FERNHILL LA
58
83
84
85

144

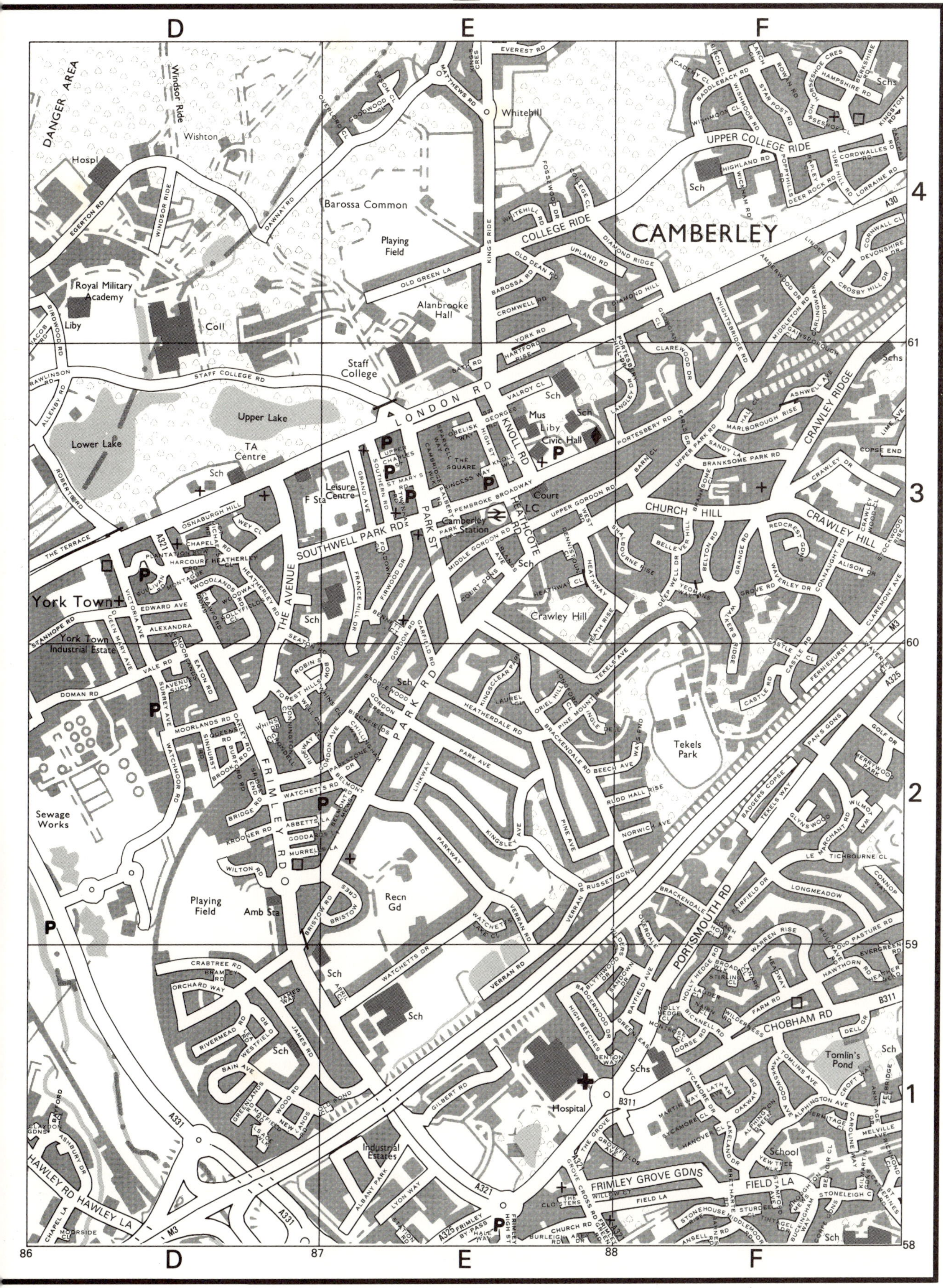

152

not continued, see key diagram

145

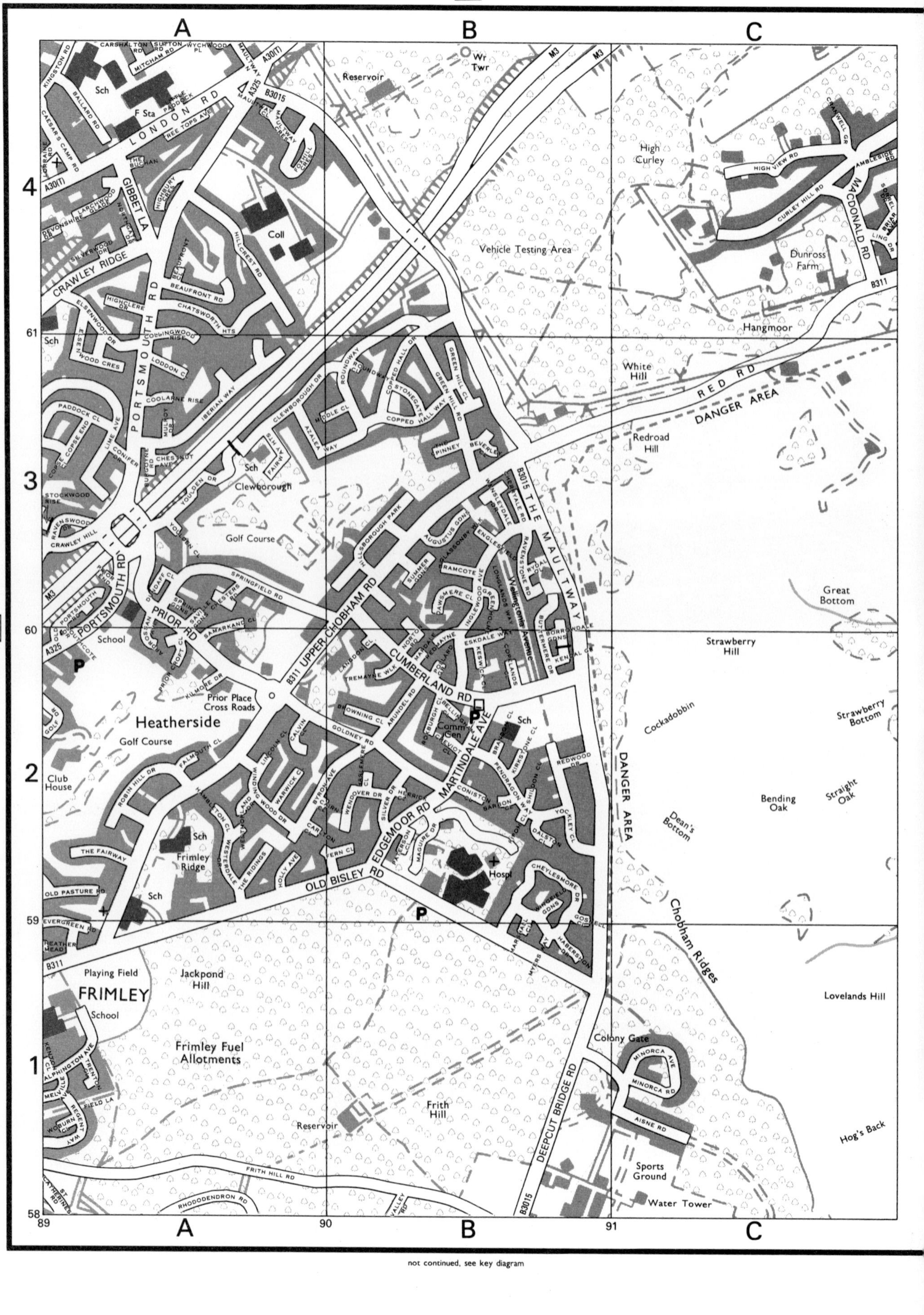
A
B
C
4
3
2
1
61
60
59
58
89
90
91
LONDON RD
GIBBET LA
CRAWLEY RIDGE
PORTSMOUTH RD
CHATSWORTH HTS
BEAUFRONT RD
HILLCREST RD
IBERIAN WAY
Sch
F Sta
Coll
Reservoir
Wr Twr
M3
A30(T)
A325
B3015
Vehicle Testing Area
High Curley
HIGH VIEW RD
CURLEY HILL RD
MACDONALD RD
AMBLESIDE RD
Dunross Farm
B311
Hangmoor
White Hill
RED RD
DANGER AREA
Redroad Hill
CLEWBOROUGH DR
COPPED HALL WAY
GREEN HILL RD
Clewborough
Golf Course
THE MAULTWAY
UPPER CHOBHAM RD
CUMBERLAND RD
SPRINGFIELD RD
PRIOR RD
School
Prior Place Cross Roads
Heatherside
Golf Course
Club House
Comm Cen
MARTINDALE AVE
EDGEMOOR RD
OLD BISLEY RD
Frimley Ridge
Hospl
THE FAIRWAY
Great Bottom
Strawberry Hill
Cockadobbin
Strawberry Bottom
Bending Oak
Straight Oak
Dean's Bottom
Chobham Ridges
Playing Field
FRIMLEY
Jackpond Hill
School
Frimley Fuel Allotments
Lovelands Hill
Colony Gate
MINORCA AVE
MINORCA RD
AISNE RD
DEEPCUT BRIDGE RD
Frith Hill
Reservoir
Hog's Back
Sports Ground
Water Tower
FRITH HILL RD
RHODODENDRON RD

151

146

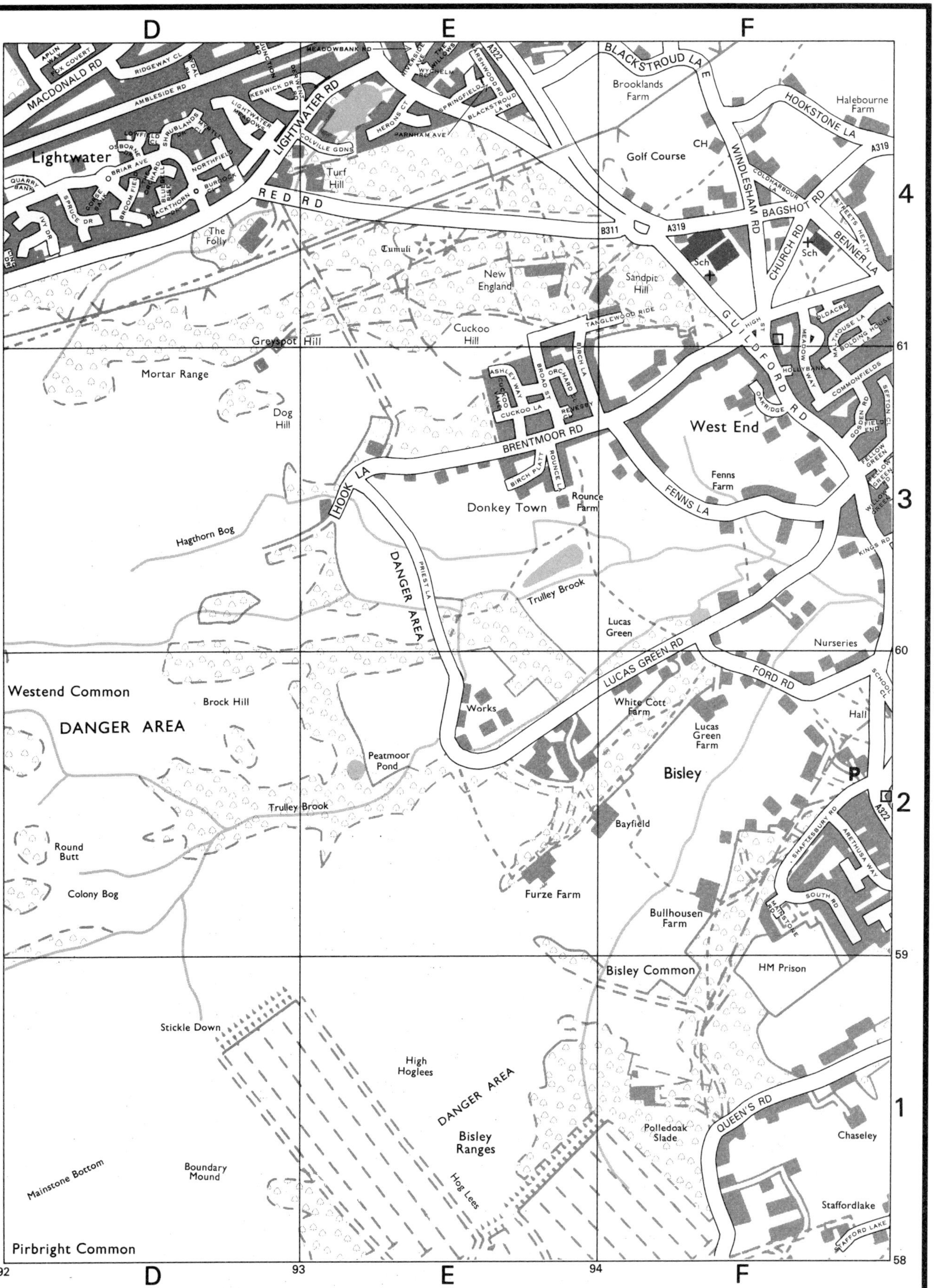

not continued, see key diagram

not continued, see key diagram

EXPLANATION OF THE STREET INDEX REFERENCE SYSTEM

Street names are listed alphabetically and show the locality, the map page number and a reference to the square in which the name falls on the map page.

Example:	Rushey Way. Read...*87* E1
Rushey Way	This is the full street name, which may have been abbreviated on the map.
Read	This is the abbreviation for the town, village or locality in which the street falls.
87	This is the page number of the map on which the street name appears.
E1	The letter and figure indicate the square on the map in which the centre of the street falls. The square can be found at the junction of the vertical column carrying the appropriate letter and the horizontal row carrying the appropriate figure.

ABBREVIATIONS USED IN THE INDEX

Road Names

Approach	App	North	N
Avenue	Ave	Orchard	Orch
Broadway	Bwy	Parade	Par
By-Pass	By-Ps	Passage	Pas
Causeway	Cswy	Place	Pl
Common	Comm	Pleasant	Plea
Corner	Cnr	Precinct	Prec
Cottages	Cotts	Promenade	Prom
Court	Ct	Road	Rd
Crescent	Cres	South	S
Drive	Dri	Square	Sq
Drove	Dro	Street, Saint	St
East	E	Terrace	Terr
Gardens	Gdns	Walk	Wlk
Grove	Gr	West	W
Heights	Hts	Yard	Yd
Lane	La		

Towns, Villages and Rural Localities

Aldermaston .... Alde 135 D4
Aldworth .... Aldw 32 C2
Arborfield .... Arbo 114 B2
Ascot .... Ascot 120 A3
Ashampstead .... Asham 54 A4
Ashford .... Ashf 97 F2
Aston Tirrold .... Ast T 12 C4
Bagshot .... Bags 145 E2
Ball Hill .... Ball H 129 E2
Barkham .... Bark 115 E1
Beech Hill .... Bee H 138 B3
Beedon .... Beed 51 E4
Beenham .... Been 108 C3
Binfield .... Binf 90 B1
Bisham .... Bish 18 C4
Bisley .... Bis 153 F2
Blackwater .... Black 150 B2
Blewbury .... Blew 12 A4
Bourne End .... Bou E 3 D1
Boxford .... Box 76 B2
Bracknell .... Brac 118 C2
Bradfield .... Brad 82 B3
Brightwalton .... Brig 28 C2
Brimpton .... Brim 133 F3
Bucklebury .... Buck 80 C1
Burchett's Green .... Bur G 38 B4
Burghfield Common .... Bur C 110 C1
Burleigh .... Burl 119 E4
Burnham .... Burn 21 E2
Camberley .... Camb 151 F4
Caversham .... Caver 59 E2
Chaddleworth .... Chadd 49 D4
Charvil .... Char 61 D3
Chertsey .... Chert 124 A1
Chieveley .... Chiev 51 D1
Chilton .... Chil 10 C4
Chilton Foliat .... Chil F 72 C1
Cholsey .... Chol 14 A4
Cold Ash .... Cold A 106 B4
Combe .... Combe 147 F4
Compton .... Comp 31 F2
Cookham .... Cook 20 A4
Crowthorne .... Crow 143 D2
Datchet .... Datch 68 B3
Dorney .... Dorn 41 D2
East Garston .... East G 47 E3
East Isley .... East I 30 C3
Englefield .... Eng G 95 E1
Eton .... Eton 67 E4
Farnborough .... Farn 8 C1
Farnham Common .... Far C 22 B3
Fawley .... Fawl 27 E4
Fawley (Bucks) .... Faw (Bu) 15 E4
Feltham .... Felt 98 C4
Finchampstead .... Felt 141 F1
Flackwell Heath .... Fla H 3 D4
Froxfield .... Frox 99 D3
Fulmer .... Fulm 23 E4
Goring .... Gori 34 B3
Great Shefford .... Gr She 48 A2
Greenham .... Gree 131 E4
Ham .... Ham 126 B1
Hambledon .... Hamb 16 B4
Hampstead Norreys .... Hamp N 52 C3
Hamstead Marshall .... Ham M 129 D4
Harlington .... Harl 71 E4
Harmonsworth .... Harm 70 B4
Headley .... Head 132 B1
Henley-On-Thames .... Hen-O-T 15 E1
Hermitage .... Herm 79 D4
Holyport .... Holy 65 D4
Horton .... Hort 69 D2
Hungerford .... Hung 100 C3
Hurley .... Hurl 17 F2
Hurst .... Hurst 88 C3
Inkpen .... Ink 127 E3
Iver .... Iver 44 C4
Iver Heath .... Iver H 23 F2
Kintbury .... Kint 102 A1
Knowl Hill .... Know H 37 F2
Lambourn .... Lamb 25 E1
Leckhampstead .... Leckh 50 A3
Letcombe Bassett .... Let B 6 C4
Lightwater .... Light 153 D4
Linkenholt .... Link 147 E1
Little Marlow .... Lit M 2 B3
Maidenhead .... Maid 39 F2
Mapledurham .... Maple 57 F3
Marlow .... Mar 1 A1
Marlow Bottom .... Mar B 1 B3
Medmenham .... Medm 17 D3
Mortimer .... Mort 137 D3
Moulsford .... Moul 13 F2
Newbury .... Newb 104 C2
Newell Green .... New G 91 E2
Newtown .... Newt 131 D2
Oakley Green .... Oak G 66 A3
Old Windsor .... Old W 95 D4
Padworth .... Padw 109 F1
Pangbourne .... Pangb 56 A3
Peasemore .... Pease 50 C4
Purley .... Purl 57 D3
Reading .... Read 85 D3
Remenham Hill .... Rem H 16 B1
Sandhurst .... Sand 150 B4
Shepperton .... Shepp 125 F2
Shinfield .... Shin 113 F3
Shiplake .... Shipl 35 F1
Silchester .... Silc 136 B1
Slough .... Slough 42 C3
Sonning .... Sonn 60 C2
South Stoke .... Sou S 14 B2
Staines .... Stai 96 C1
Stanford Dingley .... Stan D 81 E2
Stanwell .... Stan 70 B1
Stoke Poges .... Sto P 22 C2
Streatley .... Stre 34 A4
Sulham .... Sulh 56 C1
Sulhamstead .... Sulhd 110 B3
Swallowfield .... Swal 139 E3
Tadley .... Tad 134 C1
Taplow .... Tapl 20 C1
Thatcham .... That 106 C2
Theale .... Thea 83 E2
Tidmarsh .... Tidm 56 B1
Twyford .... Twyf 61 E3
Upper Basildon .... Upp B 55 D3
Virginia Water .... Vir W 122 B3
Waltham St Lawrence .... W St L 62 C3
Wargrave .... Warg 36 B1
Wentworth .... Went 121 F2
West End .... West E 153 F3
West Ilsley .... West I 10 A1
West Woodhay .... West W 128 B2
Whitchurch .... Whitc 56 B4
White Waltham .... Whi Wa 63 F4
Wickham .... Wick 75 E2
Windlesham .... Windl 146 B2
Windsor .... Wind 67 F3
Winkfield .... Wink 92 B3
Winnersh .... Winn 88 A2
Winterbourne .... Wint 77 E3
Wokingham .... Woki 116 A4
Wooburn Green .... Wood G 3 F4
Woodley .... Wood 88 A4
Woolhampton .... Wool 108 B1
Wraysbury .... Wray 95 F4
Yateley .... Yate 149 E3
Yattendon .... Yatt 53 F1

Abattoirs Rd. Read 86 A4
Abbetts La. Camb 151 D2
Abbey Cl. Brac 118 B2
Abbey Cl. Newb 131 D4
Abbey Cl. Slough 41 F3
Abbey Gdns. Chert 124 A2
Abbey Green. Chert 124 A2
Abbey Park. Bur C 110 C2
Abbey Rd. Bou E 2 C3
Abbey Rd. Chert 124 A1
Abbey Rd. Shepp 125 D1
Abbey Rd. Vir W 122 B3
Abbey Sq. Read 86 A4
Abbey St. Read 86 A4
Abbey Way. Bish 18 B3
Abbot Cl. Stai 97 E1
Abbots Dr. Vir W 122 B3
Abbot's Rd. Bur C 110 C1
Abbots Rd. Newb 105 D1
Abbot's Wlk. Read 86 A4
Abbot's Wlk. Wind 66 C3
Abbotsbury. Brac 117 F2
Abbotts Way. Slough 41 E3
Aberford Cl. Read 85 E4
Abex Rd. Newb 105 E2
Abingdon Cl. Brac 118 C2
Abingdon Dr. Caver 59 E3
Abingdon Rd. East I 30 C4
Abingdon Rd. Sand 143 E1
Abingdon Wlk. Maid 19 F2
Abney Ct Dr. Bou E 3 D1
Aborfield Cl. Slough 42 C2
Abrahams Rd. Hen-O-T 15 E2
Acacia Ave. Crow 143 E1
Acacia Ave. Stai 125 D2
Acacia Ave. Wray 68 C2
Acacia Ct. Brac 118 A3
Acacia Mews. Harm 70 B4
Acacia Rd. Read 86 B3
Acacia Rd. Stai 97 D2
Academy Cl. Camb 151 F4
Accommodation La. Harm 70 A4
Ackrells Mead. Sand 142 C1
Acorn Dr. Woki 116 B4
Acorn Gr. Harl 71 F4
Acorn Rd. Black 150 A3
Acre Pas. Wind 67 E3
Acre Rd. Read 113 D4
Acre The. Mar 1 C1
Adam Cl. Slough 42 A3
Adam Cl. Tad 134 C1
Adam Ct. Hen-O-T 15 F1
Adams Way. Read 86 C1
Addington Cl. Wind 67 D2
Addington Rd. Read 86 B3
Addiscombe Chase. Sulh 57 D2
Addiscombe Rd. Crow 143 E2
Addison Cl. Iver 44 C4
Addison Ct. Maid 20 A1
Addison Rd. Read 59 D1
Adelaide Cl. Slough 42 A2
Adelaide Rd. Ashf 97 E2
Adelaide Rd. Read 87 D3
Adelaide Sq. Wind 67 E3
Adelphi Gdns. Slough 42 C2
Adkins Rd. W St L 62 C4
Admirals Ct. Read 86 A3
Admiralty Way. Sand 150 C2
Admoor La. Been 109 E4
Adwell Dr. Winn 87 E1
Adwell Sq. Hen-O-T 15 E1
Agar Cres. Brac 91 D1
Agars Pl. Datch 68 A4
Agate Cl. Woki 115 F4
Aggisters La. Woki 115 E2
Agincourt Cl. Woki 115 F3
Agricola Way. That 106 C1
Ainsdale Cres. Read 85 D2
Aintree. Lamb 25 D1
Aintree Cl. Newb 105 E1
Aintree Cl. Stan 69 F3
Airport Way. Stan 70 A2
Aisne Rd. Camb 152 C1
Ajax Ave. Slough 42 A3
Alan Pl. Read 85 D3
Alan Way. Slough 43 F4
Alandale Cl. Read 113 E4
Albain Cres. Stan 97 F3
Albany Park. Camb 151 E1
Albany Park. Stan 69 E4
Albany Park Dr. Winn 88 A2
Albany Pl. Eng G 96 A2
Albany Rd. Old W 68 A1
Albany Rd. Read 85 E4
Albany Rd. Wind 67 E3
Alben Rd. Binf 90 B2
Albert Ave. Chert 124 A3
Albert Cl. Slough 42 C2
Albert Rd. Ashf 97 F2
Albert Rd. Bags 145 F1
Albert Rd. Brac 118 A4
Albert Rd. Camb 151 E3
Albert Rd. Caver 58 C2
Albert Rd. Crow 143 D3
Albert Rd. Eng G 95 E1
Albert Rd. Hen-O-T 15 F1
Albert Rd. Newb 105 D2
Albert Rd. Old W 68 A1
Albert Rd. Wind 67 F2
Albert Rd. Woki 116 A3
Albert St. Maid 39 F4
Albert St. Slough 42 C2
Albert St. Wind 67 D3
Albion Cl. Slough 43 D3
Albion Rd. Sand 150 A4
Albion Terr. Read 86 B4
Albury Cl. Read 58 B1
Albury Gdns. Read 84 C2
Alcot Cl. Crow 143 D2
Aldborough Spur. Slough 42 C4
Aldbourne Ave. Read 87 D2
Aldbourne Rd. Burn 41 D4
Aldeburgh Cl. Caver 59 E4
Aldebury Rd. Maid 19 F1
Alden View. Wind 66 B3
Aldenham Cl. Caver 59 E3
Aldenham Terr. Brac 118 B2
Alder Cl. Eng G 95 F2
Alder Cl. Slough 41 F3
Alder Dr. Read 84 B3
Alder Gr. Yate 149 E3
Alderbourne La. Fulm 23 F4
Alderbrook Cl. Finch 142 C3
Alderbury Rd. Slough 43 F2
Alderbury Rd W. Slough 43 F2
Alderfield Cl. Thea 83 F2
Alderley Cl. Wood 60 C1
Alderman Willey Cl. Woki 116 A3
Alders The. That 106 B2
Alderside Wlk. Eng G 95 F2
Aldin Ave S. Slough 43 D2
Aldridge Rd. Slough 22 A1
Aldwick Dr. Maid 39 E3
Aldworth Cl. Brac 118 A3
Aldworth Cl. Read 85 E3
Aldworth Gdns. Crow 143 D3
Aldworth Rd. Comp 31 F2
Aldworth Rd. Upp B 55 D3
Alexander Rd. Stai 96 B2
Alexander Rd. That 106 C1
Alexandra Ave. Camb 151 D3
Alexandra Cl. Ashf 98 B1
Alexandra Cl. Stai 97 E1
Alexandra Ct. Ashf 98 B1
Alexandra Rd. Ashf 98 C1
Alexandra Rd. Eng G 95 E1
Alexandra Rd. Maid 39 E4
Alexandra Rd. Read 86 B3
Alexandra Rd. Slough 42 B2
Alexandra Rd. Wind 67 E3
Alford Cl. Read 84 B4
Alfred St. Read 85 F4
Alice La. Burn 21 D1
Alison Cl. Bur C 110 C1
Alison Dr. Camb 151 F3
All Hallows Rd. Caver 59 E2
All Saints' Ave. Maid 39 E4
All Saints Cl. Woki 116 B4
All Saints Cres. Black 150 C1
All Saints' Rd. Light 146 B1
All Souls' Rd. Ascot 120 A3
Allanson Rd. Mar 1 C2
Allcot Cl. Felt 98 C4
Allcroft Rd. Read 86 B3
Allenby Rd. Camb 151 D3
Allenby Rd. Maid 39 D4
Allendale Cl. Sand 143 D1
Allendale Rd. Read 87 D2
Allerds Rd. Burn 22 A2
Alleyns La. Cook 19 E4
Allhusen Gdns. Fulm 23 F4
Alliance Ct. Ashf 98 B2
Allison Gdns. Purl 57 E3
Allnatt Ave. Winn 88 B1
Allonby Cl. Read 87 E1
Allyn Cl. Stai 96 C1
Alma Rd. Eton 41 F1
Alma Rd. Wind 67 E3
Alma St. Read 85 E4
Almners Rd. Chert 123 D1
Almond Ave. Newb 105 D3
Almond Cl. Eng G 95 D1
Almond Cl. Stai 125 E4
Almond Cl. Woki 115 E2
Almond Dr. Caver 59 F2
Almond Rd. Burn 21 E1
Almons Way. Slough 43 D4
Almswood Rd. Tad 135 D1
Alpha St N. Slough 42 C2
Alpha St S. Slough 42 C2
Alphington Ave. Camb 151 F1
Alphington Green. Camb 151 F1
Alpine St. Read 86 A3
Alsace Wlk. Camb 151 D1
Alston Mews. That 106 B1
Alston Wlk. Caver 59 E1
Altmore. Bur G 38 C2
Alton Ct. Stai 123 F4
Alton Ride. Black 150 B3
Altona Way. Slough 42 A4
Altwood Bailey. Maid 39 D3
Altwood Cl. Burn 41 F4
Altwood Cl. Maid 39 D3
Altwood Dr. Maid 39 D3
Altwood Rd. Maid 39 D3
Alvista Ave. Burn 41 D4
Alwyn Rd. Maid 39 D4
Alwyns Cl. Chert 124 A2
Alwyns La. Chert 123 F2
Amanda Ct. Slough 43 E2
Ambarrow Cres. Sand 142 C1
Ambarrow La. Sand 142 C1
Ambassador. Brac 117 F2
Amberley Cl. Newb 104 C2
Amberley Ct. Maid 20 B2
Amberley Dr. Twyf 61 E3
Amberley Rd. Burn 41 F4
Amberwood Dr. Camb 151 F4
Amblecote Rd. Read 85 D4
Ambleside Cl. Wood 87 F4
Ambleside Dr. Felt 98 C4
Ambleside Rd. Light 153 D4
Ambleside Way. Stai 96 A1
Ambrook Road. Read 113 D4
Ambrose Pl. Read 85 F4
Ambury Rd. Comp 32 C2
Amen Corner Business Park. Brac 117 F4
Amerden Cl. Tapl 40 B4
Amerden La. Tapl 40 B4
Amerden La. Tapl 40 C2
Amerden Way. Slough 42 A2
Amersham Rd. Caver 59 E1
Amethyst Cl. Woki 115 E4
Amherst Rd. Read 87 D3
Amity Rd. Read 86 C4
Amity St. Read 86 C4
Amners Farm Rd. Bur C 112 A4
Ampere Rd. Newb 105 D2
Ancaster Dr. Ascot 119 F4
Ancastle Gr. Hen-O-T 15 E1
Andermans. Wind 66 B3
Anderson Ave. Read 87 D3
Anderson Cres. Arbo 114 C1
Anderson Dr. Ashf 98 B2
Anderson Pl. Bags 145 F2
Andover Cl. Read 57 E1
Andover Dro. Ham M 130 A2
Andover Rd. Ball H 130 B3
Andover Rd. Black 150 B3
Andover Rd. Newb 130 B3
Andrew Cl. Woki 116 C3
Andrews Cl. Thea 83 F2
Andrews Rd. Read 87 D2
Andrews Way. Mar B 1 B4
Angel Ct. Newb 105 D2
Angel Mead. Wool 108 B1
Angel Pl. Binf 90 B1
Angle Field Rd. Caver 59 E2
Anglers Way. Read 86 B4
Anglesey Cl. Ashf 98 A3
Angus Cl. Read 84 C2
Annadale. Cold A 79 E1
Anne Cl. Maid 19 F1
Anneforde Pl. Brac 91 D1
Annesley Gdns. Winn 88 B2
Annett Cl. Shepp 125 F3
Anscuff Rd. Slough 22 A1
Ansell Rd. Camb 151 F1
Anslow Pl. Slough 41 E4
Anson Cres. Read 113 E4
Anstey Pl. Bur C 111 D2
Anstey Rd. Read 86 A4
Anston Cl. Read 114 A4
Antares Cl. Woki 115 F3
Anthony Way. Slough 41 E3
Antrim Rd. Wood 87 E3
Apex Dr. Camb 151 E1
Aplin Way. Light 146 A1
Apple Cl. Purl 57 D2
Apple Cl. Woki 115 F3
Apple Tree Cl. Newb 130 C4
Apple Tree Way. Sand 143 E1
Appleby End. Read 85 D4
Appleby Gdns. Felt 98 C4
Applecroft. Maid 39 E2
Appledore. Brac 117 F2
Appleford Cl. That 106 B1
Appleford Rd. Read 85 D3
Appletree La. Shin 113 D1
Appletree La. Slough 43 E2
Appletree Pl. Brac 118 A4
Approach Rd. Ashf 98 B1
Approach Rd. Tapl 40 C4
April Cl. Camb 151 E1
Aquila Cl. Woki 115 F3
Aragon Cl. Ashf 98 C1
Arbor La. Winn 88 A2
Arbor Meadows. Winn 88 A2
Arborfield Rd. Shin 113 F2
Arcade The. Gori 34 B3
Arcade The. Newb 105 D2
Archer Cl. Maid 39 E4
Archway Rd. Caver 59 D1
Arden Cl. Brac 119 D4
Ardingly. Brac 118 A2
Ardler Rd. Caver 59 E1
Ardrossan Ave. Camb 152 A3
Ardwell Cl. Finch 142 C3
Arenal Dr. Crow 143 E2
Arethusa Way. Bis 153 F2
Argosy Gdns. Stai 96 C1
Argosy La. Stan 97 E4
Argyle Rd. Newb 104 C1
Argyle Rd. Read 85 F4
Argyle St. Read 85 F4
Arkle Ave. That 105 F2
Arkley Ct. Holy 40 B1
Arkwright Dr. Brac 117 E4
Arkwright Rd. Read 86 A2
Arkwright Rd. Stan 69 F3
Arlington Cl. Brac 118 A4
Arlington Cl. Maid 38 C4
Arlington Rd. Ashf 97 F2
Armadale Ct. Read 85 E3
Armitage Ct. Ascot 120 B2
Armitage Dr. Camb 151 F1
Armour Hill. Read 57 E1
Armour Rd. Read 57 E1
Armstrong Rd. Eng G 95 E1
Armstrong Way. Wood 88 A4
Arncliffe. Brac 118 A2
Arndale Way. Eng G 96 A2
Arnett Ave. Woki 141 F4
Arnewood Ave. Tad 135 E1
Arnhem Rd. Newb 105 D2
Arnold Rd. Stai 97 E1
Arnside Cl. Twyf 61 E4
Aronsmead. Hen-O-T 15 E1
Arrowhead Rd. Thea 83 F1
Arrowsmith Way. That 106 C1
Arthur Cl. Bags 145 F1
Arthur Pl. Read 86 B4
Arthur Rd. Newb 104 C1
Arthur Rd. Slough 42 B2
Arthur Rd. Wind 67 D3
Arthur Rd. Woki 116 A3
Arun Cl. Winn 88 A1
Arundel Cl. Maid 39 D4
Arundel Ct. Slough 43 E1
Arundel Rd. Camb 152 B2
Arundel Rd. Wood 87 F4
Ascot Cl. Newb 131 E4
Ascot Rd. Felt 98 A3
Ascot Rd. Holy 40 A1
Ascot Rd. Holy 64 C4
Ash Cl. Brig 28 B2
Ash Cl. Sand 150 B3
Ash Cl. Slough 44 A2
Ash Gr. Felt 98 C4
Ash Gr. Stai 97 E1
Ash Gr. Sto P 22 C3
Ash La. Bur C 111 D2
Ash La. Wind 66 B3
Ash Rd. Newt 132 A2
Ash Rd. Newt 131 F2
Ash Rd. Read 84 C4
Ash Rd. Stai 125 D3
Ash Terr. Cold A 106 A4
Ash Tree Gr. Ham M 129 D4
Ash Way. Woki 115 E2
Ashampstead Rd. Brad 82 A4
Ashampstead Rd. Read 85 D2
Ashampstead Rd. Upp B 55 D3
Ashbourne. Brac 117 F2
Ashbourne Gr. Maid 39 E2
Ashbourne Way. That 106 A2
Ashbrook Rd. Old W 95 D4
Ashburton Rd. Read 86 B1
Ashbury Dr. Camb 151 D1
Ashbury Dr. Read 84 B4
Ashby Ct. Read 113 D4
Ashby Way. Harm 71 D4
Ashcroft Cl. Caver 58 C3
Ashcroft Ct. Burn 21 D2
Ashcroft Rd. Maid 39 E4
Ashdale Cl. Stan 97 F3
Ashdale Park. Brac 142 B3
Ashdene Cl. Stai 98 B1
Ashdown. Maid 20 A2
Ashdown Cl. Brac 119 D4
Ashen Cross. Slough 44 A4
Ashenden Wlk. Far C 22 B4
Asher Dr. Burl 119 E4
Ashfield Green. Yate 149 F3
Ashford Ave. Ashf 98 A1
Ashford Cl. Ashf 97 F2
Ashford Cres. Ashf 97 F3
Ashford Hill Rd. Head 132 C1
Ashford Industrial Estate. Felt 98 B2
Ashford La. Dorn 41 D2
Ashford Rd. Felt 98 C3
Ashford Rd. Stai 98 B1
Ashford Rd. Stai 97 E1
Ashgrove Rd. Ashf 98 B2
Ashleigh Ave. Stai 96 B1
Ashley Cl. Read 87 D1
Ashley Cl. Shepp 125 F1
Ashley Dr. Black 150 B2
Ashley Park. Maid 20 A1
Ashley Park Ave. Shepp 125 F1
Ashley Park Cres. Shepp 125 F1
Ashley Rd. Read 85 F3
Ashley Way. West E 153 E3
Ashman Pl. Kint 102 A1
Ashman Rd. That 107 D2
Ashmere Cl. Bur C 84 B2
Ashmore Green Rd. Cold A 106 A4
Ashmore Rd. Read 86 B1
Ashridge Green. Brac 118 A4
Ashridge Rd. Woki 116 B4
Ashton Cl. Read 84 B4
Ashton Rd. Newb 105 D1
Ashton Rd. Woki 88 C1
Ashtrees Rd. Wood 87 F4
Ashurst Dr. Stai 124 C3
Ashview Cl. Ashf 97 F2
Ashview Gdns. Ashf 97 F2
Ashville Way. Woki 116 A3
Ashwell Ave. Camb 151 F3
Ashwood. Wood 87 E2
Ashwood Cl. Read 84 A3
Ashwood Dr. Newb 105 E2
Ashwood Pl. Eng G 95 D1
Ashworth Dr. That 106 B1
Askew Dr. Shin 113 D2
Aspen Cl. Slough 42 A4
Aspen Cl. Stai 96 C3
Aspin Way. Black 150 A3
Astleham Way. Stai 124 C3
Astley Cl. Woki 115 F4
Aston Ave. Read 57 D3
Aston Cl. Pangb 56 B3
Aston Ferry La. Rem H 16 B3
Aston La. Rem H 16 B2
Aston Mead. Wind 66 C3
Aston St. Ast T 12 C4
Astor Cl. Winn 88 B2
Atfield Gr. Windl 146 B2
Atherton Cl. Read 84 C4
Atherton Cl. Stan 70 B1
Atherton Cres. Hung 100 B3
Atherton Pl. Lamb 25 D2
Atherton Rd. Hung 100 B3
Athlone Cl. Maid 19 F1
Atrebatti Rd. Sand 143 E1
Auckland Cl. Maid 40 A4
Auckland Rd. Read 87 D3
Auclum Cl. Bur C 111 D1
Auclum La. Bur C 111 D1
Audley Cl. Newb 105 E3
Audley Dr. Maid 39 D3
Audley St. Read 85 F4
Audley Way. Burl 119 E3
August End. Read 85 E4
August End. Slough 43 F4
Augustine Cl. Stan 69 F2
Augustus Gdns. Camb 152 B3
Austen Gdns. Newb 131 D4
Austin Rd. Wood 87 F3
Australia Ave. Maid 39 F4
Australia Rd. Slough 43 D2
Autumn Cl. Caver 59 E4
Autumn Cl. Slough 41 F3
Autumn Wlk. Maid 39 D3
Autumn Wlk. Warg 36 B1
Avalon Rd. Bou E 3 D3
Avalon Rd. Read 87 E2
Avebury. Brac 118 A2
Avebury. Slough 42 A3
Avebury Sq. Read 86 B3
Avenue Rd. Felt 98 C3
Avenue Rd. Maid 40 A3
Avenue Rd. Stai 96 B2
Avenue Sucy. Camb 151 D2
Avenue The. Ascot 92 C1
Avenue The. Bou E 3 D2
Avenue The. Camb 151 D3
Avenue The. Crow 143 D3
Avenue The. Eng G 96 A2
Avenue The. Far C 22 A4
Avenue The. Light 146 A1
Avenue The. Maid 20 B2
Avenue The. Mort 137 D3
Avenue The. Old W 68 A1
Avenue The. Slough 68 A3
Avenue The. Stai 124 A4
Avenue The. Wray 68 C2
Averil Ct. Slough 41 E4
Avington Cl. Read 57 D3
Avocet Cres. Sand 150 C4
Avon Cl. Read 84 C3
Avon Cl. Slough 41 F3
Avon Gr. Brac 91 E1
Avon Pl. Read 86 B4
Avon Rd. Ashf 98 C1
Avon Way. Padw 109 F3
Avondale. Maid 19 E1
Avondale Ave. Stai 96 C1
Avondale Rd. Ashf 97 E3
Avonway. Newb 105 E2
Axbridge. Brac 118 C2
Axbridge Rd. Read 86 B1
Ayebridges Ave. Stai 96 B1
Aylesbury Cres. Slough 42 B3
Aylesham Way. Yate 149 D3
Aylesworth Ave. Slough 22 A1
Aylesworth Spur. Old W 95 D4
Aylsham Cl. Read 84 C4
Aymer Cl. Stai 123 F4
Aymer Dr. Stai 123 F4
Aysgarth. Brac 118 A2
Aysgarth Park. Holy 40 A1
Azalea Way. Camb 152 A3
Azalea Way. Slough 43 F4

Babbington Rd. Read 113 E3
Bachelors Acre. Wind 67 E3
Back La. Been 109 D4
Back La. Brad 81 F2
Back La. Brim 134 B2
Back La. Kint 127 F4
Back La. Shin 139 D4
Back La. Stan D 81 F2
Back St. East G 47 E3
Backsideans. Warg 36 B1
Bacon Cl. Sand 150 B3
Bad Godesberg Way. Maid 39 F4
Baden Cl. Stai 97 D1
Bader Gdns. Slough 42 A2
Bader Way The. Wood 88 A3
Badgebury Rise. Mar B 1 B4
Badgemore La. Hen-O-T 15 E2
Badger Cl. Maid 39 E2
Badger Dr. Light 146 A1
Badger Dr. Twyf 61 E4
Badgers Copse. Camb 151 F2
Badgers Croft. Mort 137 D3
Badgers Hill. Vir W 122 B2
Badgers Holt. Yate 149 D3
Badgers Rise. Caver 59 D3
Badgers Sett. Crow 142 C3
Badgers Way. Brac 118 C4
Badgers Way. Mar B 1 B4
Badgers Wlk. Shipl 36 A2
Badgers Wood. Far C 22 B4
Badgerwood Dr. Camb 151 E1
Badminton Rd. Maid 39 D3
Bagnols Way. Newb 104 C1
Bagshot Green. Bags 145 F2
Bagshot Rd. Ascot 120 A1
Bagshot Rd. Brac 118 B2
Bagshot Rd. Eng G 95 E1
Bagshot Rd. Sunn 120 A1
Bagshot Rd. West E 153 F4
Bailey Cl. Maid 39 F4
Bailey Cl. Wind 67 D3
Baileys Cl. Black 150 B2
Bailey's La. Hurst 62 C2
Baily Ave. That 106 A2
Bain Ave. Camb 151 D1
Bainbridge Rd. Bur C 84 A2
Baird Cl. Slough 42 A2
Baird Rd. Arbo 140 C4
Baird Rd. Bark 140 C4
Bakeham La. Eng G 95 E1
Baker St. Ast T 12 C4
Baker St. Read 85 F4
Bakers La. Maid 38 C4
Baldwin Rd. Burn 21 E1
Baldwin's Shore. Eton 67 E4
Balfour Cres. Brac 118 A2
Balfour Cres. Newb 130 B3
Balfour Dr. Bur C 84 A2
Balintore Ct. Sand 150 B4

Ball Pit Rd. Beed 30 A3
Ball Pit Rd. East I 30 A3
Ballamore Cl. Bur C 84 A2
Ballard Green. Wind 66 C4
Ballard Rd. Camb 152 A4
Ballencrief Rd. Sunn 120 C1
Balliol Rd. Caver 58 B2
Balliol Way. Crow 143 F1
Balmoral. Maid 19 D1
Balmoral Cl. Slough 41 F4
Balmoral Gdns. Wind 67 E2
Balmore Dr. Caver 59 D2
Bamburgh Cl. Read 86 B2
Bamford Pl. Bur C 84 A2
Banbury. Brac 118 C1
Banbury Ave. Slough 41 F4
Banbury Gdns. Caver 59 E2
Bancroft Cl. Ashf 98 A2
Bancroft Pl. Bur C 84 A2
Band La Eng G 96 A2
Bangors Cl. Iver 44 C4
Bangors Rd S. Iver 44 C4
Bank Side. Woki 141 F3
Banks Spur. Slough 42 A2
Bankside Cl. Read 86 B1
Bannard Rd. Maid 39 D3
Bannister Cl. Slough 43 F2
Bannister Gdns. Yate 149 F3
Bannister Pl. Brim 133 F3
Bannister Rd. Bur C 110 C1
Barbara Cl. Shepp 125 D2
Barbara's Meadow. Sulh 57 D1
Barber Cl. Hurst 88 C4
Barberry Way. Black 150 C1
Barbon Cl. Camb 152 B2
Barbrook Cl. Read 57 E2
Barchester Rd. Slough 43 F2
Barclay Rd. Bur C 84 B2
Barclose Ave. Caver 59 E2
Bardney Cl. Maid 39 E2
Bardolph's Cl. Maple 58 B4
Bardown. Chiev 51 D1
Barfield Rd. That 106 A2
Barge La. Swal 139 D3
Bargeman Rd. Maid 39 F2
Bargeman Rd. Maid 39 F3
Barholm Cl. Winn 87 F1
Barkby. Read 87 E1
Barker Ct. Hurst 88 C4
Barker Green. Brac 118 A2
Barker Rd. Chert 123 F1
Barkham Rd. Bark 115 E2
Barkham Rd. Woki 115 E2
Barkham Ride. Bark 141 F4
Barkham Ride. Woki 141 F4
Barkham St. Bark 115 E1
Barkhart Dr. Woki 116 B4
Barkhart Gdns. Woki 116 B4
Barkwith Cl. Winn 87 F1
Barley Cl. That 106 C1
Barley Fields. Woo G 3 F4
Barley Mow Rd. Eng G 95 E2
Barley Mow Way. Stai 125 D3
Barley Wlk. Read 84 A3
Barn Cl. Ashf 98 A2
Barn Cl. Brac 118 B4
Barn Cl. Camb 151 F3
Barn Cl. Far C 22 A4
Barn Cl. Maid 19 F1
Barn Cl. Read 85 E2
Barn Cres. Newb 130 B4
Barn Dr. Maid 39 D2
Barn La. Hen-O-T 15 E2
Barnard Cl. Caver 59 E3
Barnards Hill. Mar 1 B1
Barnes Rd. Camb 151 F1
Barnes Way. Iver 44 C3
Barnett Green. Brac 118 A2
Barnfield. Iver 44 C4
Barnfield. Slough 41 E3
Barnhill Cl. Mar 1 B2
Barnhill Gdns. Mar 1 B2
Barnhill Rd. Mar 1 B2
Barnsdale Rd. Read 86 B2
Barnway. Eng G 95 E2
Barnwood Cl. Read 85 F4
Baron Ct. Read 85 F4
Barons Way. Stai 96 B1
Barossa Rd. Camb 151 E4
Barracane Dr. Crow 143 D3
Barrack La. Wind 67 E3
Barracks La. Shin 113 D1
Barrett Cres. Woki 116 C3
Barrington Cl. Read 87 D3
Barr's Rd. Burn 41 D4
Barry Ave. Wind 67 E4
Barry Pl. Read 86 A4
Bartelotts Rd. Slough 21 F1
Bartholomew St. Newb 104 C1
Bartlemy Cl. Newb 130 C4
Bartlemy Rd. Newb 130 C4
Barton Cl. Shepp 125 D2
Barton Rd. Read 84 A4
Barton Rd. Slough 43 F2
Bartons Dr. Yate 149 E2
Barwell Cl. Crow 142 C2
Basemoors. Brac 118 C4
Basford Way. Wind 66 B2
Basil Cl. Read 86 C1
Basingstoke Rd. Alde 109 D1
Basingstoke Rd. Read 86 A2
Basingstoke Rd. Shin 139 E3
Basingstoke Rd. Swal 139 E3
Baskerville La. Shipl 36 A2
Baslow Rd. Winn 88 A1
Basmore Ave. Shipl 36 A2
Bass Mead. Cook 19 F3
Bassett Cl. Winn 114 B4
Bassett Rd. Let B 6 C4
Bassett Way. Slough 21 F1
Batcombe Mead. Brac 118 C1
Bates Cl. Slough 43 F4
Bath Rd. Been 108 B1
Bath Rd. Brad 108 B1
Bath Rd. Bur G 38 B3
Bath Rd. Burn 41 E4
Bath Rd. Camb 151 E3
Bath Rd. Frox 99 D2
Bath Rd. Harl 71 E3
Bath Rd. Harm 70 B3
Bath Rd. Hung 100 C4
Bath Rd. Know H 38 B3
Bath Rd. Maid 38 B3
Bath Rd. Newb 104 B3
Bath Rd. Padw 108 B1
Bath Rd. Read 85 E3
Bath Rd. Slough 41 E4
Bath Rd. Sonn 60 C1
Bath Rd. That 108 B1
Bath Rd. Thea 108 B1
Bath Rd. Warg 62 A4
Bath Rd. Wool 108 B1
Bathurst Cl. Iver 44 C2
Bathurst Rd. Winn 88 A1
Bathurst Wlk. Iver 44 C2
Battery End. Newb 130 B3
Battle Cl. Newb 104 B2
Battle Rd. Gori 34 C4
Battle Rd. Newb 130 B3
Battle St. Read 85 F4
Battlemead Cl. Maid 20 B2
Batty's Barn Cl. Woki 116 B3
Baxendales The. Newb 105 E1
Bay Cl. Read 86 C1
Bay Dr. Brac 118 C4
Bay Rd. Brac 118 C4
Bay Tree Ct. Burn 21 E1
Bay Tree Rise. Read 84 B3
Baydon Dr. Read 85 F3
Baydon Rd. East G 46 B2
Baydon Rd. Gr She 46 B2
Baydon Rd. Lamb 46 B2
Bayfield Ave. Camb 151 F1
Bayford Cl. Camb 151 D1
Bayford Dr. Read 84 C2
Bayley Cres. Burn 41 D4
Bayley Ct. Winn 88 A1
Baylis Rd. Slough 42 C3
Bayliss Rd. Warg 36 B1
Baysfarm Ct. Harm 70 B3
Beacon Rd. Felt 71 D1
Beaconsfield Rd. Far C 22 B3
Beaconsfield Way. Read 87 D1
Beale Cl. Woki 116 A4
Beal's La. Sulh 84 A4
Bean Oak Rd. Woki 116 C3
Beancroft Rd. That 106 B1
Bear La. Newb 105 D2
Beard's Rd. Ashf 98 C1
Bearwood Path. Winn 88 A1
Bearwood Rd. Woki 115 E3
Beauchief Cl. Read 113 F4
Beaufield Cl. Wood 87 E4
Beaufort Cl. Mar 1 C1
Beaufort Gdns. Ascot 119 F4
Beaufort Gdns. Mar 1 C1
Beaufort Pl. Maid 40 B2
Beauforts. Eng G 95 E2
Beaufront Cl. Camb 152 A4
Beaufront Rd. Camb 152 A4
Beaulieu Cl. Brac 119 D3
Beaulieu Cl. Datch 68 A3
Beaulieu Gdns. Sand 150 B3
Beaumont Cl. Maid 39 D2
Beaumont Dr. Ashf 98 B2
Beaumont Gdns. Brac 118 C2
Beaumont Rd. Slough 42 B4
Beaumont Rd. Wind 67 E3
Beaumont Rise. Mar 1 C1
Beaver La. Yate 149 F3
Beaver Way. Wood 88 A4
Becket Cl. Woki 116 C3
Beckford Ave. Brac 118 A2
Beckford Cl. Woki 88 C1
Beckfords. Upp B 55 D3
Beckings Way. Fla H 3 E4
Bede Wlk. Read 86 B2
Bedfont Cl. Felt 71 E1
Bedfont Ct. Stan 70 A2
Bedfont La. Felt 98 C4
Bedfont Rd. Felt 98 B3
Bedfont Rd. Stan 70 C1
Bedford Ave. Slough 42 A4
Bedford Cl. Maid 39 D2
Bedford Cl. Newb 130 B3
Bedford Dr. Far C 22 A3
Bedford Gdns. Woki 115 F4
Bedford La. Sunn 121 D2
Bedford Rd. Read 85 F4
Bedfordshire Way. Woki 115 F3
Bedwins La. Cook 19 D3
Beech Ave. Camb 151 E2
Beech Cl. Ashf 98 B2
Beech Cl. Bur C 111 D2
Beech Dr. Black 150 B2
Beech Glen. Brac 118 A3
Beech Hill Rd. Bee H 138 C3
Beech Hill Rd. Sunn 120 C2
Beech La. Gori 14 C1
Beech La. Read 87 D1
Beech Rd. Felt 98 C4
Beech Rd. Maple 58 B4
Beech Rd. Newt 132 A2
Beech Rd. Purl 57 D3
Beech Rd. Read 86 C1
Beech Rd. Slough 43 F2
Beech Ride. Sand 143 D1
Beech Tree La. Stai 124 A4
Beech Wlk. That 106 C1
Beecham Rd. Read 85 E4
Beechbrook Ave. Yate 149 F3
Beechcroft. Brac 118 A3
Beechcroft. Hamp N 53 D3
Beechcroft Cl. Ascot 120 B3
Beeches Dr. Far C 22 A4
Beeches Rd. Far C 22 A4
Beeches The. Gori 34 A3
Beeches The. Read 57 E2
Beeches Way. Burn 21 D1
Beechingstoke. Mar 1 C2
Beechmont Ave. Went 122 B2
Beechnut Cl. Woki 115 F3
Beechnut Dr. Black 150 A3
Beechtree Ave. Eng G 95 D1
Beechtree Ave. Mar B 1 B3
Beechwood Ave. Read 84 B4
Beechwood Ave. Stai 97 D1
Beechwood Ave. Wood 87 E4
Beechwood Cl. Burl 92 C1
Beechwood Dr. Maid 39 D3
Beechwood Dr. Mar 18 A4
Beechwood Gdns. Slough 42 C2
Beechwood Rd. Slough 42 B4
Beechwood Rd. Went 122 A1
Beedon Dr. Brac 117 F2
Beehive La. Brac 117 E4
Beehive Rd. Brac 117 E4
Beehive Rd. Stai 96 C2
Beeston Way. Read 114 A4
Beggars Hill Rd. Char 61 D1
Beighton Cl. Read 113 F4
Beir Path The. Sou S 14 A2
Belfast Ave. Slough 42 B4
Belgrave Ct. Black 150 B2
Belgrave Rd. Slough 42 C3
Bell Cl. Slough 43 D4
Bell Corner. Chert 123 F1
Bell Ct. Hurl 17 F2
Bell Foundary La. Woki 116 B4
Bell Foundry La. Woki 116 B4
Bell Hill. Ham M 130 A2
Bell Hill. Newb 130 A2
Bell Holt. Newb 130 B3
Bell La. Eton 41 F1
Bell La. Hen-O-T 15 F2
Bell La. Ink 127 E2
Bell La. Sand 150 B3
Bell Lane. Comp 32 C2
Bell Pl. Bags 145 F2
Bell St. Hen-O-T 15 F1
Bell St. Maid 39 F3
Bell View. Wind 66 C3
Bell View Cl. Wind 66 C3
Bell Weir Cl. Wray 96 A3
Belle Ave. Read 87 D3
Belle Vue Cl. Stai 124 A4
Belle Vue Rd. Hen-O-T 35 E4
Belle Vue Rd. Read 85 F4
Bellever Hill. Camb 151 F3
Bellingham Cl. Camb 152 B2
Bellingham Wlk. Caver 59 D3
Bells Hill. Sto P 23 D2
Bells Hill Green. Sto P 23 D3
Bells La. Hort 69 D2
Bellswood La. Iver 44 A4
Belmont. Slough 42 A4
Belmont Cres. Maid 39 E4
Belmont Dr. Maid 39 E4
Belmont Mews. Camb 151 E2
Belmont Park Ave. Maid 39 E4
Belmont Park Rd. Maid 39 E4
Belmont Rd. Camb 151 E2
Belmont Rd. Crow 143 D3
Belmont Rd. Maid 39 E4
Belmont Rd. Read 85 E4
Belmont Vale. Maid 39 E4
Belton Rd. Camb 151 F3
Belvedere Ct. Black 150 B2
Belvedere Dr. Newb 131 D4
Belvedere Wlk. Winn 88 A2
Belvoir Cl. Camb 151 F1
Bembridge Ct. Slough 42 C2
Bembridge Pl. Read 86 B4
Benbricke Green. Brac 91 D1
Bence The. Stai 123 D3
Bencombe Rd. Mar B 1 C3
Benedict Dr. Felt 98 B4
Benen-stock Rd. Stan 70 A1
Benetfeld Rd. Binf 90 A1
Benham Hill. Newb 105 F2
Benham Hill. That 105 F2
Benham La. Swal 139 E2
Benhams La. Faw (Bu) 15 F4
Benner La. West E 153 F4
Bennet Rd. Read 86 A1
Bennett Cl. Newb 104 C3
Bennett Ct. Camb 151 E3
Bennetts Cl. Slough 42 A3
Bennett's Hill. Bur C 111 E4
Benning Cl. Wind 66 B2
Benning Way. Woki 116 B4
Bennings Cl. Brac 91 D1
Benson Cl. Read 86 B2
Benson Cl. Slough 43 D3
Benson Rd. Crow 142 C3
Bentley Park. Burn 21 E2
Bentley Rd. Slough 42 A3
Benyon Ct. Read 85 F3
Benyon Mews. Read 85 F3
Beomonds Row. Chert 124 A1
Bere Court Rd. Pangb 56 A2
Bere Rd. Brac 118 C2
Beresford Ave. Slough 43 E3
Beresford Rd. Read 85 F4
Berkeley Ave. Read 85 F3
Berkeley Cl. Stan 96 B3
Berkeley Gdns. Shepp 125 F1
Berkeley Mews. Mar 1 C1
Berkeley Rd. Newb 104 C1
Berkley Cl. Maid 39 D4
Berkshire Ave. Slough 42 A4
Berkshire Dr. Read 84 B4
Berkshire Rd. Camb 151 F4
Berkshire Rd. Hen-O-T 35 E4
Berkshire Way. Brac 117 E3
Berners Cl. Slough 41 F3
Bernersh Cl. Sand 143 E1
Berries Rd. Cook 20 A4
Berry Field. Slough 43 E4
Berry Hill. Tapl 40 B4
Berrybank. Sand 150 C3
Berrylands Rd. Caver 59 D2
Berrys La. Bur C 85 D1
Berrys Rd. Buck 107 E3
Berryscroft Rd. Stai 97 E1
Berstead Cl. Read 87 D1
Berwick Ave. Slough 42 A3
Berwick Cl. Mar 1 B2
Berwick La. Mar 1 B2
Berwick Rd. Mar 1 B2
Beryl Cl. Woki 115 F4
Bessel's Way. Blew 12 A4
Bestobell Rd. Slough 42 B4
Betam Rd. Read 86 B4
Betchworth Ave. Read 87 D2
Bethany Waye. Felt 98 C4
Bethesda Cl. Upp B 55 D3
Bethesda St. Upp B 55 D4
Betjeman Wlk. Yate 149 D2
Betteridge Rd. That 106 C1
Beverley Cl. Camb 152 B3
Beverley Cl. Mar 1 B1
Beverley Cl. That 106 B2
Beverley Ct. Slough 43 D2
Beverley Gdns. Maid 19 D1
Beverley Gdns. Warg 36 C1
Beverley Rd. Read 57 E1
Beverley Rd. Shepp 125 F4
Bevers The. Mort 137 D3
Bexley Ct. Read 85 E3
Bexley St. Wind 67 E3
Bibury Cl. Wood 87 E2
Bicknell Rd. Camb 151 F1
Bideford Cl. Wood 87 E3
Big La. Lamb 25 D2
Bigbury Gdns. Read 86 B2
Bigfrith La. Cook 19 D3
Biggs La. Bark 141 D4
Billet Bridge. Stai 97 D2
Billet La. Slough 44 A4
Billet Rd. Stan 97 D3
Billing Ave. Woki 141 F3
Billingbear La. Binf 90 A3
Billington Way. Cold A 106 B3
Binbrook Cl. Winn 87 E1
Binfield Rd. Binf 116 C4
Binfield Rd. Brac 118 A4
Binfield Rd. Woki 116 C4
Bingham Dr. Stai 97 E1
Bingham Rd. Burn 41 D4
Binghams The. Maid 40 A2
Bingley Gr. Wood 60 C1
Binsted Dr. Black 150 B3
Birch Ave. Read 85 D4
Birch Cl. Camb 151 F4
Birch Dr. Black 150 B2
Birch Gr. Shepp 125 F4
Birch Gr. Slough 42 A4
Birch Gr. Wind 66 B3
Birch Hill Rd. Brac 118 A1
Birch La. Burl 119 D4
Birch La. Silc 136 C3
Birch La. West E 153 E3
Birch Platt. West E 153 E3
Birch Rd. Bur C 111 D2
Birch Rd. Tad 134 C1
Birch Rd. Windl 146 C2
Birch Rd. Woki 142 A4
Birch Side. Crow 142 C3
Birch Tree View. Light 146 A1
Birches The. Black 150 A3
Birches The. Gori 34 A3
Birchetts Cl. Brac 118 A4
Birchfields. Camb 151 E2
Birchington Rd. Wind 67 D3
Birchland Cl. Silc 136 C3
Birchmead. Winn 88 B1
Birchview Cl. Yate 149 E2
Birchwood Cl. Caver 59 E3
Birchwood Dr. Light 146 B1
Birchwood Rd. Newb 105 E2
Birchwood The. Read 57 D3
Bird Mews. Woki 116 A3
Birdhill Ave. Read 86 B1
Birds La. Wool 107 F2
Birdwood Rd. Maid 39 D4
Birdwood Rd. Sand 151 D4
Birkbeck Rd. Crow 143 F1
Birkdale. Brac 117 F1
Birley Rd. Slough 42 B4
Bishop Ct. Maid 39 E3
Bishop Duppas Park. Shepp 125 F1
Bishopdale. Brac 118 A3
Bishops Dr. Felt 71 E1
Bishops Dr. Woki 116 B4
Bishops Farm Cl. Oak G 66 A3
Bishops Gr. Windl 146 B2
Bishop's La. New G 92 A4
Bishop's La. Wink 92 A4
Bishops Orch. Far C 22 A1
Bishops Rd. Brad 81 F2
Bishop's Rd. Read 87 D3
Bishops Rd. Slough 43 D2
Bishops Way. Stai 96 B1
Bishops Wlk. Bou E 3 F3
Bishopsgate Rd. Eng G 95 D2
Bishopswood La. Tad 134 C1
Bishopswood Rd. Tad 134 C1
Bissley Dr. Maid 39 D2
Bitham La. Ham 126 B3
Bitham La. Ink 127 D2
Bitham Rd. Farn 8 B4
Bittern Cl. Sand 150 B4
Bitterne Ave. Read 84 A3
Bix Hill. Faw (Bu) 15 D3
Bix La. Maid 38 C4
Black Boy La. Hurl 17 E2
Black Butts Cotts. Cook 20 A4
Black Horse Cl. Wind 66 B3
Black Park Rd. Fulm 23 F2
Black Park Rd. Iver H 23 F2
Blackamoor La. Maid 40 A4
Blackberry Cl. Shepp 125 F3
Blackbird Cl. Bur C 111 D2
Blackbird Cl. Sand 150 B4
Blackcap Pl. Sand 150 C4
Blackdown Way. That 106 B1
Blackett Cl. Stai 123 F4
Blacklands Rd. Buck 107 E3
Blackley Cl. Winn 87 F2
Blackmeadows. Brac 118 B2
Blackmoor Cl. Burl 119 E4
Blackmoor Wood. Burl 119 E4
Blacknest Rd. Went 121 F3
Blackpond La. Far C 22 A2
Blacksmith Row. Slough 44 A1
Blacksmiths La. Chert 124 A1
Blacksmith's La. Stai 124 B3
Blackstroud La E. Light 146 B1
Blackstroud La W. Light 153 E4
Blackthorn Dell. Slough 43 E2
Blackthorn Dr. Light 153 D4
Blackthorne Rd. Stan 69 F2
Blackwater Cl. Caver 59 F2
Blackwater Rise. Bur C 84 A2
Blagdon Rd. Read 86 B1
Blagrave La. Caver 58 B2
Blagrave St. Read 86 A4
Blagrove Dr. Woki 115 F2
Blagrove La. Woki 115 F2
Blair Rd. Slough 42 C3
Blaire Park. Yate 149 D4
Blake Cl. Crow 143 E2
Blake Cl. Woki 116 C4
Blakeney Fields. Gr She 48 A2
Blakes Cotts. Read 86 B4
Blake's La. Tad 135 E1
Blakes Rd. Warg 36 C2
Blakes Ride. Yate 149 D3
Blanchard Cl. Wood 88 A4
Blandford Cl. Slough 43 E2
Blandford Rd. Read 113 E4
Blandford Rd N. Slough 43 E2
Blandford Rd S. Slough 43 E2
Bland's Cl. Bur C 110 C1
Blandy Rd. Hen-O-T 35 E4
Blandys Hill. Kint 128 A4
Blandy's La. Upp B 55 D3
Blatch's Cl. Thea 83 E2
Blays Cl. Eng G 95 E1
Blay's La. Eng G 95 D1
Bledlow Cl. Newb 130 B3
Blenheim Cl. Slough 43 F3
Blenheim Cl. Woki 115 F3
Blenheim Gdns. Read 86 C3
Blenheim Rd. Caver 59 D2
Blenheim Rd. Maid 39 D4
Blenheim Rd. Newb 104 C1
Blenheim Rd. Read 86 C3
Blenheim Rd. Slough 43 E1
Bletchmore Cl. Harl 71 E4
Blewburton Wlk. Brac 118 C3
Blewbury Dr. Read 84 A4
Blewbury Hill. Blew 12 B4
Blinco La. Slough 43 F4
Blind La. Bou E 3 D3
Blind La. Fla H 3 D3
Blind La. Lamb 25 D1
Blomfield Dale. Brac 117 E4
Blomfield Dr. Brac 91 E1
Blondell Cl. Harm 70 B4
Bloomfield Rd. Maid 39 D3
Bloomfieldhatch La. Bee H 138 A4
Bloomfieldhatch La. Shin 112 C2
Bloomsbury Way. Black 150 B2
Blossom Ave. Thea 83 F2
Blossom La. Thea 83 F2
Bloxworth Cl. Brac 118 C3
Blue Ball La. Eng G 95 F2
Blue Coat Wlk. Brac 118 B2
Bluebell Dr. Bur C 110 C2
Bluebell Hill. Brac 118 C4
Bluebell Meadow. Winn 88 B2
Bluebell Rise. Light 153 D4
Bluecoats. That 106 B2
Bluethroat Cl. Sand 150 C4
Blumfield Cres. Burn 41 F4
Blumfield Ct. Slough 21 E1
Blundell's Rd. Read 84 C4
Blunts Ave. Harm 71 D4
Blyth Ave. That 106 C1
Blythe Cl. Iver 44 C4
Blythewood La. Ascot 119 F4
Blythwood Dr. Camb 151 E1
Boames La. Ham M 129 F3
Boarlands Cl. Slough 41 F3
Bobgreen Ct. Read 113 E4
Bobmore La. Mar 1 C2
Bockhampton Rd. Lamb 25 E1
Bockmer La. Medm 17 D4
Bodens Ride. Brac 119 F1
Bodmin Ave. Slough 42 A4
Bodmin Cl. That 106 B1
Bodmin Rd. Wood 87 E3
Body Rd. Read 85 F4

Bog La. Brac 119 D3
Boham's Rd. Blew 11 E3
Bolding House La. West E 153 F4
Boldrewood. Bur C 110 C1
Boleyn Cl. Stai 96 C2
Bolingbroke Way. That 106 C2
Bolney Rd. Shipl 36 A3
Bolton Ave. Wind 67 E2
Bolton Cres. Wind 67 E2
Bolton Rd. Wind 67 E2
Bolton's La. Harl 71 E4
Bolwell Cl. Twyf 61 F2
Bomer Cl. Harm 71 D4
Bond St. Eng G 95 E2
Bone La. Newb 105 E2
Bones La. Shipl 35 D2
Booth Dr. Stai 97 E1
Borderside. Slough 43 D4
Borderside. Yate 149 D3
Borrowdale Cl. Stai 96 A1
Borrowdale Gdns. Camb 152 B2
Borrowdale Rd. Winn 88 A2
Boscawen Way. That 107 D2
Boscombe Cl. Stai 123 E4
Bosham Cl. Road 114 A4
Bosman Dr. Windl 146 A3
Bostock La. Thea 83 D1
Boston Ave. Read 85 F3
Boston Gr. Slough 42 B4
Boston Rd. Hen-O-T 35 F4
Bosworth Gdns. Wood 87 F2
Botany Cl. That 106 C2
Bothy The. Warg 36 B1
Botmoor Way. Chadd 48 C4
Bottisham Cl. Winn 114 B4
Bottle La. Binf 91 D3
Bottle La. Know H 38 A2
Bottle La. New G 91 D3
Bottom La. Sulhd 110 B4
Bouldish Farm Rd. Ascot 119 F3
Boult St. Read 86 B4
Boulters Cl. Maid 20 B1
Boulters Cl. Slough 42 A2
Boulters Cl. Wood 87 F4
Boulters Ct. Maid 20 B1
Boulters Gdns. Maid 20 B1
Boulters La. Maid 20 B1
Boulton Rd. Read 86 A2
Boult's Wlk. Read 86 A3
Boundary Cl. Read 84 B3
Boundary La. Caver 58 C2
Boundary Pl. Woo G 3 E4
Boundary Rd. Newb 105 D1
Boundary Rd. Stai 97 E2
Boundary Rd. Tapl 40 C4
Boundary Rd. Woo G 3 E4
Bourn Cl. Winn 87 E1
Bourne Arch. That 106 A2
Bourne Ave. Chert 124 A3
Bourne Ave. Read 86 A2
Bourne Ave. Wind 67 E2
Bourne Cl. Bou E 3 D3
Bourne Cl. Bur C 84 A2
Bourne End Rd. Bou E 20 C4
Bourne End Rd. Tapl 20 C4
Bourne Meadow. Stai 123 D3
Bourne Rd. Pangb 56 C3
Bourne Rd. Slough 42 B2
Bourne Rd. That 106 A2
Bourne Rd. Went 122 B2
Bourne Vale. Hung 100 B3
Bourneside. Went 122 A1
Bourton Cl. Read 84 C4
Bouverie Way. Slough 43 F1
Boveney Cl. Slough 42 A2
Boveney New Rd. Eton 41 F1
Boveney Rd. Dorn 41 E1
Bovingdon Hts. Mar 1 C1
Bowden Rd. Ascot 120 B2
Bower Way. Slough 41 F3
Bowes Rd. Stai 96 C1
Bowes Rd. That 106 B1
Bowfell Cl. Read 57 E1
Bowland Drive. Brac 118 C1
Bowling Ct. Hen-O-T 15 E2
Bowling Green Rd. That 106 A3
Bowmans Cl. Burn 21 D2
Bowry Dr. Wray 68 C1
Bowyer Cres. Woki 116 B4
Bowyer Dr. Slough 41 F3
Bowyer's La. New G 91 E3
Boxford Ridge. Brac 118 A3
Boyd Ct. Brac 118 A4
Boyn Hill Ave. Maid 39 E3
Boyn Hill Cl. Maid 39 E3
Boyn Hill Rd. Maid 39 E3
Boyn Valley Rd. Maid 39 E3
Boynden Rd. Maid 39 E4
Bracken Bank. Burl 119 E4
Bracken Cl. Far C 22 B4
Bracken Cl. Read 57 E1
Bracken La. Yate 149 D3
Bracken Rd. Maid 39 E2
Bracken Way. Bur C 111 D1
Bracken Way. Fla H 3 D4
Brackendale Cl. Camb 151 F2
Brackendale Rd. Camb 151 E2
Brackenforde. Slough 43 E2
Brackens The. Brac 143 D4
Brackenwood. Bur C 110 C1
Bracknell Cl. Camb 144 C1
Bracknell Rd. Bags 145 F3
Bracknell Rd. Brac 143 F4
Bracknell Rd. Camb 145 D1
Bracknell Rd. New G 92 A3
Bracknell Rd. Wink 92 A3
Bradcutts La. Cook 19 F4
Bradenham La. Bish 18 B3
Bradfields. Brac 118 B2
Bradford Rd. Slough 42 A4
Brading Way. Purl 57 E3
Bradley Cl. Kint 102 A1
Bradley Rd. Slough 42 C3
Bradmore Way. Read 114 A4
Bradshaw Cl. Wind 66 C3
Bradwell Rd. Read 57 E2
Braemar Gdns. Slough 42 A2
Braemore Cl. That 106 B1
Brakendale Way. Read 87 D3
Bramber Ct. Slough 42 A3
Bramber Mews. Caver 59 F2
Bramble Cl. Shepp 125 E3
Bramble Cres. Read 84 C4
Bramble Dr. Maid 91 D1
Brambledown. Stai 124 A4
Bramblegate. Crow 143 D3
Brambles The. Brac 142 B3
Bramcote. Camb 152 B3
Bramley Cl. Chert 124 A1
Bramley Cl. Maid 39 E2
Bramley Cl. Read 87 D2
Bramley Cl. Stai 97 E1
Bramley Gr. Brac 142 B3
Bramley La. Black 150 A3
Bramley Rd. Camb 151 D1
Bramley Rd. Silc 136 A1
Bramling Ave. Yate 149 D3
Brammas Cl. Slough 42 B2
Bramshaw Rd. Read 58 A1
Bramshill Cl. Arbo 140 C4
Bramwell Cl. That 106 C1
Bran Cl. Read 84 C4
Brandon Ave. Wood 88 A4
Brandon Cl. Camb 152 B2
Brands Rd. Slough 69 D4
Branksome Cl. Camb 151 F3
Branksome Hill Rd. Sand 150 C4
Branksome Park Rd. Camb 151 F3
Brants Bridge. Brac 118 C3
Braunfels Wlk. Newb 104 C1
Bravington Cl. Stai 124 C2
Bray Cl. Maid 40 B2
Bray Ct. Holy 40 B1
Bray Rd. Maid 40 A3
Bray Rd. Read 85 D2
Braybank. Maid 40 B2
Braybrooke Gdns. Warg 36 B1
Braybrooke Rd. Brac 91 D1
Braybrooke Rd. Warg 36 B1
Braye Cl. Sand 143 E1
Brayfield Rd. Maid 40 B2
Brayford Rd. Read 113 E4
Braywick Rd. Maid 40 A3
Braywood Ave. Eng G 96 A1
Braziers La. Wink 92 B2
Breach Sq. Hung 100 B2
Breadcroft La. Bur G 38 C2
Breadcroft Rd. Whi Wa 38 C2
Bream Cl. Mar 18 B4
Brecon Rd. Wood 87 F4
Bredon Rd. Woki 88 C1
Bredward Cl. Burn 21 D1
Bremer Rd. Stan 97 D3
Brendon Cl. Harl 71 E4
Brendon Cl. Read 57 F1
Brent Cl. That 106 B1
Brent Gdns. Read 86 A2
Brent Rd. Bou E 3 D2
Brentmoor Rd. West E 153 E3
Brerewood. Read 86 C1
Bret Harte Rd. Camb 151 F1
Brewery Comm. Mort 137 D4
Brewhouse Hill. Frox 99 D2
Briant's Ave. Caver 59 E1
Briants Piece. Herm 79 D3
Briar Ave. Light 153 D4
Briar Cl. Burn 41 D4
Briar Cl. Caver 59 D3
Briar Dene. Maid 19 E1
Briar Glen. Cook 19 F3
Briar Rd. Stai 125 D2
Briar Way. Slough 42 A4
Briarlea Rd. Mort 136 C3
Briars Cl. Pangb 56 C3
Briars The. Slough 43 F1
Briars The. Stan 70 A1
Briarwood. Woki 141 F3
Brickfield La. Burn 21 D2
Brickfield La. Harl 71 E4
Bridge Ave. Cook 19 F3
Bridge Cl. Shepp 125 F1
Bridge Cl. Slough 41 F3
Bridge Cl. Stai 96 C2
Bridge End. Camb 151 D2
Bridge Gdns. Stai 98 B1
Bridge La. Went 122 C2
Bridge Rd. Ascot 120 B2
Bridge Rd. Bags 145 F2
Bridge Rd. Camb 151 D2
Bridge Rd. Chert 124 A1
Bridge Rd. Maid 40 A4
Bridge St. Caver 59 D1
Bridge St. Hung 100 B3
Bridge St. Iver 69 E4
Bridge St. Maid 40 A4
Bridge St. Newb 105 D2
Bridge St. Read 86 A4
Bridge St. Shepp 125 F1
Bridge St. Stai 96 C2
Bridge View. Went 121 D1
Bridge Walk. Yate 149 E4
Bridgeman Dr. Wind 67 D3
Bridges Cl. Woki 115 F4
Bridges The. Silc 136 B3
Bridgestone Dr. Bou E 3 E2
Bridgewater Cl. Read 58 B1
Bridgewater Terr. Wind 67 E3
Bridgewater Way. Wind 67 E3
Bridle Cl. Maid 19 F1
Bridle Rd. Maid 19 F1
Bridlepath Way. Felt 98 C4
Bridlington Spur. Slough 42 A2
Bridport Cl. Read 87 E1
Bridport Way. Slough 22 A1
Brierley Pl. Purl 57 E2
Briff La. Buck 107 E4
Brigham Rd. Read 59 D1
Brighton Rd. Read 87 D3
Brighton Spur. Slough 22 A1
Brightside Ave. Stai 97 E1
Brill Cl. Caver 59 D2
Brill Cl. Maid 39 E2
Brill Cl. Mar 1 B1
Brimblecombe Cl. Woki 89 D1
Brimpton Rd. Brim 133 F4
Brimpton Rd. Read 85 D2
Brimpton Rd. Tad 134 B1
Brimpton Rd. Wool 133 F4
Brinn's La. Sand 150 B3
Brisbane Rd. Read 85 D4
Bristol Cl. Stan 70 C1
Bristol Way. Slough 42 C3
Bristow Cres. Camb 151 E2
Bristow Ct. Mar 2 A2
Bristow Rd. Camb 151 D2
Britannia Way. Stan 97 E4
Britten Rd. Read 86 A3
Britwell Rd. Burn 21 E1
Brixham Rd. Read 86 A1
Broad Hinton. Twyf 61 F2
Broad La. Bou E 3 F3
Broad La. Brac 118 B3
Broad La. Buck 107 E3
Broad Oak. Slough 22 B1
Broad Oak Ct. Slough 22 B1
Broad Platts. Slough 43 E2
Broad St. East I 30 C4
Broad St. Read 86 A4
Broad St. West E 153 E3
Broad St. Woki 116 B3
Broad Street Mall The. Read 86 A4
Broad Wlk. Camb 151 F1
Broadacre. Stai 97 D2
Broadcommon Rd. Hurst 89 D4
Broadhalfpenny La. Tad 135 E1
Broadlands Ave. Shepp 125 E2
Broadlands Cl. Read 84 B3
Broadlands Dr. Sunn 120 B1
Broadley Green. Windl 146 B2
Broadmark Rd. Slough 43 D3
Broadmoor La. W St L 63 D3
Broadmoor La. Whi Wa 63 D3
Broadwater Cl. Wray 95 F4
Broadwater La. Hurst 61 F1
Broadwater Park. Holy 40 C1
Broadwater Rd. Twyf 61 F2
Broadway. Brac 118 B4
Broadway. Maid 39 F4
Broadway. That 106 B2
Broadway Rd. Light 146 B1
Broadway The. Lamb 25 D2
Broadway The. Newb 105 D2
Broadway The. Sand 150 A4
Broadway The. Stai 124 B4
Brocas Rd. Bur C 110 C1
Brocas St. Eton 67 E4
Brocas Terr. Eton 67 E4
Brock Gdns. Read 85 E4
Brock La. Maid 39 F4
Brock Way. Vir W 122 B3
Brockenhurst Dr. Yate 149 E3
Brockenhurst Rd. Ascot 120 A2
Brockenhurst Rd. Brac 119 D3
Brocklands. Yate 149 D2
Brockley Cl. Read 85 D4
Brocks La. Buck 80 A2
Brocks Way. Shipl 36 A2
Brocksby Cl. Black 150 A3
Broken Furlong. Eton 42 A1
Broken Way. Newt 131 E1
Bromley Wlk. Read 84 C4
Brompton Cl. Winn 87 E1
Brompton Dr. Maid 19 E1
Bromycroft Rd. Slough 22 A1
Brook Cl. Sand 143 F1
Brook Cl. Stan 97 F4
Brook Cl. Woki 116 A4
Brook Cres. Slough 41 F4
Brook Dr. Ashf 98 C1
Brook Dr. Brac 118 C3
Brook La. Hurst 62 C2
Brook Path. Slough 41 F3
Brook Path. Slough 41 F3
Brook Rd. Bags 145 F1
Brook Rd. Camb 151 D2
Brook St. Twyf 61 E2
Brook St. Wind 67 E3
Brook St W. Read 86 A3
Brookbank. Bou E 3 E2
Brookdene Cl. Maid 19 F1
Brooke Pl. Binf 90 B2
Brookers Cnr. Crow 143 E3
Brookers Hill. Read 113 E3
Brookers Row. Brac 143 D3
Brookfield Rd. Bou E 3 E2
Brookhouse Dr. Bou E 3 E2
Brooklands Cl. Stai 125 F4
Brooklyn Dr. Caver 59 D3
Brookmill The. Read 85 F3
Brooks Rd. That 106 C2
Brooksby Rd. Read 57 E1
Brookside. Chert 123 F1
Brookside. Iver 69 E4
Brookside. Read 84 C2
Brookside. Sand 150 B4
Brookside. Woki 115 F4
Brookside Ave. Stai 97 E2
Brookside Ave. Wray 68 C2
Brookside Cl. Read 87 E1
Brookway. Newb 105 E1
Broom Acres. Sand 143 D1
Broom Cl. Black 150 C2
Broom Cl. Read 84 B3
Broom Field. Light 153 D4
Broom Gr. Woki 115 E2
Broom Hill. Cook 19 F3
Broom Hill. Sto P 23 D3
Broome Cl. Yate 149 E4
Broomfield Cl. Went 121 D1
Broomfield Park. Went 121 D1
Broomfield Rd. Read 58 A1
Broomfield Rd. Read 84 C4
Broomhall La. Sunn 121 D2
Broomsquire Rd. Bags 145 F1
Broughton Cl. Read 58 B1
Broughton Mews. Camb 151 F1
Brownfields Gdns. Maid 39 F3
Browngraves Rd. Harl 71 E4
Browning Cl. Camb 152 B2
Browning Cl. That 106 B2
Brownlow Dr. Brac 91 E1
Brownlow Rd. Read 85 F4
Brownrigg Cres. Brac 118 C4
Brownrigg Rd. Ashf 98 A2
Brownsfield Rd. That 106 B2
Bruan Rd. Newb 130 C4
Bruce Ave. Shepp 125 E2
Bruce Cl. Slough 42 A3
Bruce Rd. Wood 87 E4
Bruce Wlk. Wind 66 B3
Brudenell. Wind 66 C2
Brummell Rd. Newb 104 C3
Brunel Cl. Maid 39 F3
Brunel Dr. Wood 60 C1
Brunel Rd. Maid 39 E3
Brunel Rd. Read 85 D2
Brunel Way. Slough 42 C3
Brunswick. Brac 118 A1
Brunswick Hill. Read 85 F4
Brunswick St. Read 85 F3
Bruton Way. Brac 118 C1
Bryant Ave. Slough 42 C4
Bryants La. Yatt 53 F1
Brybur Cl. Read 113 E4
Bryer Pl. Wind 66 B2
Buccaneer Cl. Wood 88 A4
Buccleuch Rd. Datch 68 A4
Buchan The. Camb 152 A4
Buchanan Dr. Woki 141 F4
Buchanan Sq. That 106 C1
Buck Side. Caver 59 D1
Buckden Cl. Wood 88 A3
Buckham Hill. Chadd 48 B3
Buckhurst Gr. Woki 116 C3
Buckhurst Hill. Brac 118 C3
Buckhurst La. Ascot 121 D3
Buckhurst Rd. Ascot 120 C4
Buckhurst Way. Read 87 D2
Buckingham Ave. Slough 42 A4
Buckingham Ave E. Slough 42 B4
Buckingham Dr. Caver 59 D3
Buckingham Gdns. Slough 42 C2
Buckingham Rd. Newb 104 C1
Buckingham Way. Camb 151 F1
Buckland Ave. Slough 43 D2
Buckland Cres. Wind 66 C3
Buckland Rd. Read 86 A2
Buckle La. New G 91 D3
Bucklebury. Brac 118 A1
Bucklebury Cl. Holy 40 B1
Bucknell Ave. Pangb 56 C3
Bucknell Cl. Read 84 C2
Budebury Rd. Stai 97 D2
Budge's Gdns. Woki 116 C4
Budge's Rd. Woki 116 B4
Buffins. Tapl 20 B1
Bulkeley Ave. Wind 67 D2
Bulkeley Cl. Eng G 95 E2
Bull La. Brac 118 A4
Bull La. Swal 139 D2
Bull Meadow The. Stre 33 F3
Bullbrook Dr. Brac 118 C4
Bullbrook Row. Brac 118 C4
Bullfinch Cl. Sand 150 C4
Bulmershe Rd. Read 86 C3
Bulpit La. Hung 100 B2
Bunby Rd. Sto P 22 C3
Bunces Cl. Eton 42 A1
Bunces La. Bur C 111 D1
Bundy's Way. Stai 96 C1
Bungler's Hill. Swal 140 A3
Bunkers Hill. Newb 130 B3
Bunten Meade. Slough 42 A3
Burbage Green. Brac 118 C2
Burbidge Cl. Read 84 C2
Burbidge Rd. Stai 125 D3
Burchell Rd. Newb 104 C3
Burchetts Green La. Bur G 38 B3
Burchetts Green Rd. Bur G 38 A4
Burchetts Way. Shepp 125 D2
Burcombe Way. Caver 59 D2
Burcot Gdns. Maid 19 F2
Burdett Ct. Read 86 B2
Burdock Cl. Bur C 111 D1
Burdock Cl. Light 153 D4
Burfield Rd. Old W 95 D4
Burford Cl. Mar B 1 B3
Burford Gdns. Slough 41 E4
Burford Rd. Camb 151 D2
Burford's. East G 47 E3
Burgess Cl. Wood 87 E2
Burgess La. Kint 128 B3
Burgett Rd. Slough 42 A2
Burghead Cl. Sand 150 B4
Burghfield Rd. Read 85 D2
Burgoyne Rd. Ashf 98 C1
Burgoyne Rd. Camb 152 A3
Burleigh Gdns. Ashf 98 B2
Burleigh La. Ascot 119 F4
Burleigh Mews. Caver 59 E3
Burleigh Rd. Ascot 119 F4
Burleigh Rd. Camb 151 E1
Burley Way. Black 150 B3
Burlings The. Ascot 119 F4
Burlington Ave. Slough 42 C2
Burlington Cl. Felt 98 B4
Burlington Ct. Black 150 B2
Burlington Rd. Burn 41 D4
Burlington Rd. Read 84 B4
Burlington Rd. Slough 42 C2
Burlsdon Way. Brac 118 C4
Burn Moor Chase. Brac 118 C1
Burn Wlk. Burn 21 D1
Burne-Jones Dr. Sand 150 B3
Burnetts Rd. Wind 66 C3
Burney Bit. Silc 135 F1
Burnham Cl. Bou E 3 D2
Burnham Cl. Wind 66 B3
Burnham Gr. Brac 91 E1
Burnham La. Slough 41 F4
Burnham Rd. Tad 134 C1
Burnham Rise. Caver 59 E3
Burniston Cl. Winn 87 F1
Burns Cl. Wood 87 F2
Burns Wlk. That 106 B2
Burnt Oak. Cook 19 F4
Burnt Oak. Woki 141 F4
Burnt Pollard La. West E 146 C1
Burnthouse La. BurC 112 A3
Burrcroft Rd. Read 85 D3
Burrell Rd. Comp 31 F2
Burroughs Cres. Bou E 3 D2
Burroway Rd. Slough 44 A2
Burrows Hill Cl. Stan 70 B2
Burton Cl. Windl 146 B2
Burton Way. Wind 66 C2
Burtons Hill. Kint 102 A1
Burway Cres. Chert 124 A3
Burwell Cl. Winn 87 E1
Burys Bank Rd. Gree 132 A3
Burys Bank Rd. That 132 A3
Bush Rd. Stai 125 D2
Business Centre The. Woki 116 A2
Butchers La. Whi Wa 63 E4
Bute St. Read 85 D3
Butler Ct. Mar 2 A2
Butler Rd. Bags 145 F1
Butler Rd. Crow 143 D3
Butlers Cl. Wind 66 B3
Butson Cl. Newb 104 C2
Buttenshaw Ave. Bark 141 D4
Buttenshaw Cl. Bark 141 D4
Butter Market. Read 86 A4
Butterfield. Bou E 3 E2
Buttermere Ave. Slough 41 E4
Buttermere Cl. Felt 98 C4
Buttermere Dr. Camb 152 B3
Buttermere Gdns. Brac 118 B3
Buttermere Way. Stai 96 A1
Buttersteep Rise. Brac 119 E1
Butts Hill Rd. Wood 87 F4
Buxton Ave. Caver 58 C2
Buxton Rd. Ashf 97 E2
Bybend Cl. Far C 22 A2
Byefield Rd. Read 85 D2
Byeways Cl. Warg 37 F2
Byland Dr. Holy 40 A1
Byreton Cl. Read 87 D1
Byron Ave. Camb 152 A2
Byron Cl. Mar 1 C2
Byron Cl. Newb 130 C4
Byron Cl. Twyf 61 F2
Byron Cl. Yate 149 D2
Byron Dr. Crow 143 D2
Byron Rd. Read 87 D4
Byron Rd. Twyf 61 F2
Bythorn Cl. Winn 87 F1
Byways. Burn 41 D4
Byways. Yate 149 D3
Bywood. Brac 118 A1
Byworth Cl. Read 113 D4

Cabrera Ave. Went 122 B2
Cabrera Cl. Went 122 B2
Cadbury Cl. Ashf 98 C1
Cadbury Rd. Ashf 98 C1
Caddy Cl. Eng G 96 A2
Cadogan Cl. Holy 65 D4
Cadwell Dr. Maid 39 E2
Caesar's Camp Rd. Camb 152 A4
Caesar's Way. Shepp 125 E2
Cages Wood Dr. Far C 22 A4
Cain Rd. Brac 117 F4
Cain's La. Harm 71 F1
Cairn Cl. Camb 152 A2
Cairngorm Rd. That 106 B1
Caistor Cl. Bur C 84 A2
Calard Dr. That 106 A3
Calbourne Dr. Bur C 84 B2
Calbroke Rd. Slough 21 F1
Calcot Ct. Read 84 C3
Calcot Place Dr. Read 84 C2
Caldbeck Dr. Wood 87 F4
Calder Cl. Maid 19 F1
Calder Cl. Read 84 C4
Calder Ct. Maid 19 E1
Calder Ct. Slough 43 F1
Calder Way. Stan 69 F2
Caldwell Rd. Windl 146 B3
Caledonia Rd. Stan 97 F4
Caleta Cl. Caver 59 E1
Calfridus Way. Brac 118 C3
Calleva Park. Alde 134 C1
Callington Rd. Read 86 B1
Callin's La. W St L 63 D2

Callis Farm Cl. Stan 70 C1
Callow Hill. Vir W 122 B4
Calshot Pl. Bur C 84 B2
Calshot Rd. Harm 71 D3
Calshot Way. Harm 71 D3
Calvin Cl. Camb 152 A2
Camberley Rd. Harm 71 D2
Camborne Cl. Harm 71 D2
Camborne Cl. Read 87 D1
Camborne Rd S. Harm 71 D2
Camborne Way. Harm 71 D2
Cambria Gdns. Stan 97 F4
Cambrian Way. Brac 142 A4
Cambrian Way. Bur C 84 B2
Cambridge Ave. Burn 21 D2
Cambridge Ave. Slough 42 A4
Cambridge Cl. Harm 70 B4
Cambridge Rd. Crow 143 E2
Cambridge Rd. Mar 1 B1
Cambridge Rd. Sand 143 F1
Cambridge Rd. Stai 90 B1
Cambridge St. Read 85 F4
Cambridge Wlk. Camb 151 E3
Cambridgeshire Cl. Woki 115 F3
Camden Pl. Bou E 3 D2
Camden Pl. Bur C 84 A2
Camden Rd. Maid 19 E1
Camellia Way. Woki 115 E4
Camilla Cl. Ashf 98 C1
Camley Gdns. Maid 39 D4
Camley Park Dr. Maid 38 C4
Camm Ave. Wind 66 C2
Camp Rd. Padw 110 B1
Campbell Rd. Wood 87 E3
Camperdown. Maid 20 A1
Campion Cl. Black 150 C2
Canada Rd. Slough 43 D2
Canal Walk. Hung 100 B3
Canal Way. Read 86 B4
Canal Wharf. Slough 44 A2
Canberra Cl. Yate 149 D4
Canberra Rd. Harm 71 D2
Candleford Cl. Brac 91 E1
Candover Cl. Harm 70 B4
Canford Ct. Read 85 E4
Cannock Cl. Maid 40 A3
Cannock Way. Wood 87 E1
Cannon Court Rd. Cook 19 E2
Cannon Court Rd. Maid 19 E2
Cannon Hill. Brac 118 B2
Cannon Hill Cl. Maid 40 B1
Cannon La. Maid 38 C2
Cannon La. Whi Wa 38 C2
Cannon St. Read 85 F4
Cannondown Rd. Cook 19 F3
Canon Hill Dr. Maid 40 A2
Canopus Way. Stan 97 F4
Cansfield End. Newb 104 C2
Canterbury Ave. Slough 22 B1
Canterbury Rd. Read 86 B2
Cantley Cres. Woki 116 A4
Captains Gorse. Upp B 54 C3
Caraway Rd. Read 87 D1
Carbery La. Ascot 120 A3
Carbinswood La. Buck 108 A3
Cardiff Rd. Read 58 C1
Cardigan Gdns. Read 86 C3
Cardigan Rd. Read 86 C3
Cardinal Cl. Caver 59 D1
Cardinals The. Brac 118 A3
Cardinal's Wlk. Ashf 98 C1
Cardinals Wlk. Slough 41 E4
Cardwell Cres. Ascot 120 B2
Carew Rd. Ashf 98 B1
Carey Cl. Wind 67 D2
Carey Rd. Woki 116 B3
Carey St. Read 85 F4
Cariad Ct. Gori 34 A4
Carisbrooke Cl. Caver 59 E3
Carisbrooke Cl. Maid 39 E3
Carisbrooke Ct. Slough 42 C3
Carland Cl. Read 87 D1
Carlile Gdns. Twyf 61 E3
Carlingwark Dr. Camb 151 F4
Carlisle Rd. Read 57 F2
Carlisle Rd. Slough 42 B3
Carlton Cl. Camb 152 A2
Carlton Cl. Wood 87 F3
Carlton Rd. Ashf 98 C1
Carlton Rd. Caver 58 C3
Carlton Rd. Slough 43 D3
Carlyle Rd. Stai 97 D1
Carmarthen Rd. Slough 42 C3
Carnarvon Rd. Read 86 C3
Carnation Dr. Burl 92 A1
Carnegie Rd. Newb 105 D1
Carnoustie. Brac 117 F1
Carolina Pl. Woki 141 F4
Caroline Ct. Ashf 98 A1
Caroline Ct. Mar 1 C2
Caroline Dr. Woki 116 A4
Caroline St. Read 85 F4
Caroline Way. Camb 151 F1
Carrick Gdns. Wood 87 E4
Carrick La. Yate 149 F3
Carrington Ave. Fla H 3 D4
Carrington Rd. Slough 42 C3
Carroll Cres. Ascot 119 F3
Carron Cl. Read 85 D4
Carsdale Cl. Read 85 F3
Carshalton Rd. Camb 145 D1
Carshalton Way. Wood 87 E1
Carston Gr. Read 84 C2
Carter Cl. Wind 67 D3
Carter's Hill. Binf 90 A2
Carters Rise. Read 84 C2
Cartmel Dr. Wood 87 E3
Cary Cl. Newb 130 B3
Casey Ct. Stan D 81 E2
Cassia Dr. Read 86 C1
Cassiobury Ave. Felt 98 C4
Castle Ave. Datch 68 A4
Castle Cl. Camb 151 F2
Castle Cl. Stai 98 C1
Castle Cres. Read 85 F3
Castle Ct. Maid 39 E4
Castle Dr. Maid 39 E4
Castle Gr. Newb 104 C3
Castle Hill. Maid 39 F4
Castle Hill. Read 85 F3
Castle Hill. Swal 140 B4
Castle Hill Rd. Eng G 95 E3
Castle Hill Terr. Maid 39 F4
Castle La. Wint 104 C3
Castle Mews. Maid 39 F4
Castle Rd. Camb 151 F2
Castle St. Read 86 A4
Castle St. Slough 42 C2
Castlecraig Ct. Sand 150 B4
Castleton Ct. Mar 1 C1
Castleview Rd. Slough 43 E1
Castor Ct. Yate 149 D4
Caswall Cl. Binf 90 B1
Caswall Ride. Yate 149 F3
Catalina Cl. Wood 88 A4
Catcliffe Way. Read 113 F4
Catena Rise. Light 146 A1
Catesby Gdns. Yate 149 D3
Catherine Dr. Ashf 98 C1
Catherine Rd. Newb 105 D1
Catherine St. Read 85 F4
Catlin Cres. Shepp 125 E2
Catmore Rd. Farn 29 E4
Catmore Rd. West I 29 E4
Caunter Rd. Newb 104 B2
Causeway The. Maid 40 A2
Causeway The. Maid 40 B2
Causeway The. Mar 1 C1
Causeway The. Stai 96 B2
Causmans Way. Read 57 E1
Cavalier Cl. Newb 105 E3
Cavalier Cl. Thea 83 E1
Cavalry Cres. Wind 67 E2
Cavendish Cl. Ashf 98 C1
Cavendish Cl. Burn 41 D4
Cavendish Ct. Black 150 B2
Cavendish Gdns. Winn 88 A2
Cavendish Meads. Ascot 120 B2
Cavendish Rd. Ashf 98 C1
Cavendish Rd. Caver 59 E3
Caversham Park Rd. Caver 59 F3
Caversham Rd. Caver 59 D1
Caves Farm Cl. Sand 150 A4
Cawcott Dr. Wind 66 C3
Cawsham Gdns. Caver 59 E2
Caxton Cl. Read 58 B1
Cecil Aldin Dr. Purl 57 E2
Cecil Cl. Ashf 98 B1
Cecil Rd. Ashf 98 B1
Cecil Rd. Iver 44 C4
Cecil Way. Slough 21 F1
Cedar Ave. Black 150 B3
Cedar Chase. Tapl 20 B1
Cedar Cl. Bags 145 F2
Cedar Cl. Stai 124 B3
Cedar Cl. Woki 116 B3
Cedar Ct. Eng G 96 A2
Cedar Ct. Mar 1 C1
Cedar Dr. Brac 91 E1
Cedar Dr. Mar B 1 B4
Cedar Dr. Pangb 56 B2
Cedar Dr. Windl 121 D1
Cedar Mount. Newb 130 C4
Cedar Rd. Felt 98 B4
Cedar Rd. Read 86 C1
Cedar Way. Slough 43 F1
Cedar Way. Stai 98 C1
Cedar Wood Cres. Caver 59 D2
Cedars Cl. Sand 149 F4
Cedars Rd. Maid 40 A4
Cedars The. Read 57 E1
Celandine Cl. Crow 143 E3
Celandine Ct. Yate 149 D4
Celia Cres. Stai 97 E1
Cell Farm Ave. Old W 68 A1
Celsea Pl. Chol 14 A4
Cemetery La. Shepp 125 D1
Central Dr. Slough 41 F3
Centre The. Shepp 125 F1
Centurion Cl. Read 86 A3
Centurion Cl. Sand 150 B4
Century Rd. Stai 96 B2
Cerotus Pl. Chert 123 F1
Ceviot Rd. Sand 142 C1
Chaffinch Cl. Sand 150 B4
Chaffinch Cl. Woki 115 F3
Chagford Rd. Read 86 A1
Chain St. Read 86 A4
Chainhill Rd. Farn 8 A4
Chalcraft Cl. Hen-O-T 35 E4
Chalfont Cl. Read 87 D1
Chalfont Way. Read 87 D1
Chalford. Woo G 3 F3
Chalford Rd. Newb 104 C1
Chalgrove Cl. Maid 40 A3
Chalgrove Way. Caver 59 E3
Chalk Hill. Ast T 12 C4
Chalk Hill. Shipl 35 E3
Chalk Pit La. Burn 21 D2
Chalkhousegreen La. Maples 59 D4
Chalklands. Bou E 3 D2
Chalkpit La. Mar 1 A2
Challenge Rd. Felt 98 B2
Challenor Cl. Woki 141 F4
Challow Ct. Maid 19 E1
Chalmers Rd. Ashf 98 A2
Chalmers Rd. Ashf 98 B2
Chalmers Rd. E. Ashf 98 B2
Chalvey Gdns. Slough 42 C2
Chalvey Gr. Slough 42 A2
Chalvey Park. Slough 42 C2
Chalvey Rd E. Slough 42 C2
Chalvey Rd W. Slough 42 B2
Chamberlain's Gdns. Arbo 114 C1
Champion Rd. Caver 59 E1
Chancellor's Way The. Read 86 C2
Chanctonbury Dr. Sunn 120 C1
Chandlers Cl. Felt 98 C4
Chandlers La. Yate 149 E4
Chandos Rd. Newb 131 D4
Chandos Rd. Stai 96 B2
Chantry Cl. Wind 67 D3
Chantry Mead. Hung 100 B3
Chantry Rd. Bags 145 E1
Chantry Rd. Chert 124 B1
Chapel Cl. Sou S 14 B2
Chapel Ct. That 106 C2
Chapel Hill. Read 84 B4
Chapel La. Asham 54 A4
Chapel La. Bags 145 E1
Chapel La. Binf 90 B1
Chapel La. Blew 12 A4
Chapel La. Camb 151 D1
Chapel La. Head 133 F1
Chapel La. Herm 78 C3
Chapel La. Herm 79 E4
Chapel La. Lamb 25 D2
Chapel La. Shin 113 D1
Chapel La. Silc 135 D1
Chapel La. Sto P 23 D3
Chapel La. Swal 139 E2
Chapel La. Yatt 53 F1
Chapel Rd. Camb 151 D3
Chapel Rd. Fla H 3 D4
Chapel Row. Twyf 61 E2
Chapel Sq. Sand 150 C3
Chapel St. Mar 1 C1
Chapel St. Slough 42 C2
Chapel St. That 106 B2
Chaplain's Hill. Crow 143 E2
Chaplin Cres. Ashf 98 C1
Chapman La. Bou E 3 D3
Chapman La. Fla H 3 D3
Chapter Mews. Wind 67 E4
Charadon Cl. Read 86 A3
Chard Cl. Wood 87 F3
Chard Rd. Harm 71 D3
Charlbury Cl. Brac 118 C3
Charles Evans Way. Caver 59 E1
Charles Gdns. Slough 43 D4
Charles Rd. Chol 14 A4
Charles Rd. Stai 97 E1
Charles Sq. Brac 118 B4
Charles St. Chert 123 F1
Charles St. Newb 130 B3
Charles St. Read 85 F4
Charles St. Wind 67 D3
Charlotte Cl. Herm 79 D3
Charlotte Way. Mar 1 C1
Charlton. Oak G 66 B3
Charlton Cl. Slough 42 A2
Charlton Ct. Sand 143 E1
Charlton La. Shepp 125 E3
Charlton La. Swal 139 E3
Charlton Pl. Newb 105 D2
Charlton Rd. Stai 125 E4
Charlton Sq. Oak G 66 B3
Charlton Way. Oak G 66 B3
Charlville Dr. Bur C 84 A2
Charmwood Cl. Newb 104 C3
Charnham La. Hung 100 B4
Charnham St. Hung 100 B3
Charrington Rd. Bur C 84 B2
Charta Rd (E). Stai 96 B1
Charta Rd (S). Stai 96 B1
Charta Rd (W). Stai 96 B2
Charter Cl. Slough 42 C2
Charter Rd. Newb 131 D4
Charter Rd. Slough 41 F3
Charterhouse Cl. Brac 118 C2
Charters La. Ascot 120 B2
Charters Rd. Sun 120 C1
Charters Rd. Windl 120 C1
Charters Way. Windl 120 C1
Charvil House Rd. Char 61 D3
Charvil La. Sonn 60 C2
Charwood Rd. Woki 116 C4
Chase Gdns. Binf 90 B2
Chase The. Bur C 84 B2
Chase The. Crow 143 D3
Chase The. Mar 2 A2
Chaseside Ave. Twyf 61 E4
Chaseside Gdns. Chert 124 A1
Chatfield. Slough 42 A4
Chatham St. Read 85 F4
Chatsworth Ave. Winn 88 A1
Chatsworth Cl. Caver 59 E3
Chatsworth Cl. Maid 39 E3
Chatsworth Hts. Camb 152 A4
Chatteris Way. Winn 114 B4
Chattern Hill. Ashf 98 A2
Chattern Rd. Ashf 98 B2
Chatton Cl. Read 114 A4
Chaucer Cl. Caver 59 D3
Chaucer Cl. Woki 116 C3
Chaucer Cres. Newb 104 C3
Chaucer Rd. Ashf 97 F2
Chaucer Rd. Crow 143 D2
Chaucer Way. Woki 115 F3
Chauntry Cl. Maid 40 B3
Chauntry Rd. Maid 40 A3
Chavey Down Rd. Burl 92 A1
Chawridge La. Wink 92 B4
Chazey Cl. Maple 58 B4
Chazey Rd. Caver 58 B2
Cheam Cl. Brac 118 B2
Cheap St. Comp 31 F3
Cheap St. Newb 105 D1
Cheapside. Read 86 A4
Cheapside Rd. Ascot 120 B4
Cheddar Rd. Harm 71 D3
Cheddington Cl. Read 84 C3
Cheeseman Cl. Woki 116 B4
Chelford Way. Caver 58 C2
Chelsea Cl. Read 57 F1
Chelwood Dr. Sand 142 C1
Chelwood Rd. Read 87 D1
Cheney Cl. Binf 90 B1
Cheniston Gr. Maid 38 C4
Chepstow Rd. Read 57 E1
Chequer La. Bee H 138 C1
Chequers Orchard. Iver 44 C4
Chequers Way. Wood 87 E4
Cherbury Cl. Brac 118 C3
Cherington Gate. Maid 19 D1
Cherington Way. Ascot 119 F4
Cheriton Ave. Twyf 61 E3
Cheriton Cl. Newb 131 D4
Cheriton Way. Black 150 B3
Cherries The. Slough 43 D4
Cherry Ave. Slough 43 E2
Cherry Cl. Caver 59 F4
Cherry Cl. Fla H 3 D4
Cherry Cl. Newb 104 C2
Cherry Garden La. Bur G 38 C2
Cherry Orch. Gr She 48 A2
Cherry Orch. Sto P 23 D3
Cherry Orchard. Stai 97 D2
Cherry Rise. Fla H 3 D4
Cherry Tree Ave. Stai 97 D1
Cherry Tree Cl. Sand 143 E1
Cherry Tree Dr. Brac 118 B3
Cherry Tree Gr. Woki 115 E2
Cherry Tree La. Fulm 23 F3
Cherry Tree Rd. Far C 22 B3
Cherry Way. Shepp 125 F3
Cherrydale Rd. Camb 152 B3
Cherrygarden La. Whi Wa 63 F4
Cherrywood Ave. Eng G 95 D1
Cherrywood Gdns. Fla H 3 D4
Chertsey Bridge Rd. Shepp 124 B1
Chertsey La. Stai 96 C1
Chertsey Rd. Felt 98 C2
Chertsey Rd. Shepp 124 B1
Chertsey Rd. Windl 146 C3
Chervil Way. Bur C 111 D1
Cherwell Cl. Maid 40 A4
Cherwell Cl. Slough 69 D4
Cherwell Rd. Bou E 3 D2
Cherwell Rd. Caver 59 D3
Cheseridge Rd. Comp 31 E2
Cheshire Ct. Slough 43 D2
Chessholme Ct. Ashf 98 C1
Chessholme Rd. Ashf 98 B1
Chester Cl. Ashf 98 B2
Chester Cl. Newb 105 E1
Chester Rd. Harm 71 D2
Chester Rd. Slough 42 B4
Chester St. Caver 59 D1
Chester St. Read 85 E4
Chesterblade La. Brac 118 C1
Chesterfield Rd. Ashf 97 F2
Chesterfield Rd. Newb 105 D1
Chesterman St. Read 86 A3
Chesters Rd. Camb 152 A3
Chesterton Rd. That 106 B3
Chestnut Ave. Camb 152 A3
Chestnut Ave. Caver 59 F2
Chestnut Ave. Slough 43 F2
Chestnut Ave. Went 121 F3
Chestnut Cl. Ashf 98 A2
Chestnut Cl. Ashf 98 C1
Chestnut Cl. Black 150 C3
Chestnut Cl. Eng G 95 E1
Chestnut Cl. Harl 71 D4
Chestnut Cl. Maid 20 A1
Chestnut Cl. Thea 83 F2
Chestnut Cres. Newb 105 D2
Chestnut Cres. Shin 113 F2
Chestnut Dr. Bur C 111 D2
Chestnut Dr. Eng G 95 E1
Chestnut Dr. Wind 66 C2
Chestnut Gr. Purl 57 E3
Chestnut Gr. Stai 97 E1
Chestnut La. Lamb 25 F2
Chestnut Manor Cl. Stai 97 D2
Chestnut Rd. Ashf 98 A2
Chestnut Wlk. Hung 100 B2
Chestnut Wlk. Shepp 125 F3
Chestnuts The. Shipl 36 A2
Chetwode Cl. Woki 116 C3
Cheveley Gdns. Burn 21 E2
Cheviot Cl. Camb 152 B2
Cheviot Cl. Hart 71 E4
Cheviot Cl. Maid 40 A3
Cheviot Cl. Newb 130 B3
Cheviot Dr. Char 61 D2
Cheviot Rd. Slough 44 A1
Chewter Cl. Bags 145 F2
Chewter La. Windl 146 A3
Cheylesmore Dr. Camb 152 B2
Cheyne Rd. Ashf 98 B1
Chichester Ct. Slough 43 D2
Chichester Rd. Read 84 C4
Chicory Cl. Read 86 C1
Chievley Cl. Read 84 B4
Chilcombe Way. Read 87 E1
Child St. Lamb 25 D1
Childrey Way. Read 84 B4
Chillingham Way. Camb 151 E2
Chilsey Green Rd. Chert 123 F1
Chiltern Cl. Hen-O-T 35 D4
Chiltern Cl. Newb 130 B3
Chiltern Cres. Read 87 D4
Chiltern Dr. Char 61 D2
Chiltern Green. Fla H 3 D4
Chiltern Rd. Burn 41 D4
Chiltern Rd. Caver 59 E2
Chiltern Rd. Maid 40 A3
Chiltern Rd. Mar 1 B1
Chiltern Rd. Sand 142 C1
Chiltern View. Purl 57 E3
Chiltern Wlk. Pangb 56 C3
Chilterns Cl. Fla H 3 D4
Chilterns Park. Bou E 3 D3
Chilton Way. Hung 100 B3
Chilwick Rd. Slough 21 F1
Chippendale Cl. Black 150 C2
Chippendale Cl. Tad 134 C1
Chippenham Cl. Read 113 F4
Chipstead Rd. Harm 71 D2
Chisbury Cl. Brac 118 C2
Chitterfield Gate. Harm 71 D4
Chittering Cl. Winn 87 E1
Chive Rd. Read 87 D1
Chivers Dr. Woki 141 F4
Chobham La. Went 122 A1
Chobham Rd. Camb 151 F1
Chobham Rd. Went 121 D1
Choke La. Cook 19 D2
Cholmeley Pl. Read 86 C4
Cholmeley Rd. Read 86 C4
Cholmeley Terr. Read 86 C4
Cholsey Rd. That 106 C2
Choseley Cl. Know H 37 F2
Choseley Rd. Know H 37 F2
Chrislaine Cl. Stan 70 B1
Christchurch Dr. Black 150 B3
Christchurch Gdns. Read 86 B3
Christchurch Rd. Harm 71 D2
Christchurch Rd. Read 86 B3
Christchurch Rd. Vir W 122 B3
Christie Cl. Light 146 B1
Christie Hts. Newb 131 D4
Christie Wlk. Yate 149 E2
Christmas La. Far C 22 B4
Christopher Ct. Newb 105 D1
Chudleigh Gdns. Read 86 B1
Church App. Stai 123 E3
Church Cl. Eton 67 E4
Church Cl. Ham M 129 F3
Church Cl. Lamb 25 D2
Church Cl. Maid 39 E3
Church Cl. Stai 124 B3
Church Cl. Winn 88 B1
Church Croft. Hung 100 B3
Church Dr. Maid 40 B2
Church End La. Read 84 C4
Church Farmbarns. Mort 137 E3
Church Gate. That 106 B2
Church Gr. Slough 43 E4
Church Hams. Woki 141 E3
Church Hill. Binf 90 B3
Church Hill. Camb 151 F3
Church Hill. Chil 10 B4
Church Hill. East I 30 C3
Church Hill. Hurst 88 C3
Church La. Arbo 114 B2
Church La. Ascot 120 B3
Church La. Asham 54 A3
Church La. Bark 115 E1
Church La. Binf 90 B2
Church La. Brim 133 F3
Church La. Bur C 111 F3
Church La. Chiev 51 D1
Church La. Combe 147 F3
Church La. Finch 141 F2
Church La. Ham M 129 F4
Church La. Hung 100 B3
Church La. Maid 40 B2
Church La. Newb 104 B2
Church La. Padw 110 B2
Church La. Read 113 E3
Church La. Shipl 35 F1
Church La. Silc 136 C1
Church La. Slough 43 E4
Church La. Sto P 22 C1
Church La. Swal 140 B3
Church La. That 106 B2
Church La. Twyf 61 F3
Church La. Wind 67 E3
Church La. Yatt 53 F1
Church Mews. Purl 57 E3
Church Path. Maid 40 B2
Church Rd. Alde 135 D4
Church Rd. Ascot 120 A3
Church Rd. Ashf 97 F2
Church Rd. Bags 145 E2
Church Rd. Brac 118 B4
Church Rd. Burl 119 D4
Church Rd. Camb 151 E1
Church Rd. Caver 59 D1
Church Rd. Cook 19 D3
Church Rd. Crow 143 D3
Church Rd. Eng G 96 A2
Church Rd. Far C 22 B1
Church Rd. Frox 99 D3
Church Rd. Ham 126 A1
Church Rd. Lit M 2 B3
Church Rd. Maid 40 A3
Church Rd. Newb 105 D3
Church Rd. Pangb 56 B3
Church Rd. Read 87 D3
Church Rd. Sand 143 F1
Church Rd. Shepp 125 D1
Church Rd. Silc 135 F1
Church Rd. Silc 135 F1
Church Rd. Sunn 121 D2
Church Rd. Swal 139 E3
Church Rd. West E 153 F4
Church Rd. Windl 146 B2
Church Rd. Wink 92 B3
Church Rd. Wood 87 F4
Church Rd E. Crow 143 E3
Church Rd W. Crow 143 D2

Church Side. East I 30 C3
Church Sq. Shepp 125 D1
Church St. Blew 12 A4
Church St. Burn 21 E1
Church St. Caver 59 D1
Church St. Crow 143 D3
Church St. Frox 99 D1
Church St. Gr She 48 A2
Church St. Hamp N 52 C3
Church St. Hen-O-T 15 E1
Church St. Hung 100 B3
Church St. Kint 102 A1
Church St. Read 86 A3
Church St. Slough 42 B2
Church St. Slough 42 C2
Church St. Stai 96 C2
Church St. Thea 83 F2
Church St. Twyf 61 E2
Church St. Warg 36 B1
Church St. Wind 67 E3
Church View. Been 109 D3
Church View. Whi Wa 63 F4
Church Views. Maid 39 F4
Church Way. Hung 100 B3
Churchfield Mews. Slough 43 D4
Churchill Cl. Fla H 3 D4
Churchill Cl. Fla H 3 E4
Churchill Cres. Yate 149 E3
Churchill Dr. Mar 1 C2
Churchill Dr. Winn 88 A1
Churchill Rd. Slough 43 F1
Churchward Wlk. Read 84 C2
Churchway. West I 10 A1
Churn Rd. Comp 31 E3
Cinnamon Cl. Read 86 C1
Cintra Ave. Read 86 B3
Cippenham Cl. Slough 41 F3
Cippenham La. Slough 42 A3
Circle Hill Rd. Crow 143 E3
Circuit La. Read 85 E3
City Rd. Read 84 A4
Clacy Green. Brac 91 D1
Clandon Ave. Stai 96 B1
Clanfield Cres. Read 57 E1
Clanfield Ride. Black 150 B3
Clappers Meadow. Maid 20 B1
Clapps Gate Rd. Silc 135 F1
Clapton App. Woo G 3 E4
Clare Ave. Woki 116 B4
Clare Dr. Far C 22 A4
Clare Gdns. Eng G 96 A2
Clare Rd. Maid 39 E3
Clare Rd. Slough 41 E4
Clare Rd. Stan 70 C1
Clare Rd. Stan 97 F4
Clare Wlk. Newb 130 B3
Claredon Cl. Winn 88 B1
Clarefield Cl. Maid 19 D1
Clarefield Dr. Maid 19 D1
Clarefield Rd. Maid 19 D1
Claremont Ave. Camb 151 F3
Claremont Dr. Shepp 125 D2
Claremont Gdns. Mar 1 C1
Claremont Rd. Mar 1 C1
Claremont Rd. Stai 96 B2
Claremont Rd. Wind 67 E3
Clarence Cres. Wind 67 E3
Clarence Dr. Eng G 95 E2
Clarence Rd. Hen-O-T 15 E1
Clarence Rd. Wind 67 D3
Clarence St. Eng G 95 F1
Clarence St. Stai 96 C2
Clarence Way. Read 84 A2
Clarendon Ct. Black 150 B2
Clarendon Ct. Slough 43 D3
Clarendon Gdns. Newb 105 D2
Clarendon Rd. Ashf 97 F2
Clarendon Rd. Read 87 D3
Clares Green Rd. Shin 113 D2
Clarewood Dr. Camb 151 F3
Clarke Cres. Sand 150 C4
Clark's Gdns. Hung 100 B3
Classics The. Lamb 25 D1
Claverdon. Brac 118 A1
Clay Cl. Fla H 3 D4
Clay Hill Cres. Newb 105 E3
Clay La. Been 108 C3
Claydon Gdns. Camb 151 D1
Clayhall La. Old Wind 67 F1
Clayhill Cl. Brac 119 D3
Clayton Gr. Brac 118 C4
Clayton Rd. Black 150 C1
Clayton Wlk. Read 86 B2
Claytons Meadow. Bou E 3 D2
Clearsprings. Light 146 A1
Cleaves Way. Ashf 98 C1
Cleeve Down. Gori 34 B4
Cleeve Rd. Gori 34 A4
Clements Cl. Shin 113 D1
Clements Cl. Slough 43 D2
Clements Mead. Sulh 57 D1
Clements Rd. Hen-O-T 15 E2
Clent Rd. Read 86 A2
Cleve Ct. Wind 66 C2
Clevedon Dr. Read 87 D1
Clevedon Rd. Read 57 F2
Clevehurst Cl. Sto P 23 D3
Cleveland. Char 61 D2
Cleveland Cl. Maid 40 A3
Cleveland Dr. Stai 124 A4
Cleveland Gr. Newb 104 C2
Clevemede. Gori 34 B3
Clewborough Dr. Camb 152 A3
Clewer Ave. Wind 67 D3
Clewer Ct Rd. Wind 67 D4
Clewer Fields. Wind 67 D3
Clewer Hill Rd. Wind 66 C2
Clewer New Town. Wind 67 D3
Clewer Park. Wind 67 D4
Clifford Gr. Ashf 98 A2
Clifford Way. Bou E 3 D3
Clifton Cl. Maid 40 A2
Clifton Rd. Harm 71 D2
Clifton Rd. Newb 104 C1
Clifton Rd. Slough 43 D2
Clifton Rd. Woki 116 A4
Clifton Rise. Warg 36 C1
Clifton Rise. Wind 66 B3
Clifton St. Read 85 F4
Clintons Green. Brac 118 A4
Clive Ct. Slough 42 B2
Clive Green. Brac 118 A2
Clivedale Rd. Wood 87 F2
Cliveden Mead. Maid 20 B1
Cliveden Pl. Shepp 125 E2
Cliveden Rd. Tapl 20 C2
Clivemont Rd. Maid 39 F4
Clockhouse La. Ashf 98 A3
Clockhouse La. Felt 98 A3
Clockhouse La. E. Stai 96 A1
Clockhouse La E. Stai 96 A1
Clockhouse La W. Eng G 96 A1
Cloister Mews. Thea 83 F2
Cloisters The. Camb 151 E1
Cloisters The. Caver 59 D2
Clonmel Way. Burn 21 D1
Close End. Lamb 25 D1
Close The. Bou E 3 D3
Close The. Bur C 111 D2
Close The. Burl 119 E4
Close The. Gr She 48 A2
Close The. Hamp N 52 C3
Close The. Hen-O-T 35 E4
Close The. Light 146 A1
Close The. Sand 150 C4
Close The. Slough 41 E3
Close The. That 106 A2
Close The. Vir W 122 B2
Close The. Wood 87 F3
Clove Cl. Read 86 C1
Clover La. Yate 149 D3
Club La. Crow 143 E3
Clumps The. Felt 98 B2
Clyde Rd. Stan 97 F4
Clyve Way. Stai 123 F4
Coach House Cl. Camb 151 F2
Coach Ride. Mar 1 B2
Coalport Way. Read 57 F1
Cobb Cl. Datch 68 B3
Cobbett's La. Yate 149 F3
Cobblers Cl. Far C 22 A2
Cobham Rd. Wood 87 F4
Cochrane Cl. That 106 C2
Cochrane Pl. Windl 146 B3
Cock La. Brad 82 A1
Cock-a-Dobby. Sand 143 D1
Cockett Rd. Slough 43 F2
Cockney Hill. Read 84 C3
Cock's La. New G 92 A3
Cock's La. Wink 92 A3
Coe Spur. Slough 42 A2
Coftards. Slough 43 E4
Cold Ash Hill. Cold A 106 B4
Coldharbour Cl. Hen-O-T 35 E4
Coldharbour Cl. Stai 123 E3
Coldharbour La. Stai 123 E3
Coldharbour La. West E 153 F4
Coldharbour Rd. Hung 100 B2
Coldicutt St. Caver 59 E1
Coldmoorholme La. Bou E 2 C2
Colemans Moor La. Wood 87 F3
Colemans Moor Rd. Wood 88 A3
Colenorton Cres. Eton 41 F1
Coleridge Ave. Yate 149 F3
Coleridge Cl. Crow 143 E2
Coleridge Cres. Stan 69 F3
Coleridge Rd. Ashf 97 F2
Coley Ave. Read 85 F3
Coley Hill. Read 85 F3
Coley Park Rd. Read 85 F3
Coley Pl. Read 86 A3
Colin Way. Slough 42 A2
Collaroy Rd. Cold A 106 B4
College Ave. Maid 39 F4
College Ave. Slough 42 C2
College Ave. Stai 96 A1
College Cl. Camb 151 E4
College Cres. Sand 150 C4
College Cres. Wind 67 E3
College Glen. Maid 39 E4
College Piece. Mort 136 C3
College Rd. Maid 39 F4
College Rd. Read 86 C3
College Rd. Slough 41 F3
College Ride. Bags 145 E1
College Ride. Camb 151 E4
College Rise. Maid 39 E4
Colleton Dr. Twyf 61 F2
Collier Cl. Maid 19 F1
Colliers Way. Read 85 D4
Collingwood Rise. Camb 152 A4
Collingwood Wlk. Read 84 A4
Collins Cl. Newb 105 E2
Collinswood Rd. Far C 22 B4
Collis St. Read 86 A3
Colliston Wlk. Read 84 C2
Collum Green Rd. Sto P 23 D4
Coln Cl. Maid 39 F4
Colnbrook By-Pass. Iver 69 E4
Colnbrook By-Pass. Sloug 69 E4
Colndale Rd. Stan 69 F3
Colne Bank. Hort 69 E2
Colne Orchard. Iver 44 C4
Colne Way. Wray 96 A3
Colnebridge Cl. Stai 96 C2
Colnworth Cl. Read 114 A4
Colonel's La. Chert 124 A2
Colonial Rd. Felt 98 C4
Colonial Rd. Slough 43 D2
Colston Cl. Bur C 84 B2
Colthrop La. That 107 D1
Columbia Ct. Woki 141 F4
Colville Gdns. Light 153 E4
Colwyn Cl. Yate 149 E3
Colyer Cl. Herm 79 E4
Colyton Way. Purl 57 E3
Combe Rd. Read 84 C4
Combe View. Hung 100 B2
Combermere Cl. Wind 67 D3
Comet Rd. Stan 97 E4
Comet Way. Wood 88 A4
Commercial Rd. Read 86 A1
Commercial Rd. Stai 97 D1
Common Hill. Brad 82 C2
Common La. Brig 28 B3
Common La. Eton 42 B1
Common Rd. Dorn 41 E1
Common Rd. Eton 42 A1
Common Rd. Fla H 3 D4
Common Rd. Head 132 C1
Common Rd. Slough 44 A1
Common The. Fla H 3 D4
Common Wood. Far C 22 B4
Commonfield La. Bark 141 D4
Commonfields. West E 153 F3
Commons Rd. Woki 88 C1
Compton Ave. Read 57 D3
Compton Cl. Brac 117 F2
Compton Cl. Read 87 E2
Compton Cl. Sand 143 E1
Compton Ct. Slough 41 F4
Compton Dr. Maid 39 D4
Comsaye Wlk. Brac 118 B2
Concorde Way. Slough 42 B2
Concorde Way. Wood 88 A4
Condor Cl. Sulh 57 E2
Condor Rd. Stai 124 B3
Conegar Ct. Slough 42 C3
Congreve Cl. Alde 135 D4
Conifer Cl. Tad 134 C1
Conifer Crest. Newb 130 B2
Conifer Dr. Camb 152 A3
Conifer Dr. Sulh 57 D1
Conifer La. Stai 96 B2
Conifers The. Brac 143 D4
Coningham Rd. Read 113 E3
Coningsby. Brac 118 B3
Coningsby Cl. Maid 39 E2
Coningsby La. Holy 65 E3
Conisboro Ave. Caver 58 C3
Conisboro Way. Caver 58 C3
Coniston Cl. Camb 152 B2
Coniston Cl. That 106 A2
Coniston Cl. Wood 87 F3
Coniston Cres. Slough 41 E4
Coniston Ct. Light 146 A1
Coniston Dr. Read 57 F1
Coniston Way. Stai 96 A1
Connaught Ave. Ashf 97 F2
Connaught Cl. Crow 142 C2
Connaught Cl. Maid 19 F1
Connaught Cl. Read 85 E4
Connaught Cl. Yate 149 D3
Connaught Rd. Bags 145 E2
Connaught Rd. Camb 151 F3
Connaught Rd. Newb 105 D2
Connaught Rd. Read 85 E4
Connaught Rd. Slough 43 D2
Conniston Cl. Mar 1 A1
Connop Way. Camb 151 F2
Constable Way. Sand 150 C3
Constitution Rd. Read 85 D4
Consul Cl. Wood 88 A3
Control Tower Rd. Harm 71 D2
Convent Rd. Ashf 98 A2
Convent Rd. Wind 67 D3
Conway Dr. Ashf 98 B1
Conway Dr. That 106 A3
Conway Rd. Burn 41 D4
Conway Rd. Harm 71 D2
Conway Rd. Read 84 B3
Conway Rd. Slough 41 D4
Cookham Cl. Sand 143 E1
Cookham Dean Bottom La. Cook 19 E4
Cookham Rd. Maid 19 F1
Coolarne Rise. Camb 152 A3
Coolgardie Rd. Ashf 98 B2
Coombe Ct. That 106 C2
Coombe Hill. Farn 28 A4
Coombe Pine. Brac 118 B2
Coombe Rd. Comp 31 F2
Coombe Rd. Yate 149 D4
Coombe Sq. That 106 C2
Coombe The. Stre 33 F3
Coombes La. Woki 115 E2
Coombesbury La. Box 76 B1
Cooper Cl. Read 113 E4
Cooper Rd. Hen-O-T 15 E2
Cooper Rd. Windl 146 B2
Cooper Way. Slough 42 A2
Coopers Cl. Stai 96 C2
Coopers Cres. That 106 B2
Cooper's Hill La. Eng G 95 E2
Cope Hall La. Ham M 130 B4
Copelands Cl. Camb 152 B2
Copenhagen Cl. Read 113 E4
Copped Hall Dr. Camb 152 B3
Copped Hall Way. Camb 152 B3
Copper Beech Cl. Wind 66 B3
Copperage Rd. Farn 9 D1
Copperdale Cl. Read 86 C2
Coppermill Rd. Hort 69 D1
Coppermill Rd. Wray 69 D1
Coppice Cl. Newb 131 D4
Coppice Dr. Wray 95 E4
Coppice Gdns. Crow 142 C3
Coppice Gdns. Yate 149 E3
Coppice Green. Brac 90 C1
Coppice Rd. Wood 87 F2
Coppice The. Ashf 98 A1
Coppins La. Iver 44 C4
Copse Ave. Caver 59 F2
Copse Cl. Camb 152 A3
Copse Cl. Mar 1 B1
Copse Cl. Read 57 E2
Copse Dr. Woki 116 A4
Copse End. Camb 152 A3
Copse Mead. Wood 60 C1
Copse The. Warg 36 C2
Copse Way. Woki 141 F4
Copthorn Cl. Maid 39 D2
Copthorne Cl. Shepp 125 E2
Copthorne Dr. Light 146 A1
Corbett Gdns. Wood 87 F4
Corbridge Rd. Read 86 B2
Corby Cl. Wood 61 D1
Corby Dr. Eng G 95 E1
Cordelia Gdns. Stan 97 F4
Cordelia Rd. Stan 97 F4
Corderoy Cl. That 106 C1
Cordwalles Rd. Camb 151 F4
Cordwallis Rd. Maid 39 F4
Cordwallis St. Maid 39 F4
Cores End Rd. Bou E 3 D2
Corfe Gdns. Camb 151 F1
Corfe Gdns. Slough 42 A3
Corfe Mews. Caver 59 F2
Corfield Cl. Finch 141 F2
Coriander Way. Read 86 C1
Cormorant Pl. Sand 150 C4
Cornbunting Cl. Sand 150 B4
Cornerside. Ashf 98 B1
Cornfield Green. Woki 115 F4
Cornfield Rd. Wood 88 A4
Cornfields. Yate 149 D2
Cornflower Cl. Woki 115 E4
Cornwall Ave. Slough 22 B1
Cornwall Cl. Camb 151 F4
Cornwall Cl. Eton 41 F1
Cornwall Cl. Maid 19 F1
Cornwall Cl. Purl 57 D2
Cornwall Cl. Woki 115 E3
Cornwall Way. Stai 96 C1
Cornwell Rd. Old W 68 A1
Cornwood Gdns. Read 86 B2
Coronation Ave. Slough 43 F4
Coronation Rd. Ascot 120 A1
Coronation Rd. Bish 38 A3
Coronation Rd. Brac 120 A1
Coronation Rd. Yate 149 F4
Coronation Sq. Read 85 D2
Coronation Sq. Woki 116 B4
Corrie Gdns. Went 122 B1
Corrine Cl. Read 86 A1
Corsair Cl. Stan 97 F4
Corsair Rd. Stan 97 F4
Corsham Rd. Read 84 C2
Corsham Way. Crow 143 D3
Corwen Rd. Read 84 C4
Coster Cl. Newb 104 B3
Cotswold Cl. Maid 40 A3
Cotswold Cl. Slough 42 B2
Cotswold Cl. Stai 97 D2
Cotswold Rd. Sand 142 C1
Cotswold Way. Read 57 E1
Cottage Farm Way. Stai 123 E3
Cottage La. Bur C 85 E1
Cotterell Cl. Brac 91 D1
Cottesbrooke Cl. Stan 69 E3
Cottesmore. Brac 118 A1
Cottesmore Rd. Wood 87 E3
Coulson Way. Burn 41 D4
Course Rd. Ascot 120 A3
Court Cl. Holy 40 B1
Court Cres. Slough 42 B4
Court Dr. Maid 20 B2
Court Gdns. Camb 151 E3
Court Hill Rd. Farn 7 D4
Court Hill Rd. Let B 7 D4
Court La. Burn 21 E1
Court La. Iver 44 C3
Court La. Slough 41 D2
Court Rd. Maid 20 B2
Courtenay Dr. Caver 59 D4
Courtfield Rd. Ashf 98 A1
Courtfields Dr. Maid 39 E3
Courthouse Rd. Maid 39 E4
Courtlands. Maid 39 F3
Courtlands Ave. Slough 43 E1
Courtlands Hill. Pangb 56 B2
Courtlands Rd. Newb 105 D1
Courtney Rd. Harm 71 D2
Courts Rd. Read 87 D2
Courtyard The. Thea 83 F2
Coventry Rd. Read 86 C4
Coverdale Way. Slough 21 F1
Covert The. Sunn 120 A1
Cow La. East I 30 C4
Cow La. Moul 13 F2
Cow La. Read 58 C1
Cowley Ave. Chert 123 F1
Cowley La. Chert 123 F1
Coworth Cl. Sunn 121 D2
Coworth Rd. Sunn 121 D2
Cowper Cl. Chert 123 F2
Cowper Rd. Slough 22 A1
Cowper Way. Read 85 E2
Cowslade. Newb 104 B3
Cowslip Cl. Read 84 A3
Cox Green La. Maid 39 E2
Cox Green Rd. Maid 39 E2
Coxborrow Cl. Cook 19 F4
Coxeter Rd. Newb 104 C2
Cox's La. Wool 107 E2
Crabtree Cl. Herm 78 C3
Crabtree Rd. Camb 151 D1
Crabtree Rd. Stai 123 E4
Craddock Rd. Read 86 A2
Crafts End. Chil 10 C4
Craig Ave. Read 85 D4
Craigwell Cl. Stai 123 F4
Crail Cl. Woki 116 A2
Crake Pl. Sand 150 B4
Cranborne Gdns. Read 58 A1
Cranbourne Ave. Bur C 84 B2
Cranbourne Ave. Wind 66 C3
Cranbourne Cl. Slough 42 B3
Cranbourne Hall Caravan Site. Wink 93 D4
Cranbourne Rd. Slough 42 B3
Cranbrook Dr. Maid 19 E1
Cranbury Rd. Read 85 E4
Crane Ct. Sand 150 B4
Crane Wharf. Read 86 A4
Craneswater. Harl 71 F4
Cranford Ave. Stan 97 F4
Cranford Cl. Hurst 88 C4
Cranford Cl. Stan 97 F4
Cranford La. Harl 71 F4
Cranford La. Harm 71 F2
Cranford La. Harm 71 F3
Cranford Park Dr. Yate 149 E3
Cranleigh Rd. Felt 98 C2
Cranmer Cl. Sulh 57 D2
Cranwell Gr. Light 152 C4
Cranwell Gr. Stai 124 C3
Cranwell Rd. Harm 71 D2
Craufurd Rise. Maid 39 F4
Craven Cl. Kint 102 A1
Craven Dene. Newb 105 D2
Craven Rd. Ink 127 D3
Craven Rd. Newb 104 C1
Craven Rd. Read 86 B3
Craven Way. Kint 102 A1
Crawford Cl. Read 87 D2
Crawford Gdns. Camb 151 D3
Crawford Pl. Newb 104 C2
Crawley Dr. Camb 151 F3
Crawley Hill. Camb 151 F3
Crawley Ridge. Camb 151 F3
Crawley Wood Cl. Camb 151 F3
Crawshay Dr. Caver 59 D4
Crayle St. Slough 22 A1
Crayonne Cl. Stai 125 F4
Crecy Cl. Woki 115 F3
Creden Cl. Maid 39 E4
Crediton Cl. Wood 88 A3
Crees Meadow. Windl 146 B2
Cremyll Rd. Read 58 C1
Crescent Ave. Read 86 C3
Crescent Dr. Maid 39 F4
Crescent Rd. Read 57 E1
Crescent Rd. Shepp 125 E2
Crescent Rd. Woki 116 B3
Crescent The. Ashf 97 F2
Crescent The. Chert 124 A3
Crescent The. Eng G 95 F1
Crescent The. Harl 71 E4
Crescent The. Kint 102 A1
Crescent The. Maid 39 F4
Crescent The. Mort 137 D3
Crescent The. Padw 109 E2
Crescent The. Read 87 E2
Crescent The. Shepp 125 F1
Crescent The. Shipl 36 A2
Crescent The. Slough 42 C2
Crescent The. Thea 83 F2
Cress Rd. Slough 42 A2
Cressex Cl. Binf 90 B1
Cressingham Rd. Read 86 B1
Cressington Pl. Bou E 3 D2
Cresswell Rd. Newb 105 E2
Cresswells Mead. Holy 40 B1
Crest Cl. Twyf 61 F3
Crest The. Caver 59 E3
Creswell Cl. Read 113 E3
Cricket Field Gr. Crow 143 E2
Cricket Hill. Finch 141 F1
Cricket Hill La. Yate 149 F2
Cricketers. Box 103 F3
Cricketers La. Windl 146 B2
Crimp Hill. Eng G 95 D3
Crimp Hill. Old W 95 D3
Crisp Rd. Hen-O-T 15 E2
Crispin Cl. Caver 58 B3
Crispin Way. Far C 22 B4
Crocker Cl. Ascot 119 F4
Crockhamwell Rd. Wood 87 F3
Crocus Way. Woki 115 E4
Croft Cl. Harl 71 E4
Croft Cl. Woki 116 A1
Croft La. Newb 104 C2
Croft La. Yate 149 E4
Croft Rd. Gori 34 B3
Croft Rd. Hung 100 B3
Croft Rd. Mort 136 C3
Croft Rd. Newb 130 C4
Croft Rd. Woki 116 A1
Croft Road. Shin 113 E1
Croft The. Brac 91 D1
Croft The. Kint 102 A1
Croft The. Maid 39 E3
Croft The. Mar 2 A2
Croft Way. Camb 151 F1
Crofthill Rd. Slough 22 A1
Crofton Cl. Brac 118 C2
Crofts The. Shepp 125 F3
Cromer Cl. Read 57 E1
Cromer Rd. Harm 71 D3
Cromer Rd W. Harm 71 D2
Cromwell Cl. Hen-O-T 35 F4
Cromwell Dr. Slough 42 C4
Cromwell Gdns. Mar 1 C1
Cromwell Rd. Ascot 120 A3
Cromwell Rd. Camb 151 E4
Cromwell Rd. Caver 59 D1

Cromwell Rd. Hen-O-T 35 F4
Cromwell Rd. Maid 39 E4
Cromwell Rd. Mar 1 C1
Cromwell Rd. Newb 105 E3
Crondall End. Yate 149 E4
Crondell Ct. Camb 151 D2
Cropper Cl. That 107 D2
Crosby Gdns. Yate 149 D4
Crosby Hill Dr. Camb 151 F4
Cross Fell. Brac 118 A3
Cross Gates Cl. Brac 118 C3
Cross Keys Rd. Sou S 14 B2
Cross La. Bee H 138 B4
Cross Oak. Wind 67 D3
Cross Rd. Windl 121 D1
Cross St. Read 86 A4
Cross St. Woki 116 B3
Crossfields Cl. Read 113 F4
Crossland Rd. Read 86 A4
Crossways. Stai 96 B1
Crossways. Stai 98 C1
Crossways. Wood 87 F3
Crosswell Cl. Stai 125 E4
Crosthwaite Way. Slough 41 E4
Crouch La. Wink 92 C4
Crow Piece La. Burn 21 F2
Crowfield Dr. That 106 A2
Crowle Rd. Lamb 25 D1
Crown Acre Cl. That 106 B2
Crown La. Burn 22 A2
Crown La. Maid 40 A4
Crown La. Mar 1 B1
Crown La. Thea 83 F2
Crown La. Went 122 B2
Crown Meadow. Iver 69 D4
Crown Pl. Read 86 B3
Crown Pl. Sand 143 F1
Crown Rd. Mar 1 B1
Crown Rd. Went 122 B2
Crown Row. Brac 118 B2
Crown St. Eng G 96 A2
Crown St. Read 86 A3
Crowsley Rd. Shipl 36 A2
Crowthorne Rd. Brac 118 A2
Crowthorne Rd. Brac 117 F1
Crowthorne Rd. Sand 143 D1
Crowthorne Rd N. Brac 118 A3
Croxley Rise. Maid 39 E3
Croydon Rd. Harm 71 D2
Crummock Cl. Slough 41 E4
Crutchley Rd. Woki 116 B4
Cuckoo La. West E 153 E3
Cuckoo Pound. Shepp 125 F2
Cuckoo Vale. West E 153 E3
Culford Cl. Winn 87 E1
Culham Dr. Maid 19 F1
Cullen Cl. Yate 149 E3
Cullern's Pas. Maid 39 F3
Culley Way. Maid 39 D2
Culloden Way. Woki 115 F3
Culver La. Read 87 D4
Culver Rd. Newb 130 C4
Culver Rd. Read 86 C3
Culver Rd. Sand 143 E1
Cumberland Ave. Slough 22 B1
Cumberland Dr. Brac 118 B4
Cumberland Rd. Ashf 97 D3
Cumberland Rd. Camb 152 B2
Cumberland Rd. Read 86 C4
Cumberland St. Stai 96 B2
Cumberland Way. Woki 115 E3
Cumbernauld Gdns. Ashf 98 C2
Cumbria Cl. Maid 39 E2
Cumnor Way. Brac 118 C3
Curl Way. Woki 116 A3
Curlew Cl. That 106 B2
Curlew Dr. Read 84 B3
Curley Hill Rd. Light 152 C4
Curling Way. Newb 105 E2
Curls Rd. Maid 39 E2
Curridge Green. Herm 78 C2
Curridge Piece. Herm 78 C3
Curridge Rd. Herm 78 B2
Curriers La. Burn 21 F4
Curtis Rd. Read 84 B2
Curzon St. Read 85 F4
Cutbush Cl. Read 114 A4
Cutbush La. Read 114 A4
Cutting Hill. Ham 126 A2
Cygnet Cl. That 106 A2
Cypress Cl. Brac 142 A4
Cypress Rd. Stai 125 F4
Cypress Rd. Wood 88 A3
Cypress Way. Black 150 A3
Cypress Wlk. Eng G 95 D1
Cyril Vokins Rd. Gree 105 F1

Dacre Ave. Caver 59 F2
Dagmar Rd. Wind 67 E3
Dairy La. Hamb 16 A4
Dalby Cres. Newb 131 E4
Dalcross. Brac 118 C2
Dale Cl. Sunn 121 D2
Dale Ct. Slough 42 B2
Dale Gdns. Sand 150 A4
Dale Lodge Rd. Sunn 121 D2
Dale Rd. Ashf 98 C1
Dale Rd. Read 86 A3
Dale Rd. Shepp 125 F1
Daleham Ave. Eng G 96 A1
Dalston Cl. Camb 152 B2
Dalton Cl. Read 84 C4
Damar Gdns. Hen-O-T 35 F4
Dandridge Cl. Slough 43 E1
Dandridge Dr. Bou E 3 E2
Dane Rd. Ashf 98 B1
Danehill. Read 114 A4
Danvers Cl. That 106 B1
Danywern Dr. Winn 88 B1
Darby Green La. Black 150 A3
Darby Green Rd. Black 150 A3
Darby La. Upp B 55 D3
Darell Rd. Caver 58 C2
Dark La. Brad 82 B4
Dark La. Read 57 D1
Dark La. Warg 36 B1
Dark La. Wick 101 D4
Darleydale Cl. Crow 143 E1
Darling's La. Bish 18 C1
Darrell Cl. Slough 43 F1
Dart Cl. Slough 69 D4
Dart Cl. That 106 A3
Dart Cl. Woki 141 F3
Dartington Ave. Wood 87 E2
Dartmouth Cl. Brac 118 C3
Darvill's La. Slough 42 B2
Darvills La. W St L 62 C1
Darwall Dr. Burl 119 E4
Darwin Cl. Read 86 A1
Darwin Rd. Slough 43 F2
Dashwood Cl. Brac 118 B4
Dashwood Cl. Slough 43 E1
Datchet Pl. Slough 68 A3
Datchet Rd. Datch 42 C1
Datchet Rd. Hort 68 C2
Datchet Rd. Old W 68 A2
Datchet Rd. Slough 42 C1
Datchet Rd. Wind 67 E4
Dauntless Rd. Bur C 111 D2
Davenport Rd. Brac 118 C4
Daventry Cl. Stan 69 F3
Daventry Ct. Brac 118 A4
David Cl. Harl 71 E4
David Rd. Stan 69 F3
David Smith Ct. Read 84 C3
Davis Cl. Mar 1 C1
Davis Cl. Winn 88 A1
Davis St. Hurst 88 B3
Davis Way. Hurst 88 A2
Dawes East Rd. Burn 21 E1
Dawes Moor Cl. Slough 43 E4
Dawley Ride. Stan 69 F3
Dawlish Rd. Read 86 B1
Dawn Redwood Cl. Hort 69 D2
Dawnay Cl. Ascot 119 F4
Dawnay Rd. Sand 151 D4
Dawsmere Cl. Camb 152 B3
Dawson Cl. Wind 67 D3
De Beauvoir Rd. Read 86 C3
De Bohun Rd. Read 86 A4
De Havilland Way. Stan 70 C1
De Montfort Gr. Hung 100 B2
De Montfort Rd. Newb 104 C3
De Montfort Rd. Read 59 D1
De Vitre Green. Woki 116 C4
Deacon Cl. Woki 116 B4
Deacon Way. Read 58 A1
Deaconfield. Sou S 14 B2
Deacons La. Herm 79 E4
Deadmans La. Gree 131 D4
Deadman's La. Thea 83 E2
Deadmoor La. Ball H 130 C1
Deadmoor La. Newt 130 C1
Deal Ave. Slough 41 F4
Dean Cl. Wind 66 B2
Dean La. Cook 19 E4
Dean St. Mar 1 B1
Deanfield Ave. Hen-O-T 15 E1
Deanfield Cl. Mar 1 B2
Deanfield Rd. Hen-O-T 15 E1
Deans Cl. Sto P 23 D2
Deans Ct. Windl 146 B2
Deansgate. Brac 118 A1
Deansgate Rd. Read 86 A3
Decies Way. Sto P 23 D2
Dedmere Ct. Mar 1 C1
Dedmere Rd. Mar 1 C1
Dedmere Rise. Mar 1 C1
Dedworth Dr. Wind 66 C3
Dedworth Rd. Wind 66 B3
Dee Rd. Read 85 D4
Deena Cl. Slough 41 F3
Deep Field. Datch 68 A4
Deep Well Dr. Camb 151 F3
Deepcut Bridge Rd. Camb 152 B1
Deepdene Cl. Read 85 F4
Deepfield Rd. Brac 118 B4
Deer Rock Hill. Brac 118 B2
Deer Rock Rd. Camb 151 F4
Deerhurst Ave. Winn 88 B1
Deerhurst Cl. Read 84 C2
Deerswood. Maid 20 A1
Defford Cl. Woki 88 C1
Delafield Dr. Bur C 84 B2
Delaford Cl. Iver 44 C4
Delamere Rd. Read 87 D4
Delane Dr. Winn 88 A1
Delaney Cl. Read 84 C4
Delft Cl. Read 84 C4
Dell Cl. Far C 22 B4
Dell Gr. Camb 151 F1
Dell Rd. Finch 142 A2
Dell Rd. Read 57 E1
Dell The. Whi Wa 38 C2
Dell The. Yate 149 E3
Dellars Hill. Hurl 38 A4
Delph The. Winn 87 E1
Delta Way. Stai 123 E4
Denbury Gdns. Read 113 E4
Denby Way. Read 57 F1
Dene Cl. Brac 118 B4
Dene Cl. Read 87 D2
Dene Hollow. Chil 10 C4
Dene Way. Newb 105 D3
Denford La. Hung 101 D4
Denford La. Wick 101 D4
Denham Cl. Maid 39 E3
Denham Dr. Yate 149 F3
Denham Gr. Brac 118 B2
Denham Rd. Eng G 96 A2
Denhose Cl. Read 87 D1
Denison Rd. Felt 98 C2
Denly Way. Light 146 B1
Denman Dr. Ashf 98 A1
Denmark Ave. Wood 61 D1
Denmark Rd. Newb 105 D2
Denmark Rd. Read 86 B3
Denmark St. Maid 39 F4
Denmark St. Woki 116 B3
Denmead Ct. Brac 118 C2
Dennis Cl. Ashf 98 B1
Dennis Way. Slough 41 E3
Dennisford Rd. East I 31 D3
Dennistoun Cl. Camb 151 E3
Denny Rd. Slough 43 F1
Denton Cl. That 106 B1
Denton Rd. Woki 116 B3
Denton Way. Camb 151 E1
Depot Rd. Maid 40 A3
Deppdale. Brac 118 A3
Derby Cl. Lamb 25 D1
Derby Rd. Caver 59 D2
Derby Rd. Newb 104 C1
Derby St. Read 85 F4
Derek Rd. Maid 40 B4
Deri Dene Cl. Stan 70 C1
Derrick Cl. Bur C 84 B2
Derry Rd. Black 150 C1
Derwent Ave. Read 57 F1
Derwent Cl. Felt 98 C4
Derwent Cl. Woki 115 F3
Derwent Dr. Maid 39 E4
Derwent Dr. Slough 41 E4
Derwent Rd. Light 153 D4
Derwent Rd. Stai 96 A1
Derwent Rd. That 106 A2
Desborough Cl. Shepp 125 D1
Desborough Cres. Maid 39 E3
Deseronto Wharf. Slough 43 F2
Desford Way. Ashf 97 F3
Devenish La. Sunn 120 B1
Devenish Rd. Ascot 120 B1
Devenish Rd. Sunn 120 B1
Devereux Rd. Wind 67 E3
Deveron Dr. Read 85 D4
Devil's Highway The. Brac 142 C3
Devil's Highway The. Finch 142 C3
Devil's La. Stai 96 B1
Devitt Cl. Read 86 C1
Devon Ave. Slough 42 B4
Devon Cl. Sand 150 B4
Devon Cl. Woki 115 F3
Devon Dr. Caver 59 F2
Devonshire Cl. Slough 22 A2
Devonshire Dr. Camb 151 F4
Devonshire Gdns. Sulh 57 D2
Devonshire Green. Far C 22 A2
Devonshire Park. Read 86 C1
Dhoon Rise. Maid 39 F3
Diamedes Ave. Stan 97 E4
Diamedes Cres. Stan 97 E4
Diamond Hill. Camb 151 F4
Diamond Rd. Slough 43 D2
Diamond Ridge. Camb 151 F4
Diamond Way. Woki 115 F4
Diana Cl. Slough 43 F4
Dianthus Cl. Chert 123 F1
Dick Turpin Way. Harm 71 F2
Dickens Way. Yate 149 E3
Dickens Wlk. Newb 131 D4
Dido Rd. Chil 9 F4
Dieppe Cl. Woki 115 F3
Digby Rd. Newb 104 C2
Dines Way. Herm 79 E4
Dingle Rd. Ashf 98 A2
Disraeli Ct. Slough 69 D4
Ditchfield La. Woki 141 F4
Ditchling. Brac 118 A1
Ditton Park Rd. Datch 68 C4
Ditton Rd. Datch 68 B4
Ditton Rd. Slough 68 C4
Dobson's La. Faw (Bu) 15 E4
Dockett Eddy La. Shepp 124 C1
Doctors La. Herm 79 D3
Doddington Cl. Winn 87 E1
Doddsfield Rd. Slough 22 A1
Dog La. Asham 54 A3
Doghurst Ave. Harl 71 D4
Doghurst Dr. Harl 71 D4
Dogkennel La. Fawl 27 E2
Doles Hill. Woki 115 E2
Doles La. Woki 115 F2
Dolman Rd. Newb 105 D2
Dolphin Ct. Slough 43 D2
Dolphin Ct. Stan 97 D3
Dolphin Rd. Slough 43 D2
Dolphin Rd. Stai 125 F4
Dolphin Rd N. Stai 125 F4
Dolphin Rd S. Stai 125 F4
Dolphin Rd W. Stai 125 F4
Doman Rd. Camb 151 D2
Domoney Cl. That 106 C2
Don Cl. Read 85 D4
Doncastle Rd. Brac 117 F3
Donegal Cl. Caver 59 E2
Donkin Hill. Caver 59 E2
Donnington Cl. Buck 108 B4
Donnington Cl. Camb 151 D2
Donnington Gdns. Read 86 C3
Donnington Pl. Winn 88 B1
Donnington Rd. Read 86 B3
Donnington Sq. Newb 104 C3
Donnybrook. Brac 118 A1
Dorchester Cl. Maid 19 D1
Dorchester Ct. Read 85 E3
Dorchester Dr. Felt 71 F1
Dorian Dr. Ascot 120 C4
Doris Rd. Ashf 98 B1
Dorking Way. Bur C 84 A2
Dorly Cl. Shepp 125 F2
Dormer Cl. Crow 143 D3
Dormer Cl. Newb 130 C3
Dornels. Slough 43 E4
Dorney Reach Rd. Dorn 40 C2
Dorney Wood Rd. Burn 21 E3
Dorothy St. Read 86 A3
Dorset Rd. Ashf 97 E3
Dorset Rd. Wind 67 E3
Dorset St. Read 85 E4
Dorset Way. Woki 115 F3
Doublet Cl. That 106 A2
Douglas Ct. Mar 2 A2
Douglas Grange. Hurst 88 A2
Douglas La. Wray 68 C1
Douglas Rd. Caver 59 E1
Douglas Rd. Slough 42 B4
Douglas Rd. Stan 70 B1
Douro Cl. Tad 134 B1
Dove Cl. Read 113 F4
Dove House Cres. Slough 21 F1
Dovecote Rd. Read 113 D4
Dovedale Cl. Caver 58 C2
Dovedale Cl. Crow 143 E1
Dover Rd. Slough 41 F4
Dover St. Read 86 A3
Doveton Way. Newb 105 D2
Dowding Cl. Wood 88 A4
Dower Park. Wind 66 C2
Down Pl. Oak G 66 A4
Downend La. Chiev 51 D1
Downfield La. W St L 63 D3
Downfield Rd. W St L 63 D2
Downing Path. Slough 21 F1
Downing Rd. Read 84 B4
Downlands. East G 47 E3
Downmill Rd. Brac 117 F4
Downs Cl. Lamb 46 C4
Downs Rd. Comp 32 A2
Downs Rd. Slough 43 E2
Downs Way. Chil 9 F4
Downs Way. Read 57 E1
Downshire Cl. Gr She 48 A2
Downshire Sq. Read 85 F3
Downshire Way. Brac 118 A3
Downside. Chert 123 F1
Downside. Chil 10 B4
Doyle Gdns. Yate 149 E2
Drake Ave. Slough 43 E1
Drake Ave. Stai 96 C2
Drake Cl. Brac 118 A2
Drake Cl. Woki 141 F4
Draper Cl. That 106 B1
Drawback Hill. Shipl 35 E3
Draycott. Brac 118 C2
Drayhorse Dr. Bags 145 F1
Drayton Cl. Brac 118 B4
Drayton Rd. Read 85 D4
Dresden Way. Read 57 F1
Drew Meadow. Far C 22 B4
Drewett Cl. Read 113 E3
Drift Rd. Holy 65 E2
Drift Rd. Wink 93 D4
Drift Way. Iver 69 E4
Driftway Cl. Winn 87 E1
Drill Hall Rd. Chert 124 A1
Drive The. Ashf 98 B1
Drive The. Bou E 2 C2
Drive The. Newb 130 C4
Drive The. Read 87 D4
Drive The. Slough 68 A3
Drive The. Slough 43 F2
Drive The. Vir W 122 C2
Drive The. Wray 68 B1
Droitwich Cl. Brac 118 C3
Dromepath. Winn 88 A2
Dropmore Rd. Burn 21 E3
Drove La. Herm 79 E1
Drovers Way. Brac 118 C3
Drovers Way. Wood 87 F3
Druce Way. That 106 B2
Drummond Cl. Brac 118 C4
Drury La. Mort 137 D2
Dry Arch Rd. Sunn 120 C2
Dryden. Brac 118 A1
Dryden Cl. That 106 B3
Du Pre Wlk. Bou E 3 E2
Dudley Cl. Read 57 F1
Dudley Mews. Read 57 F1
Dudley Rd. Ashf 97 F2
Dudley Rd. Felt 98 B4
Duffield La. Sto P 22 C3
Duffield Park. Sto P 23 D1
Duffield Rd. Wood 60 C1
Duke Of Cornwall Ave. Camb 144 B1
Duke St. Hen-O-T 15 F1
Duke St. Read 86 A4
Duke St. Wind 67 E4
Dukes Cl. Ashf 98 B2
Dukes Covert. Bags 145 F3
Dukes Pl. Mar 1 B1
Duke's Ride. Crow 143 D3
Duke's Ride. Finch 143 D3
Dukes Ride. Silc 136 A1
Dukes Wood. Crow 143 D3
Dukeshill Rd. Brac 118 A4
Dulnan Cl. Read 85 D4
Dulverton Gdns. Read 86 B1
Dumas Cl. Yate 149 E3
Dumbarton Way. Caver 59 F3
Dunally Park. Shepp 125 E1
Dunaways Cl. Read 87 E2
Dunbar Dr. Wood 88 A3
Dunboe Pl. Shepp 125 E1
Duncan Dr. Woki 116 C3
Duncan Gdns. Purl 57 E2
Duncan Rd. Wood 87 F3
Duncannon Cres. Wind 66 B2
Duncroft. Wind 66 C2
Dundaff Cl. Camb 152 A3
Dundas Cl. Brac 118 A3
Dundee Rd. Slough 42 A4
Dundela Cl. Wood 87 F3
Dungells Farm Cl. Yate 149 E2
Dungells La. Yate 149 E2
Dungrovehill La. Bish 18 B2
Dunholme Cl. Winn 87 F1
Dunhome End. Maid 39 E2
Dunkirk Cl. Woki 115 F3
Dunluce Gdns. Pangb 56 C3
Dunn Cres. Kint 102 A1
Dunnock Way. Warg 36 C2
Dunoon Cl. Read 84 C2
Dunsfold Rd. Read 84 C4
Dunsmore Gdns. Yate 149 D3
Dunstall Cl. Read 84 B4
Dunstan Rd. That 106 C2
Dunster Cl. Caver 59 E3
Dunster Gdns. Slough 42 A3
Dunt Ave. Hurst 88 C2
Dunt La. Hurst 88 C2
Duppas Cl. Shepp 125 E2
Durand Rd. Read 87 D1
Durham Ave. Slough 42 A4
Durham Cl. Read 113 E4
Durham Cl. Woki 115 F3
Durham Rd. Sand 143 F1
Durley Mead. Brac 118 C2
Durrell Way. Shepp 125 E2
Dutch Barn Cl. Stan 70 B1
Dutton Way. Iver 44 C4
Duval Pl. Bags 145 F2
Dwyer Rd. Read 85 D2
Dyer Straits. Chil 9 F4
Dyson Cl. Wind 67 D2
Dysonswood La. Maple 58 C4

Eagle Cl. Brac 143 D4
Eagle Cl. Woki 115 F3
Earley Hill Rd. Read 87 D3
Earley Pl. Read 86 A4
Earleydene. Sunn 120 A1
Earls Gr. Camb 151 F3
Earlsfield. Holy 40 B1
Earlsfield Cl. Caver 59 F2
Earlswood. Brac 118 A1
Easby La. Winn 87 E1
Easington Dr. Winn 87 F1
East Burnham La. Burn 22 A2
East Cres. Wind 66 C3
East Dr. Read 84 C3
East Dr. Sto P 22 C1
East Dr. Vir W 122 A2
East Green. Black 150 B2
East La. Chiev 51 D1
East La. Twyf 62 B3
East Paddock. Bish 18 C3
East Ramp. Harm 71 D3
East Rd. Felt 98 B4
East Rd. Maid 39 F3
East Rd. Maid 39 F4
East Ridge. Bou E 3 D2
East St. Read 86 A4
East Stratton Cl. Brac 118 C2
East View Cl. Warg 36 C1
East View Rd. Warg 36 C1
Eastbourne Rd. Slough 42 A4
Eastbridge. Slough 43 D3
Eastbury Ave. Read 57 D3
Eastbury Park. Winn 88 B1
Eastbury Shute. Lamb 46 C1
Eastchurch Rd. Harm 71 F2
Eastcourt Ave. Read 87 D3
Eastcroft. Slough 22 A1
Easterfield La. Whitc 56 B4
Eastern Ave. Chert 124 A3
Eastern Ave. Read 86 C3
Eastern Dr. Bou E 3 E2
Eastern La. Crow 143 F2
Eastern Perimeter Rd. Harm 71 F3
Eastern Rd. Brac 118 B4
Eastfield. Blew 12 A4
Eastfield Cl. Slough 43 D2
Eastfield La. White 56 B4
Eastfield Rd. Burn 41 D4
Easthampstead Rd. Brac 118 A4
Easthampstead Rd. Brac 116 C2
Eastheath Ave. Woki 116 A2
Eastheath Gdns. Woki 116 A2
Eastleigh Rd. Harm 71 F2
Eastlyn Rd. Silc 135 F1
Easton Hill. Wick 76 A3
Eastwood Rd. Wood 87 F2
Eastworth Rd. Chert 124 A1
Eaton Pl. Read 85 F4
Eaton Rd. Camb 151 D2
Ebborn Sq. Winn 114 B4
Ebsworth Cl. Maid 20 B2
Eccles Cl. Caver 59 E1
Echelforde Dr. Ashf 98 A2
Eddington Hill. Hung 100 C4
Eddington Rd. Brac 117 F2
Eddystone Wlk. Stan 97 F4
Eden Cl. Slough 44 A1
Eden Way. Winn 88 A1
Edenhall Cl. Read 57 E2
Edenham Cl. Winn 87 F1
Edenham Cres. Read 85 F3
Edgar Milward Cl. Read 58 A1
Edgbarrow Rise. Sand 143 D1
Edgcumbe Park Dr. Crow 143 D3
Edgecombe La. Newb 105 E3
Edgedale Cl. Crow 143 D3
Edgehill St. Read 86 A3
Edgell Cl. Vir W 122 C3
Edgell Rd. Stai 96 C2

Edgemoor Rd. Camb 152 B2
Edgewood Cl. Brac 143 D4
Edinburgh Ave. Slough 42 A4
Edinburgh Dr. Stai 97 E1
Edinburgh Gdns. Wind 67 E3
Edinburgh Rd. Maid 19 F1
Edinburgh Rd. Mar 1 C2
Edinburgh Rd. Read 85 F4
Edith Rd. Maid 39 D4
Edmunds Way. Slough 43 D4
Edney's Hill. Woki 115 E1
Edward Ave. Camb 151 D3
Edward Ct. Stai 97 E1
Edward Rd. Harm 71 F1
Edward Rd. Twyf 61 D3
Edward Rd. Windl 146 B2
Edward Way. Ashf 97 F3
Edwards Ct. Slough 42 C2
Edwards Hill. Lamb 25 D1
Edwin Cl. That 106 C2
Eeklo Pl. Newb 105 D1
Egerton Rd. Read 86 C1
Egerton Rd. Sand 150 C4
Egerton Rd. Slough 21 F1
Egham By-Pass. Eng G 96 A2
Egham Hill. Eng G 95 E1
Egremont Dr. Read 87 E2
Egremont Gdns. Slough 42 A3
Egypt La. Far C 22 A4
Eight Acres. Burn 21 D1
Elan Cl. Read 84 C4
Elbow Meadow. Stan 69 F3
Eldart Cl. Read 85 D4
Elder Cl. Read 57 E1
Elderfield Cres. Chil 10 B4
Elderfield Rd. Sto P 22 C3
Eldon Pl. Read 86 B4
Eldon Rd. Read 86 B4
Eldon Sq. Read 86 B4
Eldon St. Read 86 B4
Eldon Terr. Read 86 B4
Elford Cl. Wood 87 E1
Elgar Ave. Crow 143 D4
Elgar Rd. S. Read 86 A2
Elgar Rd. Read 86 A3
Elgarth Dr. Woki 141 F4
Elgin Ave. Ashf 98 B1
Elgin Cres. Harm 71 F3
Eliot Cl. Caver 59 D2
Eliot Cl. That 106 B3
Eliot Dr. Mar 1 C2
Elizabeth Ave. Bags 145 F1
Elizabeth Ave. Newb 130 B4
Elizabeth Ave. Stai 97 E1
Elizabeth Cl. Brac 118 B3
Elizabeth Cl. Hen-O-T 35 D4
Elizabeth Ct. Read 85 F4
Elizabeth Gdns. Ascot 120 A2
Elizabeth Rd. Hen-O-T 35 D4
Elizabeth Rd. Mar 1 C2
Elizabeth Rd. Woki 116 B3
Elizabeth Rout Cl. Shin 113 E1
Elizabeth Way. Sto P 22 C2
Elizabethan Cl. Stan 97 E4
Elizabethan Way. Stan 97 E4
Ellesfield Ave. Brac 117 F3
Ellesmere Cl. Caver 59 D2
Elliman Ave. Slough 42 C3
Ellington Ct. Tapl 40 B4
Ellington Gdns. Tapl 40 B4
Ellington Park. Maid 19 F1
Ellington Rd. Felt 98 C2
Ellington Rd. Tapl 40 B4
Elliott Gdns. Stai 125 D3
Elliott Rise. Burl 119 E4
Ellis Ave. Slough 42 C2
Ellis Rd. Crow 143 D3
Ellison Cl. Wind 66 C2
Ellison Way. Woki 116 A3
Elm Bank. Yate 149 E4
Elm Cl. Far C 22 B3
Elm Cotts. Ball H 129 F1
Elm Croft. Datch 68 B3
Elm Dr. Bur C 111 D3
Elm Gr. Maid 39 F4
Elm Gr. That 106 A3
Elm La. Bou E 2 C3
Elm La. Read 86 C1
Elm Lodge Ave. Read 85 E4
Elm Park. Windl 120 C1
Elm Park Rd. Read 85 E4
Elm Rd. Felt 98 B4
Elm Rd. Maple 58 B4
Elm Rd. Read 86 C1
Elm Rd. Wind 67 D2
Elm Tree Cl. Ashf 98 A2
Elmar Green. Slough 22 A1
Elmbank Ave. Eng G 95 D1
Elmcroft. Gori 34 B3
Elmcroft Cl. Felt 71 F1
Elmcroft Dr. Ashf 98 A2
Elmdon Rd. Harm 71 F2
Elmhurst Rd. Gori 34 B4
Elmhurst Rd. Read 86 B3
Elmhurst Rd. Slough 44 A2
Elmhurst Rd. That 106 A3
Elmleigh Ct. Caver 59 E2
Elmley Cl. Woki 88 C1
Elms Ave. That 106 C2
Elms Dr. Bou E 3 E2
Elms Rd. Woki 116 A3
Elmshott La. Slough 41 F3
Elmsleigh Rd. Stai 96 C2
Elmstone Dr. Read 57 E1
Elmsway. Ashf 98 A2
Elmwood. Maid 20 A2
Elmwood Rd. Slough 43 D3
Elsenwood Cres. Camb 152 A3
Elsenwood Dr. Camb 152 A4
Elsinore Ave. Stan 97 F4
Elsley Rd. Read 57 F2
Elstow Ave. Caver 59 E3
Elstree Cl. Read 57 E1
Eltham Ave. Caver 59 F3
Elton Dr. Maid 39 E4
Elvaston Way. Read 85 D4
Elvedon Cl. Winn 87 F1
Elvendon Rd. Gori 34 B4
Elwell Cl. Eng G 96 A1
Ely Ave. Slough 42 B4
Ely Rd. Harm 71 F3
Ely Rd. Thea 83 F2
Embankment The. Wray 95 E4
Ember Rd. Slough 44 A2
Emblem Cres. Arbo 114 C1
Embrook Way. Read 84 A2
Emerald Cl. Woki 115 F4
Emerald Ct. Slough 42 C2
Emery Acres. Upp B 55 D3
Emery Down Cl. Brac 119 D3
Emlyns Bldgs. Eton 67 E4
Emm Cl. Woki 115 F4
Emmbrook Gate. Woki 115 F4
Emmbrook Rd. Woki 115 F4
Emmbrook Vale. Woki 89 D1
Emmer Green Ct. Caver 59 E3
Emmets Nest. Binf 90 B1
Emmets Park. Binf 90 B1
Emmview Cl. Woki 115 F4
Empress Rd. Read 84 B3
Enborne Cl. Read 84 B4
Enborne Gr. Newb 104 C1
Enborne Pl. Newb 104 C1
Enborne Rd. Ham M 104 C1
Enborne Rd. Newb 104 C1
Enborne St. Ham M 130 B3
Enborne St. Newb 130 B3
Enborne Way. Brim 133 F3
Enfield Rd. Harm 71 F3
Englefield Cl. Eng G 95 E1
Englefield Rd. Thea 83 E2
Engleheart Dr. Felt 71 F1
Englehurst. Eng G 95 E1
Englemere Rd. Brac 90 C1
Englesfield. Camb 152 B3
English Gdns. Wray 68 B1
Ennerdale. Brac 118 A3
Ennerdale Cl. Felt 98 C4
Ennerdale Cres. Slough 41 E4
Ennerdale Rd. Read 86 B2
Ennerdale Way. That 106 A2
Ensign Cl. Stan 97 E4
Ensign Way. Stan 97 E4
Enstone Rd. Wood 88 A4
Enterprise Way. That 107 D1
Epping Cl. Read 85 F4
Epping Way. Brac 118 C3
Epsom Cl. Camb 151 E4
Epsom Cres. Newb 105 D1
Epsom Ct. Read 85 F3
Epson Sq. Harm 71 F3
Eric Ave. Caver 59 D3
Erica Cl. Slough 41 F3
Eriswell Cl. Winn 87 F1
Erkenwald Cl. Chert 123 F1
Erleigh Court Dr. Read 87 D4
Erleigh Court Gdns. Read 87 D4
Erleigh Dene. Newb 104 C1
Erleigh Rd. Read 86 B3
Ermin Wlk. That 106 A2
Erskine Cl. Silc 135 F1
Esher Cres. Harm 71 F3
Esher Rd. Camb 145 D1
Eskdale Gdns. Holy 40 A1
Eskdale Rd. Winn 88 A2
Eskdale Way. Camb 152 B2
Eskin Cl. Read 85 D4
Essex Ave. Slough 42 A4
Essex Pl. Lamb 25 D2
Essex St. Newb 130 B4
Essex St. Read 86 A3
Ethel Rd. Ashf 97 F2
Eton Cl. Datch 68 A4
Eton Ct. Eton 67 E4
Eton Ct. Stai 96 C2
Eton Pl. Mar 1 B1
Eton Rd. Datch 68 A4
Eton Rd. Harl 71 F4
Eton Sq. Eton 67 E4
Eton Wick Rd. Eton 42 A1
Eustace Cres. Woki 116 B4
Evedon. Brac 118 A1
Evelyn Cres. Shepp 125 F4
Evelyn Ct. Wood 87 F3
Evelyn Way. Shepp 125 F4
Evendons Cl. Woki 116 A2
Evendon's La. Bark 115 F1
Evenlode. Maid 39 F4
Evenlode Rd. Bou E 3 D2
Evenlode Way. Sand 150 B4
Everard Ave. Slough 42 C2
Everest Rd. Camb 151 E4
Everest Rd. Crow 143 D3
Everest Rd. Stan 97 F4
Evergreen Dr. Read 84 C2
Evergreen Rd. Camb 152 A1
Evergreen Way. Woki 115 F3
Everington La. Yatt 53 D1
Everland Rd. Hung 100 B3
Eversley Rd. Arbo 114 C1
Eversley St. Finch 141 D1
Eversley Way. Stai 123 E4
Evesham Rd. Caver 59 D3
Evesham Wlk. Crow 143 E1
Evreham Rd. Iver 44 C4
Evreux Cl. That 106 C1
Ewing Way. Newb 131 D4
Exbourne Rd. Read 113 E4
Exchange Rd. Ascot 120 B2
Exeforde Ave. Ashf 98 A2
Exeter Ct. Read 113 D4
Exeter Gdns. Yate 149 D4
Exeter Rd. Thea 83 F2
Exmoor Rd. That 106 B2
Explorer Ave. Stan 97 F4
Exwick Sq. Read 113 E4
Eynsford Cl. Caver 59 F3
Eynsham Rd. Wood 87 F4
Fagg's Rd. Harm 71 F2
Fair Lawn Green. Read 86 C1
Fair Mile. Hen-O-T 15 E2
Fairacre. Maid 39 E3
Fairacres Industrial Estate. Wind 66 B3
Faircroft. Slough 22 A1
Faircross. Brac 118 A3
Faircross Quarters. Herm 78 C3
Faircross Rd. Read 85 E3
Fairfax. Brac 118 A4
Fairfield. Comp 31 E2
Fairfield App. Wray 68 B1
Fairfield Ave. Datch 68 B4
Fairfield Ave. Stai 96 C2
Fairfield Cl. Datch 68 B4
Fairfield Dr. Camb 151 F2
Fairfield La. Far C 22 A2
Fairfield Rd. Burn 21 E1
Fairfield Rd. Gori 34 B4
Fairfield Rd. Wray 68 B1
Fairfields. Hung 100 B3
Fairford Rd. Maid 39 F4
Fairford Rd. Read 57 E1
Fairhaven. Eng G 95 F2
Fairholme. Felt 98 C4
Fairholme Rd. Ashf 97 F2
Fairlawn Park. Wind 66 C2
Fairlawns Cl. Stai 97 D1
Fairlea. Maid 39 D2
Fairlie Rd. Slough 42 A4
Fairlight Ave. Wind 67 E3
Fairlop Cl. Bur C 84 B2
Fairmead Cl. Sand 150 C4
Fairmead Rd. Shin 113 F3
Fairoak Way. Tad 134 B1
Fairsted Cl. Read 85 D4
Fairview Ave. Read 87 D3
Fairview Dr. Stai 124 C2
Fairview Estate. Hen-O-T 35 F4
Fairview Rd. Burn 41 D4
Fairview Rd. Hung 100 B3
Fairview Rd. Slough 21 F1
Fairview Rd. Woki 116 B3
Fairwater Dr. Wood 87 E3
Fairway. Chert 124 A1
Fairway Ave. Read 84 B3
Fairway Dr. Char 61 D3
Fairway Hts. Camb 152 A3
Fairway The. Burn 21 E2
Fairway The. Camb 152 A2
Fairway The. Fla H 3 E4
Fairway The. Maid 39 D2
Fairways. Ashf 98 A1
Fakenham Cl. Read 114 A4
Fakenham Way. Crow 143 E1
Falaise. Eng G 95 F2
Falcon Ave. Read 86 C1
Falcon Dr. Stan 70 C1
Falcon House Gdns. Ball H 129 F1
Falcon Way. Shepp 125 F4
Falcon Way. Woki 115 F3
Falcon Way. Yate 149 D3
Falcons Croft. Woo G 3 F4
Falconwood. Eng G 95 F2
Falkland Dr. Newb 130 C4
Falkland Garth. Newb 130 B4
Falkland Rd. Caver 59 D1
Falkland Rd. Newb 130 B3
Fallowfield. Yate 149 D4
Fallowfield Cl. Caver 59 D2
Falmouth Cl. Camb 152 A2
Falmouth Rd. Read 113 E4
Falmouth Rd. Slough 42 A4
Falmouth Way. That 106 C2
Falstaff Ave. Read 86 C1
Fane Way. Maid 39 E3
Fanes Cl. Brac 117 F4
Faraday Cl. Arbo 140 C4
Faraday Cl. Slough 42 A4
Faraday Rd. Bark 141 D4
Faraday Rd. Newb 105 D2
Faraday Rd. Slough 42 A4
Farcrosse Cl. Sand 150 B4
Fareham Dr. Yate 149 D4
Faringdon Cl. Sand 143 E1
Faringdon Dr. Brac 118 B2
Faringdon Wlk. Read 85 D2
Farleigh Mews. Caver 59 F3
Farley Copse. Brac 117 F4
Farm Cl. Ascot 120 B2
Farm Cl. Brac 143 E4
Farm Cl. Brac 117 F4
Farm Cl. Chert 123 D2
Farm Cl. Holy 40 B1
Farm Cl. Maid 39 D4
Farm Cl. Purl 57 E3
Farm Cl. Shepp 125 D1
Farm Cl. Stai 96 C2
Farm Cl. Yate 149 E3
Farm Cres. Slough 43 E4
Farm Dr. Read 84 A3
Farm Lea. Woo G 3 F4
Farm Rd. Bou E 2 C2
Farm Rd. Burn 41 D3
Farm Rd. Camb 151 F1
Farm Rd. Hen-O-T 35 F4
Farm Rd. Maid 39 D4
Farm Rd. Stai 97 D1
Farm View. Yate 149 E3
Farm Way. Stan 69 F1
Farm Yd. Wind 67 E4
Farman Cl. Wood 88 A4
Farmers Cl. Maid 39 D2
Farmers Cl. Read 113 E3
Farmer's Rd. Stai 96 C2
Farmers Way. Maid 39 D2
Farmiloe Cl. Purl 57 E2
Farnburn Ave. Slough 42 A4
Farnell Rd. Stan 97 D3
Farnham Cl. Brac 118 B4
Farnham Dr. Caver 59 F2
Farnham La. Slough 22 A2
Farnham Park La. Far C 22 B2
Farnham Rd. Slough 42 B4
Farningham. Brac 118 C2
Farnsfield Cl. Read 114 A4
Farriers Cl. Wood 87 F4
Farrowdene Rd. Read 113 E4
Farthing Green La. Sto P 23 D2
Farthingales The. Maid 40 A4
Fatherson Rd. Read 86 B4
Faulkner Pl. Bags 145 F2
Faversham Rd. Crow 143 E1
Fawcett Cres. Wood 87 E3
Fawcett Rd. Wind 67 D3
Fawler Mead. Brac 118 C3
Fawley Bottom La. Faw (Bu) 15 E4
Fawley Cl. Maid 19 E1
Fawley Rd. Read 85 E3
Fawns Manor Cl. Felt 98 B4
Fawns Manor Rd. Felt 98 B4
Fawsley Cl. Stan 69 F4
Faygate Way. Read 87 D1
Feathers La. Wray 96 A3
Felbridge Cl. Camb 151 F1
Felix La. Shepp 125 F2
Felixstowe Cl. Winn 87 E1
Fellow Green. West E 153 F3
Fellow Green Rd. West E 153 F3
Fells The. Read 84 A3
Felstead Cl. Read 86 C2
Feltham Hill Rd. Ashf 98 A2
Feltham Rd. Ashf 98 A2
Felthorpe Cl. Read 114 A4
Felton Way. Read 84 B4
Fencote. Brac 118 B2
Fennel Cl. Newb 105 E3
Fennel Cl. Read 86 C1
Fenns La. West E 153 F3
Fenton Ave. Stai 97 E2
Fern Cl. Camb 152 B2
Fern Cl. Read 84 B3
Fern Dr. Burn 41 D4
Fern Glen. Read 57 E1
Fern La. Lit M 2 C3
Fern Wlk. Ashf 97 E2
Fernbank. Woki 141 E4
Fernbank Cres. Burl 119 E4
Fernbank Pl. Burl 119 E4
Fernbank Rd. Burl 119 E4
Fernbrook Rd. Caver 58 C3
Ferndale Ave. Read 85 D2
Ferndale Cl. Read 57 E2
Ferndale Rd. Ashf 97 F2
Ferne Cl. Gori 34 B4
Fernery The. Stai 96 C2
Fernhill Cl. Black 150 C1
Fernhill Cl. Brac 90 C1
Fernhill La. Black 150 C1
Fernhill Rd. Black 150 C1
Fernhill Wlk. Black 150 C1
Fernhurst Rd. Ashf 98 B2
Fernhurst Rd. Bur C 84 B2
Ferniehurst. Camb 151 F2
Fernley Ct. Maid 19 E1
Ferrard Cl. Burl 119 E4
Ferrier Gr. Newb 131 D4
Ferry Ave. Stai 96 C1
Ferry La. Bou E 3 D1
Ferry La. Gori 34 A3
Ferry La. Hamb 16 B3
Ferry La. Medm 17 D3
Ferry La. Shepp 125 D1
Ferry La. Sou S 14 A2
Ferry La. Stai 124 B3
Ferry La. Warg 36 B1
Ferry La. Wray 96 A3
Ferry Rd. Maid 40 B2
Ferry Rd. Sou S 14 B2
Fettiplace. Gr She 48 A2
Fetty Pl. Maid 39 E2
Fidler's La. East I 30 C4
Fidlers Wlk. Warg 36 C1
Field Cl. Bur C 111 D1
Field Cl. Harl 71 E4
Field End. West E 153 F3
Field Farm Rd. Bur C 84 C1
Field House Cl. Brac 120 A1
Field Hurst. Slough 43 F1
Field La. Camb 151 F1
Field Rd. Black 150 C1
Field Rd. Pease 29 E1
Field Rd. Read 86 A3
Field View. Caver 59 D2
Field View. Felt 98 B2
Field View. Stai 96 B2
Fielden Pl. Brac 118 B4
Fieldfare Ave. Yate 149 D3
Fieldhead Gdns. Bou E 3 D2
Fieldhouse Industrial Estate. Mar 1 C1
Fieldhouse La. Mar 1 C1
Fieldhouse Way. Mar 1 C1
Fielding Gdns. Crow 143 D2
Fielding Rd. Maid 39 D4
Fielding Rd. Sand 150 C3
Fieldings The. Holy 65 D4
Fieldridge. Newb 105 E3
Fields The. Slough 42 B2
Fieldway. Winn 88 B1
Fifehead Cl. Ashf 97 F1
Fifield La. Holy 65 E2
Fifield Rd. Holy 65 E4
Fifth Rd. Newb 104 C1
Filbert Dr. Read 84 B4
Filey Rd. Read 86 C4
Filey Spur. Slough 42 A2
Filmer Rd. Wind 66 B3
Finbeck Way. Read 113 F4
Finch Ct. Maid 39 E3
Finch Rd. Read 87 E2
Fincham End Dr. Crow 142 C2
Finchampstead Rd. Finch 142 A4
Finchampstead Rd. Woki 142 A4
Findhorn Cl. Sand 150 B4
Finmere. Brac 118 B1
Finney Dr. Windl 146 B2
Finstock Cl. Winn 87 E1
Finstock Green. Brac 118 C3
Fir Cottage Rd. Bark 141 F4
Fir Cottage Rd. Woki 141 F4
Fir Dr. Black 150 B2
Fir Tree Ave. Sto P 22 C1
Fir Tree Cl. Ascot 120 A1
Fir Tree La. Newb 105 F2
Fir Tree Paddock. West I 10 A1
Firbank Pl. Eng G 95 D1
Fircroft Cl. Read 57 E1
Fircroft Cl. Sto P 23 D3
Fireball Hill. Sunn 120 B1
Firglen Dr. Yate 149 E4
Firgrove Rd. Yate 149 D3
Firlands. Brac 118 B2
Firlands Ave. Camb 151 E3
Firmstone Cl. Winn 87 E1
Firs Ave. Wind 66 C2
Firs Cl. Woki 141 F4
Firs Dr. Slough 43 F3
Fir's End. Bur C 111 D1
Firs La. Maid 38 C2
Firs Rd. Read 84 B3
Firs The. That 106 A2
First Ave. Mar 2 A1
First Cres. Slough 42 B4
Firtree Cl. Sand 142 C1
Firview Cl. Mar 1 C1
Firwood Dr. Camb 151 E3
Firwood Rd. Went 121 F2
Fisher Green. Binf 90 A1
Fisherman's La. Alde 135 D4
Fishermans Retreat. Mar 1 C1
Fisherman's Way. Bou E 3 D2
Fishers Ct. Caver 59 E3
Fisher's La. Cold A 79 D1
Fishers Wood. Went 121 E1
Fishery Rd. Maid 40 B3
Fishponds Cl. Woki 116 A2
Fishponds Rd. Woki 116 A2
Fitzrobert Pl. Eng G 96 A1
Fitzroy Cres. Wood 88 A3
Five Acre. Read 57 E1
Five Acres. Woo G 3 F4
Flag Staff Sq. That 106 C1
Flamborough Cl. Winn 87 F1
Flamborough Spur. Slough 42 A2
Flamingo Cl. Woki 115 F3
Flanders Ct. Stai 96 B2
Flats The. Black 150 B2
Flaxman Cl. Read 86 C1
Flecker Cl. That 106 B3
Fleet Cl. Woki 115 F3
Fleet Hill. Finch 141 E1
Fleet St. Finch 141 D1
Fleetham Gdns. Wood 87 E1
Fleetway. Stai 123 E3
Fleetwood Rd. Slough 42 C3
Fleming Cl. Arbo 140 C4
Fleming Rd. Newb 105 D2
Flemish Fields. Chert 124 A1
Fletcher Gdns. Brac 117 E4
Flexford Green. Brac 117 F2
Flintgrove. Brac 118 B4
Flintlock Cl. Stan 70 A2
Flodden Dr. Bur C 84 B2
Florence Ave. Maid 40 A4
Florence Ave. Maid 39 F4
Florence Cl. Yate 149 E3
Florence Gdns. Stai 97 D1
Florence Rd. Sand 150 C4
Florence Wlk. Read 86 B4
Florian Gdns. Read 85 D3
Flower's Hill. Pangb 56 B2
Flowers Piece. Asham 54 A3
Fobney St. Read 86 A4
Fokerham Rd. That 106 C1
Folder's La. Brac 91 E1
Foliejohn Way. Whi Wa 38 C1
Folkestone Ct. Slough 44 A1
Follet Cl. Old W 68 A1
Folly La. Bur 110 C3
Folly La. Sulhd 110 C3
Folly Rd. Ink 127 F3
Folly Rd. Lamb 25 D2
Folly The. Newb 105 D1
Fontmell Cl. Ashf 98 A2
Fontmell Park. Ashf 98 A2
Fontwell Cl. Maid 39 D4
Fontwell Dr. Read 84 C3
Fontwell Rd. Newb 105 D1
Forbes Chase. Sand 150 B4
Forbury La. Kint 128 B4
Forbury Rd. Read 86 B4
Forbury The. Read 86 A4
Ford Cl. Ashf 97 F1
Ford Cl. Stai 125 D2
Ford La. Swal 140 A2
Ford Rd. Ashf 97 F2

Ford Rd. Bis 153 F2
Ford Rd. Chert 124 A1
Ford Rd. West E 153 F2
Fordbridge Cl. Chert 124 A1
Fordbridge Rd. Ashf 97 F2
Fordbridge Rd. Shepp 125 F2
Fordham Way. Winn 87 E1
Fordwater Rd. Chert 124 A1
Fordwells Dr. Brac 118 C3
Forehead The. Bee H 137 F2
Forest Cl. Brac 119 E3
Forest Cl. Tad 134 C1
Forest Dr. Stai 98 C1
Forest End Rd. Sand 150 A4
Forest Green. Brac 118 B4
Forest Green Rd. Holy 65 D3
Forest Hill. Read 57 F1
Forest Hills. Camb 151 D2
Forest Rd. Ascot 92 C1
Forest Rd. Binf 90 B2
Forest Rd. Burl 92 C1
Forest Rd. Crow 143 E3
Forest Rd. New G 92 C1
Forest Rd. Wind 66 C3
Forest Rd. Woki 88 C1
Foresters Sq. Brac 118 C3
Forge Cl. Caver 59 E1
Forge Dr. Far C 22 B3
Forge Hill. Hamp N 53 D3
Forge The. Hung 100 B3
Forlease Cl. Maid 40 A3
Forlease Dr. Maid 40 A3
Forlease Rd. Maid 40 A3
Formby Cl. Winn 87 F2
Forndon Cl. Winn 87 F1
Fortrose Cl. Sand 150 B4
Fortrose Wlk. Read 84 C2
Forty Green Dr. Mar 1 A1
Fosseway. Crow 143 D3
Fossewood Dr. Camb 151 E4
Foster Ave. Wind 66 C2
Fosters Gr. Windl 146 A3
Fosters La. Wood 87 F3
Fosters Path. Slough 21 F1
Fotherby Ct. Maid 40 A3
Fotheringay Gdns. Slough 42 A3
Foundation Park. Maid 38 C2
Foundry La. Hort 69 D2
Fountain Gdns. Wind 67 E2
Fountains Garth. Brac 118 A3
Fourth Ave. Mar 2 A1
Fowler Cl. Read 87 D2
Fowlers La. Brac 118 A4
Fox Cl. Bur C 111 D2
Fox Covert. Light 153 D4
Fox Covert Cl. Ascot 120 B2
Fox Dr. Yate 149 E4
Fox La. Yate 149 D4
Fox Lane N. Chert 123 F1
Fox Lane S. Chert 123 F1
Fox Rd. Slough 43 E1
Foxborough. Swal 139 E3
Foxborough Cl. Slough 44 A1
Foxbury. Lamb 25 D1
Foxcombe Dr. Read 84 B4
Foxcote. Woki 142 A4
Foxdown Cl. Camb 151 E3
Foxes Piece. Mar 1 C2
Foxes Wlk. Char 61 D2
Foxglove Cl. Woki 115 E4
Foxhays Rd. Read 113 E4
Foxherne. Slough 43 E2
Foxhill Cl. Caver 60 A3
Foxhill Cres. Camb 152 A4
Foxhill La. Caver 59 F3
Foxhill Rd. Read 86 C3
Foxhollow Dr. Far C 22 B4
Foxhunt Gr. Read 84 C2
Foxhunter Way. That 105 F2
Foxley Cl. Sand 150 B3
Foxley La. Binf 90 B1
Framewood Rd. Sto P 23 E3
Framlingham Dr. Caver 59 F3
Frampton Cl. Wood 60 C1
France Hill Dr. Camb 151 E3
Frances Ave. Maid 20 B1
Frances Rd. Wind 67 E3
Frances The. That 106 B2
Francis Chichester Cl. Ascot 120 A2
Francis Cl. Stai 125 D3
Francis St. Read 86 A3
Francis Way. Slough 41 E3
Frank London Cl. Bou E 3 E2
Franklin Ave. Slough 42 A4
Franklin Ave. Tad 135 D1
Franklin St. Read 85 F4
Franklyn Cres. Wind 66 B2
Frascati Way. Maid 39 F4
Fraser Ave. Caver 59 E3
Fraser Rd. Brac 118 A4
Frederick Pl. Woki 116 A3
Free Prae Rd. Chert 124 A1
Freeborn Way. Brac 118 C4
Freeman Cl. Shepp 125 F3
Freemans Cl. Hung 100 B3
Freemans Cl. Sto P 23 D3
Freemantle Rd. Bags 145 F2
Freesia Cl. Woki 115 E4
French Gdns. Black 150 B2
Frenchum Gdns. Slough 41 F3
Frensham. Brac 118 B2
Frensham Cl. Yate 149 D3
Frensham Green. Read 86 C1
Frensham Rd. Crow 143 D4
Frensham Wlk. Far C 22 B3
Freshfield Cl. Winn 87 F2
Freshwater Rd. Read 86 C4
Freshwood Dr. Yate 149 E2
Friar St. Read 86 A4
Friars Keep. Brac 118 A3
Friars Rd. Newb 131 D4
Friars Rd. Vir W 122 B3
Friars Way. Chert 124 A2
Friary Rd. Ascot 120 A2
Friary Rd. Wray 68 B1
Friary Rd. Wray 95 E4
Friary The. Old W 68 B1
Friday St. Hen-O-T 15 F1
Frieth Cl. Read 87 D1
Frilsham Rd. Read 85 D2
Frimley By-Pass. Camb 151 E1
Frimley Cl. Wood 87 E4
Frimley Green Rd. Camb 151 E1
Frimley Grove Gdns. Camb 151 F1
Frimley High St. Camb 151 E1
Frimley Rd. Camb 151 D2
Fringford Cl. Winn 87 E1
Frith Hill Rd. Camb 152 A1
Frithe The. Slough 43 D4
Frithwald Rd. Chert 123 F1
Frobisher. Brac 118 B1
Frobisher Cres. Stan 97 F4
Frobisher Gdns. Stan 97 F4
Frodsham Way. Sand 143 F1
Frog Hall Dr. Woki 116 C3
Frog La. Brac 118 A3
Frogmill. Hurl 17 E2
Frogmore Cl. Slough 42 A2
Frogmore Gr. Black 150 B2
Frogmore Park Dr. Black 150 B2
Frogmore Rd. Sand 150 B3
Frogmore Way. Read 85 D3
Fromer Rd. Bou E 3 E2
Fromont Dr. That 106 B2
Fromow Gdns. Windl 146 B2
Front St. East G 47 E3
Froxfield Ave. Read 85 F3
Froxfield Down. Brac 118 C2
Fruen Rd. Felt 98 C4
Fry Rd. Ashf 97 E2
Frymley View. Wind 66 B3
Fry's La. Bags 145 E1
Fry's La. Yate 149 F4
Fuchsia Cl. Read 84 B3
Fullbrook Cl. Maid 40 A4
Fullbrook Cl. Woki 89 D1
Fullbrook Cres. Read 57 E2
Fuller Cl. That 106 C1
Fullers La. Ball H 129 E1
Fuller's La. Bur C 112 A2
Fulmead Rd. Read 85 E4
Fulmead Rd. Read 85 E4
Fulmer Cl. Read 87 D1
Fulmer Common Rd. Fulm 23 F3
Fulmer Rd. Fulm 23 F4
Furlong Cl. Bou E 3 D2
Furlong Rd. Bou E 3 D2
Furness. Oak G 66 B3
Furness Sq. Oak G 66 B3
Furness Way. Oak G 66 B3
Furnival Ave. Slough 42 A4
Furnival Cl. Went 122 B2
Furrow Way. Maid 39 D2
Furze Hill Cres. Crow 143 E2
Furze Platt Rd. Maid 19 E1
Furze Rd. Maid 19 E1
Furze Rd. Tad 134 C1
Furzebank. Ascot 120 B3
Furzemoors. Brac 118 A2
Furzen Cl. Slough 22 A1
Fuzzens Wlk. Wind 66 C3
Fydlers Cl. Ascot 93 D1
Fyfield Cl. Black 150 B3
Fyfield Rd. That 106 B1
Fylingdales. That 106 B2

Gables Ave. Ashf 97 F2
Gables Cl. Datch 68 A4
Gables Cl. Maid 40 A4
Gabriels The. Newb 130 B3
Gage Cl. Maid 39 F2
Gainsborough. Brac 118 B2
Gainsborough. Cook 19 F3
Gainsborough Ave. Kint 102 A1
Gainsborough Cl. Camb 151 F4
Gainsborough Cl. Wood 88 A3
Gainsborough Cres. Hen-O-T 35 E4
Gainsborough Dr. Ascot 119 E4
Gainsborough Dr. Maid 39 E2
Gainsborough Hill. Hen-O-T 35 E4
Gainsborough Rd. Hen-O-T 35 E4
Gainsborough Rd. Read 85 D3
Gairn Cl. Read 85 D4
Galahad Cl. Slough 42 A2
Gale Dr. Light 146 A1
Galley La. Head 132 B1
Galleymead Rd. Stan 69 F3
Gallop The. Yate 149 E4
Gallys Rd. Wind 66 B3
Galsworthy Dr. Caver 59 F3
Galsworthy Rd. Chert 124 A1
Galton Rd. Sunn 120 C2
Galvin Rd. Slough 42 B3
Garde Rd. Sonn 60 C2
Garden Cl. Ashf 98 B1
Garden Cl. Maid 39 D3
Garden Close La. Newb 130 B2
Gardeners La. Brad 55 E2
Gardens The. Harm 71 E1
Gardens The. Sou S 14 B2
Gardner Rd. Maid 19 F1
Garfield Rd. Camb 151 E3
Garford Cres. Newb 130 B4
Garlands Cl. Bur C 111 D1
Garnet Cl. Slough 42 A2
Garnet Ct. Mar 1 B1
Garnet Field. Yate 149 D3
Garnet Hill. Read 86 A3
Garnet St. Read 86 A3
Garrard Rd. Slough 21 F1
Garrard St. Read 86 A4
Garrett Rd. Woki 141 F4
Garrick Cl. Stai 97 D1
Garson La. Wray 95 E4
Garson's La. New G 92 A4
Garston Cl. Read 85 D2
Garston Cres. Read 84 A3
Garswood. Brac 118 B2
Garth Cl. Winn 88 B1
Garth Rd. Mort 137 D3
Garth Sq. Brac 91 D1
Garthlands. Maid 19 E1
Gas Works Rd. Read 86 B4
Gascon's Gr. Slogh 22 A1
Gaskell Mews. Newb 131 D4
Gaskells End. Maple 58 B4
Gaston Bridge Rd. Shepp 125 E2
Gaston Way. Shepp 125 E2
Gatcombe Cl. Read 84 B2
Gatehampton Rd. Gori 34 B3
Gatewick Cl. Slough 42 C3
Gatward Ave. Maid 39 D2
Gaveston Rd. Slough 21 F1
Gayhurst Cl. Caver 59 E3
Geffers Ride. Ascot 119 F4
Geneva Cl. Shepp 125 F4
Geoffreyson Rd. Caver 58 C3
George Cl. Mar 1 C2
George Green Rd. Slough 43 F4
George St. Caver 59 D1
George St. Read 85 F4
George St. Stai 96 C2
Georgeham Rd. Crow 143 E1
Georges Dr. Fla H 3 E4
Georgian Cl. Camb 151 F4
Georgian Cl. Stai 97 D2
Gerrards Cross Rd. Sto P 23 D4
Gibbet La. Camb 152 A4
Gibbons Cl. Sand 150 B4
Gibbs Cl. Woki 141 F3
Gibbs Way. Yate 149 D2
Gibraltar La. Cook 2 B1
Gibson Ct. Slough 43 F1
Gibson Pl. Stan 70 B1
Gifford Cl. Caver 59 F3
Gilbert Rd. Camb 151 E1
Gilbey Wlk. Bou E 3 E2
Gilchrist Way. Bish 38 A3
Giles Travers Cl. Stai 123 E3
Gillette Way. Read 86 A1
Gilliat Rd. Slough 42 C3
Gilliatt Cl. Iver 44 C4
Gillotts Cl. Hen-O-T 35 D4
Gillott's La. Shipl 35 E4
Gilman Cres. Wind 66 B2
Gilmore Cl. Slough 43 E2
Gilmore Cres. Ashf 98 A2
Gilpin Way. Harl 71 E4
Gilroy Cl. Newb 130 B3
Gingells Farm Rd. Char 61 D3
Gipsy La. Brac 118 B4
Gipsy La. Hung 100 C4
Gipsy La. Read 87 E2
Gipsy La. Read 57 F1
Gipsy La. Woki 116 B2
Gipsy La. Woki 114 B4
Girton Cl. Crow 143 F1
Glade Rd. Mar 1 C1
Glade The. Ascot 120 B2
Glade The. Newb 130 C4
Glade The. Purl 57 E2
Glade The. Stai 97 D1
Gladridge Cl. Read 87 E2
Gladstone Cl. Kint 102 A1
Gladstone La. Cold A 106 B4
Gladstone Way. Slough 42 A3
Glaisdale. That 106 B1
Glamis Way. Read 84 A2
Glanmor Rd. Slough 43 D3
Glanty The. Stai 96 A2
Glasgow Rd. Slough 42 A4
Glassonby Wlk. Camb 152 B3
Glebe Cl. Dorn 40 C2
Glebe Cl. Light 146 B1
Glebe Cl. Moul 13 F3
Glebe Gdns. Sonn 60 C2
Glebe La. Sonn 60 C2
Glebe Rd. Maid 40 A3
Glebe Rd. Old W 68 A1
Glebe Rd. Purl 57 D3
Glebe Rd. Read 86 B3
Glebe Rd. Stai 96 B1
Glebe Rd. Stai 97 D2
Glebe Ride. Gori 34 A3
Glebe The. Aldw 32 C2
Glebe The. Black 150 C2
Glebefields. Newb 105 D3
Glebeland Gdns. Shepp 125 E2
Glebeland Rd. Sand 150 C2
Glebelands Rd. Woki 116 B4
Glebewood. Brac 118 B2
Glen Ave. Ashf 98 A2
Glen Cl. Stai 125 D3
Glen Innes. Sand 143 F1
Glen The. Silc 135 F1
Glen The. Slough 43 E1
Glenapp Grange. Mort 136 C3
Glenavon Gdns. Slough 43 E2
Glenavon Gdns. Yate 149 E2
Glenbeigh Terr. Read 85 F3
Glendale Ave. Newb 130 B3
Glendale Rd. Tad 135 D1
Glendevon Rd. Wood 87 F4
Gleneagles Cl. Stan 70 B1
Glenfield Rd. Ashf 98 B1
Glenhurst Cl. Black 150 C2
Glenmore Cl. That 106 B1
Glennon Cl. Read 85 E2
Glenrosa Rd. Read 85 D4
Glentworth Pl. Slough 42 B3
Glenwood. Brac 118 B3
Glenwood Dr. Read 84 B4
Globe Farm La. Black 150 A3
Glory Cl. Woo G 3 F4
Glory Mill La. Woo G 3 F4
Gloucester Ave. Slough 42 B4
Gloucester Cres. Stai 97 E1
Gloucester Ct. Read 85 E4
Gloucester Dr. Stai 96 B3
Gloucester Gdns. Bags 145 F2
Gloucester Pl. Wind 67 E3
Gloucester Rd. Bags 145 F2
Gloucester Rd. Maid 19 F1
Gloucester Rd. Newb 104 C1
Gloucester Rd. Read 85 E4
Glyme Wlk. Read 84 C2
Glynswood. Camb 151 F2
Goaters Rd. Burl 119 E4
Goddard Cl. Shin 113 F3
Goddard Cl. Stai 124 C3
Goddard Ct. Winn 88 A1
Goddards La. Camb 151 D2
Goddington Rd. Bou E 3 D3
Godolphin Rd. Slough 42 B3
Godstow Cl. Wood 87 F4
Goffs Rd. Ashf 98 B2
Gogmore Farm Cl. Chert 123 F1
Gogmore La. Chert 124 A1
Gold Cup La. Burl 119 E4
Goldcrest Cl. Yate 149 D3
Goldcrest Way. Read 84 A3
Golden Ball La. Cook 19 D2
Golden Oak. Far C 22 B3
Golden Orb Wood. Brac 117 E4
Goldfinch La. Newt 131 F2
Golding Cl. That 106 C2
Goldney Rd. Camb 152 B2
Goldsmid Rd. Read 85 F4
Goldsmith Cl. That 106 B3
Goldsmith Way. Crow 143 D2
Goldsworthy Way. Slough 41 E4
Goldthorpe Gdns. Read 113 F4
Goldwell Dr. Newb 104 C2
Golf Dr. Camb 152 A2
Goodboy's La. Bur C 112 A1
Goodboy's La. Mort 112 A1
Goodchild Rd. Woki 116 B3
Goodings Green. Woki 116 C3
Goodliffe Gdns. Purl 57 E2
Goodman Park. Slough 43 E3
Goodman Pl. Stai 96 C2
Goodrich Cl. Caver 59 F3
Goodways Dr. Brac 118 B4
Goodwin Cl. Bur C 84 C2
Goodwin Meadows. Woo G 3 F3
Goodwin Rd. Slough 21 F1
Goodwin Wlk. Newb 130 B3
Goodwood Cl. Bur C 111 D1
Goodwood Cl. Camb 151 E4
Goodwood Rise. Mar B 1 B4
Goodwood Way. Newb 105 E1
Goose Cnr. New G 91 F2
Goose Green. Far C 22 A2
Goose Green. Lamb 25 D2
Goose Green Way. That 106 C2
Goose La. Leckh 49 F3
Goose Pool. Chert 123 F1
Gordon Ave. Camb 151 E2
Gordon Cl. Stai 97 D1
Gordon Cres. Camb 151 E2
Gordon Cres. Comp 31 F2
Gordon Dr. Shepp 125 E1
Gordon Pl. Read 85 E4
Gordon Rd. Ashf 97 F3
Gordon Rd. Camb 151 E3
Gordon Rd. Crow 143 E2
Gordon Rd. Maid 39 E4
Gordon Rd. Newb 105 D1
Gordon Rd. Shepp 125 E2
Gordon Rd. Stai 96 B2
Gordon Rd. That 106 A3
Gordon Rd. Wind 66 C3
Gordon Wlk. Yate 149 F3
Gore End Rd. Ball H 129 D2
Gore Rd. Burn 21 D1
Goring La. Bur C 111 F2
Goring Rd. Stai 96 C2
Gorrick Sq. Brac 116 A2
Gorse Bank. Light 153 D4
Gorse Dr. Wood 88 A4
Gorse Hill La. Vir W 122 B3
Gorse Hill Rd. Vir W 122 B3
Gorse Meade. Slough 42 A3
Gorse Rd. Camb 151 F1
Gorse Rd. Cook 19 F3
Gorse Ride N. Woki 141 F4
Gorse Ride S. Woki 141 F3
Gorselands. Caver 59 D3
Gorselands. Newb 130 B3
Gorselands. Tad 135 E1
Gorselands. Yate 149 E2
Gosbrook Rd. Caver 59 D1
Gosden Rd. West E 153 F3
Gosforth Cl. Read 87 E1
Goslar Way. Wind 67 D3
Gosling Green. Slough 43 F2
Gosling Rd. Slough 43 F2
Gosnell Cl. Camb 152 B2
Gossmore Cl. Mar 1 C1
Gossmore La. Mar 1 C1
Goswell Hill. Wind 67 E3
Goswells Rd. Wind 67 E3
Gothic Ct. Harl 71 E4
Gothic Ct. Sand 150 A4
Gough's La. New G 91 E1
Gough's Meadow. Sand 150 A4
Gould Rd. Felt 98 C4
Govenor's Rd. Sand 150 C3
Govett Ave. Shepp 125 E2
Govett Gr. Windl 146 B3
Gower St. Read 85 F4
Gower The. Stai 123 D3
Graces La. Chiev 78 A4
Graffham Cl. Read 114 A4
Grafton Cl. Maid 19 F1
Grafton Cl. Slough 43 F4
Grafton Rd. Read 84 B4
Graham Cl. Blew 12 A4
Graham Cl. Maid 39 E3
Graham Cl. Read 84 C2
Graham Rd. Cook 19 F3
Graham Rd. Windl 146 B2
Grahame Ave. Pangb 56 B3
Grampian Cl. Harl 71 E4
Grampian Rd. Sand 143 D1
Grampian Way. Slough 44 A1
Gramp's Hill. Let B 6 C3
Granby Ct. Read 86 C4
Granby End. Bur C 111 D2
Granby Gdns. Read 86 C4
Grand Ave. Camb 151 E3
Grange Ave. Crow 143 D3
Grange Ave. Read 87 D3
Grange Cl. Gori 34 A3
Grange Cl. Wray 68 C1
Grange Dr. Bou E 3 E2
Grange Gdns. Far C 22 B4
Grange La. Cook 19 F4
Grange Pl. Stai 124 B4
Grange Rd. Brac 118 B4
Grange Rd. Camb 151 F3
Grange Rd. Cook 19 F4
Grange Rd. Eng G 95 F2
Grange Rd. Hen-O-T 15 F1
Grange The. Burn 21 E1
Grange The. Old W 68 A1
Grange Way. Iver 44 C4
Grangely Cl. Bur C 84 B2
Grant Ave. Slough 42 C4
Grant Cl. Shepp 125 D2
Grant Rd. Crow 143 E2
Grant Wlk. Sunn 120 C1
Grantham Cl. Sand 143 F1
Grantham Rd. Read 84 C2
Granthams The. Lamb 25 D2
Granville Ave. Slough 42 B4
Granville Rd. Read 85 D3
Grasmere Ave. Read 57 F1
Grasmere Ave. Slough 43 D3
Grasmere Cl. Felt 98 C4
Grasmere Cl. Stai 96 A1
Grasmere Par. Slough 43 D3
Grasmere Rd. Light 146 A1
Grass Hill. Caver 58 C2
Grassington Pl. That 106 B2
Grassmead. That 106 C1
Grassmere Cl. Winn 88 A1
Grassy La. Maid 39 F4
Grattan Ct. Mar 2 A2
Gratton Dr. Wind 66 C2
Gratton Rd. Read 113 E4
Gratwicke Rd. Read 84 C4
Gravel Hill. Box 103 F3
Gravel Hill. Caver 59 D3
Gravel Hill. Hen-O-T 15 E1
Gravel Rd. Caver 35 D1
Gravelly Cl. Ball H 129 D2
Graveney Dr. Caver 58 C2
Gravett Cl. Hen-O-T 35 E4
Grayling Cl. Mar 18 B4
Grays Cres. Wood 87 E4
Grays La. Ashf 98 A2
Grays Park Rd. Sto P 23 D2
Gray's Pl. Slough 42 C3
Gray's Rd. Slough 42 C3
Grayshot Dr. Sand 150 B3
Grazeley Rd. Shin 113 D2
Great Hill Cres. Maid 39 E3
Great Hollands Rd. Brac 117 F2
Great Hollands Sq. Brac 117 F2
Great Knollys St. Read 85 F4
Great South West Rd. Felt 71 F1
Great South West Rd. Harm 71 F1
Green Acre Mount. Read 84 B4
Green Cl. Burn 41 D4
Green Cl. Maid 19 F1
Green Cres. Fla H 3 E4
Green Croft. Woki 116 C4
Green Dragon La. Fla H 3 D4
Green End. Yate 149 E4
Green End Cl. Shin 113 D1
Green Farm Rd. Bags 145 F2
Green Finch Cl. Brac 142 C3
Green Hill Cl. Camb 152 B3
Green Hill Rd. Camb 152 B3
Green La. Ascot 120 C4
Green La. Ashf 98 C1
Green La. Bags 145 F1
Green La. Black 150 C2
Green La. Bur C 85 D1
Green La. Bur G 38 A3
Green La. Burn 221 E2
Green La. Caver 35 D1
Green La. Far C 22 A3
Green La. Hen-O-T 35 E4
Green La. Holy 64 A3
Green La. Hurst 88 C2
Green La. Maid 40 A3
Green La. Newb 104 C1
Green La. Padw 110 B1
Green La. Pangb 56 B2
Green La. Sand 150 B3
Green La. Sand 150 B4
Green La. Shepp 125 E2
Green La. Slough 68 A3

Green La. Stai 96 A2
Green La. Stai 123 F4
Green La. That 106 B2
Green La. Wind 67 D3
Green La. Woki 88 B1
Green La. Yate 149 D4
Green Lane Ct. Burn 21 E1
Green Leas. Ashf 98 C1
Green Leas Cl. Ashf 98 C1
Green Park. Stai 96 C3
Green Rd. Read 87 D3
Green Rd. Vir W 123 F4
Green The. Brac 118 A3
Green The. Burn 21 D1
Green The. Chil 10 C4
Green The. Datch 68 A4
Green The. Slough 42 B2
Green The. Thea 83 E1
Green The. Woki 115 F4
Green The. Woo G 3 F3
Green The. Wray 68 C1
Green Verges. Mar 1 C2
Green Way. Burn 21 D2
Green Wood. Burl 119 E4
Greenacre. Wind 66 C3
Greenacre Ct. Eng G 95 E1
Greenacres. Ball H 129 F1
Greenacres. Sand 150 A4
Greenacres Ave. Winn 88 A2
Greenacres La. Winn 88 A2
Greencroft Gdns. Read 84 C3
Greene Fielde End. Stai 97 E1
Greenfell Ave. Maid 39 F3
Greenfern Ave. Slough 41 E4
Greenfield Way. Brac 143 D4
Greenfields. Maid 40 A3
Greenfields Rd. Read 113 D4
Greenfinch Cl. Read 84 A3
Greenham Cl. Wood 88 A3
Greenham Mill. Newb 105 D2
Greenham Rd. Newb 105 D1
Greenham Wood. Brac 118 B2
Greenhaven. Yate 149 D3
Greenholme. Camb 152 B3
Greenhow. Brac 118 A3
Greenlands. Ball H 129 F1
Greenlands. Fla H 3 D4
Greenlands Rd. Camb 151 D1
Greenlands Rd. Newb 105 D1
Greenlands Rd. Stai 97 D2
Greenleas. Camb 151 F1
Greenleas Ave. Caver 59 D4
Greenleas Cl. Yate 149 E4
Greeno Cres. Stai 125 D2
Greenock Rd. Slough 42 A4
Greenside. Bou E 3 D3
Greenside. Crow 142 C3
Greenside. Slough 42 A4
Greensward La. Arbo 114 B1
Greenway Dr. Stai 124 A4
Greenway The. Fawl 27 E4
Greenway The. Slough 41 E3
Greenways. Ball H 129 F1
Greenways. Eng G 95 F2
Greenways. Lamb 25 D1
Greenways. Sand 143 D1
Greenways Dr. Maid 39 D4
Greenways Dr. Sunn 120 C1
Greenwood Gr. Winn 88 B2
Greenwood Rd. Crow 143 D3
Greenwood Rd. Read 84 C3
Gregory Cl. Winn 114 B4
Gregory Dr. Old W 68 A1
Grenfell Pl. Maid 39 F3
Grenfell Rd. Maid 39 F3
Grenville Cl. Burn 21 D2
Gresham Rd. Slough 42 A4
Gresham Rd. Stai 96 C2
Gresham Rd. Stai 97 D2
Gresham Way. Read 58 A1
Greyberry Copse Rd. Gree 131 E4
Greyfriars Dr. Ascot 120 A2
Greyfriars Rd. Read 86 A4
Greys Ct. Read 86 B4
Greys Hill. Hen-O-T 15 E1
Grey's Rd. Hen-O-T 35 E4
Greystoke Ct. Crow 143 D2
Greystoke Rd. Caver 59 E2
Greystoke Rd. Slough 41 F4
Griffin Cl. Maid 39 F3
Griffin Cl. Slough 42 B2
Griffiths Cl. That 106 C1
Grindle Cl. Cold A 106 B3
Gringer Hill. Maid 39 F4
Grosvenor Ct. Black 150 B2
Grosvenor Dr. Maid 40 B4
Grosvenor Rd. Caver 59 E2
Grosvenor Rd. Stai 97 D1
Grove Cl. Brac 142 C4
Grove Cl. Old W 95 D4
Grove Cl. Slough 43 D2
Grove Cotts. Caver 59 D3
Grove Cross Rd. Camb 151 E1
Grove Ct. Eng G 96 A2
Grove End. Windl 145 F3
Grove Hill. Caver 59 D2
Grove La. Wink 92 A2
Grove Rd. Burn 21 F2
Grove Rd. Camb 151 F3
Grove Rd. Caver 59 D3
Grove Rd. Chert 123 F2
Grove Rd. Hen-O-T 15 F1
Grove Rd. Maid 39 F4
Grove Rd. Newb 104 C3
Grove Rd. Shepp 125 E2
Grove Rd. Wind 67 E3
Grove The. Burl 119 E4
Grove The. Camb 151 E1
Grove The. Eng G 96 A2
Grove The. Read 86 B4
Grove The. Slough 43 D2
Grove The. That 106 B2
Grove The. Twyf 61 E3
Grovefields Ave. Camb 151 E1
Groveland Rd. Newb 104 C3
Grovelands Ave. Winn 88 B1
Grovelands Cl. Winn 88 B2
Grovelands Rd. Read 85 D4
Grovelands Rd. Shin 113 E1
Groveley Rd. Ashf 98 C2
Groves Way. Cook 19 F3
Grovestile Waye. Felt 98 B4
Grubwood La. Cook 19 D4
Guards Club Rd. Maid 40 B4
Guards Rd. Oak G 66 B3
Guildford Ave. Felt 98 C3
Guildford Rd. Bags 145 F2
Guildford Rd. Bis 153 F4
Guildford Rd. Light 153 F4
Guildford Rd. West E 153 F4
Guildford St. Chert 124 A1
Guildford St. Stai 97 D1
Gun St. Read 86 A4
Gunthorpe Rd. Mar 2 A2
Gurney Cl. Caver 58 B3
Gurney Dr. Caver 58 B3
Gwendale. Maid 19 E1
Gweneth Ct. Mar 1 B2
Gwent Cl. Maid 39 D2
Gwyn Cl. Newb 130 C4
Gwynne Cl. Read 57 E2
Gwynne Cl. Wind 66 C3
Gwyns Piece. Lamb 25 D2
Gypsy La. Mar 1 C2
Gypsy La. Sto P 22 C4
Habershon Dr. Camb 152 B1
Haddon Dr. Wood 87 F4
Haddon Rd. Maid 39 E3
Hadfield Rd. Stan 70 B1
Hadfield Rd. Stan 97 E4
Hadleigh Rise. Caver 59 F3
Hadlow Ct. Slough 42 B3
Hadrian Cl. Stan 97 F4
Hadrian Way. Stan 97 F4
Hadrian Wlk E. Read 86 B2
Hag Hill La. Burn 41 D4
Hag Hill Rise. Burn 41 D4
Hagley Rd. Read 86 A2
Haig Dr. Slough 42 A2
Haig Rd. Sand 150 C3
Hailey La. Beed 29 F1
Hailsham Cl. Crow 143 E1
Haldane Rd. Caver 58 C3
Hale End. Brac 118 C3
Hale St. Stai 96 C2
Hale Way. Camb 151 E1
Halewood. Brac 117 F2
Half Mile Rd. Lamb 46 A1
Half Moon St. Bags 145 F2
Halfacre Cl. Shin 113 D2
Halfpenny La. Chol 13 F3
Halfpenny La. Went 121 D1
Halifax Cl. Maid 39 D4
Halifax Rd. Maid 39 D4
Halifax Way. Maid 39 D4
Halkingcroft. Slough 43 E2
Hall Cl. Camb 151 F3
Hall Ct. Datch 68 A4
Hall Farm Cres. Yate 149 E3
Hall La. Harl 71 E4
Hall La. Yate 149 E3
Hall Meadow. Burn 21 E2
Hall Place La. Bur G 38 A4
Halldore Hill. Cook 19 F4
Halley Dr. Ascot 119 E4
Hallgrove Bottom. Windl 145 F3
Halliford Cl. Shepp 125 F3
Halliford Rd. Shepp 125 F3
Halls La. Read 86 C1
Halls La. W St L 63 D3
Halls Rd. Read 84 B3
Halpin Cl. Read 84 B2
Halstead Cl. Wood 87 F4
Ham La. Eng G 95 D2
Ham La. Old W 68 B2
Ham Rd. Ham 126 A2
Hamble Ave. Black 150 B3
Hambleden Wlk. Maid 19 F2
Hambledon Cl. Winn 87 F1
Hambleton Cl. Camb 152 A2
Hambridge La. Gree 105 F1
Hambridge Rd. Newb 105 E1
Hamilton Ave. Hen-O-T 15 F1
Hamilton Cl. Chert 123 F1
Hamilton Cl. Felt 98 C2
Hamilton Ct. Black 150 C1
Hamilton Ct. Newb 131 D4
Hamilton Dr. Sunn 120 C1
Hamilton Gdns. Burn 21 D1
Hamilton Rd. Felt 98 C2
Hamilton Rd. Read 86 C3
Hamilton Rd. Slough 42 A4
Hamilton Rd. Warg 36 C1
Hammond Cl. That 106 C1
Hammond End. Far C 22 B4
Hammond Way. Light 146 A1
Hammonds Heath. Mort 137 D3
Hampden Cl. Sto P 23 D1
Hampden Rd. Caver 59 D1
Hampden Rd. Maid 39 D4
Hampden Rd. Slough 43 F2
Hampdens The. Newb 130 B3
Hampshire Ave. Slough 42 B4
Hampshire Rd. Camb 151 F4
Hampshire Way. Woki 115 E3
Hampstead Hill. Caver 60 B4
Hampstead Norreys Rd. Herm 79 D4
Hampton Rd. Newb 104 C1
Hanbury Cl. Burn 41 D4
Hanbury Dr. Bur C 84 B2
Hancocks Mount. Ascot 120 B2
Hancombe Rd. Sand 143 D1
Handford La. Yate 149 E3
Hanger Rd. Tad 134 C1
Hangerfield Cl. Yate 149 E3
Hangman's Stone La. Chadd 49 D3
Hanley Cl. Wind 66 B3
Hannibal Rd. Stan 97 F4
Hanover Cl. Camb 151 F1
Hanover Cl. Eng G 95 D1
Hanover Cl. Slough 43 D2
Hanover Cl. Wind 66 C3
Hanover Gdns. Brac 117 F1
Hanover Way. Wind 66 C3
Hanwood Cl. Wood 87 E4
Hanworth Cl. Brac 118 B2
Hanworth La. Chert 123 F1
Hanworth Rd. Brac 118 A1
Harcourt Cl. Dorn 40 C2
Harcourt Cl. Hen-O-T 15 E1
Harcourt Cl. Stai 96 B1
Harcourt Dr. Read 86 C2
Harcourt Rd. Brac 118 A2
Harcourt Rd. Camb 151 D3
Harcourt Rd. Dorn 40 C2
Harcourt Rd. Wind 66 C3
Hardell Cl. Eng G 96 A2
Harding Rd. Wood 87 E4
Hardwell Way. Brac 118 C3
Hardwick Cl. Maid 39 D4
Hardwick La. Chert 123 E1
Hardwick Rd. Read 84 C4
Hardwick Rd. Whitc 56 B4
Hardy Ave. Yate 149 E2
Hardy Cl. Caver 59 E1
Hardy Cl. Slough 42 A3
Hardy Cl. That 106 B3
Hardy Green. Crow 143 D2
Hare Shoots. Maid 39 F3
Harefield Cl. Winn 88 B1
Harefield Rd. Maid 39 D4
Harewood Dr. Cold A 106 B4
Harewood Pl. Slough 43 D2
Hargrave Rd. Maid 39 E4
Hargreaves Way. Read 84 C2
Harkness Rd. Burn 41 D4
Harlech Ave. Caver 59 E3
Harlech Rd. Black 150 B2
Harley Rd. Caver 59 D1
Harlington Cl. Harl 71 E4
Harlton Cl. Winn 114 B4
Harmans Water Rd. Brac 118 B2
Harmar Cl. Woki 116 C3
Harmondsworth La. Harm 70 C4
Harness Cl. Read 113 D3
Harold Rd. Kint 102 A1
Harpesford Ave. Went 122 B2
Harpton Cl. Yate 149 E4
Harrier Cl. Wood 88 A3
Harrington Cl. Read 87 E1
Harrington Cl. Wind 66 C2
Harris Cl. Lamb 25 D2
Harris Way. Stai 125 F4
Harrison Cl. Twyf 61 F2
Harrison Ct. Stai 125 D2
Harrison Way. Slough 41 E3
Harrogate Ct. Slough 44 A1
Harrogate Rd. Caver 58 C2
Harrow Bottom Rd. Went 122 C2
Harrow Cl. Maid 19 F1
Harrow Ct. Read 85 F3
Harrow La. Maid 19 F1
Harrow Rd. Ashf 98 A3
Harrow Rd. Slough 43 F2
Harrow Way. Stai 125 E4
Hart Cl. Brac 91 D1
Hart Dyke Cl. Brac 116 A1
Hart St. Hen-O-T 15 F1
Hart St. Read 85 F4
Hartford Rise. Camb 151 E3
Hartland Cl. Slough 42 B3
Hartland Rd. Read 86 B1
Hartley Cl. Black 150 A3
Hartley Cl. Sto P 23 E2
Hartley Court Rd. Shin 112 C3
Hartley Way. That 106 C2
Hartmead Rd. That 106 C2
Harts Cl. Arbo 114 C1
Harts Hill Rd. That 106 B2
Hart's La. Sulhd 110 B3
Harts Leap Cl. Sand 143 D1
Harts Leap Rd. Sand 150 A4
Hartsbourne Rd. Read 87 D2
Hartshill Rd. Tad 134 C1
Hartslock Ct. Pangb 56 A3
Hartslock Way. Read 57 E1
Hartstock View. Upp B 34 C1
Harvard Cl. Wood 88 A4
Harvard Rd. Crow 143 F1
Harvest Cl. Read 84 A3
Harvest Cl. Yate 149 D2
Harvest Ct. Stai 125 D3
Harvest Green. Newb 104 C1
Harvest Hill. Bou E 3 E1
Harvest Hill Rd. Maid 39 F2
Harvest Rd. Eng G 95 E1
Harvey Rd. Shepp 125 F1
Harvey Rd. Slough 44 A2
Harwich Cl. Winn 87 E1
Harwich Rd. Slough 42 A4
Harwood Gdns. Old W 95 D4
Harwood Rd. Mar 1 B1
Harwood Rise. Ball H 129 F1
Haslemere Cl. Camb 152 B2
Haslemere Rd. Wind 67 D3
Haslett Rd. Shepp 125 F4
Hasting Cl. Maid 40 B1
Hatch Cl. Buck 108 B4
Hatch End. Windl 146 B2
Hatch Gate La. Know H 37 D3
Hatch La. Buck 108 B4
Hatch La. Bur C 111 E3
Hatch La. Harm 70 B4
Hatch La. Wind 67 D3
Hatch Ride. Brac 142 C4
Hatch Ride. Brac 143 D4
Hatch The. Oak G 66 C4
Hatchet La. Ascot 93 D2
Hatchet La. Old W 93 D2
Hatchet La. Wink 93 D2
Hatchets La. Buck 80 B4
Hatchett Rd. Felt 98 B4
Hatchgate Cl. Cold A 106 B4
Hatchgate Copse. Brac 117 F2
Hatchgate Gdns. Burn 21 E1
Hatfield Cl. Maid 39 E3
Hatfield Ct. Bur C 84 A2
Hatfield Rd. Slough 43 D2
Hatford Rd. Read 85 D2
Hatherley Rd. Read 86 C3
Hatherwood. Yate 149 F3
Hatton Ave. Far C 22 B1
Hatton Ct. Wind 67 E3
Hatton Hill. Asham 54 A4
Hatton Hill. Windl 146 B3
Hatton Rd. Felt 98 B4
Hatton Rd. Harm 71 F1
Havelock Cres. Maid 39 D4
Havelock Rd. Maid 39 D4
Havelock Rd. Woki 116 A3
Havelock St. Woki 116 A3
Haven Rd. Ashf 98 A3
Haven The. Kint 102 A1
Haversham Dr. Brac 118 A2
Haw La. Asham 53 F4
Hawkchurch Rd. Read 113 E4
Hawkedon Way. Winn 87 F1
Hawker Way. Wood 88 A4
Hawkes Cl. Woki 116 A4
Hawkes Leap. Windl 146 A3
Hawkesbury Dr. Bur C 84 C2
Hawkesworth Dr. Bags 145 F1
Hawkins Cl. Brac 119 D4
Hawkins Way. Woki 116 C3
Hawks Hill. Bou E 3 E1
Hawkshill Rd. Slough 22 A1
Hawksway. Stai 96 C3
Hawkswood Ave. Camb 151 F1
Hawkswood La. Fulm 23 F4
Hawksworth Rd. Bur C 111 D2
Hawley Cl. Bur C 84 B2
Hawley La. Camb 151 D1
Hawley Rd. Black 150 C2
Hawley Way. Ashf 98 A2
Haws La. Stan 70 A1
Hawthorn Cl. Brac 118 A4
Hawthorn Cl. Mar 1 C2
Hawthorn Gdns. Read 86 C1
Hawthorn La. Burn 22 A3
Hawthorn Rd. Camb 151 F1
Hawthorn Rd. Newb 105 D2
Hawthorn Way. Shepp 125 E3
Hawthorn Way. Sonn 60 C1
Hawthorne Cres. Black 150 C2
Hawthorne Cres. Slough 42 C4
Hawthorne Rd. Caver 59 F2
Hawthorne Rd. Stai 96 B2
Hawthorne Way. Gr She 48 A2
Hawthornes. Sulh 57 D2
Hawthorns The. Char 61 D2
Hawthorns The. Stan 69 F3
Hawtrey Cl. Slough 43 D2
Hawtrey Rd. Wind 67 E3
Hay La. Fulm 23 E4
Hay Rd. Read 85 F3
Hayes La. Bark 115 E2
Hayes Pl. Mar 1 B1
Hayfield Cl. Read 84 B4
Haymill Rd. Slough 21 E1
Haynes Cl. Slough 43 F1
Hayse Hill. Wind 66 B3
Haywards Cl. Hen-O-T 15 E1
Haywards Mead. Eton 41 F1
Haywards The. That 106 B2
Haywood. Brac 118 B1
Haywood Ct. Read 86 C4
Haywood Way. Read 84 C3
Hazel Cl. Bur C 111 D3
Hazel Cl. Eng G 95 D1
Hazel Cl. Mar B 1 B3
Hazel Cl. Woki 115 F3
Hazel Cres. Read 86 C1
Hazel Dr. Wood 87 E3
Hazel Gr. Stai 97 E1
Hazel Gr. That 106 B3
Hazel Green. Tad 134 B1
Hazel Rd. Purl 57 E2
Hazelbank. Woki 141 F3
Hazelbank Rd. Chert 124 B1
Hazeldene. Chiev 51 D1
Hazelhurst Rd. Burn 21 E2
Hazell Cl. Maid 39 F4
Hazell Hill. Brac 118 B3
Hazell Way. Sto P 22 C3
Hazelmere Cl. Harm 71 F1
Hazelwood Cl. Read 57 E1
Hazelwood La. Binf 90 C2
Hazlemere Rd. Slough 43 D3
Heacham Cl. Read 114 A4
Headington Cl. Maid 39 D4
Headington Cl. Woki 116 B4
Headington Dr. Woki 116 B4
Headington Rd. Maid 39 D4
Headley Cl. Wood 88 A4
Headley Park Industrial Estate. Wood 87 F4
Headley Rd. Wood 87 F4
Headley Rd E. Wood 88 A4
Heads La. Ink 128 A3
Heads La. West W 128 A3
Heardman Cl. That 106 C1
Hearmon Cl. Yate 149 F3
Hearn Rd. Wood 87 F3
Hearn Wlk. Brac 118 C4
Hearne Dr. Holy 40 A1
Hearsey Gdns. Black 150 A3
Heath Cl. Harl 71 E4
Heath Cl. Stan 70 B1
Heath Cl. Vir W 122 B3
Heath Cl. Woki 116 A2
Heath Dr. Caver 35 D1
Heath End Rd. Tad 134 C1
Heath Gr. Ashf 98 C1
Heath Hill Rd. Crow 143 D3
Heath Hill Rd S. Crow 143 D2
Heath La. That 106 B3
Heath Rd. Bags 145 F2
Heath Rd. Beac 3 F4
Heath Rd. Brad 82 A1
Heath Rd. Read 87 D3
Heath Rd. Silc 135 F1
Heath Ride. Finch 142 B3
Heath Ride. Woki 142 B3
Heath Rise. Camb 151 E3
Heath Rise. Vir W 122 B3
Heathcote Rd. Camb 151 E3
Heathcroft Ave. Ashf 98 C1
Heather Cl. Woki 141 F4
Heather Dr. Tad 134 C1
Heather Dr. Went 121 D1
Heather Mead. Camb 151 F1
Heatherdale Rd. Camb 151 E2
Heatherden Cl. Read 113 E4
Heatherdene Ave. Finch 142 C2
Heatherley Cl. Camb 151 D3
Heatherley Rd. Camb 151 D3
Heathermount. Brac 118 C3
Heathermount Dr. Crow 143 D3
Heathers The. Stan 97 F4
Heatherside Dr. Vir W 122 A2
Heatherway. Crow 143 D3
Heathfield Ave. Ascot 120 C2
Heathfield Ave. Read 84 B3
Heathfield Ave. Shipl 35 D1
Heathfield Cl. Shipl 35 D1
Heathfield Rd. Bou E 20 C4
Heathfield Rd. Tapl 20 C4
Heathlands. Tad 134 C1
Heathlands Dr. Maid 39 D3
Heathlands Rd. Woki 116 C1
Heathmoors. Brac 118 B2
Heathpark Dr. Windl 146 C2
Heathrow Cl. Harm 70 A3
Heathway. Burl 119 F4
Heathway. Camb 151 E3
Heathway. Read 84 B4
Heathway Cl. Camb 151 E3
Heathwood Cl. Yate 149 E4
Heavens Lea. Bou E 3 E1
Hebden Cl. That 106 B1
Hedge Lea. Woo G 3 E4
Hedgeway. Newb 105 E2
Hedley Rd. Fla H 3 D4
Hedsor Hill. Bou E 3 E1
Hedsor La. Bou E 3 F1
Hedsor Rd. Bou E 3 D1
Heelas Rd. Woki 116 A3
Helena Rd. Wind 67 E3
Helgiford Gdns. Ashf 98 C1
Hellyer Way. Bou E 3 E2
Helmsdale. Brac 118 C2
Helmsdale Cl. Read 85 D4
Helston Gdns. Read 86 A1
Helston La. Wind 67 D3
Helvellyn Cl. Stai 96 B1
Hemdean Hill. Caver 59 D2
Hemdean Rd. Caver 59 D2
Hemdean Rise. Caver 59 D2
Hempson Ave. Slough 43 E2
Hemsdale. Maid 19 D1
Hemwood Rd. Wind 66 B2
Hencroft St N. Slough 42 C2
Hencroft St S. Slough 42 C2
Hendon Way. Stan 70 B1
Hendons Way. Holy 40 A1
Hengrave Cl. Winn 87 F1
Hengrove Cres. Ashf 97 E3
Henley Gdns. Yate 149 E3
Henley Rd. Bur G 18 A1
Henley Rd. Caver 60 B4
Henley Rd. Hurl 18 A1
Henley Rd. Maid 18 A1
Henley Rd. Mar 18 A4
Henley Rd. Shipl 60 B4
Henley Rd. Slough 41 F4
Henley Wood Rd. Read 87 E2
Henry Rd. Slough 42 B2
Henry St. Read 86 A3
Henrys The. That 106 B2
Henshaw Cres. Newb 130 B4
Hensworth Rd. Stai 97 E2
Henwick Cl. That 106 A3
Henwick La. That 106 A2
Henwood Copse. Upp B 55 D3
Hepplewhite Cl. Tad 134 C1
Hepworth Way. Shepp 125 F1
Herald Way. Wood 88 A3
Herbert Cl. Brac 118 A2
Hereford Cl. Stai 124 A4
Herewood Cl. Newb 104 C2
Heriot Rd. Chert 124 A1
Hermitage Cl. Camb 151 F1
Hermitage Cl. Slough 43 E2
Hermitage Cl. Stai 125 D3
Hermitage Dr. Ascot 119 F4

Hermitage Dr. Twyf 61 E3
Hermitage La. Wind 67 D2
Hermitage Rd. Cold A 79 D1
Hermitage Rd. Herm 79 D1
Hermitage The. Lamb 46 C4
Hermits Cl. Bur C 111 D2
Hermit's Hill. Bur C 111 E2
Heroes Wlk. Read 113 D4
Heron Cl. Burl 119 E4
Heron Dr. Twyf 61 F3
Heron Island. Caver 59 E1
Heron Rd. Woki 115 F3
Heron Shaw. Gori 34 B4
Heron Way. Bur C 85 F2
Heron Way. That 106 A2
Herondale. Brac 118 B1
Heronfield. Eng G 95 D1
Herons Ct. Light 153 E4
Herons Pl. Mar 1 C2
Heron's Way. Woki 116 C4
Herrick Cl. Camb 152 B2
Herrings La. Chert 124 A2
Herrings La. Windl 146 B2
Herriot Cl. Yate 149 E2
Herschel Park Dr. Slough 42 C2
Herschel St. Slough 42 C2
Hertford Cl. Caver 59 E3
Hertford Cl. Woki 115 F3
Hetherington Cl. Slough 21 F1
Hetherington Rd. Stai 125 E4
Hever Cl. Maid 39 E3
Hewett Ave. Caver 58 B2
Hewett Cl. Caver 58 B2
Hewlett Pl. Bags 145 F2
Hexham Cl. Crow 143 E1
Hexham Rd. Read 86 B2
Heywood Ave. Whi Wa 39 D1
Heywood Court Cl. Whi Wa 39 D1
Heywood Gdns. Whi Wa 39 D1
Hibbert Rd. Maid 40 A2
Hibbert's Alley. Wind 67 E3
Hicks La. Black 150 A3
Higgs La. Bags 145 E2
High Beech. Brac 118 C3
High Beeches. Camb 151 E1
High Fields. Sunn 120 C2
High Heavens Wood. Mar B 1 B4
High Meadow. Caver 58 B2
High Rd. Cook 19 F3
High St. Ascot 120 A3
High St. Ascot 120 B2
High St. Bags 145 F2
High St. Box 76 A2
High St. Brac 118 A4
High St. Brac 118 B4
High St. Burn 21 E1
High St. Camb 151 E3
High St. Chiev 51 D1
High St. Comp 31 E2
High St. Cook 20 A4
High St. Crow 143 E2
High St. Datch 68 A3
High St. East I 30 C4
High St. Eng G 96 A2
High St. Eton 67 E4
High St. Felt 98 C3
High St. Gori 34 B3
High St. Harl 71 E4
High St. Harm 70 B4
High St. Hung 100 B3
High St. Iver 44 C4
High St. Iver 69 E4
High St. Kint 102 A1
High St. Lamb 24 C3
High St. Lamb 25 D1
High St. Maid 40 A2
High St. Maid 40 B2
High St. Maid 39 F4
High St. Mar 1 C1
High St. Pangb 56 B3
High St. Read 86 A4
High St. Sand 143 D1
High St. Sand 149 F4
High St. Shepp 125 E2
High St. Slough 44 A1
High St. Slough 42 B2
High St. Slough 42 C2
High St. Sonn 60 B2
High St. Stai 96 C2
High St. Stan 70 B1
High St. Stre 34 A3
High St. Sunn 121 D2
High St. Tapl 20 C1
High St. That 106 B2
High St. Thea 83 F2
High St. Twyf 61 E2
High St. Warg 36 B1
High St. West E 153 F4
High St. Whitc 56 B4
High St. Wick 76 A2
High St. Wind 67 E3
High St. Wray 68 C1
High St Harlington. Harl 71 E4
High Town Rd. Maid 39 F3
High Tree Dr. Read 87 D3
High View Cl. Mar B 1 B4
High View Rd. Light 152 C4
Highbeeches Cl. Mar B 1 B3
Highbridge Cl. Caver 59 F2
Highbridge Wharf. Read 86 A4
Highbury Cres. Camb 152 A4
Highbury Rd. Read 84 A4
Highclere. Ascot 120 B2
Highclere Cl. Brac 118 C4
Highclere Dr. Camb 152 A4
Highdown Ave. Caver 59 F4
Highdown Hill Rd. Caver 59 D4
Highdown Hill Rd. Maple 59 D4
Higher Alham. Brac 118 C1
Highfield. Brac 117 F2
Highfield. Read 87 D1
Highfield Ave. Newb 105 D1
Highfield Cl. Woki 116 A3
Highfield Ct. Bur C 111 D2
Highfield La. Maid 39 D2
Highfield Park. Mar 18 A4
Highfield Park. Warg 36 C1
Highfield Rd. Bou E 3 D2
Highfield Rd. Chert 124 A1
Highfield Rd. Fla H 3 D4
Highfield Rd. Maid 39 D4
Highfield Rd. Newb 104 C1
Highfield Rd. Purl 57 E2
Highfield Rd. Shepp 125 F2
Highfield Rd. Wind 66 C2
Highgate Rd. Wood 87 E3
Highgrove Park. Maid 39 F4
Highgrove St. Read 86 B3
Highgrove Terr. Read 86 A3
Highland Ave. Woki 115 F4
Highland Park. Felt 98 C2
Highland Rd. Camb 151 F4
Highlands. Fla H 3 D4
Highlands La. Shipl 35 D4
Highlea Ave. Fla H 3 D4
Highmead Cl. Read 86 C1
Highmoor Rd. Caver 58 C2
Highview. Read 84 A3
Highview Cres. Camb 144 C1
Highway. Crow 143 D3
Highway Ave. Maid 39 D3
Highway Rd. Maid 39 D3
Highwayman's Ridge. Windl 146 A3
Highwood Cl. Newb 105 E3
Highwood Cl. Yate 149 E2
Highwoods Cl. Mar B 1 B4
Highwoods Dr. Mar B 1 B4
Highworth Way. Sulh 57 D1
Hilary Cl. Read 113 E4
Hilborne Way. Bark 115 D1
Hilbury Rd. Read 87 D2
Hilcot Rd. Read 85 E4
Hildens Dr. Read 84 B4
Hilfield. Yate 149 F3
Hill Cl. Newb 130 B4
Hill Cl. Woo G 3 F4
Hill Copse View. Brac 118 C4
Hill Farm App. Woo G 3 F4
Hill Farm Rd. Mar B 1 C3
Hill Farm Rd. Tapl 20 C1
Hill Gdns. Stre 34 A3
Hill Lands. Warg 36 B1
Hill Piece. Chil 10 C4
Hill Rd. Bark 114 C1
Hill Rd. Newb 104 C2
Hill St. Read 86 A3
Hill Top Dr. Mar 1 A1
Hill View Rd. Wray 68 B1
Hillary Dr. Crow 143 D3
Hillary Rd. Slough 43 F2
Hillberry. Brac 118 B1
Hillborn Rd. Bark 140 C4
Hillbrow. Read 86 C1
Hillcrest. Tad 135 D1
Hillcrest Ave. Cook 19 F3
Hillcrest Rd. Camb 152 A4
Hillersdon. Slough 43 D4
Hillgreen La. Pease 50 B4
Hillhouse La. Head 133 E1
Hillingdon Ave. Stan 97 F4
Hillmead Ct. Tapl 40 C4
Hillrise. Slough 69 D4
Hills La. Cook 19 E4
Hillsborough Park. Camb 152 B3
Hillside. Bur C 111 E2
Hillside. East G 47 E3
Hillside. Maid 39 E3
Hillside. Sand 150 C4
Hillside. Slough 42 C2
Hillside. Went 122 B2
Hillside. Whitc 56 B4
Hillside Dr. Binf 90 B1
Hillside Park. Windl 120 C1
Hillside Rd. Hung 100 B2
Hillside Rd. Mar 1 C2
Hillside Rd. Read 87 E2
Hilltop Cl. Ascot 120 C4
Hilltop Rd. Caver 58 B3
Hilltop Rd. Read 87 D4
Hilltop Rd. Twyf 61 F4
Hilltop View. Yate 149 D3
Hillview Cl. Read 57 D1
Hilmanton. Read 113 F4
Hilperton Rd. Slough 42 C2
Hindhead Rd. Read 87 D2
Hinksey Cl. Slough 44 A2
Hinton Cl. Crow 143 D4
Hinton Dr. Crow 143 D4
Hinton Rd. Hurst 62 A1
Hinton Rd. Hurst 88 C4
Hinton Rd. Slough 41 F3
Hintonhatch Cnr. Hurst 62 A1
Hirtes Ave. Shin 113 F3
Hitcham La. Tapl 20 C1
Hitcham Rd. Burn 41 D4
Hitchcock Cl. Stai 124 C3
Hithermoor Rd. Stan 70 A1
Hobart Ct. Mar 2 A2
Hobbis Dr. Maid 39 D3
Hockett La. Bish 19 D3
Hockett La. Cook 19 D3
Hockford La. Head 134 A2
Hockham Rd. Comp 31 F3
Hockley La. Sto P 23 D3
Hodges Cl. Bags 145 F1
Hodsoll Rd. Read 85 F4
Hoe Benham La. Wick 102 C3
Hogarth Ave. Ashf 98 B1
Hogarth Ave. Read 84 C3
Hogarth Cl. Slough 41 F3
Hogfair La. Burn 21 E1
Hogmoor La. Hurst 61 F1
Hogwood La. Bark 141 D3
Holbeche Cl. Yate 149 D3
Holbeck. Brac 117 F2
Holberton Rd. Read 113 E4
Holborn Hill. Let B 6 B4
Holborne Cl. Newb 130 B3
Holford Cl. Read 84 B4
Holkam Cl. Read 57 F1
Holland Gdns. Stai 123 F4
Holland Pines. Brac 117 F1
Holland Rd. Mar 1 C2
Holland Rd. Read 84 B4
Hollands The. That 106 C2
Hollicombe Cl. Read 84 C4
Hollies The. Newb 130 B3
Hollins Wlk. Read 85 E3
Hollow Hill La. Iver 44 B3
Hollow La. Shin 113 F3
Hollow La. Vir W 122 B3
Holloway La. Harm 70 C4
Holly Ave. Camb 152 A2
Holly Cl. Eng G 95 D1
Holly Cl. Far C 22 B4
Holly Cres. Wind 66 B3
Holly Dr. Maid 39 F4
Holly Dr. Old Wind 67 F1
Holly Hedge Cl. Camb 151 F1
Holly Hedge Rd. Camb 151 F1
Holly La. Asham 54 B3
Holly Rd. Wood 88 A3
Holly Spring La. Brac 118 B4
Holly Way. Black 150 B2
Hollybank. West E 153 F3
Hollybush Hill. Sto P 23 D3
Hollybush La. Cook 19 D3
Hollybush La. Iver 44 A3
Hollybush La. Sulhd 110 C2
Hollybush Ride. Brac 142 B3
Hollybush Ride. Finch 142 B3
Hollycombe. Eng G 95 E2
Hollycroft Cl. Harm 71 D4
Hollycroft Gdns. Harm 71 D4
Hollydale Cl. Read 86 C1
Hollyfields Cl. Camb 151 D3
Hollyhook Cl. Brac 143 D3
Hollym Cl. Winn 87 F1
Holmanleaze. Maid 40 A4
Holmbank Dr. Shepp 125 F3
Holmbury Ave. Brac 143 D4
Holmdale. Slough 43 E3
Holmdene. Bur C 111 D2
Holme Cl. Brac 143 D4
Holmemoor Dr. Sonn 60 C1
Holmes Cl. Ascot 120 B2
Holmes Cl. Woki 116 A2
Holmes Cres. Woki 116 A2
Holmes Rd. Read 87 D3
Holmewood Cl. Woki 116 A1
Holmlea Rd. Datch 68 B3
Holmlea Rd. Gori 34 B3
Holmlea Wlk. Datch 68 B3
Holmsdale Cl. Iver 44 C4
Holmwood Ave. Read 84 C2
Holmwood Cl. Maid 39 D3
Holsworthy Cl. Winn 87 F2
Holt La. Brig 49 F4
Holt La. Woki 116 A4
Holt Rd. Kint 102 A1
Holt The. Purl 57 E2
Holton Heath. Brac 118 C3
Holtspur Ave. Woo G 3 F4
Holtspur La. Woo G 3 F3
Holtwood Rd. Ham M 129 D3
Holybrook Cres. Read 85 D2
Holybrook Rd. Read 85 F3
Holyport St. Holy 65 D4
Holyrood Cl. Caver 59 E3
Holywell Cl. Stan 97 F4
Holywell Way. Stan 97 F4
Hombrook Dr. Brac 117 F4
Home Croft. Sulh 57 D1
Home Farm Cl. Read 86 B2
Home Farm Cl. Shepp 125 F3
Home Farm Way. Sto P 23 E2
Home Mead Cl. Newb 130 C4
Home Meadow. Far C 22 B2
Home Meadow Dr. Fla H 3 D4
Home Park Farm La. Sonn 60 B1
Home Park Rd. Yate 149 E3
Homefield Way. Hung 100 B3
Homers Rd. Wind 66 B3
Homestead Rd. Maid 39 E2
Homestead Rd. Stai 97 D1
Homewaters Ave. Shepp 125 E4
Homewood. Slough 43 E4
Hone Hill. Sand 150 A4
Honesty Bottom. Brig 28 B1
Honey End La. Read 85 D3
Honey Hill. Brac 117 D1
Honey Hill. Lamb 25 D2
Honey La. Hurl 17 F1
Honeybottom Rd. Tad 135 D1
Honeyfields. Hung 100 B3
Honeyhill Rd. Brac 118 A4
Honeysuckle Cl. Brac 143 D4
Honeysuckle Cl. Yate 149 D3
Honiton Rd. Read 86 B1
Honnor Rd. Stai 97 E1
Hook End La. Upp B 34 A1
Hook La. West E 153 E3
Hook Mill La. Light 146 B1
Hookstone La. West E 153 F4
Hop Gdns. Hen-O-T 15 E1
Hope Ave. Brac 118 C1
Hopeman Cl. Sand 150 B4
Hopwood Cl. Newb 105 E2
Horewood Rd. Brac 118 A2
Hormer Cl. Sand 143 E1
Horn St. Comp 31 F3
Hornbeam Cl. Purl 57 E3
Hornbeam Cl. Sand 143 E1
Hornbeam Cl. Woki 115 E2
Hornbeam Gdns. Slough 43 D2
Hornbeams. Swal 139 E3
Horncastle Dr. Read 84 C3
Horne Rd. Stai 125 D3
Horne Rd. That 106 C1
Hornsea Cl. Read 57 F1
Horse Cl The. Caver 59 E2
Horse Gate Ride. Ascot 120 A2
Horsebrass Dr. Bags 145 F1
Horseguards Dr. Maid 40 A4
Horsell Ct. Chert 124 A1
Horsemoor Cl. Slough 44 A1
Horseshoe Cl. Camb 151 F4
Horseshoe Cres. Camb 151 F4
Horseshoe Hill. Burn 21 E4
Horseshoe Park. Pangb 56 B3
Horseshoe Rd. Pangb 56 B3
Horsham Rd. Crow 143 E1
Horsham Rd. Felt 71 E1
Horsnape Gdns. Binf 90 A1
Horsneile La. Brac 118 A4
Horton Cl. Maid 20 B1
Horton Rd. Datch 68 B3
Horton Rd. Hort 69 D3
Horton Rd. Stan 70 A2
Hose Hill. Bur C 111 D4
Hosier St. Read 86 A4
Houlton Ct. Bags 145 F1
Houston Way. Finch 142 B3
How La. Holy 64 A2
Howard Ave. Slough 42 C4
Howard Cl. Ashf 98 C1
Howard Rd. Ashf 97 E2
Howard Rd. Newb 105 D1
Howard Rd. Woki 116 B3
Howard St. Read 85 F4
Howarth Rd. Maid 40 A3
Howgate Dr. Gori 34 B4
Howth Dr. Wood 87 E4
Hubberholme. Brac 118 A3
Hubert Rd. Slough 43 E2
Huckleberry Cl. Purl 57 E2
Huddington Glade. Yate 149 D3
Hudson Rd. Harl 71 E4
Hudson Rd. Wood 87 F3
Hugh Fraser Dr. Read 84 B3
Hughenden Cl. Maid 39 E3
Hughenden Rd. Slough 42 B4
Hughes Rd. Ashf 98 B1
Hughes Rd. Woki 116 C4
Humber Cl. That 106 A3
Humber Cl. Woki 115 F4
Humber Way. Sand 150 B4
Humber Way. Slough 44 A1
Hummer Rd. Eng G 96 A2
Humphrey's La. East G 47 E3
Hungerford Ave. Slough 42 C4
Hungerford Cl. Sand 150 B4
Hungerford Dr. Maid 19 F2
Hungerford Dr. Read 85 F3
Hungerford Hill. East G 47 F1
Hungerford Hill. Lamb 25 D1
Hungerford La. Hurst 62 C1
Hungerford La. W St L 62 C1
Hungerford Rd. Kint 101 F2
Huntercombe Cl. Burn 41 E4
Huntercombe Cl. Slough 41 E4
Huntercombe La N. Slough 41 E4
Huntercombe La S. Burn 41 E3
Huntercombe La S. Slough 41 E3
Hunter's Hill. Bur C 110 C2
Hunters Meadow. Gr She 48 A2
Hunters Mews. Wind 67 E3
Hunters Way. Shin 113 D1
Huntingdonshire Cl. Woki 115 E3
Huntingfield Way. Stai 96 B1
Huntington Cl. Winn 87 F1
Huntley Ct. Read 86 C3
Hunt's La. Tapl 20 C2
Huntsmans Meadow. Ascot 119 F4
Huntsmoor Rd. Tad 135 D1
Huntswood La. Burn 20 C2
Huntswood La. Tapl 20 C2
Hurley High St. Hurl 17 F2
Hurley La. Bish 18 A2
Hurley La. Hurl 18 A2
Hurricane Way. Wood 88 A4
Hursley Cl. Read 84 C4
Hurst Gr. Shepp 125 F1
Hurst La. Vir W 123 D4
Hurst Park Rd. Twyf 61 F1
Hurst Rd. Slough 41 E4
Hurst Rd. Twyf 61 F2
Hurstdene Ave. Stai 97 D1
Hurstfield Dr. Burn 41 D4
Hurstwood. Ascot 120 A2
Huscarle Way. Purl 57 E2
Hutsons Cl. Woki 116 B4
Hutton Cl. Newb 105 D2
Hutton Cl. Read 87 D1
Hutton Cl. Windl 146 B2
Hyde End La. Brim 133 E3
Hyde End La. Shin 113 E2
Hyde End Rd. Shin 113 E1
Hyde Green. Mar 1 C1
Hyde La. Newt 132 A1
Hyde Terr. Ashf 98 C1
Hydes The. Purl 57 E2
Hylle Cl. Wind 66 C3
Hyperion Way. Read 86 A2
Hythe Cl. Brac 118 C2
Hythe End Rd. Wray 96 A3
Hythe Field Ave. Stai 96 B1
Hythe Park Rd. Stai 96 B2
Hythe Rd. Stai 96 B2
Hythe The. Stai 96 C2

Ian Mikardo Way. Caver 59 E1
Iberian Way. Camb 152 A3
Ibstock Cl. Read 85 D4
Ibstone Ave. Caver 59 F3
Icknield Pl. Gori 34 B4
Icknield Rd. Gori 34 B4
Ilbury Cl. Shin 113 F3
Ilchester Cl. Maid 39 E3
Ilchester Mews. Caver 59 F3
Ilex Cl. Eng G 95 D1
Ilex Cl. Silc 135 F1
Ilex Cl. Yate 149 D3
Ilfracombe Way. Winn 87 F2
Ilkley Rd. Caver 58 C2
Ilkley Way. That 106 B1
Illingworth. Wind 66 C2
Illingworth Ave. Caver 59 F3
Illingworth Gr. Brac 118 C4
Ilsley Rd. Comp 31 E2
Imperial Rd. Felt 98 C4
Imperial Rd. Wind 67 D3
Imperial Way. Read 113 D4
Impstone Rd. Silc 135 F1
In The Ray. Maid 40 A4
Inchwood. Brac 118 B1
India Rd. Slough 43 D2
Ingle Dell. Camb 151 E2
Ingle Glen. Woki 142 A4
Ingleglen. Far C 22 A4
Ingleside. Stan 69 F3
Ingleton. Brac 118 A3
Inglewood Ave. Camb 152 B3
Inglewood Ct. Read 85 E3
Inglewood Rd. Kint 101 F1
Inhurst Way. Tad 134 C1
Inkerman Rd. Eton 41 F1
Inkpen Cl. Read 85 D2
Inkpen Rd. Hung 100 C2
Inkpen Rd. Kint 102 A1
Inkpen Rd. Kint 127 D4
Inner Ring E. Harm 71 D2
Inner Ring W. Harm 71 D2
Innings La. Whi Wa 63 E4
Institute Rd. Burn 40 C4
Institute Rd. Mar 1 C1
Institute Rd. Tapl 40 C4
Instow Rd. Read 87 D1
Invergordon Cl. Read 84 C2
Inverness Way. Sand 150 B4
Inwood Cl. Cook 19 D3
Iona Cres. Slough 41 F4
Ipswich Rd. Slough 42 A4
Irish Hill Rd. Kint 102 A1
Irvine Pl. Vir W 122 C2
Irvine Way. Winn 114 B4
Isaac Newton Rd. Bark 115 D1
Isis Cl. Winn 88 A1
Isis Way. Bou E 3 D2
Isis Way. Sand 150 B4
Island Cl. Stai 96 C2
Island Farm Rd. Bur C 110 B1
Island Farm Rd. Bur C 136 C4
Island Farm Rd. Sulhd 110 B1
Island Rd. Bur C 85 F1
Island Rd. Read 85 F1
Islandstone La. Hurst 89 D3
Islet Park. Maid 20 B2
Islet Park Dr. Maid 20 B2
Islet Rd. Maid 20 B2
Iver La. Iver 44 C4
Iverdale Cl. Iver 44 B3
Iverna Gdns. Harm 71 E1
Ives Cl. Yate 149 D4
Ives Rd. Slough 44 A2
Ivy Cl. Holy 65 D4
Ivy Cres. Slough 41 F3
Ivy Dr. Light 153 D4
Ivybank. Read 57 E1
Ivydene Rd. Read 58 B1

Jack St. Newb 105 D2
Jackson Cl. Brac 118 A2
Jacob Cl. Brac 117 E4
Jacob Cl. Wind 66 C3
Jacob Rd. Sand 151 D4
James Butcher Dr. Thea 83 F2
James Cl. Mar 1 C2
James Rd. Camb 151 D1
James St. Read 85 F4
James St. Wind 67 E3
James Watt Rd. Bark 140 C4
James Way. Camb 151 D1
James's La. Bur C 111 F2
Jameston. Brac 118 B1
Jamnagar Cl. Stai 96 C1
Janson Ct. Read 85 F3
Japonica Cl. Woki 115 E2
Jaques's La. Sulhd 110 C3
Jarry Ct. Mar 1 C2
Jasmine Cl. Woki 115 E4
Jays Nest Cl. Black 150 B2
Jedburgh Cl. That 106 C2
Jefferson Cl. Slough 44 A1
Jeffries Ct. Bou E 3 D1
Jellicoe Cl. Slough 42 A2
Jenkins Hill. Bags 145 E1
Jennery La. Burn 21 E1
Jennetts Cl. Brad 81 F2
Jennings Field. Fla H 3 E4
Jennings Wharf. Wind 67 E4
Jenny's Wlk. Yate 149 F3
Jerome Cl. Mar 1 C2
Jerome Rd. Wood 87 F3
Jerrymoor Hill. Woki 141 F4

Jesmond Dene. Newb 104 C2
Jesse Cl. Yate 149 F3
Jesse Terr. Read 85 F4
Jessiman Terr. Stai 125 D2
Jevington. Brac 118 B1
Jig's La. New G 91 E1
Job's La. Cook 19 D4
Jock's La. Binf 90 C1
Joel Cl. Read 87 D2
John Childs Cl. Newb 105 D1
John Hunt Cl. That 106 C1
John Nike Way. Binf 117 E4
John Taylor Ct. Slough 42 B3
John's Cl. Ashf 98 B2
Johnson's La. Cold A 106 B4
Jonathan Hill. Newt 131 D2
Jordan Cl. Caver 59 F3
Jordans Cl. Stan 97 E4
Jordan's La. Bur C 110 C1
Josephine Ct. Read 85 F3
Jouldings La. Swal 140 B2
Jourdelay's Pas. Eton 67 E4
Journeys End. Slough 42 C4
Jubilee Ave. Burl 119 F4
Jubilee Ave. Woki 116 A4
Jubilee Cl. Burl 119 F4
Jubilee Cl. Silc 135 F1
Jubilee Cl. Stan 97 E4
Jubilee Rd. Bish 38 A3
Jubilee Rd. Finch 141 F2
Jubilee Sq. Read 86 A3
Judy's Pas. Eton 42 B1
Julkes La. Arbo 114 B4
Junction Rd. Ashf 98 B2
Junction Rd. Light 146 A1
Junction Rd. Read 86 C3
Juniper. Brac 118 B1
Juniper Dr. Maid 40 A4
Juniper La. Fla H 3 E4
Juniper La. Woo G 3 E4
Juniper Rd. Mar B 1 B3
Juniper Way. Read 57 E1
Junnipers The. Woki 115 E2
Jupiter Way. Woki 115 F3
Justice Cl. That 106 C1
Jutland Cl. Woki 115 F3
Jutland Pl. Stai 96 B2

Katesgrove La. Read 86 A3
Kathleen Saunders Ct. Thea 83 F2
Kaywood Cl. Slough 43 E2
Keane Cl. Wood 87 F4
Kearsley Rd. Read 85 E3
Keates Green. Brac 118 A4
Keats Cl. Wood 87 F2
Keats La. Eton 67 E4
Keats Rd. Wood 87 F2
Keats Way. Crow 143 D3
Keats Way. Yate 149 D2
Keble Rd. Maid 39 F4
Keble Way. Crow 143 F1
Keel Dr. Slough 42 B2
Keeler Cl. Wind 66 C2
Keepers Combe. Brac 118 B2
Keepers Farm Cl. Wind 66 C2
Keepers Farm Cl. Wind 66 C3
Keepers Wlk. Vir W 122 B2
Keephatch Rd. Woki 116 C4
Keighley Cl. That 106 B1
Kelburne Cl. Winn 88 B2
Keldholme. Brac 118 A3
Kelly Cl. Shepp 125 F4
Kelmscott Cl. Caver 58 C2
Kelpatrick Rd. Slough 41 E4
Kelsey Ave. Woki 141 F3
Kelsey Cl. Maid 39 E2
Kelsey Gr. Yate 149 F3
Kelso Mews. Caver 59 F3
Kelton Cl. Winn 87 F1
Kelvedon Way. Caver 58 C3
Kelvin Cl. Arbo 140 C4
Kelvin Rd. Newb 105 D2
Kemble Ct. Bur C 84 B2
Kemerton Cl. Bur C 84 B2
Kemp Ct. Bags 145 F1
Kempton Cl. Newb 105 E1
Kenavon Dr. Read 86 B4
Kendal Ave. Caver 59 F3
Kendal Ave. Shin 113 F3
Kendal Cl. Felt 98 C4
Kendal Cl. Slough 43 D3
Kendal Cl. That 106 B2
Kendal Dr. Slough 43 D3
Kendal Gr. Camb 152 B2
Kendrick Cl. Woki 116 B3
Kendrick Rd. Newb 130 B3
Kendrick Rd. Read 86 B3
Kendrick Rd. Slough 43 D2
Kenilworth Ave. Brac 118 B4
Kenilworth Ave. Read 85 E3
Kenilworth Ct. Slough 42 C2
Kenilworth Gdns. Stai 97 E2
Kenilworth Rd. Ashf 97 D3
Kenneally. Oak G 66 B3
Kennedy Cl. Far C 22 B3
Kennedy Cl. Maid 39 E3
Kennedy Cl. Mar 1 C2
Kennedy Cl. Newb 130 B3
Kennedy Dr. Pangb 56 C3
Kennedy Gdns. Read 87 D2
Kennel Ave. Ascot 119 F4
Kennel Cl. Ascot 92 C1
Kennel Green. Ascot 119 F4
Kennel La. Brac 91 D1
Kennel La. Cook 19 E4
Kennel La. Windl 146 B3
Kennel Ride. Ascot 92 C1
Kennel Wood. Ascot 119 F4
Kennet Cl. That 106 C2
Kennet Ct. Woki 115 F3
Kennet Pl. Bur C 111 D2
Kennet Rd. Kint 102 A1
Kennet Rd. Maid 39 F4
Kennet Rd. Newb 104 C2
Kennet Side. Newb 105 E2
Kennet Side. Read 86 B4
Kennet St. Read 86 B4
Kennett Rd. Bou E 3 D2
Kennett Rd. Slough 44 A2
Kensington Rd. Read 85 E4
Kent Ave. Slough 42 B4
Kent Cl. Stai 97 E1
Kent Cl. Woki 115 E3
Kent Rd. Read 85 E4
Kent Rd. Windl 146 B3
Kent Way. Maid 19 F1
Kentigern Dr. Brac 143 F3
Kenton Cl. Brac 118 B4
Kenton Cl. Camb 152 A1
Kenton Cl. Mar 1 C1
Kenton Rd. Read 87 E2
Kenton's La. Warg 36 B4
Kenton's La. Wind 66 C3
Kentwood Cl. Read 57 F1
Kentwood Hill. Read 57 F1
Kenwood Cl. Harm 71 D4
Kenwood Cl. Maid 39 D4
Keppel Spur. Old W 95 D4
Keppel St. Wind 67 E3
Kepple Pl. Bags 145 F2
Kernham Dr. Purl 57 E2
Kerris Way. Read 87 D1
Kersey Cres. Newb 104 C3
Kesteven Way. Woki 115 F3
Keston Cl. Caver 59 E1
Kestrel Ave. Stai 96 C3
Kestrel Cl. That 106 A2
Kestrel Path. Slough 21 F1
Kestrel Way. Read 85 D2
Kestrel Way. Woki 115 F3
Keswick Cl. Camb 152 B2
Keswick Cl. Read 84 B4
Keswick Cl. Slough 42 C3
Keswick Dr. Light 153 D4
Keswick Gdns. Wood 87 F3
Keswick Rd. Stai 96 A1
Kettering Cl. Bur C 84 C2
Kevins Dr. Yate 149 F4
Keynsham Way. Crow 143 E1
Keys La. Maid 39 F3
Kibble Green. Brac 118 B2
Kibblewhite Cres. Twyf 61 E3
Kidderminster Rd. Slough 22 A1
Kidmore End Rd. Caver 59 D4
Kidmore End Rd. Maple 59 D4
Kidmore Rd. Caver 58 C3
Kidwells Cl. Maid 39 F4
Kidwells Park Dr. Maid 39 F4
Kier Park. Ascot 120 B3
Kilburn Cl. Bur C 84 B2
Kildare Gdns. Caver 59 E2
Killarney Dr. Maid 39 F4
Kilmartin Gdns. Camb 151 F1
Kilmington Cl. Brac 118 C1
Kilmiston Ave. Shepp 125 E2
Kilmore Dr. Camb 152 A2
Kilmuir Cl. Sand 150 B4
Kiln Cl. Harl 71 E4
Kiln Cl. Herm 79 E4
Kiln Dr. Herm 78 C3
Kiln La. Ascot 93 D1
Kiln La. Bou E 3 E2
Kiln La. Brac 118 A4
Kiln La. Mort 137 E3
Kiln La. Shipl 35 E1
Kiln La. Sulh 84 A4
Kiln La. Sunn 121 D2
Kiln Rd. Caver 59 E4
Kiln Rd. Newb 105 E3
Kiln Ride. Upp B 54 C3
Kiln Ride. Woki 142 A4
Kiln Ride Extension. Woki 142 A3
Kiln View Rd. Read 86 B1
Kilnsea Dr. Read 87 E1
Kilnsea Dr. Winn 87 E1
Kilowna Cl. Char 61 D2
Kilross Rd. Felt 98 C4
Kimber Cl. Wind 67 D2
Kimberley. Brac 118 B1
Kimberley Cl. Read 85 F3
Kimberley Cl. Slough 43 F1
Kimber's Cl. Newb 104 C2
Kimbers Dr. Burn 21 E1
Kimbers Dr. Newb 104 B3
Kimber's La. Maid 39 F2
Kimmeridge. Brac 118 C2
Kimpton Cl. Read 113 F4
King Edward St. Slough 42 B2
King Edward VII Ave. Wind 67 F4
King Edwards Rd. Burl 119 F4
King Edwards Rise. Burl 92 C1
King Edwards Rise. Burl 119 F4
King James Way. Hen-O-T 35 E4
King John's Cl. Wray 68 B1
King St. Chert 124 A1
King St. Maid 39 F3
King St. Mort 137 D3
King St. Read 86 A4
King Stable St. Eton 67 E4
King Street La. Winn 88 B1
Kingfisher Ct. Twyf 61 F2
Kingfisher Dr. Stai 96 C2
Kingfisher Dr. Wood 87 E3
Kingfisher Dr. Yate 149 D3
Kingfisher Pl. Read 86 A4
Kinghorn Park. Maid 19 E2
King's Ave. Ashf 98 C1
Kings Cl. Hen-O-T 15 E1
King's Cl. Stai 97 E1
King's Cres. Camb 151 E4
King's Gr. Maid 39 F3
King's Keep. Sand 143 D1
Kings La. Cook 19 D4
Kings La. Eng G 95 D1
Kings La. Windl 146 C3
Kings Mead. Newb 130 B3
King's Meadow Rd. Read 86 A4
King's Rd. Ascot 120 B2
King's Rd. Caver 59 E1
King's Rd. Crow 143 E3
King's Rd. Eng G 96 A2
King's Rd. Hen-O-T 15 E1
Kings Rd. Newb 105 D1
King's Rd. Read 86 B4
Kings Rd. Silc 136 A1
King's Rd. Slough 42 C2
Kings Rd. West E 153 F3
King's Rd. Wind 67 E2
Kings Rd W. Newb 105 D1
King's Ride. Ascot 119 E3
King's Ride. Brac 119 E3
King's Ride. Camb 151 E4
King's Wlk. Sand 150 C3
Kingsbridge Cotts. Brac 142 C4
Kingsbridge Hill. Swal 139 D3
Kingsbridge Rd. Newb 104 C1
Kingsbridge Rd. Read 86 B1
Kingsbury Dr. Old W 68 A1
Kingsclear Park. Camb 151 E2
Kingsdown Cl. Read 87 D1
Kingsfield. Wind 66 B3
Kingsford Cl. Wood 88 A3
Kingsgate St. Read 86 B4
Kingshorn La. Maid 19 E2
Kingsland Grange. Newb 130 C4
Kingsley Ave. Camb 151 E2
Kingsley Ave. Eng G 95 D1
Kingsley Cl. Char 61 D3
Kingsley Cl. Crow 143 D2
Kingsley Cl. Newb 105 D3
Kingsley Cl. Read 113 D4
Kingsley Dr. Mar B 1 B3
Kingsmere Rd. Brac 117 F4
Kingston Ave. Felt 71 F1
Kingston Cres. Stai 97 E2
Kingston Gdns. Read 86 B1
Kingston La. Sulhd 110 B3
Kingston Rd. Camb 152 A4
Kingston Rd. Stai 97 E1
Kingsway. Black 150 C3
Kingsway. Caver 59 F3
Kingsway. Far C 22 B3
Kingsway. Iver 44 C4
Kingsway. Stan 97 E4
Kingsway. That 106 C1
Kingswick Cl. Ascot 120 B3
Kingswick Dr. Ascot 120 B3
Kingswood Cl. Eng G 95 E2
Kingswood Creek. Wray 68 B1
Kingswood Ct. Maid 39 F3
Kingswood Rise. Eng G 95 E2
Kinross Ave. Ascot 119 F2
Kinross Cl. Ashf 98 C2
Kinross Ct. Ascot 119 F2
Kinross Dr. Ashf 98 C2
Kinson Rd. Read 58 A1
Kintbury Rd. Kint 127 E3
Kipling Cl. That 106 B3
Kipling Cl. Yate 149 E2
Kirkfell Cl. Read 57 E1
Kirkham Cl. Caver 59 F3
Kirkham Cl. Crow 143 E1
Kirkstall Ct. Bur C 84 B2
Kirkstone Cl. Camb 152 B2
Kirkwood Cres. Bur C 110 C2
Kirton Cl. Read 85 D4
Kirtons Farm Rd. Bur C 85 E1
Kitsmead La. Went 122 B1
Kittiwake Cl. Wood 88 A4
Kitwood Dr. Winn 87 F1
Klondyke. Mar 1 B1
Knapp Rd. Ashf 97 F2
Knapp The. Read 87 D2
Knappe Cl. Hen-O-T 35 E4
Knighton Cl. Caver 59 D2
Knights Cl. Stai 96 B1
Knights Cl. Wind 66 B3
Knights La. Ball H 129 E2
Knights Way. Caver 59 D3
Knightsbridge Cres. Stai 97 D1
Knightsbridge Dr. Head 132 A2
Knightsbridge Rd. Camb 151 F4
Knightswood. Brac 118 A1
Knoll Cl. Let B 6 C4
Knoll Rd. Camb 151 E3
Knoll Wlk. Camb 151 E3
Knollmead. Bur C 84 B2
Knollys Rd. Silc 135 F1
Knolton Way. Slough 43 E4
Knossington Cl. Read 87 E1
Knott La. Been 109 D2
Knowle Cl. Caver 58 B2
Knowle Gr. Went 122 B1
Knowle Green. Stai 97 D2
Knowle Grove Cl. Went 122 B1
Knowle Hill. Went 122 B1
Knowle Park Ave. Stai 97 D2
Knowle Rd. Wood 87 F2
Knowles Ave. Finch 142 C3
Knowles Ave. Finch 142 C3
Knowsley Cl. Maid 19 D1
Knowsley Rd. Sulh 57 E2
Knox Green. Binf 90 B2
Korda Cl. Stai 124 C3
Krooner Rd. Camb 151 D2
Kybes La. Shin 112 B3
Kyle Cl. Brac 118 A3
La Roche Cl. Slough 43 E2
Laburnam Pl. Eng G 95 D1
Laburnham Rd. Maid 39 F3
Laburnum Cl. Mar 1 C2
Laburnum Gdns. Read 86 C1
Laburnum Gr. Newb 105 D2
Laburnum Gr. Slough 69 D4
Laburnum Rd. Chert 124 A1
Laburnum Way. Stan 97 F4
Laburnums The. Black 150 A3
Lacey Cl. Stai 96 B1
Ladbroke Cl. Wood 87 F3
Ladbrooke Rd. Slough 42 B2
Ladwell Cl. Newb 130 B3
Lady Jane Ct. Caver 59 E2
Lady Margaret Rd. 120 C1
Ladybank. Brac 118 A1
Ladymask Cl. Read 84 C2
Laffords The. Brad 82 A1
Laggan Rd. Maid 19 F1
Laggan Sq. Maid 19 F1
Laigents La. Windl 146 B2
Laird Ct. Bags 145 F1
Lake Ave. Slough 42 B3
Lake End Rd. Burn 41 D3
Lake End Rd. Dorn 41 D2
Lake End Way. Crow 143 D2
Lake Rd. Vir W 122 A3
Lake Side The. Black 150 B2
Lakeland Dr. Camb 151 F1
Lakeside. Brac 91 E1
Lakeside. Maid 20 A1
Lakeside. Read 87 D2
Lakeside Dr. Sto P 22 C2
Lakeside Rd. Iver 69 F4
Lalande Cl. Woki 115 F3
Laleham Rd. Shepp 125 D2
Laleham Rd. Stai 96 C1
Laleham Rd. Stai 125 D2
Laleys Green. Herm 78 C2
Lamb Cl. That 106 B3
Lambert Ave. Slough 43 F2
Lambert Cres. Black 150 B2
Lambfields. Thea 83 E2
Lambourn Pl. Lamb 25 D2
Lambourn Rd. Newb 104 B3
Lambourne Cl. Read 84 B4
Lambourne Dr. Bags 145 E1
Lambourne Dr. Maid 39 E2
Lambourne Gdns. Read 87 E2
Lambourne Gr. Brac 118 C4
Lambridge La. Hen-O-T 15 E2
Lambridge La. Shipl 15 E2
Lambridge Wood Rd. Hen-O-T 15 D2
Lambs La. Shin 139 D4
Lambwood Hill. Shin 112 B1
Lamerton Rd. Read 86 B1
Lammas Ave. Wind 67 E3
Lammas Ct. Wind 67 E3
Lammas Dr. Wray 96 B2
Lammas Rd. Slough 41 E4
Lamorna Cres. Read 57 E1
Lamp Acres. Newb 105 D3
Lamplighters Wlk. Read 84 C2
Lamsden Way. Bur C 111 D2
Lanark Cl. Camb 151 F1
Lanark Cl. Wood 88 A3
Lancaster Ave. Slough 22 B1
Lancaster Cl. Hung 100 B2
Lancaster Cl. Read 86 B3
Lancaster Cl. That 106 B2
Lancaster Gdns. Read 87 D2
Lancaster Rd. Maid 39 D4
Lancaster Sq. Hung 100 B2
Lancastria Mews. Maid 39 E4
Lancelot Cl. Slough 42 A2
Lancing Cl. Read 85 E4
Lancing Rd. Felt 98 C3
Landen Ct. Woki 116 A2
Landon Way. Ashf 98 A1
Landrake Cres. Read 86 B1
Landseer Cl. Sand 150 C3
Landsend La. Char 61 D1
Lane End Cl. Shin 113 F3
Lane The. Chert 124 A3
Lane The. Chil 10 C4
Lane The. Silc 136 A1
Lane The. Vir W 122 C3
Langborough Rd. Woki 116 B3
Langdale Cl. Maid 40 A3
Langdale Dr. Ascot 119 F4
Langdale Gdns. Read 86 C1
Langdon Cl. Camb 152 B2
Langford Cl. Caver 59 E3
Langham Pl. Eng G 95 F2
Langhams Way. Warg 36 C1
Langley Broom. Slough 43 F1
Langley Common Rd. Arbo 114 C1
Langley Common Rd. Bark 114 C1
Langley Cres. Harl 71 F4
Langley Dr. Camb 151 E3
Langley Hill. Read 84 B3
Langley Hill Cl. Read 84 B3
Langley Park Rd. Iver 44 B3
Langley Park Rd. Slough 44 B3
Langley Rd. Slough 43 E2
Langley Rd. Stai 96 C1
Langley Way. Mar 1 B1
Langton Cl. Maid 39 E4
Langton Way. Stai 96 B1
Langton's Meadow. Far C 22 B3
Langworthy End. Holy 65 D4
Langworthy La. Holy 65 D4
Laniver Cl. Read 87 D1
Lansdowne Ave. Slough 42 C3
Lansdowne Ct. Slough 42 C3
Lansdowne Rd. Read 84 B4
Lansdowne Rd. Stai 97 D1
Lapwing Cl. Read 84 B3
Larch Ave. Ascot 120 C2
Larch Ave. Sunn 120 C2
Larch Ave. Woki 116 A4
Larch Cl. Bur C 111 D2
Larch Cl. Camb 151 F4
Larch Cl. Slough 42 A4
Larch Dr. Wood 87 F3
Larches Way. Black 150 A3
Larchfield Rd. Maid 39 F3
Larchwood Dr. Eng G 95 D1
Larchwood Glade. Camb 152 A4
Larges Bridge Dr. Brac 118 B3
Larges La. Brac 118 B4
Larissa Cl. Read 57 F1
Lark Ave. Stai 96 C3
Larkings La. Sto P 23 D2
Larksfield. Eng G 95 E1
Larks-Meade. Read 87 D1
Larkspur Cl. Woki 115 E4
Larkswood Cl. Read 57 E2
Larkswood Cl. Sand 143 D1
Larkswood Dr. Crow 143 D3
Lascelles Rd. Slough 43 D2
Lashbrook Mead. Shipl 36 A2
Lashbrook Rd. Shipl 36 A2
Lassell Gdns. Maid 40 A4
Lasswade Rd. Chert 123 F1
Latham Ave. Camb 151 F1
Latimer. Brac 118 A1
Latimer Dr. Bur C 84 B2
Latimer Rd. Woki 116 A3
Latton Cl. Chil 10 C4
Laud Way. Woki 116 C3
Laud's Cl. Hen-O-T 15 E1
Launceston Ave. Caver 59 F3
Launcestone Cl. Read 87 D1
Launder Cl. Camb 151 F1
Laundry La. Sand 150 C3
Lauradale. Brac 118 A3
Laurel Ave. Eng G 95 D2
Laurel Ave. Slough 43 F2
Laurel Cl. Camb 151 E2
Laurel Cl. Stan 69 F4
Laurel Cl. Woki 115 F3
Laurel Dr. Read 57 D3
Laurence Cres. Windl 146 B2
Lauser Rd. Stan 97 E4
Lavenham Dr. Wood 87 F4
Lawford Cres. Yate 149 E3
Lawkland. Far C 22 A1
Lawn Cl. Datch 68 B4
Lawrence Cl. Woki 116 B3
Lawrence Ct. Wind 67 E3
Lawrence Gr. Binf 117 E4
Lawrence Mead. Kint 102 A1
Lawrence Rd. Read 85 D4
Lawrence Way. Sand 150 C2
Lawrence Way. Slough 41 E4
Lawrences La. Cold A 106 B3
Lawson La. Chil 10 B4
Lawson Way. Windl 121 D2
Laxton Green. Maid 39 E2
Layburn Cres. Slough 69 D4
Layland's Green. Kint 102 A1
Laytm Rise. Sulh 57 E2
Layton's La. Shepp 125 F4
Le Marchant Rd. Camb 151 F2
Lea Cl. Mar B 1 B3
Lea Cl. Read 85 D2
Lea Croft. Crow 143 D3
Lea Rd. Camb 151 D1
Lea The. Stai 96 B1
Leacroft. Stai 97 D2
Leacroft. Sunn 121 D2
Leacroft Cl. Stai 97 D2
Leacroft Rd. Iver 44 C4
Leafield Copse. Brac 118 C3
Leaholme Gdns. Slough 41 E4
Leas Dr. Iver 44 C4
Leaver Rd. Hen-O-T 15 E1
Leaves Green. Brac 118 B2
Ledbury Cl. Read 58 A1
Ledbury Dr. Bur C 84 B2
Ledger La. Holy 65 E3
Ledger's Rd. Slough 42 B2
Ledran Cl. Winn 87 E1
Lee La. Bish 18 C1
Lee La. Maid 18 C1
Leeds Rd. Slough 42 C3
Lees Cl. Maid 39 D3
Lees Gdns. Maid 39 D3
Lees Wlk. Mar 1 B1
Leeson Gdns. Eton 41 F1
Leicester. Brac 118 C1
Leicester Cl. Hen-O-T 15 E2
Leigh Field. Mort 136 C3
Leigh Park. Datch 68 B4
Leigh Rd. Slough 42 A3
Leigh Sq. Wind 66 B3
Leighton Gdns. Maid 20 A1
Leiston Cl. Winn 87 E1
Leiston Spur. Slough 42 C4
Leith Cl. Brac 143 D4
Lemart Cl. Read 84 C4
Lemington Gr. Brac 118 A2
Leney Cl. Woki 116 B4
Lenham Cl. Woki 88 C1
Lennox Cl. Bur C 84 A2
Lennox Rd. Read 87 D3
Lent Green La. Burn 21 D1
Lent Rise Rd. Burn 41 D4
Leopold Wlk. Read 86 B4
Leppington. Brac 118 A1
Lesford Rd. Read 85 F3
Leslie Southern Ct. Newb 105 D2
Lesters Rd. Cook 19 D3
Letchworth Ave. Felt 98 C4
Letcombe Sq. Brac 118 C3
Letcombe St. Read 86 A4

Leverton La. Hung 73 D1
Lewendon Rd. Newb 104 C3
Lewins Way. Slough 41 F3
Lewis Wlk. Newb 130 B3
Lewisham Way. Crow 143 E1
Lexington Ave. Maid 39 E3
Lexington Gr. Read 113 E3
Leyburn Cl. Wood 88 A4
Leycester Cl. Windl 146 A3
Leyland Gdns. Shin 113 F3
Leylands La. Stan 69 F2
Leys Gdns. Newb 104 C2
Leyside. Crow 143 D3
Lichfield Cl. Wood 87 E1
Lichfields. Brac 118 C4
Liddel Way. Ascot 119 F2
Liddell. Oak G 66 B2
Liddell Cl. Finch 141 F2
Liddell Sq. Oak G 66 B3
Lido Rd. Chil 9 F4
Lidstone Cl. Winn 114 B4
Liebenrood Rd. Read 85 E3
Lightlands La. Cook 19 F3
Lightwater Meadows. Light 153 D4
Lightwater Rd. Light 153 E4
Lightwood. Brac 118 B2
Lilac Cl. Purl 57 E3
Lilacs The. Woki 115 E2
Lillibrooke Cres. Maid 39 D2
Lily Hill Dr. Brac 118 C4
Lily Hill Rd. Brac 118 C4
Lima Ct. Read 85 F3
Lime Ave. Camb 152 A3
Lime Cl. Newb 105 E2
Lime Cl. Woki 115 F3
Lime Tree Rd. Gori 34 A3
Lime Wlk. Brac 118 B3
Lime Wlk. Maid 39 D4
Limecroft. Yate 149 E3
Limefield Cl. Winn 87 F2
Limerick Cl. Brac 118 A4
Limes Cl. Ashf 98 A2
Limes Rd. Eng G 95 F2
Limmer Cl. Woki 115 E2
Limmerhill Rd. Woki 115 F3
Linchfield Rd. Datch 68 B3
Lincoln Cl. Camb 152 A2
Lincoln Cl. Winn 88 A2
Lincoln Gdns. Twyf 61 E3
Lincoln Hatch La. Burn 21 E1
Lincoln Rd. Maid 39 D4
Lincoln Rd. Read 86 B2
Lincoln Way. Slough 41 E3
Lincoln Way. Stai 125 F4
Lind Cl. Read 87 D1
Lindale Cl. Went 121 F3
Lindale Rd. Crow 143 E1
Linden Ave. Maid 19 E1
Linden Cl. Holy 65 D4
Linden Cl. Newb 104 C2
Linden Cl. Woki 115 F2
Linden Ct. Camb 151 F4
Linden Ct. Eng G 95 D1
Linden Dr. Far C 22 B2
Linden Rd. Newt 131 F2
Linden Rd. Read 86 C1
Linden Rd. Wood 87 E2
Linden Way. Shepp 125 E2
Lindenhill Rd. Brac 117 F4
Lindores Rd. Holy 65 D4
Lindsay Cl. Stan 70 B1
Lindsay Dr. Shepp 125 E2
Lindsey Cl. Woki 115 F3
Lindsey Gdns. Felt 98 B4
Lines Rd. Hurst 88 C3
Ling Dr. Light 152 C4
Lingfield Rd. Newb 131 E4
Lingholm Cl. Maid 39 E3
Lingholm Cl. Read 84 C3
Lingwood. Brac 118 B2
Link Rd. Datch 68 B3
Link Rd. Felt 98 C4
Link Rd. Newb 105 D1
Link The. Slough 43 D4
Link The. Yate 149 E4
Link Way. Arbo 114 C1
Link Way. Stai 97 D1
Link Way. That 106 A2
Links App. Fla H 3 D4
Links Dr. Read 85 D4
Links Rd. Ashf 97 F2
Links Rd. Fla H 3 E4
Links Way. Fla H 3 D4
Linkscroft Ave. Ashf 98 A1
Linkswood Rd. Burn 21 E2
Linkway. Camb 151 E2
Linkway. Crow 142 C3
Linnet Ave. Newt 131 F2
Linnet Cl. Read 84 A3
Lintott Ct. Stan 70 B1
Lion Cl. Stai 124 C3
Lip La. Wick 75 F2
Lipscomb Cl. Herm 79 D3
Lipscombe Cl. Newb 104 C2
Liscombe. Brac 118 A1
Lisle Cl. Newb 104 C3
Lismore Cl. Wood 87 F2
Lisset Rd. Maid 40 A3
Lister Cl. Purl 57 E3
Liston Rd. Mar 1 B1
Litcham Spur. Slough 42 B4
Lithgow's Rd. Harm 71 F2
Littington Cl. Winn 114 B4
Little Bowden La. Pangb 55 F2
Little Buntings. Wind 66 C2
Little Cl. Fla H 3 D3
Little Croft. Yate 149 E3
Little Croft Rd. Gori 34 B3
Little Elms. Harl 71 E4
Little Glebe. Sonn 60 C2
Little Heath Rd. Read 84 A4
Little Hill Rd. Hurst 88 A2
Little John's La. Read 85 E4
Little La. Buck 107 E3
Little London Rd. Silc 136 A1
Little Marlow Rd. Mar 1 C2
Little Moor. Sand 143 E1
Little Oak Dr. Read 84 B4
Little Paddock. Camb 152 A4
Little Ringdale. Brac 118 C3
Little St. Read 85 F4
Little Sutton La. Iver 44 B1
Little Sutton La. Slough 69 D4
Little Vigo. Yate 149 D2
Little Woodlands. Wind 66 C2
Littlebrook Ave. Slough 21 F1
Littlecote Dr. Read 85 F3
Littlecote Rd. Frox 99 D3
Littlecroft Rd. Eng G 95 F2
Littledale Cl. Brac 118 C3
Littledown Rd. Slough 42 C3
Littlefield Green. Whi Wa 63 F3
Littlejohn's La. Read 58 B1
Littleport Spur. Slough 42 C4
Littlestead Cl. Caver 59 F3
Littleton La. Stai 124 C2
Littleton Rd. Stai 98 B1
Liverpool Rd. Read 86 C4
Liverpool Rd. Slough 42 A4
Livery Cl. Read 86 B4
Livingstone Gdns. Wood 87 F3
Livingstone Rd. Newb 105 D1
Llangar Gr. Crow 143 D3
Llanvair Cl. Ascot 120 A2
Llanvair Dr. Ascot 119 F2
Lochinvar Cl. Slough 42 A2
Lochinver. Brac 118 A1
Lock Ave. Maid 20 B1
Lock La. Maid 39 E2
Lock Mead. Maid 20 B1
Lock Path. Dorn 66 B4
Lock Pl. Read 86 B4
Lock Rd. Mar 1 C1
Lockbridge Rd. Bou E 3 D2
Locke Gdns. Slough 43 E2
Lockets Cl. Wind 66 B3
Lockram Rd. Bur C 111 E1
Lockram Rd. Mort 111 E1
Locks Ride. Burl 92 B1
Lockstile Mead. Gori 34 B3
Lockstile Way. Gori 34 B3
Lockton Chase. Ascot 119 E3
Loddon Bridge Rd. Winn 87 F3
Loddon Bridge Rd. Wood 87 F3
Loddon Cl. Camb 152 A3
Loddon Dr. Char 61 D4
Loddon Dr. Maid 39 E4
Loddon Hall Rd. Twyf 61 F3
Loddon Rd. Bou E 3 D2
Loddon Spur. Slough 42 C4
Lodge Cl. Eng G 95 E2
Lodge Cl. Mar 1 C1
Lodge Gr. Yate 149 F3
Lodge Rd. Hurst 88 C4
Lodge Way. Ashf 97 F3
Lodge Way. Stai 125 E4
Lodge Way. Wind 66 C2
Logan Cl. Read 84 C4
Lois Dr. Shepp 125 D2
Lomond Ave. Caver 59 F3
London Rd. Ascot 119 F3
London Rd. Ashf 97 E3
London Rd. Bags 145 F2
London Rd. Binf 117 E4
London Rd. Black 150 B2
London Rd. Blew 11 F4
London Rd. Brac 118 C3
London Rd. Camb 151 E3
London Rd. Datch 68 B4
London Rd. Eng G 95 E1
London Rd. Newb 105 E2
London Rd. Read 86 B4
London Rd. Read 87 D4
London Rd. Slough 43 F1
London Rd. Stan 97 E3
London Rd. Sunn 121 E3
London Rd. That 106 C2
London Rd. That 105 E2
London Rd. Twyf 61 F3
London Rd. Went 121 E2
London Rd. Windl 146 B4
London St. Chert 124 A1
London St. Read 86 A4
Lone Acre. Windl 146 C2
Long Barn La. Read 86 B2
Long Cl. Far C 22 A3
Long Cl. Kint 102 A1
Long Dr. Burn 21 E1
Long Furlong Dr. Slough 21 F1
Long Gr. Tad 134 B1
Long Grove. Buck 107 E3
Long Hedge. Lamb 25 E1
Long Hill Rd. Burl 119 D4
Long La. Brig 28 C2
Long La. Cold A 78 C1
Long La. Cook 19 E3
Long La. Herm 78 C1
Long La. Holy 64 C3
Long La. Purl 57 D2
Long La. Stan 97 F4
Long La. Sulh 57 D2
Long La. Wint 78 C1
Long Mickle. Sand 143 D1
Long Readings La. Slough 22 A1
Longacre. Newb 130 B4
Longbourne Way. Chert 123 F2
Longbridge Rd. That 106 C1
Longcroft Rd. That 106 C1
Longdon Rd. Winn 88 B1
Longdown Rd. Sand 143 D1
Longfield Rd. Twyf 61 E3
Longford Ave. Felt 71 F1
Longford Ave. Stan 97 F4
Longford Cl. Camb 151 E2
Longford Way. Stan 97 F4
Longhurst Cl. Caver 59 E2
Longlands Way. Camb 152 B3
Longleat Dr. Sulh 57 D2
Longleat Gdns. Maid 39 E3
Longleat Way. Felt 98 B4
Longmead. Ball H 129 F1
Longmead. Wind 66 C3
Longmead La. Burn 21 E3
Longmeadow. Camb 151 F2
Longmoor La. Mort 137 D4
Longmoors. Brac 117 F4
Longmore Rd. Read 113 E3
Longridge Cl. Read 85 D4
Long's Way. Woki 116 C4
Longshot Industrial Estate. Brac 117 F4
Longshot La. Brac 117 F4
Longside Cl. Stai 123 E4
Longview. Beac 3 F4
Longwater La. Finch 141 F2
Longwater Rd. Brac 118 B2
Longwater Rd. Finch 141 F1
Longworth Ave. Read 84 A4
Longworth Dr. Maid 20 B1
Lonsdale Cl. Maid 20 A1
Lonsdale Way. Holy 40 B1
Loosen Dr. Maid 39 D2
Lord Knyvett Cl. Stan 70 B1
Loring Rd. Wind 66 C3
Lorne Cl. Slough 42 A2
Lorne St. Read 85 F4
Lorraine Rd. Camb 151 F4
Lory Hill La. Beac 3 F4
Losfield Rd. Wind 66 C3
Lossie Dr. Iver 44 A3
Loughborough. Brac 118 C2
Loundyes Cl. That 106 A2
Lovatt Cl. Read 84 A4
Love Green La. Iver 44 C4
Love Hill La. Slough 44 A3
Love La. Iver 44 B4
Love La. Newb 105 D3
Love La. Yate 149 D4
Lovedean Ct. Brac 118 C2
Lovejoy La. Wind 66 B3
Lovel La. Wink 93 D2
Lovel Rd. Wink 93 D2
Lovelace Cl. Hurl 17 F2
Lovelace Rd. Brac 117 F3
Lovell Cl. Hen-O-T 35 E4
Lovells Cl. Light 146 A1
Loverock Rd. Read 58 B1
Loverock Rd. Read 58 B1
Love's Cl. Bur C 111 D2
Loves Wood. Mort 136 C3
Lovett Gdns. Maid 20 B2
Lovett Rd. Stai 96 B2
Lowbrook Dr. Maid 39 D2
Lowbury. Brac 118 C3
Lower Armour Rd. Read 57 E1
Lower Boyndon Rd. Maid 39 F3
Lower Britwell Rd. Slough 21 E1
Lower Broadmoor Rd. Crow 143 E2
Lower Brook St. Read 86 A3
Lower Bungalows. Gori 34 B4
Lower Church Rd. Sand 149 F4
Lower Cippenham La. Slough 41 F3
Lower Common. Finch 140 C1
Lower Cookham Rd. Maid 20 B1
Lower Earley Way. Read 114 B4
Lower Earley Way. Winn 114 B4
Lower Earley Way (W). Read 113 F4
Lower Early Way (N). Winn 87 F1
Lower Elmstone Dr. Read 57 E1
Lower Field Rd. Read 86 A3
Lower Henley Rd. Caver 59 E2
Lower Lees Rd. Slough 22 A1
Lower Mill Field. Bags 145 E1
Lower Nursery. Sunn 121 D2
Lower Pound La. Mar 18 B4
Lower Rd. Chil 10 B4
Lower Rd. Cook 19 F4
Lower Ridge. Bou E 3 D2
Lower Sandhurst Rd. Finch 142 B1
Lower Sandhurst Rd. Sand 142 B1
Lower Village Rd. Ascot 120 B2
Lower Way. That 106 A2
Lower Way. That 105 F2
Lower Wokingham Rd. Brac 142 B3
Lower Wokingham Rd. Finch 142 B3
Lowes Comm. Finch 140 C1
Lowestoft Cl. Winn 87 E1
Lowfield Cl. Light 153 D4
Lowfield Green. Caver 59 F2
Lowfield Rd. Caver 59 E3
Lowlands Rd. Black 150 B2
Lowry Cl. Sand 150 B3
Lowther Cl. Woki 115 F4
Lowther Rd. Woki 115 F4
Loxwood. Read 87 E1
Loxwood Cl. Felt 98 B4
Lucan Dr. Stai 97 E1
Lucas Cl. Yate 149 E3
Lucas Green Rd. West E 153 F2
Lucey Cl. Sulh 57 D2
Lucie Ave. Ashf 98 A1
Luckley Rd. Brac 116 A2
Luckley Wood. Brac 116 A2
Luckmore Dr. Read 87 D2
Luddington Ave. Vir W 122 C4
Ludlow. Brac 118 A1
Ludlow Rd. Felt 98 C3
Ludlow Rd. Maid 39 F3
Luff Cl. Wind 66 C2
Luker Ave. Hen-O-T 15 E2
Lulworth Rd. Read 113 E4
Lunds Farm Rd. Wood 88 A4
Lundy La. Read 85 E4
Lupin Cl. Bags 145 E1
Luscombe Cl. Caver 59 E2
Lutman's Haven. Know H 37 F3
Lutterworth Cl. Brac 91 E1
Lutton Cl. Read 113 F4
Lych Gate Cl. Sand 149 F4
Lycroft Cl. Gori 34 B4
Lydbury. Brac 118 C3
Lydford Ave. Slough 42 B4
Lydford Rd. Read 86 C3
Lydney. Brac 118 A1
Lydsey Cl. Slough 22 A1
Lyefield Ct. Caver 59 D3
Lyell. Oak G 66 B2
Lyme Gr. Read 57 E1
Lymington Ave. Yate 149 E3
Lymington Gate. Caver 58 C3
Lynch Hill La. Slough 21 F1
Lyndhurst Ave. Black 150 B3
Lyndhurst Ave. Cook 19 F3
Lyndhurst Cl. Brac 119 D3
Lyndhurst Rd. Ascot 120 A3
Lyndhurst Rd. Gori 34 B3
Lyndhurst Rd. Read 58 A1
Lyndwood Dr. Old W 68 A1
Lyne Cl. Went 122 C2
Lyne Crossing Rd. Chert 123 D2
Lyne La. Chert 123 D1
Lyne Rd. Went 122 C2
Lynegrove Ave. Ashf 98 B2
Lyneham Gdns. Maid 19 D1
Lyneham Rd. Crow 143 D3
Lynmouth Rd. Read 59 D1
Lynn Cl. Ashf 98 B2
Lynton Cl. Wood 87 E3
Lynton Ct. Newb 105 D2
Lynton Green. Maid 39 F4
Lynwood Ave. Eng G 95 F1
Lynwood Ave. Slough 43 E2
Lynwood Chase. Brac 91 E1
Lynwood Cres. Sunn 120 C2
Lyon Cl. That 106 C1
Lyon Rd. Crow 143 E3
Lyon Sq. Read 85 D4
Lyon Way. Camb 151 E1
Lysander Cl. Wood 88 A4
Lytham. Brac 117 F2
Lytham Cl. Read 85 E2
Lytham End. Sulh 57 D2
Lytham Rd. Wood 87 F4

Macdonald Rd. Light 153 D4
Mace Cl. Read 87 D1
Mackay Cl. Read 84 C2
Mackenzie St. Slough 42 C2
Macklin Cl. Hung 100 B3
Macrae Rd. Yate 149 E3
Maddle Rd. Lamb 24 B4
Madeira Wlk. Wind 67 E3
Madingley. Brac 118 A1
Mafeking Rd. Wray 96 A3
Magdalen Rd. Stai 124 C3
Magdalene Rd. Crow 143 F1
Magill Cl. Shin 113 D1
Magna Carta La. Wray 95 F4
Magna Rd. Eng G 95 D1
Magnolia Cl. Sand 143 E1
Magnolia Gdns. Slough 43 E2
Magnolia Way. Woki 115 F3
Magpie Cl. That 106 A2
Magpie Way. Read 84 A3
Magpie Way. Slough 21 F1
Maguire Dr. Camb 152 B2
Maiden Erlegh Dr. Read 87 D2
Maiden Lane Centre. Read 87 E1
Maiden Pl. Read 87 E1
Maidenhead Court Park. Maid 20 A2
Maidenhead Rd. Binf 89 E2
Maidenhead Rd. Cook 19 F3
Maidenhead Rd. Oak G 66 C4
Maidenhead Rd. Wind 66 C4
Maidensfield. Winn 88 B1
Main Dr. Burl 119 D4
Main St. Chil 10 B4
Main St. Yate 149 E4
Mainprize Rd. Brac 118 C4
Mainstone Rd. Bis 153 F2
Maise Webster Cl. Stan 97 E4
Maitland Rd. Read 85 F4
Majendie Cl. Newb 104 B3
Major's Farm Rd. Datch 68 C4
Makepiece Rd. Brac 91 D1
Maker Cl. Read 85 D2
Makins Rd. Hen-O-T 35 E4
Malders La. Cook 19 E2
Malders La. Maid 19 E2
Maldon Cl. Read 85 E3
Malet Cl. Stai 96 B1
Malham Fell. Brac 118 A3
Malham Rd. That 106 B2
Mallard Cl. Read 87 D2
Mallard Cl. Twyf 61 F2
Mallard Dr. Slough 41 F3
Mallard Row. Read 86 A4
Mallard Way. Yate 149 D3
Mallards The. Stai 124 A4
Mallory Ave. Caver 59 E3
Mallow Park. Maid 19 E1
Mallowdale Rd. Brac 118 C1
Malone Rd. Wood 87 E3
Malpas Rd. Slough 43 D3
Malt Hill. Eng G 95 F2
Malt House. Old W 95 D4
Malt Shovel La. Lamb 24 C2
Maltby Way. Read 114 A4
Malthouse Cl. That 106 C1
Malthouse La. Read 85 F4
Malthouse La. West E 153 F4
Maltings Pl. Read 86 A4
Maltings The. West I 10 A1
Malton Ave. Slough 42 A3
Malvern Cl. Wood 87 F3
Malvern Ct. Newb 104 C1
Malvern Rd. Harl 71 F4
Malvern Rd. Maid 19 E1
Malvern Way. Twyf 61 E4
Malyons The. Shepp 125 E2
Manchester Rd. Read 86 C4
Mandeville Cl. Read 84 C3
Mandeville Ct. Eng G 96 A2
Mandeville Rd. Stai 125 D2
Manea Cl. Winn 114 B4
Manfield Cl. Slough 22 A1
Manners Rd. Wood 87 E4
Manor Cl. Brac 91 D1
Manor Cres. Comp 31 E2
Manor Ct. Mar 1 B2
Manor Farm Ave. Shepp 125 D2
Manor Farm Cl. Wind 66 C2
Manor Farm Cotts. Old W 68 A1
Manor Farm La. Eng G 96 A2
Manor Farm La. Tidm 56 B1
Manor Farm Rd. Read 86 A1
Manor Gr. Holy 65 E3
Manor House Ct. Shepp 125 D1
Manor House Dr. Ascot 93 D1
Manor House La. Slough 68 A3
Manor La. Chiev 51 D1
Manor La. Harl 71 E4
Manor La. Herm 79 D4
Manor La. Leckh 49 F3
Manor La. Maid 39 F2
Manor La. Newb 105 F3
Manor La. That 105 F3
Manor Leaze. Stai 96 A2
Manor Park. Frox 99 D2
Manor Park Dr. Woki 141 F3
Manor Park Dr. Yate 149 E3
Manor Pl. Newb 104 B3
Manor Pl. Stai 97 D2
Manor Rd. Ashf 98 A2
Manor Rd. Farn 7 D4
Manor Rd. Gori 34 A3
Manor Rd. Hen-O-T 35 E4
Manor Rd. Maid 39 F2
Manor Rd. Shepp 125 F1
Manor Rd. Whitc 56 B4
Manor Rd. Wind 66 C3
Manor Rd. Woki 116 A1
Manor Way. Bags 145 F2
Manor Way. Eng G 95 F1
Manor Way. Holy 65 D4
Manorcrofts Rd. Eng G 96 A1
Man's Hill. Bur C 111 E1
Manse Cl. Harl 71 E4
Mansel Cl. Slough 43 D4
Mansell Cl. Wind 66 C3
Mansell Dr. Newb 130 B3
Mansfield Cl. Burl 119 E4
Mansfield Cres. Brac 118 A2
Mansfield Pl. Burl 119 E4
Mansfield Rd. Read 85 F3
Mansfield Rd. Woki 115 F3
Mansion House St. Newb 105 D2
Mansion La. Iver 44 B3
Manston Dr. Brac 118 B2
Mant Cl. Wick 75 E3
Manygate La. Shepp 125 E2
Maple Cl. Maid 39 E3
Maple Cl. Sand 150 B3
Maple Cl. Sand 142 C1
Maple Cl. Winn 88 B2
Maple Cres. Newb 105 D2
Maple Cres. Slough 43 D3
Maple Ct. Eng G 95 D1
Maple Ct. Gori 34 A3
Maple Dr. Brac 143 E4
Maple Gdns. Read 86 C1
Maple Gdns. Stan 97 F3
Maple Gdns. Yate 149 E3
Maple La. Upp B 55 D3
Maple Rise. Mar 1 C2
Mapledurham Dr. Purl 57 E3
Mapledurham View. Read 57 E1
Mapledurham Wlk. Maid 19 F2
Marbeck Cl. Wind 66 B3
Marchant Ct. Mar 2 A2
Marchwood Ave. Caver 59 E4
Marconi Rd. Newb 105 D2
Marcus Cl. Read 85 D4
Mardale. Camb 152 B2
Mare La. Whi Wa 63 F2
Marefield. Read 87 E1
Marefield Rd. Mar 1 B1
Marescroft Rd. Slough 41 F4
Marfleet Cl. Winn 87 F1
Margaret Cl. Read 113 E4
Margaret Cl. Stai 97 E1
Marigold Cl. Brac 142 C3
Marina Way. Iver 44 C3
Marina Way. Slough 41 E3
Mariners La. Brad 82 A2
Marion Ave. Shepp 125 D2
Marish Wharf. Slough 43 F2
Markby Way. Winn 87 F1
Market La. Slough 44 B2
Market Pl. Brac 118 A4
Market Pl. Hen-O-T 15 E1
Market Pl. Newb 105 D2
Market Pl. Read 86 A4
Market Pl. Woki 116 B3
Market Sq. Mar 1 B1
Market Sq. Stai 96 C2

Market St. Brac 118 A4
Market St. Gree 105 F1
Market St. Maid 39 F4
Market St. Newb 105 D1
Market St. Wind 67 E3
Markham Centre (Trading Estate)
The. Thea 83 F1
Marks Rd. Woki 116 A4
Marlborough Ave. Read 86 B3
Marlborough Cl. Maid 39 D3
Marlborough Ct. Read 85 F3
Marlborough Rd. Ashf 97 F2
Marlborough Rd. Maid 39 D3
Marlborough Rd. Slough 43 F1
Marlborough Rise. Camb 151 F3
Marlborough Way. Read 84 A2
Marlin Ct. Mar 1 B1
Marling Cl. Read 57 E1
Marlow Bottom. Mar B 18 B2
Marlow Bridge La. Bish 18 C4
Marlow Mill. Mar 1 C1
Marlow Rd. Bish 18 C2
Marlow Rd. Bou E 2 B3
Marlow Rd. Hen-O-T 15 F2
Marlow Rd. Lit M 2 B3
Marlow Rd. Maid 39 F4
Marlow Rd. Mar B 1 A3
Marlowes The. Newb 130 C4
Marlston Rd. Herm 79 E3
Marmion Rd. Hen-O-T 35 F4
Marriott Cl. Harm 71 E1
Mars Cl. Woki 115 F3
Marsack St. Caver 59 E1
Marsh La. Herm 78 B2
Marsh La. Hung 100 A3
Marsh La. Newb 105 D2
Marsh La. Tapl 40 C3
Marsh Rd. That 106 C2
Marshall Cl. Camb 152 B2
Marshall Cl. Read 57 E2
Marshall Rd. Sand 150 B3
Marshalls Ct. Newb 104 B3
Marshland Sq. Caver 59 D3
Marshwood Rd. Light 153 E4
Marston Way. Ascot 119 F4
Marten Pl. Sulh 57 D2
Martin Cl. Wind 66 B3
Martin Cl. Wood 87 F3
Martin Rd. Maid 39 F4
Martin Rd. Slough 42 C2
Martin Way. Camb 151 F1
Martindale Ave. Camb 152 B2
Martineaux La. Hurst 88 C4
Martins Cl. Black 150 B2
Martins Dr. Woki 116 A4
Martins La. Brac 118 C3
Martin's Plain. Sto P 22 C2
Martins The. That 106 C1
Marunden Green. Slough 21 F1
Maryland. Woki 141 F4
Maryside. Slough 43 F2
Mascoll Path. Slough 21 F1
Masefield Rd. That 106 B2
Mason Cl. Yate 149 F3
Mason Pl. Sand 149 F4
Mason St. Read 85 F4
Masonic Hall Rd. Chert 123 F2
Masons Rd. Slough 41 F3
Matlock Rd. Caver 58 C2
Matson Dr. Rem H 15 F1
Mattewsgreen Rd. Woki 116 A4
Matthews La. Stai 96 C2
Matthews Rd. Camb 144 B1
Maultway Cl. Camb 152 A4
Maultway Cres. Camb 152 A4
Maultway N. Camb 145 D1
Maultway The. Camb 152 B3
Mawbray Cl. Read 87 E1
Maxine Cl. Sand 143 D1
Maxwell Cl. Wood 87 F4
Maxwell Rd. Ashf 98 B1
May Cl. Sand 143 E1
May Fields. Woki 115 D4
May Tree Cl. Mar B 1 B3
Maybrick Cl. Sand 142 C1
Maybury Cl. Slough 41 E4
Mayfair. Read 84 B4
Mayfair Dr. Newb 104 C1
Mayfield Ave. Read 84 A2
Mayfield Cl. Ashf 98 A1
Mayfield Dr. Caver 59 E2
Mayfield Gdns. Stai 96 C1
Mayfield Rd. Camb 151 D1
Mayfield Rd. Woo G 3 F3
Mayflower Dr. Yate 149 D4
Mayflower Way. Far C 22 B4
Maynard Cl. Cold A 106 B3
Mayo Rd. Shepp 125 F1
Mayow Cl. That 106 C1
Maypole Rd. Burn 41 D4
Mays Cl. Read 87 D3
May's La. Padw 136 A4
Mays La. Read 87 D3
Mays Rd. Woki 116 C3
Mc Carthy Way. Woki 141 F4
McCrae's Wlk. Warg 36 B1
Mead Ave. Slough 44 A2
Mead Cl. Mar 1 C2
Mead Cl. Pease 50 B4
Mead Cl. Read 84 A3
Mead Cl. Slough 44 A2
Mead Cl. Stai 96 A1
Mead La. Chert 124 A1
Mead La. Upp B 55 F4
Mead The. Gr She 48 A2
Mead Way. Slough 41 E4
Mead Wlk. Slough 44 A2
Meadfield Ave. Slough 44 A2
Meadfield Rd. Slough 44 A2
Meadhurst Rd. Chert 124 A1
Meadow Cl. Black 150 B2
Meadow Cl. Gori 34 B3
Meadow Cl. Mar 1 C1
Meadow Cl. Moul 13 F2
Meadow Cl. Old W 68 A1
Meadow Cl. That 106 B2
Meadow Cres. Comp 31 F3
Meadow Ct. Stai 96 C3
Meadow Gdns. Stai 96 B2
Meadow La. Eton 67 E4
Meadow Rd. Ashf 98 B2
Meadow Rd. Hen-O-T 15 F1
Meadow Rd. Newb 130 C4
Meadow Rd. Read 58 C1
Meadow Rd. Read 87 E2
Meadow Rd. Slough 43 F2
Meadow Rd. Went 121 F2
Meadow Rd. Woki 116 A3
Meadow View. Mar B 1 C3
Meadow View. Winn 88 B2
Meadow View La. Holy 64 C4
Meadow Walk. Woki 116 A3
Meadow Way. Bou E 3 D3
Meadow Way. Brac 91 D1
Meadow Way. Dorn 40 C2
Meadow Way. Holy 65 E3
Meadow Way. Old W 68 A1
Meadow Way. Sand 150 B3
Meadow Way. Thea 83 F2
Meadow Way. West E 153 F3
Meadow Way. Woki 116 A3
Meadowbank Rd. Light 146 B1
Meadowbrook Cl. Stan 69 F3
Meadowcroft Rd. Read 113 E4
Meadows The. Fla H 3 D4
Meadowside Rd. Pangb 56 B3
Meadway. Ashf 98 A2
Meadway. Camb 151 F1
Meadway. Stai 97 D1
Meadway Cl. Stai 97 D1
Meadway The. Read 84 C4
Meare Estate. Woo G 3 F4
Mearings The. Bur C 111 F3
Measham Way. Read 87 E1
Meashill Way. Chil 9 F4
Meavy Gdns. Read 86 A1
Medallion Pl. Maid 40 A4
Medina Cl. Woki 115 F4
Medlake Rd. Stai 96 B1
Medlar Dr. Black 150 C2
Medway Cl. That 106 A3
Medway Cl. Woki 115 F4
Melbourne Ave. Slough 42 B4
Melbourne Ave. Winn 88 B1
Melbury Cl. Chert 124 A1
Meldreth Way. Winn 87 E1
Meldrum Cl. Newb 130 B3
Melford Green. Caver 59 F3
Melksham Cl. Read 113 F4
Melling Cl. Winn 87 F2
Melody Cl. Winn 88 B2
Melrose. Brac 118 A1
Melrose Ave. Read 87 D3
Melrose Gdns. Arbo 114 C1
Melton Ct. Maid 39 F3
Melville Ave. Camb 151 F1
Membury Wlk. Brac 118 C3
Memorial Ave. Shipl 35 F1
Menair Cl. Read 87 D1
Mendip Cl. Char 61 D2
Mendip Cl. Harl 71 E4
Mendip Cl. Slough 44 A1
Mendip Rd. Brac 118 C2
Menpes Rd. Purl 57 E2
Meon Cl. Tad 135 D1
Merchants Pl. Read 86 A4
Mercia Rd. Maid 39 E2
Mercian Way. Slough 41 E3
Mercury Ave. Woki 115 F3
Mere Cl. Mar 1 C1
Mere Rd. Shepp 125 D2
Mere Rd. Slough 42 C2
Mereoak La. Shin 112 C2
Merlewood. Brac 118 B2
Merlin Cl. Slough 69 D4
Merrifield Cl. Winn 114 B4
Merrivale Gdns. Read 86 A1
Merron Cl. Yate 149 E3
Merryhill Green Hill. Winn 88 B2
Merryhill Rd. Brac 118 A4
Merryman Dr. Brac 143 D3
Merrywood Park. Camb 151 F2
Mersey Way. That 106 A3
Merton Cl. Maid 39 E2
Merton Rd. Crow 143 F1
Merton Rd. Read 86 A1
Merton Rd. Slough 43 D2
Merton Rd. Slough 43 D2
Mervyn Rd. Shepp 125 E1
Merwin Way. Wind 66 B2
Metcalf Rd. Ashf 98 A2
Meteor Cl. Wood 88 A4
Mews The. Read 86 C3
Meyrick Dr. Newb 130 B3
Michael Cl. Maid 39 E3
Michaelmas Cl. Yate 149 E2
Micheldever Way. Brac 118 C2
Michelet Cl. Light 146 A1
Micklands Rd. Caver 59 F2
Mickle Hill. Sand 143 D1
Midcroft. Slough 22 A1
Middle Cl. Camb 152 B3
Middle Cl. Newb 130 B4
Middle Gordon Rd. Camb 151 E3
Middle Green. Slough 43 F3
Middle Hill. Eng G 95 E2
Middle Wlk. Burn 21 E1
Middlefields. Twyf 61 F3
Middlegreen Rd. Slough 43 E3
Middlemoor Rd. Camb 151 F1
Middleton Rd. Camb 151 F4
Midway Ave. Chert 124 A3
Midway Ave. Stai 123 D3
Midwinter Cl. Read 84 C4
Milbanke Ct. Brac 117 F4
Milbanke Way. Brac 117 F4
Mildenhall Cl. Winn 87 E1
Mildenhall Rd. Slough 42 C4
Mile Elm. Mar 2 A2
Miles Way. Wood 88 A4
Milestone Ave. Char 61 D3
Milestone Cres. Char 61 D2
Milestone Way. Caver 59 E3
Milford Rd. Read 58 C1
Milkhouse Rd. Box 103 E2
Mill Bank. Kint 102 A2
Mill Cl. Woki 115 F4
Mill Farm Ave. Stai 98 C1
Mill Field. Bags 145 E2
Mill Green. Caver 59 E1
Mill House La. Stai 123 D3
Mill La. Ascot 121 D4
Mill La. Brac 117 F3
Mill La. Bur C 84 C2
Mill La. Cook 20 B4
Mill La. Hen-O-T 35 F4
Mill La. Hort 69 D2
Mill La. Hurl 17 F2
Mill La. Lamb 25 E2
Mill La. Newb 105 D2
Mill La. Padw 109 E1
Mill La. Read 86 A4
Mill La. Read 87 F2
Mill La. Sand 149 E4
Mill La. Shipl 36 A1
Mill La. Stai 123 E3
Mill La. Tapl 40 B4
Mill La. Wind 67 D4
Mill La. Winn 87 F1
Mill La. Winn 87 F1
Mill La. Yate 149 E4
Mill Mead. Stai 96 C2
Mill Pl. Datch 68 B3
Mill Pond Rise. Windl 146 A3
Mill Rd. Bur C 84 C1
Mill Rd. Caver 59 E1
Mill Rd. Gori 34 B4
Mill Rd. Mar 1 C1
Mill Rd. Shipl 36 A2
Mill Reef Cl. That 105 F2
Mill Ride. Burl 119 E4
Mill St. Iver 69 E4
Mill St. Slough 42 C3
Millbank. Mar 1 C1
Millbank Cres. Wood 87 F3
Millboard Rd. Bou E 3 D2
Millbridge Rd. Yate 149 D4
Milldown Ave. Gori 34 B4
Milldown Rd. Gori 34 B4
Millers Cl. Gori 34 A4
Millers Cl. Stai 97 D2
Miller's Field. Gr She 48 A2
Millers Gr. Read 84 C2
Milley La. Warg 62 A4
Milley Rd. W St L 62 C3
Millfield. Lamb 25 D1
Millgreen La. Head 132 C2
Millins Cl. Sand 143 F1
Millmead. Woki 116 A4
Millmere. Yate 149 E4
Mills Spur. Old W 95 D4
Millside. Bou E 3 E2
Millstream La. Slough 41 F3
Millstream Way. Woo G 3 F4
Millworth La. Shin 113 F2
Milman Cl. Brac 119 D4
Milman Rd. Read 86 A3
Milner Rd. Burn 41 D4
Milsom Cl. Shin 113 F3
Milton Cl. Brac 118 A2
Milton Cl. Hen-O-T 15 E1
Milton Cl. Hort 69 D2
Milton Dr. Stai 124 C3
Milton Dr. Woki 116 A3
Milton Gdns. Woki 116 A3
Milton Rd. Eng G 95 F2
Milton Rd. Far C 22 B1
Milton Rd. Read 87 D4
Milton Rd. Woki 116 A4
Milton Way. Twyf 61 F3
Milverton Cl. Maid 39 D2
Mina Ave. Slough 43 E2
Minchin Green. Binf 90 B2
Minden Cl. Woki 115 F3
Minley Rd. Yate 149 F1
Minniecroft Rd. Burn 21 D1
Minorca Ave. Camb 152 C1
Minorca Rd. Camb 152 C1
Minstead Cl. Brac 118 C3
Minstead Dr. Yate 149 E3
Minster St. Read 86 A4
Minster Way. Slough 43 F2
Minsterley Ave. Shepp 125 F3
Mint Cl. Read 86 C1
Minton Cl. Read 84 C4
Minton Rise. Burn 41 D4
Mirador Cres. Slough 43 E3
Mire La. W St L 62 B2
Mistletoe Rd. Yate 149 E2
Mitcham Cl. Read 86 A3
Mitcham Rd. Camb 145 D1
Mitcham Rd. Camb 145 D1
Mitchell Cl. Slough 42 A2
Mitchell Way. Wood 88 A4
Mitford Cl. Read 113 E4
Mitre Cl. Shepp 125 E2
Moat Dr. Slough 43 E4
Modbury Gdns. Read 86 B1
Moffatts Cl. Sand 150 A4
Moffy Hill. Maid 19 F1
Mohawk Way. Wood 88 A4
Mole Rd. Arbo 114 C3
Moles Cl. Woki 116 B3
Mollison Cl. Wood 88 A4
Molly Millar Bridge. Woki 116 A2
Molly Millar's La. Woki 116 A2
Molyneux Rd. Windl 146 B2
Monarch Cl. Felt 98 C4
Moneyrow Green. Holy 65 D4
Monkey Island La. Holy 40 C1
Monks Cl. Ascot 120 A2
Monks Dr. Ascot 120 A2
Monks Hollow. Mar B 1 C3
Monk's La. Newb 130 C4
Monks Rd. Vir W 122 B3
Monks Rd. Wind 66 B3
Monks Way. Harm 70 C4
Monks Way. Read 85 E3
Monks Way. Stai 97 E1
Monks Wlk. Ascot 120 A2
Monksfield Way. Slough 22 A1
Monkswood Cl. Newb 130 C4
Mons Cl. Woki 115 F3
Mons Wlk. Stai 96 B2
Monsell Gdns. Stai 96 C2
Montacute Dr. That 106 C1
Montagu Rd. Slough 68 A3
Montague Cl. Camb 151 D3
Montague Cl. Light 146 A1
Montague Rd. Slough 42 C3
Montague St. Caver 59 E1
Montague St. Read 86 B4
Montague Terr. Newb 131 D4
Monteagle La. Yate 149 D3
Montem La. Slough 42 B2
Montgomery Cl. Sand 150 A4
Montgomery Dr. Shin 113 D1
Montgomery Pl. Slough 43 E4
Montgomery Rd. Newb 130 C4
Montpelier Ct. Wind 67 E3
Montpelier Dr. Caver 59 E3
Montrose Ave. Datch 68 B4
Montrose Ave. Slough 42 A4
Montrose Cl. Ashf 98 B2
Montrose Cl. Camb 151 F1
Montrose Dr. Maid 39 D3
Montrose Rd. Felt 71 E1
Montrose Way. Datch 68 B4
Montrose Wlk. Read 84 C2
Monument Cl. Newb 130 B4
Monycrower Dr. Maid 39 F4
Moor Cl. Sand 143 F1
Moor Cl. Woki 141 F4
Moor Copse Cl. Read 87 D2
Moor End. Holy 40 B1
Moor La. Harm 70 B4
Moor La. Maid 19 F1
Moor La. Newb 104 C2
Moor La. Stan 96 B3
Moor Pl. Windl 146 A3
Moorbridge Rd. Maid 40 A4
Moordale Ave. Brac 90 C1
Moore Cl. Slough 42 A2
Moore Grove Cres. Eng G 95 F1
Moores Green. Woki 116 C4
Moores La. Eton 41 F1
Moores Pl. Hung 100 B3
Moorfield Terr. Maid 40 A4
Moorfields Cl. Stai 123 F4
Moorhayes Dr. Stai 124 B3
Moorland Rd. Harm 70 B4
Moorlands Dr. Maid 38 C4
Moorlands Pl. Camb 151 D2
Moorlands Rd. Camb 151 D2
Moormede Cres. Stai 96 C2
Moors The. Pangb 56 B3
Moors The. That 106 B1
Moorside. Woo G 3 F4
Moorside Cl. Camb 151 D1
Moorside Cl. Maid 19 F1
Moorstown Ct. Slough 42 C2
Moray Ave. Sand 150 B4
Mordaunt Dr. Crow 143 D2
Morden Cl. Brac 118 C3
Moreau Wlk. Slough 43 F4
Morecambe Ave. Caver 58 C3
Moreland Ave. Iver 69 E4
Moreleigh Cl. Read 113 E4
Morella Cl. Vir W 122 B3
Morello Dr. Slough 43 F3
Moretaine Rd. Ashf 97 E3
Moreton Way. Slough 41 E3
Morgan Rd. Read 86 B3
Moriston Cl. Read 85 D4
Morlands Ave. Read 85 D3
Morley Cl. Slough 43 F2
Morley Cl. Yate 149 D3
Morley Pl. Hung 100 B3
Mornington Ave. Woki 141 F4
Mornington Cl. Tad 134 C1
Mornington Rd. Ashf 98 B2
Morpeth Cl. Read 86 B2
Morrice Cl. Slough 44 A1
Mortimer Cl. Read 113 E4
Mortimer La. Mort 137 E3
Mortimer Rd. Slough 43 E2
Morton Rd. Hort 69 D3
Moss Cl. Caver 59 E2
Mossy Vale. Maid 19 E1
Moulsham Copse La. Yate 149 D4
Moulsham La. Yate 149 D4
Mount Cl. Far C 22 B4
Mount Cl. Newb 105 D1
Mount Cl The. Went 122 B2
Mount Felix. Shepp 125 F1
Mount La. Brac 118 B4
Mount La. Chadd 49 D4
Mount Lee. Eng G 95 F2
Mount Pleasant. Brac 118 B3
Mount Pleasant. Read 86 A3
Mount Pleasant. Sand 143 D1
Mount Pleasant. Tad 135 D1
Mount Pleasant. Woki 116 A3
Mount Pleasant Cl. Light 146 A1
Mount Pleasant Gr. Read 86 A3
Mount Rd. That 106 C2
Mount St. Read 86 A3
Mount The. Caver 58 C2
Mount The. Caver 59 D2
Mount The. Read 86 B3
Mount The. Went 122 B2
Mount View. Hen-O-T 15 E1
Mountain Ash. Mar B 1 B3
Mountbatten Cl. Newb 105 E3
Mountbatten Cl. Slough 43 D2
Mountbatten Rise. Sand 142 C1
Mountfield. Gori 34 B4
Mounts Hill. Old W 93 E3
Mounts Hill. Wink 93 E3
Mountsfield Cl. Stan 70 A1
Mowbray Cres. Eng G 96 A2
Mowbray Dr. Read 85 D4
Mower Cl. Woki 116 C4
Moyleen Rise. Mar 1 B1
Muckhatch La. Stai 123 D4
Mud La. Finch 140 C1
Mud La. Pease 50 B3
Muirfield Cl. Read 86 B4
Mulberry Ave. Stan 97 F4
Mulberry Cl. Crow 143 E2
Mulberry Cl. Sand 143 E1
Mulberry Cl. Wood 87 F3
Mulberry Dr. Slough 43 F1
Mulberry Trees. Shepp 125 E1
Mulberry Way. Thea 83 F2
Mulfords Hill. Tad 135 D1
Mullins Rd. Stai 96 B2
Mulroy Dr. Camb 152 A3
Mumbery Hill. Warg 36 C1
Muncaster Cl. Ashf 98 A2
Muncaster Rd. Ashf 98 A2
Munces Rd. Mar B 1 B3
Mundaydean La. Mar 1 A2
Mundesley Spur. Slough 42 C4
Mundesley St. Read 86 A3
Munkle Marsh. That 107 D2
Munnings Dr. Sand 150 C3
Munro Ave. Wood 87 F2
Murdoch Cl. Stai 97 D2
Murdoch Rd. Woki 116 B3
Murray Ct. Ascot 120 B2
Murray Rd. Woki 116 A3
Murrellhill La. Binf 117 E4
Murrells La. Camb 151 D2
Murrin Rd. Maid 39 E4
Mushroom Castle La. Burl 92 A1
Mustard La. Sonn 60 C1
Mustard Mill Rd. Stai 96 C2
Muswell Cl. Thea 83 F2
Myers Way. Camb 152 B1
Myline Sq. Woki 116 B3
Myrke The. Datch 42 C1
Myrke The. Slough 42 C1
Myrtle Ave. Harm 71 F1
Myrtle Cl. Bur C 111 D2
Myrtle Cl. Light 153 D4
Myrtle Cl. Stan 69 F3
Myrtle Cl. Sulh 57 E2
Myrtle Cres. Slough 42 C3
Myrtle Dr. Black 150 B3
Myton Wlk. Thea 83 F2

Nairn Cl. Camb 151 F1
Nalderhill Rd. Box 103 D3
Napier Cl. Crow 143 E3
Napier Rd. Ashf 98 B1
Napier Rd. Crow 143 E2
Napier Rd. Harm 70 B3
Napier Rd. Maid 39 D3
Napier Rd. Read 86 B4
Napier Wlk. Ashf 98 B1
Napper Cl. Burl 119 E4
Narromine Dr. Read 84 C2
Naseby. Brac 118 A1
Nash Cl. Read 87 D2
Nash Gdns. Ascot 119 F4
Nash Grove La. Woki 115 F1
Nash Park. Binf 90 A1
Nash Rd. Slough 44 A1
Nashdom La. Burn 21 D3
Natalie Cl. Felt 98 B4
Neath Gdns. Read 84 C4
Needham Cl. Wind 66 C3
Neil Cl. Ashf 98 B2
Nell Gwynn Ave. Shepp 125 E2
Nell Gwynne Ave. Ascot 120 B3
Nell Gwynne Cl. Ascot 120 B3
Nelson Cl. Brac 118 C4
Nelson Cl. Slough 43 E1
Nelson Rd. Ashf 97 F2
Nelson Rd. Caver 59 E1
Nelson Rd. Harm 70 C3
Nelson Rd. Wind 66 C2
Nelson Way. Sand 150 C2
Nelson's La. Hurst 89 D3
Nene Rd. Harm 71 D3
Neptune Cl. Woki 115 F3
Neptune Rd. Harm 71 E3
Netherton. Brac 118 A3
Netley Cl. Caver 59 F3
Netley Rd (N). Harm 71 E3
Nettlecombe. Brac 118 C2
Nettleton Rd. Harm 71 D3
Neville Cl. Binf 117 E4
Neville Cl. Sto P 22 C3

Neville Cl. W St L 62 C3
Neville Dr. That 106 C2
Nevis Rd. Read 57 E2
New Bath Rd. Char 61 E3
New Bath Rd. Twyf 61 E3
New Bath Rd. Warg 61 E3
New Bright St. Read 86 A3
New Ct. Mar 1 B1
New Forest Ride. Brac 118 C2
New Ham Rd. Harm 71 E3
New Hill. Purl 57 E3
New Lane Hill. Read 84 C3
New Meadow. Burl 119 E4
New Mile Rd. Ascot 120 B4
New Mill La. Finch 140 C1
New Mill Rd. Bark 140 C2
New Park Rd. Ashf 98 B2
New Rd. Black 150 C2
New Rd. Bou E 3 D2
New Rd. Brac 118 B4
New Rd. Bur C 111 F1
New Rd. Burl 92 C1
New Rd. Cook 19 F4
New Rd. Crow 143 E3
New Rd. Datch 68 B3
New Rd. Felt 71 E1
New Rd. Harl 71 E4
New Rd. Holy 65 D4
New Rd. Hurl 17 F2
New Rd. Mar B 1 B3
New Rd. Mort 111 F1
New Rd. Newb 105 E1
New Rd. Read 86 B3
New Rd. Sand 150 A4
New Rd. Shipl 36 A2
New Rd. Slough 44 A2
New Rd. Stai 96 B2
New Rd. Stai 125 D3
New Rd. Twyf 61 E4
New Rd. Twyf 61 F3
New Rd. Windl 146 A2
New Road. Woki 115 D4
New St. Bee H 138 A1
New St. Hen-O-T 15 F1
New St. Stai 97 D2
New Way. Brad 82 A1
New Wickham La. Eng G 96 A1
New Wickham La. Stai 96 A1
New Wokingham Rd. Crow 143 F4
New Zealand Ave. Shepp 125 F1
Newall Rd. Harm 71 E3
Newalls Rise. Warg 36 C1
Newark Rd. Windl 146 A3
Newark St. Read 86 A3
Newber 42 B2
Newberry Cres. Wind 66 B3
Newbery Cl. Read 57 E1
Newbold Rd. Newb 104 B3
Newbolt Cl. That 106 B3
Newbury Dr. Maid 40 A3
Newbury Hill. Hamp N 52 C3
Newbury La. Comp 31 E2
Newbury Rd. Gr She 48 A1
Newbury Rd. Harm 70 C3
Newbury Rd. Herm 79 D3
Newbury Rd. Lamb 25 E1
Newbury St. Kint 102 A1
Newbury St. Lamb 25 D1
Newcastle Rd. Read 86 B2
Newchurch Rd. Slough 41 F4
Newchurch Rd. Tad 135 D1
Newfield Gdns. Mar 1 C2
Newfield Rd. Mar 1 C2
Newfield Way. Mar 1 C1
Newhaven Cres. Ashf 98 B2
Newhaven Spur. Slough 22 A1
Newhurst Gdns. New G 91 E2
Newlands Ave. Caver 59 D2
Newlands Cl. Yate 149 E3
Newlands Dr. Maid 39 D4
Newlands Dr. Stan 69 F2
Newlyn Gdns. Read 86 A1
Newlyn Rd. Harm 71 D3
Newman Rd. Harm 71 D3
Newmarket Cl. Winn 87 E1
Newport Cl. Newb 105 D2
Newport Rd. Harm 71 D3
Newport Rd. Newb 105 D2
Newport Rd. Read 59 D1
Newport Rd. Slough 21 F1
Newquay Dr. Read 87 D1
Newton Ave. Caver 59 E3
Newton Cl. Slough 43 F2
Newton Ct. Old W 68 A1
Newton La. Old W 68 A1
Newton Rd. Harm 70 C3
Newton Rd. Hen-O-T 35 F4
Newton Rd. Mar 1 C2
Newtown. Tad 135 D1
Newtown Gdns. Hen-O-T 35 F4
Newtown Rd. Newb 131 D4
Newtown Rd. Sand 150 A4
Niagara Rd. Hen-O-T 35 F4
Nicholas Rd. Hen-O-T 35 D4
Nicholls. Oak G 66 B2
Nicholson Wlk. Eng G 96 A2
Nicholsons La. Maid 39 F4
Nideggen Cl. That 106 B2
Nightingale Cres. Brac 118 B2
Nightingale Gdns. Sand 150 A4
Nightingale La. Mort 137 E3
Nightingale Park. Burn 21 F3
Nightingale Rd. Wood 87 E2
Nightingales The. Newb 131 D4
Nimrod Cl. Wood 88 A4
Nimrod Rd. Harm 71 D3
Nimrod Way. Harm 71 D3
Nimrod Way. Read 86 A3
Nine Mile Ride. Bark 142 B4
Nine Mile Ride. Brac 142 B4
Nine Mile Ride. Woki 142 B4
Nixey Cl. Slough 43 D2
Noakes Hill. Asham 54 A4
Nobles Way. Eng G 95 F1
Norcot Rd. Read 84 C4
Norden Cl. Maid 39 E2
Norden Rd. Maid 39 E3
Norelands Dr. Burn 21 E2
Nores Rd. Read 113 E4
Norfolk Ave. Slough 42 B4
Norfolk Cl. Woki 115 F3
Norfolk Park Cotts. Maid 39 F4
Norfolk Rd. Maid 39 F4
Norlands. That 106 B3
Norlands La. Stai 123 F4
Norman Ave. Hen-O-T 15 F1
Norman Rd. Ashf 98 B1
Norman Rd. Caver 59 E2
Normandy Wlk. Stai 96 B2
Normanhurst. Ashf 98 A2
Normans The. Slough 43 D4
Normanstead Rd. Read 84 B4
Normay Rise. Newb 130 B3
Normoor Rd. Bur C 110 C1
Norreys Ave. Woki 116 B4
Norreys Dr. Maid 39 E2
Norris Field. Chadd 49 D4
Norris La. Chadd 49 D4
Norris Rd. Read 87 D3
Norris Rd. Stai 96 C2
North Burnham Cl. Burn 21 D2
North Cl. Felt 71 E1
North Cl. Medm 17 E4
North Cl. Wind 66 C3
North Croft. Woo G 3 F3
North Dr. Sulhd 110 B4
North Dr. Went 121 F2
North End La. Went 121 D1
North Fryerne. Yate 149 E4
North Gr. Chert 123 F2
North Green. Brac 118 B4
North Green. Maid 19 F1
North Green. Slough 42 C3
North Hatton Rd. Harm 71 E3
North Links Rd. Fla H 3 D4
North Lodge Dr. Burl 119 E4
North Park. Iver 44 B2
North Rd. Burl 119 D4
North Rd. Felt 71 E1
North Rd. Maid 39 F4
North Rd. Moul 13 F2
North St. Caver 59 D1
North St. Eng G 95 F1
North St. Read 85 F4
North St. Wink 93 D3
North Standen Rd. Hung 100 A2
North Star La. Maid 39 E3
North Town Cl. Maid 19 F1
North Town Mead. Maid 19 F1
North Town Moor. Maid 19 F1
North Town Rd. Maid 19 F1
North Wlk. Thea 83 F2
Northam Cl. Winn 87 F2
Northampton Ave. Slough 42 B4
Northampton Cl. Brac 118 C3
Northborough Rd. Slough 22 A1
Northbourne Cl. Read 87 D1
Northbrook Rd. Caver 59 E3
Northbrook St. Newb 105 D2
Northbury Ave. Twyf 61 F3
Northbury La. Twyf 61 F3
Northcott. Brac 118 A1
Northcourt Ave. Read 86 B2
Northcroft. Slough 22 A1
Northcroft Cl. Eng G 95 D2
Northcroft Gdns. Eng G 95 D2
Northcroft La. Newb 104 C2
Northcroft Rd. Eng G 95 D2
Northcroft Villas. Eng G 95 D2
Northdean. Maid 19 F1
Northend Cl. Fla H 3 E4
Northern Ave. Newb 105 D3
Northern Hts. Bou E 3 D3
Northern Perimeter Rd. Harm 71 E3
Northern Perimeter Rd (w). Harm 70 C3
Northern Rd. Slough 22 B1
Northern Woods. Fla H 3 E4
Northfield. Light 153 D4
Northfield Ave. Shipl 36 A2
Northfield End. Hen-O-T 15 E2
Northfield Rd. Eton 41 F1
Northfield Rd. Maid 19 F1
Northfield Rd. Read 59 D1
Northfield Rd. Shipl 36 A2
Northfield Rd. Stai 124 A4
Northfield Rd. That 106 A2
Northfields. Chiev 51 D2
Northfields. Lamb 25 D2
Northgate Dr. Camb 152 A4
Northington Cl. Brac 118 C2
Northmead Rd. Slough 41 F4
Northolt Rd. Harm 70 C3
Northrop Rd. Harm 71 F3
Northumberland Ave. Read 86 B2
Northumberland Cl. Stan 70 C1
Northumberland Cres. Felt 71 F1
Northumbria Rd. Maid 39 D2
Northview. Hung 100 B3
Northway. Newb 105 D1
Northway. That 106 B3
Northway. Woki 115 F4
Northwood Dr. Newb 105 E2
Northwood Rd. Harm 70 B3
Norton Cl. Newb 130 B3
Norton Park. Ascot 120 B2
Norton Rd. Camb 152 B3
Norton Rd. Read 86 C4
Norton Rd. Swal 139 E2
Norton Rd. Woki 116 B3
Norton Rd. Wood 87 F3
Norway Dr. Slough 43 D4
Norwich Ave. Camb 151 F2
Norwich Dr. Wood 87 E4
Norwood Cres. Harm 71 E3
Norwood Rd. Read 86 C4
Notley End. Eng G 95 E1
Notton Way. Read 113 F4
Nuffield Dr. Crow 143 F1
Nuffield Rd. Bark 140 C4
Nugee Ct. Crow 143 D3
Nugent Ct. Mar 1 C2
Nuneaton. Brac 118 C2
Nunhide La. Sulh 83 F3
Nun's Acre. Gori 34 A4
Nuns Wlk. Vir W 122 B2
Nursery Gdns. Purl 57 D3
Nursery Gdns. Shepp 125 F4
Nursery Gdns. Stai 97 D1
Nursery La. Burl 119 F4
Nursery La. Slough 43 E3
Nursery Rd. Burn 41 D4
Nursery Rd. Shepp 125 F4
Nursery Way. Wray 68 B1
Nursery Wlk. Mar 1 A1
Nut La. W St L 62 C3
Nutbean La. Swal 139 F3
Nuthatch Dr. Read 87 D2
Nuthurst. Brac 118 C2
Nutley. Brac 118 A1
Nutley Cl. Yate 149 E3
Nutmeg Cl. Read 86 C1
Nutter's Hill. Swal 140 A4
Nutty La. Stai 125 E3

Oak Ave. Sand 143 E1
Oak Ave. Stai 96 B1
Oak Dr. Bur C 110 C1
Oak Dr. Wood 88 A3
Oak End Way. Padw 109 E2
Oak Farm Cl. Sand 150 B3
Oak Grove Cres. Sand 150 C3
Oak Hill. Frox 99 E2
Oak La. Eng G 95 F4
Oak La. Wind 67 D3
Oak Stubbs La. Dorn 40 C2
Oak Tree Ave. Mar 1 C2
Oak Tree Cl. Mar 1 B2
Oak Tree Cl. Tad 135 D1
Oak Tree Cl. Went 122 B2
Oak Tree Copse. Read 57 F2
Oak Tree Dr. Eng G 95 E2
Oak Tree Rd. Mar 1 B2
Oak Tree Rd. Read 57 E1
Oak Tree Rd. That 106 C1
Oak Tree Wlk. Purl 57 E3
Oak View. Read 84 B4
Oak Way. Felt 98 C4
Oak Way. Wood 87 E2
Oakdale. Brac 118 B2
Oakdale Cl. Read 84 B4
Oakdale Wlk. Wood 88 A4
Oakdene. Bur C 111 D1
Oakdene. Sunn 120 C2
Oaken Gr. Maid 19 E1
Oaken Gr. Newb 130 B4
Oakengates. Brac 118 A1
Oakfield Ave. Slough 42 A3
Oakfield Rd. Ashf 98 A2
Oakfield Rd. Black 150 C2
Oakfield Rd. Bou E 3 D2
Oakfield Rd. Silc 135 F1
Oakhall Dr. Ashf 98 C2
Oakham Cl. Read 57 E1
Oakhurst. Maid 20 A2
Oaklands. Yate 149 E3
Oaklands Cl. Ascot 92 C1
Oaklands Dr. Ascot 92 C1
Oaklands Dr. Woki 116 A3
Oaklands La. Crow 143 D4
Oaklea Dr. Finch 140 C1
Oakley Cres. Slough 42 C3
Oakley Green Rd. Holy 66 A3
Oakley Green Rd. Oak G 66 A3
Oakley Rd. Camb 151 D2
Oakley Rd. Caver 58 C2
Oakley Rd. Newb 105 E2
Oakridge. West E 153 F3
Oaks Rd. Shipl 36 A2
Oaks Rd. Stan 70 B1
Oaks The. Brac 118 B4
Oaks The. Yate 149 E3
Oakside Way. Read 113 F4
Oaktree Way. Sand 143 D1
Oakway Dr. Camb 151 F1
Oakwood Rd. Brac 118 C4
Oakwood Rd. Vir W 122 B2
Oakwood Rd. Windl 146 C2
Oareborough. Brac 118 C3
Oast House Cl. Wray 95 F4
Oatlands Dr. Shepp 125 F1
Oatlands Dr. Slough 42 B4
Oatlands Rd. Shin 113 F3
Oban Ct. Slough 42 B2
Oban Gdns. Wood 87 F2
Obelisk Way. Camb 151 E3
Oberon Way. Stai 124 C3
Ockwells Rd. Maid 39 E2
Octavia. Brac 118 A1
Octavia Way. Stai 97 D1
Oddfellows Rd. Newb 104 C1
Odell Cl. Read 114 A4
Odencroft Rd. Slough 22 A1
Odiham Ave. Caver 59 F3
Odiham Rd. Swal 139 E1
Odney La. Cook 20 A4
Ogmore Cl. Read 84 C4
Old Barn Cl. Caver 59 D3
Old Bath Rd. Char 61 D3
Old Bath Rd. Newb 104 C2
Old Bath Rd. Sonn 60 B1
Old Bisley Rd. Camb 152 B2
Old Bracknell Cl. Brac 118 A3
Old Bracknell La. Brac 118 A3
Old Bracknell La E. Brac 118 A3
Old Bracknell La W. Brac 118 A3
Old Charlton Rd. Shepp 125 E2
Old Court Cl. Maid 39 D2
Old Dean Rd. Camb 151 E4
Old Elm Dr. Read 84 B4
Old Farm Cres. Read 57 E1
Old Farm Dr. Brac 91 E1
Old Ferry Dr. Wray 68 B1
Old Forge Cl. Maid 40 A2
Old Forge Cres. Shepp 125 D2
Old Green La. Camb 151 E4
Old Hayward La. Hung 73 E2
Old Kiln Rd. Fla H 3 D4
Old La. Ham M 102 C1
Old La. Head 133 F1
Old La The. Read 85 F3
Old Marsh La. Dorn 40 C2
Old Mill La. Maid 40 B2
Old Newtown Rd. Newb 104 C1
Old Orchard The. Bur C 84 C2
Old Pasture Rd. Camb 151 F2
Old Pond Cl. Camb 151 E1
Old Portsmouth Rd. Camb 152 A3
Old Post Office La. Maid 39 F4
Old Sawmill La. Crow 143 E3
Old School Ct. Wray 95 F4
Old School La. Yate 149 E3
Old Slade La. Iver 44 C1
Old St. Chiev 51 E3
Old St. Chiev 51 F1
Old St. Herm 78 C4
Old Station La. Wray 69 D1
Old Station Way. Bou E 3 F3
Old Vicarage Way. Bou E 3 E2
Old Watery La. Woo G 3 F4
Old Welmore. Yate 149 F3
Old Whitley Road La. Read 113 E3
Old Wokingham Rd. Brac 143 E3
Oldacre. West E 153 F4
Oldacres. Maid 40 A4
Oldbury. Brac 117 F3
Oldbury Rd. Chert 123 F1
Oldcorne Hollow. Yate 149 D3
Olde Farm Dr. Black 150 A3
Oldershaw Mews. Maid 39 D4
Oldfield Cl. Read 87 D4
Oldfield Rd. Maid 40 A4
Oldhouse La. Light 146 B1
Oldstead. Brac 118 B2
Oldway La. Slough 41 E3
Oleander Cl. Brac 143 D4
Oliver Dr. Read 84 B3
Oliver Rd. Ascot 120 A3
Oliver's Paddock. Mar B 1 B3
Ollerton. Brac 118 A1
Omer's Rise. Bur C 110 C2
One Pin La. Far C 22 B4
Onslow Dr. Ascot 93 D1
Onslow Gdns. Caver 59 E2
Onslow Mews. Chert 124 A2
Onslow Rd. Went 121 D1
Opal Way. Woki 115 F4
Opendale Rd. Burn 41 D4
Opladen Way. Brac 118 C2
Orbit Cl. Woki 141 F3
Orchard Ave. Ashf 98 B1
Orchard Ave. Harm 71 E1
Orchard Ave. Slough 41 E4
Orchard Ave. Wind 67 D3
Orchard Chase. Hurst 88 C4
Orchard Cl. Ashf 98 B1
Orchard Cl. Black 150 C1
Orchard Cl. Hen-O-T 15 F1
Orchard Cl. Herm 79 E4
Orchard Cl. Maid 40 A2
Orchard Cl. Newb 105 E3
Orchard Cl. Purl 57 E2
Orchard Cl. Shin 113 D1
Orchard Cl. Shipl 35 F1
Orchard Cl. West E 153 E3
Orchard Cl. Woki 116 B3
Orchard Cl. Wool 108 B1
Orchard Ct. Harm 70 B4
Orchard Ct. Read 113 E4
Orchard Dr. Bou E 3 E2
Orchard Estate. Twyf 61 F3
Orchard Gate. Far C 22 B4
Orchard Gate. Sand 150 A4
Orchard Gr. Fla H 3 D4
Orchard Gr. Maid 39 E4
Orchard Hill. Windl 146 B2
Orchard Park Cl. Hung 100 B2
Orchard Pl. Woki 116 B3
Orchard Rd. Hurst 88 C4
Orchard Rd. Mort 137 D3
Orchard Rd. Old W 68 A1
Orchard St. Read 86 A3
Orchard The. Fla H 3 D4
Orchard The. Light 153 D4
Orchard The. Mar 1 C2
Orchard The. Thea 83 F2
Orchard The. Vir W 122 C2
Orchard Way. Ashf 97 F3
Orchard Way. Camb 151 D1
Orchard Way. Slough 43 F3
Orchardene. Newb 105 D2
Orchardville. Burn 21 D1
Orchids The. Chil 10 B4
Oregon Ave. Read 57 E2
Oregon Wlk. Woki 141 F4
Oriel Hill. Camb 151 E2
Oriental Rd. Ascot 120 B3
Orion. Brac 118 A1
Orkney Cl. Bur C 84 C2
Ormonde Rd. Woki 116 A3
Ormsby St. Read 85 F4
Orrin Cl. Read 85 D4
Orts Rd. Newb 105 D1
Orts Rd. Read 86 B4
Orville Cl. Wood 88 A4
Orwell Cl. Caver 58 C2
Orwell Cl. Wind 67 E2
Osborne Ave. Stan 97 F4
Osborne Dr. Light 153 D4
Osborne La. New G 91 E2
Osborne Mews. Wind 67 E3
Osborne Rd. Eng G 95 F1
Osborne Rd. Read 85 D4
Osborne Rd. Wind 67 E2
Osborne Rd. Woki 116 B3
Osborne St. Slough 42 C2
Osbourne Ct. Wind 67 E3
Osman's Cl. Burl 92 A1
Osnaburgh Hill. Camb 151 D3
Osney Rd. Maid 19 F1
Osterley Cl. Woki 116 C3
Osterley Dr. Caver 59 F3
Ostler Gate. Maid 19 E1
Otter Cl. Brac 143 D4
Ouseley Rd. Old W 95 E4
Overbury Ave. Woki 88 C1
Overdale Rise. Camb 151 F2
Overdown Rd. Read 57 E1
Overlanders End. Read 57 F2
Overlord Cl. Camb 151 E4
Owen Rd. Newb 105 D3
Owen Rd. Windl 146 B3
Owl Cl. Woki 115 F3
Owlsmoor Rd. Sand 143 E1
Owston. Read 87 E1
Oxenhope. Brac 118 A3
Oxford Ave. Burn 21 D2
Oxford Ave. Harl 71 F4
Oxford Ave. Slough 41 F4
Oxford Cl. Stai 98 B1
Oxford Rd. Mar 1 B1
Oxford Rd. Newb 104 B3
Oxford Rd. Read 58 A1
Oxford Rd. Sand 143 F1
Oxford Rd. Wind 67 D3
Oxford Rd. Woki 116 A3
Oxford Rd E. Wind 67 E3
Oxford St. Caver 59 D1
Oxford St. Hung 100 C4
Oxford St. Lamb 25 D2
Oxford St. Newb 104 C2

Pack and Prime La. Hen-O-T 15 E1
Padbury Cl. Felt 98 C4
Paddick Cl. Sonn 60 C2
Paddock Cl. Camb 152 A3
Paddock Cl. Whi Wa 39 D1
Paddock Hts. Twyf 61 F2
Paddock Rd. Caver 59 E1
Paddock Rd. Newb 130 C4
Paddock The. Crow 143 D3
Paddock The. Maid 19 E1
Paddock The. Newb 105 E1
Paddock The. Slough 68 A3
Paddocks The. Fla H 3 D4
Paddocks Way. Chert 124 A1
Padstow Cl. Slough 43 F2
Padstow Gdns. Read 86 A1
Padworth Rd. Mort 136 B4
Padworth Rd. Silc 136 B4
Page Rd. Felt 98 B4
Page's Croft. Woki 116 B3
Paget Cl. Mar 1 C2
Paget Dr. Maid 39 D2
Paget Rd. Slough 43 F1
Pagoda The. Maid 20 A1
Paice Green. Woki 116 B4
Paices Hill. Alde 135 D3
Paley St. Holy 64 A3
Palmer Cl. Brac 143 D4
Palmer Park Ave. Read 87 D3
Palmer School Rd. Woki 116 B3
Palmera Ave. Bur C 84 B2
Palmers Cl. Maid 39 D2
Palmer's Hill. Asham 54 B3
Palmer's La. Bur C 112 A2
Palmer's La. Bur C 111 D1
Palmerston Ave. Slough 43 D2
Palmerstone Rd. Read 87 D3
Pamber Heath Rd. Silc 135 F1
Pamela Row. Holy 65 D4
Panbourne Hill. Pangb 56 B3
Pangbourne Rd. Upp B 55 E2
Pangbourne St. Read 58 A1
Pankhurst Dr. Brac 118 B2
Pan's Gdns. Camb 151 F2
Pantile Row. Slough 44 A1
Papist Way. Chol 14 A4
Paprika Cl. Read 86 C1
Parade The. Ashf 98 C1
Parade The. Bou E 3 D2
Parade The. Wood 87 F4
Paradise Rd. Hen-O-T 15 E1
Paradise Way. Buck 108 B4
Park Ave. Camb 151 E2
Park Ave. Stai 96 B1
Park Ave. Stai 97 D1
Park Ave. That 106 B2
Park Ave. Woki 116 A3
Park Ave. Wray 68 B2
Park Cres. Read 85 D3
Park Cres. Sunn 120 C2
Park Crnr. Wind 66 C2
Park Dr. Sunn 120 C2
Park End. Newb 105 D2
Park Gr. Read 85 D3

Park La. Bark 141 D3
Park La. Bee H 137 E1
Park La. Box 103 D1
Park La. Burn 21 F4
Park La. Camb 151 E3
Park La. Char 61 D2
Park La. Hort 69 D2
Park La. Newb 105 D2
Park La. Read 84 B4
Park La. Slough 43 D2
Park La. That 106 B2
Park Rd. Ashf 98 A2
Park Rd. Brac 118 B4
Park Rd. Camb 151 E2
Park Rd. Eng G 96 A2
Park Rd. Far C 22 B2
Park Rd. Hen-O-T 15 F1
Park Rd. Sand 150 B4
Park Rd. Shepp 125 D1
Park Rd. Stan 70 B1
Park Rd. Sto P 22 B2
Park Rd. Woki 116 A3
Park St. Bags 145 E2
Park St. Bags 145 F2
Park St. Camb 151 E3
Park St. Hung 100 B3
Park St. Maid 39 F4
Park St. Newb 105 D2
Park St. Slough 42 C2
Park St. Stan 69 E3
Park St. Wind 67 E3
Park The. Lamb 25 D2
Park View Dr N. Char 61 D3
Park View Dr S. Char 61 D2
Park Wall La. Upp B 34 B1
Park Way. Hung 100 C2
Park Way. Newb 105 D2
Park Wlk. Purl 57 E3
Parkcorner La. Arbo 114 C3
Parkgate. Burn 21 E1
Parkhill Cl. Black 150 B2
Parkhill Dr. Read 57 E1
Parkhill Rd. Black 150 B2
Parkhouse La. Read 85 E3
Parkland Ave. Slough 43 E1
Parkland Dr. Brac 118 C4
Parkland Gr. Ashf 98 A2
Parkland Rd. Ashf 98 A2
Parkside. Maid 19 E1
Parkside Rd. Read 85 E3
Parkside Rd. Sunn 121 D2
Parkside Rd. That 106 B3
Parkstone Dr. Camb 151 E2
Parkview. Fla H 3 D4
Parkview Chase. Slough 41 F4
Parkway. Camb 151 E2
Parkway. Crow 143 D3
Parkway. Mar 2 A2
Parkway Dr. Sonn 60 C2
Parlaunt Rd. Slough 44 A1
Parliament La. Burn 20 C3
Parnham Ave. Light 153 E4
Parry Green N. Slough 43 F1
Parry Green S. Slough 44 A1
Parsley Cl. Read 86 C1
Parsonage Gdns. Mar 1 C1
Parsonage La. Far C 22 B2
Parsonage La. Hung 100 B3
Parsonage La. Lamb 25 D1
Parsonage La. Wind 67 D3
Parsonage Pl. Lamb 25 D2
Parsonage Rd. Eng G 95 E2
Parsons Cl. Bark 141 D4
Parsons Cl. Newb 104 C1
Parsons Field. Sand 150 A4
Parson's Wood La. Far C 22 B3
Part La. Swal 139 F2
Parthia Cl. Read 86 A3
Partridge Ave. Yate 149 D3
Partridge Dr. Read 84 B3
Partridge Mead. Maid 19 F1
Paschal Rd. Camb 151 F4
Patches Field. Mar B 1 C3
Paterson Cl. Camb 152 B2
Paterson Rd. Ashf 97 E2
Pates Manor Dr. Felt 98 B4
Patricia Cl. Slough 41 F3
Patrick Rd. Caver 59 D1
Patriot Pl. Read 86 B4
Patten Ash Dr. Woki 116 C4
Patten Ave. Yate 149 E3
Pavenham Cl. Read 114 A4
Pavilion Gdns. Stai 97 D1
Pavy Cl. That 106 C1
Paxton Ave. Slough 42 B2
Paynesdown Rd. That 106 A2
Peace La. Cook 19 F3
Peach St. Woki 116 B3
Peachy Dr. That 106 C1
Peacock Ave. Felt 98 B4
Peacock La. Brac 117 E3
Peacock Rd. Mar 2 A2
Pear Tree La. Newb 105 E3
Pear Tree Rd. Ashf 98 B2
Pearce Cl. Maid 19 F1
Pearce Rd. Maid 19 F1
Pearces Orch. Hen-O-T 15 E2
Pearl Gdns. Slough 42 A3
Pearmain Cl. Shepp 125 D2
Pearman's Glade. Read 113 F4
Pearson Rd. Sonn 60 B2
Pearson Way. Wood 87 F3
Peascod Pl. Wind 67 E3
Peascod St. Wind 67 E3
Pease Hill. Buck 107 F4
Peasemore Hill. Pease 50 A4
Pebble Hill. Kint 128 A3
Peddlars Gr. Yate 149 F3
Peel Cl. Caver 59 E1
Peel Cl. Wind 67 D2
Peel Ct. Slough 42 A4
Pegasus Cl. That 106 A2
Peg's Green Cl. Read 85 D3
Peket Cl. Stai 123 F4
Pelican La. Newb 105 D2
Pelican Rd. Alde 135 F1
Pell St. Read 86 A3
Pelling Hill. Old W 95 D4
Pemberton Gdns. Bur C 84 B2
Pemberton Rd. Slough 21 F1
Pembroke. Brac 118 A1
Pembroke Broadway. Camb 151 E3
Pembroke Cl. Ascot 120 B2
Pembroke Cl. Bur C 111 E2
Pembroke Pl. Caver 59 E2
Pembroke Rd. Newb 105 D2
Pembury Ct. Harl 71 E4
Pendals Cl. Hamp N 52 C3
Pendell Ave. Harl 71 F4
Pendennis Ave. Caver 59 F3
Pendine Pl. Brac 118 A2
Pendlebury. Brac 118 A1
Pendragon Way. Camb 152 B2
Pendred Rd. Read 113 E3
Peninsular Cl. Felt 71 F1
Penling Cl. Cook 19 F3
Penn Cl. Caver 59 D3
Penn Meadow. Sto P 22 C2
Penn Rd. Datch 68 B3
Penn Rd. Farc 22 B1
Penn Rd. Newb 104 B3
Pennfields. Twyf 61 F3
Pennine Cl. Read 84 A3
Pennine Rd. Slough 42 A4
Pennine Way. Char 61 D2
Pennine Way. Harl 71 E4
Pennylets Green. Sto P 23 D3
Pennypiece. Gori 34 B4
Penroath Ave. Read 85 E3
Penrose Ave. Wood 87 F3
Penrose Cl. Newb 104 C3
Penrose Ct. Eng G 95 E1
Penry La. Shepp 125 F1
Pensford Cl. Crow 143 D4
Penshurst Rd. Maid 39 E3
Pentland Ave. Stai 125 D2
Pentland Cl. Read 84 C3
Pentland Pl. That 106 B1
Pentland Rd. Slough 42 A4
Pentlands The. Kint 102 B1
Penton Ave. Stai 123 F4
Penton Hall Dr. Stai 124 A4
Penton Hook Rd. Stai 124 A4
Penton Rd. Stai 96 C1
Penwood Ct. Maid 39 D4
Penwood Gdns. Brac 117 E2
Penwood La. Mar 1 B1
Penwood Rd. Ball H 130 B2
Penyston Rd. Maid 39 E4
Peppard La. Hen-O-T 35 F4
Peppard Rd. Caver 59 E3
Pepper La. Read 86 B2
Pepys Cl. Slough 69 D4
Perch Cl. Mar 18 B4
Percival Rd. Felt 98 C3
Percy Ave. Ashf 98 A2
Percy Bryant Rd. Stai 98 C1
Percy Pl. Slough 68 A3
Peregrine Cl. Brac 118 A2
Peregrine Cl. Woki 115 F3
Peregrine Rd. Shepp 125 F4
Periam Cl. Hen-O-T 35 E4
Perkins Way. Woki 116 A3
Perrin Cl. Ashf 97 F2
Perry Oaks. Brac 118 C4
Perry Oaks Dr. Harm 70 B3
Perry Way. Brac 118 C4
Perrycroft. Wind 66 C2
Perryhill Dr. Sand 142 C1
Perryman Way. Slough 21 F1
Perserverance Hill. Hen-O-T 35 D3
Perth Ave. Slough 42 A4
Perth Cl. Wood 61 D1
Peterhouse Cl. Crow 143 F1
Petersfield Ave. Slough 43 D3
Petersfield Ave. Stai 97 E1
Petersfield Rd. Stai 97 E2
Petrel Cl. Woki 115 F3
Petts La. Stai 125 D3
Petworth Ave. Read 84 C2
Petworth Ct. Wind 67 D3
Pevensey Ave. Caver 59 F3
Pevensey Rd. Slough 42 A4
Pewsey Vale. Brac 118 C2
Pheasant Cl. Winn 88 B1
Pheasants Croft. Maid 39 D3
Philip Dr. Fla H 3 E4
Philip Rd. Stai 97 E1
Phillimore Rd. Caver 59 E4
Phipps Cl. Whi Wa 39 D1
Phipps Rd. Burn 41 F4
Phoebe Ct. Read 86 A3
Phoenix Cl. Woki 115 F3
Phoenix Wlk. Newb 130 B3
Phyllis Court Dr. Faw (Bu) 15 F2
Phyllis Ct. Dr. Hen-O-T 15 F2
Pickering. Brac 118 A3
Picket Post Cl. Brac 118 C3
Picketts La. Pangb 55 F2
Pickford Dr. Slough 43 F3
Pickins Piece. Hort 69 D3
Pickwell Cl. Wood 87 E1
Picton Way. Caver 59 D2
Piercefield. Bur C 84 B2
Pierce's Hill. Read 57 E1
Pierson Rd. Wind 66 B3
Pigeonhouse La. Wink 92 C2
Piggott's Rd. Caver 59 E1
Pigott Rd. Woki 116 C4
Pike Cl. Mar 18 B4
Pike St. Newb 105 D2
Pikeshaw Way. Read 57 E1
Pimento Dr. Read 86 C1
Pincents La. Sulh 84 A3
Pinchcut. Bur C 111 D2
Pinchington La. Gree 131 D4
Pine Ave. Camb 151 E2
Pine Cl. Maid 39 D4
Pine Cl. Sand 150 C4
Pine Croft Rd. Woki 116 A1
Pine Dr. Black 150 C2
Pine Dr. Mort 136 C3
Pine Dr. Woki 142 A4
Pine Gr. Twyf 61 E3
Pine Gr. Windl 146 B2
Pine Mount Rd. Camb 151 E2
Pine Ridge. Newb 105 E3
Pine Ridge Rd. Bur C 111 D2
Pine Way. Eng G 95 D1
Pinecote Dr. Sunn 120 C1
Pinecroft. Mar 1 B2
Pinefields Cl. Crow 143 D2
Pinehill Rd. Crow 143 E2
Pinehill Rise. Sand 150 B4
Pinetree Ct. Caver 59 D3
Pinewood Ave. Crow 143 E3
Pinewood Cl. Tad 134 B1
Pinewood Dr. Stai 97 D2
Pinewood Gdns. Bags 145 E2
Pinewood Rd. Vir W 122 A3
Pinewood Rd. Went 122 A3
Pingewood Rd. Bur C 85 D1
Pingewood Rd S. Bur C 112 B4
Pingewood Rd S. Shin 112 B4
Pinglestone Cl. Harm 70 C4
Pink La. Burn 21 D2
Pinkneys Dr. Maid 38 C4
Pinkneys Rd. Maid 39 D4
Pinks La. Tad 134 C1
Pipers Cl. Burn 21 E1
Pipers Ct. That 107 D1
Pipers End. Vir W 122 B3
Pipers Way. That 107 D1
Pipit Cl. That 106 A2
Pippins Ct. Ashf 98 A1
Pippins The. Slough 43 F3
Pitcroft Ave. Read 87 D3
Pitfield La. Mort 137 E2
Pitfield La. Silc 137 E2
Pitford Rd. Wood 88 A4
Pitts Cl. Binf 90 B1
Pitt's La. Read 87 D4
Pitts Rd. Slough 42 B3
Plackett Way. Slough 41 E3
Plaitinson Rd. Read 113 E3
Planes The. Chert 124 B1
Plantation Cl. Herm 78 C3
Plantation Rd. Camb 151 D3
Plantation Rd. Chil 9 F4
Plantation Rd. Tad 134 C1
Plantation Row. Camb 151 D3
Platt La. Lamb 45 E3
Play Platt. Thea 83 F2
Players Green. Wood 87 F3
Playhatch Rd. Caver 60 A3
Plough La. Sto P 23 D2
Plough La. Woki 116 C3
Plough Rd. Yate 149 F4
Ploughlands. Brac 117 F4
Ploughlees La. Slough 42 C3
Plover Cl. Stai 96 C3
Plover Cl. Woki 115 F3
Plowden Way. Shipl 35 F1
Plumpton Rd. Newb 105 E1
Plumtrees. Read 87 D1
Pluto Rd. Chil 9 F4
Plymouth Ave. Wood 87 E3
Plympton Cl. Winn 87 F2
Pococks La. Eton 42 C1
Poffley Pl. That 107 D2
Pointers Cl. Chiev 51 D1
Points The. Maid 39 D2
Polehampton Cl. Twyf 61 E2
Pollard Cl. Old W 68 A1
Pollard Gr. Camb 152 B2
Pollardrow Ave. Brac 117 F4
Polsted Rd. Read 57 E1
Pond Cl. Newb 130 B4
Pond Croft. Yate 149 F3
Pond Head La. Read 87 E2
Pond La. Herm 79 E4
Pond La. Maple 57 F4
Pond Moor Rd. Brac 118 A2
Pond Rd. Stai 96 B1
Pondside Cl. Harl 71 E4
Pool La. Slough 42 C3
Poole Cl. Read 85 D4
Pooley Ave. Stai 96 A2
Pooley Green Cl. Stai 96 B2
Pooley Green Rd. Stai 96 B2
Poolmans Rd. Wind 66 B2
Pope Cl. Felt 98 C4
Popes Cl. Iver 69 E4
Popes La. Cook 19 E4
Popeswood Rd. Binf 117 E4
Popham Cl. Brac 118 C2
Poplar Ave. Read 84 C3
Poplar Ave. Windl 146 A3
Poplar Cl. Stan 69 F3
Poplar Gdns. Read 86 C1
Poplar La. Hurst 62 A1
Poplar La. Winn 88 B2
Poplar Rd. Ashf 98 B2
Poplars Rd. Maid 20 A1
Poplars The. Ascot 120 A2
Poppy Way. Read 84 B3
Poppyhills Rd. Camb 151 F4
Porchester. Ascot 120 A3
Porchester Rd. Newb 105 D1
Porchfield Cl. Read 87 D1
Porlock Cl. That 106 B1
Porlock Pl. Bur C 84 B2
Porter Cl. Winn 114 B4
Porter End. Newb 131 D4
Portesbery Hill Dr. Camb 151 F3
Portesbury Rd. Camb 151 F3
Portland Cl. Slough 21 E1
Portland Cres. Felt 98 B2
Portland Gdns. Read 84 B4
Portland Rd. Ashf 97 F3
Portlands. Mar 1 B1
Portlock Rd. Maid 39 E4
Portman Cl. Brac 118 A4
Portman Rd. Read 58 B1
Portnall Dr. Went 121 F2
Portnall Rd. Went 121 F2
Portnall Rise. Went 121 F2
Portrush Rd. Wood 87 E3
Portsmouth Rd. Camb 152 A4
Portway. Swal 139 E1
Portway. Tad 134 C1
Portway Cl. Read 85 F3
Post Horn Pl. Read 84 C2
Post Office La. Slough 43 E4
Post Office Rd. Ink 127 F3
Posting House Mews. Newb 104 C2
Potley Hill Rd. Yate 149 F3
Pottery La. Ink 127 F3
Pottery Rd. Read 57 F1
Potts Pl. Mar 1 B1
Poulcott. Wray 68 C1
Pound Cres. Mar 1 B1
Pound La. Hurst 89 D3
Pound La. Lit M 2 B2
Pound La. Mar 1 B1
Pound La. Newb 104 B2
Pound La. Sonn 60 C1
Pound La. That 106 A2
Pound La. Windl 146 B2
Pound Piece. Hung 100 B3
Pound Rd. Chert 124 A1
Pound St. Newb 104 C1
Pound The. Cook 19 F4
Poundfield La. Cook 19 F4
Powis Cl. Maid 39 D2
Powney Rd. Maid 39 E4
Poyle La. Burn 21 D2
Poyle Rd. Stan 69 F3
Poynings. Iver 44 C1
Precincts The. Burn 21 E1
Prescott. Brac 117 F1
Prescott Rd. Stan 69 F3
Preston Rd. Read 86 A3
Preston Rd. Slough 43 E3
Preston Rd. Stai 125 D2
Prestwood. Slough 43 D4
Pretoria Rd. Chert 123 F1
Priest Ave. Woki 116 C3
Priest Hill. Caver 59 D2
Priest Hill. Eng G 95 E3
Priest La. West E 153 E3
Priestwood Ave. Brac 117 F4
Priestwood Court Rd. Brac 118 A4
Primrose Cl. Purl 57 E3
Primrose La. Winn 88 B2
Primrose Lea. Mar 1 B1
Primrose Way. Sand 143 D1
Primrose Wlk. Brac 118 B2
Prince Albert Dr. Brac 119 E2
Prince Andrew Cl. Maid 20 A1
Prince Andrew Rd. Maid 20 A1
Prince Andrew Way. Burl 119 E4
Prince Consort Cotts. Wind 67 E3
Prince Consort Dr. Brac 119 E3
Prince Dr. Sand 143 D1
Prince Hold Rd. That 106 A2
Prince of Wales Ave. Read 85 E4
Prince William Dr. Read 57 E1
Princes Cl. Eton 41 F1
Prince's La. Pease 50 B3
Princes Rd. Ashf 97 F2
Princes Rd. Bou E 3 E2
Princes Rd. Eng G 95 F1
Princes Rd. Felt 98 C3
Prince's St. Read 86 B4
Princes St. Slough 43 D2
Princes Way. Bags 145 F1
Princess Ave. Wind 67 D2
Princess Marina Dr. Bark 140 C4
Princess Marina Dr. Bark 115 D1
Princess St. Maid 39 F3
Princess Way. Camb 151 E3
Prior Croft Cl. Camb 152 A2
Prior End. Camb 152 A3
Prior Rd. Camb 152 A3
Priors Cl. Maid 40 A1
Priors Cl. Slough 43 D2
Priors Court Rd. Chiev 78 C4
Prior's La. Black 150 A3
Priors Rd. Tad 135 D1
Priors Rd. Wind 66 B2
Priors Way. Maid 40 A1
Priory Ave. Caver 59 D1
Priory Ave. Hung 100 B2
Priory Cl. Hung 100 B2
Priory Cl. Went 121 D1
Priory Ct. Winn 88 B2
Priory Green. Stai 97 D2
Priory La. New G 91 E1
Priory Mews. Stai 97 D2
Priory Rd. Burl 119 D4
Priory Rd. Hung 100 B2
Priory Rd. Newb 105 D1
Priory Rd. Slough 41 E4
Priory Rd. Went 121 D1
Priory The. Winn 88 B2
Priory Way. Datch 68 A4
Priory Way. Harm 70 C4
Priory Wlk. Brac 118 C3
Proctors Rd. Woki 116 C3
Promenade. Wind 67 E4
Promenade Rd. Caver 59 D1
Prospect Ct. Read 85 D3
Prospect La. Eng G 95 D2
Prospect Pl. Hurl 17 F2
Prospect Pl. Newb 105 D1
Prospect Pl. Stai 96 C2
Prospect Rd. Hung 100 B3
Prospect Rd. Mar 1 B1
Prospect St. Caver 59 D1
Prospect St. Read 85 F4
Providence La. Harl 71 E4
Providence Pl. Maid 39 F4
Prune Hill. Eng G 95 E1
Pudding Hill. Know H 37 E3
Pudding La. Brig 28 C1
Puffers Way. Newb 104 C1
Pump La. Shin 112 B1
Pump La. Wink 120 C4
Pump La N. Lit M 1 C3
Pump La s. Lit M 2 A2
Pumpkin Hill. Burn 21 F3
Pundles La. Whi Wa 63 E3
Purbrook Ct. Brac 118 C2
Purcell Rd. Crow 143 D4
Purfield Dr. Warg 36 C1
Purley La. Purl 57 E3
Purley Rise. Purl 56 C3
Purley Village. Purl 57 E3
Purley Way. Pangb 56 C3
Purssell Cl. Maid 39 D2
Purton Ct. Far C 22 B3
Purton La. Far C 22 B3
Putman Pl. Hen-O-T 15 F1
Pyegrove Chase. Brac 118 C1
Pyke's Hill. Asham 54 B2
Pyle Hill. Newb 105 D1
Pyrcroft Rd. Chert 123 F1

Quadrant Ct. Brac 118 C3
Quadrant The. Maid 40 A3
Qualitas. Brac 117 F1
Quantock Ave. Caver 59 E3
Quantock Cl. Char 61 D2
Quantock Cl. Harl 71 E4
Quantock Cl. Slough 44 A1
Quantocks The. That 106 B1
Quarrington Cl. That 106 C1
Quarry Bank. Light 153 D4
Quarry La. Yate 149 F3
Quarrydale Dr. Mar 1 C1
Quartz Cl. Woki 115 E4
Quaves Rd. Slough 43 E2
Quebec Gdns. Black 150 B2
Quebec Rd. Hen-O-T 35 F4
Queen Anne's Cl. Old W 94 A3
Queen Annes Gate. Caver 59 E2
Queen Anne's Rd. Wind 67 E2
Queen Charlotte St. Wind 67 E3
Queen Cl. Hen-O-T 15 F1
Queen Elizabeth Rd. Camb 144 B1
Queen Mary Ave. Camb 151 D3
Queen Mary Rd. Stai 125 E4
Queen St. Caver 59 D2
Queen St. Chert 124 A1
Queen St. Hen-O-T 15 F1
Queen St. Maid 39 F4
Queen Victoria St. Read 86 A4
Queens Acre. Wind 67 E2
Queens Cl. Burl 119 F4
Queen's Cl. Old W 68 A1
Queen's Cotts. Read 86 B4
Queen's Ct. Slough 42 C3
Queen's Dr The. Read 86 B2
Queens Gate. Wind 67 E2
Queens Hill Rise. Ascot 120 B3
Queen's La. Maid 39 F4
Queen's Mead. Datch 68 A3
Queens Park Gdns. Felt 98 C3
Queens Pine. Brac 118 C2
Queen's Pl. Ascot 120 A3
Queen's Rd. Ascot 120 B2
Queen's Rd. Bis 153 F1
Queens Rd. Camb 151 D2
Queen's Rd. Caver 59 E1
Queen's Rd. Datch 68 A4
Queen's Rd. Eng G 95 F1
Queens Rd. Eton 41 F1
Queen's Rd. Mar 1 B1
Queen's Rd. Newb 105 D1
Queen's Rd. Read 86 B4
Queen's Rd. Slough 42 C3
Queen's Rd. Wind 67 E3
Queens Way. Kint 102 A1
Queens Wlk. Ashf 97 E2
Queensborough Dr. Caver 58 C3
Queensbury Pl. Black 150 B2
Queenshill Lodge. Ascot 120 A3
Queensmere Rd. Slough 43 D2
Queensway. Caver 59 E3
Queensway. Maid 19 F1
Quentin Rd. Wood 87 E3
Quentin Way. Vir W 122 A3
Quinbrookes. Slough 43 E4
Quince Cl. Ascot 120 B3
Quincy Rd. Eng G 96 A2
Quintilis. Brac 117 F1
Quoiting Sq. Mar 1 B1
Quoitings Dr. Mar 1 B1

Rackstraw Rd. Crow 143 E1
Radbourne Rd. Bur C 84 B2
Radcliffe Way. Brac 117 F4
Radcot Ave. Slough 44 A2
Radcot Cl. Maid 19 F2

Radcot Cl. Wood 87 F4
Radical Ride. Woki 141 F4
Radley Bottom. Wick 101 E4
Radnor Cl. Hen-O-T 15 F1
Radnor Rd. Brac 118 C3
Radnor Rd. Read 87 E2
Radnor Way. Slough 43 F1
Radstock La. Read 87 D1
Radstock Rd. Read 86 C4
Raeburn Way. Sand 150 B3
Ragdale. Bur C 111 D2
Raggleswood Cl. Read 87 E2
Raghill. Alde 135 E3
Raglan Gdns. Caver 59 E2
Ragley Mews. Caver 59 E3
Ragmans Cl. Mar B 1 B4
Ragstone Rd. Slough 42 C2
Railside. Wool 108 C1
Railton Cl. Read 113 E4
Railway App. Chert 123 F1
Railway Rd. Newb 105 D1
Railway Terr. Slough 42 C3
Railway Terr. Stai 96 B2
Railways Cotts. Gori 34 B3
Rainworth Cl. Read 114 A4
Raleigh Cl. Slough 42 A3
Raleigh Cl. Wood 87 F3
Raleigh Ct. Stai 97 D2
Raleigh Rd. Felt 98 C3
Ralphs Ride. Brac 118 C3
Rambler Cl. Burn 41 D4
Rambler La. Slough 43 E2
Rambury Cl. Brac 117 F2
Ramptons La. Silc 136 A3
Ramsay Rd. Windl 146 C3
Ramsbury Dr. Read 87 D2
Ramsey Cl. Winn 87 F1
Rances La. Woki 116 C3
Randall Cl. Slough 43 F1
Randall Mead. Binf 90 A1
Randell Cl. Black 150 C1
Randolph Rd. Read 59 D1
Randolph Rd. Slough 43 F2
Ranelagh Cres. Burl 119 E4
Ranelagh Dr. Brac 118 B3
Range Rd. Brac 142 A4
Range Ride. Sand 150 C4
Range View. Sand 150 C4
Range Way. Shepp 125 D1
Rangewood Ave. Read 84 C2
Rapley Cl. Camb 151 F4
Rapley Green. Brac 118 B2
Ratby Cl. Read 87 E1
Raven Cl. Yate 149 D3
Ravendale Rd. Shepp 125 F4
Ravenglass Cl. Read 87 E2
Ravens Field. Slough 43 E2
Ravensbourne Ave. Stan 97 F4
Ravensbourne Dr. Wood 87 F4
Ravenscourt. Shepp 125 F4
Ravenscroft Rd. Hen-O-T 15 E1
Ravensdale Rd. Ascot 120 A2
Ravensfield. Eng G 95 E1
Ravenshoe Cl. Bou E 3 D2
Ravenstone Rd. Camb 152 B3
Ravenswood Ave. Crow 142 C3
Ravenswood Ave. Finch 142 C3
Ravenswood Dr. Camb 152 A3
Ravensworth Rd. Silc 136 C3
Ravensworth Rd. Slough 22 A1
Rawlinson Rd. Camb 151 D3
Ray Dr. Maid 40 A4
Ray Lea Cl. Maid 40 A4
Ray Lea Rd. Maid 40 A4
Ray Lodge Mews. Maid 40 A4
Ray Mead Ct. Maid 20 B1
Ray Mead Rd. Maid 40 A4
Ray Mill Rd E. Maid 20 A1
Ray Mill Rd W. Maid 40 A4
Ray Park Ave. Maid 40 A4
Ray Park La. Maid 40 A4
Ray Park Rd. Maid 40 A4
Ray St. Maid 40 A4
Raymond Cl. Stan 69 F3
Raymond Rd. Maid 39 E4
Raymond Rd. Slough 44 A2
Rayners Cl. Iver 69 E4
Rays Ave. Wind 66 C4
Raywood Cl. Harl 71 E4
Reading Bridge. Read 86 A4
Reading Rd. Aldw 33 D1
Reading Rd. Arbo 114 B2
Reading Rd. Bark 140 C2
Reading Rd. Black 150 A2
Reading Rd. Bur C 111 E2
Reading Rd. Chol 14 A4
Reading Rd. Finch 140 C2
Reading Rd. Gori 34 C3
Reading Rd. Moul 14 A4
Reading Rd. Pangb 56 B3
Reading Rd. Purl 57 D3
Reading Rd. Stre 34 A3
Reading Rd. Woki 115 F4
Reading Rd. Wood 87 E4
Recreation La. Shin 113 D1
Recreation Rd. Bou E 3 D2
Recreation Rd. Bur C 111 D1
Recreation Rd. Read 84 C4
Recreation Rd. Warg 36 C1
Rectory Cl. Brac 118 B3
Rectory Cl. Far C 22 A1
Rectory Cl. Newb 104 C1
Rectory Cl. Sand 149 F4
Rectory Cl. Stai 125 D3
Rectory Cl. Wind 67 D3
Rectory Cl. Woki 116 B3
Rectory La. Blew 12 C4
Rectory La. Brac 118 A3
Rectory La. Windl 146 B2
Rectory Rd. Caver 59 D1
Rectory Rd. Padw 135 F4
Rectory Rd. Stre 33 E4
Rectory Rd. Tapl 20 C1
Rectory Rd. Woki 116 B3
Red Cottage Mews. Slough 43 E2
Red Cross Rd. Gori 34 B3
Red Ct. Slough 42 C3
Red Hill. Shipl 35 D3
Red House Cl. Read 114 A4
Red La. Alde 135 E3
Red Leaf Cl. Slough 43 F3
Red Lion Way. Woo G 3 F3
Red Rd. West E 152 C4
Red Rose. Binf 90 B2
Red Shute Hill. Herm 79 D2
Redberry Cl. Caver 59 E3
Redcrest Gdns. Camb 151 F3
Reddington Dr. Slough 43 F1
Redditch. Brac 118 B1
Redfield Ct. Newb 105 E2
Redford Rd. Wind 66 B3
Redhatch Dr. Read 87 D1
Redlands Rd. Read 86 B3
Redlane Hill. Alde 135 E3
Redleaves Ave. Ashf 98 A1
Redmayne. Camb 152 B2
Redriff Cl. Maid 39 E3
Redruth Gdns. Read 86 A1
Redshots Cl. Mar 1 C2
Redvers Rd. Brac 118 A2
Redwood. Burn 21 D2
Redwood. Stai 123 F4
Redwood Ave. Wood 88 A3
Redwood Dr. Camb 152 B2
Redwood Dr. Windl 121 D2
Redwood Gdns. Slough 42 B3
Redwood Way. Read 57 E2
Reed Cl. Iver 44 C4
Reed Wlk. Newb 105 E2
Reeds Ave. Read 86 C2
Reed's Hill. Brac 118 A2
Reedsfield Rd. Ashf 98 A2
Reeve Rd. Holy 65 D4
Reeves Way. Woki 116 A2
Reform Rd. Maid 40 A4
Regency Hts. Caver 58 C2
Regent Cl. Hung 100 B3
Regent Ct. Bags 145 F1
Regent Ct. Maid 39 F4
Regent Ct. Read 86 A4
Regent St. Read 86 C4
Regent Way. Camb 152 A1
Regents Pl. Sand 150 B4
Regents Wlk. Ascot 120 B1
Regis Cl. Read 113 E4
Regnum Dr. Newb 105 D3
Reid Ave. Maid 39 F3
Rembrant Cl. Woki 115 E3
Remembrance Rd. Newb 104 C1
Remenham Church La. Rem H 16 A2
Remenham La. RemH 15 F2
Renault Rd. Wood 88 A3
Renfree Way. Shepp 125 D1
Rennie Cl. Ashf 97 E3
Repton Cl. Maid 39 E2
Repton Rd. Read 87 E2
Restwold Cl. Read 85 E2
Retford Cl. Wood 60 C1
Retreat The. Eng G 95 F2
Retreat The. Holy 65 E4
Revel Rd. Woo G 3 E4
Revesby Cl. Maid 39 E2
Revesby Cl. West E 153 E3
Rex Ave. Ashf 98 A2
Reynards Cl. Winn 88 B1
Reynolds Green. Sand 150 B3
Rhodes Cl. Winn 87 F2
Rhododendron Cl. Burl 92 C1
Rhododendron Rd. Camb 152 A1
Rhododendron Wlk. Burl 92 C1
Ribbleton Cl. Winn 87 F2
Ribstone Rd. Maid 39 D2
Ricard Rd. Old W 68 A1
Richards Cl. Harl 71 E4
Richborough Cl. Read 87 D1
Richfield Ave. Read 58 C1
Richings Way. Iver 44 C2
Richmond Ave. Felt 71 F1
Richmond Cl. Camb 151 F1
Richmond Cres. Slough 43 D3
Richmond Cres. Stai 96 C2
Richmond Dr. Shepp 125 E2
Richmond Rd. Caver 58 C2
Richmond Rd. Read 85 E4
Richmond Rd. Sand 150 C4
Richmond Rd. Stai 96 C2
Richmond Rise. Woki 115 F4
Richmondwood. Went 121 D1
Rickman Cl. Arbo 114 C1
Rickman Cl. Brac 118 B2
Rickman Cl. Wood 87 E3
Rickman's La. Sto P 22 C3
Riddings La. Head 133 E1
Rider's La. Bur C 112 A2
Rideway Cl. Camb 151 D2
Ridge Hall Cl. Caver 58 C2
Ridge Mount Rd. Windl 121 D1
Ridge The. Cold A 106 B4
Ridge The. Upp B 55 F4
Ridge Way. Warg 36 C1
Ridgebank. Slough 41 F3
Ridgemead Rd. Eng G 95 D3
Ridgemount Cl. Sulh 57 D1
Ridgeway. Iver 44 C3
Ridgeway. Shepp 125 F1
Ridgeway Cl. Light 153 D4
Ridgeway Cl. Mar 1 C2
Ridgeway The. Brac 118 B3
Ridgeway The. Caver 59 D2
Ridgeway The. Light 146 A1
Ridgeway The. Mar 1 C2
Ridgeway The. Wood 87 F3
Riding Court Rd. Datch 68 C4
Riding Way. Woki 115 F3
Ridings The. Camb 152 A2
Ridings The. Caver 59 E4
Ridings The. Iver 44 C1
Ridings The. Maid 39 D3
Ridlington Cl. Winn 87 F1
Riley Rd. Mar 1 B1
Riley Rd. Read 84 C4
Ring The. Brac 118 B4
Ringmead. Brac 117 F2
Ringwood. Brac 117 F1
Ringwood Cl. Ascot 120 A3
Ringwood Rd. Black 150 B3
Ringwood Rd. Read 58 A1
Ripley Ave. Eng G 95 F1
Ripley Cl. Slough 43 F1
Ripley Rd. Read 58 A1
Ripon Cl. Camb 152 B2
Ripplesmere. Brac 118 B3
Ripplesmore Cl. Sand 150 A4
Ripston Rd. Ashf 98 B2
Risborough Rd. Maid 39 F4
Rise Rd. Sunn 120 C2
Rise The. Caver 59 D2
Rise The. Cold A 106 B4
Rise The. Crow 142 C3
Rise The. Crow 143 D3
Rise The. Finch 141 D1
Rise The. Woki 116 A4
Riseley Rd. Maid 39 E4
Rissington Cl. Read 57 F2
River Gdns. Maid 40 B2
River Gdns. Purl 57 E3
River Mount. Shepp 125 F1
River Park. Newb 105 D2
River Park Ave. Stai 96 B2
River Rd. Caver 58 B2
River Rd. Read 86 A3
River Rd. Stai 123 F4
River Rd. Tapl 40 B4
River Rd. Yate 149 D4
River St. Wind 67 E4
River View. Fla H 3 D4
River Wlk. Newb 105 E2
Riverbank. Stai 96 C1
Riverdene Dr. Winn 88 A2
Riverfield Rd. Stai 96 C1
Rivermead Cl. Bish 18 C4
Rivermead Rd. Camb 151 D1
Rivermead Rd. Wood 87 F3
Riverpark Dr. Mar 1 C1
Riversdale Ct. Read 86 C4
Riversdell Cl. Chert 123 F1
Riverside. Bou E 3 E2
Riverside. Eng G 96 A3
Riverside. Shepp 125 F1
Riverside. Wray 95 E4
Riverside Ave. Light 153 E4
Riverside Cl. Stai 123 F4
Riverside Dr. Stai 96 C2
Riverside Dr. Stai 123 F4
Riverside Pl. Stan 70 C1
Riverside Rd. Stai 96 C1
Riverside Rd. Stan 70 B1
Riverside Rd. Stan 70 C1
Riverview Rd. Pangb 56 B3
Riverway. Gr She 48 A2
Riverway. Stai 124 A4
Riverwoods Ave. Mar 2 A1
Riverwoods Dr. Mar 2 A1
Rixman Cl. Maid 39 E3
Rixon Cl. Slough 43 F4
Road Hill. Box 76 B2
Roasthill La. Dorn 41 E1
Roberts Cl. Stan 70 B1
Roberts Rd. Camb 151 D3
Roberts Rd. Sand 151 D3
Roberts Way. Eng G 95 E1
Robertsfield. That 105 F2
Robertson Cl. Newb 131 D4
Robin Cl. Bur C 111 D2
Robin Hill Dr. Camb 152 A2
Robin Hood Cl. Slough 41 F3
Robin Hood Way. Winn 88 B2
Robin La. Sand 143 E1
Robin Way. Read 84 A3
Robin Way. Stai 96 C3
Robindale Ave. Read 87 E2
Robinhood La. Winn 88 B2
Robin's Bow. Camb 151 D2
Robins Cl. Newb 130 C4
Robins Grove Cres. Yate 149 D3
Robins Hill. Ink 127 F3
Robinson Ct. Read 87 D1
Rochester Ave. Felt 98 C3
Rochester Ave. Wood 60 C1
Rochford Way. Burn 41 D4
Rochfords Gdns. Slough 43 E3
Rockbourne Gdns. Read 58 A1
Rockfield. Lamb 25 D1
Rockfield Way. Sand 150 B4
Rockingham Rd. Newb 104 C1
Rockmoor La. Link 147 D1
Rodney Way. Stan 69 F3
Rodway Rd. Read 57 F1
Roebuck Estate. Binf 90 B1
Roebuck Green. Slough 41 F3
Roebuts Cl. Newb 130 C4
Rogers La. Sto P 22 C2
Rogers's La. East G 47 E3
Rokeby Cl. Brac 118 B4
Rokeby Cl. Newb 131 D4
Rokeby Dr. Maple 58 B4
Rokes Pl. Yate 149 D3
Rokesby Rd. Slough 21 F1
Rolls La. Holy 64 C4
Roman Fields. Silc 136 A1
Roman Lea. Cook 19 F4
Roman Ride. Finch 142 B3
Roman Way. Bou E 3 D2
Roman Way. Read 87 E2
Roman Way. That 106 A3
Romans Gate. Silc 135 F1
Romany Cl. Read 58 A1
Romany La. Read 58 A1
Romney Cl. Ashf 98 B2
Romney Ct. Mar 1 C2
Romsey Cl. Black 150 B3
Romsey Cl. Slough 43 F2
Romsey Rd. Read 58 A1
Rona Ct. Read 85 D4
Rood Hill. Wick 76 B2
Rook Cl. Woki 115 F3
Rook Rd. Bou E 3 E2
Rookery Ct. Mar 1 B1
Rookery Rd. Stai 97 D2
Rooksfield. Newt 132 A1
Rooksmead Rd. Shepp 125 F4
Rooksnest La. Kint 128 A3
Rookswood. Brac 91 D1
Rookwood Ave. Sand 143 F1
Rope Wlk. That 106 B2
Rosa Ave. Ashf 98 A2
Rosary Gdns. Ashf 98 A2
Rosary Gdns. Yate 149 E3
Rose Cl. Wood 88 A4
Rose Hill. Binf 90 B2
Rose Hill. Burn 21 D3
Rose Kiln La. Bur C 86 A2
Rose Kiln La. Read 86 A2
Rose La. Know H 37 D4
Rose St. Woki 116 B3
Rose Wlk. Read 86 A4
Rose Wlk. Slough 42 A4
Roseacre Cl. Stai 125 D2
Rosebank Cl. Cook 19 F4
Rosebery Rd. Maple 58 B4
Rosecroft Way. Shin 113 F3
Rosedale. Binf 90 B2
Rosedale Cres. Read 87 D4
Rosedale Gdns. Brac 118 A2
Rosedale Gdns. That 106 B1
Rosedene La. Sand 150 B3
Rosefield Rd. Stai 97 D2
Rosehill Park. Caver 59 E4
Roseleigh Cl. Maid 39 D4
Rosemary Ave. Read 86 C1
Rosemary Gdns. Black 150 B3
Rosemary La. Sand 150 B3
Rosemary La. Stai 123 D3
Rosemead Ave. Felt 98 C3
Rosemead Ave. Sulh 57 D2
Rosery The. Bou E 3 D2
Roses La. Wind 66 B3
Rosewood. Wood 87 E2
Rosewood Dr. Stai 124 C2
Rosewood Way. Far C 22 B4
Rosier Cl. That 106 C1
Rosken Gr. Far C 22 A2
Roslyn Rd. Wood 87 E3
Ross Rd. Maid 39 F2
Ross Rd. Read 58 C1
Ross Rd. Read 59 D1
Rossendale Rd. Caver 59 E2
Rossett Cl. Brac 118 A3
Rossey Pl. Eton 42 B1
Rossington Pl. Read 113 E4
Rossiter Cl. Slough 43 F1
Rother Cl. Sand 150 B4
Rotherfield Ave. Woki 116 A4
Rotherfield Cl. Thea 83 F2
Rotherfield Rd. Hen-O-T 35 F4
Rotherfield Way. Caver 59 D2
Rothwell Gdns. Wood 61 D1
Rothwell Wlk. Caver 59 E1
Rotton Row Hill. Brad 81 F2
Roughgrove Copse. Binf 90 A1
Rounce La. West E 153 E3
Round Cl. Yate 149 F3
Round End. Newb 130 B3
Roundabout La. Woki 115 E4
Roundfield. Buck 107 D3
Roundhead Rd. Thea 83 E2
Roundway. Camb 152 B3
Roundway. Stai 96 B2
Roundway Cl. Camb 152 B3
Routh La. Read 84 C3
Row La. Caver 59 F4
Rowallan Cl. Caver 59 E3
Rowan Ave. Stai 96 B2
Rowan Cl. Woki 115 F3
Rowan Dr. Brac 143 E4
Rowan Dr. Crow 143 E3
Rowan Dr. Newb 105 D3
Rowan Dr. Wood 87 F4
Rowan Rd. Camb 151 F4
Rowan Way. Bur C 111 D3
Rowan Way. Slough 42 A4
Rowanhurst Dr. Far C 22 B4
Rowans Cl. Black 150 C1
Rowans The. Ashf 98 C2
Rowcroft Rd. Arbo 140 C4
Rowland Cl. Wind 66 B2
Rowland Way. Read 86 C1
Rowland Way. Stai 98 B1
Rowley Cl. Brac 118 C3
Rowley La. Sto P 23 E2
Rowley Rd. Read 86 A2
Roxburgh Cl. Camb 152 B2
Roxford Cl. Shepp 125 F2
Roxwell Cl. Slough 41 F3
Royal Ave. Read 84 B3
Roycroft La. Woki 141 F4
Royston Cl. Read 84 C4
Royston Way. Slough 41 E4
Ruby Cl. Slough 42 A2
Ruby Cl. Woki 115 F4
Rudd Hall Rise. Camb 151 F2
Ruddlesway. Wind 66 B3
Rudland Cl. That 106 B1
Rugby Cl. Sand 143 F1
Ruggles-Brise Rd. Ashf 97 E2
Rumsey's La. Blew 12 A4
Runnemede Rd. Eng G 96 A2
Runnymede Ct. Eng G 96 A2
Rupert Cl. Hen-O-T 15 F2
Rupert Rd. Newb 130 C4
Rupert St. Read 86 B4
Rupert's La. Hen-O-T 15 F2
Ruscombe Gdns. Datch 68 A4
Ruscombe La. Twyf 61 F3
Ruscombe Park. Twyf 61 F3
Ruscombe Rd. Twyf 61 F3
Ruscombe Way. Felt 98 C4
Rushall Cl. Read 113 F4
Rusham Park Ave. Eng G 95 F1
Rusham Rd. Eng G 95 F1
Rushbrook Rd. Wood 87 E4
Rushburn. Woo G 3 F3
Rushden Dr. Read 86 C1
Rushes The. Maid 40 A3
Rushes The. Mar 18 B4
Rushey Way. Read 87 E1
Rushington Ave. Maid 39 F3
Rushmoor Gdns. Bur C 84 A2
Ruskin Ave. Felt 71 F1
Ruskin Rd. Stai 96 C1
Ruskin Way. Woki 115 E3
Russell Ct. Maid 39 F4
Russell Dr. Stan 70 B1
Russell Rd. Maple 58 B4
Russell Rd. Newb 104 C1
Russell Rd. Shepp 125 E1
Russell St. Read 85 F4
Russell St. Wind 67 E3
Russell Way. Winn 88 A1
Russet Cl. Stan 69 F1
Russet Gdns. Camb 151 E2
Russet Glade. Bur C 111 D1
Russet Glade. Caver 59 E4
Russet Rd. Maid 39 E2
Russington Rd. Shepp 125 E2
Russley Green. Woki 116 A1
Rustington Cl. Read 87 D1
Ruston Way. Ascot 119 F4
Rutherford Wlk. Read 84 A4
Rutherwyk Rd. Chert 123 F1
Rutland Pl. Maid 39 E3
Rutland Rd. Maid 39 E3
Rutland Rd. Read 85 E4
Ruxbury Rd. Chert 123 E2
Ryan Mount. Sand 150 A4
Ryans Mount. Mar 1 B1
Rycroft. Wind 66 C2
Rydal Ave. Read 57 F1
Rydal Cl. Camb 152 B3
Rydal Dr. That 106 A2
Rydal Pl. Light 153 D4
Rydal Way. Stai 96 A1
Ryde The. Stai 124 A4
Rydings. Wind 66 C2
Rye Cl. Maid 39 D2
Rye Ct. Slough 43 D2
Rye Gr. Light 146 C1
Ryecroft Cl. Warg 36 C1
Ryecroft Cl. Wood 60 C1
Ryecroft Gdns. Black 150 C2
Ryehurst La. Binf 90 C3
Ryeish La. Shin 113 E2
Ryemead La. Wink 92 B3
Ryhill Way. Read 113 F4
Ryland Cl. Felt 98 C2
Rylstone Cl. Maid 39 E2
Rylstone Rd. Read 85 E4
Ryvers Rd. Slough 43 F2
Ryves Ave. Yate 149 D3

Sackville St. Read 86 A4
Saddleback Rd. Camb 151 F4
Saddlewood. Camb 151 E2
Sadlers Ct. Woki 88 B1
Sadler's La. Woki 115 E4
Sadlers Rd. Ink 127 D3
Saffron Cl. Datch 68 A3
Saffron Cl. Newb 104 C2
Saffron Cl. Read 87 E2
Saffron Rd. Brac 118 A3
Sage Cl. Read 87 D1
Sage Rd. Sulh 57 E2
Sagecroft Rd. That 106 B3
St. Mary's Gdns. Bags 145 F2
St. Mary's Rd. Newb 105 D2
St Adrian's Cl. Maid 39 D2
St Agnes Terr. Lamb 25 D1
St Albans St. Wind 67 E3
St Andrews. Brac 117 F2
St Andrew's Ave. Wind 66 C3
St Andrew's Cl. Old W 68 A1
St Andrew's Cl. Shepp 125 E3
St Andrew's Cl. Wray 68 C1
St Andrew's Cres. Wind 66 C3
St Andrew's Rd. Caver 58 C2
St Andrew's Rd. Hen-O-T 35 E4
St Andrew's Way. Slough 41 E3
St Annes Ave. Stan 97 E4
St Anne's Cl. Hen-O-T 15 E1
St Annes Glade. Bags 145 E2
St Anne's Rd. Caver 59 D1
St Ann's Cl. Chert 123 F2
St Ann's Hill Rd. Chert 123 E2
St Ann's Rd. Chert 123 F2
St Anthonys Cl. Brac 118 A4

St Anthony's Way. Harm 71 F2
St Barnabas Rd. Caver 59 D3
St Barnabas Rd. Read 86 C1
St Bartholomews Rd. Read 86 C4
St Bernards Rd. Slough 43 E2
St Birinus Rd. Read 84 B3
St Catherine's Cl. Woki 88 A1
Saint Catherine's Hill. Silc 136 C3
St Catherines Rd. Camb 151 F1
St Chad's Rd. Maid 39 D2
St Christophers Gdns. Burl 119 E4
St Clements Cl. Wood 87 E1
St Columba's Cl. Maid 39 D2
St David's Cl. Caver 58 C3
St David's Cl. Maid 39 D2
St David's Rd. Newb 104 C1
St Donats Pl. Newb 105 D1
St Dunstan's Rd. Felt 98 C3
St Edward's Rd. Read 87 D3
St Elizabeth Cl. Read 113 D4
St Elmo Cres. Far C 22 B1
St George's Ave. Newb 104 C1
St George's Cl. Wind 66 C3
St George's Cres. Slough 41 E3
St George's La. Ascot 120 A3
St Georges Rd. Camb 151 E3
St George's Rd. Read 85 E4
St George's Terr. Read 85 D4
St Giles Cl. Read 86 A3
St Helens Cres. Sand 150 A4
St Helier Cl. Woki 116 A2
St Hilda's Ave. Ashf 97 F2
St Ives Cl. Thea 83 E1
St Ives Rd. Maid 40 A4
St James Cl. Pangb 56 B3
St James Cl. Twyf 61 F3
St James Rd. Woki 141 F4
St James Wlk. Iver 44 C2
St Johns Ct. Eng G 96 A2
St Johns Dr. Wind 67 D3
St John's Hill. Read 86 B4
St John's Rd. Ascot 92 C1
St John's Rd. Caver 59 E1
St John's Rd. Mort 137 D3
St John's Rd. Newb 105 D1
St John's Rd. Read 86 B4
St John's Rd. Sand 150 B4
St Johns Rd. Slough 43 D3
St John's Rd. That 106 B2
St Johns Rd. Wind 67 D3
St John's St. Read 86 B4
St Jude's Cl. Eng G 95 E2
St Jude's Rd. Eng G 95 E2
St Katherine's Rd. Hen-O-T 35 E4
St Laurence Way. Slough 43 D2
St Leonard's Ave. Wind 67 E3
St Leonard's Hill. Wind 66 C2
St Leonards Rd. Wind 66 B1
St Leonard's Rd. Wind 67 E2
St Leonards Wlk. Iver 44 C2
St Luke's Rd. Maid 39 F4
St Luke's Rd. Old W 68 A1
St Margarets Ave. Ashf 98 A2
St Margaret's Rd. Maid 39 D4
St Mark's Cl. Brad 83 D3
St Marks Cl. That 106 B2
St Marks Cres. Maid 39 D4
St Mark's Pl. Wind 67 E3
St Marks Rd. Binf 90 B1
St Mark's Rd. Binf 117 E4
St Mark's Rd. Hen-O-T 35 E4
St Mark's Rd. Maid 39 E4
St Mark's Rd. Wind 67 E3
St Martins Cl. Wood 87 E1
St Martin's Ct. Stai 97 E2
St Mary's Ave. Purl 57 E3
St Mary's Ave. Stan 97 E4
St Mary's Butts. Read 86 A4
St Mary's Cl. Hen-O-T 35 D4
St Mary's Cl. Maid 40 A4
St Marys Cl. Sand 150 B4
St Mary's Cl. Stan 97 E4
St Mary's Cres. Stan 97 E4
St Mary's Dr. Felt 98 B4
St Mary's Gdns. Bags 145 F2
St Mary's Hill. Ascot 120 B2
St Marys La. Wink 92 B3
St Mary's Rd. Ascot 120 A2
St Mary's Rd. Camb 151 E3
St Mary's Rd. Mort 137 D3
St Mary's Rd. Newb 105 D2
St Mary's Rd. Slough 43 E2
St Mary's Rd. Woki 88 A1
St Mary's Way. Bur C 111 D2
St Mary's Wlk. Maid 39 F4
St Michael's Ct. Slough 21 E1
St Michaels Rd. Camb 151 D3
St Michael's Rd. Newb 104 C1
St Michael's Rd. Read 84 B4
St Michael's Rd. Sand 149 F4
St Micheals Rd. Ashf 98 A2
St Nazaire Cl. Stai 96 B2
St Nicholas Dr. Shepp 125 D1
St Nicholas' Rd. Newb 104 C1
St Olave's Cl. Stai 96 C1
St Patrick's Ave. Char 61 D3
St Patrick's Cl. Maid 39 D2
St Pauls Ave. Slough 43 D3
St Paul's Cl. Ashf 98 B2
St Paul's Ct. Read 86 A3
St Paul's Gate. Woki 116 A3
St Paul's Rd. Stai 96 B1
St Peter St. Mar 1 C1
St Peter's Ave. Caver 58 C2
St Peter's Cl. Burn 21 D1
St Peter's Cl. Old W 68 A1
St Peter's Cl. Stai 96 C1
St Peter's Gdns. Yate 149 E3
St Peter's Hill. Caver 58 C2
St Peter's Rd. Maid 19 E1
St Peter's Rd. Read 87 D3
St Pinnock Ave. Stai 124 A4
St Ronan's Rd. Read 85 D4
St Saviour's Rd. Read 85 F3
St Stephens Cl. Caver 59 D1
St Swithins Cl. Wick 75 E2
St Theresa's Rd. Harm 71 F2
St Thomas Ct. That 106 C2
Saint-Cloud Way. Maid 40 A4
Salamanca. Finch 142 C3
Salcombe Dr. Read 87 D2
Salcombe Rd. Ashf 97 F3
Salcombe Rd. Newb 104 C1
Salcombe Rd. Read 86 B2
Sale Garden Cotts. Woki 116 B3
Saleby Cl. Winn 87 F1
Salford Cl. Read 113 E4
Salisbury Ave. Slough 42 B4
Salisbury Cl. Woki 116 A1
Salisbury Rd. Harm 71 E1
Salisbury Rd. Hung 100 B2
Salisbury Rd. Read 85 F4
Salisbury Rd. Sand 150 B3
Salmon Cl. Shin 113 D1
Salmond Rd. Read 113 E3
Salt Hill Ave. Slough 42 B3
Salt Hill Dr. Slough 42 B3
Salt Hill Way. Slough 42 B3
Salters' Rd. Maid 40 A4
Saltersgate Cl. Winn 87 E1
Salwey Cl. Brac 118 A2
Samarkand Cl. Camb 152 A2
Sampage Cl. Read 113 E3
Sampsons Green. Slough 21 F1
Sanctuary Cl. Read 84 C4
Sanctuary Rd. Stan 71 D1
Sandcroft Rd. Caver 58 C3
Sandell's Ave. Ashf 98 B2
Sanden Cl. Hung 100 B3
Sandford Down. Brac 118 C2
Sandford Dr. Wood 60 C1
Sandford La. Hurst 88 B3
Sandgate Ave. Read 57 F1
Sandhills Ct. Vir W 122 C2
Sandhills La. Vir W 122 C2
Sandhills Way. Read 84 C2
Sandhurst La. Black 150 A3
Sandhurst Rd. Brac 142 A4
Sandhurst Rd. Crow 143 D2
Sandhurst Rd. Yate 149 F4
Sandisplatt Rd. Maid 39 D3
Sandleford Cl. Read 113 E3
Sandleford Rise. Newb 131 D4
Sandlers End. Slough 22 A1
Sandown Ave. Read 84 A2
Sandown Cl. Black 150 B3
Sandown Dr. Camb 151 F1
Sandown Rd. Slough 41 F4
Sandown Way. Newb 105 E1
Sandpit Hill. Newb 130 B2
Sandpit La. Swal 140 A3
Sandringham Ct. Slough 41 E4
Sandringham Dr. Ashf 97 E2
Sandringham Rd. Maid 19 F1
Sandringham Rd. Stan 70 C1
Sandringham Way. Read 84 A2
Sands Farm Dr. Burn 21 E1
Sandstone Cl. Winn 88 B1
Sandy Cl. Herm 79 D2
Sandy Dr. Felt 98 C4
Sandy La. Brac 118 B4
Sandy La. Camb 151 F3
Sandy La. Herm 78 C2
Sandy La. Sand 143 D1
Sandy La. Sunn 121 D2
Sandy La. Vir W 122 C3
Sandy La. Woki 115 E2
Sandy Mead. Holy 40 B1
Sandy Way. Shepp 125 F1
Sandygate Cl. Mar 1 B2
Sandygate Rd. Mar 1 B2
Sapgood Cl. That 106 C1
Sapphire Cl. Woki 115 F4
Sarsby Dr. Wray 96 A3
Sarum. Brac 117 F1
Sarum Cres. Woki 116 B4
Sarum Rd. Tad 135 D1
Sarum Way. Hung 100 B2
Saturn Cl. Woki 115 F3
Saunton Ave. Harl 71 F4
Savernake Cl. Read 84 C4
Savernake Way. Brac 118 C2
Savill Way. Mar 1 C1
Saville Cres. Ashf 98 B1
Saville Gdns. Camb 152 A3
Savory Wlk. Binf 90 B1
Savoy Gr. Black 150 B2
Sawmill Rd. Herm 79 D2
Sawpit Rd. Hurst 88 C4
Sawtry Cl. Winn 87 F1
Sawyers Cl. Whi Wa 39 D1
Sawyer's Cl. Wind 66 C4
Sawyers Cres. Whi Wa 39 D1
Saxe Cl. Bur C 111 D2
Saxon Cl. Slough 43 F2
Saxon Gdns. Tapl 20 B1
Saxon Rd. Ashf 98 B1
Saxon Way. Harm 70 B4
Saxon Way. Old W 68 A1
Sayers Cl. Gree 131 D4
Scafell Cl. Read 57 E1
Scafell Rd. Slough 41 F4
Scampton Rd. Stan 70 C1
Scarborough Rd. Stan 71 E1
Scarborough Way. Slough 42 A2
Scholars Cl. Caver 58 C2
School Green. Shin 113 F2
School Hill. Crow 143 E2
School Hill. Sand 143 D1
School Hill. Warg 36 B1
School La. Bags 145 F1
School La. Box 76 C2
School La. Bur C 111 D1
School La. Caver 59 D1
School La. Caver 59 D3
School La. Cook 20 A4
School La. Cook 19 D4
School La. East G 47 E3
School La. Eng G 96 A2
School La. Frox 99 D1
School La. Lit M 2 B3
School La. Maid 19 F1
School La. Medm 17 D3
School La. Padw 109 F1
School La. Shepp 125 D2
School La. Sto P 23 D2
School La. Warg 36 B1
School La. Windl 146 B2
School La. Yate 149 D3
School Rd. Ascot 120 B2
School Rd. Ashf 98 A1
School Rd. Bark 114 C1
School Rd. Bis 153 F2
School Rd. Bur C 111 E3
School Rd. Chiev 78 A4
School Rd. Comp 31 F2
School Rd. Harm 70 B4
School Rd. Hurst 88 C4
School Rd. Read 84 B4
School Rd. Read 114 C1
School Rd. Swal 139 F2
School Rd. Windl 146 A3
School Rd. Woki 116 B3
School Rd. Woo G 3 F3
School Terr. Read 86 C4
Schroder Ct. Eng G 95 D2
Scotland Hill. Sand 143 D1
Scotlands Dr. Far C 22 A3
Scots Cl. Stan 97 E4
Scots Dr. Woki 115 F4
Scott Cl. Caver 59 D3
Scott Cl. Far C 22 B4
Scott Cl. Wood 88 A4
Scott Terr. Brac 118 C4
Scottalls La. Hamp N 52 C3
Scott's Ave. Ashf 98 C1
Scott's Way. Ashf 97 C1
Scours La. Read 58 A1
Scratchface La. Brad 81 F3
Scrivens Mead. That 106 C2
Scylla Cres. Felt 98 A4
Scylla Rd. Felt 71 D1
Seacourt Rd. Slough 44 A1
Seaford Gdns. Wood 87 F3
Seaford Rd. Stan 70 B1
Seaford Rd. Woki 116 B3
Sealand Rd. Stan 71 D1
Searles Farm La. Bur C 85 D1
Seaton Dr. Ashf 97 F3
Seaton Gdns. Read 86 B1
Seaton Rd. Camb 151 D3
Second Cres. Slough 42 B4
Sedgefield Rd. Newb 131 E4
Sedgmoor Gdns. Fla H 3 D4
Sedgmoor La. Fla H 3 D4
Sedgmoor Rd. Fla H 3 D4
Sefton Cl. Sto P 22 C2
Sefton Cl. West E 153 F3
Sefton Paddock. Sto P 23 D3
Segsbury Gr. Brac 118 C3
Selborne Gdns. Read 58 A1
Selbourne Cl. Black 150 B3
Selby Rd. Ashf 98 B1
Selcourt Cl. Wood 87 E4
Sellafield Way. Read 87 E1
Selsdon Ave. Wood 87 F4
Selsey Way. Read 114 A4
Selwood Cl. Stan 70 B1
Selwood Gdns. Stan 70 B1
Selwyn Dr. Yate 149 D3
Send Rd. Caver 59 E1
Setley Way. Brac 119 D3
Seton Dr. Read 84 C3
Sett The. Yate 149 D3
Sevenoaks Rd. Read 87 D2
Severn Cl. Sand 150 B4
Severn Cl. That 106 A3
Severn Cres. Slough 69 D4
Severn Way. Read 84 C3
Sewell Ave. Woki 116 A4
Sewell Cl. Cold A 79 D1
Seymour Ave. Shin 113 F3
Seymour Cl. Maid 39 D2
Seymour Court Rd. Mar 1 B2
Seymour Court Rd. Mar B 1 B2
Seymour Ct La. Mar B 1 A3
Seymour Park Rd. Mar 1 B2
Seymour Plain. Mar 1 B3
Seymour Plain. Mar B 1 B3
Seymour Rd. Slough 42 B2
Seymour Way. Ashf 98 C1
Shackleton Rd. Slough 42 C3
Shackleton Way. Wood 88 A4
Shaftesbury Cres. Stai 97 E1
Shaftesbury Mount. Black 150 B2
Shaftesbury Rd. Bis 153 F2
Shaftesbury Rd. Read 85 D4
Shaftsbury Cl. Brac 118 B2
Shaggy Calf La. Slough 43 F4
Shakespeare Cl. Caver 59 E3
Shakespeare Rd. That 106 B2
Shalbourne Cl. Hung 100 A3
Shalbourne Rise. Camb 151 E3
Sharney Ave. Slough 44 A2
Sharnwood Dr. Read 84 C3
Sharpethorpe Cl. Read 87 D1
Shaw Hill. Newb 105 D3
Shaw Park. Crow 143 D2
Shaw Rd. Newb 105 D2
Shaw Rd. Read 85 F3
Shaw The. Cook 19 F3
Sheehy Way. Slough 43 D3
Sheep Leaze La. Pease 29 E1
Sheep Wlk. Caver 59 D2
Sheepcote La. Bou E 3 F1
Sheepcote La. Holy 64 B2
Sheepcote Rd. Eton 42 A1
Sheepcote Rd. Wind 66 C3
Sheepdrove Rd. Lamb 25 E2
Sheephouse Rd. Maid 20 A1
Sheephouse Way. Chadd 49 D3
Sheepridge La. Bou E 2 C4
Sheepridge La. Fla H 2 C4
Sheepwalk. Shepp 124 C2
Sheepwalk. Stai 124 C2
Sheepwash. Newt 131 D1
Sheepways La. Maple 58 A4
Sheerlands Rd. Arbo 140 C4
Sheerlands Rd. Bark 140 C4
Sheet St. Wind 67 E3
Sheet Street Rd. Old W 94 A4
Sheet Street Rd. Wind 94 A4
Sheet Street Rd. Wind 67 E1
Sheffield Rd. Harm 71 E1
Sheffield Way. Harm 71 E1
Shefford Cres. Woki 116 B4
Sheldon Gdns. Read 86 B1
Shelgate Wlk. Wood 87 E4
Shelley Ave. Brac 118 C4
Shelley Cl. Slough 43 F1
Shelley Cl. Wood 87 F2
Shelley Rd. Mar 1 C2
Shelley Rd. That 106 B2
Shelley Walk. Yate 149 D3
Shelson Ave. Felt 98 C2
Shelton Ct. Slough 43 E2
Shenstone Cl. Woki 142 A4
Shenstone Dr. Burn 21 E1
Shenstone Park. Ascot 120 C3
Shenstone Rd. Read 86 A2
Shephards La. Brac 91 D1
Shephards Way. Finch 142 C3
Shepherds Ave. Read 87 D4
Shepherds Chase. Bags 145 F1
Shepherds Cl. Hurl 17 F2
Shepherds Cl. Shepp 125 D2
Shepherds Hill. Brac 118 B4
Shepherds Hill. Comp 31 F2
Shepherds Hill. Wood 87 E4
Shepherd's House La. Read 87 D4
Shepherds La. Caver 58 B3
Shepherds La. Hurl 17 F2
Shepherds Mount. Comp 31 F2
Shepherds Rise. Comp 31 F2
Shepherds Wlk. Wood 87 E4
Shepley Dr. Read 85 E2
Shepley Dr. Went 121 E2
Shepley End. Went 121 E2
Shepperton Court Dr. Shepp 125 D2
Shepperton Rd. Stai 124 B3
Sheraton Cl. Black 150 C2
Sheraton Dr. Read 57 E1
Sherborne Cl. Stan 69 F3
Sherborne Rd. Felt 98 B4
Sherbourne Dr. Went 121 E2
Sherbourne Dr. Wind 66 C2
Sherbourne Dr. Wood 87 F4
Sherbourne Wlk. Far C 22 B4
Shergold Way. Cook 19 F3
Sheridan Ave. Caver 59 D2
Sheridan Cres. Tad 134 C1
Sheridan Way. Woki 115 F3
Sherman Rd. Read 86 A3
Sherman Rd. Slough 42 C4
Sherrardmead. Newb 105 D3
Sherring Cl. Brac 91 E1
Sherwood Cl. Brac 119 D4
Sherwood Cl. Slough 43 F2
Sherwood Dr. Maid 39 D3
Sherwood Gdns. Hen-O-T 35 E4
Sherwood Rd. Winn 88 B1
Sherwood St. Read 85 E4
Shield Rd. Felt 98 B2
Shifford Cres. Maid 19 F2
Shildon Cl. Camb 152 B2
Shinfield Rd. Read 86 C2
Shinfield Rise. Read 86 C1
Shipley Cl. Wood 61 D1
Shipton Cl. Read 57 E1
Shire Cl. Bags 145 F1
Shire's Head Cl. Read 85 E3
Shires The. Woki 115 F2
Shires Way. Yate 149 E4
Shirley Ave. Read 113 E4
Shirley Ave. Wind 66 C3
Shirley Rd. Maid 39 E3
Sholto Rd. Stan 97 F3
Shooter's Hill. Pangb 56 A3
Shop La. Leckh 49 F3
Shop La. Newb 104 C3
Shoppenhanger's Rd. Maid 39 F2
Shoreham Rd (E). Stan 70 C1
Shoreham Rd (W). Stan 70 C1
Short La. Stan 97 F4
Short Rd. Stan 70 C1
Short St. Caver 59 D1
Short St. Pangb 56 B3
Short St. Read 86 A3
Short The. Purl 57 E3
Shortfern. Slough 43 E4
Shortheath La. Sulhd 110 C2
Shortland. Harl 71 E4
Shortlands Hill. Moul 13 E2
Shortwood Ave. Ashf 97 D2
Shrewsbury Rd. Harm 71 E1
Shrivenham Cl. Sand 150 B4
Shrubbs Hill La. Went 121 E2
Shrubland Dr. Read 85 D2
Shrublands Dr. Light 153 D4
Shute End. Woki 116 A3
Shyshack La. Tad 134 C1
Sibley Park Rd. Read 87 D1
Sibson. Read 87 E1
Sidbury Cl. Sunn 121 D2
Sidestrand Rd. Newb 130 C4
Sidmouth Grange Cl. Read 87 D4
Sidmouth Grange Rd. Read 87 D4
Sidmouth St. Read 86 B4
Sidney Rd. Stai 97 D2
Silbury Cl. Bur C 84 A2
Silchester Rd. Read 85 E2
Silchester Rd. Tad 135 E1
Silco Dr. Maid 39 F3
Silver Birches. Woki 115 E2
Silver Cl. Maid 39 D3
Silver Dr. Camb 152 B2
Silver Fox Cres. Wood 87 E3
Silver Hill. Sand 150 C4
Silver La. Padw 136 A4
Silver St. Read 86 A3
Silverdale Rd. Read 87 E2
Silverdale Rd. Tad 135 D1
Silverdale Rd. Warg 36 C1
Silverglades. Yate 149 E2
Silverthorne Dr. Caver 58 C3
Silvertrees Dr. Maid 39 D3
Silverwood Dr. Camb 152 A4
Silwood. Brac 117 F1
Silwood Cl. Ascot 120 B4
Silwood Rd. Sunn 120 C3
Simkins Cl. Burl 92 A1
Simmonds Cl. Brac 117 F4
Simmonds St. Read 86 A4
Simmons Cl. Slough 44 A1
Simmons Rd. Hen-O-T 15 E2
Simms Farm La. Silc 136 C3
Simons Cl. Purl 57 E2
Simon's La. Woki 115 E4
Simons Wlk. Eng G 95 E1
Simpson Cl. Maid 40 A4
Sindlesham Rd. Arbo 114 C2
Singer La. Hen-O-T 15 F1
Singers Cl. Hen-O-T 35 F4
Sinhurst Rd. Camb 151 D2
Sipson Cl. Harm 71 D4
Sipson La. Harl 71 D4
Sipson Rd. Harm 71 D4
Sipson Way. Harm 71 D4
Sirius Cl. Woki 115 F3
Six Acre La. Ham 126 A3
Skeffling Cl. Winn 87 F1
Skelmerdale Way. Winn 87 F2
Skerrit Way. Read 57 E2
Skillman Dr. That 106 C2
Skilton Rd. Read 57 E2
Skimpedhill La. Brac 118 A4
Skinners Green La. Ham M 130 A4
Skippons Cl. Newb 130 B3
Skydmore Path. Slough 21 F1
Skye Cl. Read 84 C2
Skyes Dr. Stai 97 D2
Skylings. Newb 105 E2
Skyport Dr. Harm 70 B4
Slaidburn Green. Brac 118 C1
Slanting Hill. Herm 79 D3
Sloan Ct. Gori 34 B3
Slopes The. Caver 59 E1
Slough Rd. Datch 68 A4
Slough Rd. Eton 42 C1
Slough Rd. Slough 42 C1
Smallmead Rd. Bur C 85 E1
Smallmead Rd. Read 86 A1
Smith Sq. Brac 118 B4
Smitham Bridge Rd. Hung 100 B3
Smithfield Cl. Whi Wa 39 D2
Smithfield Rd. Maid 39 D2
Smith's Hill. Let B 6 C3
Smith's La. Wind 66 C3
Smithy's Green. Windl 146 B2
Snape Spur. Slough 42 C4
Snipe La. Newt 131 F1
Snowball Hill. Whi Wa 64 A4
Snowberry Cl. Woki 115 F3
Snowden Cl. Wind 66 B2
Snowden Dr. Read 84 A3
Snowdon Cl. That 106 B1
Snowdon Rd. Harm 71 E1
Snowdon Rd W. Harm 71 E1
Snowdrop Gr. Winn 88 B2
Snow's Paddock. Windl 146 A4
Snows Ride. Windl 146 A3
Soham Cl. Winn 114 B4
Soho Cres. Bou E 3 E2
Soke Rd. Alde 135 F2
Soke Rd. Silc 135 F2
Soldiers Rise. Brac 142 B4
Solent Rd. Stan 70 C1
Somerford Cl. Maid 40 A4
Somersby Cres. Maid 39 F2
Somerset Cl. Hung 100 B3
Somerset Cl. Woki 115 E3
Somerset Way. Iver 44 C2
Somerset Wlk. Read 84 A3
Somerton Gdns. Read 87 D1
Somerton Gr. That 106 B1
Somerville Cres. Yate 149 F3
Somerville Gr. Woki 115 E2
Somerville Rd. Eton 42 B1
Sonning La. Sonn 60 B1
Sonning Meadows. Sonn 60 B1
Sonninge Cl. Sand 150 B4
Sopwith Cl. Wood 88 A4
Sorrel Cl. Bur C 111 D2
Sorrel Cl. Newb 105 E3
Sorrel Dr. Light 152 C4

Sospel Ct. Far C 22 B2
South Ave. Hen-O-T 35 F4
South Ave. Stai 96 B1
South Cl. Medm 17 E4
South Cl. Slough 41 E3
South Cl. Woki 116 B2
South Dr. Read 86 C1
South Dr. Sulhd 110 B4
South Dr. Went 122 A1
South Dr. Woki 116 B3
South End Rd. Brad 82 A1
South Field Cl. Dorn 41 E2
South Gate Ave. Felt 98 B2
South Gr. Chert 123 F2
South Green. Slough 42 C3
South Hill Rd. Brac 118 A2
South Lake. Wood 87 F3
South Lynn Cres. Brac 118 A2
South Meadow. Crow 143 E2
South Meadow La. Eton 67 E4
South Path. Wind 67 E3
South Pl. Mar 117 F3
South Rd. Bis 153 F2
South Rd. Crow 143 F2
South Rd. Eng G 95 E1
South Rd. Maid 39 F3
South Row. Chil 10 B4
South St. Blew 12 A4
South St. Caver 59 D1
South St. Read 86 B4
South St. Stai 96 C2
South View. Hung 100 B3
South View Ave. Caver 59 E1
South View Park. Caver 59 E1
Southampton Cl. Black 150 B3
Southampton Rd. Stan 70 C1
Southampton St. Read 86 A3
Southampton Way. Stan 70 C1
Southbourne Dr. Bou E 3 D2
Southcote Ave. Felt 98 C3
Southcote Dr. Camb 152 A3
Southcote Farm La. Read 85 E2
Southcote La. Read 85 E2
Southcote Rd. Read 85 E3
Southcroft. Slough 22 A1
Southdown Rd. Caver 59 D3
Southdown Rd. Tad 135 D1
Southdown Rd. That 105 F2
Southend. That 106 B3
Southern Hill. Read 86 B3
Southern Perimeter Rd. Harm 71 E1
Southern Perimeter Rd. Stan 70 B1
Southern Rd. Camb 151 E3
Southerndene Cl. Read 57 E1
Southfield Gdns. Burn 41 D4
Southfields Ave. Ashf 98 A1
Southlands Cl. Woki 116 B3
Southlands Rd. Woki 116 B2
Southlea Rd. Datch 68 A3
Southside. Chert 124 A3
Southview Cl. Twyf 61 F3
Southview Rd. Mar 1 C2
Southville Cl. Felt 98 C4
Southville Cres. Felt 98 C4
Southville Rd. Felt 98 C4
Southwark Cl. Yate 149 E3
Southwell Park Rd. Camb 151 E3
Southwick. Bags 145 F1
Southwick Ct. Brac 118 C2
Southwold. Brac 117 F1
Southwold Cl. Winn 87 E1
Southwood. Woki 116 B2
Southwood Gdns. Bur C 111 D2
Southwood Gdns. Cook 19 F3
Southwood Rd. Cook 19 F3
Spackman Cl. That 106 B1
Spackmans Way. Slough 42 B2
Spade Oak Meadows. Bou E 2 C2
Span Hill. Caver 60 B4
Sparrow Cl. Woki 115 F3
Sparrowbill. Brig 28 C1
Sparvell Way. Camb 151 E3
Speen Hill Cl. Newb 104 C2
Speen La. Newb 104 B2
Speen Lodge Ct. Newb 104 C2
Speen Pl. Newb 104 C2
Spelthorne Gr. Stai 98 C1
Spelthorne La. Stai 125 E4
Spencer Cl. Silc 135 F1
Spencer Cl. Woki 115 E3
Spencer Gdns. Eng G 95 E2
Spencer Rd. Brac 117 F4
Spencer Rd. Newb 130 B3
Spencer Rd. Read 113 D4
Spencer Rd. Slough 43 F2
Spencers Cl. Maid 39 E4
Spencers La. Cook 19 F3
Spencers Rd. Maid 39 E4
Spenwood Cl. Shin 113 D1
Sperling Rd. Maid 19 F1
Spey Rd. Read 85 D4
Spinfield La. Mar 1 A1
Spinfield La W. Mar 1 B1
Spinfield Mount. Mar 1 A1
Spinfield Park. Mar 1 B1
Spinis. Brac 117 F1
Spinner Green. Brac 118 A2
Spinners Wlk. Mar 1 B1
Spinners Wlk. Wind 67 E3
Spinney. Slough 42 A3
Spinney Cl. Caver 59 D4
Spinney Dr. Felt 98 B4
Spinney The. Camb 152 B3
Spinney The. Read 84 C2
Spinney The. Sunn 120 C2
Spinney The. Woki 141 F4
Spinney The. Yate 149 E4
Spinningwheel La. Binf 90 B4
Spitfire Way. Wood 88 A4
Spittal St. Mar 1 B1
Spode Cl. Read 84 C4
Spout La. Stan 70 A2
Spout La N. Stan 70 A2
Spray La. Brig 28 B1
Spray Rd. Ham 126 C2
Spray Rd. Ink 127 D2
Spriggs Cl. That 106 B1
Spring Ave. Eng G 95 F1
Spring Cl. Maid 19 F1
Spring Cl. Pangb 55 E3
Spring Gdns. Ascot 120 A3
Spring Gdns. Bou E 3 D2
Spring Gdns. Burl 92 C1
Spring Gdns. Camb 152 A3
Spring Gdns. Mar 1 C2
Spring Gdns. Shin 113 D1
Spring Gdns. Woo G 3 F4
Spring Gr. Read 86 A3
Spring Hill. Maid 39 F2
Spring La. Alde 135 E4
Spring La. Ast T 12 C4
Spring La. Caver 60 A3
Spring La. Cold A 106 B4
Spring La. Cook 19 E3
Spring La. Far C 22 B3
Spring La. Mort 137 D3
Spring La. Slough 41 F3
Spring La. Swal 139 D2
Spring Meadow. Brac 118 B4
Spring Meadows. Gr She 48 A2
Spring Rd. Felt 98 C3
Spring Rise. Eng G 95 F1
Spring Wlk. Warg 36 B1
Spring Wood La. Bur C 111 D1
Spring Woods. Sand 143 E1
Spring Woods. Vir W 122 A3
Springate Field. Slough 43 F2
Springcross Ave. Black 150 B2
Springdale. Read 87 D1
Springdale. Woki 141 F4
Springfield. Light 153 E4
Springfield Cl. Wind 67 D3
Springfield End. Gori 34 B4
Springfield Gr. Shepp 125 F4
Springfield La. Newb 131 D4
Springfield Park. Holy 40 B1
Springfield Park. Twyf 61 F2
Springfield Rd. Ashf 97 F2
Springfield Rd. Binf 117 E4
Springfield Rd. Camb 152 A3
Springfield Rd. Silc 135 F1
Springfield Rd. Slough 69 D4
Springfield Rd. Wind 67 D3
Springhill Rd. Gori 34 B4
Spruce Dr. Light 153 D4
Spruce Rd. Wood 88 A3
Spur The. Slough 41 E4
Spur The. Warg 36 C2
Spurcroft Rd. That 106 C1
Square The. Bags 145 F2
Square The. Camb 151 E3
Square The. Harm 70 C4
Square The. Pangb 56 B3
Square The. Shin 113 D1
Squire's Bridge Rd. Stai 124 C3
Squires Rd. Stai 125 D3
Squires Wlk. Ashf 98 B1
Squirrel Cl. Sand 150 A4
Squirrel Rise. Mar B 1 B3
Squirrels Drey. Crow 142 C3
Squirrels Way. Read 87 D1
Stable Cl. Bur C 111 D2
Stable Croft. Bags 145 E1
Stable Ct. Newb 105 D3
Stable View. Yate 149 E4
Stables Ct. Mar 1 A1
Staddlestone Cl. Read 57 E1
Stadium Way. Read 58 A1
Staff College Rd. Camb 151 D3
Staff College Rd. Sand 151 D3
Stafferton Way. Maid 40 A3
Stafford Ave. Slough 22 B1
Stafford Cl. Burn 41 D4
Stafford Cl. Wood 87 F4
Stafford Lake. Bis 153 F1
Staffordshire Cl. Read 57 F1
Stag Hill. Chil F 73 D1
Stainash Cres. Stai 97 D2
Staines By-Pass. Stai 97 E2
Staines La. Chert 124 A2
Staines Lane Cl. Chert 123 F2
Staines Rd. Felt 98 B4
Staines Rd. Stai 123 F2
Staines Rd. Wray 95 F4
Staines Rd W. Ashf 98 B1
Stainford Cl. Ashf 98 B2
Stamford Ave. Camb 151 F1
Stamford Rd. Maid 39 E3
Stanfield. Tad 135 D1
Stanham Rd. Read 84 C4
Stanhope Heath. Stan 70 B1
Stanhope Rd. Read 86 B2
Stanhope Rd. Sand 150 C2
Stanhope Rd. Slough 41 E4
Stanhope Way. Stan 70 B1
Stanlake La. Twyf 61 F2
Stanley Cl. Mar 1 C2
Stanley Cotts. Slough 42 C3
Stanley Gr. Read 85 F4
Stanley Green E. Slough 43 F1
Stanley Green W. Slough 43 F1
Stanley Rd. Ashf 97 F2
Stanley Rd. Newb 105 D1
Stanley Rd. Woki 116 C3
Stanley St. Read 85 F4
Stanmore Cl. Ascot 120 A3
Stanmore Gdns. Mort 136 C3
Stanmore Rd. Beed 30 B1
Stanmore Rd. East I 30 C4
Stanshawe Rd. Read 86 A4
Stanstead Rd. Stan 70 C1
Stanton Cl. Read 87 E2
Stanton Way. Slough 43 F1
Stanwell Cl. Stan 70 B1
Stanwell Gdns. Stan 70 B1
Stanwell Moor Rd. Harm 70 A2
Stanwell Moor Rd. Stan 70 A2
Stanwell Moor Rd. Stan 97 D4
Stanwell Rd. Ashf 97 F2
Stanwell Rd. Felt 98 A4
Stanwell Rd. Felt 71 D1
Stanwell Rd. Hort 69 E2
Stanwell Rd. Stan 69 E2
Stapleford Rd. Read 85 E2
Staplehurst. Brac 117 F1
Stapleton Cl. Mar 1 C2
Stapleton Cl. Newb 130 B3
Star La. Know H 37 F2
Star La. Read 86 A4
Star Post Rd. Camb 151 F4
Star Rd. Caver 59 E1
Starling Cl. Woki 115 F3
Starlings Dr. Read 84 A3
Starmead Dr. Woki 116 C3
Starting Gates. Newb 105 E1
Startins La. Cook 19 E4
Starwood Ct. Slough 43 E2
Statham Ct. Brac 117 F4
Station App. Ashf 97 F2
Station App. Mar 1 C1
Station App. Read 86 A4
Station App. Shepp 125 E2
Station App. Stai 97 D2
Station App. Vir W 122 B3
Station Cres. Ashf 97 F2
Station Hill. Ascot 120 A3
Station Hill. Cook 19 F4
Station Hill. Read 86 A4
Station Par. Vir W 122 B3
Station Rd. Ashf 97 F2
Station Rd. Bags 145 F2
Station Rd. Ball H 130 A2
Station Rd. Bou E 3 D2
Station Rd. Brac 118 A4
Station Rd. Camb 151 E1
Station Rd. Chert 124 A1
Station Rd. Cook 19 F4
Station Rd. East G 47 E3
Station Rd. Eng G 96 A2
Station Rd. Gori 34 B3
Station Rd. Gr She 48 A2
Station Rd. Hen-O-T 15 F1
Station Rd. Hung 100 B3
Station Rd. Kint 102 A1
Station Rd. Lamb 25 D1
Station Rd. Mar 1 C1
Station Rd. Newb 104 B3
Station Rd. Newb 105 D1
Station Rd. Pangb 56 B3
Station Rd. Read 86 A4
Station Rd. Read 87 E2
Station Rd. Shepp 125 E2
Station Rd. Shipl 36 A2
Station Rd. Slough 44 A2
Station Rd. Slough 41 F4
Station Rd. Sunn 121 D2
Station Rd. Tapl 40 C4
Station Rd. That 106 C1
Station Rd. Thea 83 F1
Station Rd. Twyf 61 E2
Station Rd. Warg 36 B1
Station Rd. Woki 116 A3
Station Rd. Wool 108 B1
Station Rd. Wray 69 D1
Station Rise. Mar 117 F3
Staunton Rd. Slough 42 B4
Staveley Rd. Ashf 98 B1
Staverton Cl. Brac 91 D1
Staverton Cl. Woki 116 C3
Staverton Rd. Read 86 B2
Stayne End. Went 122 A3
Steam Farm La. Harm 71 F2
Steeple Wlk. Read 113 F4
Stepgates. Chert 124 A1
Stephen Cl. Stai 96 B1
Stephen Rd. Mort 136 C3
Stephen's Cl. Mort 136 C3
Stephens Firs. Mort 136 C3
Stephenson Cl. That 106 B2
Stephenson Rd. Bark 141 D4
Stephenson Rd. Wind 67 D4
Sterling Way. Read 58 A1
Stevens Hill. Yate 149 F3
Stevenson Dr. Binf 90 B2
Stewart Ave. Slough 42 C4
Stewart Ave. Stai 125 D3
Stewart Cl. Holy 65 E3
Stewarts Dr. Far C 22 A4
Stewarts Way. Mar B 1 B4
Stile Rd. Slough 43 E2
Stilton Cl. Winn 87 F1
Stilwell Cl. Yate 149 F3
Stirling Cl. Camb 151 F1
Stirling Cl. Caver 59 E3
Stirling Cl. Wind 66 B3
Stirling Rd. Slough 42 A4
Stirling Rd. Stan 70 C1
Stockbridge Way. Yate 149 E2
Stockbury Cl. Read 87 D1
Stockdales Rd. Eton 41 F1
Stockton Rd. Read 86 B1
Stockwells. Tapl 20 B1
Stockwood Rise. Camb 151 F3
Stoke Common Rd. Fulm 23 D4
Stoke Common Rd. Sto P 23 D4
Stoke Court Dr. Sto P 22 C2
Stoke Gdns. Slough 42 C3
Stoke Green. Sto P 23 D1
Stoke Park Ave. Far C 22 A1
Stoke Poges La. Slough 42 C4
Stoke Rd. Slough 42 C4
Stoke Wood. Sto P 22 C4
Stokeford Cl. Brac 118 C2
Stomp Rd. Burn 41 D4
Stomp Rd. Burn 21 E1
Stomp Rd. Slough 41 D4
Stompits Rd. Holy 65 E4
Stone Cres. Felt 98 C4
Stone House La. Cook 2 B1
Stone St. Read 58 A1
Stonea Cl. Winn 114 B4
Stonecroft Ave. Iver 44 C4
Stonegate. Camb 152 B3
Stoneham Cl. Read 85 D3
Stonehaven Dr. Wood 88 A3
Stonehill Rd. Light 146 A1
Stonehouse Rise. Camb 151 F1
Stoneleigh Ct. Camb 151 F1
Stoney Cl. Yate 149 E2
Stoney La. Burn 22 A2
Stoney La. Cold A 105 E3
Stoney La. Newb 105 E3
Stoney La. That 106 C2
Stoney Meade. Slough 42 A3
Stoney Rd. Brac 118 A4
Stoney Ware. Bish 18 C4
Stoney Ware Cl. Bish 18 C4
Stoneyfield. Been 109 D3
Stoneyland Ct. Eng G 95 F2
Stoneylands Rd. Eng G 95 F2
Stookes Way. Yate 149 D2
Stour Cl. Read 85 D4
Stour Cl. Slough 42 A2
Stovell Rd. Wind 67 D4
Stowe Rd. Slough 41 F3
Straight Bit. Fla H 3 D4
Straight La. Lamb 46 C3
Straight Mile The. Hurst 89 E3
Straight Mile The. W St L 62 C1
Straight Rd. Old W 68 A1
Strand La. Cook 19 F3
Strand Way. Wood 87 E1
Stranraer Rd. Stan 70 C1
Stratfield. Brac 117 F1
Stratfield Rd. Slough 43 D2
Stratford Cl. Slough 21 E1
Stratford Dr. Bou E 3 E2
Stratford Gdns. Maid 39 E2
Stratford Rd. Harm 71 E1
Stratford Way. Read 84 A3
Strathcona Cl. Fla H 3 E4
Strathcona Way. Fla H 3 E4
Strathearn Ave. Harl 71 F4
Stratheden Pl. Read 85 F4
Strathmore Dr. Char 61 D2
Strathy Cl. Read 85 D4
Stratton Gdns. Read 86 B1
Stratton Rd. Shepp 125 F4
Strawberry Hill. Newb 104 C2
Streatley and Goring Bridge. Gori 34 A3
Streatley Hill. Stre 33 F3
Street The. Alde 135 D4
Street The. Brad 83 D3
Street The. Mort 137 E3
Street The. Moul 14 A3
Street The. Sou S 14 A2
Street The. Swal 139 E4
Street The. Tidm 56 B1
Streets Heath. West E 153 F4
Strode St. Eng G 96 A2
Strode's Cres. Stai 97 E2
Stroller Cl. That 105 F2
Strongrove Hill. Hung 100 B3
Stroud Cl. Wind 66 B2
Stroud Farm Rd. Holy 65 D4
Stroud Way. Ashf 98 A1
Stroude Rd. Vir W 122 C3
Stroude Rd. Vir W 123 D4
Strouds Meadow. Cold A 106 B4
Strouds The. Been 108 C3
Stuart Cl. Caver 59 D3
Stuart Cl. Wind 66 C3
Stuart Rd. Newb 130 B3
Stuart Way. Stai 97 D1
Stuart Way. Vir W 122 A3
Stuart Way. Wind 66 C3
Stubbles La. Cook 19 D3
Studios Rd. Stai 124 C3
Studland Cl. Read 113 E4
Sturbridge Cl. Wood 87 E1
Sturdee Cl. Camb 151 F1
Sturges Rd. Woki 116 B3
Sturt Green. Holy 64 C4
Styventon Pl. Chert 123 F1
Suck's La. Asham 54 B2
Suffolk Cl. Slough 41 F4
Suffolk Cl. Woki 115 E3
Suffolk Rd. Maid 39 E2
Suffolk Rd. Read 85 E4
Suffork Cl. Bags 145 F1
Sulham La. Pangb 56 C2
Sulham La. Purl 56 C2
Sulham La. Sulh 56 C2
Sulham Wlk. Read 85 D2
Sulhamstead Hill. Sulhd 110 B3
Sulhamstead La. Sulhd 110 B2
Sulhamstead Rd. Bur 111 D3
Sulhamstead Rd. Sulhd 111 D3
Sullivan Rd. Camb 151 D3
Summer Gdns. Camb 152 B3
Summerfield Cl. Woki 88 C1
Summerfield Rise. Gori 34 B4
Summerhouse La. Harm 70 B4
Summerlea. Slough 42 A3
Summerleaze Rd. Maid 20 A1
Summers Rd. Burn 21 E1
Summit Cl. Woki 141 F4
Sun Gdns. Bur C 111 D1
Sun La. Maid 39 F4
Sun Pas. Wind 67 E3
Sun Ray Estate. Sand 150 A4
Sun St. Read 86 B4
Sunbury Cres. Felt 98 C3
Sunbury Rd. Eton 67 E4
Sunbury Rd. Felt 98 C3
Sunderland Cl. Wood 88 A4
Sunderland Rd. Maid 39 D4
Sundon Cres. Went 122 B2
Sundown Rd. Ashf 98 B2
Sunley Cl. Newb 130 B3
Sunmead Rd. Shepp 125 F3
Sunning Ave. Sunn 120 C1
Sunninghill Rd. Ascot 120 B3
Sunninghill Rd. Windl 146 A4
Sunninghill Rd. Wink 93 E1
Sunnybank. Mar 1 B2
Sunnyside. Newb 104 C3
Surbiton Rd. Camb 145 D1
Surley Row. Caver 59 D3
Surly Hall Wlk. Wind 66 C3
Surrey Ave. Camb 151 D2
Surrey Ave. Slough 22 B1
Surrey Rd. Read 86 A2
Surridge Ct. Bags 145 F1
Sussex Cl. Slough 43 D2
Sussex Gdns. Wood 87 F4
Sussex La. Shin 113 E1
Sussex Pl. Slough 43 D2
Sutcliffe Ave. Read 87 E2
Sutherland Ave. Shepp 125 F4
Sutherland Chase. Ascot 119 F4
Sutherland Gdns. Shepp 125 F4
Sutherland Gr. Read 84 C2
Sutherlands. Newb 130 C4
Sutherlands Ave. Read 86 B3
Sutton Ave. Slough 43 E2
Sutton Cl. Cook 20 A4
Sutton Cl. Maid 39 E3
Sutton La. Slough 44 B1
Sutton Pl. Slough 69 D4
Sutton Rd. Camb 145 D1
Sutton Rd. Cook 20 A3
Sutton Rd. Newb 104 B3
Sutton Wlk. Read 86 B3
Suttons Park Ave. Read 86 C4
Swabey Rd. Slough 44 A1
Swainstone Rd. Read 86 A3
Swaledale. Brac 118 A2
Swallow Cl. Read 84 B3
Swallow Cl. Stai 96 C2
Swallow Cl. Yate 149 D3
Swallow St. Iver 44 B4
Swallow Way. Woki 115 F3
Swallowfield. Eng G 95 D1
Swallowfield Dr. Read 113 E3
Swallowfield Gdns. Thea 83 F2
Swallowfield Rd. Arbo 114 B1
Swan La. Sand 150 A4
Swan Pl. Read 86 A4
Swan Rd. Iver 44 C4
Swancote Green. Brac 118 A2
Swanholm Gdns. Read 84 C2
Swanmore Cl. Winn 87 F1
Swanscourt. Twyf 61 F2
Swansdown Wlk. That 106 A2
Swansea Rd. Harm 71 E1
Swansea Rd. Read 59 D1
Swansea Terr. Read 57 E1
Swanston Field. Whitc 56 B4
Sweeps La. Eng G 95 F2
Sweet Briar Dr. Bur C 84 B2
Sweetbriar. Brac 143 D4
Sweetzer's Piece. Silc 136 C3
Swepstone Cl. Read 87 E1
Swift Cl. Woki 115 F3
Swift La. Windl 145 F2
Swinbrook Cl. Read 57 E2
Swindon Rd. Harm 71 E1
Swinley Rd. Brac 119 E2
Swiss Cottage Cl. Read 84 B4
Switchback Cl. Maid 19 E1
Switchback Rd. Cook 19 F2
Switchback Rd. S. Maid 19 E1
Switchback Rd N. Cook 19 F2
Switchback Rd N. Maid 19 F2
Switchback Rd S. Maid 19 E1
Switchback The. Maid 19 E1
Sycamore Cl. Bur C 111 D2
Sycamore Cl. Camb 151 F1
Sycamore Cl. Sand 150 A4
Sycamore Cl. Wood 87 E3
Sycamore Ct. Wind 67 E2
Sycamore Dr. Camb 151 F1
Sycamore Dr. Mar B 1 B3
Sycamore Dr. Twyf 61 E3
Sycamore Rd. Read 86 C1
Sycamore Rise. Brac 118 B3
Sycamore Rise. Newb 105 E3
Sycamore Wlk. Eng G 95 D1
Sycamore Wlk. Slough 43 F4
Sycamores The. Black 150 A3
Sydings The. Newb 104 B3
Sydney Cl. Brac 143 E4
Sydney Cres. Ashf 98 A1
Sydney Gr. Slough 42 B4
Syke Cluan. Iver 44 C2
Syke Ings. Iver 44 C2
Sykes Rd. Slough 42 A4
Sylvan Ridge. Sand 143 D1
Sylvan Wlk. Read 85 E2
Sylvanus. Brac 117 F1
Sylvester Cl. Newb 104 C3
Sylvester Rd. Maid 19 F1
Sympson Rd. Tad 135 E1

Tachbrook Rd. Felt 98 C4
Tadcroft Wlk. Read 84 C2
Tadham Pl. That 106 B1
Tadley Common Rd. Tad 135 E1
Tadmor Cl. Shepp 125 F3
Taff Way. Read 85 D4
Tag La. Warg 37 D1
Talbot Ave. Slough 43 F2
Talbot Cl. Caver 59 E1
Talbot Cl. Newb 104 C3
Talbot Ct. Read 86 A4
Talbot Pl. Bags 145 F2
Talbot Pl. Datch 68 B3
Talbot Rd. Ashf 97 F2
Talbot Way. Sulh 57 E2
Talbots Dr. Maid 39 D3
Talfour Ave. Read 87 D3
Tall Trees. Stan 69 F3
Tallis La. Read 85 E2
Tamar Gdns. Read 86 B2
Tamar Way. Slough 44 A1
Tamar Way. Woki 115 F4
Tamarind Way. Read 86 C1
Tamarisk Ave. Read 86 C1
Tamarisk Rise. Woki 116 B4
Tamworth. Brac 118 B1
Tamworth Cl. Wood 87 E1
Tangier La. Eton 67 E4
Tanglewood. Woki 142 A4
Tanglewood Ride. West E 153 F4
Tangley Dr. Brac 116 A2
Tanglyn Ave. Stai 125 D2
Tanhouse La. Woki 116 A3
Tank Rd. Sand 150 C3
Tanner Ct. Newb 105 D2
Tanners La. Maple 58 C4
Tape La. Hurst 88 C4
Taplow Common Rd. Burn 21 D2
Taplow Common Rd. Tapl 21 D2
Taplow Rd. Burn 41 D4
Tarbat Ct. Sand 150 B4
Tarbay La. Oak G 66 B2
Target Cl. Felt 71 F1
Targett Ct. Winn 88 A1
Tarlton Ct. Read 84 C3
Tarmac Way. Harm 70 A4
Tarn La. Newb 130 C4
Tarnbrook Way. Brac 118 C1
Tarragon Cl. Read 86 C1
Tarragon Way. Bur C 111 D2
Tarrants Hill. Hung 100 B3
Tasker Cl. Harl 71 E4
Tatchbrook Cl. Maid 40 A4
Tattersall Cl. Woki 116 C3
Tavistock Cl. Maid 39 D4
Tavistock Cl. Stai 97 E1
Tavistock Rd. Read 86 A2
Tawfield. Brac 117 F1
Tay Rd. Read 85 D4
Taylor's Cl. Mar 1 C1
Tazewell Ct. Read 85 F3
Tebbit Cl. Brac 118 B4
Teesdale Rd. Slough 41 F4
Tekels Ave. Camb 151 E2
Tekels Way. Camb 151 F2
Telford Cres. Wood 60 C1
Telford Dr. Slough 42 A2
Telston Cl. Bou E 3 D3
Tempest Rd. Stai 96 B1
Templar Cl. Sand 150 A4
Templars Pl. Mar 1 C1
Temple Gdns. Stai 123 F4
Temple La. Bish 18 B3
Temple Mill Island. Bish 18 B3
Temple Park. Hurl 17 F2
Temple Pl. Read 86 A3
Temple Rd. Wind 67 E3
Temple Way. Far C 22 B4
Templecroft. Ashf 98 B1
Templedene Ave. Stai 97 E1
Templeton Gdns. Read 86 B1
Templewood La. Far C 22 B4
Ten Acre La. Stai 123 E4
Tenaplas Dr. Upp B 54 C3
Tenby Ave. Caver 59 E3
Tenby Dr. Ascot 120 B2
Tennyson Rd. Ashf 97 F2
Tennyson Rd. That 106 B2
Tennyson Rd. Wood 87 F2
Tennyson Way. Slough 21 F1
Tern Cl. Read 85 D3
Terrace Rd N. Binf 90 B2
Terrace Rd S. Binf 90 B1
Terrace The. Ascot 120 B2
Terrace The. Crow 143 E3
Terrace The. Maid 40 B2
Terrace The. Woki 116 A3
Terrington Hill. Mar 1 B1
Terry's La. Cook 19 F4
Tesimond Dr. Yate 149 D3
Tessa Rd. Read 58 C1
Test Cl. Read 85 D4
Testwood Rd. Wind 66 B3
Teviot Rd. Read 84 C4
Thakerays The. That 106 B1
Thames Ave. Chert 124 A3
Thames Ave. Pangb 56 B3
Thames Ave. Read 59 D1
Thames Ave. Wind 67 E4
Thames Cl. Bou E 3 D2
Thames Cl. Chert 124 B1
Thames Cres. Maid 20 A1
Thames Dr. Char 60 C4
Thames Industrial Estate. Mar 1 C1
Thames Mead. Wind 66 C3
Thames Rd. Gori 34 A3
Thames Rd. Slough 44 A2
Thames Rd. That 106 A3
Thames Reach. Purl 55 E3
Thames Side. Chert 124 B1
Thames Side. Hen-O-T 15 F1
Thames Side. Read 59 D1
Thames Side. Stai 96 C1
Thames Side. Wind 67 E4
Thames Side Prom. Read 59 D1
Thames St. Shepp 125 F1
Thames St. Sonn 60 B2
Thames St. Stai 96 C2
Thames St. Wind 67 E4
Thamesfield Ct. Shepp 125 E1
Thamesfield Gdns. Mar 1 C1
Thanington Way. Read 87 D1
Thatchers Dr. Maid 39 D3
Theal Cl. Sand 150 B4
Theale Rd. Bur C 111 E3
Theobald Dr. Read 57 E2
Thetford Mews. Caver 59 E3
Thetford Rd. Ashf 97 F3
Thibet Rd. Sand 150 B4
Thicket Gr. Maid 38 C4
Thicket Rd. Read 84 C4
Thickthorne La. Stai 97 E1
Third Ave. Mar 1 C1
Third Cres. Slough 42 B4
Thirkleby Cl. Slough 42 B3
Thirlmere Ave. Read 57 F1
Thirlmere Ave. Slough 41 E4
Thirlmere Cl. Stai 96 A1
Thirtover. Cold A 79 D1
Thistledown. Read 57 E1
Thistleton Way. Winn 87 F1
Thomas La. Woki 141 F4
Thomas Rd. Bou E 3 E2
Thompkins La. Burn 22 A3
Thompson Cl. Slough 44 A1
Thompson Dr. That 106 C1
Thomson Wlk. Bur C 84 C2
Thone Cl. Brac 143 D4
Thorn Dr. Slough 43 F4
Thorn La. Read 86 A4
Thorn St. Read 86 A4
Thornbank Cl. Stan 70 A1
Thornbers Way. Char 61 D3
Thornbridge Rd. Read 113 D4
Thornbury Cl. Crow 143 D3
Thorncroft. Eng G 95 E1
Thorndike. Slough 42 A4
Thorndown La. Windl 146 B2
Thorne Cl. Stai 98 B1
Thorne Cl. Woki 115 E2
Thorney Cl. Winn 87 F1
Thorney La N. Iver 44 C3
Thorney La S. Iver 44 C3
Thornfield. Head 132 B2
Thornfield Green. Black 150 C2
Thornford Rd. Gree 132 B2
Thornford Rd. Head 132 C2
Thornford Rd. That 132 B2
Thornhill. Brac 118 C3
Thornhill Way. Stai 125 D2
Thorningdown. Chil 10 B4
Thornton Mews. Read 85 E4
Thornton Rd. Read 85 E4
Thorp Cl. Binf 90 B2
Thorpe By Pass. Stai 123 D3
Thorpe Cl. Woki 116 A2
Thorpe Lea Rd. Stai 96 A1
Thorpe Rd. Chert 123 E2
Thorpe Rd. Stai 96 B2
Thorpe Rd. Stai 123 E2
Three Acre Rd. Newb 130 C4
Three Firs Way. Bur C 110 C1
Three Gables La. Stre 34 A4
Three Post La. Lamb 25 D1
Threshfield. Brac 118 A2
Thrift La. Holy 64 B4
Throgmorton Rd. Yate 149 D3
Thrush Cl. Bur C 111 D2
Thurlby Way. Maid 39 E2
Thurlestone Cl. Shepp 125 E2
Thurlestone Gdns. Read 86 B1
Thurnscoe Cl. Read 113 F4
Thurso Cl. Read 85 D4
Thurston Rd. Slough 42 C4
Thyme Cl. Read 87 D1
Tichborne Cl. Black 150 B3
Tichbourne Cl. Camb 151 F2
Tickenor Dr. Woki 141 F4
Tickhill Cl. Read 113 F4
Tidmarsh La. Pangb 56 A1
Tidmarsh La. Tidm 56 A1
Tidmarsh Rd. Pangb 56 B2
Tidmarsh Rd. Tidm 56 B2
Tidmarsh St. Read 58 A1
Tiffany Cl. Woki 115 E3
Tiger Cl. Wood 88 A4
Tigerseye Cl. Woki 115 E4
Tilbury Cl. Caver 59 E2
Tile Barn Row. Ball H 129 F1
Tilecotes Cl. Mar 1 B1
Tilehurst La. Binf 90 B2
Tilehurst Rd. Read 85 E4
Tilling Cl. Read 57 D1
Tilly's La. Stai 96 C2
Tilney Way. Read 113 F4
Tilstone Ave. Eton 41 F1
Tilstone Cl. Eton 41 F1
Timbers Wlk. Maid 39 D3
Timline Green. Brac 118 C4
Timsway. Stai 96 C2
Tindal Cl. Yate 149 E3
Tinkers La. Wind 66 B3
Tinkers La. Windl 121 D2
Tinsey Cl. Stai 96 A2
Tinsley Cl. Read 113 F4
Tintagel Dr. Camb 151 F1
Tintagel Rd. Brac 142 A4
Tintern Cl. Slough 42 B2
Tintern Cres. Read 85 F3
Tinwell Cl. Winn 87 F1
Tippett Rise. Read 86 A3
Tippings La. Wood 88 A4
Tippits Mead. Brac 117 E4
Tiptree Cl. Read 113 F4
Titcombe Way. Kint 102 A1
Tite Hill. Eng G 95 E2
Tithe Barn Dr. Holy 40 B1
Tithe Cl. Holy 40 B1
Tithe Ct. Slough 44 A1
Tithe La. Wray 69 D1
Tithe Meadows. Went 122 B2
Tithebarn Gr. Read 84 C2
Titlarks Hill Rd. Went 121 D1
Tiverton Cl. Wood 60 C1
Toad La. Black 150 C2
Tockley Rd. Burn 21 D1
Tofrek Terr. Read 85 E4
Tokers Green Rd. Maple 58 C4
Tokersgreen La. Caver 58 B3
Tokersgreen La. Maple 58 B3
Toll Gdns. Brac 118 C3
Tollgate. Maid 39 D3
Tolpuddle Way. Yate 149 F3
Tomlin Cl. That 106 C1
Tomlin Rd. Slough 21 F1
Tomlins Ave. Camb 151 F1
Tomlinson Dr. Brac 142 A4
Topaz Cl. Slough 42 A3
Topaz Cl. Woki 115 F4
Tope Cres. Bark 140 C4
Tope Rd. Bark 140 C4
Torcross Gr. Bur C 84 A2
Torin Ct. Eng G 95 E2
Torridge Rd. Slough 69 D4
Torrington Rd. Read 86 B1
Toseland Way. Winn 87 F2
Totnes Rd. Read 86 B1
Tottenham Wlk. Crow 143 E1
Totterdown. Bur C 110 C1
Toutley Cl. Woki 88 C1
Toutley Rd. Woki 89 D1
Tower Cl. Caver 59 E4
Tower Cl. Fla H 3 E4
Tower Hill. Chadd 49 D4
Towers Dr. Crow 143 D2
Town La. Bou E 3 E2
Town La. Stan 70 B1
Town La. Stan 97 E4
Town Sq. Brac 118 B4
Town Tree Rd. Ashf 98 A2
Townsend Cl. Brac 118 C2
Townsend Rd. Aldw 32 C2
Townsend Rd. Ashf 97 F2
Townsend Rd. Stre 34 A4
Towpath. Shepp 124 C1
Trafalgar Cl. Woki 115 F3
Trafalgar Ct. Read 85 F3
Trafalgar Way. Sand 150 C2
Trafford Rd. Read 58 C1
Travic Rd. Slough 21 F1
Travis Ct. Slough 22 A1
Travis La. Sand 150 B4
Tredegar Rd. Caver 59 D3
Tree Cl. Read 84 B4
Tree Tops Ave. Camb 152 A4
Trees Rd. Bou E 3 D2
Treesmill Dr. Maid 39 E2
Treeton Cl. Read 113 F4
Trelawney Ave. Slough 43 F2
Trelawney Dr. Read 57 E1
Trelleck Rd. Read 85 F3
Tremayne Wlk. Camb 152 B2
Trenchard Rd. Holy 65 D4
Trenches La. Slough 44 A3
Trent Cl. Woki 115 F4
Trent Cres. That 106 A3
Trent Rd. Slough 69 D4
Trenton Cl. Camb 152 A1
Trevelyan. Brac 117 F1
Triangle The. Read 84 B4
Trindledown. Brac 91 D1
Tring Rd. Read 57 E1
Trinity. Crow 143 F1
Trinity Ave. Mar 1 B2
Trinity Cl. Stan 70 B1
Trinity Cl. Sunn 121 D2
Trinity Pl. Read 85 F4
Trinity Pl. Wind 67 E3
Trinity Rd. Mar 1 B1
Triumph Cl. Harl 71 E3
Troon Ct. Brac 117 F2
Trotsworth Ave. Vir W 122 C3
Trout Cl. Mar 18 B4
Trout Wlk. Newb 105 E2
Troutbeck Cl. Twyf 61 E3
Trowe's La. Bee H 138 B2
Trowe's La. Swal 139 E3
Trumbull Rd. Brac 91 D1
Trumps Mill La. Went 122 C2
Trumpsgreen Ave. Went 122 B2
Trumpsgreen Rd. Went 122 B2
Truro Cl. Maid 39 D4
Truss Hill Rd. Ascot 120 B2
Trust Cnr. Hen-O-T 35 F4
Trusthorpe Cl. Winn 87 F1
Tubbs Farm Cl. Lamb 25 D1
Tubwell Rd. Sto P 23 D2
Tudor Cl. Ashf 97 F2
Tudor Cl. Woki 116 C3
Tudor Dr. Woo G 3 E4
Tudor Dr. Yate 149 E2
Tudor Gdns. Slough 41 E4
Tudor La. Old W 95 E4
Tudor Rd. Ashf 98 B1
Tudor Rd. Newb 105 D1
Tudor Rd. Read 86 A4
Tudor Way. Wind 66 C3
Tunnel Rd E. Harm 71 D3
Tunnel Rd W. Harm 71 D3
Tuns Hill Cotts. Read 87 D3
Tuns La. Hen-O-T 15 F1
Tuns La. Slough 42 B2
Tupsley Rd. Read 85 F3
Turf Hill Rd. Camb 151 F4
Turk's La. Silc 137 D2
Turmeric Cl. Read 86 C1
Turnberry. Brac 117 F1
Turner Pl. Sand 150 B3
Turner Rd. Slough 43 E2
Turners Cl. Stai 97 D2
Turners Dr. That 106 C1
Turnfields. That 106 B2
Turnpike Rd. Brac 117 F4
Turnpike Rd. Newb 105 F2
Turnpike Rd. That 105 F2
Turnstone Cl. Winn 88 A2
Turnstone End. Yate 149 D3
Turnville Cl. Light 146 A1
Turpin Rd. Felt 71 F1
Turpins Gr. Maid 39 D3
Turpins Rise. Windl 146 A3
Turton Way. Slough 42 B2
Tuscam Way. Sand 150 C2
Tuscan Cl. Read 57 F1
Tuxford Mews. Read 85 D4
Tweed Ct. Read 85 D4
Tweed Rd. Slough 69 D4
Twin Oaks. Caver 59 D3
Twinches La. Slough 42 A3
Two Tree Hill. Hen-O-T 35 D4
Twyford Rd. Binf 89 D1
Twynham Rd. Camb 151 E3
Twynham Rd. Maid 39 D4
Tyberton Pl. Read 85 F3
Tydehams. Newb 130 C4
Tyle Pl. Old W 68 A1
Tyle Rd. Read 84 B4
Tyler Cl. Caver 58 C3
Tyler's La. Buck 80 A1
Tylers Pl. Read 84 C4
Tyne Way. That 106 A3
Tyrell Gdns. Wind 66 C2
Tytherton. Brac 118 B4

Ubilee Rd. Read 87 D3
Uffington Cl. Read 84 B4
Uffington Dr. Brac 118 C3
Uffoott Cl. Read 113 F4
Ullswater. Brac 117 F1
Ullswater Cl. Light 146 A1
Ullswater Cl. Slough 41 E4
Ullswater Cl. That 106 A2
Ullswater Dr. Read 57 E2
Ullswater Rd. Light 146 A1
Ulster Cl. Caver 59 E3
Umberville Way. Slough 21 F1
Underhill. Moul 14 A2
Underhill Cl. Maid 39 F3
Underwood. Brac 117 F2
Underwood Rd. Read 85 D2
Union Cl. Sand 143 F1
Union Rd. Brad 82 B2
Union St. Read 86 A4
Unity Cl. Caver 59 D3
Unwin Ave. Harm 71 E1
Upavon Dr. Read 85 F3
Upavon Gdns. Brac 118 C2
Upcroft. Wind 67 D2
Updown Hill. Windl 146 B2
Upland Rd. Camb 151 E4
Uplands. Hung 100 B3
Uplands. Mar B 1 B3
Uplands Cl. Sand 150 A4
Uplands Rd. Caver 58 C3
Upper Bray Rd. Maid 40 B2
Upper Broadmoor Rd. Crow 143 E3
Upper Charles St. Camb 151 E3
Upper Chobham Rd. Camb 152 A2
Upper College Ride. Camb 151 F4
Upper Crown St. Read 86 A3
Upper End. Chadd 49 D4
Upper Gordon Rd. Camb 151 E3
Upper Halliford Rd. Shepp 125 F3
Upper Lambourn Rd. Lamb 25 D2
Upper Lees Rd. Slough 22 A1
Upper Nursery. Sunn 121 D2
Upper Park Rd. Camb 151 F3
Upper Red Cross Rd. Gori 34 B3
Upper Redlands Rd. Read 86 C3
Upper Village Rd. Ascot 120 B2
Upper Warren Ave. Caver 58 B2
Upper Woodcote Rd. Caver 58 B3
Uppingham Dr. Wood 60 C1
Uppingham Gdns. Caver 59 E3
Upshire Gdns. Brac 118 C3
Upton Cl. Hen-O-T 15 F1
Upton Cl. Slough 42 C2
Upton Court Rd. Slough 43 D1
Upton Lea Par. Slough 43 D3
Upton Park. Slough 42 C2
Upton Rd. Read 85 D4
Upton Rd. Slough 43 D2
Urquhart Rd. That 106 C1
Usk Rd. Read 84 C3
Uxbridge Rd. Slough 43 E3

Vachel Rd. Read 86 A4
Vale Cres. Read 57 F1
Vale Gr. Slough 42 C2
Vale Rd. Camb 151 D2
Vale Rd. Wind 66 C3
Valentia Rd. Read 85 E4
Valentine Cres. Caver 59 E2
Valeview Dr. Bee H 138 B3
Valley Cl. Caver 59 D2
Valley Cl. Gori 34 B3
Valley Cres. Woki 116 A4
Valley End. Iver H 23 E1
Valley Rd. Bur C 111 D2
Valley Rd. Camb 152 B1
Valley Rd. Hen-O-T 35 D4
Valley Rd. Newb 130 C4
Valley Way. Silc 135 F1
Valon Rd. Arbo 140 C4
Valpy St. Read 86 A4
Valroy Cl. Camb 151 E3
Vandyke. Brac 117 F2
Vanlore Way. Read 84 B3
Vanners La. Ham M 129 E3
Vansittart Rd. Bish 18 C4
Vansittart Rd. Wind 67 D3
Vantage Rd. Slough 42 A3
Vanwall Business Park. Maid 39 E3
Vanwall Rd. Maid 39 E2
Vastern Rd. Caver 59 D1
Vaughan Copse. Eton 42 B1
Vaughan Way. Slough 21 F1
Vauxhall Dr. Wood 88 A3
Vegal Cres. Eng G 95 E2
Venetia Cl. Caver 59 E4
Venning Rd. Bark 140 C4
Ventnor Rd. Read 57 E1
Venus Cl. Woki 115 F3
Verey Cl. Twyf 61 F2
Vermont Rd. Slough 21 F1
Vermont Woods. Woki 141 F4
Verney Cl. Mar 1 B1
Verney Mews. Read 85 E4
Verney Rd. Slough 44 A1
Vernon Cres. Read 113 D4
Vernon Dr. Ascot 119 F4
Vernon Rd. Felt 98 C3
Verran Rd. Camb 151 E2
Versley Rd. Bark 140 C3
Vicarage Ave. Stai 96 A2
Vicarage Cl. Cook 20 A4
Vicarage Cres. Stai 96 A2
Vicarage Ct. Felt 98 B4
Vicarage Ct. Stai 96 A1
Vicarage Dr. Maid 40 B2
Vicarage Gdns. Ascot 120 A2
Vicarage La. Cold A 106 B4
Vicarage La. Stai 124 B3
Vicarage La. Wray 95 F4
Vicarage La. Yate 149 E4
Vicarage Rd. Ashf 98 C1
Vicarage Rd. Bags 145 E2
Vicarage Rd. Black 150 C2
Vicarage Rd. Hen-O-T 35 F4
Vicarage Rd. Maid 39 F4
Vicarage Rd. Read 86 B3
Vicarage Rd. Stai 96 A1
Vicarage Rd. Stai 96 C3
Vicarage Rd. Yate 149 E4
Vicarage Way. Iver 69 E4
Vicarage Wlk. Maid 40 B2
Vickers Cl. Shin 113 F2
Vickers Cl. Wood 88 A4
Victor Rd. That 106 C2
Victor Rd. Wind 67 E2
Victor Way. Wood 88 A4
Victoria Ave. Camb 151 D3
Victoria Cres. Iver 44 C3
Victoria Ct. Bags 145 F1
Victoria Dr. Black 150 B2
Victoria Gdns. Newb 105 D2
Victoria La. Harl 71 E4
Victoria Rd. Ascot 120 A2
Victoria Rd. Caver 59 D2
Victoria Rd. Eton 41 F1
Victoria Rd. Far C 22 B3
Victoria Rd. Mar 1 C1
Victoria Rd. Mort 136 C3
Victoria Rd. Read 84 B4
Victoria Rd. Sand 143 F1
Victoria Rd. Slough 43 D3
Victoria Rd. Stai 96 C3
Victoria Rd. Warg 36 C1
Victoria St. Eng G 95 E1
Victoria St. Read 86 B4
Victoria St. Slough 42 C2
Victoria St. Wind 67 E3
Victory Rd. Chert 124 A1
Vigo La. Yate 149 E2
Viking. Brac 117 F2
Village Cl. Read 113 D3
Village Rd. Dorn 41 E2
Village Rd. Stai 123 E3
Village The. Finch 141 F2
Village The. Old W 94 A3
Village Way. Ashf 98 A2
Village Way. Yate 149 E4
Villiers Mead. Woki 116 A3
Villiers Rd. Slough 42 B4
Villiers Way. Newb 130 B3
Villiers Wlk. Newb 130 B3
Vincent Cl. Chert 123 F1
Vincent Cl. Harm 71 D4
Vincent Cl. Wood 87 F3
Vincent Dr. Shepp 125 F3
Vincent Rd. Chert 123 F1
Vincent Rd. That 106 C2
Vincent Rise. Brac 118 C3
Vine Cl. Stan 70 A1
Vine Cres. Read 85 D2
Vine Rd. Sto P 22 C3
Vineries Cl. Harm 71 D4
Vines The. Woki 115 E2
Vineyard Dr. Bou E 3 D3
Viola Ave. Stan 97 F4
Virginia Ave. Vir W 122 B2
Virginia Cl. Stai 124 B3
Virginia Dr. Vir W 122 B3
Virginia Way. Read 85 D3
Viscount Rd. Stan 97 F4

Viscount Way. Harm 71 F2
Viscount Way. Wood 88 A4
Vivien Cl. Cook 19 F3
Volunteer Rd. Thea 83 E1
Vulcan Cl. Sand 150 A4
Vulcan Way. Sand 150 A4

Wabone Rd. Bou E 3 D2
Wade Dr. Slough 42 A3
Wadham. Crow 143 F1
Wadham Cl. Shepp 125 E1
Wagbullock Rise. Brac 118 B2
Waggoners Hollow. Bags 145 F1
Wagner Cl. Whi Wa 38 C2
Wagtail Cl. Twyf 61 F2
Waingels Rd. Char 61 D1
Waingels Rd. Wood 61 D1
Wakefield Cres. Sto P 22 C3
Wakeford Cl. Silc 135 F1
Wakelins End. Cook 19 F4
Wakeman Rd. Bou E 3 D2
Wakemans. Pangb 55 E2
Walbury. Brac 118 C3
Waldeck Rd. Maid 40 A4
Waldeck St. Read 86 A3
Waldegrave Pl. Newb 105 D2
Walden Ave. Arbo 114 B2
Waldens Cl. Bou E 3 D2
Waldorf Hts. Black 150 B2
Waldron Hill. Brac 118 C4
Walgrove Gdns. Whi Wa 63 F4
Walk The. Ashf 98 C1
Walk The. Eton 42 A1
Walker Rd. Maid 40 A2
Walker's La. Lamb 25 D2
Walkers Pl. Read 85 E4
Walker's Ridge. Camb 151 F3
Wall La. Silc 136 B1
Wallace Cl. Mar 1 C2
Wallace Cl. Shepp 125 E3
Wallace Cl. Wood 87 E3
Walled Gdn The. Warg 36 B1
Wallingford Cl. Brac 118 C3
Wallingford Rd. Comp 31 F3
Wallingford Rd. Gori 14 B3
Wallingford Rd. Sou S 14 B3
Wallingford Rd. Stre 34 A4
Wallington Rd. Camb 145 D1
Wallington's Rd. Kint 101 F1
Wallis Ct. Slough 43 D2
Wallner Way. Woki 116 C3
Walmer Cl. Crow 143 E3
Walmer Cl. Read 85 D3
Walmer Rd. Wood 60 C1
Walnut Cl. Woki 115 F3
Walnut Cl. Yate 149 E2
Walnut Tree Cl. Bou E 3 D1
Walnut Tree Ct. Gori 34 B3
Walnut Tree Rd. Stai 125 E3
Walnut Tree Rd. Stai 125 E4
Walnut Way. Bou E 3 D1
Walnut Way. Read 84 B4
Walpole Rd. Old W 95 D4
Walpole Rd. Slough 41 E4
Walrus Cl. Wood 88 A4
Walter Rd. Woki 115 F4
Walters Cl. Cold A 106 B4
Waltham Cl. Crow 143 E1
Waltham Cl. Whi Wa 38 C1
Waltham Rd. Twyf 61 F2
Waltham Rd. Twyf 61 F3
Waltham Rd. Whi Wa 38 C1
Walton Ave. Hen-O-T 35 F4
Walton Bridge Rd. Shepp 125 F1
Walton Cl. Wood 87 E4
Walton Dr. Ascot 119 F4
Walton Gdns. Felt 98 C2
Walton La. Burn 21 F2
Walton La. Shepp 125 F1
Walton Way. Newb 105 E2
Wandhope Way. Read 57 E1
Wanstraw Gr. Brac 118 C1
Wantage Cl. Brac 118 C2
Wantage Rd. Gr She 48 B3
Wantage Rd. Lamb 25 E3
Wantage Rd. Read 85 E4
Wantage Rd. Sand 150 B4
Wantage Rd. Stre 33 F4
Wapshott Rd. Stai 96 C2
Waram Cl. Hung 100 C4
Warbler Cl. Read 84 A3
Warborough Ave. Read 57 D3
Warborough Rd. Let B 7 D4
Warbreck Dr. Sulh 57 D4
Warbrook La. Finch 141 D1
Ward Cl. Iver 44 C3
Ward Cl. Woki 116 B4
Ward Gdns. Slough 41 F3
Ward Royal. Wind 67 D3
Wardle Ave. Read 57 E1
Wardle Cl. Bags 145 F2
Wareham Rd. Brac 118 C2
Warfield Rd. Brac 91 E1
Warfield Rd. Felt 98 C4
Warfield St. New G 91 E2
Wargrave Hill. Warg 36 B1
Wargrave Rd. Rem H 36 A4
Wargrave Rd. Twyf 61 E3
Wargrove Dr. Sand 150 B4
Waring Cl. Winn 114 B4
Warley Rise. Sulh 57 E2
Warner Cl. Harl 71 E4
Warner Cl. Slough 41 F3
Warners Hill. Cook 19 E4
Warnford Rd. Read 84 C4
Warnsham Cl. Read 87 D1
Warren Cl. Bur C 111 D2
Warren Cl. Sand 150 A4
Warren Cl. Slough 43 F2
Warren Down. Brac 117 F4
Warren End. Newb 130 B3
Warren House Rd. Bint 89 E1
Warren House Rd. Woki 116 B4
Warren La. Woki 141 F3
Warren Rd. Ashf 98 C1
Warren Rd. Wood 60 B1
Warren Rise. Camb 151 F2
Warren Row. Burl 119 E4
Warren Row Rd. Know H 37 E3
Warren The. Caver 58 C2
Warrington Ave. Slough 42 B4
Warrington Spur. Old W 95 D4
Warwick. Brac 118 C2
Warwick Ave. Slough 22 B1
Warwick Ave. Stai 97 E1
Warwick Ave. Stai 123 E4
Warwick Cl. Camb 152 A2
Warwick Cl. Maid 39 D2
Warwick Dr. Newb 105 D1
Warwick Rd. Ashf 97 F2
Warwick Rd. Read 86 B2
Wasdale Cl. Crow 143 E1
Wash Hill. Bou E 3 F2
Wash Hill Lea. Bou E 3 E2
Wash Water. Ham M 130 A2
Wash Water. Newb 130 A2
Washing La. Brim 134 B3
Washington Ct. Mar 2 A2
Washington Dr. Slough 41 E3
Washington Dr. Wind 66 C2
Washington Rd. Caver 59 D1
Watchetts Dr. Camb 151 E1
Watchetts Lake Cl. Camb 151 E2
Watchetts Rd. Camb 151 D2
Watchmoor Rd. Camb 151 D2
Water La. Gree 131 E4
Water Rd. Read 85 D4
Water St. Hamp N 52 C3
Waterbeach Rd. Slough 42 B4
Waterfall Cl. Vir W 122 A3
Waterford Way. Woki 116 B3
Waterham Rd. Brac 118 A2
Waterloo Cres. Woki 116 C3
Waterloo Rd. Crow 143 D2
Waterloo Rd. Read 86 A3
Waterloo Rd. Woki 116 C3
Waterman Pl. Read 59 D1
Waterman's Rd. Hen-O-T 35 F4
Waterman's Way. Warg 36 B1
Watermead. Felt 98 C4
Watermill Ct. Wool 108 B1
Waters Dr. Stai 96 C2
Watersfield Cl. Read 87 D1
Waterside. Woo G 3 F4
Waterside Ct. Newb 105 D2
Waterside Dr. Purl 57 E3
Waterside Dr. Slough 44 A2
Waterside Gdns. Read 86 A4
Waterside Park Industrial Estate. Brac 117 F4
Watersplash La. Ascot 120 C4
Watersplash La. Wink 120 C4
Watersplash Rd. Stai 125 D3
Watery La. Chert 123 E1
Watery La. Kint 128 C3
Watery La. Woo G 3 F4
Watkins Cl. Woki 141 F4
Watlington St. Read 86 B4
Watmore La. Winn 88 B1
Watt's La. Blew 12 A4
Wavell Cl. Read 86 C1
Wavell Gdns. Slough 21 F1
Wavell Rd. Maid 39 D3
Wavendene Ave. Stai 96 B1
Waverley. Brac 117 F2
Waverley Cl. Camb 151 F2
Waverley Dr. Camb 151 F3
Waverley Dr. Vir W 122 A3
Waverley Rd. Bags 145 F2
Waverley Rd. Read 85 E4
Waverley Rd. Slough 42 B4
Waverleys The. That 106 B2
Waybrook Cres. Read 86 C3
Wayland Cl. Brac 118 C3
Waylen St. Read 85 F4
Ways End. Camb 151 F2
Wayside Mews. Maid 39 F4
Weald Rise. Read 57 F1
Wealden Way. Read 84 C4
Wealden Way. Read 57 F1
Weavers La. Ink 127 E3
Weavers Wlk. Newb 105 D2
Webb Cl. Bags 145 F1
Webb Cl. Slough 43 E1
Webbs Acre. That 106 C1
Webbs La. Been 109 D4
Webster Cl. Maid 39 D3
Wedderburn Cl. Winn 88 B1
Wedgewood Way. Read 57 F1
Weekes Dr. Slough 42 A2
Weighbridge Row. Read 58 C1
Weir Cl. Read 84 C2
Weir Pl. Stai 123 F4
Weir Rd. Chert 124 A1
Welbeck. Brac 117 F2
Welbeck Rd. Maid 39 E3
Welby Cl. Maid 39 D2
Welby Cres. Winn 88 A1
Weldale St. Read 85 F4
Welford Rd. Wood 88 A4
Well Cl. Camb 151 D2
Well House La. Swal 140 B2
Well Meadow. Newb 105 D3
Welland Cl. Read 57 E1
Welland Cl. Slough 69 D4
Wellbank. Tapl 20 C1
Wellcroft Rd. Slough 42 A3
Weller's La. New G 91 E4
Wellesley Ave. Iver 44 C2
Wellesley Cl. Bags 145 E2
Wellesley Dr. Brac 142 C3
Wellesley Dr. Finch 142 C3
Wellesley Rd. Slough 43 D2
Welley Ave. Wray 68 C2
Welley Rd. Hort 68 C1
Welley Rd. Wray 68 C1
Wellfield Cl. Read 84 B4
Wellhill Rd. Fawl 27 E3
Wellhouse La. Buck 79 F3
Wellhouse La. Herm 79 F3
Wellhouse Rd. Maid 19 F1
Wellington Ave. Read 86 B2
Wellington Ave. Vir W 122 A2
Wellington Ave. Went 122 A2
Wellington Cl. Newb 105 E3
Wellington Cl. Sand 150 B4
Wellington Cl. Shepp 125 F1
Wellington Cres. Tad 134 B1
Wellington Dr. Brac 118 C2
Wellington Dr. Brac 118 C3
Wellington Rd. Ashf 97 F2
Wellington Rd. Crow 143 E2
Wellington Rd. Harm 71 F1
Wellington Rd. Maid 39 E4
Wellington Rd. Sand 150 B4
Wellington Rd. Woki 116 A3
Wellington St. Slough 43 D2
Wellingtonia Ave. Finch 142 B2
Wells Cl. Wind 67 D4
Wells La. Ascot 120 A3
Welsh La. Swal 139 D1
Welshman's Rd. Silc 136 A3
Welwick Cl. Winn 87 F1
Welwyn Ave. Felt 71 F1
Wendan Rd. Newb 130 C4
Wendover Dr. Camb 152 B2
Wendover Pl. Stai 96 B2
Wendover Rd. Bou E 3 D3
Wendover Rd. Burn 41 D4
Wendover Rd. Slough 41 D4
Wendover Rd. Stai 96 B2
Wendover Way. Read 84 B4
Wenlock Edge. Char 61 D2
Wenlock Way. That 106 B1
Wensley Cl. Twyf 61 E3
Wensley Rd. Read 85 F3
Wensleydale Dr. Camb 152 B3
Wentworth Ave. Burl 119 E4
Wentworth Ave. Read 113 E4
Wentworth Ave. Slough 22 A1
Wentworth Cl. Ashf 98 A2
Wentworth Cl. Yate 149 E3
Wentworth Cres. Maid 39 E3
Wentworth Ct. Newb 105 D1
Wentworth Dr. Vir W 122 A2
Wentworth Way. Burl 119 E4
Wescott Rd. Woki 116 B3
Wesley Dr. Eng G 96 A1
Wessex Cl. Hung 100 B3
Wessex Gdns. Twyf 61 F2
Wessex Rd. Bou E 3 D1
Wessex Rd. Harm 70 C2
Wessex Way. Maid 39 D2
Wessons Hill. Cook 19 E4
West Cl. Ashf 97 F2
West Cl. Medm 17 E4
West Cres. Wind 66 C3
West Dean. Maid 39 F4
West Dr. Read 84 C3
West Dr. Sonn 60 C1
West Dr. Went 122 A1
West Dr. Went 121 F1
West End Ct. Sto P 22 C2
West End La. Hart 71 E4
West End La. Sto P 22 C2
West End Rd. Silc 136 C3
West Fryerne. Yate 149 E4
West Green. Yate 149 D4
West Green Ct. Read 85 F3
West Hill. Read 86 A3
West Mead. Maid 19 F1
West Mills. Newb 104 C2
West Point. Slough 41 E3
West Ramp. Harm 71 D3
West Rd. Camb 151 E3
West Rd. Felt 98 B4
West Rd. Maid 39 F4
West Ridge. Bou E 3 D2
West Sq. Iver 44 C4
West St. Hen-O-T 15 E1
West St. Maid 39 F4
West St. Mar 1 B1
West St. Newb 104 C2
West St. Read 86 A4
West View. Felt 98 B4
West View. Pease 50 B4
West Way. Shepp 125 E2
Westborough Ct. Maid 39 E3
Westborough Rd. Maid 39 E3
Westbourne Rd. Felt 98 C3
Westbourne Rd. Sand 150 C4
Westbourne Rd. Stai 97 D1
Westbourne Terr. Read 85 E4
Westbrook. Holy 40 C1
Westbrook Cl. Hung 100 B3
Westbrook Gdns. Brac 118 B4
Westbrook Green. Blew 11 F4
Westbrook Rd. Read 58 B1
Westbrook Rd. Stai 96 C2
Westbrook St. Blew 11 F4
Westbury Cl. Crow 143 D3
Westbury Cl. Shepp 125 D2
Westbury La. Purl 57 D3
Westcombe Cl. Brac 118 C1
Westcote Rd. Read 85 E3
Westcroft. Slough 22 A1
Westdene Cres. Caver 58 C2
Westerdale. That 106 B2
Westerdale Dr. Camb 152 A2
Western Ave. Chert 124 A3
Western Ave. Hen-O-T 35 F4
Western Ave. Newb 104 C2
Western Ave. Stai 123 D3
Western Ave. Wood 60 C1
Western Cl. Chert 124 A3
Western Dr. Bou E 3 F3
Western Dr. Shepp 125 E2
Western Elms Ave. Read 85 F4
Western End. Newb 104 C1
Western Oaks. Read 57 F1
Western Perimeter Rd. Harm 70 A2
Western Perimeter Rd. Stan 70 A2
Western Rd. Brac 117 F4
Western Rd. Hen-O-T 35 F4
Western Rd. Read 85 F3
Westfield Cotts. Medm 16 C3
Westfield Cres. Shipl 36 A2
Westfield Cres. That 106 A2
Westfield Rd. Camb 151 D1
Westfield Rd. Caver 59 D1
Westfield Rd. Chol 13 E4
Westfield Rd. Maid 39 D4
Westfield Rd. Slough 22 A1
Westfield Rd. That 106 A3
Westfield Rd. Winn 88 A1
Westfield Way. Newb 104 C1
Westfields. Comp 31 E2
Westgate Cres. Slough 41 F3
Westgate Rd. Newb 104 C1
Westhatch Cnr. New G 91 E3
Westhope Rd. Mar 1 C2
Westland. That 106 A2
Westland Cl. Stan 70 C1
Westlands Ave. Read 86 C1
Westlands Ave. Slough 41 E4
Westlands Cl. Slough 41 E4
Westlands Rd. Newb 131 D4
Westlyn Rd. Silc 135 F1
Westmacott Dr. Felt 98 C4
Westmead. Wind 67 D2
Westmead Dr. Newb 130 C4
Westminster Way. Wood 87 E1
Westmorland Cl. Woki 115 E3
Westmorland Dr. Camb 152 A2
Westmorland Rd. Maid 39 E3
Weston Rd. Slough 41 F4
Westonbirt Dr. Caver 58 C2
Westons. Beed 51 E4
Westridge Ave. Purl 57 E3
Westview Dr. Twyf 61 F3
Westward Rd. Woki 115 F4
Westway. Gori 34 B4
Westwood Glen. Read 57 E1
Westwood Green. Cook 19 F3
Westwood Rd. Mar 1 B1
Westwood Rd. Newb 105 E1
Westwood Rd. Read 57 E1
Westwood Rd. Windl 146 C3
Westwood Row. Read 57 E1
Wetherby Cl. Caver 59 E3
Wethered Dr. Burn 41 D4
Wethered Rd. Mar 1 B1
Wexham Park La. Iver H 23 E1
Wexham Park La. Sto P 23 E1
Wexham Rd. Slough 43 D3
Wexham St. Sto P 23 D2
Wexham Woods. Slough 43 E4
Wey Ave. Chert 124 A3
Wey Cl. Camb 151 D3
Weybridge Mead. Yate 149 F4
Weycrofts. Brac 90 C1
Weymead Cl. Chert 124 B1
Whaley Rd. Woki 116 B4
Wharf La. Bou E 3 D2
Wharf La. Hen-O-T 15 F1
Wharf Rd. Newb 105 D2
Wharf Rd. Wray 95 E4
Wharf St. Newb 105 D2
Wharf The. Newb 105 D2
Wharfdale Rd. Winn 88 A2
Wharfside. Padw 109 E2
Whatley Green. Brac 118 A2
Whatmore Cl. Stan 70 A1
Wheatbutts Meadow. Eton 41 F1
Wheatfield Cl. Maid 39 D2
Wheatfields Rd. Shin 113 F3
Wheatlands Cl. Read 84 C2
Wheatlands La. Ham M 130 A3
Wheatlands Rd. Slough 43 E2
Wheatley. Brac 117 F2
Wheatley Cl. Read 86 C1
Wheatsheaf La. Newb 105 D2
Wheatsheaf La. Stai 96 C1
Wheble Dr. Wood 87 E4
Wheeler Cl. Bur C 111 D2
Wheelers Green Way. That 106 C1
Wheelton Cl. Winn 87 F2
Whins Cl. Camb 151 D2
Whins Dr. Camb 151 D2
Whistler Gr. Sand 150 B3
Whistley Cl. Brac 118 C3
Whitamore Row. Hen-O-T 35 F4
Whitby Dr. Read 86 B3
Whitby Green. Caver 59 E3
Whitby Rd. Slough 42 B3
Whitchurch Cl. Maid 19 F2
Whitchurch Rd. Pangb 56 B3
White Bridge Cl. Felt 71 F1
White City. Crow 143 E3
White Cl. Slough 42 B3
White Gates. Wick 75 E3
White Hart Rd. Maid 39 F4
White Hart Rd. Slough 42 B2
White Hart Row. Chert 124 A1
White Hill. Beac 3 F4
White Hill. Rem H 16 A1
White Hill. Shipl 35 D3
White Hill. Windl 146 A3
White Hill. Woo G 3 F4
White Horse La. Finch 141 E3
White Horse Rd. Wind 66 B3
White House Gdns. Yate 149 E4
White Lilies Island. Wind 67 D4
White Lion Way. Yate 149 E4
White Lodge. Mar B 1 B3
White Lodge Cl. Sulh 57 D2
White Paddock. Whi Wa 39 D1
White Rd. Chil 10 B4
White Rd. Sand 150 C3
White Shoot. Blew 12 A3
White Waltham Airfield Estate. Whi Wa 38 C2
Whitebeam Cl. Woki 115 E2
Whiteford Rd. Slough 42 C4
Whitegates La. Read 87 D4
Whitehall Dr. Arbo 140 C4
Whitehall Farm La. Vir W 122 C3
Whitehall La. Eng G 95 F1
Whitehall La. Wray 69 D1
Whitehill Cl. Mar B 1 B3
Whitehill Rd. Camb 151 E4
Whitehills Green. Gori 34 B3
Whiteknights Rd. Read 86 C3
Whitelands Dr. Burl 119 E4
Whitelands Rd. That 106 B2
Whiteley. Wind 66 C4
Whitemoor La. Upp B 54 C3
Whitepit La. Fla H 3 E4
Whites Hill. Sulhd 110 C3
White's La. Been 109 D4
Whites La. Datch 68 A4
Whitestone Cl. Winn 87 F2
Whiteways Ct. Stai 97 D1
Whitley Cl. Stan 70 C1
Whitley Park La. Read 86 B2
Whitley Rd. Yate 149 E2
Whitley St. Read 86 A3
Whitley Wood La. Read 113 E4
Whitley Wood Rd. Read 113 E4
Whitmoor Rd. Bags 145 F1
Whitmore Cl. Sand 143 E1
Whitmore La. Sunn 121 D2
Whitstone Gdns. Read 86 B1
Whittaker Rd. Slough 21 F1
Whittenham Cl. Slough 43 D3
Whittle Cl. Woki 141 F4
Whittle Parkway. Slough 41 E4
Whitton Cl. Brac 118 C3
Whitton Cl. Winn 87 E1
Whitworth Rd. Bark 141 D4
Whurley Way. Maid 19 F1
Whynstones Rd. Ascot 120 A2
Whyteladyes La. Cook 19 F3
Wick Hill La. Woki 142 A3
Wick La. Eng G 94 C1
Wick Rd. Eng G 95 D1
Wickford Way. Read 113 F4
Wickham La. Eng G 96 A1
Wickham Rd. Camb 151 F4
Wickham Rd. Winn 87 F1
Wickham Vale. Brac 117 F2
Wick's Green. Binf 90 A2
Widbrook Rd. Maid 20 A2
Widecroft Rd. Iver 44 C4
Widmere La. Mar B 1 A4
Wield Ct. Winn 87 F1
Wiggett Gr. Binf 90 B1
Wigmore La. Read 58 A1
Wigmore La. Read 58 B1
Wigmore La. Thea 83 E1
Wigmore Rd. Tad 134 C1
Wilberforce Way. Brac 118 B2
Wilcox Gdns. Stai 124 C3
Wild Briar. Woki 141 F4
Wild Cl. Winn 114 B4
Wildcroft Dr. Woki 116 A1
Wilder Ave. Pangb 56 C3
Wilderness Ct. Read 87 D2
Wilderness Rd. Camb 151 F1
Wilderness Rd. Read 87 D2
Wilders Cl. Brac 91 D1
Wilders Cl. Camb 151 F2
Wildgreen N. Slough 44 A1
Wildgreen S. Slough 44 A1
Wildridings Rd. Brac 118 A3
Wildridings Sq. Brac 118 A3
Wildwood Dr. Tad 134 B1
Wilford Rd. Slough 43 F1
Wilfred Way. That 107 D2
Wilfrids Wood Cl. Bou E 3 D3
Willats Cl. Chert 124 A2
William Cl. That 106 B1
William Ellis Cl. Old W 68 A1
William St. Read 85 F4
William St. Slough 42 C3
William St. Wind 67 E3
Williant Cl. Whi Wa 38 C1
Willoners. Slough 42 A4
Willoughby Rd. Brac 117 F3
Willoughby Rd. Slough 44 A2
Willow Cl. Bur C 111 D3
Willow Cl. Fla H 3 E3
Willow Cl. Iver 69 E4
Willow Cl. Newb 104 C1
Willow Ct. Camb 151 E1
Willow Dr. Brac 118 B4
Willow Dr. Maid 40 A1
Willow Dr. Twyf 61 E3
Willow Gdns. Read 86 C1
Willow Green. West E 153 F3
Willow La. Black 150 B2
Willow La. Warg 36 B2
Willow Park. Sto P 23 D3
Willow Pl. Eton 67 E4
Willow Rd. Newt 131 F1
Willow Rd. Stan 68 F3

Willow St. Read 86 A3
Willow Tree Glade. Bur C 84 B2
Willow Way. Sand 142 C1
Willow Wlk. Chert 124 A1
Willow Wlk. Eng G 95 E2
Willowbrook. Eton 42 B1
Willowbrook Rd. Stan 97 F3
Willowdale. Woki 141 F4
Willowford. Yate 149 E3
Willowmead. Stai 124 A4
Willowmead Cl. Mar 1 C2
Willowmead Cl. Newb 130 B3
Willowmead Gdns. Mar 1 C2
Willowmead Rd. Mar 1 C2
Willowmead Sq. Mar 1 C2
Willows End. Sand 150 A4
Willows Rd. Bou E 3 D2
Willows The. Caver 59 D1
Willows The. Light 146 B1
Willowside. Wood 60 C1
Willson Rd. Eng G 95 D2
Wilmington Cl. Wood 87 F4
Wilmot Cl. Binf 90 B1
Wilmot Rd. Burn 21 D1
Wilmot Way. Camb 151 F2
Wilmot Wlk. Newb 130 B3
Wilmott Cl. Winn 88 A1
Wilsford Cl. Read 113 F4
Wilson Ave. Hen-O-T 35 F4
Wilson Cl. Comp 31 F2
Wilson Ct. Winn 88 A1
Wilson Rd. Read 85 E4
Wilton Cl. Harm 70 B4
Wilton Cres. Wind 66 B2
Wilton Rd. Camb 151 D2
Wilton Rd. Read 85 E4
Wiltshire Ave. Crow 143 D3
Wiltshire Ave. Slough 22 B1
Wiltshire Dr. Woki 116 B4
Wiltshire Rd. Mar 1 C2
Wiltshire Rd. Woki 116 B4
Wiltshire Wlk. Read 84 A3
Wilwood Rd. Brac 117 F4
Wilwyne Cl. Caver 59 E2
Wimbledon Cl. Camb 144 C1
Wimbledon Rd. Camb 144 C1
Wimblington Dr. Winn 114 B4
Wimborne Gdns. Read 58 A1
Wimbushes. Woki 141 E3
Winbury Ct. Maid 39 F4
Wincanton Rd. Read 113 E4
Winchbottom La. Lit M 2 A3
Winchcombe Rd. Newb 105 D1
Winchcombe Rd. Twyf 61 F2
Winchester Cl. Stan 69 F3
Winchester Dr. Maid 39 D2
Winchester Rd. Harl 71 F4
Winchester Rd. Read 86 A2
Winchester Way. Black 150 B3
Winchgrove Rd. Brac 91 D1
Winchstone Cl. Stai 124 C3
Wincroft Rd. Caver 58 C3
Windermere Cl. Stai 96 A1
Windermere Rd. Light 146 A1
Windermere Rd. Read 86 B2
Windermere Way. Slough 41 E4
Windermere Way. That 106 A2
Winding Wood Dr. Camb 152 A2
Windle Cl. Windl 146 B2
Windlebrook Green. Brac 118 A4
Windlesham Ct. Windl 146 B4
Windlesham Rd. Brac 117 F4
Windlesham Rd. West E 153 F4
Windmill Ave. Woki 115 F4
Windmill Cl. Stai 98 C1
Windmill Cl. Wind 67 D3
Windmill Cl. Woki 115 F4
Windmill Cnr. Mort 137 D3
Windmill Field. Windl 146 B2
Windmill La. Buck 108 A3
Windmill La. Wool 108 A3
Windmill Rd. Brac 118 A4
Windmill Rd. Cook 19 F3
Windmill Rd. Fulm 23 E4
Windmill Rd. Mort 137 D3
Windmill Rd. Slough 42 B3
Windmill Rd. Stai 125 F4
Windmill Rd W. Stai 125 F4
Windrush Ave. Slough 44 A2
Windrush Hts. Sand 150 A4
Windrush Way. Maid 39 F4
Windrush Way. Read 85 D4
Windsor Dr. Ashf 97 E2
Windsor Hill. Bou E 3 F3
Windsor La. Burn 21 E1
Windsor Park Rd. Harl 71 F4
Windsor Rd. Ascot 120 A4
Windsor Rd. Datch 68 A4
Windsor Rd. Eng G 95 F3
Windsor Rd. Holy 40 B1
Windsor Rd. Maid 40 B1
Windsor Rd. Oak G 40 B1
Windsor Rd. Slough 42 C2
Windsor Rd. Sto P 23 D4
Windsor Rd. Wray 68 C1
Windsor Ride. Sand 151 D4
Windsor Ride. Woki 142 A4
Windsor Rise. Newb 131 E4
Windsor St. Chert 124 A2
Windsor Way. Read 84 A2
Wing Cl. Mar 1 B1
Wingate Rd. Wood 87 F3
Wingfield Gdns. Camb 152 B2
Wingrove Rd. Read 85 E3
Winkfield Cl. Woki 116 A2
Winkfield La. Wink 92 B4
Winkfield Rd. Ascot 120 A4
Winkworth La. Alde 135 E1
Winnersh Gate. Winn 88 B1
Winnersh Gr. Winn 88 B1
Winscombe. Brac 117 F2
Winser Dr. Read 85 E3
Winston Way. Purl 57 D3
Winston Way. That 105 F2
Winter Hill. Cook 2 B1
Winter Hill. Cook 19 D2
Winter Hill. Cook 19 D4
Winter Hill. Maid 19 D2
Winterbourne Rd. Box 76 C2
Winterbourne Rd. Wint 76 C2
Winterton Dr. Newb 104 B3
Winton Cres. Yate 149 E3
Winton Rd. Read 113 E4
Wintoun Path. Slough 21 F1
Wintringham Way. Purl 57 E3
Winvale. Slough 42 C2
Winwood. Slough 43 E4
Wise's Firs. Sulhd 110 B2
Wishmoor Cl. Camb 151 F4
Wishmoor Rd. Camb 151 F4
Wispington Cl. Winn 87 E1
Wistaria La. Yate 149 E3
Wisteria Cl. Woki 115 F3
Wiston Terr. Read 86 A4
Witcham Cl. Winn 114 B4
Withey Cl. Wind 66 C3
Witheygate Ave. Stai 97 D1
Withy Cl. Light 146 B1
Withy Croft. Slough 43 F4
Withybed La. Kint 101 F2
Wittenham Ave. Read 57 D3
Wittenham Rd. Brac 118 C4
Woburn Cl. Camb 152 A1
Woburn Cl. Caver 58 C2
Wokingham Rd. Brac 117 F4
Wokingham Rd. Hurst 88 C4
Wokingham Rd. Read 87 E2
Wokingham Rd. Sand 142 C1
Wolf La. Wind 66 C2
Wolseley St. Read 86 A3
Wolsey Rd. Ashf 98 C1
Wolsey Rd. Ashf 97 F2
Wolsey Rd. Caver 59 D1
Wolsingham Way. That 106 B1
Wooburn Manor Park. Bou E 3 F3
Wooburn Mews. Bou E 3 F3
Wood Cl. Wind 67 E2
Wood End. Crow 142 C2
Wood Green Cl. Read 85 F4
Wood La. Arbo 114 C2
Wood La. Binf 90 B1
Wood La. Iver 44 B4
Wood La. Slough 42 A2
Wood Moor. Finch 141 F1
Wood Rd. Camb 151 D1
Wood Rd. Stai 125 D3
Wood Ridge. Newb 130 C4
Woodberry Cl. Caver 59 D2
Woodbine Cl. Sand 150 B4
Woodbine Cl. Winn 87 E1
Woodbine La. Newt 130 C1
Woodbourne Cl. Yate 149 E3
Woodbridge Rd. Black 150 A3
Woodbridge Rd. Read 84 A3
Woodbury. Lamb 25 E1
Woodby Dr. Sunn 120 C1
Woodcote. Maid 39 E3
Woodcote Rd. Caver 58 C2
Woodcote Rd. Sou S 14 B2
Woodcote Way. Caver 58 B3
Woodend Cl. Burl 119 F4
Woodend Dr. Ascot 120 A2
Woodenhill. Brac 117 F1
Woodfield Dr. Maid 39 D3
Woodfield Way. Thea 83 F2
Woodford Cl. Caver 58 C2
Woodford Green. Brac 118 C3
Woodford Way. Slough 22 A1
Woodhall La. Windl 146 C4
Woodhaw. Stai 96 A2
Woodhouse La. Head 133 E1
Woodhurst La. Woki 115 F4
Woodhurst Rd. Maid 20 A1
Woodies Cl. Binf 90 B1
Woodland Ave. Slough 42 B3
Woodland Ave. Wind 66 C2
Woodland Ave. Woki 115 F4
Woodland Cl. Mar 1 C2
Woodland Cres. Brac 91 E1
Woodland Dr. Read 84 B4
Woodland Way. Mar 1 C2
Woodlands. Yate 149 E2
Woodlands Ave. Bur C 111 D2
Woodlands Ave. Wood 87 E4
Woodlands Cl. Ascot 119 F2
Woodlands Cl. Black 150 C1
Woodlands Ct. Crow 143 F1
Woodlands Gr. Caver 59 F2
Woodlands La. Windl 146 C2
Woodlands Parade. Ashf 98 B1
Woodlands Park Ave. Whi Wa 39 D1
Woodlands Park Rd. Maid 39 D2
Woodlands Park Rd. Whi Wa 39 D2
Woodlands Rd. Camb 151 D3
Woodlands Rd. Shipl 35 F2
Woodlands Rd. Tad 134 B1
Woodlands Rd. Vir W 122 B3
Woodlands Rd E. Vir W 122 B3
Woodlands Rd W. Vir W 122 B3
Woodlands Ride. Ascot 120 A2
Woodlands The. Woki 115 E2
Woodlands Wlk. Black 150 C1
Woodlee Cl. Vir W 122 B4
Woodley Green. Wood 87 F4
Woodman Cl. Read 113 E3
Woodmancott Cl. Brac 118 C2
Woodman's La. Bur C 110 C2
Woodmere. Brac 118 C3
Woodmere Cl. Read 87 D1
Woodmoor End. Cook 20 A4
Woodpecker Cl. Twyf 61 F2
Woodridge Cl. Brac 118 B3
Woodrow Dr. Woki 116 C3
Woods Rd. Caver 59 F2
Woodsend Cl. Read 113 E4
Woodshore Cl. Vir W 122 A2
Woodside. Black 150 B2
Woodside. Fla H 3 E3
Woodside. Newb 130 B4
Woodside. Sand 150 C4
Woodside Ave. Fla H 3 E4
Woodside Cl. Buck 107 E3
Woodside Cl. Woki 141 F4
Woodside La. Wink 93 E2
Woodside Rd. Ascot 93 D1
Woodside Way. Read 113 E4
Woodside Way. Vir W 122 A3
Woodstock Ave. Slough 43 E1
Woodstock Cl. Maid 19 F1
Woodstock St. Read 86 C4
Woodthorpe Rd. Ashf 97 E2
Woodthorpe Rd. Stai 97 E2
Woodview Rd. Pangb 56 B3
Woodville Cl. Black 150 A3
Woodward Cl. Winn 88 B1
Woodway. Camb 151 D3
Woodway Rd. Blew 12 A4
Woodwaye. Wood 87 E4
Woodyer Cl. Wood 87 F3
Woolacombe Dr. Read 86 C1
Woolford Cl. Burl 92 B1
Woolhampton Hill. Wool 108 B2
Woolhampton Way. Brac 118 B2
Woosehill. Woki 115 F3
Woosehill La. Woki 115 F3
Woosehill La. Woki 115 F4
Wootton Cl. Read 84 B4
Wootton Rd. Hen-O-T 35 E4
Wootton Way. Maid 39 E3
Worcester Cl. Maid 39 E2
Worcester Cl. Read 85 D3
Worcester Dr. Ashf 98 A2
Wordsworth. Brac 117 F2
Wordsworth Ave. Yate 149 D2
Wordsworth Ct. Caver 59 E4
Wordsworth Rd. Slough 21 E1
Wordsworth Rd. That 106 B2
Worlds End Hill. Brac 118 C2
Worple Ave. Stai 97 D1
Worple Rd. Stai 97 D1
Worple The. Wray 68 C1
Worrall Way. Read 113 F4
Worster Rd. Cook 19 F3
Worton Dr. Read 113 D4
Wrabness Way. Stai 124 A4
Wraysbury Rd. Stai 96 B3
Wraysbury Rd. Wray 96 B3
Wren Cl. Woki 115 F3
Wren Cl. Yate 149 D3
Wren Ct. Slough 44 A2
Wrenfield Dr. Caver 58 C3
Wren's Ave. Ashf 98 B2
Wrensfield. Mar 1 B1
Wrenswood Cl. Read 113 D4
Wright. Oak G 66 B2
Wright Cl. Wood 88 A4
Wroxham. Brac 117 F2
Wroxham Rd. Wood 87 E4
Wurford Dr. That 106 C2
Wyatt Rd. Stai 97 D2
Wyatt Rd. Wind 66 B2
Wychcotes. Caver 58 C2
Wychelm Rd. Light 153 E4
Wychelm Rd. Shin 113 F3
Wychwood Ave. Brac 118 C3
Wychwood Cl. Read 86 C1
Wychwood Cres. Read 86 C2
Wychwood Pl. Camb 152 A4
Wycombe La. Woo G 3 F4
Wycombe Rd. Mar 1 C2
Wycombe Rd. Mar B 1 C3
Wye Cl. Ashf 98 A2
Wye Cl. Read 84 C3
Wye Rd. Woo G 3 E4
Wykeham Cl. Harm 71 D4
Wykeham Rd. Read 87 D3
Wylam. Brac 117 F2
Wylands Rd. Slough 44 A1
Wyld Court Hill. Hamp N 53 E3
Wymers Cl. Burn 21 D2
Wymers Wood Rd. Burn 21 D2
Wyncote Cl. Read 86 C1
Wyndale Cl. Hen-O-T 15 F1
Wyndham Cl. Yate 149 E4
Wyndham Cres. Burn 21 D2
Wyndham Cres. Wood 60 B1
Wyndham Rd. Newb 105 E3
Wynford Cl. Read 85 E2
Wynnstay Gdns. Mar B 1 C3
Wynsham Way. Windl 146 A3
Wyre Ct. Sulh 57 E2
Wyres Dale. Brac 118 C1
Wythe Mead. Binf 90 A1
Wyvern Cl. Brac 118 A3

Yale Cl. Crow 143 F1
Yard Mead. Eng G 96 A3
Yardley. Brac 117 F2
Yarnold Cl. Woki 116 C4
Yarnton Cl. Caver 59 E3
Yateley Dr. Yate 149 D1
Yateley Rd. Sand 149 F4
Yattendon La. Asham 54 B1
Yattendon La. Yatt 54 B1
Yattendon Rd. Herm 79 D4
Yaverland Dr. Bags 145 E1
Ye Meads. Tapl 40 C3
Yelverton Rd. Read 86 B2
Yeomans La. Newt 131 D1
Yeomans Way. Camb 151 F3
Yeosfield. Swal 139 E2
Yeoveney Cl. Stan 96 B3
Yeovil Rd. Burn 41 F4
Yeovil Rd. Sand 143 F1
Yew Cl. Woki 115 F3
Yew Gate. Newb 104 C3
Yew La. Read 85 F3
Yew Tree Cl. Maid 39 F4
Yew Tree Ct. Gori 34 B3
Yew Tree Rd. Slough 43 D2
Yew Tree Rise. Read 84 B3
Yew Tree Wlk. Camb 151 F1
Yewhurst Cl. Twyf 61 E3
Yewtrees. Stai 123 E3
Yield Hall La. Read 86 A4
Yield Hall Pl. Read 86 A4
Yockley Cl. Camb 152 B2
Yoreham Cl. Winn 87 F1
York Ave. Slough 42 B4
York Ave. Wind 67 D3
York Cl. Newb 105 D1
York Rd. Binf 90 B2
York Rd. Camb 151 E4
York Rd. Hen-O-T 15 E1
York Rd. Hung 100 B2
York Rd. Maid 40 A4
York Rd. Mar 1 B1
York Rd. Newb 105 D1
York Rd. Read 59 D1
York Rd. Wind 67 D3
York Way. Sand 150 A4
Yorktown Rd. Sand 150 B4
Youlden Cl. Camb 152 A3
Youlden Dr. Camb 152 A3

Zealand Ave. Harm 70 C4
Zinnia Cl. Woki 115 E4
Zinzan St. Read 85 F4